ARTIFICIAL INTELLIGENCE
An Engineering Approach

D0146884

Also Available from McGraw-Hill

Schaum's Outline Series in Computers

Most outlines include basic theory, definitions, and hundreds of solved problems and supplementary problems with answers.

Titles on the Current List Include

Advanced Structured Cobol
Boolean Algebra
Computer Graphics
Computer Science
Computers and Business
Computers and Programming
Data Processing
Data Structures
Digital Principles, 2d Edition
Discrete Mathematics
Essential Computer Mathematics
Mathematical Handbook of Formulas & Tables
Matrix Operations
Microprocessor Fundamentals, 2d Edition
Programming with Advanced Structured Cobol
Programming with Assembly Language
Programming with Basic, 3d edition
Programming with C
Programming with Fortran
Programming with Pascal
Programming with Structured Cobol

Schaum's Solved Problems Books

Each title in this series is a complete and expert source of solved problems containing thousands of problems with marked out solutions.

Related Titles on the Current List Include
3000 Solved Problems in Calculus
2500 Solved Problems in Differential Equations
3000 Solved Problems in Linear Algebra
2000 Solved Problems in Numerical Analysis

Available at your college bookstore. A complete listing of Schaum titles may be obtained by writing to: Schaum Division
McGraw-Hill Publishing Co.
Princeton Road, S-1
Hightstown, NJ 08520

ARTIFICIAL INTELLIGENCE
An Engineering Approach

Robert J. Schalkoff
Clemson University

McGraw-Hill Publishing Company

New York St. Louis San Francisco Auckland Bogotá Caracas Hamburg
Lisbon London Madrid Mexico Milan Montreal New Delhi Oklahoma City
Paris San Juan São Paulo Singapore Sydney Tokyo Toronto

CREDITS

Quote, p. 1: From THE LORAX, by Dr. Seuss. Copyright ©1971 by Dr. Seuss and A. S. Geisel. Reprinted by permission of Random House, Inc.

Fig. 7.2: Roads, C., *Foundations of Computer Music*, MIT Press, copyright 1979.

Fig. 13.2, 13.3: Harmon, P., and King, D., *Expert Systems*, copyright 1985, John Wiley and Sons, reprinted by permission.

Fig. 13.4: Barker, V., and O'Connor, D., "Expert Systems for Configuration at Digital: XCON and Beyond," *Comm. of the ACM*, March 1989.

Fig. 13.15: Hayes-Roth, F., "Rule-Based Systems," in *Encyclopedia of Artificial Intelligence* (Shapiro, S., ed), copyright 1987, John Wiley and Sons, reprinted by permission.

Figs. 13.16, 13.17: copyright 1984, IEEE.

Figs. 13.19, 13.20, 16.10: copyright 1986, Academic Press.

Fig. 15.1: copyright 1983, SIAM.

Fig. 16.3: copyright 1987, IEEE.

Fig. 16.12: Clancy, W. J., "From Guidon to Neomycin," *AI Magazine*, August 1986, page 53, copyright 1986, American Association for Artificial Intelligence.

Fig. 18.2: Carbonell, J., and Langley, P., "Machine Learning," in *Encyclopedia of Artificial Intelligence* (Shapiro, S., ed.), copyright 1987, John Wiley and Sons, reprinted by permission.

Fig. 19.1: copyright 1987, IEEE.

ARTIFICIAL INTELLIGENCE
An Engineering Approach

Copyright ©1990 by McGraw-Hill, Inc. All rights reserved.
Printed in the United States of America. Except as permitted under the United States Copyright Act of 1976, no part of this publication may be reproduced or distributed in any form or by any means, or stored in a data base or retrieval system, without the prior written permission of the publisher.

1 2 3 4 5 6 7 8 9 0 DOC DOC 9 5 4 3 2 1 0

ISBN 0-07-055084-0

This book was set in Times Roman by Publication Services.
The editor was David M. Shapiro;
the production supervisor was Denise L. Puryear.
The cover was designed by Albert M. Cetta.
Project supervision was done by Publication Services.
R. R. Donnelley & Sons Company was printer and binder.

Library of Congress Cataloging-in-Publication Data

Schalkoff, Robert J.
   Artificial intelligence: an engineering approach / Robert J.
   Schalkoff
     p.   cm.
   Includes bibliographical references.
   ISBN 0-07-055084-0
   1. Artificial intelligence   2. Artificial intelligence—Data
   processing.   3. Prolog (Computer program language)   I. Title.
Q335.S37   1990
006.3—dc20   89-13682

ABOUT THE AUTHOR

Robert J. Schalkoff received the Ph.D. degree in Electrical Engineering from the University of Virginia. Currently, he is a Professor of Electrical and Computer Engineering at Clemson University in Clemson, South Carolina. His primary research interests are in artificial intelligence and computer vision with special emphasis on model-based image understanding, motion and stereo vision, and associated computer architectures. He is also the author of *Digital Image Processing and Computer Vision* (John Wiley and Sons, 1989).

TO LESLIE AND KATIE

CONTENTS

Preface   **xxi**

1   Introduction   **1**

Background and History   1
    What is AI?   2
    Emulating Human Cognitive Processes   6
    Why Is AI Difficult?   7
Central Themes in AI   8
    Overview of Concepts   8
    To Search or Not to Search (The Knowledge-Search Tradeoff)   9
Mathematical Preliminaries   10
    Stored Knowledge, Descriptions, and Relations   10
    Semantic Nets   13
    Representations That Attempt to Convey "Meaning"   16
The Role of Knowledge Representations and Computational Models in AI   17
    Why Models?   17
    Representation Characteristics   22
    An Abstract View of Modeling   23
    The Frame Problem in AI   24
Elementary Knowledge Representation Approaches   26
    Procedural versus Declarative Schemes   26
    Selection of Representation Primitives   27
    State Space Representations and Control   29
    Characteristics of AI Algorithms   31
Topical Outline   31
Ancillary References   32
References   33
Problems   34

2   Symbolic (Computational) Logic   37

Introduction	37
The Use of Logic in AI	38
Relation to "Classical" Logics and Extensions	38
Inference	38
The Vocabulary of Logic	39
The Mathematics of Logic	39
Statements	39
Analysis of Compound Statements Using Simple Logical Connectives	41
Implication	41
A Further Look at Implication	43
Deduction Using Propositional Logic	45
Predicate Logic	48
Introduction	48
Predicates and Variables	48
Quantified Predicates, Equivalences, and Manipulations	50
The Language of First Order Logic	53
Manipulation of WFFS	55
Resolution (Proof by Refutation)	55
Unification	57
Extending Modus Ponens to Statements with Variables (and Unification)	63
Summary and Limitations of Logic-Based Representations	65
References	66
Problems	66

3   AI Programming Languages and Development Systems—"The Tools of the Trade"   73

Programming Languages Overview	73
Languages for AI Implementation	74
"Conventional" and Symbolic Computing	74
Coupled Computing Systems	75
Manipulabe Representations and Data Structures	76
The LISP and PROLOG Distinction	77
The Distinction (What's Different?)	77
The PROLOG Programming Concept as Description	78
The LISP Programming Concept	78
Data Directed Processing	79
AI Development Environments and Systems	79
Desirable AI Software Capabilities	79
Desirable AI Software Enviornments	80
Programming Language Classifications	81
Introduction and Definitions	81
Examples of Pascal, LISP and PROLOG	82
Control Structures	84
Alternative Languages	85
Recursion	85
Implementation of Recursion	86
Tail Recursion	87

Variables and Scoping (Programming Point of View)   88
    Variable Scope   88
    Binding   88
    Pascal Example   89
LISP and PROLOG Variable Scoping   89
    The Binding Environment   90
    Dynamic and Lexical Scoping of LISP Variables   90
References   90

4   Fundamentals of PROLOG   91

PROLOG Background   91
    Introduction   91
    Unification—the Basis of PROLOG   92
    PROLOG "Standards," Compatibility and C + M   92
    Logical Connections and PROLOG Syntax   93
Clauses, Facts, Goals, and Rules   93
    Clauses   93
    Facts   93
    Goals   94
    Rules   94
    PROLOG and Modus Ponens   96
    More Comprehensive Examples   96
The Syntax and Characteristics of PROLOG   98
    PROLOG Syntax Basics   99
    Lists in PROLOG   101
    Goals and the PROLOG Unification Mechanism   103
Potential Unification Circularities with Symmetric and Transitive Relations   107
Constraints Using Variables in PROLOG   109
Creating, Modifying and Examining PROLOG Databases (Database Management)   109
    Consult   109
    Reconsult   111
    Retract and Listing   112
A Detailed Look at the Unification Process and Search   112
References   115
Problems   115

5   Constraint Satisfaction Problems and PROLOG Application to Image Labeling   124

Constraint Satisfaction Problems   124
    Constraint Satisfaction Problem Formulations   125
    Relation to Numerical Constraint Satisfaction Problems   125
    Interpretation as Search   126
Region Labeling and Segmentation in Image Processing   127
    General Labeling Formulation   127
    Image Labeling Example   128
    Constraint Determination   129
PROLOG Implementation of Constraint Satisfaction   130
    The Positive Approach   130
    The Negative Approach (Coding What Is Not Allowed in PROLOG)   135

References 139
Problems 139

6 An AI Application Using PROLOG: Electric Power System Protection Analysis **144**

Overview 144
    Objectives 144
    Simple Power Protection Background 145
Problem Formulation 146
    Overall Goals 146
    PROLOG Description of System Topology 147
    Breaker Backup 148
    An Extended Example of PROLOG Description Derivation 148
    General Network Topology Description 149
Significant Rules in Description 151
    Connectivity Rules 151
    Locating Corresponding Breakers via Rules 151
    Generation Rules 151
    Review of the PROLOG Cut Predicate 152
    Backup Breaker Description 152
Determination of Fault Locations through Electrical Isolation 155
Rules for Interpretation and Display 155
    Overall Goal (Incorporated in Database, for Simplicity) 156
    Sample Results 158
Conclusions 158
References 159
Problems 160

7 PROLOG Application to Structural Object Description, Formal Languages, and Parsing **163**

Introduction 163
Parsing and Applications 164
    Compilation of High Level Languages 164
    Understanding of Natural Language 165
    Description and Interpretation of Image (Visual) Data 168
    Syntactic Pattern Classification 168
Formal Language Theory 170
    Formal Definitions 170
    Example of a 2-D Language Application—A Line Drawing
      Description Grammar [Shaw 1970] 172
Sentence Generation and Parsing in PROLOG 174
    PROLOG Sentence Generation 174
    Context-Free Parsing In PROLOG 177
    Graphical Constructs: The Derivation Tree 178
    An Abstract View of the Parsing Problem 178
    Top-Down versus Bottom-Up Parsing 179
    Development of the G1 Parser 179
    Parser/Generator Similarities 179
    Desired Parser Input Structure 180

(Augmented) Transition Networks (ATN's) 185
 Transition Networks 185
 Augmented Transition Nets (ATNs) 188
Concluding Remarks 189
 Parsing Computational Complexity 189
 From Parsing to Meaning 190
References 190
Problems 191

8 Fundamentals of LISP 194

Introduction 194
 Getting Started in LISP 194
Basic LISP Concepts and Examples (Eval, Lists, and Function Definitions) 196
 The Eval Function 197
 Elementary List Manipulation 197
 Function Definition 200
 (FranzLISP) Help 201
 Simple LISP Assignment and I/O 201
LISP Syntax in General 203
 The Basic Function Groups 204
 Functions and Variables 204
 Control Functions 205
 List Manipulation (Construction) Functions (and Distinctions) 210
 Properties and Property Lists 212
 Scoping of LISP Variables 215
Extended Example of Recursion Using LISP 216
References 221
Problems 221

9 List Structures—Rationale and Computer Representations 228

Introduction 228
Why Graphs, Relations, and Lists? 229
Operations on Stored Representation(s) Desired 230
Trees 233
Computer Memory Model(s) 234
Computer Representation of Graphs and Relational Information 234
 Conversion of Graphical Representations into Trees and Lists 236
The cons Cell and Building Lists 237
 The cons Cell 238
 Extensions Using the cons Cell 240
References 244
Problems 244

10 Matching and Unification in LISP—A Prelude to Rule-based Inference 248

Introduction 248
 The Need for Matching 248
 A Hierarchy of Matching Problems 249

The Simplest Matcher in LISP 250
Matching with "Don't Cares" 252
Matching with Variables and Bindings 255
    Limited Matching Using match-var without Checking Prior Bindings 258
    Matching with Checking and Adding of Bindings 260
The General Unifier 266
Matching of Lists with Lists of Lists 271
    Constants Only (Case 4) 271
    List Matching with Variables 272
    Summary 274
References 275
Problems 275

11 Rule-based Inference Systems Part I—Production Systems, Forward Chaining, and LISP Implementations   279

Production Systems 279
    Overview and Basic Structure 279
    Features of Rule-based Production Systems 282
Theoretical Aspects of the Production System Structure and Inference Strategy 283
    Significant Aspects of the Inference Engine (Inference Control Strategies) 283
    Problem Solving, the State Space, and the Inference Engine 284
    Production System Properties 284
Rule-based Chaining Inference Approaches 287
    Rule-based Systems as Production Systems and Control Paradigms 287
    Review of the Logical Basis for Forward Chaining 288
Implementation of a Simple Forward Chaining System in LISP 289
    Overall System Structure 289
    Database Structure 290
    Rule Representation and Rulebase Structure 291
    Forward Chaining Inference Engine Main Function "Chainforward" 295
    Examples 296
    Image Motion Description Example 300
Extensions to the Simple Forward Chaining Inference System 303
    Rule Selection, Specificity and the Conflict Set 304
Forward Chaining with Variables in Rules 308
    Examples of Conflict Resolution Strategies and Resulting Rule
        Firing Sequences 314
Summary 319
References 319
Problems 319

12 Rule-based Inference Systems Part II—Backward Chaining with LISP Implementation   325

Backward Chaining 325
    The Basis for Backward Chaining 327
    Hypothesis Generation and Application to Intelligent Systems 330
    Abduction 331

LISP Implementations of Backward Chaining 334
Derivation of the Inference Engine 334
LISP Implementation of Basic Backward Chaining Algorithm 334
Extensions to the Backward Chaining Algorithm 342
Backward Chaining with Variables in Rules (Optional) 348
Backward versus Forward Chaining (Choosing "Directions") 352
References 353
Problems 354

13 Inference Systems—A Further Look **359**

Expert Systems 359
Introduction and Examples 359
Expert System Limitations 363
Expert System Development 364
Expert Systems Summary 366
Reasoning with Uncertainty 367
Incorporating Uncertainty in the Inference Process 368
Types of Uncertainties and Their Propagation 369
Probability Review 372
Simple Example of Two-Antecedent Rule Using Probability 374
Probabilistic Extensions (Optional) 376
Heuristic Approaches Derived from Probabilistic Reasoning
(Confidence Factors) 378
Many Valued Logics 381
LISP Implementations 386
Example of Numerical Confidence Propagation and Conflict Resolution
in Forward Chaining 387
A Commercial Rule-based System Example: OPS5 390
The OPS5 Production System Programming Language 390
OPS5 Program Structure 392
Conflict Resolution in OPS5 395
OPS5 Examples 395
Additional Inference Approaches and Applications 406
Approaches Based upon Model Unification 406
Using a Forward Chaining System for Backward Chaining (Optional) 411
References 415
Problems 417

14 Planning in AI Systems **424**

The Significance of Planning 424
Background 424
Planning Examples 425
Representational Issues in Planning 426
Representation, Operator Specification, and Search 428
Developing a Representation 428
Search and Potential Computational Complexity 429
Operators and Representations 430
Planning Difficulties (Local Actions and Global Objectives) 431

Planning Related to a Production System   432
    The Non-Commutative Nature of Planning Systems   432
    Plan Generation as a Control Problem   432
Blocks-World System Representation   434
    Problem Specification, Assumptions and Operator Representations   434
Plan Generation Algorithms   436
    Cycles in Plans   436
    Forward State Propagation Using Generate-and-Test   436
    Backward State Propagation   437
Advanced Planning Strategies   444
    Generation of Expertise (Remembering a Plan)   444
    The Triangle Table   445
    Example of Plan and Corresponding Triangle Table Formation   446
LISP Implementation of Plan Generators   448
    Forward State Propagation Using Generate-and-Test
        (Checkerboard)   448
Incorporating "Means-End" in the Operator Selection (Search) Strategy   463
    Operator (and State) Evaluation Functions and
        Problem-Solving Heuristics   463
    Forward State Propagation (Blocks-World) LISP Implementation
        Using Action Ordering (Means-End)   464
    LISP Implementation of Backward State Propagation   476
Planning Extensions   481
    Hierarchical Planning and Macro-Operators (Considering
        More Than One State Change)   481
    Planning in a Changing Environment   481
    Simultaneous Application of Operators and Parallel Planning   482
References   486
Problems   486

15   Search and Computational Complexity in AI Systems   493

Computational Complexity   493
    Quantifying Computational Complexity   494
Search in AI Problems   496
    A Formal Representation for Search Problems   496
    Problem Decomposition and Searching with AND-OR Trees   499
    Incorporating Search in AI   502
    Search Computational Complexity and Trade-offs   503
Search Algorithms   505
    Trial-and-Error Approaches   505
    Breadth-First Search   506
    Depth-First Search   507
    Forward-Backward (Bidirectional) Search   507
    Other Search Approaches (Including Heuristic
        Search Techniques)   507
References   508
Problems   509

16 Structured Knowledge Representation and Manipulation (Frames, Blackboards, and Advanced Control Concepts) 513

Representational Structures 514
    Structured Knowledge Representations and "Focusing" Inference 514
    Classes, Structural Links, and Hierarchical Representations 515
    Inheritance 516
Frames 518
    Frame Concept 518
    Slot Types 519
    Inheritance with Exceptions 520
    Frame Networks 521
Frame Implementation and Examples 524
    PROLOG Frame Implementation 524
    LISP Frame Implementation Example 525
    Frame Manipulation Primitives 529
    An Example of Frame-based Inference (SIGMA) 529
Other Representation Partitions 529
    Blackboard (Theoretical Concept) 531
    Blackboard Operation 532
Advanced IE Control Concepts 533
    Metarules and Demons 533
Verifying Knowledge-Base Consistency 535
    Description and Identification of Six Types of Rule-Base Problems 535
Nonmonotonic Reasoning 536
    Situations Involving Nonmonotonic Reasoning 537
    Nonmonotonic Reasoning Formalisms 537
References 538
Problems 538

17 Temporal Logic and Reasoning in Artificial Intelligence 543

Introduction 543
    Time and Logic 543
Concepts and Approaches for Reasoning with Time (RWT) 546
    Time Concepts 546
    Graphical Representations for RWT 549
    Simple PROLOG Example of RWT Implementation 551
A RWT Theoretical Framework 551
    Modal Logic as a RWT Framework (Optional) 559
References 560
Problems 560

18 Learning in AI Systems 564

Introduction 564
The Concept of Learning 564
Historical Learning Research 565
Learning Definitions 566
Examples of Current Automated Learning Research Paradigms 566

Learning Approaches	567
Learning Algorithms	569
Learning through Description; Generalization/Specialization	570
General-to-Specific (G-S) and Specific-to-General (S-G) Approaches	570
A Detailed Look at G-S and S-G Algorithmic Approaches	571
Inductive Reasoning and Truth/Falsity Preservation	577
Generalization Operators	578
Sample Non-Constructive Generalization Operators	580
Constructive Inductive Generalization	582
Learning through Building Models and Structural Links	582
References	582
Problems	583

19   AI System Architectures — 586

Introduction	586
AI System Architecture Components	586
Levels of Architectural Concern	588
A General Need for Parallel Computing Architectures	588
Examples of Current AI-Machine Architectural Features	589
General Concepts of Parallel Processing	590
Parallel Computer Architecture, Decompositions, and Algorithms	590
Area/Time Trade-offs and Decompositions	590
Algorithm Decomposition Tools (Flow Graphs)	592
Do We Need a Specific Architecture for AI?	593
Symbolic Processing Benchmarks	594
Parallel Implementations Using PROLOG	595
Types of PROLOG Parallelism	595
Implementing PROLOG Unification (Search) in Parallel	597
Concurrent PROLOG	599
Parallel Implementations Using LISP	601
Parallel LISP Implementation Examples	602
Parallelism in LISP Using the "Future" Construct	604
Other Parallel Implementations	605
Parallel Implementation of Production Systems	605
Distributed Artificial Intelligence (DAI)	606
References	607
Problems	608

Appendices — 613

Appendix 1: Discrete Mathematics Review	613
Relations	613
Logic	616
Appendix 2: PROLOG Syntax Summary	624
Basic Program Elements	624
Unification	625
Lists	625
Special Symbols and Operators	625
Database Creation and Editing	625
Noteworthy Built-in Predicates	626

Appendix 3: Commonly Used LISP Functions and Examples   627
    Predicates   627
    List Manipulation   628
    Assignment   630
    Property and Association Lists   630
    Arithmetic and Logical Functions   630
    Printing Functions   631
    Function Definition and Application   632
    Control Functions   633
    Debugging and Tracing Functions   634
    System Functions   634
Appendix 4: Elementary UNIX Commands and vi   635
    Basic UNIX Use   635
    Elements of the Visual Editor (vi)   637
References   641

Epilogue   **642**

Index   **643**

PREFACE

"All men by nature desire knowledge."

Metaphysics, bk. I, ch. 1

ARISTOTLE
384–322 B.C.

This book explores the theoretical and practical underpinnings of Artificial Intelligence (AI) and provides an introductory-level "hands-on," engineering-oriented perspective on AI technology. No previous experience in this area is assumed, although readers are expected to have minimal familiarity with discrete mathematics and some exposure to modern programming languages, such as Pascal. Since this is a teaching text dedicated to those new to the field, efforts have been made to provide the reader a "soft start."

Artificial Intelligence may be the Rodney Dangerfield of scientific disciplines. Only recently has AI begun to receive serious, widespread attention (respect?). This is due partially to the fact that many visible and important AI successes exist. These include expert systems, natural-language and speech-understanding systems, and computer vision systems. Although many issues in AI are still "open" or unresolved, most optimistic observers predict new successes are just beyond the horizon. Indeed, the expectations from Artificial Intelligence may be at an all-time peak. Perhaps we should modify the common expression "knowledge is power" to "representation and autonomous manipulation of knowledge is *real* power."

The book presents topics that are generally considered "core " AI concepts; it does not attempt to be an encyclopedia or bibliographic summary of all AI-related research work ever produced. Emphasis on the conceptual approach explains the organization of the text (i.e., the partitioning of topics). In addition, the book attempts to make the important distinctions between theory and practice that are often major factor's in the choice and implementation of AI algorithms.

The area of Artificial Intelligence is becoming more important in both undergraduate and graduate curricula in Computer Science and Engineering. In fact, it represents a major elective area in the IEEE Model Curriculum. There is little doubt that AI techniques will become more commonplace in other engineering and scientific disciplines. In this text, extensive use of detailed PROLOG and LISP examples of AI implementation allows the design of an AI system to be treated with an engineering approach and in a "symbolically quantitative" manner. In addition, the AI theory presented is merged with practical aspects of software engineering.

Although the primary objective of the text is to provide a teaching tool, it is quite likely that practicing engineers and scientists will also find the clear, concept-based treatment useful in updating their backgrounds. Hopefully, this will provide the fundamental conceptual and algorithmic tools necessary to confront the industrial application-driven challenges of this rapidly expanding and emerging field.

Here are two things a reader should consider before entering into a study of AI.

1. AI embodies an *inexact form of computation,* which appears, at best, to be based on an *ambiguous model* (similar to human reasoning). This contrasts with numerical computation, where algorithm behavior typically is explicitly developed a priori and (numerical) answers are known to many decimal places. Some aspects of AI are therefore close to "exploratory programming."
2. AI is a *rapidly maturing discipline* with a strong *interdisciplinary nature*. Algorithms and data structures that were in vogue yesterday are now considered obsolete. Today's algorithms are under scrutiny, and tomorrow's algorithms are on the horizon.

In research, it has been found that a theoretical understanding of AI concepts (e.g., unification, first-order predicate logic), while desirable, is not sufficient. A capability to develop, analyze, and implement knowledge databases; design, analyze, and modify inference engines; develop large-scale systems; and interface AI systems to the "real," or outside, world is also necessary. As a consequence, both theoretical and practical aspects are explored in this text using straightforward examples in the LISP and PROLOG programming languages. The Clocksin and Mellish syntax is used for PROLOG. The LISP constructs used are those typically found in a "pure" LISP dialect. For the most part, they are a subset of those available in Franz or Common LISP. At this point in history, it is *not clear whether PROLOG or LISP will become the AI language of choice*; each has its strengths, weaknesses, and preferred applications. Since both languages are currently enjoying popularity, and often the representation or manipulation desired is more naturally suited for one, both are included in this book. The use of these languages as an integral part of the presentation helps make illustration of concepts unambiguous and concise.

It is possible to use this text while de-emphasizing programming aspects. In the author's opinion, however, the hands-on, or practical, experience gained by developing and modifying working systems in AI languages is an invaluable aspect of any AI course. Learning the jargon of AI is one thing; development of an ability to appreciate and experiment with the underlying concepts is a higher goal. Many of the ideas in AI are in fact fully understood only when the complexities and limitations of underlying data structures and inference mechanisms themselves are familiar to the student through hands-on experience. Table P.1 summarizes options for the use of this text in courses with differing orientations.

Clearly, there is more material than can be covered in one semester—the choice of specific topics is left to individual instructors. Given students with significant logic, LISP, and PROLOG background, it is possible to cover many of the later chapters on advanced topics (e.g., learning, temporal reasoning, architectures) in a single semester. Alternatively, Chapters 1 through 13 provide the basis for a comprehensive one-semester introduction, which then could be followed by a second course based Chapters 14 through 19, supplemented with readings from the current AI literature and possibly a comprehensive project. Many of the problems at the end of each chapter, combined with the implementation examples in the text, serve as good starting points for projects or extended self-study.

TABLE P.1
Suggested use of text in courses with different orientations/objectives

Orientation/Objective	Chapters/Sequence
2-semester AI course (with or without projects)	Ch. 1–13 (first semester) Ch. 13–19 (second semester) Supplement with outside reading/programming/project
1-semester course with programming emphasis	Ch. 1–5, 7–12; selected portions of Ch. 13, 14
1-semester course without programming emphasis	Ch. 1, 2, 4 (lightly), 5, 8 (lightly), 11–14 (without LISP examples)
1-semester course with project	Ch. 1–5, 7–12; selected portions of Ch. 13, 14, with projects chosen from Ch. 13–19
1-semester course with PROLOG and LISP programming background required	Ch. 1, 2, 5, 7, 11–15; selected portions of Ch. 16–19

It is difficult to specify the intended audience of this text on the basis of the descriptors "graduate" or "undergraduate." It is accurate to term the material "introductory," that is, suitable for a first course in AI. This first exposure may occur anywhere from the junior level undergraduate to first year graduate level.

The book is structured in the following order:

1. Introduction to logic, representation, and AI languages.
2. AI concepts and examples in PROLOG.
3. AI concepts and examples in LISP.
4. Advanced AI concepts.

This structure has suited teaching needs well, since some underlying theory may be presented while the students are becoming familiar with the particular PROLOG or LISP development systems to be used. Additionally, the first examples are shown in PROLOG since this language has a built-in unification mechanism; this allows concentration on *problem specification* or representation, without worrying about the solution procedure. It is also a natural extension of the logic-based representation considered early in Chapter 2. Having developed some dexterity in setting up AI (symbolic manipulation) problems, students are then ready to tackle LISP and explicitly develop their own representations and solution procedures.

There is no single, unique, or generally agreed upon set of algorithms for AI. In this book many of the algorithms shown or developed are shown in *skeletal form*. They constitute a general approach, and possible variants, options, or extensions are indicated.

This book reflects the contribution of numerous individuals. Comments and questions from many students led to subsequent revisions that improved overall quality. The efforts of students in solving early versions of the problems and debugging and revising LISP and PROLOG code are also reflected.

An accompanying instructor's manual is available from the publisher. It contains problem solutions as well as IBM-format diskettes containing all the PROLOG and LISP examples shown in the text. Both Common and Franz LISP versions are provided.

REFERENCES

Leitch, R. R., "Artificial Intelligence: The Emergence of a Formal Basis for Engineering," *IEE Proc. (Part D: Control Theory and Application),* Institution of Electrical Engineers (London), Vol. 132, No. 4, July 1987, p. 216.

"Model Program in Computer Science and Engineering" (Model Program Committee, Educational Activities Board, IEEE), *IEEE Computer Society, December 1983.*

ACKNOWLEDGMENTS

I would like to thank my wife Leslie for her support throughout this project. The quality and accuracy of the text reflects her careful word processing, editing, and proofreading assistance.

McGraw-Hill and the author would like to thank the following reviewers for their many helpful comments and suggestions: Seth Hutchinson, Purdue University; Robert McCoard, California State University–Northridge; Dennis E. Ray, Old Dominian University; Kathleen Swigger, North Texas State University.

Robert J. Schalkoff

"It is impossible for a man who takes a survey of what is already known, not to see what an immensity in every branch of science yet remains to be discovered."

THOMAS JEFFERSON

Monticello, June 18, 1799

ARTIFICIAL INTELLIGENCE
An Engineering Approach

CHAPTER

1

INTRODUCTION

Intelligence . . . is the faculty of making artificial objects, especially tools to make tools.

Henri Bergson 1859–1941
L'Evolution Creatrice [Creative Evolution] (1907), ch. 2

"It was sort of a man. Describe him? . . . That's hard. I don't know if I can."

Dr. Seuss
The Lorax, Random House, 1971

BACKGROUND AND HISTORY

This book concerns the foundations of a new generation of computing technology and capability, most commonly referred to as Artificial Intelligence (AI). The new generation of AI computing is decidedly different in the sense that it is characterized not by its hardware (although this also may differ from past generations) but by its *capabilities*. Previous computer generations have emphasized numerical computations for business or scientific applications. The work of Church, Turing, and others [Pylyshya 1984] proved that the notion of a computation goes far beyond numerical calculation. The decade of the 90s is likely to be the era of

1. Symbolic (as opposed to numerical) manipulation, with the goal of emulating "intelligent" behavior. This does not preclude the use of numerical information as part of AI.
2. Parallel computations, to enable the results (either symbolic or numerical) to be produced in a timely (or "real-time") fashion.

This book emphasizes the first topic (although we take a brief look at AI systems architectures in Chapter 19) from an *AI engineering* point of view. The desired predominant capability of this new generation is the ability to emulate (and perhaps in some cases surpass) human intelligence functions. This new generation is often referred to as the "Fifth Generation." In some sense, AI represents a natural evolution of computing. Whether this will lead to a new information revolution that parallels the industrial revolution in impact (or leads to, as Feigenbaum claims, "the only revolution of significance" [Feigenbaum/McCorduck 1983]) is a subject of considerable philosophical and economic concern; it is also presently an unanswerable question.

INTELLIGENCE THROUGH COMPUTATION. AI seeks to achieve *intelligence through computation*. Any computation requires a *representation* of some entity (e.g., as a numerical quantity) as well as a procedure for *manipulation*. (This ignores the possibility of nonalgorithmic computing.) Representation and manipulation are key elements of AI. Obviously, we cannot manipulate knowledge unless it is adequately represented. Thus, representation and manipulation are not separate issues; they are addressed concurrently in the chapters that follow.

AI has reached a point where we realize that the general problems are very difficult, whereas certain well-focused application-specific problems are solvable. The AI "theory" community seems to be concentrating on fundamental issues of intelligence. The AI "applications" community is involved in the reduction of existing AI principles to practice and the identification of suitable new problem domains for AI. This book attempts to reflect this balance of theory versus practice, or AI as "science" versus AI as "engineering." We explore underlying theory, implementations and computational issues, and unsolved problems.

What is AI?

A GENERAL DEFINITION. Widely accepted definitions of AI are both controversial and elusive [Schank 1987]. This is not surprising, considering the difficulty in defining natural intelligence (NI). It is probably better, however, to attempt a definition of AI than to assume that an all-encompassing, universally accepted definition exists. It appears that the origins of AI may be traced back to a conference at Dartmouth College in the summer of 1956. Perhaps the broadest definition is that

- AI is a field of study that seeks to explain and emulate intelligent behavior in terms of computational processes. (1-1)

Thus, AI is neither a pure science (the explanation part) nor solely a novel engineering discipline (the emulation part). This explains the cross-disciplinary nature of AI, involving cognitive scientists, computer scientists, engineers, and mathematicians.

AN ENGINEERING DEFINITION. From an engineering viewpoint, we might argue that AI is about *generating representations and procedures that automatically (au-tonomously) solve problems heretofore solved by humans*. This aspect is repeatedly enforced throughout the text by the many appearances of the terms *knowledge representation* and *manipulation*. The reader should note that *manipulation* includes the creation of new facts, concepts, structures, and so on.

The two viewpoints are easily unified if we adopt the philosophy that *the goal of AI is the understanding of intelligence as a feasible computation*. This distinguishes AI from the development of "conventional" software for narrowly defined tasks, as encountered in *expert systems* (Chapter 13). The preponderance of expert systems, which are often mistakenly taken to be synonymous with artificial intelligence, is a principal source of confusion about what constitutes AI.

The methodology and terminology of AI is still developing. AI is decomposing into and finding related subfields: logic, neural networks, object-oriented programming, formal languages, and so forth. This explains why the study of AI is not confined to mathematics, computer science, engineering, or psychology departments. Rather, each of these disciplines is a potential contributor.

ENGINEERING VERSUS COGNITIVE SCIENCE. Applied AI is the engineering counterpart of cognitive science. Cognitive science is a blend of philosophy, linguistics, and psychology.

An engineering approach to AI requires the development of programs; that is, algorithms and databases that exhibit intelligent behavior. Figure 1.1 shows a characterization of intelligent behavior without defining intelligence. Since this autonomous capability is a form of advanced computation, an alternative descriptor might be *machine intelligence*. This reinforces our previous definitions since

1. Mechanization of intelligence implies the need for an explicit and quantitative description.

2. Codifying expert knowledge is articulating intelligence.

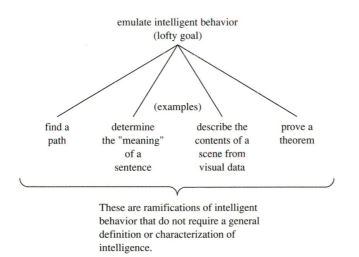

FIGURE 1.1
AI goals via examples of intelligent behavior.

Certain aspects of AI are not new. AI researchers have theorized, axiomized, developed heuristics, and demonstrated prototype systems of some complexity for several decades. For example, considerable resources were expended in early AI efforts in the late 50s and early 60s. It turned out that seemingly easy problems were, after closer examination, actually quite difficult. Results were less than spectacular, and the field quietly subsided.

THREE MAJOR QUESTIONS (REPRESENTATION AND MANIPULATION). From an engineering viewpoint, much of the work in developing AI systems is based upon the development of explicit and comprehensive *knowledge representations* and corresponding effective, versatile and practical *manipulation strategies*.

Therefore, three questions may guide our study of AI. They are

1. What is knowledge? $\qquad$ (1-2*a*)

2. (How) can it be represented? $\qquad$ (1-2*b*)

3. (How) can it (should it) be manipulated? $\qquad$ (1-2*c*)

The remainder of the text seeks to provide partial answers to these questions.

AI ECONOMICS AND INCENTIVES. Recently, AI has become one of the "hot" areas of research and development. AI is expected to become a leading force in software technology in the 1990s. This is due to a number of causes, including commercial and governmental interest. For example, the return on investment at IBM on a series of expert systems costing $2.5 million was estimated at $37.5 million. Another cause is the exponentially increasing capability of computing technology. We see a doubling of "speed" measured in IPS (instructions/sec) or MFLOPS (millions of floating point operations/sec) about every five years. The realization of AI potential by countries other than the United States is also significant. The current AI research budgets of DARPA, NSF, NASA, and NIH combined are over $100 million [Reddy 1988]. Indeed, AI (among other technologies) has become recognized as a potential cure for lagging productivity. In the 1980s, average hourly wages have risen 3.9 percent per year, but factory output has only risen by $\frac{1}{3}$ of this amount. As the following table shows, U.S. productivity gains have been overshadowed by those of other countries, prompting a search for a "technological edge" in this important competition. AI technology may be that edge. Figure 1.2 lists typical AI application domains.

AI GROWING PAINS. Artificial intelligence is not without its critics and has experienced "growing pains." AI confuses some, excites some, and threatens the livelihood

Productivity gains 1973–1984 (source: U.S. Labor Department study [Rukeyser 1988])

U.S.	2.1%
Japan	5.9%
Great Britain	2.3%

Robotics	• Path and motion planning (Navigation)
	• Computer vision
	• Manufacturing control (CAM)
	• Manufacturing diagnostic systems
	• Manufacturing scheduling
Expert systems	• Medical diagnosis (MYCIN)
	• Battlefield management (Pilot's Associate)
	• Geological prospecting (PROSPECTOR)
	• Computer configuration (XCON)
	• Power system control
	• Production planning and scheduling
	• Design

Game playing

Natural language understanding

Theorem proving

Computer-assisted education/learning

Automated decision making

Automated software generation

FIGURE 1.2
Sample AI application domains.

of some. The gross exaggerations of AI system capability (driven by both commercial and military interests), the claims of impending AI breakthroughs in the late 1960s (which never materialized), and the preponderance of simplistic "expert systems" are partially to blame. The lack of detailed theoretical tools for the study of AI is another area that fuels criticism. Indeed it is possible that AI is in a "pretheoretical" stage, just as aviation was in the days of the Wright brothers. Another of the perplexing problems AI researchers face, one which fuels the fires of critics, is the lack of a suitable definition of the field. However, the lack of a universal agreement on the definition of a research area is not necessarily bad. For example, how many readers could unambiguously and uncontroversially define "Electrical Engineering"?

Another problem, again related to the definitional problem, is the uncertainty about what constitutes an AI system. Generally, we see wholesale linking of the phrase "AI" with anything computer- or information-related, particularly in the commercial sector. The mandatory inclusion of the descriptor "AI-based" parallels the marketing strategy of the early 1970s, when "microcomputer-based" was a prerequisite for product description. Furthermore, some might claim that anything written in LISP or PROLOG is an AI application. We note immediately that AI languages are tools, not AI itself, just as a gun is not law enforcement. One could just as well claim that any program containing IF-THEN constructs is an example of a rule-based system. If a program checks for reasonability of its values, is it an "expert system?" Does an adaptive Kalman filter exhibit intelligence? Is any system with tables of situations and corresponding actions a production system? The examples could continue; time will determine whether AI is a bonafide, significant, and emerging field or a marketing tool for relatively insignificant concepts.

Emulating Human Cognitive Processes

A PSYCHOLOGIST'S VIEWPOINT. The study of the mind is probably almost as old as man. Certainly, psychologists have studied human reasoning and behavior since the time of Aristotle. One particularly important psychologist was William James, many of whose basic insights into human behavior have survived the test of time. His two-volume *Psychology* [James 1890] is considered a research milestone and gives some indication of how an engineering approach to AI might proceed. Lest we anticipate that this work will answer all questions regarding human behavior and, more naively still, assume that algorithms will result, we need to note that, according to James, "thought works under strange conditions."

James noted that high-level biological reasoning systems, including the human brain, are not designed principally to think abstractly. Rather, they are designed to *facilitate the survival of the overall system*. Thus, an engineering characterization of human cognitive ability is that of a system that performs reasonably well, according to some performance criteria, with reasonable resources, and in a timely fashion. A corollary to James's philosophy is that the human brain is only as well-developed as it needs to be.

Another important result from James's work is that mental concepts *need to be studied in the context or environment in which they occur*. Consider, for example, these ideas:

- Reasoning processes are not developed in a vacuum. (This is a consequence of nature and man, including man's reasoning and survival ability, evolving together.)

  (1-3*a*)
- Reasoning processes may be adaptations of previous strategies. (1-3*b*)
- Reasoning processes are often application-dependent. (1-3*c*)

DISCRIMINATION AND ASSOCIATION. Furthermore, James surmised that the principles of *discrimination* and *association* are of paramount importance in exploring human reasoning, which involves breaking down and building up concepts. This is recognized as one of the basic strategies for AI knowledge representation development. This in turn

- Suggests the utility of hierarchical structures. (1-4*a*)
- Invokes the principle of connections or associations between thoughts. (1-4*b*)

James also noted that there seem to be "mechanical" conditions upon which thoughts depend. This suggests a sequence or time-varying pattern to thoughts, not unlike the formulation of plans. Of course, this sequence may be dictated by the causal aspects of the problem under consideration. Furthermore, the repeated co-occurrence of two "things thought of" tends to reinforce a link between these entities. This, as we see in later chapters, is one version of learning.

Finally, it is worth noting that human intelligence is not based upon immutable facts, or truths, and logic. Rather, experience and intuition (instinct) may also play roles. This is particularly evident in situations where humans develop (sometimes clever) problem-solving "shortcuts" that circumvent the computational complexity of brute-force automated solutions.

Why is AI Difficult?

AN ELUSIVE MODEL. AI concerns *relating mental models to real-world computation*. We temporarily defer a basic question in AI research: how closely should human intelligence paradigms be simulated? The precise form of internal representations used by humans is vague and often dependent upon the specific concept. Furthermore, humans record visual or iconic images of many concepts, and can recall such images from sentences. For example, the phrase "at the beach" may generate a different recalled iconic image for each imaginer. Surprisingly, we appear to know a great deal more about our physiological functioning (e.g., operation of the heart, immune systems and nutrition) than the underlying operation of our conscious and subliminal mental processes. These cognitive processes are complex (why do we need twelve years of schooling after we have reached the age of five?) and not always quantifiable or logical. For example, few human cognitive processes appear to be entirely representable by simple IF, THEN, ELSE structures familiar to programmers.

Another complication is the significant distinction between data and knowledge. There are also numerous examples of successful managers (including presidents and coaches) who consistently make correct decisions based upon unexplainable inner (or "gut") "feelings." The clear need is for *algorithms* that describe the reasoning process and thereby facilitate the mechanization of reasoning. Thus, we are faced with what may be one of the most significant "system identification" problems of all time.

- Underlying Artificial Intelligence (AI) research efforts is an implicit assumption that human-like reasoning is a form of computation that may be identified and consequently automated. (1-5)

The goals of *identification* and *automation* of intelligent behavior give rise to the two major impediments to success in AI:

1. It is difficult, at best, to identify or, more specifically, *quantify* human intellectual capability in a form that lends itself to direct computer implementation. Abstraction of brain functions is an endeavor that has kept psychologists and cognitive scientists busy for decades. In other words, a "knowledge calculus" does not presently exist. Another way to express this is to claim that what is lacking is the model for intelligence, from which algorithmic emulations may be developed. Unfortunately, it appears that intelligence is an elusive and subjective concept, whose instantiations are not easily or directly converted into a model-based response. While we may describe facets of intelligent behavior, such as reasoning capability,

interpretation of visual information, and learning, the exact description of the mechanisms underlying these facets are elusive. Humans often muddle through a number of vague knowledge forms, employing subliminal processes, analogy, "common sense," heuristics, or even "intuition" to arrive at "intelligent" solutions to problems. Our inability to accurately define and quantify broad areas of "natural intelligence" suggests that the development of any "artificial intelligence" system will be, at the very least, challenging. Nonetheless, numerous examples of successful autonomous systems that exhibit human-like behavior provide an impetus for further development.

2. Even with current computing resources, the implementation of simplistic AI systems often yields problems of tremendous complexity. This remark will be amply verified in our exploration of algorithms that rely on *recursion and search*. Thus, languages and architectures that facilitate these operations are of fundamental interest.

PUZZLE SOLVING, (RIDDLES) AND INTELLIGENCE. There is a spectrum of opinion concerning what constitutes (automated) intelligent behavior. We digress briefly to evaluate the utility of approaching AI systems development using problem domains taken from well-known puzzles and games. Examples are the games of tic-tac-toe and chess, the "fox and chickens" puzzle, the Tower of Hanoi puzzle, and a plethora of similar "brain teasers."

Explicit formulations and solutions to many of these puzzles are complex. Solving these puzzles indicates some level of autonomous problem-solving capability; however,   (1-6)

1. The solution to many typical puzzles may be accomplished by an exhaustive (but relatively unsophisticated) search procedure, whereas humans often formulate a more elaborate or "clever" solution.

2. The representation of many real-world AI problems is considerably more complex than that of puzzles. For example, in practical problems, many more constraints are applicable, uncertainty is present, and conflicts may arise requiring further definition of the problem. The representation for a puzzle, however, may be as simple as the state of a chessboard.

3. It is not clear that solutions to puzzles extrapolate to solutions to realistic problems.

Nevertheless, the study of AI solutions to puzzle-like problems has merit. One benefit is that solutions to puzzles illustrate important concepts such as search. Furthermore, these solutions provide vehicles to explore the representation and programming details of more realistic problems. Finally, they may be used to illustrate the utility of heuristic-based solutions.

CENTRAL THEMES IN AI

Overview of Concepts

A number of themes recur in the study of AI systems. Fundamental to AI system development is the concept of

- Knowledge representation, structure, "meaning," and acquisition.

  Other basic and related themes are

- Inference/control (manipulation) strategies.
- Ability to learn/adapt (from experience, examples, or a "teacher").
- Representation of uncertainty and incomplete reasoning.
- Search and matching techniques
- Unification and resolution.
- Nonmonotonic reasoning (retracting conclusions based on newly revised information or beliefs).
- Empiricism ("generate and test").
- Problem decomposition, or reducing overall goals to subgoals.
- Problem dynamics (changes with time).
- Types of reasoning (e.g., deduction, induction, common sense).
- Satisfaction with "good" versus optimal solutions; also, questions concerning the existence of a solution.
- Relevant programming/representation languages for implementation and associated architectures.

To Search or Not to Search
(The Knowledge-Search Tradeoff)

We acknowledge a ubiquitous problem in AI systems development:

- Problems associated with computational complexity and search are (typically) inherent in the implementation of AI systems.   (1-7)

    The potential database size and associated computational complexity of realistic AI implementations have been projected. One assertion is that a minimum of 10^6 "elements of knowledge" would be required for "very great intelligence" [Minsky 1968]. This estimated volume of "facts" or knowledge has been corroborated by those attempting medical applications [Pauker 1976], as well as by others [Anderson 1983, Lenat 1984, Lenat/Prakash/Shepherd 1986].

    As we show in Chapter 15, most AI problems exhibit characteristics of exponential growth and combinatorial explosion. This is especially apparent in empirical solution approaches employing trial-and-error (e.g., generate-and-test) or random selection. To avoid this pitfall, the formulation of solution strategies to search-based problems using an intelligent component is desirable. This may be viewed as trading brute-force computation for "insight" or "cleverness" in the solution procedure. Thus, *knowledge facilitates efficient search.* Surprisingly, however, we may also assert that *search facilitates incomplete knowledge.* An example is the previously mentioned trial-and-error solution.

MATHEMATICAL PRELIMINARIES

There are several areas of mathematics that provide useful tools for the study of AI. For example, the theory of logic is addressed in Chapter 2. Presently, we develop the mathematical basis of both symbolic and numerical relations, which in turn introduces the concepts of functions, graphs, digraphs, and semantic networks. Appendix 1 ("Discrete Mathematics Review") provides a more in-depth look at these and related topics.

Stored Knowledge, Descriptions, and Relations

We begin by considering the linguistic relation between two entities, x and y, which may be symbols, numbers, actions, or concepts. Consider, for example,

$$\text{attribute } R \text{ of object } x \text{ has value } y \tag{1-8}$$

For modeling purposes one view of (1-8) might be that x and R are arguments to a function, denoted f_y, that returns y; that is,

$$y = f_y(x, R) \tag{1-9}$$

If the domains of x and R are finite sets, we can represent this linguistic relation as the ordered triple

$$(R, x, y) \tag{1-10}$$

which is in the (attribute, object, value), or (A, O, V), format. This is read as

$$\text{"the } A \text{ of } O \text{ is } V." \tag{1-11}$$

An alternative is to view this as a *relation* (in a more strict mathematical sense); that is,

$$\text{"}x \text{ is related to } y \text{ by } R\text{"} \tag{1-12}$$

or graphically,

$$\begin{array}{c} R \\ x \ \rightarrow \ y \end{array} \tag{1-13}$$

Representation and manipulation of relations among entities are fundamental to AI. Certain representations are perceived as being more natural in given situations. As we see in the semantic net section that follows, descriptions used in a representation are often relations. Furthermore, the ability to characterize relations and relation properties mathematically often leads to concise and tractable representations.

RELATIONS AND EXAMPLES.

• If A and B are sets, a **relation** from A to B is a subset of $A \times B$. (1-14)

Here $A \times B$ denotes the Cartesian product of the sets A and B.

This definition is mathematically precise and somewhat esoteric. It is referred to as a *binary relation* since it only involves two sets, and provides a way of "connecting" members of the sets. Exactly how the sets are connected and the properties of this connection, or relation, are of interest. We investigate this concept via several examples.

Relations that involve symbolic quantities are of significant interest in AI. Relations between entities may involve *positional*, *temporal* or *procedural aspects*. For example, suppose we have been given a pre-processed image with several extracted regions, as shown in Fig. 1.3. The regions are given symbol labels, which are elements of the set

$$L = \{a, \ b, \ c, \ d\}$$

We proceed to develop a relationship between these labels (a subset of $L \times L$) that denotes "contained inside of" or "enclosed within." This is shown in Fig. 1.3(*b*) using a *directed graph* or *digraph*. In Chapter 5 this image processing formulation is extended using constraint satisfaction and the PROLOG language.

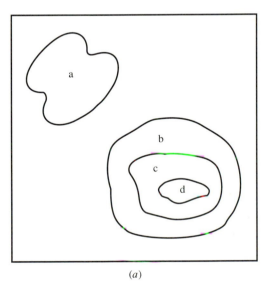

(*a*)

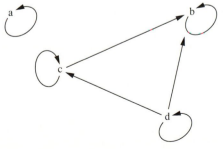

(*b*)

FIGURE 1.3
Simple example of a relation using processed image data: (*a*) image data (Regions), (*b*) relation "contained in," for regions depicted in (*a*), shown as Digraph.

RELATIONS AND PROPERTIES. The concept of an entity possessing a property or attribute is important in modeling. Properties may include color, age, function, application, and so forth. For example, we may wish to represent the fact that a "computer has chips." In terms of the previously defined *relation*, we could merely note that the relation "has" or, more specifically, "has-attribute" includes the *ordered pair* (computer, chips). This representation, although correct, is somewhat cumbersome. Instead, we often loosely speak of chips as one value of a *property* ("has" or "part-of") attributed to computer. Furthermore, this type of property representation may loosely be called a *unary relation*, although it does not fit the previous definition. The use of relations represented as properties, such as "has," "is-a," and "could-be," forms an important part of the semantic net representational scheme, explored later.

The inherent directionality or ordering of relations gives rise to a number of relation properties. We consider three properties of prime importance for a relation R, which form a mapping from sets A to B.

1. *reflexive*: R is reflexive if, for all $a \in A$, $(a,a) \in R$.   (1-15*a*)

2. *symmetric*: R is symmetric if, for all $(a,b) \in R$, $(b,a) \in R$.   (1-15*b*)

3. *transitive*: R is transitive if, for all $(a,b) \in R$ and $(b,c) \in R$, $(a,c) \in R$.   (1-15*c*)

TERNARY (AND HIGHER ORDER) RELATIONS AND CONSTRAINTS. The binary relations previously considered form an important structure for studying constraint satisfaction problems. Whereas binary relations describe relationships between objects on a pairwise basis, the reader may wonder about relations (or perhaps constraints) among triples of objects, quadruples of objects, and so on. In other words, the representation of ordinarily encountered *non-binary relations* is of interest. Fortunately, two things occur:

1. Ternary and quarternary (and higher order) relations may be shown to be defined via a straightforward extension of the set-based derivation for the binary case.

2. Ternary and quarternary (and higher order) relations, as will be shown, may be cast in terms of ordered n-tuples, which in turn may be viewed as ordered pairs (each pair consisting of an $(n - 1)$-tuple and a single element), and therefore may be studied within the framework of binary relations.

A ternary relation among objects of the three sets A, B, and C is defined as a subset of the Cartesian product of the two sets $(A \times B) \times C$, and described by ordered triples of the form $((a,b),c)$. Note that each element of the relation may be viewed as an ordered pair where the first term itself is an ordered pair. Similarly, a quarternary relation among four sets A,B,C, and D is defined as a subset of $(((A \times B) \times C) \times D)$, and described by ordered quadruples of the form $(((a,b),c),d)$. Again, we may view the description of this relation in terms of ordered pairs, the first element being $((a,b),c)$ and the second, d.

RELATIONAL TABLES. Binary and higher-order relations, such as ternary and quarternary, are more conveniently described by *relational tables*. These tables enumerate

TABLE 1.1
Relational table for the relation of Fig. 1.4

Set *A* element	Set *B* element
a	*b*
b	*c*
b	*d*
b	*a*
c	*c*
d	*a*

the relation as ordered *n*-tuples in tabular form. Table 1.1 shows a relational table corresponding to the binary relation of Fig. 1.4.

Finally, a non-binary relation is representable using a graphical approach (cf. semantic nets in the following section). For example, the ternary relation

the road, trees, and car are adjacent

may be depicted by a graph with nodes composed of the representational primitives "road," "trees," "car," and "adjacent," with an arc from each of the first three to the "adjacent" node.

Semantic Nets

FROM DIGRAPH TO SEMANTIC NET. The use of graphical constructs to specify both numerical and symbolic relations among sets of entities is fundamental to many knowledge representation approaches. In fact, the careful structuring of this construct (e.g., such that it may be efficiently decomposed into tightly coupled subgraphs) is fundamental to many efficient schemes for knowledge manipulation.

- A semantic network, or simply **semantic net**, is a labeled digraph used to describe relations (including properties) of objects, concepts, situations, or actions.   (1-16)

Semantic nets are ideal visualization tools, widely used in AI to provide a mechanism to "get started" in the development of a knowledge representation. Knowledge in a semantic net may be naturally organized to reflect hierarchies and enable inheritance (Chapter 16). Because a semantic net representation denotes relations as labeled

FIGURE 1.4
Digraph for $R = \{ (a,b), (b,c), (b,d), (b,a), (c,c), (d,a) \}$.

arcs, an algorithm for reasoning using semantic nets may make relevant associations simply by matching observed (or stored) evidence with the graphical structure.

Unfortunately, for most reasonable representations of our knowledge about even a very restricted subject, the overall semantic net is usually a large and highly interconnected entity. This causes major difficulty in the *matching*, or unifying, of observed features or entities and their properties in accordance with the structure indicated by the semantic net. Considering the possible numbers of matches for each node, it is easy to see how combinatorial explosion may occur.

SEMANTIC NET EXAMPLES. A semantic net represents *objects as nodes* (shown as circles) and *relations as labeled arcs* (or edges). For "real-world" entities, the nets are usually quite complicated. A relatively simple semantic net for a "blocks world" problem is shown in Fig. 1.5. Figure 1.6 shows a portion of a semantic net for a typical vehicle description. Here are some remarks concerning these figures:

1. Often, the semantic net consists of many different edge types, or relations; examples include "is-a," "has-attribute," "used-for," "adjacent-to."
2. The semantic network may contain redundant or "derivable" information. For example, the "left-of" and "right-of" arcs between nodes A and B in Fig. 1.5(*b*), while both correct, are redundant, since given one, the other may be deduced. This requires, for example, an explicit rule indicating that the existence of an arc labeled "right" allows the inference of a converse arc labeled "left." In addition, the enumeration of other information, such as the transitivity of the relation "on-

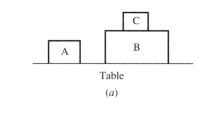

(*a*)

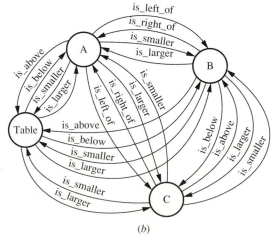

(*b*)

FIGURE 1.5
Semantic net representation of "Blocks World" (*a*) system, (*b*) semantic net.

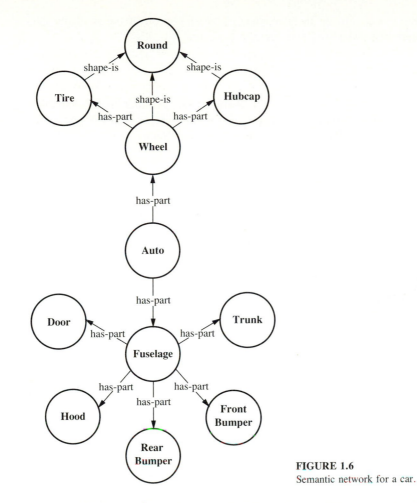

FIGURE 1.6
Semantic network for a car.

top-of," allows the deduction of additional arcs. This approach often allows the semantic net to be written in an uncluttered form while retaining the desired representation in the form of a "skeletal" semantic net and a set of underlying explicit rules.

3. The type of representation shown in Fig. 1.5, when practical, is of fundamental importance when designing knowledge-based systems. We note that our objective is to reduce the information in this semantic net (and any other information, such as properties of the network relations) into a *symbolically tractable* representation.[1]

---

[1]The meaning of the phrase "symbolically tractable" is not universally agreed upon. It facilitates our discussions by providing a reminder that a fundamental subgoal of AI systems development is to develop representations for the knowledge underlying a system in a form that is primarily *symbolic* and that, in order to be useful, must lend itself to *manipulation*. The phrase does not conflict with the concept of mathematical tractability, which means "manipulable with known and valid mathematical tools" (e.g., calculus is mathematically tractable). Mathematically tractable models form the basis of many engineering subject areas.

For example, as we will see in later chapters, a subportion of the semantic net may be represented using predicate logic in the form

```
on_top_of(B,  table)
```

4. The type of representation in Fig. 1.5 is useful in our exploration of *planning*, where a set of operators may be applied to the entities (blocks) in the system to change the state of the system, that is, to change the relations among the blocks and, consequently, the semantic net.

Representations That Attempt to Convey "Meaning"

AN EXAMPLE OF THE DIFFICULTY. Consider the fragment of music notated in Fig. 7.2 (Chapter 7). This symbolic representation illustrates the difficulty in representing "deep" meaning or even intensional knowledge, since

- To a nonmusician, the notes are mere symbols on a page. The information on the page could be scanned or converted to other (e.g., MIDI) representations.
- To an experienced musician, the data represented can be "interpreted" or "heard," and therefore may contain emotions, through the sequence of various dissonances and resolutions. This representation therefore evokes a deeper set of "moods."

CONCEPTUAL GRAPHS. Conceptual graphs are used, like semantic nets, to represent concepts, actions, and situations using *conceptual relations*, thus forming a *conceptualization*. At the very least, the conceptualization involves an *agent* and an *act*. An example is shown in Fig. 1.7. Note that boxes represent concepts and circles indicate conceptual relation(s). Conceptual relations indicate the role that an entity plays in the representation, and thus facilitate the determination of "who does what to whom." Hence, in conceptualizations, *causal interactions* as well as general relations are shown. Conceptual graphs offer an advantage over semantic nets in that semantics, or meaning, may be explicitly represented.

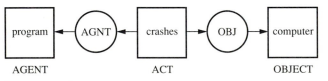

AGENT   ACT   OBJECT

boxes: concepts
circles: conceptual relations

FIGURE 1.7
Conceptual graph for "the program crashes the computer."

THE ROLE OF KNOWLEDGE REPRESENTATIONS AND COMPUTATIONAL MODELS IN AI

Why Models?

In most scientific or engineering disciplines, it would be foolhardy to seek meaningful solutions to a problem for which there was not an explicit or approximate model. For example, few control engineers would attempt to develop control strategies for electrical, mechanical, or chemical systems for which models, consisting of circuit relations, differential equations, chemical reaction equations, material stress-strain characteristics, and so on, were not available or derivable. In fact, the first part of the engineering process would be a careful characterization of the underlying model. Thus, we would call any algorithmic results "model-based."

"THE MODEL CONSTRUCTION BOTTLENECK." Interestingly, this engineering tenet is not directly transferable, via analogy, to AI system development efforts. Although it may seem strange or even heretical to suggest, there may not always be an explicit model underlying the development of an AI system. However, what does exist is *a large body of knowledge related to the application at hand*, including input-output or cause-effect relationships, a priori information, heuristics, and so forth. This situation is akin to the approach taken in nonparametric (statistical) pattern-recognition designs: a great deal of information (labeled "samples" or "training sets") is available, from which an underlying model may be estimated. However, we may choose to use the information directly rather than through the auspices of a formal model. Note that this would not preclude the employment of a formal representation for this information, if one may be derived.

LEVELS OF AI MODEL DEVELOPMENT. In any attempt at modeling and implementing high level conceptual processes, we identify three development stages, as shown in Fig. 1.8. These are the *conceptual (M)*, *representational (R)*, and *implementational (I)* levels. As will be shown later, a formal relation between M and R, denoted $\mathscr{S}$, exists. Note also that Fig. 1.8 indicates that a practical model is incomplete, that is, it is not possible to model exhaustively all aspects of a situation. The level of completeness for the model is a function of the available features, and determines to some extent the range of applicability of the model. We will examine this from an abstract viewpoint.

Model-based reasoning (MBR) examples. The dichotomy between model-based and intuitive reasoning strategies may be shown via simple examples.

> **Example 1.1   Intuitive versus model-based reasoning.** People usually duck to avoid being hit by flying objects. This is an intelligent, but more importantly, nonmodel-based response. The stored knowledge leading up to this response might be a sequence of reasoning steps involving the observation that an object is on a trajectory that passes through their current location, the fact that if they get hit with this object it will probably hurt, and the recollection that being hurt is an unfavorable situation. Note that nowhere

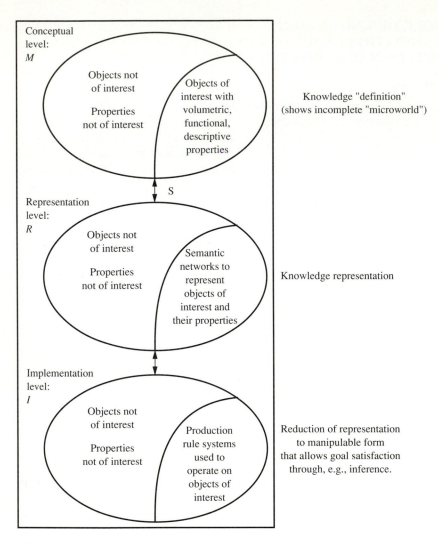

FIGURE 1.8
Stages of model development.

in this reasoning chain is there reference to an explicit model including the motion parameters of the object and all the associated laws of physics connected with objects in motion, nor all the physiological models associated with the effects of projectile impact upon human tissue.

Example 1.2   MBR in diagnosis. A second example of this difference may be presented in the following way: Suppose you take your car to an automobile repair facility, knowing that it is not operating correctly. Two mechanics are independently assigned the problem of fixing the vehicle.

The first, the model-based mechanic, immediately refers to the shop manuals (i.e., the documentation composing a model of the automobile, subdivided by component subsystems and functions) and, in parallel, connects the automobile to complex instrumentation apparatus, which indicates engine parameters (air/fuel ratio, vacuum, wheel alignment, etc.). Using the information from this equipment, together with the repair manualbased model, the mechanic first determines that the air/fuel ratio is incorrect and, further, that this is a function of a number of parameters and possible maladies. The various possible underlying problems (e.g., fouled fuel injectors) are tested individually. After determining that the solution to this problem merely involves the periodic adjustment of this engine parameter by screw S1 (located in an obscure and unreachable location under the hood), the mechanic makes the adjustment and the car runs properly.

The second mechanic, immediately upon seeing the automobile symptoms, remarks: "Oh yeah—we had Mr. Bennett's car in here yesterday with the same problem. All we need to do is turn screw S1 on the fuel injector unit half a turn." Whereupon the mechanic performs the service, the car runs well, a large repair bill is written up, and the problem is solved.

Note the first mechanic alone actually *diagnosed* the problem; the second mechanic merely fixed it. It was not necessary for the second mechanic to *understand* the reason underlying the vehicle problem. Bear in mind, however, that if several different maladies can yield the same symptom, it is only accidental that in this instance the second mechanic solved the problem. The first mechanic compared the state of the system with the model-specified state in order to ascertain the repair that made the states coincident; the second mechanic, on the other hand, employed a knowledge representation of the form

```
IF
     car behaves in specific way
         AND
     it is desired to make it run in a desired way
         AND
     the symptom is a ....

THEN
     turn screw S1 1/2 turn.
```

The example illustrates the fact that "intelligent" responses may be evoked with varying levels of underlying "understanding."

AI AS REPRESENTATION AND MANIPULATION. We adopt an "engineering approach" to AI by assuming for the majority of the text that the objective is to *construct a model or representation* of the underlying domain and then to *design one or more reasoning mechanisms* that can be used, together with the model, to *achieve a specific goal*. Achieving this objective with current technology requires that we adopt relatively modest goals. First, let us define a representation:

- A (knowledge) **representation** is a scheme or device used to capture the essential elements of a problem domain. A **manipulable representation** is one that facilitates computation. In manipulable representations, the information is accessible to other entities (e.g., inference engines or unifiers), which use the representation as part of a computation. (1-17)

Due to the variety of forms knowledge may assume, the issues involved in the development of a knowledge representation are complex, interrelated, and goal-dependent. A methodology for building models, which comprise knowledge representations and algorithmic strategies and which are to be used to obtain "intelligent" behavior, addresses the following questions:

- Is the model easily extendable in the current application domain and/or to others?
- Where are the model limitations?
- Does the model efficiently store the desired information?
- Can a human explore or inspect the model easily?
- Does the model contain conflicting or inconsistent information?

Figure 1.9 typifies the steps used in representation development.

OTHER KNOWLEDGE REPRESENTATION CLASSIFICATIONS.

- **Intensional knowledge** is knowledge about connotation, abstract meaning, or utility of a concept. This is often embedded in the inference process.   (1-18a)

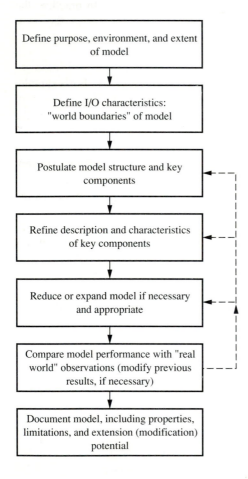

FIGURE 1.9
Steps in AI model development.

- **Extensional knowledge** is knowledge about the set of things denoted by a concept.

  (1-18*b*)
- **Meta-knowledge** is knowledge about knowledge. (1-18*c*)
- **Domain knowledge** is a collection of specific facts (including concepts and relations) and procedures related to the solution of a specific problem; **domain-independent knowledge**, in contrast, consists of more general, problem-independent facts and procedures.
- **Hierarchical representations** allow the modeling of the structure and complex relations among entities. Frames (Chapter 16) are an example. (1-18*d*)

Two additional themes in model-building or representation that should be considered are

1. The determination of the *ideal level of abstraction* of the model. Abstraction allows information to be stored and retrieved from a knowledge structure at different levels of detail and from different perspectives. This is often application-dependent.
2. The *resolution* (or "granularity") and *completeness* of the model. In practice, the failure of a particular AI system might be attributed to this concept (in the sense that adding more knowledge might have led to the correct behavior).

While model-based reasoning is a major theme of this text, we note that model-based achievement of intelligent behavior is not the only approach. For example, the non-algorithmic approach of *neural computing* represents a potentially important paradigm for achieving intelligent behavior. In this approach, the "model" of the environment under consideration is seldom, if at all, explicit.

REPRESENTATIONAL LIMITATIONS. Many of the philosophical questions inherent in cognitive science, such as the achievability of complete emulation of human behavior, are unanswered. Implicitly, we are assuming that psychological processes are typically computational in nature, and therefore that a computational model of cognition can be used to emulate human behavior [Fodor 1983]. The successes achieved to date in AI implementation suggest that, with modest application objectives, this is a reasonable assumption. However, several generic and difficult representation issues remain unresolved; for example,

- What are the trade-offs between the sophistication of control structures and knowledge bases? For example, can a relatively simple control strategy in conjunction with a complex knowledge base achieve the same performance as a sophisticated control strategy and a simplistic knowledge base? (1-19*a*)
- (How) can an initial representation and control strategy be systematically refined on the basis of new knowledge, experience (learning), and perhaps recognition of mistakes? (1-19*b*)

REPRESENTATIONS FOR EXPLANATIONS OF OBSERVED DATA. As shown in Chapter 13 (Fig. 13.15), one of the major roles of a representation is the *explanation* *of observations or unification of observed data* with one or more representations. From an alternative, pattern-recognition-based viewpoint, we seek to determine

- Which representation best explains the observed data? (1-20)

Representation Characteristics

Model-based reasoning (MBR) necessitates developing an explicit, symbolically tractable representation of the structure, principles, and characteristics of the concept for which or about which "intelligence" is desired. The system model may include

- *Concepts*, such as logical subdivisions of the overall system into subsystems.
- *Entities*, such as individual components, or what are often referred to as objects. Objects, at the lowest level, may be decomposed into *primitives*, or atomic elements, which form an elemental basis for a model.
- *Properties, attributes*, and *values* of entities or concepts, such as the color of an object, the function of a subsystem, the response of a sensor, etc. Some of these properties are easy to define and quantify (e.g., weight, age), whereas others defy accurate quantification (e.g., "tall," "smart").
- *Constraints* and *associations* (including relations and causal interactions) among entities. These include things like "contained-in," "causes," etc.

    In addition to these components of a good *knowledge representation*, we note that other desirable characteristics include

- *Applicability*—The model or representation accurately characterizes the system or environment for which AI capability is desired.
- *Completeness* (descriptive adequacy)—The model or representation comprehensively and completely characterizes the system. Often, this is called a *closed* system description, meaning that all the relations and causal interactions between system elements are represented. This property is generally difficult to achieve. Thus, most AI systems are designed for application in a domain-specific "microworld." Note this property could be achieved without exhaustive enumeration of a large number of facts if the relations (and properties) may be cast succinctly in terms of a set of productions, that is, in a manner that allows generation of new relational or property information. This may involve entities "inheriting" properties.
- *Flexibility* and *extendibility*—The model or representation should in general be applicable to a range of situations and changes in, or exceptions to, these situations. Equivalently, it should not necessarily be so tightly focused that a relatively insignificant and perhaps anticipated change in the situation causes complete rejection of the model applicability. For example, an AI medical diagnosis system should be applicable to a range of patients, not just those of a particular sex or age group. In addition, as new diseases become known, it should be possible to add this information to the system. The ease with which modifications may be made to the representation is often referred to as "plasticity."

- *Consistency*—The model or representation should not aid in the production of conflicting conclusions, nor employ a knowledge base with contradictory facts or relations. This is a difficult situation to prevent.
- *Tractability* or *manipulability* (procedural adequacy)—It is of relatively little use to have a model or representation that precludes manipulation of the knowledge in order to achieve some goal (e.g., unification of a structure, confirmation or denial of a hypothesis). This requirement forces, to some extent, the model or representation to straddle the "completely conceptual—completely representable" boundary in order to facilitate computation.
- *Integrability* with observable environment data—Some of the knowledge in the model or representation, embedded as entities, relations, properties, and so on, consists of measurable or observable quantities. For example, in vision applications, the color of a certain object, or its 3-D spatial extent, or its spatial relation (e.g., "left-of") to other objects may be a significant part of the model. Thus, object color must be observable or measurable.
- *Practicality*—This may be the most difficult requirement of all. A model or representation that satisfies all the requirements above may be hopelessly complex.

Notice we did not include the descriptor "robust" in the above model/representation characterization. If a model were to be "robust," we would need to specify some standard with respect to which the model should be robust.

An Abstract View of Modeling

An abstract view of the modeling problem is developed in Brown [1981] for solid modeling applications. We modify these concepts here and apply the definitions to the more abstract representations used in AI.

A **modeling space**, M, is an entity whose elements are abstract entities that capture the relevant aspects of the class of objects for which a model (and consequently a representation) is desired. In the case of a simplistic fluid flow problem, for example, this space includes the laws of physics and differential equations. In the AI case, this space is generally poorly defined, if at all.

Representations, as typified by Fig. 1.10, are symbolic structures that obey syntactic rules. R denotes the space of all representations. A **representation scheme**, S, is a **relation** between M and R. The **domain**, D, of the representational scheme is a subset of M, and characterizes the descriptive power of the scheme. A **valid representation** is one that is a member of the range of a representation scheme. An example of an invalid representation is a nonsensical semantic net; note it has no basis in M.

If S is a function, the representation is unique. A representational scheme is **unambiguous** if S^{-1} (the inverse of the relation) is a single-valued function. Similarly, a representation is **unique** if S is a function. Two representations, r_1 and r_2 in R, determined by respective representation schemes S_1 and S_2 are **consistent** if there exists at least one element, m, of the modeling space M, such that

$$S_1(m) = r_1 \qquad (1\text{-}21a)$$

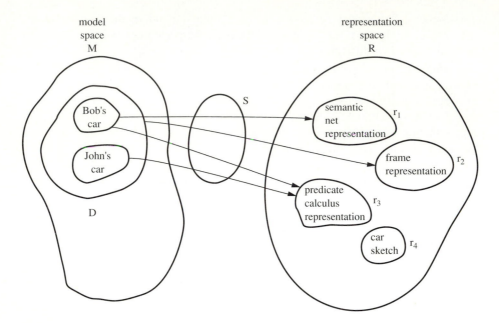

FIGURE 1.10
Abstract view of models and representations.

and

$$S_2(m) \;=\; r_2 \tag{1-21b}$$

Figure 1.10 depicts a simple example of this abstract concept.

The Frame Problem in AI

One of the most fundamental representational problems in AI is the so-called *frame problem* (not to be confused with the concept of the related *frames* data structure). The frame problem is related to the "all-inclusive" requirement of an AI system database. The basis of the frame problem is that it is unreasonable to enumerate exhaustively how a set of facts (the system state) changes as actions or events occur. Most of the difficulty arises in the *persistence* of properties or truth values, which are implicit assumptions in human reasoning. Thus, one succinct definition of the frame problem is [McCarthy/Hayes 1969]

- "The frame problem is that of specifying what doesn't change when an event occurs."   (1-22)

The frame problem has a strong link to other high-level AI topics, such as temporal reasoning, planning, and common-sense reasoning.

    Example 1.3   The "Pool-Table" Scenario. Consider the scenario of Fig. 1.11(*a*). Suppose one objective is to develop a system that, given this initial information, is able

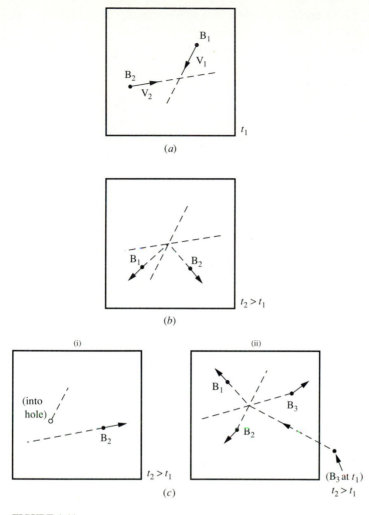

FIGURE 1.11
Illustration of the "Frame Problem" using the "Pool-Table" example: (*a*) initial condition, (*b*) one possible prediction (with implicit assumptions), (*c*) alternate scenarios.

to "reason" about later states of the system. For example, a human observer, schooled in the laws of physics (or a frequent visitor to pool halls!), might predict the scenario shown in Fig.1.11(*b*). Under some (unstated) set of assumptions, the system state in part (*b*) may actually come to pass. This includes assumptions as to uniform friction on the table, lack of significant "crosswinds," lack of other balls (not observed or modeled at t_1) that may cross paths with B_1 and B_2, a level table, no holes in the table into which balls may fall, and so forth. Figure 1.11(*c*) shows other possible scenarios, each the result of different assumptions or a priori information.

Significant characteristics of this example:

1. Predictions were based upon incomplete information (and a hope that ignored factors were insignificant).
2. Humans tend to solve the problem by "visualization."
3. Both symbolic (e.g., existence of holes, other balls) and numerical (e.g., laws of physics) quantitative information was used.
4. Events (such as discovering the presence of a hole in the table) cause a revision of initial assumptions.
5. Predictions of future scenarios for time t close to t_1 (i.e. short time intervals) appear to be more accurate than those for longer time intervals.
6. Fortunately, most facts in real-world reasoning situations are *persistent*, to the extent that they remain unchanged as the result of many actions. For example, the action of painting the exterior of one's house seldom results in rearrangement of the interior furniture [McCarthy/Hayes 1969]. If most facts were not persistent, the world would appear quite chaotic.

SITUATIONS. One formalism for knowledge representations that address the frame problem is the notion of *situations*. Situations are instantaneous snapshots of the system state [McCarthy/Hayes 1969]. They are analogous to individual still frames of a movie. In a movie, adjacent still frames are highly related, whereas frames separated by hundreds of feet of film are not. Clearly, little change between consecutive frames occurs. Thus, the information is persistent. An **action** transfers the system from one situation to another. Situations may be implemented via *frames*, which are described in Chapter 16. Through a set of **frame axioms**, frames are mapped into new frames. It is the axioms that convey the **persistence** of various facts.

ELEMENTARY KNOWLEDGE REPRESENTATION APPROACHES

Procedural versus Declarative Schemes

Knowledge-representation approaches may be subdivided into *declarative* (meaning the representation of facts and assertions) and *procedural* (meaning the storing of actions or consequences) approaches. An alternative characterization of this dichotomy is *knowing what* (declarative) versus *knowing how* (procedural). At this time it appears that AI research emphasis is divided more or less equally between these approaches. In addition, the dichotomy between procedural and declarative representations is no longer considered as clear cut as it once was. The specifics of an application may dictate a preferred approach. A reasonable postulate is that versatile, intelligent machines may need to use both procedural and declarative representations.

Declarative schemes include *logic-based* and *relational* approaches. Relational models may lead to representations in the form of trees, graphs, or semantic networks. Logical representation schemes include the use of propositional logic and, more importantly, predicate logic.

Procedural models and representational schemes store knowledge in *how* to do things. They may be characterized by formal grammars and usually implemented via *procedural* or *rule-based (production) systems*. These are often structured as IF (condition) THEN (action). We explore both of these representational schemes in the examples that follow.

> **Example 1.4 Declarative versus procedural knowledge.** The difference between declarative and procedural schemes may be illustrated by a simple example. A table of logarithms is an *explicit enumeration* of this (numerical) domain knowledge and would be considered a *declarative representation*. On the other hand, a stored sequence of *actions* indicating *how to compute* the logarithm of a number might be considered a procedural representation.

TRADE-OFFS. The preceding example illustrates the trade-offs in using declarative or procedural knowledge representations. Declarative representations are usually more expansive (and expensive), in the sense that enumeration may be redundant and inefficient. However, modification of declarative representations is usually quite easy; one merely adds or deletes the knowledge. Procedural representations, on the other hand, may be more compact, at the expense of flexibility. Practical representations may include both declarative and procedural elements. For example, in subsequent chapters we consider a database consisting of a *list of facts* (declarative) and a related *set of rules* (procedural) to manipulate the fact list.

Selection of Representation Primitives

Manipulation of knowledge involves the *judicious selection of objects, entities or features* that are central to the representations. At the lowest level of knowledge representation, these entities may consist of the raw input data (e.g., digitalized and quantized speech recordings, image data, sensor values, switch settings, or elementary facts). These basic building blocks of the representation are often referred to as **primitives**. The choice of representation primitives may determine system capabilities, success, correctness, and expansion capability.

> **Example 1.5 "Automobile" representation.** The typical American (male or female) is quite adept at the identification and classification of automobiles. Consider the representation of knowledge in an "auto-identification" system. A representation of "auto" could include

$$
\begin{array}{lll}
\text{auto} & \text{HAS-PART} & \text{wheels} \\
& \text{HAS-ID} & \text{owner} \\
& \text{HAS-LOCATIONS} & \text{exterior and interior} \\
& \text{HAS-PART} & \text{roof} \\
& \text{HAS-FOR-PROPULSION} & \text{engine} \quad\quad (1\text{-}23)
\end{array}
$$

> Notice relations between the object *auto* and a spectrum of other objects (wheels, owner,...). Furthermore, each of these objects may itself be a part of other relations:

```
wheel       HAS-PART                  tire
            MAY-HAVE-PART             spokes
            MAY-HAVE-PART             fancy-hub-cap
            IS                        round
                UNLESS
                     IS flat
```

and

```
roof
            LOCATION-IS               (usually) highest-point
            MAY-BE-TYPE               convertible                    (1-24)
```

Thus, the representation of "auto" is generally quite complicated and somewhat hierarchical. Note the use of specific relations such as HAS-PART and HAS-LOCATION tend to reduce ambiguity compared with simply using HAS.

An alternative representation includes a rule-based approach. The logical basis for rule-based representations is reviewed in Chapter 2. For example, the relations postulated in (1-23) and (1-24) may be encoded as a set of rules in antecedent-consequent form. An example of this, using the variable (? entity), might be

Example 1.6   Abstract rule representation.

```
IF    (? entity)      HAS-PART spokes AND IS round
OR    (? entity)      HAS-PART fancy-hub-cap AND IS round
THEN  (? entity) MAY BE wheel.
```

and

```
IF (? entity)
       HAS-ATTRIBUTES wheels owner roof . . .
THEN (? entity) ISA auto
     OR (? entity) ISA mobile-home
     OR (? entity) ISA . . .
     OR (? entity) IS unknown.                                      (1-25)
```

REPRESENTATIONS FOR MATCHING/RECOGNITION. Identification of the variable (? entity), in the representation of (1-25), necessitates some type of matching process. Similarly, an *inference mechanism* may be used in conjunction with the rule-based system to conclude (or hypothesize and prove) that the entity under observation belongs to the class "auto." More importantly (and practically), problem ambiguity and feature uncertainty may necessitate *reasoning with uncertainty* (Chapter 13). Furthermore, we may be more concerned with input structure and relations than numerical values of features, thus necessitating a study of *structural object description* (Chapter 7). Note that the concept of an "object" is quite general. For example, an object might be a musical composition, a 3-D scene, or a sentence.

INTRODUCTION TO FRAME REPRESENTATIONS. We have seen previously the utility of a network knowledge representation, leading to the semantic net. The concept of frames allows a structured and somewhat higher-level abstracted knowledge representation. Frames, and their corresponding properties, allow the system attention to remain focused. From the implementation viewpoint, frames are related to generalized property lists, or association lists.

> **Example 1.7 Blocks World frame fragment.** We may alternatively represent the information shown in Fig. 1.5 as an extension of a set of "combined" tables, as shown:

```
Frame:  Block  A
slots:                         values:
        is-left-of             Block B*
                               Block C*
        is-above               Table
        is-smaller             Block B
         .
         .
         .

*Note these entities are also frames.                    (1-26)
```

State Space Representations and Control

THE CONCEPT OF A SYSTEM STATE SPACE. For a given concept, the choice of a model and especially the corresponding representation is not unique; the options include clauses, predicate calculus, lists, vector-matrix forms, and so on. Once a representation is chosen, we are able to describe the interrelated concepts of *state representation*, *system state*, *system state-space*, and *problem space*. These concepts are fundamental to analysis of puzzle solving, rule-based inference, and planning. Furthermore, they indicate the potential problems associated with *search* and computational complexity, which are treated throughout the text and emphasized in Chapter 15.

The **system state**, or **state description**, contains the set of all information, in the context of the chosen representation, that describes the current status of the system. It is a somewhat abstract concept until we consider specific examples of *state representations*. States S_i and S_g denote the initial and goal states, respectively, of a system. The **system state-space**, or **problem space**, is the domain of all possible system states. This is shown in Fig. 1.12 for the "checkerboard" problem (Chapters 14 and 15). Each state is designated by the location of blocks A and B (i.e., the initial state is ($A4$, $B8$)). Operators such as "move up" and "move left" are used to modify the state of the system. Often the state-space is infinite or practically infinite.

SATISFYING GOALS VIA STATE MANIPULATION WITH OPERATORS. Figure 1.13 indicates the overall objective of many AI systems where S_i and S_g are shown abstractly. Mechanisms for state modification or transformation are identified as *operators*, *productions*, or *actions* and are used *to link the initial and goal states*. Thus,

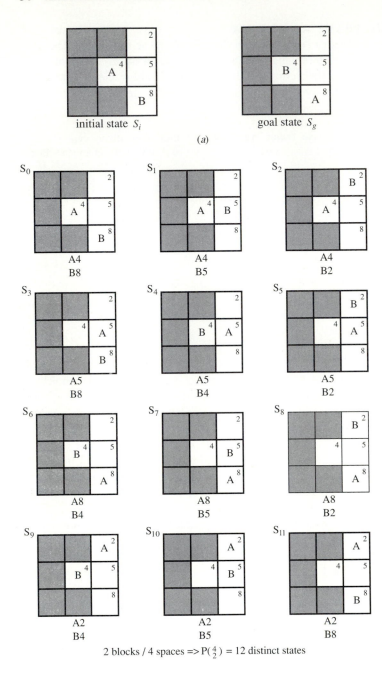

FIGURE 1.12
Sample problem and state space (graphical representation): (a) S_i and S_g (b) state space.

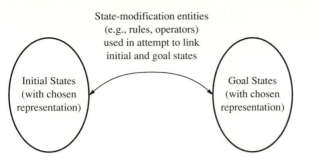

FIGURE 1.13
Generalized view of AI problems as prelude to search.

- Operators (or productions or actions) are a means to control or change the system state. Operator application is constrained by appropriate system states and generally changes the system state. Typical examples of operators are rules (Chapters 11–13) and planning actions (Chapter 14). (1-27)

When solutions or sequences of operators linking S_i with S_g exist, it is desirable to develop AI algorithms such that these sequences are identified. Since the number of possible operator sequences to be explored in the development of a solution is usually large, solution methods that do not require enumeration of all possible sequences are desirable. This again suggests a problem in searching for a sequence of solution steps. If we begin at S_i and proceed (we hope) towards S_g, *data-driven search* may be employed. Conversely, working from S_g to S_i ("backward") exemplifies *goal-directed search*. While many AI texts choose to begin with the subject of search, it is deferred here until we consider logic programming, rule-based approaches, and planning, in order to appreciate more fully the need for search techniques. Search problems are closely related to those of optimization.

Characteristics of AI Algorithms

Certain fundamental questions regarding the relation between the existence and multiplicity of AI problem solutions and the "quality" of AI algorithms used to generate these solutions arise. These include the following:

- Does a solution to the problem exist?
- If so, is a particular algorithm certain to find it?
- Will this algorithm find the "good" solution if more than one exists?
- Can the algorithm (be modified to) find all solutions to the problem?
- How complex is the solution algorithm?
- Does a simpler solution procedure exist?
- Is there a choice of problem representation that leads to a better/simpler solution? (1-28)

TOPICAL OUTLINE

Many of the questions raised in this introduction will be taken up again in later chapters. The following outline gives an overview of the text (in three parts) by topic.

PART I:

> what is AI?
>
> knowledge representation
>
> symbolic logic and variables
>
> predicate functions
>
> relations and graphs
>
> unification
>
> applicative, declarative, and imperative languages
>
> constraint-satisfaction problems
>
> PROLOG
>
> predicate-based databases (PROLOG)
>
> labeling, language understanding, and power examples

PART II:

> symbolic matching
>
> LISP
>
> list-based-representations manipulation
>
> problem decomposition
>
> production systems and structures
>
> rule-based systems
>
> "expert" systems
>
> inference (forward and backward) techniques
>
> inference engine control mechanisms
>
> OPS5 production system language
>
> reasoning with uncertainty

PART III:

> search
>
> planning
>
> is-a hierarchies, frames, and blackboards
>
> learning
>
> temporal reasoning
>
> AI system architectures

ANCILLARY REFERENCES

Throughout the study of AI, a number of topics arise that may readily be explored in more depth. We cite here references that give a good introductory treatment of these topics or that elaborate on the coverage herein. Specifically, those references forming the core of an "AI library" might be categorized as follows:

Programming language references

1. Brooks, Programming in Common LISP, Wiley, 1985.
2. Clocksin and Mellish, Programming in PROLOG, Springer Verlag, 1984.
3. Willinsky, LISPCRAFT, Norton, 1984.

AI references (books)

1. Charniak and McDermott, *Introduction to Artificial Intelligence: Concepts, Techniques, and Applications*, Wiley, 1982.
2. *The Encyclopedia of Artificial Intelligence*, (Shapiro, Ed.), Wiley, 1987.
3. Feigenbaum and Barr, *Handbook of Artificial Intelligence*, William Kaufman, 1982.
4. Genesereth and Nilsson, *Logical Foundations of Artificial Intelligence*, Morgan Kaufman, 1988.
5. Nilsson, *Principles of Artificial Intelligence*, Tioga, 1980.
6. Rich, *Artificial Intelligence*, McGraw-Hill, 1983.
7. Rose, *Into the Heart of the Mind* (a layman's introduction), Harper and Row, 1984.
8. Shirai and Tsujii, *Artificial Intelligence: Concepts, Techniques, and Applications*, Wiley, 1984.
9. Tanimoto, *The Elements of Artificial Intelligence*, Computer Science Press, 1987.
10. Winston, *Artificial Intelligence*, Addison-Wesley, 1984.

AI references (periodicals)

1. *ACM (Association for Computing Machinery) Transactions and Special Interest Group (SIG) Proceedings.*
2. *AI Magazine* (a publication of the American Association for Artificial Intelligence (AAAI)).
3. *Artificial Intelligence Journal*, Elsevier Science Publication.
4. *Cognitive Science.*
5. *Computational Intelligence.*
6. *Computational Linguistics.*
7. *Computer Vision, Graphics, and Image Processing* (for image processing-related work).
8. *IEEE Transactions on Pattern Analysis and Machine Intelligence.*

REFERENCES

[Anderson 1983] Anderson, J., *The Architecture of Cognition*, Harvard University Press, Cambridge, MA, 1983.
[Brown 1981] Brown, C.M., "Some Mathematical and Representational Aspects of Solid Modeling," *IEEE Transactions PAMI*, Vol. PAMI-3, No. 4, July 1981, pp. 444–453.
[Carnap 1956] Carnap, R., *Meaning of Necessity*, University of Chicago Press, Chicago, 1956.
[Feigenbaum/McCorduck 1983] Feigenbaum, E.A., and P. McCorduck, *The Fifth Generation: Artificial Intelligence and Japan's Challenge to the World*, Addison-Wesley, Reading, MA., 1983.
[Fodor 1983] Fodor, J., *The Modularity of Mind*, MIT Press, Cambridge, MA, 1983.
[Gevarter 1985] Gevarter, W. B., *Intelligent Machines: An Introductory Perspective on Artificial Intelligence and Robotics*, Prentice Hall, 1985.
[James 1890] James, William, *Psychology (Briefer Course)*, Holt, New York., 1890, (esp. Chapter XVI, "Association").
[Johnsonbaugh 1986] Johnsonbaugh, R., *Discrete Mathematics*, Macmillan, New York, 1986.
[Leitch 1987] Leitch, R. R., "Artificial Intelligence: The Emergence of a Formal Basis for Engineering," *IEEE Proc. Part D: Control Theory and Application*, Institution of Electrical Engineers (London), Vol. 132, No. 4, July 1987, p. 216.
[Lenat 1984] Lenat, D., "Computer Software for Intelligent Systems," *Scientific American*, Vol 251, 1984, pp. 204–213.
[Lenat 1986] Lenat, D., M. Prakash, and M. Shepherd, "CYC: Using Common Sense Knowledge to Overcome Brittleness and Knowledge Acquisition Bottlenecks," *AI Magazine*, Vol. 6, 1986, pp. 65–85.
[Liu 1977] Liu, C. L., *Elements of Discrete Mathematics*, McGraw-Hill, New York, 1977.

[Mackworth 1977] Mackworth, A. K., "Consistency in Networks of Relations," *Artificial Intelligence*, Vol. 8, 1977, pp. 99–118.

[McCarthy/Hayes 1969] McCarthy, J., and P. J. Hayes, "Some Philosophical Problems From the Standpoint of Artificial Intelligence," *Machine Intelligence 4*, Meltzer/Michie, Eds., Edinburgh University Press, Edinburgh, 1969.

[Minsky 1968] Minsky, M., Ed., *Semantic Information Processing*, MIT Press, Cambridge, MA, 1968.

[Pauker 1976] Pauker, S., G. Gorry, J. Cassirer, and H. Schwarz, "Toward the Simulation of Clinical Cognition: Taking a Present Illness by Computer," *American Journal of Medicine*, Vol. 60, 1976, pp. 981–996.

[Pylyshyn 1984] Pylyshyn, W., *Computation and Cognition: Toward a Foundation for Cognitive Science*, MIT Press, 1984.

[Reddy 1988] Reddy, Raj, "Foundations and Grand Challenges of Artificial Intelligence," *AI Magazine*, Vol. 9, No. 4, Winter 1988, pp. 9–21.

[Rukeyser 1988] Rukeyser, L., *Business Almanac*, Simon and Schuster, New York, 1988, p. 5.

[Schank 1987] Schank, R. C., "What is AI, Anyway," *AI Magazine*, Vol. 8, No. 4, Winter 1987, pp. 59–65.

[Sowa 1984] Sowa, J. F., *Conceptual Structures*, Addison-Wesley, Reading, MA, 1984.

[Topa/Kegley/Schalkoff 1987] Topa, L. C., K. A. Kegley, and R. J. Schalkoff, "High-Level Models for Image Representations," *Proceedings 19th Southeastern Symposium on Systems Theory*, Clemson, SC, March 1987, pp. 144–149.

PROBLEMS

1.1. Formulate a typical and reasonably detailed semantic net for the concept "Engineering Course."

(*a*) Include relations such as "meets," "has," "is-a," "value," and entities such as "homework," "students," "teacher," "classroom," and "time."

(*b*) Describe the properties of the relations used.

(*c*) Consider the use of relations such as "part-of" and "is-a" and comment on the inheritance of properties. Is a hierarchical semantic net representation possible?

1.2. (*a*) Determine a representational structure for a car using the "part-of" relation. For example, consider the entities car, engine, and piston. What properties does this relation have?

(*b*) Use the relation "bordering" to describe the major countries of North America. What properties does this relation have?

1.3. Discuss the representation of ternary constraints using binary relations. In particular, consider the relation "nearby(a,b,c)" as an example. How could properties of the ternary relation be related to binary relation properties?

1.4. For each of the following relations, determine whether the symmetric, reflexive, and/or transitive properties hold.

(i) "derived from"

(ii) "comprised of"

(iii) "near"

(iv) "above"

(v) "larger than"

(vi) "not related to"

(vii) "not larger than"

(viii) "not equal to"

(ix) "not smaller than"

(x) "same size as"

(xi) "uses" (verb)

1.5. Referring to Fig. 1.5,

(*a*) Develop a *complete* semantic net for the blocks world example shown, using the relations

is-left-of
is-right-of
is-on-top-of
is-below
is-larger-than
is-smaller-than
is-adjacent-to

(*b*) Recall that information in a semantic net may be redundant. In the semantic net developed in part (*a*), which arcs (members of a given relation) are derivable from others? Consider both the derivation of additional members of a relation as well as members of other relations.

(*c*) Can the absence of information in a semantic net be used to infer additional relations? For example, suppose we do not have an arc labeled "is-smaller-than" relating blocks A and B. Can we conclude "is-larger-than" holds between blocks B and A? Consider first the case where the semantic net is complete, that is, it enumerates all members of a given relation. (This part of the problem alludes to the concept of *negation-as-failure*, addressed in Chapter 4.)

1.6. Is the relation shown in Fig. 1.4
(i) transitive?

(ii) symmetric?

(iii) reflexive?

1.7. Is a symmetric and transitive relation necessarily reflexive? Show your reasoning and cite examples.

1.8. Describe the difference between knowledge and data; that is, if data is the static encoding of facts, how is knowledge different?

1.9. Discuss situations where abstraction is desirable in the knowledge base, and others where the representation should be explicit.

1.10. Does a conceptual graph (CG) exist for every semantic net? Can a semantic net be derived for every CG?

1.11. Which of the following are declarative representations? Which are procedural? Why?
(i) a cake recipe

(ii) an auto repair manual

(iii) a computer language reference manual

(iv) a set of images of a car acquired from every possible viewing orientation.

(v) $\sqrt{3} = 1.713$

(vi) $\sqrt{x} = \{y \mid y^2 = x\}$

(vii) an iterative algorithm for part (vi).

1.12. Suppose you are sitting at a computer terminal and conversing with a system that is supposedly "intelligent." An example might be Eliza, as shown in Chapter 7. How would you converse with the system to determine intelligent behavior as opposed to a "smart" natural language interface? (Hint: the "Turing Test" is one possibility).

1.13. Cite two examples of a representation, one of which is manipulable and one which is not.

1.14. For the semantic net of a car, shown in Fig. 1.6, develop a frame representation.

1.15. Repeat Problem 1.14 for the descriptions (1-23) and (1-24).

1.16. For the image region data shown in Fig. 1.3(a), show a graphical representation using the relation "larger than."

1.17. The concepts of graphical representation of a (single) relation, a semantic net, and the frame seem to follow a natural, evolutionary sequence in the development of a representation. Using the "blocks" and "car" examples, show how this might occur.

1.18. In the graphical description of a system state shown in Fig. P 1.18, each state is designated by the location of blocks A, B, and C, (i.e., the state shown is (A0, B7, C14)). Assuming that only one block may reside in an unblocked location (blocked locations are shown crosshatched), draw all possible system states.

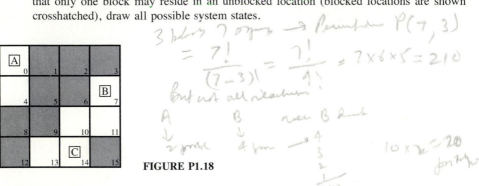

FIGURE P1.18

1.19. Often, problem decomposition and the conversion of goals into subgoals are used to generate solutions to AI problems. Show how an overall goal such as

"make it through the week"

may be recursively decomposed into smaller, less ambitious subgoals.

1.20. How can the granularity of a representation affect the results of reasoning based upon it? For example, consider the following two statements:

- water boils at 100°C   (P1-20a)
- touching objects above 60°C is uncomfortable   (P1-20b)

Suppose we quantify our temperature measure in discrete intervals of

(a) 1°C

(b) 10°C

(c) 50°C

How will conclusions using (P1-20a) and (P1-20b) be affected by each of these granularities?

1.21. (a) Develop suitable definitions and show the distinctions between knowledge, beliefs, hypotheses, and assertions.

(b) How are knowledge and ignorance related?

1.22. (a) How does a model differ from a representation?

(b) Can an explicit model incorporate heuristic knowledge?

1.23. Show an example of a problem with

(a) A simple knowledge representation and a sophisticated control strategy.

(b) A simple control strategy and a sophisticated control mechanism.

CHAPTER 2

SYMBOLIC (COMPUTATIONAL) LOGIC

If in other sciences we should arrive at certainty without doubt and truth without error, it behooves us to place the foundations of knowledge in mathematics.

Roger Bacon   c. 1214–c. 1294
Opus Majus, bk. I, ch. 4

The whole machinery of our intelligence . . . are so many symbolic, algebraic expressions. They stand for experience. . . . We would flounder hopelessly . . . did we not . . . direct our course by these intellectual devices.

George Santayana [1896]

INTRODUCTION

The discipline of *mathematical logic*, in particular *symbolic logic*, is a subset of the discipline of discrete mathematics. A systematic study of symbolic logic dates back to Aristotle (384–322 B.C.). The subject of symbolic logic is only one component of AI and has some limitations. It is presented first for several reasons. In the first place, logic is familiar to most engineers and computer scientists. Second, and more importantly, symbolic logic facilitates knowledge-manipulation strategies with solid mathematical underpinnings.

37

The Use of Logic in AI

Logic can be used *to express statements*, *to validly infer additional statements*, and *to rigorously prove (or disprove) statements*. At first glance, it appears that if the concepts of reasoning and intelligent behavior could be formalized using mathematical logic, AI implementation would be straightforward. Unfortunately, this is not the case. The application of logic in AI systems development is actually quite controversial. Critics of logic point out that

- Humans do not always reason by making logical inferences.
- Logic is too rigorous, and inflexible, to be of use in all AI problem domains.

These arguments, although somewhat true, are not sufficient reason to dismiss logic as useless for AI system development. There seems to be little reason to develop AI systems that formulate illogical conclusions.

Nonetheless, mathematical logic, especially *modus ponens* (developed later), provides a rigorous and justifiable mechanism for making inferences. Furthermore, using the rules of logic for inference is mathematically sound. In fact *logic forms the basis of rule-based systems* (see Chapters 11, 12, 13). Extensions to classical logic such as multivalued logic (Chapter 13), nonmonotonic logic (Chapter 16), and temporal logic (Chapter 17), provide many useful tools for the design of realistic AI systems.

Relation to "Classical" Logics and Extensions

As noted in the preceding section, classical logic exhibits several shortcomings as a complete foundation for AI. For example, in the classical formulation, anything that follows from a set of facts also follows from an expanded set of facts. Another way of saying this is that classical logic is *monotonic*. Unfortunately, everyday experience indicates that this property is probably not enforceable; observation of new facts often causes humans to revise a set of previous facts (or "beliefs"). This is the domain of *nonmonotonic logic*.

Furthermore, the concept of time is often very significant to human reasoning. Classical logic may be extended to include *temporal logics* (Chapter 17). Finally, in reasoning with uncertainty, classical logic may be modified to embody *fuzzy logics*, *probabalistic logic*, and *multivalued logic* (Chapter 13).

The broad objective in considering mathematical formalisms of logic is to develop mechanisms to represent and manipulate entities known as statements, facts, or (stretching things) knowledge. Since statements have a deeper meaning than groups of words or logic values, at this stage the representations are considered "shallow." They do not allow the explicit integration of "common sense," nor do they invoke broad concepts or well-known scenarios related to the statements.

Inference

After developing representations for knowledge (or facts), a (goal-specific) manipulation capability for the representation is desired. This manipulation may involve determining actions, proving or disproving facts (hypotheses), or, quite frequently, generating new knowledge. This leads to an important objective, namely that of *inference*.

DEFINITIONS

Inference is the process of deducing (new) facts from (other) existing facts.   (2-1)

Deduction is a logically sound and systematic inference procedure.   (2-2*a*)

Induction is reasoning from a part to the whole, which, in the context of learning, may involve agglomeration or classification of new information into larger entities.   (2-2*b*)

In logic-based representations, facts are stored as *axioms*. An axiom is a statement that is always true. Typically, a logic-based inference procedure begins with a set of axioms and a theorem to be proved (or refuted). If a logical representation is *complete*, all the logical consequences that follow from the axioms are derivable (as theorems); this is shown in Fig. 2.1. Whereas this chapter concerns *first-order logic*, other logics, including extensions to first-order logic, may be developed.

THE VOCABULARY OF LOGIC

Books on AI and mathematical logic include a plethora of terms such as "statement," "clause," "expression," "proposition," "sentence," and so on. In this and the following section we develop a consistent terminology as we explore the ramifications of increasingly complex and versatile formulations of logic. Figure 2.2 summarizes the vocabulary of logic and provides a road map for our study.

THE MATHEMATICS OF LOGIC

Statements

Symbolic propositional logic uses mathematical symbols to represent statements. Appendix 1 shows a number of illustrative examples.

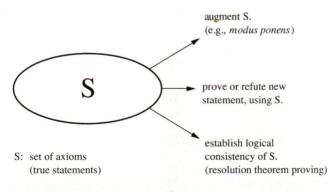

augment S.
(e.g., *modus ponens*)

prove or refute new statement, using S.

establish logical consistency of S.
(resolution theorem proving)

S: set of axioms
     (true statements)

FIGURE 2.1
Deductive reasoning using logic.

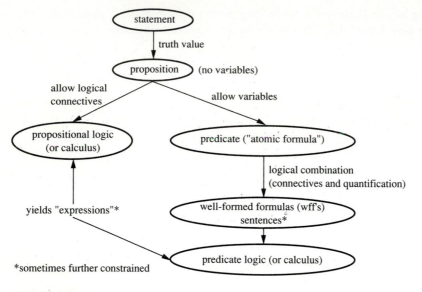

FIGURE 2.2
Vocabulary of logic.

A **statement** (or a **proposition** or an **assertion**) is a declarative sentence that is either TRUE or FALSE. (2-3)

Example 2.1   Representation forms for statements. Throughout this text, we indicate statements in various forms, ranging from English-like sentences to abstraction as a single variable. For example, the following forms are used:

"the car is moving to the left"	(English-like sentence)	(2-4a)
(car moving left)	(List-based, suited for LISP)	(2-4b)
moving (car, left)	(functional notation using predicate "moving"; well suited for PROLOG)	(2-4c)
p	(This is an abstraction; p may represent (2-4a)–(2-4c). The truth value of p is established via logic, unification, etc.)	(2-4d)
$p(X, Y)$	(same as (2-4d) except X and Y are variables)	(2-4e)

In our development of manipulation techniques using propositional logic, we implicitly map the truth value of statements into the values of logical variables, as shown in the (2-4d) and (2-4e). More importantly, in the study of AI we care about *compound statements*.

A compound statement is formed by using logical *connectives*, such as "and," "not," and "if," to connect statements. (2-5)

Analysis of Compound Statements
Using Simple Logical Connectives

SIMPLE LOGICAL CONNECTIVES. Appendix 1 illustrates the use of the simple logical connectives, such as AND ($\cap$), OR ($\cup$), and NOT ($\neg$), and equality ($=$ or $\equiv$). These are used to link other (simple or compound) statements to form compound statements. Readers unfamiliar with these connectives may wish to pause here to explore Appendix 1.

EQUALITY OF TRUTH VALUES VERSUS EQUALITY OF MEANING. We must be careful in interpreting the concept of the equality of two statements. *A compound statement based upon equality* does not mean that the component statements are in any way *equal in meaning*, but rather it means that they have *the same truth value*.

Implication

In developing knowledge representations, one of the most useful logical connectives is the implication (IF) operator.

The implication operator is used to formulate *conditional statements*, that is, statements of the form

$$\begin{array}{ll} \text{IF} & \text{antecedent} \\ & \text{THEN} \quad \text{consequent} \end{array} \qquad (2\text{-}6)$$

Symbolic information encoded via (possibly compound) "antecedent" and "consequent" statements, together with the implication connective, form the basis for many AI implementations, including rule-based systems. (2-7)

The implication or conditional operator is written as $\leftarrow$ or $\rightarrow$ depending upon the direction of the implication. When written as

$$p \quad \rightarrow \quad q \qquad (2\text{-}8)$$

the term on the left (the antecedent, i.e., p) *implies* the term on the right (the consequent, i.e., q). If the implication is TRUE when the term on the left is TRUE, the term on the right must also be TRUE. The implication operator is so fundamental to AI, and so often conceptually misunderstood, that its characteristics are presented in depth in Appendix 1.

LOGICAL PROPERTIES OF IMPLICATION. The logical properties of implication are summarized in the following truth table (Table 2.1).

Simplification of Table 2.1 via a Karnaugh map (see Fig. 2.3) yields the useful result

$$(p \ \rightarrow \ q) \ \equiv \ \neg p \ \cup \ q \qquad (2\text{-}9a)$$

Alternately interpreting this result yields

$$(p \ \rightarrow \ q) \text{ is TRUE when either } p \text{ is FALSE OR } q \text{ is TRUE.} \qquad (2\text{-}9b)$$

TABLE 2.1
Implication truth table

p	q	$p \rightarrow q$
T	T	T
T	F	F
F	T	T
F	F	T

IMPLICATION AND RULE-BASED SYSTEMS. Implication yields a fundamental basis for rule-based inference systems. If we assume that implication is TRUE, this knowledge may be used to constrain the allowable truth values of the antecedent and consequent. Consider the entries in the implication truth table that correspond to antecedent p assuming the value TRUE and the value of the implication $(p \rightarrow q)$ also being TRUE. (This is the first row of Table 2.1.) This constrains or forces q to assume the value of TRUE.

Another way to verify this important constraint is to consider Eq. 2-2a. The compound statement represented by $(\neg p \cup q)$ must be TRUE. Since p is TRUE, $\neg p$ is FALSE, and therefore q must be TRUE. The significance of this result is that, given an implication statement (of the form of (2-7)) known to have the value TRUE, the fact that the antecedent is also TRUE forces the consequent to be TRUE. This is the logical basis for *forward chaining* in a rule-based system. The antecedent statement may, however, be itself a compound statement, usually involving the conjunction (AND-ing) of a number of simpler statements.

THE "WEAK" REPRESENTATIONAL CAPABILITY OF IMPLICATION. It is important to note that implication is used in a weak sense in logic. For example,

1. p and q together do not need to make sense. For example, the following assertion is TRUE:

$$p \rightarrow q$$
(a) Form

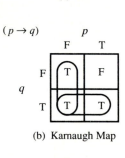

(b) Karnaugh Map

$$(p \rightarrow q) \equiv (\neg p) \cup q$$
(c) Result

FIGURE 2.3
Karnaugh map for implication statement: (*a*) form, (*b*) Karnaugh map, (*c*) result.

IF $4 + 2 = 3$

THEN   Dogs are smarter than people.

This is row 4 from the implication truth table (Table 2.1).

2. A FALSE hypothesis implies any conclusion. (See the preceding example and the truth table.)

3. The implication or assertion statement

$$p \; \rightarrow \; q$$

does not signify that "p causes q"; that is, there is not a cause-effect relationship. We are merely relating, via the implication connective, the *truth values* of the antecedent and the consequent with the truth value of the implication. From the truth table, the fact that this implication is TRUE signifies that

i. p implies q.
ii. q is TRUE if p is TRUE.
iii. p is TRUE only if q is TRUE.
iv. p is a sufficient condition for q.
v. q is a necessary condition for p.

4. A simple statement (i.e., containing no connectives) could be viewed as an implication with no antecedents.

Three additional logic forms that are related to the implication statement ($p \rightarrow q$) are

1. The *converse*, written as ($q \rightarrow p$).   (2-10*a*)
2. The *inverse*, written as (($\neg p$) $\rightarrow$ ($\neg q$)).   (2-10*b*)
3. The *contrapositive*, written (($\neg q$) $\rightarrow$ ($\neg p$)).   (2-10*c*)

IMPLICATION AND EQUALITY. Logical properties of the forms given in Table 2.1 are considered in the exercises.

If an implication and its converse are both TRUE, then the assertion may be replaced by an *equality connective*.   (2-11)

A Further Look at Implication

Up to this point we have shown the logic of assertions using single logical variables that took on the truth values of corresponding statements. This needs to be examined more fully for two reasons:

1. It is often necessary to determine *the logical consequences of assertion-based statements where the antecedents and the consequents themselves are compound statements.* Parentheses are used to indicate the precedence of connectives in these formulations.

2. The mapping of the logic incorporated in a complex statement into a simple logical variable masks a great deal of knowledge representation and manipulation difficulties. Questions that arise include the following:

a. How do we determine the "meaning" of and consequently the truth of a statement entered in English?

b. Is the knowledge in a relatively complex sentence best coded in a single, two-value logical variable?

c. What modifications in the statement would lead to a change in the truth value of the statement?

Example 2.2   Forward chaining using implication. Consider a series of assertions or IF-THEN statements. Variables p_i and q_i are used to represent the truth values of the antecedents and consequents, respectively, in the following implications:

implication 1

p_1 A college professor teaches in the summer
q_1 The professor can't do anything but teach

implication 2

p_2 The professor can't do anything but teach (same as q_1)
q_2 The professor does not have time to do research

implication 3

p_3 The professor does not have time to do research (same as q_2)
q_3 The professor is unhappy   (2-12a)

Notice that the consequents of some implications in (2-12a) are the same as the antecedents of others. We use this information to develop the following set of assertions (each of which we assume to be TRUE), which form a rule base, or perhaps a crude "knowledge base."

$$p_1 \rightarrow q_1$$
$$p_2 \rightarrow q_2$$
$$p_3 \rightarrow q_3$$
$$p_2 = q_1$$
$$q_2 = p_3 \qquad (2\text{-}12b)$$

This knowledge base may be rewritten using variable substitution and simplifies to

$$p_1 \rightarrow q_1$$
$$q_1 \rightarrow q_2$$
$$q_2 \rightarrow q_3 \qquad (2\text{-}13)$$

It is assumed that the assertions (not the component statements) in (2-13) are all TRUE. To determine the truth of statement q_3 ("the professor is unhappy"), given the fact that statement p_1 is TRUE ("the professor teaches in the summer"), we employ two things:

1. The implication truth table (Table 2.1) which indicates that if $(p \rightarrow q)$ is TRUE, AND p is TRUE, then q must be TRUE.

2. A mechanism to "chain" production of new (TRUE) facts from knowledge that p_1 is TRUE to arrive at a truth value for q_3.

Using a paradigm known as *forward chaining*, we develop the following logical sequence:

1. $((p_1 \rightarrow q_1) \cap p_1$ being TRUE$) \rightarrow (q_1$ is TRUE$)$
2. $(q_1$ is TRUE$)$ and $(q_1 = p_2)$ being TRUE yields p_2 is TRUE
3. [Similar to step 1] $((p_2 \rightarrow q_2) \cap p_2$ being TRUE$) \rightarrow (q_2$ is TRUE$)$
4. [Similar to step 2] $(q_2$ is TRUE$)$ and $(q_2 = p_3)$ being TRUE yields p_3 is TRUE
5. [Similar to steps 1 and 3] $((p_3 \rightarrow q_3) \cap p_3$ being TRUE$) \rightarrow (q_3$ is TRUE$)$

$$(2\text{-}14)$$

INFERENCE NETS AND RULE FIRINGS. The sequence of productions employed in deduction of "the professor is unhappy" from "a college professor teaches in the summer" is shown in Fig. 2.4. This type of diagram is referred to as an *inference net*. Inference nets are seldom as simple as that shown; for example, in databases containing 10,000 rules, it may not even be practical to view the inference net. The action indicated by following an arrow from the antecedent of a rule to the consequent (and thus producing a statement whose truth value is known to be TRUE) is shown. This is also referred to as *firing the rule*. The process of deciding which rule to fire is fundamental to our inference control strategy. We will examine both of these concepts more fully in our treatment of rule-based systems.

DEDUCTION USING PROPOSITIONAL LOGIC

The connectives considered previously allow generation or deduction of new information using the rules of logic. Logic enables a rigorous and formal method to create new knowledge (phrased as statements in logic) from existing knowledge via design of one or more proofs. Several useful graphical constructs are employed to show our derivations.

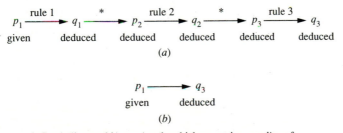

* Symbolic matching approach, which ascertains *equality* of statement truth-values (could be considered addenda to fact base or procedure invoked by inference mechanism).

FIGURE 2.4
Inference net for three-rule deduction example (given p_1 is TRUE): (*a*) forward chaining sequence, (*b*) result.

Example 2.3 Deduction involving conjunction. In the case of the conjunction (the AND operator, $\cap$), we may show that if proposition p is TRUE AND proposition q is TRUE, the conjunction of p and q is also TRUE. We designate this with a graphical construct that bears some resemblance to "longhand" arithmetic:

$$
\begin{array}{ll}
p & \text{(premise is TRUE)} \\
\underline{q \qquad\qquad\quad} & \underline{\text{(premise is TRUE)}} \\
p \,\cap\, q & \text{(conclusion is TRUE)}
\end{array}
\qquad (2\text{-}15)
$$

DEDUCTIVE REASONING USING LOGIC. The process of reaching a conclusion from a set of propositions is called *deductive reasoning*. Logic enables the development of mathematically justifiable approaches to automating deduction. Specifically, we develop approaches for manipulation of symbolic statements such that a set, S, of *axioms* (statements that are assumed TRUE) or premises, may be used to

Augment set S, by deriving additional TRUE statements from those in S. $\qquad (2\text{-}16a)$

Verify the truth of a given statement, using S. $\qquad (2\text{-}16b)$

Determine if any logical inconsistency (such as a contradiction) exists in S (or an augmented version of S). This is the basis of proof by refutation. $\qquad (2\text{-}16c)$

The ordinary concept of "justification of an argument" or "proof of a principle" is therefore extended on a rigorous mathematical basis. Not surprisingly, the implication connective is both the basis for some of the fundamental data structures in S and also a proof of the validity of a logically consistent knowledge-augmentation strategy. To see the later application, note that we seek to rigorously prove that *a new statement, n, logically follows* from S. Statement n is the *conclusion*. In other words, we seek to establish that the compound implication-based statement (the *argument*)

$$
\{S\} \;\rightarrow\; n \qquad (2\text{-}17)
$$

which represents a deductive argument, is TRUE. $\{S\}$ denotes the conjunction of the statements in S. Note that this is more than a proof that n is TRUE, it is a proof that the *reasoning mechanism* (phrased as a statement itself) used to derive n is logically valid (or TRUE). In fact, we must prove that this statement is a *tautology*, that is, it is TRUE for all values of the arguments. With this in mind, we return to the implication concept and note that there may be many logically justifiable ways to prove n is TRUE using S. When cast as an implication we are explicitly allowing this, since $\{S\}$ (the antecedent) merely provides a *sufficient condition* for n to be TRUE. An alternative way to remember this is that we do not seek to prove equality, but rather that the statement logically follows.

MODUS PONENS (MP). A second example of deduction may be written as the compound statement involving implication:

$$
(p \,\cap\, (p \;\rightarrow\; q)) \;\rightarrow\; q \qquad (2\text{-}18a)
$$

If we have a statement p (an axiom) that is known to have the truth value TRUE, and if we also have an implication involving p as the antecedent that is known to have the truth value TRUE, we may establish that statement q is TRUE using the principles of logic. This is an example of *modus ponens* (MP), which is represented graphically as

$$
\begin{array}{ll}
p & \text{(premise is TRUE)} \\
\underline{p \;\rightarrow\; q} & \text{(premise is TRUE)} \\
q & \text{(conclusion is TRUE)}
\end{array}
\qquad (2\text{-}18b)
$$

Again, this representation provides a useful mnemonic since it is similar to the representation of an arithmetic statement.

VERIFICATION OF MODUS PONENS. In a formal mathematic sense, in order to prove the validity of arguments based upon modus ponens, we must prove that the compound statement (2-18a) is a tautology. Algebraic manipulation easily confirms this; details are left to the exercises. Alternatively, we may rigorously verify that (2-18) is logically sound by examination of the truth table, as shown in Table 2.2. The first row of this table establishes the validity of 2-18.

OTHER DEDUCTION STRATEGIES. The logical validity of other commonly used deduction strategies may be investigated similarly. We show one of the most popular here. Consider the following argument:

$$
\begin{array}{ll}
\neg p \;\rightarrow\; q & \text{is TRUE} \\
\underline{p \;\rightarrow\; r} & \text{is TRUE} \\
q \;\cup\; r & \text{is TRUE (?)}
\end{array}
\qquad (2\text{-}19)
$$

This commonly employed argument is intuitively plausible. Statement p must be either TRUE or FALSE. If p is TRUE then, from the second argument, r must be TRUE. If p is FALSE, then, from the first argument, q must be TRUE. Thus, regardless of the truth value of p, $(q \cup r)$ is TRUE.

Formally, to prove

$$
((\neg p \;\cup\; r) \;\cap\; (p \;\cup\; q)) \;\rightarrow\; (q \;\cup\; r) \qquad (2\text{-}20)
$$

is a tautology, we could again convert the implication into one using OR and NOT:

$$
\begin{aligned}
[\neg \;((\neg p \;\cup\; r) \;\cap\; (p \;\cup\; q)) \;\cup\; (q \;\cup\; r)] \;\equiv\; \\
((p \;\cap\; \neg r) \;\cup\; (\neg p \;\cap\; \neg q)) \;\cup\; (q \;\cup\; r) \qquad (2\text{-}21)
\end{aligned}
$$

and verify this is TRUE. A truth table-based proof, however, involves less effort, and is left to the exercises.

TABLE 2.2
Implication and modus ponens

p	q	$(p \rightarrow q)$	$(p \cap (p \rightarrow q))$
T	T	T	T
T	F	F	F
F	F	T	F
F	T	T	F

PREDICATE LOGIC

Introduction

Propositional logic simply maps the truth value of a statement into TRUE or FALSE. The statements or propositions are *variable-free*. As mentioned, there was no other explicit dependence of the truth of the statement on the individual contents (i.e., words or phrases) of the statement. In this sense, there was no mechanism that allowed the possibility of a substitution of an element in the statement with another, with the consequent mapping of the statement truth value as a function of this substitution. In other words, in propositional logic there is no ability to relate the contents of a portion of a statement with the statement truth value.

Predicates and Variables

PREDICATES, PREDICATES AS FUNCTIONS, AND PREDICATE FUNCTIONS. The discrete mathematics and AI literature is somewhat inconsistent in usage of the terms "predicate" and "predicate functions." Some books [Wand 1980] [Winston 1984] consider predicates as functions, whereas many others generalize propositions into predicates and avoid the connotation of a function. The latter approach may yield some additional flexibility; this is explored in Problem 2.35. In an attempt to avoid confusion, we define two separate entities.

A **predicate** is a parameterized proposition, that is, a proposition with variables.

(2-22*a*)

Thus, a statement that would otherwise be a proposition, except that it involves variables, is a predicate.

A **predicate function** on a set A is a function that maps elements of A into the set {TRUE, FALSE}.

(2-22*b*)

In our case, the set A is taken to include statements containing variables (i.e., predicates), or simply variables.

For example, if A is the set of integers, we could define the *odd* predicate function, P_{odd}, as

$$P_{odd}\ (n) = \begin{cases} \text{TRUE if } n \text{ is odd} \\ \text{FALSE otherwise} \end{cases}$$

(2-23)

Predicate logic is a branch of logic that allows modeling of the truth of statements based upon the values assumed by specific portions (or phrases) of the statements. (2-24)

The set of values that a variable in a predicate may assume is called the **universe** of the variable. (2-25)

In a manner analogous to propositions, two predicates are said to be equivalent if they assume the same truth value for all possible values of their variables. Again, the reader should distinguish between *truth value* and *meaning*.

Example 2.4 Numerically based predicate. We can relate the concept of predicates to that of a more familiar mathematical formulation. (This example is examined in more detail in the constraint-satisfaction section of Chapter 5.) Consider the algebraic statement

$$y^2 - 3 = 6 \qquad (2\text{-}26a)$$

We view this as a predicate, with variable y. The universe of y is assumed to be the set of real numbers. The values $y = 3$ and $y = -3$ cause this predicate to be true. Note that an equivalent predicate is

$$(y + 3)(y - 3) = 0 \qquad (2\text{-}26b)$$

It is common to represent variables in predicates by capitalizing their first letter; values of variables are shown in lowercase. (2-27)

We adopt this convention as shown in examples (2-28)–(2-34). It is also useful since this is consistent with the syntax of most PROLOG implementations.

If the universe of each variable in a predicate function is finite, we may express the predicate function in tabular form.   In fact, if we simply enumerate all the values of variables that make the function TRUE, this is a sufficient representation. Unfortunately, if we only list some of the value permutations that are TRUE, this forces a consideration of *negation as failure* (Chapter 4).

Predicates with a single variable or argument are often used to represent *unary relations*, which are commonly referred to as **properties**. For example, the one-place predicate

$$may\_move \ (Object) \qquad (2\text{-}28)$$

is a property where the single variable *Object* may take on values

$$Object \ = \ \{car, \ horse, \ nuclear\text{-}power\text{-}plant, \ blue\text{-}ridge\text{-}mountains\} \qquad (2\text{-}29)$$

Clearly, "*may_move*" is TRUE for the first two values of *Object*, whereas it is FALSE for the latter two.

An *n-place predicate* is shown as *an n-tuple preceded by an n-ary predicate name*. Multiple argument predicates may be used to represent relations, such as the binary relation

$$next\_to \ (Region1, \ Region2) \qquad (2\text{-}30)$$

where *Region1* and *Region2* are variables whose values are the locations of certain regions. Another example is

$$on\_top\_of \ (Support, \ Object) \qquad (2\text{-}31)$$

where *Support* represents the class of entities that may have something on top of them, and *Object* represents the class of objects that may be placed on the *Support* entities.

CHOOSING PREDICATE REPRESENTATIONS. Let us consider coding the statement "the circuit breaker in line 4 is open."   In predicate calculus we could write this statement as

$$is\text{-}open(circuit\text{-}breaker, \ line\text{-}4) \qquad (2\text{-}32a)$$

Alternatively, this might be expressed as

$$circuit\text{-}breaker(line\text{-}4, \ open) \qquad (2\text{-}32b)$$

or perhaps even

$$line\text{-}4(circuit\text{-}breaker, \ open) \qquad (2\text{-}32c)$$

All three are valid interpretations in predicate logic, with corresponding general two-place relations:

$$is\text{-}open(What, \ Where) \qquad (2\text{-}33a)$$
$$circuit\text{-}breaker(Where, \ Status) \qquad (2\text{-}33b)$$
$$line\text{-}4(Protection, \ Status) \qquad (2\text{-}33c)$$

Examples of the corresponding universes of the preceding variables are

$$What \ = \ \{circuit\text{-}breaker, \ disconnect\text{-}switch, \ line\text{-}itself\} \qquad (2\text{-}34a)$$
$$Where \ = \ \{line\text{-}1, \ line\text{-}2, \ line\text{-}3, \ line\text{-}4\} \qquad (2\text{-}34b)$$
$$Status \ = \ \{open, \ closed, \ inoperable\} \qquad (2\text{-}34c)$$
$$Protection \ = \ \{relay, \ circuit\text{-}breaker, \ recloser\} \qquad (2\text{-}34d)$$

Often, the predicate name is chosen as the verb; that is, formulation (2-32a) is preferred. This distinction will become more significant when we define and consider the limitations of *first order predicate calculus*.

Example 2.5 Compound statement involving predicates. Predicates together with their arguments are statements, and therefore they may be used together with previously defined connectives to form complex statements.

Consider the following compound statement:

$$p(X, \ Y) \ \cap \ p(Y, \ Z) \ \rightarrow \ s(X, \ Z) \qquad (2\text{-}35)$$

Here $p(X, Y)$ is an abstract representation of "person X is the parent of person Y" and $s(X, Z)$ is an abstract representation of "person X is the grandparent of person Z."

Statement (2-35) is an example of using implication and variables to form a general *rule*, where the use of variables leads to an efficient representation. Note that universal quantification on variables X, Y, and Z, as described in the following section, is implied in (2-35).

Quantified Predicates, Equivalences, and Manipulations

EXTENSIONS OF LOGIC TO CATEGORICAL PROPOSITIONS AND QUANTIFIED SENTENCES. Categorical propositions enable the practical representation of more general relations. They quantify a great deal of knowledge, and thus lead to our interest in manipulation of quantified statements. For example, numerous modeling applications require that we formulate a predicate whose truth value is unchanged *regardless* of the values of its variables. In this sense, the predicate's variables are used as "place holders." (PROLOG uses an underbar, e.g., _, to signify this.) For example, the predicate

All professors are underpaid.

relates an entire set or class of objects (*professors*) with the concept of *underpaid*, and is an example of a categorical proposition.

The statement

Some professors are engineers.

is somewhat general, but it provides useful information if we need to establish, as part of a proof, that there exists at least one professor who has an engineering background. In this statement, class C_1 is the class of professors and class C_2 is the class of engineers. The above categorical proposition relates membership in C_1 to C_2, since some members of C_1 are in C_2. Categorical propositions are of four forms:

1. All (every) C_1 is a C_2. (2-36*a*)

2. No C_1 is a C_2. (2-36*b*)

3. Some (at least one) C_1 is a C_2. (2-36*c*)

4. Some (at least one) C_1 is not a C_2. (2-36*d*)

The quantifiers "all" and "no" in statements (2-36*a*) and (2-36*b*) are **universal quantifiers**, since they apply to all members of C_1. The quantifier "some" in statements (2-36*c*) and (2-36*d*) is an **existential quantifier**, since it constrains at least one member of C_1 to be related to C_2. The importance of statements in these forms is that there are logically equivalent formulations that we can investigate further. In addition, there are manipulation techniques [Johnsonbaugh 1986] for conversion between categorical proposition forms.

QUANTIFICATION EXAMPLES. It is often required in the use of logic to formulate statements that are satisfied by all of some entity, or statements where it is necessary to refer to the existence of some (one or more) entities, as in the preceding categorical examples. Predicate logic allows this by the *quantification of variables* in statements. Thus, quantified statements provide flexibility and conciseness in our logic-based descriptions. Two quantifiers exist: the universal quantifier ("for all") and the existential quantifier ("there exists").

> The *quantification of variables* in conjunction with predicates is perhaps most useful when we assume, as we did in demonstrating modus ponens, that the *truth value of the statement containing a quantified variable is TRUE*. Henceforth, we will make that assumption. (2-37)

Suppose we wish to incorporate in our symbolic logic database the fact that any object that we observe moving cannot be stationary. Thus, we wish to represent

"any object that is observed to be moving cannot be stationary." (2-38*a*)

Given the set of objects of interest, we could use a predicate-logic representation containing the variable *Object* and the predicate names "observed-moving" and "stationary." (A cumbersome alternative would be to enumerate all possibilities for the objects of interest.) This representation could be accomplished via the compound statement

$$observed\text{-}moving(Object) \rightarrow (\neg\, stationary(Object)) \tag{2-38b}$$

To achieve the desired representation in (2-38a), we need to specify that statement (2-38b) is TRUE for any value assigned to variable Object. This is an example of *implicit universal quantification.*

The general syntax for the universally quantified predicate is

$$\forall X \;\; p(X) \tag{2-39}$$

where one (or more) of the arguments of predicate p is X. This is read as "for all X, p," meaning the truth value of p is independent of the value of X used in the argument. In accordance with our previous assumption, this is taken to mean that the statement is TRUE for all values of the particular variable.

The companion to the universal quantifier is the *existential quantifier*, which specifies that there exists at least one instantiation of the existentially quantified variable that, according to the previous convention, makes this predicate TRUE. This quantifier is denoted $\exists$ and written with a syntax similar to that for the universal quantifier. The form is

$$(\exists X) \;\; p(X) \tag{2-40}$$

which is read "for some X, p," or alternately, "there exists an X such that p" is TRUE.

An important concept is the **scope** of these quantifiers, which essentially "links" the instantiation of the variables to the predicate function in which they are quantified. The scope of a quantified variable is the statement to which it is prefixed. In other words, the (perhaps compound) statement appearing enclosed in brackets (or parentheses) and prefixed by a quantified variable, is said to be within the scope of that variable.

EQUIVALENCE OF QUANTIFIED PREDICATES. Consider the example of a universally quantified predicate with truth value F (false). The categorical proposition "No X is a . . ." exemplifies this. This yields the following equivalences:

$$\neg\,(\forall X \;\; p(X)) \;\; \equiv \;\; \exists X \; \neg p(X) \tag{2-41}$$

and

$$\neg\,(\exists X \;\; p(X)) \;\; \equiv \;\; \forall X \; \neg p(X) \tag{2-42}$$

Other useful rules that combine quantification and implication are

$$\forall X \;\; p(X) \;\; \rightarrow \;\; p(a) \tag{2-43}$$

where a is in the universe of X, and

$$p(a) \;\; \rightarrow \;\; \exists X \;\; p(X) \tag{2-44}$$

Having developed the basic conceptual framework for mathematical logic, we now seek to employ these concepts to generate new facts, prove or disprove hypotheses, and prove theorems. Thus, the "computational" capabilities of logic are used to develop a toolbox of *inference techniques*.

TAUTOLOGIES. A disjunctive expression containing a pair of complementary predicates is a *tautology*. For example,

$$\neg p \cup p \qquad (2\text{-}45)$$

is a tautology. Note that *a tautology is always true*, regardless of the truth value of p.

As an aside, notice that the complement of the above tautology, viz.,

$$p \cap \neg p \qquad (2\text{-}46)$$

is *always FALSE*. It is a *contradiction* and is of interest to us for two reasons:

i. If it were contained in an AI database, we would need to question the integrity of the database.

ii. It is used in proof by refutation (resolution theorem proving).

QUANTIFICATION SUMMARY

1. *The universal quantifier*

$$\forall X \; p(X)$$

means that, for all values in the universe of X, $p(X)$ is TRUE.

2. *The existential quantifier*

$$\exists Y \; q(Y)$$

means that at least one value in the universe of Y causes $q(Y)$ to be TRUE.

3. The scope of a quantifier is delineated with parentheses.

4. The order in which quantifiers occur in nested statements is significant.

5. Changes in the scope of a quantifier may affect the interpretation of a statement.

The Language of First Order Logic

In order to proceed formally with our objective of exploring first order logic, the following additional definitions are necessary.

A **term** is either a constant, a variable, or an n-variable function. (2-47)

A **function** is an n-tuple of terms prefixed by a function symbol or a name (also referred to as a *functor*) that satisfies the definition of a function. (2-48)

The notion of a predicate was introduced in (2-23a). A more formal representation is given here.

A **predicate** is an n-tuple of terms, prefixed by a predicate symbol on name. (2-49)

Constraining our logical constructs to those permitted by these definitions forces us to generate what are known as well-formed formulae, abbreviated as wffs.

A (**well-formed**) **formula** is either a predicate or a (possibly compound) statement.

(2-50)

For example, formulae we have considered include

a (also called an atomic formula or a literal; note *a* may be either a statement in propositional logic or a predicate.)

$\neg a$

$a \cap b$

$a \cup b$

$a \rightarrow b$

$b \rightarrow a$

$q(a)$ (where q is any quantifier and a is any formula)

Thus, in considering the operations that could be applied using this set of formulae, we have formulae based upon

1. *n*-place predicates.
2. Simple statements.
3. Negation.
4. Conjunction.
5. Disjunction.
6. Implication.
7. Quantification.

A *sentence* (or a *closed formula*) is a well-formed formula in which every occurrence of a variable (if any) is within the scope of a quantifier for that variable.   (2-51)

Thus, sentences do not contain free variables.

$$(\forall X) \ (\text{computer } (X) \ \cap \ \neg \text{terminal } (Y))$$

is an expression, not a sentence. Variable X is bound, whereas Y is free.

A **bound occurrence of a variable** in a formula is an occurrence within the scope of a quantifier for that variable. Otherwise, a variable is said to be **free**.   (2-52)

Thus, **closed formulae** (or sentences) contain no free variables. **Ground formulae** contain neither free nor bound variables.

Notice that definitions (2-50)–(2-52) are necessary to ensure that quantified statements (including those implicitly universally quantified, as indicated earlier) make sense. Also note that this is a different concept from the English-like sentence we used to define a statement.

In much of what follows we drop the cumbersome quantification symbols and assume all wffs are sentences.

Finally, we come to the desired result:

If we restrict the universe of variables in sentences to exclude function and predicate names, the set of all derivable sentences is the language of **first order logic**.   (2-53)

HIGHER ORDER PREDICATE LOGIC. The previous definitions introduced first order logic. The reader may be curious about the descriptor "first order." That is, what are the representational limitations "first order" logic imposes? This is a significant mathematical concept, and we merely indicate one restriction here. Notice that (2-53) does not allow predicates to be denoted by variable names; that is, we cannot write (much less interpret)

$$\text{Variable\_predicate\_name}(\text{Arg1, Arg2}, \ldots, \text{Arg}n) \qquad (2\text{-}54)$$

Although a simple representation of the form of (2-54) is possible, the consequences of the manipulation of an entity of this type are significant. Without further constraints, it is quite easy to derive paradoxes in higher-order logic.

MANIPULATION OF WFFS

We now explore the utility of using logic as a mechanism for problem solving. Examples were shown previously using MP and the design of an implication-based rule base; here we will be more general. Of particular interest are these topics:

• Resolution.
• Unification.

Resolution (Proof by Refutation)

INTRODUCTION TO RESOLUTION. The *resolution* approach yields new clauses from an initial set. In fact, it may be shown that all logically consistent clauses may be obtained using resolution. Thus, we say resolution is logically complete. Resolution is a powerful and "indirect" method of inference, and is often misunderstood.

The utility of resolution in inference applications is subtle. Often, resolution is used to show that a set of clauses is *inconsistent*, in the sense that the resolution process produces a logical *contradiction*. While this may seem like a very "negative" approach to inference, it is quite useful, provided the set of clauses is formulated in a special way. As will be shown,

A clause may be proven to be true, in the context of a set of clauses known to be true, by appending the logical NOT of this clause to the set and seeking a contradiction.

(2-55a)

If the resolution process fails to find a contradiction, the negative of what we seek to prove is *logically consistent* with the database, thus the clause cannot be TRUE.

Thus, resolution is a means of verifying the validity (i.e., truth value) of new statements by refutation, or contradiction. It is based upon the following structure:

$$a \qquad \text{(premise is TRUE)}$$
$$\underline{\neg a \qquad \text{(premise is TRUE)}}$$

contradiction or empty clause (cannot deduce from premises)   (2-55*b*)

Since a and $\neg a$ cannot assume the same truth value, $a \cap (\neg a)$ is a contradiction, which cannot possibly be TRUE. By arranging the original database facts as wffs in clause form together with the negated new fact (actually a hypothesis), the truth of the hypothesis is tested by seeking a contradiction.

IMPLEMENTING RESOLUTION. The goal is to develop a systematic procedure to show, given an existing logic database, that a given wff is *unsatisfiable*, that is, there is no interpretation of the wff that makes sense. To do this, it is necessary first to convert statements in the logical database and the hypothesis into *clause form*, involving the disjunction of literals. Considering that we are given general wffs, which include implication and quantification, converting the wffs to the desired form suitable for resolution involves some work before the actual resolution procedure may be employed.

Resolution proceeds by augmenting the database with the negation of the desired hypothesis. Then clauses are resolved pairwise in the augmented database until a contradiction is found. If none is generated, we conclude that the situation is consistent, and therefore the hypothesis is, in fact, FALSE. First, we remove implication and equality from the wffs. This is relatively simple:

$$(p \rightarrow q) \text{ is replaced with } ((\neg p) \cup q)$$
$$(p \equiv q) \text{ is replaced with } ((\neg p) \cup q) \cap (p \cup (\neg q)) \qquad (2\text{-}56)$$

Pairwise resolution of clauses uses the following strategy:

$$
\begin{array}{cc}
a \cup b & T \\
\underline{\neg a \cup c} & \underline{T} \\
b \cup c & T
\end{array}
\qquad (2\text{-}57)
$$

which is equivalent to showing that

$$(a \cup b) \cap (\neg a \cup b) \rightarrow (b \cup c) \qquad (2\text{-}58)$$

is a tautology. Proof of (2-58) is left to the exercises.

Consider the following example of resolution-based inference:

Example 2.6   Resolution application. The initial database (D_1) contains the following statements (all statements assumed T; database assumed consistent):

1. p_1
2. $p_1 \rightarrow q_1$
3. $q_1 \rightarrow q_2$

The goal is to prove, using D_1, that q_2 is TRUE. Therefore, $\neg q_2$ is added to

D_1, clauses are converted to a form that facilitates resolution, and pairwise resolution proceeds.

The modified data base D_2, is then

(1) p_1
(2) $\neg p_1 \cup q_1$
(3) $\neg q_1 \cup q_2$
(4) $\neg q_2$

Resolution of (2) with (3), that is,

$$
\begin{array}{c}
q_1 \ \cup \ \neg p_1 \\
\underline{\neg q_1 \ \cup \ q_2} \\
\neg p_1 \ \cup \ q_2
\end{array}
$$

yields D_3:

(1) p_1
(2) $\neg p_1 \cup q_1$
(3) $\neg q_1 \cup q_2$
(4) $\neg q_2$
(5) $\neg p_1 \cup q_2$

Resolution of (4) with (5)

$$
\begin{array}{c}
\neg q_2 \\
\underline{q_2 \ \cup \ \neg p_1} \\
\neg p_1
\end{array}
$$

yields D_4:

(1) p_1
(2) $\neg p_1 \cup q_1$
(3) $\neg q_1 \cup q_2$
(4) $\neg q_2$
(5) $\neg p_1 \cup q_2$
(6) $\neg p_1$

Notice that resolution of (1) with (6) produces a contradiction ($\neg p_1 \cap p_1$). Therefore, $\neg q_2$ is inconsistent with D_1; hence q_2 is TRUE. Alternate sequences of clause resolution are possible and will be explored in the problems.

Unification

Unification is a systematic procedure for instantiation of variables in wffs. Since the truth value of predicates is a function of the values assumed by their arguments, the controlled instantiation of values thus provides a means of validating the truth values of (compound) statements containing predicates. Unification is fundamental to most inference strategies in AI. For example, the heart of PROLOG execution is the unification mechanism. The basis of unification is *substitution*.

> **Unification** is the process of attempting to make two expressions *identical* ("unify them") by finding *appropriate substitutions* or *bindings of variables* in these expressions. (2-59)
>
> A **substitution** is a set of *assignments of terms* to variables, with no variable being assigned more than one term. (2-60)
>
> A set of expressions is **unifiable** if and only if there exists (iff ∃) one or more (unifying) substitutions that make the expressions identical. (2-61)

Interestingly, substitution does not imply that all variables are assigned constant values (to produce grounded predicates), but rather allows the assignment of (other) variables to a variable. The astute reader should suspect that one needs to be careful in this process to avoid circularity in the assignment process; PROLOG's lack of a test for circularity leaves this responsibility to the programmer.

In unification applications, a simple yes/no answer on the unifiability of two expressions is often desired. In other cases, obtaining the set(s) of unifying substitutions (if they exist) is most important.

SIMPLE VARIABLE SUBSTITUTIONS. Prior to developing unification algorithms, we consider three valid substitutions that may occur:

1. A variable may be replaced by a constant. (2-62*a*)

2. A variable may be replaced by a variable. (2-62*b*)

3. A variable may be replaced by a function that does not contain the variable. (This avoids circularities). (2-62*c*)

The substitutions in (2-62) form the basis for the rules for unification shown in Table 2.3. Note that Table 2.3 does not address the case of the "don't care" or "wild-card" variable, which may always be unified. This variable is denoted by the underbar (_) in PROLOG (Chapter 4) and the (* any) list notation (Chapter 10).

DENOTING SUBSTITUTIONS. A single substitution of term "substitution" for term "substituted-for" is represented using the syntax

$$(\text{substitution/substituted-for})$$

For example, we denote a substitution of the variable R with the constant value t using the (reasonably standard) notation (t/R). This indicates that the value of R is bound to t. An easy way to remember the notation is that (t/R) is equivalent to the assignment statement $R := t$ in Pascal or (setq R t) in LISP.

Similarly, substitution of the variable V_1 for variable G_1 is denoted (V_1/G_1). This indicates that the value of variable G_1 is determined by variable V_1, which may or may not currently have a value. We might say G_1 is bound to V_1. A list of all current variable substitutions, or bindings, is called the *substitution* or *binding environment*.

TABLE 2.3
Rules for unification

1. Two atoms (constants or variables) that are identical unify.

2. Two identical lists, or expressions converted to list form, unify (although certain algorithms will use Rule 1 repeatedly to ascertain this).

3. A constant and an unbounded variable unify, with the variable becoming bound to the constant.

4. An unbound variable unifies with a bound variable, with the unbound variable becoming bound to the bound variable.

5. A bound variable unifies with a constant if the binding on the bound variable does not conflict with the constant.

6. Two unbound variables unify. If either variable becomes bound in subsequent unification steps, the other also becomes bound to the same atom (variable or constant).

7. Two bound variables unify if they are both bound (perhaps through intermediate bindings) to the same atom (variable or constant).

SUBSTITUTION (BINDING) CONSISTENCY. The difficult aspect of unification is achieving a set of *consistent* substitutions, in the sense that if we come to a unification step where a constant c_1 has replaced a variable V_1, that is, (c_1/V_1) is on the list of substitutions, then we cannot substitute another constant for V_1. We could use V_1 in other substitutions: (V_1/V_2) makes sense. It might be more efficient, however, if V_1 is already bound to c_1 to bind (or substitute) c_1 directly to (for) V_2. To accomplish unification on lists of elements, rather than single terms, we first determine how to accomplish unification on a single term, and then consider the extension of this to the remainder of the list such that consistency is achieved.

The unification strategies developed hereafter are suitable for fairly complex cases. The second example serves as a prelude to the LISP implementation of the general unifier of Chapter 10. An alternative, but equivalent, approach to unification is shown in Shirai [1984]. This approach is based upon finding the *disagreement set* between two sets of literals, and applying substitution in an attempt to reduce the disagreement set to an empty set.

UNIFICATION ALGORITHM(S): DERIVATION AND SAMPLE RESULTS. The derivations and applications of two unification algorithms are shown next. Both algorithms assume that the wffs are entered in list form, and each returns one of two things:

A list of the substitutions, including the NIL, or empty, list if there are no valid substitutions. (2-63*a*)

A report of failure (FAIL) if unification is not possible (e.g., attempted replacement of a variable by a function that contains the variable). (2-63*b*)

UNIFY1 (rewriting) and UNIFY2 (checks binding list). Both algorithms are recursive and attempt to unify the input lists element-by-element. The first algorithm, denoted UNIFY1, achieves the necessary consistent substitutions through rewriting the remainder of the list(s) to be unified. In the rewriting, all occurrences of a bound variable are replaced by the current binding. In UNIFY2, rewriting is not employed; rather a *binding list* is used to record the current binding environment. Whenever matches involving variables occur, the binding list, together with the rules of Table 2.3, are used to determine (partial) unification results. A flow chart for UNIFY1 is shown in Fig. 2.5. The corresponding algorithm is shown in Pascal-like notation in Fig. 2.6.

Examination of unification algorithm UNIFY1. Several aspects of UNIFY1 are noteworthy. First, the *unifier employs recursion*. The development of this algorithm is based upon the development of a unifier for atomic (i.e., single element) terms. Its

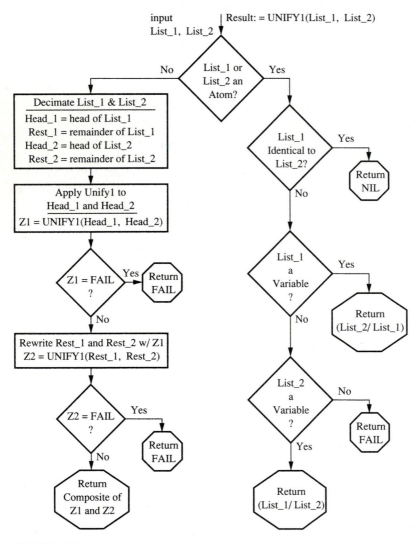

FIGURE 2.5
Unification procedure UNIFY1 (uses rewriting for consistency).

Input: Two wffs, in list form
Output: List of substitutions (note the empty list, NIL, does not indicate failure, but rather success without substitution). The list FAIL indicates failure.

```
PROCEDURE UNIFY1(List1, List2);
BEGIN
IF List1 or List2 consist of a single element (an atom)
    THEN
        IF List1 and List2 are identical
            THEN return empty list, NIL {no substitutions}
            ELSE
                IF List1 is a variable
                        THEN return (List2/List1)
                            ELSE IF List2 is a variable
                            THEN return (List1/List2)
                        ELSE return FAIL
    ELSE {not atoms; must be in lists}
        BEGIN
        Head1 := 1st element of List1;
        Rest1 := rest of List1;
        Head2 := 1st element of List2;
        Rest2 := rest of List2;
        Z1 := UNIFY1 (Head1, Head2);
        IF Z1 = FAIL
            THEN return FAIL
            ELSE
                BEGIN
                Rest1 := apply (Z1, Rest1); apply substitution Z1
                Rest2 := apply (Z1, Rest2); to Rest1 and Rest2
                Z2 := UNIFY1 (Rest1, Rest2);

                IF Z2 = FAIL
                    THEN return FAIL
                    ELSE return composite of Z1 and Z2
        END;
        END;
END. {UNIFY}
```

FIGURE 2.6
Unification algorithm UNIFY1 (rewriting).

operation is extended to lists by successive decimation of the list into single elements (atoms) and a careful assessment of previous substitutions. The right half of the flow chart indicates the procedure for unification of atomic terms; this is a straightforward and decision-laden branch that determines which, if either, of the atoms is a variable, and so forth. If both are non-variables (i.e., constants), then the procedure either returns NIL (an as yet empty binding list), if they are the same, or FAIL (since they are not the same and no substitution is possible). Note also that if the atoms under consideration are both the same variable, the procedure returns success and a NIL list of substitutions, since it makes little sense to record the substitution of a variable for itself.

Alternatives for consistent substitution. The more significant aspect of UNIFY1 concerns the left hand path of the flow chart in Fig. 2.5. Here, List_1 and List_2 are not atoms: they have more than one element. UNIFY1 extracts the first (leftmost) element of each list and proceeds to apply itself to these atoms, thereby invoking the right hand side of the flow chart. The situation then becomes more complex, due to our interest in achieving a *consistent* set of substitutions. In successive unification steps, *the results of previous substitutions must be used.* In general, this may be accomplished in several ways, among them

1. Preprocessing (rewriting) the remainder of the lists by replacing variables remaining on the lists (i.e, Rest_1 and Rest_2) with any previous substitutions.   (2-64)
2. Modifying the comparison steps involving values of variables List_1 and List_2. Instead of blindly substituting variables and constants for variables, we would need to check the list of previous substitutions to determine which new substitutions are consistent (in the sense previously described). UNIFY2, described later, accomplishes this.   (2-65)

Denoting Z_1 as the list of previous substitutions, the steps are

$$\text{Apply Z1 to Rest\_1} \tag{2-66a}$$
$$\text{Apply Z1 to Rest\_2} \tag{2-66b}$$
$$Z2 = \text{UNIFY1 (Rest\_1, Rest\_2)} \tag{2-66c}$$

This approach thus involves explicit substitution prior to further unification and is probably simpler. This is the basis of UNIFY1.

Example 2.7   Unification of two simple lists using UNIFY1. Suppose we are attempting to unify the lists (which are assumed to be wffs in list form)

$$\text{List1} = \text{(question What is)}$$
$$\text{List2} = \text{(question has What)}$$

Note the variable "What" appears in both wffs. Algorithm UNIFY1 has no trouble with the head of each list, since they are grounded and identical. Therefore, NIL, or the empty list, is returned in the first unification step. Applying the empty list of substitutions to the remainder (second and third elements) of each of these lists leaves them unchanged.
The next step in the unification process involves the decimated lists

$$\text{Rest\_1} = \text{(What is)}$$
$$\text{Rest\_2} = \text{(has What)}$$

UNIFY1, working on the first element of each, returns the list of substitutions

$$Z1 \; = \; \{(\text{has} \, / \, \text{What})\}$$

Then Rest_1 and Rest_2 are decimated to yield the remaining lists: (is) and (What), respectively.

Applying $Z1$ to each of these, as

$$Z1 \; (\text{is})$$
$$Z1 \; (\text{What})$$

produces the new lists

(is)

(has)

respectively, where the previously substituted value of What is used in the second list. Finally, applying UNIFY1 to these atoms returns FAIL, thus signifying the unification process cannot be successfully applied to the original lists. The reader should verify that this makes sense, since there is no substitution for What in the original lists that makes them equal.

Unification algorithm UNIFY2. UNIFY2 proceeds using the strategy of (2-65). It is somewhat more complex than UNIFY1, and serves as the basis for LISP implementation of the general unifier in Chapter 10 (see Example 10.36 and Fig. 10.2). A flow chart, similar to Fig. 2.6, is shown in Fig. 2.7. Rather than complicate the pseudo listing with a multitude of nested IFs, we show a number of cases to be checked, in accordance with Table 2.3. This description is easy to formulate in LISP using the COND function.

> **Example 2.8   Application of UNIFY2.** Using the same input lists as Example 2.7 we show the operation of UNIFY2.

> **Step 1.** Initialize the binding list to the empty list.
> **Step 2.** Unify "question" with "question"; return success but no bindings $Z1 = \{\phi\}$.
> **Step 3.** (Successfully) unify "What" with "has"; augment binding list $Z1 = \{(\text{has/What})\}$
> **Step 4.** Unify "is" with "What." Check binding list for binding on "What." From unification rule five, Table 2.3, *unification fails*.

Extending Modus Ponens to Statements with Variables (and Unification)

One of the most important and logically sound inference techniques involves using MP with statements (especially rules) containing variables. In this way, knowledge may be represented as more general statements involving implication.

Recall a single substitution is represented by a pair of the form (t_i/R_i). We denote application of a set of substitutions $\theta = (t_i/R_i)$, $i = 1, 2, \ldots, n$, to a statement p, as $p\theta$, where every occurrence of variable R_i in p is replaced by t_i. Two statements, p and p_1 are unifiable (i.e., they have a *unifying substitution*, θ) if

$$p\theta \; = \; p^1\theta \tag{2-67}$$

In other words, a set of substitutions, θ, exists that makes p and p_1 identical.

```
PROCEDURE unify2(List1, List2);
BEGIN
IF List1 or List2 consist of a single element (an atom)
    THEN
      IF List1 and List2 are identical {indicates same variables
      case}
        THEN return empty list, NIL {no substitutions}
        ELSE
          IF List1 or List2 are variables {logical OR}
                THEN sequentially check the following cases and take the
                corresponding action;
          CASE:
          1. List1 unbound variable: return (List2/List1)
          2. List2 unbound variable: return (List1/List2)
          {Otherwise List1 and List2 must either be bound or not variables}
          3. (List1 or binding on List1) consistent with (List2 or binding
          on List2): return NIL
          4. return FAIL
        ELSE return FAIL {not identical and neither is a variable}
    ELSE {not atoms; must be lists}
      BEGIN {decimate input lists}
      Head1 := 1st element of List1;
      Rest1 := rest of List1;
      Head2 := 1st element of List2;
      Rest2 := rest of List2;
      Z1 := unify2 (Head1, Head2);
      IF Z1 = FAIL
        THEN return FAIL
        ELSE
          BEGIN
          Z2 := unify2 (Rest1, Rest2);

          IF Z2 = FAIL
            THEN return FAIL
            ELSE form new binding list as composite of Z1 and Z2 and return it
          END;
      END;
END. {UNIFY}
```

FIGURE 2.7
UNIFY2: Unification via checking the binding list at each step. (Compare with Fig. 10.2.)

Example 2.9   Determining a unifying substitution. We show a simple example using list notation, where variables (e.g., X) are denoted by capital letters. Note that if statement p^1 contains no variables, then

$$p^1 \; = \; p\theta$$

represents a unifying substitution. For example, the two statements

$$p_1 \; = \; (block\_1 \; left\_of \; block\_2)$$
$$p \; = \; (A \; left\_of \; B)$$

unify with

$$\theta = \{(block\_1/A), (block\_2/B)\}$$

In using MP in this manner, we assume that one or more unifying substitutions, θ, exist, and revise our notation for MP as follows:

$$
\frac{\begin{array}{c} p_1 \\ (\exists \theta) \ (p\theta = p^1\theta) \\ p \to q \end{array}}{q^1}
\tag{2-68}
$$

where q^1 is the result of applying the substitution θ to q (i.e., $q^1 = q\theta$). Example 2.10 helps clarify the concept of extended MP.

Example 2.10   Example of extended MP. The (axioms) in the initial database (assuming universal quantification) are

$$(A \ \text{left\_of} \ B) \to (B \ \text{right\_of} \ A) \tag{2-69}$$
$$(block\_1 \ \text{left\_of} \ block\_2) \tag{2-70}$$

We use the following logically valid inference procedure:

• Unify antecedent of implication statement (2-69) with fact (2-70).

$$(A \ \text{left\_of} \ B) \ \text{and}$$
$$(block\_1 \ \text{left\_of} \ block\_2)$$

These unify with $\theta = \{(block\_1/A), (block\_2/B)\}$.
  Thus, (2-69) and MP allow deduction of the new fact

$$(B \ \text{left\_of} \ A)\theta \tag{2-71a}$$

or, with substitution

$$(block\_2 \ \text{right\_of} \ block\_1) \tag{2-71b}$$

SUMMARY AND LIMITATIONS OF LOGIC-BASED REPRESENTATIONS

As shown in this chapter, there is no question but that the mathematical theory of logic is useful in AI. In fact, it forms part of the underpinnings of AI. It would be misleading, however, to claim that logic representations and manipulation lead to complete and general AI solutions. Some limitations of logic are

1. Logic does not allow subtlety of expression. While we can allow entities to be other than TRUE and FALSE (such as through multivalued logic, Chapter 13), the manipulation of these entities is not nearly as straightforward as the previous strategies.

2. Logic restricts our range of expression and may not fully extract *meaning*. Consider, for example, the development of "although" used in the following statement:

the car runs although it is old

The statement seems to indicate contradiction while relating two separate facts. A strictly logical interpretation of this sentence fails to convey some of the additional inherent meaning.

3. Logic, by itself, is not able to invoke knowledge scenarios, or what will later be termed "frames." This precludes the representation of logical entities that may be TRUE in some context, yet FALSE in another.

4. Logic restricts our inferences to those that are "logical," that is, founded in logic. This is a serious limitation given the following assertion: illogical behavior may lead to useful goals. For example, it often occurs that a person makes an apparently illogical statement, only to discover, in retrospect, that the statement contains truth. Additionally, it is claimed that many significant discoveries in mathematics, medicine, and other fields have been made by mistake. On the basis of this claim, it may not be bad to allow our knowledge inference mechanism occasionally to "freelance" in its production of new facts.

Perhaps the most succinct appraisal of logic limitations in AI is from Von Neumann [1958]:

> Whatever language the central nervous system is using, it is characterized by less logical and arithmetic depth than what we are normally used to. . . . Thus the outward forms of our mathematics are not absolutely relevant from the point of view of evaluating what the mathematical or logical language truly used by the central nervous system is.

REFERENCES

[Genesereth 1987] Genesereth, M.R., and N.J. Nilsson, *Logical Foundations of Artificial Intelligence,* Morgan Kaufmann, Los Altos, CA, 1987.

[Gevarter 1985] Gevarter, W.B., *Intelligent Machines: An Introductory Perspective of Artificial Intelligence and Robotics,* Prentice Hall, Englewood Cliffs, NJ, 1985.

[Hogger 1984] Hogger, C.J., *Introduction to Logic Programming,* Academic Press, New York, 1984.

[Johnsonbaugh 1986] Johnsonbaugh, R., *Discrete Mathematics,* MacMillan, New York, 1986.

[Kolman 1984] Kolman and Busby, *Discrete Mathematical Structures for Computer Science,* Prentice Hall, Englewood Cliffs, NJ, 1984.

[Miller 1973] Miller, C.D., and V.E. Heeren, *Mathematical Ideas,* Scott, Foresman and Company, Glenview, IL, 1973.

[Nilsson 1980] Nilsson, N.J., *Principles of Artificial Intelligence,* Tioga Publications, Palo Alto, CA, 1980.

[Shirai 1984] Shirai, Y., and J. Tsujii, *Artificial Intelligence: Concepts, Techniques and Applications,* Wiley, New York, 1984.

[Von Neumann 1958] Von Neumann, J., *The Computer and the Brain,* Yale University Press, New Haven, CT, 1958.

[Wand 1980] Wand, M., *Induction, Recursion, and Programming,* Elsevier, New York, 1980.

[Winston 1984] Winston, P.H., *Artificial Intelligence,* (2nd Edition), Addison-Wesley, Reading, MA, 1984.

PROBLEMS

2.1. A knowledge engineer is seeking alternative strategies for the production of new facts. Which of the following formulations are logically valid? Show your reasoning in detail.

(a) $p \rightarrow (p_2 \rightarrow q_2)$ true

     p_2 true

     p true

---

     q_2 true

(b) $p \rightarrow (p_2 \rightarrow q_2)$ false

     p_2 false

---

     q_2 true

(c) $(p \rightarrow q) \rightarrow q_2$ true

     p false

---

     q_2 false

(d) $a \rightarrow b$ true

     $b \cap \neg c$ false

     $a \rightarrow c$ true

2.2. Determine the logical significance of the math-oriented "if and only if" (iff) connective. How does it relate to other connectives, such as implication and equality?

2.3. Use resolution (not chaining) to verify the logical soundness of the following inference technique:

     $a \rightarrow b$ true

     $b \rightarrow c$ true

     $a \rightarrow c$ true

2.4. Derive the truth table for the converse, inverse, and contrapositive of the assertion $(p \rightarrow q)$.

2.5. The connective "unless" has been used to represent compound statements of the form

Unless something (event 1) happens, something else (event 2) will happen.

(a) Write this in terms of p and q.

(b) Show the truth table for the "unless" connective.

(c) Relate this to the implication connective.

(d) Develop an example of this using English statements; for example, "Unless I do this homework I will fail my ECE class."

2.6. Consider the development of a "liar's rule base." In other words, assume we have set up a rule base (like that in Example 2.2) where each rule is assumed to be FALSE.

(a) Can we develop an approach that allows us to develop new facts from some statement known to be true and the (all FALSE) assertions in the rule base?

(b) If so, show this for the situation in Example 2.2 involving "the professor is unhappy."

2.7. Recall our derivation, using logic, of a "forward chaining" rule base paradigm. Derive, again with respect to the mathematics of logic, a paradigm that allows "backward chaining." Assume you are given a database of TRUE implication statements and assertions, and a hypothesis or goal to be proved TRUE. This goal is the consequent of one or more statements, s_i, of the implications. How can we prove or disprove the hypothesis by moving through the database starting with one of the s_i?

2.8. Redo the forward chaining example "the professor is unhappy" (Example 2.2) by employing backward reasoning. Assume the assumption that "a college professor teaches in the summer" is TRUE and work backwards to verify "the professor is unhappy."

2.9. We wish to explore the properties of a new connective, "because." For example, consider the logic associated with

The circuit board failed because integrated circuit IC5 was faulty.

(a) Can the "because" operator be used in logic? If so, develop a truth-functional interpretation.

(b) Relate this operator to the implication operator.

2.10. Which of the following are logically correct?

(a) $(p \rightarrow q) = ((\neg q) \rightarrow (\neg p))$

(b) $(p \cap p) = p$

(c) $(p \cup p) = p$

(d) $\neg (p \cap q) = ((\neg p) \cup (\neg q))$

2.11. Show, strictly by using algebra, that

$$(p \rightarrow q) \cap (q \rightarrow p)$$

is equivalent to the equality connective. Could this equivalence, if properly identified, be of use in rule-based inference?

2.12. Verify one of the fundamental tools for clause resolution, viz.,

$(a \cup b)$	T
$(\neg a \cup c)$	T
$(b \cup c)$	T

Hint: You may choose to view this alternately as the first row of the implication truth table for

$$[(a \cup b) \cap (\neg a \cup c)] \rightarrow (b \cup c)$$

Note also that $b =$ FALSE yields modus ponens.

2.13. What is the result of the unification algorithm on the following lists:

(this What Is What)

(What Class is thing)

2.14. A knowledge engineer suggests the following basis for an IE:

$\neg q \rightarrow \neg p$	T
p	T
q	T (?)

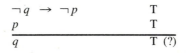

(a) Explain why or why not this strategy does or doesn't have a valid basis in symbolic logic.

(b) Discuss how a chaining-based inference strategy could be implemented using this approach.

2.15. The order of nesting is important in quantified statements. Show this by contrasting the meaning of these two statements:

$$(\forall X \ (\exists Y \ hates \ (X,Y)))$$

$$(\exists Y \ (\forall X \ hates \ (X,Y)))$$

(Assume *hates* (X, Y) is interpreted as X hates Y.)

2.16. The purpose of this problem is to consider manipulations with the implication operator. Specifically, we wish to consider whether implication may be distributed over other statements.

(*a*) Determine the truth value of the following sentence:

$$(a \rightarrow (b \rightarrow c)) \rightarrow ((a \rightarrow b) \rightarrow (a \rightarrow c))$$

(*b*) Could such a scheme, if logically correct, be of use in rule-based inference? Show your answer in detail.

2.17. Predicate logic even finds its way into rock music. For example, the 1966 Buffalo Springfield hit "For What It's Worth" contains the (assumed true) statement

"Nobody's right if everybody's wrong."

Assuming that the following is TRUE,

$$(\forall Y) \ \{(\text{right} \ (Y)) \equiv (\neg \text{wrong} \ (Y))\}$$

formulate this statement using logical connectives and quantification.

2.18. Repeat the resolution in Example 2.6, attempting pairwise clause resolution in at least two different sequences.

2.19. A three-valued logic is to be developed to enable "fuzzy" inferences. A statement may assume truth values of TRUE (T), FALSE (F), or MAYBE (M).

(*a*) Construct a truth table for each of the following logical connectives:

$\neg$

$\cap$

$\cup$

This three-valued logic should be consistent with classical propositional logic (*hint*: what if no statement ever has the value M?) and intuition. Justify each entry in the truth tables.

(*b*) Develop a truth table for the implication operator in this logic. How does it differ from two-valued logic?

(*c*) Develop the equivalent of modus ponens (MP) for this logic. How does it differ from two-valued logic?

2.20. (*a*) What is the result of unifying the following lists:

(i) (*X a Y*)
    (*Y Z b*)

(ii) (*A B C D*)
    (*a b c A*)

Use both UNIFY1 and UNIFY2 (see Examples 2.7 and 2.8).

(*b*) Which of the following list of substitutions may result from unification?

(i) (*Y/X , a/Z , Y/Z , a/X*)
(ii) (*Y/Z , a/Z , a/X , X/Y*)
(iii) (*a/Z , Z/Y , a/Y*)
(iv) (*X/Y , a/Z , Y/Z , a/Y*)

In part (*b*), assume the unification algorithm is based upon UNIFY2; that is, a binding list is created and checked to enforce consistent bindings.

2.21. Show why the basic axiom of resolution, viz.,

$$((a \cup b) \cap (\neg a \cup c)) \rightarrow (b \cup c)$$

involves *implication*; that is, show that it is *not* equality

$$((a \cup b) \cap (\neg a \cup c)) \equiv (b \cup c)$$

2.22. A function, as described in Appendix 1, is a special relation. In definitions (2-23a) and (2-23b), we distinguished the concept of *predicates* from *predicate functions*. Using these three definitions, are predicates necessarily functions? Justify your answer, and use examples where possible.

2.23. Chapter 2 considered the unification of two literals. Many AI problems require the unification of more than two literals; unification of a set of literals may be necessary. Discuss how this may be done using
(*a*) Pairwise unification of statements.
(*b*) Parallel unification of more than two statements.
Show an example of each extension.

2.24. Use *resolution* to prove the logical correctness of the following inference technique:

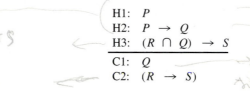

H1: P
H2: $P \rightarrow Q$
H3: $(R \cap Q) \rightarrow S$

C1: Q
C2: $(R \rightarrow S)$

2.25. Using the rule (2-35) in Example 2.5, together with the grounded predicates

$$p(r_1, \ r_2) \ \text{and} \ p(r_2, \ r_3)$$

show the logical proof of

$$s(r_1, \ r_3)$$

using unification and MP. Explicitly, show the substitution θ.

2.26. Prove the logical correctness of modus tollens:

$$a \rightarrow b$$
$$\neg b$$
$$\overline{\neg a}$$

and show an example of its use.

2.27. Which of the following are (*a*) wffs? (*b*) sentences?
(i) $(\forall X) \ ((p(X) \ \rightarrow \ p(Y)) \ \rightarrow \ q(X))$
(ii) $a \cup \ \rightarrow \ b$
(iii) $(\forall X) \ p(\neg X)$
(iv) $(\forall X) \ \neg p(X)$
(v) $\neg (\exists X) \ \neg p(X)$
(vi) $p(X \ \rightarrow \ Y)$
(vii) $(\forall X) \ \text{status} \ (X, \ \text{closed}) \ \equiv \ \neg \text{status} \ (X, \ \text{open})$

2.28. Consider the following wff:

$$(\forall X) \ (\forall Y) \ (\forall W) \ (p(X, \ Y) \cap p(Y, \ W) \ \rightarrow \ q_1 \ (X))$$

(*a*) Is it a sentence?
(*b*) Give one English language interpretation.
Compare your interpretation in part (b) with that of

[handwritten: for all X,Y,W If X rel't to Y by p, then X rel to W by q₂ and Y rel to W]

$$(\forall X)\ (\forall Y)\ (\forall W)\ (p(X,\ Y) \cap p(Y,\ W) \rightarrow q_2\ (X,\ W))$$

2.29. Show, using *both* algebraic and truth-table approaches, why

$$a \cap b \rightarrow b \qquad\qquad \text{(P2-29)}$$

is a tautology. State, in words, why the result of (P2-29) must hold, and cite an example.

2.30. Given

$$(r \cap q)\ \rightarrow\ s \qquad\qquad \text{[handwritten: } \cap \text{ not distributive wrt} \rightarrow]$$

does

$$(r\ \rightarrow\ s) \cap (q\ \rightarrow\ s) \qquad \text{NO}$$

logically follow?   *[handwritten: but $(r \rightarrow s) \cup (q \rightarrow s)$ yes]*

2.31. If the following two inferences hold:

$$a$$
$$\underline{a \rightarrow b}$$
$$b$$

$$c$$
$$\underline{c \rightarrow d}$$
$$d$$

does

$$a \cap c$$
$$a \rightarrow b$$
$$\underline{c \rightarrow d}$$
$$b \cap d$$

logically follow?   *[handwritten: Yes]*   *[handwritten: p.65]*

2.32. Repeat the derivation of Example 2.10 with the following database (recall variables are denoted with uppercase letters). Explicitly show the unifying substitution(s) and the new (derived) statements.

The axioms in the initial database are

$$(\text{moonies member\_of unification church})$$
$$(\text{prolog is\_based\_on unification})$$
$$(X\ \text{member\_of}\ Y\text{church})\ \cap\ (\text{prolog is\_based\_on}\ Y)\ \rightarrow\ (X\ \text{likes\_to\_program\_in}\ Y)$$

2.33. As noted in the text, the unification algorithm of Fig. 2.5 requires modification to form recursive procedure UNIFY1.

(*a*) One approach, indicated by (2-64) is to "preprocess" the remainder of the lists prior to further unification attempts. Show this approach using the following lists:

$$\text{List\_1}\ =\ (\text{What has Does When}) \qquad \text{(P2-33}a)$$
$$\text{List\_2}\ =\ (\text{predicate has What What}) \qquad \text{(P2-33}b)$$

(*b*) Repeat part (*a*), but instead develop a procedure based upon (2-65).

(*c*) In the right hand side of Fig. 2.5, what is the effect of interchanging the order in which List_1 and List_2 are checked to see if either is a variable? Modify the algorithm, and show the effect in unifying (P2-33*a*) and (P2-33*b*).

2.34. Given your current perspective on AI, comment on the truth value of each of the following statements:

(*a*) AI $\neq$ logic

(*b*) logic $\rightarrow$ AI

(*c*) AI $\rightarrow$ logic

(*d*) expert systems $\rightarrow$ AI

(*e*) AI $\rightarrow$ expert systems

2.35. Convert the pseudo code description of Fig. 2.7 (with the "cases" shown) into one consisting only of nested IFs.

CHAPTER 3

AI PROGRAMMING LANGUAGES AND DEVELOPMENT SYSTEMS— "THE TOOLS OF THE TRADE"

"Nothing astonishes men so much as common sense and plain dealing."

Ralph Waldo Emerson 1803–1882
Essays: First Series [1841]. Art

PROGRAMMING LANGUAGES OVERVIEW

Languages for AI Implementations

There is no *perfect* computer programming language. A useful programming language must facilitate both description (in the sense that programs may be written and read by programmers) and computations. Other features, such as portability and efficiency, are also important.

In this chapter specialized high-level languages for AI applications are considered. Salient characteristics, the distinctions between AI languages and more "conventional" languages (which we assume are familiar to most programmers), and the requirements of development environments which facilitate the AI system development are considered. These requirements may lead to specialized hardware, I/O (input/output), and debugging facilities, as described in Chapter 19 (AI architectures).

One (modest) objective of this chapter is to partially answer the question: "Why are PROLOG and LISP the 'languages of choice' for AI programmers?"

Like any sort of tool, a programming language is probably used most efficiently if it is well suited for a specific task. For example, business applications are often written in Cobol, beginners to programming often choose BASIC, and scientific processing is often undertaken with either FORTRAN, Pascal, or C. Few people would cut their lawns with sewing scissors when a lawnmower is available; similarly, few AI applications are written in Cobol.

"Conventional" and Symbolic Computing

Artificial intelligence research has spawned a resurgence in languages which allow the manipulation of (generally non-numeric) symbolic entities and the representation of concepts.

> The AI programmer has minimal interest in bits, bytes and numerical precision, but rather cares about symbolic structure, the manipulation of objects, constraint satisfaction and entity relationships. (3-1)

Figure 3.1(*a*) depicts the relationship between "conventional" (numeric, text) processing languages and AI computing languages.

"Conventional" (Numerical) Computing	*AI Computing*
• bits, bytes, numbers, functions, formatted output	• symbols, concepts, rules, relationships
• procedural algorithms to solve problems	• descriptive languages (describe known facts and relationships)
• specified sequences of steps to solution	• search/heuristics used to find solutions
• overall deterministic conclusion	• not known if algorithms converge
• data types: number character	• data types: atoms, objects, lists (programs)
• predeclared and (optional) typed variables (à la Pascal)	• not useful to predeclare or type variables (variables of certain types may be created as needed in the solution process)
• fixed dimension variables	• "dimension" of data structure may grow or shrink as solution proceeds
• exact/precise representation of information	• imprecise representation of information
• exact/precise answers sought	• any *satisfactory* answer sought

FIGURE 3.1(*a*)
AI vs. "conventional" programming.

The use of AI languages in knowledge representation and manipulation is intended to reduce the semantic gap between an implementation and the higher-level conceptual process. For example, before the availability of high-level programming languages, there was a considerable semantic gap between the concept of a matrix and its implementation, for example, via various addressing schemes in assembly language. Thus, the semantic gap may be reduced by the use of abstraction mechanisms. The complexity or efficiency of the implementation, however, is a function of the underlying algorithms, as described in Chapter 15. Note also that a range of sophistication of AI languages exists, from the elementary "pure" LISP (Chapter 8) to "canned" systems such as OPS5 (Chapter 13).

Coupled Computing Systems

In many practical AI applications, it is necessary to merge both symbolic and numerical computing procedures. In many applications, such as intelligent control, testing, database management and design, both are required. For example, in AI power systems applications (Chapter 6), often a numerical algorithm (a "load-flow" that determines system operational parameters, such as voltages, currents and power flows) provides input to a symbolic computing algorithm, for example, to assess overall system security and possible actions. Conversely, a symbolic algorithm may "trigger," initiate, or oversee one or more numerical algorithm modules. An example is a top-down approach to image analysis, where high-level expectations of a symbolic, model unification-oriented, algorithm invoke numerical procedures for low-level feature extraction from input image data.

These types of algorithmic interactions lead to the concept of **coupled computing systems** as shown in Fig. 3.1(*b*). Note that coupled computing, while merging symbolic and numerical approaches, does not require that the symbolic process is the "top-level" process, that is, controlling the numeric procedure. For example, the outcome of a numeric process could be used to trigger or invoke a specific expert system.

The most popular programming styles for AI implementation are logic programming and functional programming. Our objective in this chapter is to characterize and

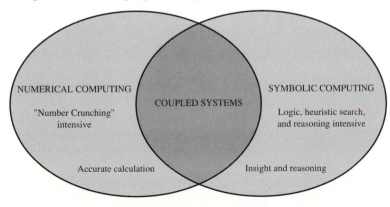

FIGURE 3.1(*b*)
Merging AI and conventional computing to form "coupled" systems.

emphasize the utility of LISP and PROLOG in AI system development. In addition, we contrast these programming paradigms with more familiar languages, such as Pascal or FORTRAN. LISP and PROLOG are not difficult to learn if the reader approaches their study systematically and rigorously follows a few simple guidelines.

Manipulable Representations and Data Structures

An elementary objective of AI programming is to define "manipulable" data objects as abstract representations of real-world entities. Examples of entities are "Bob," "Riggs Hall," and "Electrical Engineering." In this example, "Bob" is an **instance** of the entity type **person**. We may think of person as a variable, that is, the entity person may have instances (from its universe of values) of "Bob," "Sam," "Ernie," and so on. More specifically, "Bob" is the symbolic **value** (or simply value) assigned to a specific person. This person, "Bob," may have other characteristics or properties relevant to symbolic manipulation requirements, such as age and education level. More importantly, "Bob" may have properties or characteristics that are **inherited** from the class of persons, since Bob is an instance of a member of that class. This representation may be achieved in languages such as Pascal via TYPE and VAR declarations of the following form:

```
TYPE
    person_type = record
                    name: string[14];
                    age: [0..125];
                    education: set of (High School, College);
VAR
    person : ARRAY [1..N] OF person_type;                    (3-2)
```

Notice the data structure of (3-2) incorporates both symbolic (name and education) as well as numerical (age) information. To extract information relevant to the particular person "Bob," the Pascal assignment operator is used in conjunction with the above data structure. For example:

```
IF
  person.name[j] = 'Bob'
        THEN
            bobs_age := person.age[j];                    (3-3)
```

This type of "manipulable" representation is easily achieved in LISP, via the built-in structure constructs. Peeking ahead to Chapter 8, we see this can be achieved in LISP via the constructs:

```
(putprop 'Bob 'age 33)                                    (3-4a)
```

and

```
(get 'Bob 'age)                                           (3-4b)
```

Similarly, in Common LISP the Pascal code fragment of (3-4) becomes

```
(setf (get 'Bob 'age) 33)
```
(3-5*a*)

and

```
(get 'Bob 'age).
```
(3-5*b*)

THE LISP AND PROLOG DISTINCTION

The need for symbolic representation and manipulation spawned by AI has led to the popularity of several languages, notably PROLOG (PROgramming in LOGic) and LISP (LISt Processing*). Commercial interest in both languages is very high at this time. To some extent, both languages share common features, yet applications (and personal prejudices) exist where one is preferred over the other. The syntax of PROLOG is (intentionally) simpler than that of LISP. Also, in contrast to conventional languages, "pure" versions of PROLOG and LISP were designed around a small set of primitives or building blocks (predicates and functions, respectively) which could be extended to provide higher-level functionality.

Both LISP and PROLOG originated in academia. LISP origins generally may be traced to universities in the United States, whereas PROLOG has origins in Canada, France, and Great Britain. Putting aside national prejudices, we note that almost anything that can be done in one language can also be accomplished in the other, if efficiency of programming and/or execution is neglected.

The Distinction (What's Different?)

> Programming in the AI languages of PROLOG and LISP is fundamentally different from programming in an imperative language such as FORTRAN or Pascal. (3-6)

In fact, the ability to program in the latter languages, due to the aforementioned difference, many times presents an obstacle to the novice LISP or PROLOG programmer. This obstacle is especially likely to present itself when programmers attempt to write LISP and PROLOG programs using the same approach as for an imperative language. Thus, it is extremely important to note (perhaps even memorize) the following distinctions in AI language programming methodology:

> In LISP, the programmer does not emphasize the flow of program control, but rather concentrates on the application of functions to data, and the values returned from these applications. Not surprisingly, a LISP program consists of functions applied to data and the values returned by other function applications. (3-7)

> In PROLOG, the programmer does not concentrate on the specification of program execution sequence, but rather attempts to specify the problem (or situation) through

---

* Alternately, novice LISP programmers often come to believe that the acronym LISP stands for "Lots of Irritating, Silly Parentheses."

development of a database consisting of facts and rules. It is left for the PROLOG unification mechanism to employ this database to generate solutions. Not surprisingly, a PROLOG program consists of a problem description in PROLOG rule and fact-based syntax. (3-8)

The PROLOG Programming Concept as Description

In the development of PROLOG programs (or PROLOG problem descriptions) the user need not construct a flowchart or logic diagram. In fact, a flowchart, due to the declarative nature of PROLOG and the manner in which predicate logic-based unification proceeds, is meaningless. Instead, PROLOG programs concentrate on **description**. The programmer merely enumerates: (1) known facts; (2) rules (which allow combinations of facts or derivation of new facts); and (3) a goal. The overall execution sequence of the PROLOG program is handled by the PROLOG system (either interpreter or compiler). Thus, compared with imperative languages, PROLOG, by exploring possible variable bindings, determines the sequence of execution (unification) steps.

PROLOG programming is based upon **problem specification**, which parallels the concept of program specification in software engineering. The specification of a program, without indicating a solution algorithm, typically consists of high-level constructs that are not directly computable, but intuitively convey the desired meaning and reflect human reasoning constructs. For example, specification of a procedure to find the square root of a number is shown below.

> **Example 3.1 (Integer) Square root program specification.** To find the integer square root of an integer n, when $n \geq 0$, find an integer r such that
>
> $$r^2 \leq n \leq (r + 1)^2 \qquad (3-9)$$

Notice the specification does not indicate how to compute r, but rather what r is . It also does not guarantee that a solution exists. Furthermore, to a beginning programmer, particularly one familiar with imperative languages, the most startling discovery about PROLOG is the following observation:

> It is fundamental to note that there is no emphasis placed on the assignment operator (e.g., the " = " or " : = " symbol) in PROLOG. The "is" infix operator, which forces assignment, is available, but is generally used only to facilitate evaluation of arithmetic expressions. Assignment of values to variables in PROLOG takes place principally through the *unification* mechanism, the operation of which is, in the execution of a PROLOG program, left to the PROLOG system. (3-10)

The LISP Programming Concept

We now introduce LISP programming in a similar manner. In LISP, assignment of values (either numerical or symbolic) to variables is possible in a variety of ways using a variety of LISP functions. In LISP, the crucial distinction between the name variable and its value forces the programmer to carefully invoke assignment, as shown in the introductory programming examples. For example, there is a significant difference between the effect of the assignment functions "set" and "setq" (Chapter 8 explores this further). In addition, the introduction of a single quote mark preceding a LISP expression may make all the difference in the world as far as the actual assignment that takes place!

Data Directed Processing

AI applications typify the need for **data-directed processing**, in that how the data is processed is a strong function of what the data is. For example, in an image-processing application the processing focus of attention may be determined by extraction of preliminary regions of interest or other salient features from the data. This, in turn, may determine the particular algorithms which are subsequently used and thus typifies data-directed processing. By contrast, a numerical algorithm for inversion of an arbitrary matrix consists of a sequence of steps which (ignoring pivoting) are relatively insensitive to a particular matrix of data.

AI DEVELOPMENT ENVIRONMENTS AND SYSTEMS

The development of AI systems for specific applications usually involves symbolic (and, secondarily, numerical) quantification of known relations among entities that comprise the system model. While the algorithmic development task is often fundamental and of primary importance, the efficient processing of the typically voluminous (and often expanding) amount of data in symbolic models is also a concern to researchers and developers, particularly since many of the advances in AI implementation are based upon significant amounts of extensive empirical research.

Desirable AI Software Capabilities

In addition to the characteristics cited in Fig. 3.1, desirable features of AI software development systems include:

1. The ability to develop models and reasoning mechanisms *incrementally*, by decomposing the problem solution into smaller, interrelated solution units.
2(*a*). Flexible control structures to facilitate goal-directed programming.
2(*b*). Flexible control structures to facilitate data-directed programming.
2(*c*). Flexible control structures to facilitate recursion.
3. Flexible control structures to facilitate parallel programming.
4. Interactive system communication capability.
5. Debuggers that facilitate program checking, particularly with respect to unification, recursion, etc.
6. Built-in list or other symbolic data representation facilities, and the means to extend these representations into complex knowledge structures (frames).
7. Pattern matching facilities.
8. Variable binding strategies such that search and trial and error solution approaches are facilitated.

Advances of VLSI fabrication are helping to drive down symbolic processing computer costs to the point where they are economically feasible for use by small groups of researchers. Specialized machines (and even chips) are becoming available for LISP and PROLOG programming and execution (Chapter 19).

Desirable AI Software Environments

The unconventional nature of programming in AI languages and the development of AI systems generates a need for "user-friendly" development environments. For example, it would be quite cumbersome if the development cycle consisted of generating the entire program, (attempted) compiling, debugging, application (execution using data) and then modification. Instead, most AI development environments provide several useful features, including

1. *Incremental program development.* The program is developed a segment at a time, for example, in LISP a function at a time; in PROLOG a rule at a time. This segment is then tested and modified; the final version is integrated into the present state of the overall program. This capability facilitates the emerging "structural" development paradigm for programs in other languages as well, for example, ADA.

2. *Integral (intelligent) editors* as a part of the system. The source code is not developed independently of the AI language system, but rather proceeds incrementally in the sense that syntax errors are corrected in the editing or creation of the segment.

3. *Incremental compilers/interpreters.* These facilities make the debugging of programs easier; the system runs in interpreter mode until the program segment is fully developed. Then it is (incrementally) compiled for speed and memory savings. In addition, the knowledge database and inference approach may be developed and modified incrementally. For example, clauses (in PROLOG) may be added or deleted via (usually) built-in assert ( ) and retract ( ) predicates. Similarly, function definitions and variable assignments (e.g., database facts) may be modified in LISP.

4. *Intelligent and user-friendly debuggers.* Most PROLOG and LISP development environments provide a "trace" facility wherein a program may be executed in single step mode, arguments to and from functions as well as variable bindings are explicitly shown, the level of recursion or function nesting is indicated, and break points for certain conditions during the execution may be set.

5. *High resolution, high speed display capabilities.* AI development system output capabilities, particularly with respect to graphics, are often greater than those available on minicomputer and mainframe displays. Since our objective is to manipulate (generally) symbolic objects and their corresponding properties, and relations among objects, the graphical construct of a digraph or semantic net proves useful. In the specification, debugging, and output phases of AI system development, it may be quite useful to be able to display these graphical constructs. A graphical description is favored over some type of text-based listing of these relations. In addition, the interactive nature of the development process, and the need for good debugging capabilities, also support a requirement for higher resolution displays. The use of multiple display windows for program listing, program tracing, system resource

information and perhaps I/O necessitates a high resolution display that, when partitioned into windows, yields adequate resolution. In addition, the debugging of AI system code is aided by the graphical display of the order in which functions (or predicates) were invoked, current variable bindings, the current level of recursion, etc. To this end, many current AI development systems, for example, Lisp Machines, Inc. or LMI, and Symbolics provide bit-mapped displays with spatial resolution on the order of 1000×1000 pixel elements, or pixels. This is also a feature of several non-dedicated but powerful AI platforms such as Sun or MacInctosh workstations. While perhaps useful, the need for color display capability does not appear as significant.

6. *Specialized and dedicated (perhaps electrical) interfaces to instrumentation.* A good example of this requirement is the ability to acquire and perhaps output image or speech data.

7. *Large memory spaces and large amounts of (single user) memory*, particularly for the implementation of AI languages such as LISP and PROLOG, which extensively use recursion, and consequently are "stack intensive."

PROGRAMMING LANGUAGE CLASSIFICATIONS

Introduction and Definitions

A fundamental programming concept is the assignment of a value to a variable.

> Languages that are organized around assignment are referred to as imperative languages. (3-11)

In most cases, FORTRAN is a good example of a language of this type. In imperative languages, the programmer typically specifies a sequence of steps leading to a problem solution, for example, FOR i :=1 TO n DO. . . .
Alternately,

> Languages that are organized upon the application of functions to arguments are termed applicative languages. (3-12)

LISP is a good example of an applicative language. Applicative languages, which only consist of functions and arguments to these functions that uniquely define program output, are often referred to as functional languages. HOPE is an example of this type of "purely functional" language. LISP, although not purely a functional language, is often loosely referred to as such. In functional languages, as opposed to imperative languages, we concentrate on the problem formulation and results and ignore the details of how they are computed.

> Another type of language wherein program output is specified in terms of an argument and some property of this argument (usually in the form of a relationship with other arguments) is termed a relational language. (3-13)

PROLOG is currently one of the best examples of this type of language.

Both relational and applicative (functional) languages are usually applied to problems in a manner different from that of imperative languages. Not surprisingly, they are therefore applied to a different class of problems, specifically, many AI problems. Imperative languages may be used to solve a particular problem without describing anything about the solution other than the set of steps necessary to find it. Applicative/relational languages, on the other hand, are used to find a problem solution through a process of defining the desired solution form, and then allowing the program to apply this solution definition to input data to determine the solution. Since they are based upon the user describing or declaring the solution as a part of the program, applicative (functional) and relational languages are categorized as declarative languages. This descriptive-based solution property of declarative languages explains their popularity in AI applications, since often we know the characteristics of the result we are seeking; we are usually unable (or find it cumbersome) to specify a set of steps leading to the solution.

A graphical taxonomy of higher-level programming languages is shown in Fig. 3.2. The taxonomy shown conveys the typical use of each of the languages shown, and does not imply that a language cannot be used in several modes. For example, iteration is possible in LISP, and Pascal programs may be written with a functional structure.

Examples of Pascal, LISP and PROLOG

A simple example is presented to illustrate the different programming styles and provide a "soft start" introduction to PROLOG and LISP programming. Suppose we desire the factorial of an integer. (This is perhaps one of the most worn examples in

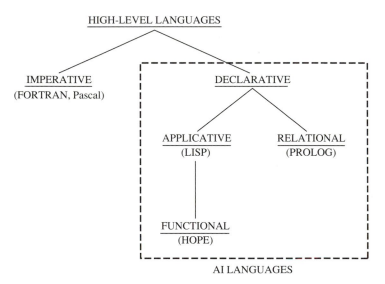

FIGURE 3.2
Programming language taxonomy.

the literature, but it does illustrate the situation.) The factorial of a number is naturally defined using recursion; however, for illustration we define it as follows:

$$n! = n(n-1)(n-2) \cdots [n-(n-2)]\,1 \qquad (3\text{-}14)$$

In Pascal, we could define this numerical operation as shown in the following program segment.

Example 3.2   Pascal "factorial" function definition (nonrecursive).

```
FUNCTION factorial(n:integer): integer;
VAR
i,accum,nm1 : integer;
BEGIN
IF n =1 THEN factorial:=n
          ELSE
                BEGIN
                accum:=n;
                nm1:=n−1;
                FOR i:=1 TO (n−1) DO
                   BEGIN
                   accum:=accum*nm1;
                   nm1:=nm1−1;
                   END;
                END;
factorial:=accum;
END;                                              (3-15)
```

The factorial function defined in (3-14) could be defined in LISP as follows.

Example 3.3   LISP "factorial" function definition (recursive).

```
(defun factorial (arg)
(cond
(= arg 1) 1)
(t (* arg (factorial (− arg 1)))))        (3-16)
```

Although we have yet to explore the details, the apparent distinction between the two programming styles is evident from the radically different syntaxes.

Several facts are worth noting:

1. It may be that the actual, machine level, computation of $n!$, using either of the above languages, is identical. This is a consequence of the compiler or interpreter used for each language, and the architecture of the processor that executes the respective machine-level programs. What is significant, however, is the important distinction between the programs, as reflected in the high-level language description.

2. The use of LISP to illustrate functional and recursive programming vis-a-vis Pascal is slightly misleading. Pascal also allows the application of functions to a spectrum

of arguments, and most Pascal environments also support recursion. In fact, (3-17) shows the equivalent Pascal definition of the factorial function using recursion:

Example 3.4   Alternate Pascal "factorial" function definition (recursive).

```
FUNCTION factorial (n: integer): integer;
BEGIN
IF n=1 THEN factorial:= n
       ELSE factorial:=n*factorial(n-1);
END; {factorial}                                          (3-17)
```

The similarity between the recursive Pascal definition and the LISP function is evident. Notice the use of Pascal's **passing by value** parameter interface. This allows recursion since a local copy of the argument is made each time function factorial is invoked (by itself). Although Pascal provides recursive capability, LISP is the language of choice for many AI applications due to other built-in features, such as variable bindings and scope as well as list manipulation capabilities.

The factorial function in (3-14) may also be described in PROLOG. For example, a recursive of (3-14) consists of a PROLOG rule (which handles the case where $n > 1$) and a fact (for the case where $n = 1$). A sample description is shown in Example 3.5.

Example 3.5   PROLOG "factorial" function description (recursive).

```
factorial(1,1).
factorial(Input,Result) :-
                          Imin1 is Input-1,
                          factorial(Imin1,Facmin1),
                          Result is Input*Facmin1.        (3-18)
```

(Note: this simple program may not be used directly due to infinite recursion problems when the input is less than 1.)

While certain AI applications may greatly necessitate one of these organizations, most programming languages have a combination of imperative and applicative features. For example, Pascal, due to the availability of recursion and procedures (functions), may be thought of as an applicative language.

Control Structures

In an imperative or applicative programming environment some type of control mechanism is necessary to allow sequencing, recursion (of either assignment or function application), conditionals and looping. These types of control structures, while often syntactically different, are common to both organizations. In a relational language such as PROLOG, limited control structures (for example, the "cut") are provided. However, the control structure of PROLOG is almost exclusively embedded in the (built-in) unification or goal satisfaction procedure.

A summary of example languages and their specific features useful for AI is shown in Table 3.1.

TABLE 3.1
Sample AI languages

Desired representation	Manipulation technique	Language(s)
Predicate logic	Unification for goal satisfaction	PROLOG
Rule-based	Forward/backward chaining	OPS5, LISP

ALTERNATIVE LANGUAGES

Other suitable languages for AI implementations exist. Some are extensions or variants of LISP and PROLOG. In addition, there are languages that combine the features of Pascal (which includes readability) with those of LISP. An excellent example of this is the language POP-11 [Barrett/Ramsey/Sloman 1985]. POP-11 is a high-level programming language developed for research and teaching in Artificial Intelligence. POP-11 is derived from POP-2, a language originally developed by Robin Popplestone at Edinburgh University. The language is a subset of a more comprehensive multi-language system called POPLOG, marketed commercially by Systems Designers International. POP-11 also bears some resemblance to sophisticated versions of LISP; its clearer syntax makes learning and reading it somewhat easier. Most installations of the language are on larger machines (for example, VAX) and contain an interactive editor and incremental compiler, thus providing the type of desirable development environment cited earlier. The POP-11 system normally runs in interpreted mode. The structure and scope of variables and the declaration of procedures are very similar to Pascal. POP-11 has a rich set of list-manipulation capabilities similar to LISP; for example, the built-in procedures "hd" and "tl" emulate the LISP "car" and "cdr" functions. Other, more advanced, built-in procedures with LISP analogies are also available. POP-11 permits recursion. One of the most useful built-in procedures of POP-11 is the **pattern matcher**, a predicate function that enables a matching of two lists. This capability is essential for rule-based inference systems and database searching.

RECURSION

A function (or procedure) that calls or invokes itself is said to be **recursive**. The previous programming examples (3-16) – (3-18) introduced programming using recursion. As noted, recursion is a capability provided by many programming languages, including Pascal, LISP and PROLOG.

Most programmers are more familiar with the concept of **iteration** than with recursion. Computer hardware architectures (described in Chapter 17) are often designed to directly support recursion via stacks. In the following programming examples in both PROLOG and LISP, we show significant use of recursion.

Example 3.6   Recursive definition (Fibonacci sequence).   Recursion examples are typically found in the syntax descriptions of programming languages. A familiar numerical example is that of the definition of the Fibonacci sequence:

$$F_1 = 1$$
$$F_2 = 1$$
$$F_n = F_{n-1} + F_{n-2} \qquad \text{if } n > 2 \tag{3-20}$$

As we shall see, recursion needs to be carefully applied to problems. The generation of infinite recursion is frequently a consequence of either improperly applied recursion or faulty unification strategies. Often, this is a consequence of the computation never encountering a termination condition.

Example 3.7 Infinite recursion. Suppose we wished to implement the binary relationship "next_to" in PROLOG. To indicate the truth of object1 being next_to object2 we would enter the fact

```
next_to(object1, object2).                        (3-21)
```

in the PROLOG database. However, we might assume that the relationship "next to" is symmetric; that is, the truth value of

```
next_to(object2, object1).                        (3-22)
```

is the same as that of statement (3-21). We might therefore attempt to embody the symmetric property of the relationship "next_to" in the PROLOG database with the rule

```
next_to (A,B) :- next_to (B,A).                   (3-23)
```

This recursively defined rule completely satisfies the syntax of PROLOG, and is a valid PROLOG clause. However, as shown in Chapter 4, the PROLOG inference mechanism attempts infinite recursion in attempting to unify this rule.

IMPLEMENTATION OF RECURSION

The use of recursion in most languages necessitates a replication of the function(s) that are used recursively. Replication of the machine-level instructions and related intermediate results (values of memory locations) is often necessary. Thus, in the implementation of a function that recursively calls itself, the need to "save" the intermediate values of variables in the current function invocation, and the need to later restore or recover these variables must be provided. Arguments and internal variables are reserved memory space in a **stack frame**. A stack frame is created for every level of recursion. Thus, large and numerous stack frames may yield problems in memory management. Figure 3.3 shows a simple graphical interpretation of a recursive function execution. Notice how the function graphically "unwinds" or "unfolds" until the deepest level of recursion is reached. Note that seldom is recursion as clear as in Fig. 3.3, since often a recursively defined function invokes other (different) recursively defined functions. Thus, the graphical interpretation yields a much more complicated

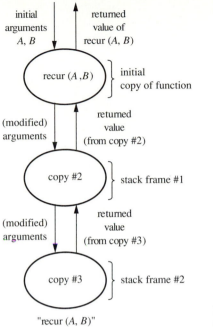

FIGURE 3.3
Graphical description of recursion.

"audit trail" of the process. In addition, circularities may be difficult to identify. Thus, it is not surprising that recursion, viewed from the machine hardware level, is a stack-intensive operation.

TAIL RECURSION

Many recursive procedures that occur naturally in the formulation of AI algorithms have a special characteristic that eliminates the need for creation of new stack frames during execution. Suppose, for example, that the returned value of the function (at the top level) is the returned value of (a copy of) the function at the deepest level of recursion. This is shown in Fig. 3.4. In this case, each of the function copies, according to Fig. 3.4, would merely serve to pass this result "upward," without modification, to the top-most level. Thus, once this value is calculated, no further need for the stack frames exists. Such a process is called **tail-recursive**. In tail recursion, it is not necessary to create new stack frames to be used as the recursive "unwinds," but rather only to pass modified function arguments to a single copy of the function. Thus, the previous stack frame may be replaced with the next deeper stack frame. Such a process uses memory efficiently. For this reason, many interpreters and compilers attempt to identify tail recursion in the user's source code. Note also that the effective result of identifying tail recursion is the replacement of recursion with iteration, since we merely invoke the function n times (with modified arguments), and return the last value.

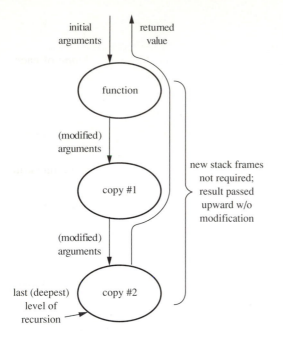

initial
arguments

returned
value

function

(modified)
arguments

copy #1

new stack frames
not required;
result passed
upward w/o
modification

(modified)
arguments

last (deepest)
level of
recursion

copy #2

FIGURE 3.4
Tail recursion (new stack frames not required).

VARIABLES AND SCOPING (PROGRAMMING POINT OF VIEW)

Variable Scope

In most programming languages, values may be *passed to* procedures and functions through parameters or variables. In addition, variables may be defined and modified during the course of execution of a procedure or a function evaluation. The way in which values of variables are passed to a procedure or function, and the subsequent overall effect of changes in the value of a variable, are a function of the scope of the variable. Thus, **scoping of variables** indicates the context in which values may be assigned to the variable. This assignment is also referred to as **binding**.

Binding

In the execution of a program, a particular variable may take on many values, as a function of the variable scope. This scope may be within certain program blocks (or portions) whose text refers to (and defines) the variable (**lexical scoping**). Alternately, if the scope of a variable is not constrained to program text (the so-called "definition" environment), but rather is determined by the history of function or procedure activations (which result in the current environment), **dynamic binding** is said to exist. The scope of a variable is particularly important when recursion of functions and the process of unification or matching of symbolic entities occurs.

Pascal Example

Pascal is a strongly typed language. Every variable in a Pascal program must be declared before use. This declaration indicates, to the compiler, the TYPE and *scope* of each variable. Thus, one way to define the scope of a variable is in the variable declaration part of a block. Defining a variable, for example,

```
VAR
is_true:boolean;
```
(3-24)

in a certain program block indicates the scope of the variable "is_true" is the block in which the variable is defined (and also any block contained within that block). Variables declared in the main program block are said to be global, and accessible to any procedure or sub-block in the program. An alternative way to scope a variable in Pascal is to tie its scope to a procedure, as a part of the procedure declaration. For example, the following procedure declaration

```
procedure part_of(wheels, roof:component);
```
(3-25a)

indicates that two variables, "wheels" and "roof," are of type "component" (which itself may be a complex type). More importantly, this declaration of variables in the formal parameter list of the procedure makes the scope of these variables local to the procedure (and any procedures contained within it). They may also be referred to as **local variables**. Changes or different value assignments to variables "wheels" and "roof" do not "propagate backwards" in the program; that is, when procedure "part_of" is invoked, *local copies* of these variables are created and used in "part_of." The reader should contrast this scoping with the program behavior if the variable declaration in the procedure is changed to

```
procedure part_of( VAR: wheels, roof:component);
```
(3-25b)

LISP AND PROLOG VARIABLE SCOPING

In PROLOG, the scope of a variable is related to its use in a rule. Since rules are based upon implication, variables are scoped using universal quantification; that is, the PROLOG rule

$$r(X) : - p(X)$$
(3-26)

is logically equivalent to

$$\forall(X)(p(X) \rightarrow r(X))$$
(3-27)

The quantification in (3-27) defines the scope of variable X. By contrast, given the database

$$(\forall X)(p_1(X) \rightarrow r_1(X))$$
(3-28a)

and

$$(\forall X)(p_2(X) \rightarrow r_2(X)) \tag{3-28b}$$

the bindings on variable X in (3-28a) and (3-28b) are completely independent.

In LISP, the scoping of variables is related to their origin in function definitions. This is insufficient, however, to fully describe the manner in which variables are assigned values, since the concept of time or order of procedure execution may enter the binding process.

The Binding Environment

In LISP and PROLOG, variables may be either *free* or *bound*. A collection of bindings of variables to values is referred to as an **environment**. Thus, to determine the current binding of a variable, one looks at the current environment. Dynamic binding assigns values depending upon the current program execution sequence; lexical binding assigns values based upon the variable scope in the program text.

Dynamic and Lexical Scoping of LISP Variables

LISP binding of variables may take place either using lexical or dynamic scoping. FranzLISP employs dynamic scoping. CommonLISP employs lexical scoping. We note

1. Dynamic binding is particularly useful in developing matching algorithms.
2. Lexical scoping is somewhat easier to trace in the debugging process.

More is said in detail about LISP scoping in Chapter 8.

REFERENCES

[Grogono 1980] Grogono, P., *Programming in PASCAL*, Addison-Wesley, Reading, MA, 1980.
[Tennent 1981] Tennent, R.D., *Principles of Programming Languages*, Prentice-Hall, N.Y., 1981.

CHAPTER
4

FUNDAMENTALS OF PROLOG

"Contrariwise," continued Tweedledee, "if it were so, it might be; and if it were so, it would be; but as it isn't, it ain't. That's logic."

Lewis Carroll
Through the Looking Glass

PROLOG BACKGROUND

Introduction

Choosing a knowledge representation based upon predicate calculus, we explore an implementation using the declarative language **PRO**gramming in **LOG**ic (PROLOG).

> The underlying concept of PROLOG is quite simple—PROLOG implements a subset of first-order logic restricted to Horn clauses. (4-1a)

Whereas PROLOG interest has been heretofore concentrated in the European community, especially Edinburgh, Scotland, PROLOG achieved much international attention when it was chosen by the Japanese as the language for the Fifth Generation computing project.

Recall that PROLOG is a declarative language, as opposed to the more traditional imperative programming languages, for example, Pascal. This often causes some difficulty for beginners since good PROLOG programmers have mastered the art of letting the unification mechanism in PROLOG solve the problem, without forcing the solution, as in imperative approaches. It is a straightforward process to learn PROLOG; the unification mechanism is transparent to the user. However, like LISP, the concepts become more complex when actually employing PROLOG for AI system development. At that point, consequences of the unification mechanism including backtracking and the computational requirements of depth-first search (Chapter 15), as well as advanced PROLOG constructs such as lists, need to be considered.

Unification—the Basis of PROLOG

PROLOG is a useful language when the solution to a problem involves satisfaction of a number of symbolic constraints relating problem variables. A good example is the labeling of objects with compatibility constraints on the labels of adjacent objects (Chapter 5). Although we considered the theoretical basis of logic, an introduction to the operation of PROLOG is presented here in a more informal approach. The relationship between first order predicate logic and PROLOG will then be developed.

> The only significant data manipulation primitive in logic programming is unification. Understanding PROLOG means understanding unification.   (4-1b)

The basis for applications implemented in PROLOG is a set of statements or clauses comprising rules, facts and goals. Often this is viewed as the "database" of problem information. PROLOG's main utility is in searching this database with the objective of satisfying one or more goals through a unification process. When one or more consistent solutions are found; that is, bindings yield facts that are either logically provable or derivable from the database, the PROLOG system reports success and returns these bindings.

PROLOG "Standards," Compatibility and C+M

The definition of a standard is a relatively significant aspect of any programming language, and tends to spawn controversy (particularly from vendors whose products do not conform to the standard). No official standard exists for the PROLOG language, although the syntax developed at the University of Edinburgh (in Scotland) or so-called "Edinburgh" syntax is almost universally accepted by the research community. This standard is described in the book Clocksin and Mellish, *Programming in Prolog,* (Springer Verlag) [Clocksin Mellish 1987], hence the so-called "C+M" designation of the standard. It is important to note that C+M describe a so-called "conversational" language, which implies an interpreted version of the language. Many PROLOG software vendors claim their products are a "superset" of this standard specification. Often (in spite of the well-understood meanings of a language adhering to a specified standard and the concept of a superset) what the vendors mean is that their product comes close to meeting the standard and has additional features not governed by the standard. The PROLOG syntax we study is that given in C+M.

TABLE 4.1
Relating logical connectives to PROLOG syntax

Connective	Logical symbol	PROLOG symbol
Negation (not)	⌐	not( )
Conjunction (and)	∩	,
Disjunction (or)	∪	;
Implication[1] (if-then)	→	:-

[1]Note the reversing of the order of arguments (see (4–6) and (4–7)).

Logical Connectives and PROLOG Syntax

For illustration, the mapping between the logical connectives explored in Chapter 2 and the syntax of PROLOG is shown in Table 4.1. Note also that variables in PROLOG are denoted by symbols beginning with an uppercase letter.

CLAUSES, FACTS, GOALS, AND RULES

Clauses

First, we consider PROLOG clauses that comprise rules and facts. A PROLOG program is a sequence of PROLOG clauses. **Clauses** in PROLOG are analogous to sentences [refer to (2-54)] in first order logic. Clauses are built using predicates and logical connectives and are allowed to contain variables that are assumed universally quantified.

> A PROLOG clause is comprised of a head and an (optional) body or tail.   (4-1c)

> If the tail or body of the clause is omitted (forming a "unit clause"), the clause is a PROLOG fact, which is interpreted to be TRUE.   (4-1d)

As shown in the following, other clauses in the body of a clause become subgoals.

Facts

PROLOG facts are introduced with the sample clause:

$$has(house, roof).   (4-2)$$

Recalling our previous study of predicates, grounded (i.e., without any variables) predicates are examples of facts. The English-language interpretation of the PROLOG statement in (4-2) is that there is a relation between two objects, roof and house, and this relation is "has"; that is, (4-2) is interpreted as "a house has a roof." More specifically, "has" is termed a predicate or a functor with nonvariable arguments "house" and "roof". The arity (number of arguments) to this predicate function is two. In addition, it is a predicate that is assumed TRUE in the PROLOG database. The entities "has," "roof," and "house" are PROLOG **atoms.**

We may represent a situation by a series of fact statements. For example, additional descriptors of a house, using additional predicates, may be incorporated in the database as

Example 4.1   Sample PROLOG database.

```
has(house,  door).
has(house,  window).
has(door,  knob).
has(window,  glass_panes).
(etc.)
```
                                                                    (4-3*a*)

In PROLOG, facts do not have to be grounded predicates. This leads to the definition:

A PROLOG clause that is unconditionally TRUE is a fact.   (4-3*b*)

The following are examples of PROLOG facts:

```
is_fact (arg1, arg2).
a_fact_too (Y).
equal (X, X).
another_fact.
wheel_is_round.
round (wheel).
wheel (round).
```
                                                                    (4-3*c*)

Goals

Another basic PROLOG construct is the goal statement. For example, we might query the PROLOG system with:

$$? - has(What, door).$$ (4-4)

indicating we are interested in having the system search the database and indicate what type of object satisfies this relationship; that is, in English, "What (in the database) has a door?" In the simplest case (temporarily neglecting the power of rules) the PROLOG system then attempts to unify statement (4-4) with one in the database (4-3*a*), by finding a substitution for the variable "What." This process typically involves search. If the process is successful, the system responds with the binding or substitution of the variable "What." If the process is not successful, we must be careful to interpret the results accurately. Lack of success in the unification process does not necessarily prove the negation of the goal, but rather may indicate simply that the database is incomplete.

All variables in PROLOG begin with a capital letter. This convention was used in our development of predicate-based logic.   (4-5)

Rules

We now turn our attention to the most significant clause in PROLOG—the concept of a rule. Rule clauses are typified by the following example:

$$has(X, door) :- is\_house (X). \tag{4-6}$$

The above statement is known as a Horn clause in predicate calculus, and forms the basis for PROLOG rule-based inference. In some PROLOG systems, the symbol :- may be replaced by the reserved word "IF," yielding a more apparent interpretation, and one entirely consistent with our development of the implication operator and the concept of a predicate function in Chapter 2. The left side of the statement, sometimes referred to as the "head" or consequent, is TRUE if the right side of the rule, (the body tail or antecedent) may be shown to be TRUE. Thus, from the first row of the implication truth table the truth of the right side of the rule implies the truth of the left side, which may be visualized by

$$is\_house (X) \rightarrow has(X, door) \tag{4-7a}$$

Note the reversing of the predicate order, since the :- connective represents "IF." Thus, the English interpretation of the above rule is:

> "If an entity is a house, then it has a door." (4-7b)

We must be particularly careful to interpret the above format according to the rules of predicate calculus. For example, entities other than houses may have doors; an automobile is a good example. In other words, the consequent may be true even if the antecedent is not true. This is shown below.

> A rule is a clause with a nonempty head and tail. PROLOG clauses comprising rules are assumed to be TRUE, therefore the head of a rule is TRUE if the tail or body may be proved TRUE. (4-8)

The following preliminary note regarding the PROLOG inference mechanism is of utmost importance:

> PROLOG seeks to verify the truth of predicates by unification with the given database. (4-9)

Thus, in the example above, to unify is_house (X) with one (or more) database statements, a variable substitution for X is sought. If the database contains

$$is\_house (my\_house). \tag{4-10a}$$

the substitution (using the notation of Chapter 2)

$$my\_house / X \tag{4-10b}$$

results, and PROLOG verifies the antecedent of rule (4-6) is TRUE. This binding also allows PROLOG to logically infer that the predicate has(my_house, door)   (4-10*c*)

is TRUE.

PROLOG and Modus Ponens

It was shown, from (4-6) and (4-8), that the database used for Modus Ponens (MP), namely,

$$p \rightarrow q \qquad (4\text{-}11a)$$

$$p \qquad (4\text{-}11b)$$

is equivalent to the PROLOG database

$$q:-p. \qquad (4\text{-}12a)$$

$$p. \qquad (4\text{-}12b)$$

Notice that a PROLOG database containing only statement (4-12*a*) excluding (4-12*b*) does not allow verification that $q = $ T or $q = $ F. The formulation of (4-12) thus reinforces the notion that in the implication of (4-12*a*) the failure to prove the truth of statement q from statement p does not constrain the truth value of q (see also Appendix 1).

It is entirely reasonable to allow the antecedent to be a compound statement; in particular, we consider the case where the conjunction of a number of predicates is used.

More Comprehensive Examples

Rules are seldom as simple as the previous example. If, as noted, predicate p represents the conjunction of a number of predicates, then the truth value of p is conditioned upon the truth of the logical AND of the component predicates. For example, in PROLOG this is denoted by a clause with a body of the form:

$$\text{pc(Arg)} :- \text{pa}_1(\text{Arg}),\text{pa}_2(\text{Arg}), \ldots, \text{pa}_n(\text{Arg}). \qquad (4\text{-}13a)$$

where the "," indicates conjunction. To logically infer that pc(Arg) (the head) in (4-13) is TRUE therefore requires PROLOG to verify that

$$\text{pa}_1(\text{Arg}) \cap \text{pa}_2(\text{Arg}) \ldots \cap \text{pa}_n(\text{Arg}) \equiv \text{T} \qquad (4\text{-}13b)$$

Predicates $\text{pa}_1 \ldots \text{pa}_n$ therefore become subgoals, each of which must be proved TRUE.

> **Example 4.2   Interrogation of an "expert" by a knowledge engineer as a prelude to PROLOG representation.** Consider the development of a PROLOG "expert" system to replace a college dean. The dean, among other things, is charged with determining which faculty members in his/her college receive tenure, or lifetime employment. We begin the development of a PROLOG implementation of this decision capability with the following dialog between a typical dean (DEAN) and the knowledge engineer (KE):
>
> KE: Dean, tell me how you decide who gets tenure.   (4-14*a*)

DEAN: That's easy. I award tenure to my faculty who publish, get research and teach well. (4-14*b*)

KE: Am I correct in my understanding that they must do all three of these? (4-14*c*)

DEAN: That's right. (4-14*d*)

KE: How does a faculty member "publish"? (4-14*e*)

DEAN: The faculty member conducts research and documents the research. (4-14*f*)

KE: How does the faculty member get research? (4-14*g*)

DEAN: The faculty member writes research proposals which subsequently become funded. (4-14*h*)

KE: What does it mean for a faculty member to teach well? (4-14*i*)

DEAN: That's easy. A good teacher prepares lectures, delivers the lecture well, and gets good evaluations from the students. (4-14*j*)

KE: Is that all there is to it?

DEAN: That's right.

KE: Thanks for your time and expertise, Dean.

Example 4.3   PROLOG representation strategy corresponding to example 4.2. On the basis of the dialog in Example 4.2, one rule for obtaining tenure which corresponds to the information obtained in (4-14*a*) and (4-14*b*) may be represented as

```
gets_tenure(Faculty) IF publishes(Faculty) AND
                        gets_research (Faculty) AND
                        teaches_well(Faculty).
```
(4-15*a*)

or, presented in PROLOG (4-15*a*) becomes:

```
gets_tenure(Faculty) :- publishes(Faculty),
                        gets_research (Faculty),
                        teaches_well(Faculty).
```
(4-15*b*)

In (4-15*b*) IF has been replaced by :-, and the conjunction operator "," replaces the more familiar logical AND operator. In this case to prove the consequent of (4-15*b*) is TRUE, the PROLOG system would need to search the database for instances of the variable "Faculty" in three subgoal predicates: publishes, gets_research and teaches_well. The implied quantification and scoping of variables in (4-15*b*) requires that the variable "Faculty" be bound to the same value in all three subgoal clauses.

The PROLOG rule of (4-15*b*) represents a fairly high level conclusion. The predicates comprising the body of (4-15*b*) may be further represented in the PROLOG database via other rules derived from the dialog of Example 4.2. For example, the PROLOG rulebase also contains the following clauses:

```
publishes(Professor)  :- does_research(Professor),
                          documents_research(Professor).
```
$$(4\text{-}16a)$$

(derived from (4-14e) and (4-14f)) as well as

```
gets_research(Researcher)
                        :- writes_proposals(Researcher),
                           gets_funded(Researcher).
```
$$(4\text{-}16b)$$

(derived from (4-14g) and (4-14h)) and

```
teaches_well(Educator)  :- prepares_lectures(Educator),
                           lectures_well(Educator),
                           gets_good_evaluations(Educator).
```
$$(4\text{-}16c)$$

(derived from (4-14i) and (4-14j)).

We return to a detailed examination of the operation of the PROLOG unification mechanism using this example in example 4.61. First, we digress to consider the syntax of PROLOG more fully.

THE SYNTAX AND CHARACTERISTICS
OF PROLOG

We are now in a position to formalize the preceding informal introduction to PROLOG and to consider in detail the nature of AI applications in PROLOG.

A PROLOG term is either a variable, a constant, or a structure. Terms are used as arguments to predicates. Structures are either functors or lists. $\qquad$ (4-17)

PROLOG restricts rules to the form:

$$p: - q, r, s \qquad (4\text{-}18)$$

where q, r and s are predicates that may contain terms, including constants, variables, functors and lists.

(4-18) may be rewritten as

$$(q \cap r \cap s) \rightarrow p \qquad (4\text{-}19)$$

Recalling our derivation of the clause form of implication, notice (4-19) may be written:

$$\neg q \cap \neg r \cap \neg s \cap p \qquad (4\text{-}20)$$

Restricting our productions to those of the form of (4-20) yields a subset of logic known as Horn set logic. This is precisely what PROLOG implements.

PROLOG implements a subset of first order logic known as Horn set logic. $\qquad$ (4-21)

PROLOG Syntax Basics

The statements that form the database in PROLOG are appropriately termed *clauses*. They consist of rules and facts. (4-22)

Facts have the general form:

$$\text{predicate\_name } (\text{term}_1, \text{term}_2, \dots, \text{term}_n). \tag{4-23a}$$

Rules have the general form (logical representation):

$$\text{pedicate\_name}_1(\text{term}_1, \text{term}_2, \dots) : -$$

$$\text{predicate\_name}_2(\text{term}_1, \text{term}_2, \dots),$$

$$\dots$$

$$\text{predicate\_name}_R(\text{term}_1, \text{term}_2, \dots). \tag{4-23b}$$

In both (4-23a) and (4-23b), the entity "term_i" may be a constant, a variable (capitalized), a list, or a functor.

AND-ed AND OR-ed CLAUSES. Recall the use of the "," in PROLOG to separate clauses and specify that the conjunction of these goals must be satisfied, for example,

$$a, b$$

forces both subgoals a AND b to succeed. C+M-based PROLOG systems also provide the disjunction (OR) operator ";", that allows the disjunction of two predicates in the form

$$a; b$$

This allows alternatives to be specified directly. We note, however, that this may also be achieved in the database by rewriting the second statement. The specification of subgoals using conjunction and disjunction operators has an impact on the decomposability of the inference system. We explore parallel processing in AI in Chapter 19.

Facts and rules in PROLOG may be related via the following observation:

A fact is a rule whose tail (antecedent) is the predicate TRUE (true). For example:

(4-24)

```
a_fact(term) :- true.
```
(4-25a)

that may be simply rewritten as

```
a_fact(term).
```
(4-25b)

THE ANONYMOUS VARIABLE. An **anonymous variable** is used to indicate that any instantiation of a variable will suffice. It is not necessary to give this variable a name, instead the underbar or "_" is used. It is noteworthy that several anonymous variables in the same clause need not be given consistent interpretations. In PROLOG the statement `pred_name(_)` is equivalent to the predicate logic statement $(\forall X)$ pred_name(X).

STRUCTURES. PROLOG allows two types of structures, namely the compound object and the list. **Compound objects** allow objects (in relations) to be comprised of other objects and relations. An example is

$$\texttt{owns(bob, shotgun(browning, target)).} \tag{4-26}$$

The object `shotgun` in the above example is a **functor**.

Recursion is permitted in PROLOG; that is, the name of a rule's consequent predicate may appear in the rule antecedent. This was shown in Chapter 3, example 3.18.

GOAL SPECIFICATION. Finally, a PROLOG program is incomplete without specification of a goal. A **goal**, entered at the interpreter prompt ("?-" in what follows), is a PROLOG clause. Typically, goals are the conjunction of subgoals, and contain variables. The PROLOG system attempts to unify the goal with the database. An example of a simple goal might be:

$$\texttt{?-has(wheel,What),has(driver,What).} \tag{4-27}$$

DATABASE MODIFICATION. PROLOG provides several built-in predicates for the modification of the database. For example,

$$\texttt{?-consult('<a\_file\_name>').} \tag{4-28}$$

causes the PROLOG system to enter the contents of ‹a_file_name› into the current PROLOG database. `Consult` is considered in more detail in a following section. If the contents of this file are syntactically correct, consult succeeds, that is, returns TRUE. Similarly,

```
assert('<a_clause>').
asserta('<a_clause>').
assertz('<a_clause>').                                    (4-29)
```

are used to enter individual PROLOG clauses (here denoted ‹a_clause›) in the database (notice this may be done during the execution of a PROLOG program). In addition

```
retract('<a_clause>').
```

removes ‹a_clause› from the PROLOG database.

Notice the use of retract is (without other coding) "unrecoverable" in the sense that PROLOG does not keep a copy of anything that is deleted. As will be noted in Chapter 11, the use of predicate `retract` leads to an irrevocable control strategy.

Lists in PROLOG

Lists are a useful and popular data structure. In PROLOG, a **list** is one form of **structure**. PROLOG permits through unification, the manipulation of data in list format.

- Lists are permitted in PROLOG and consist of elements separated by commas and enclosed in brackets [ ], i.e.,

$$[a, b, c, d] \tag{4-30a}$$

  is a list of the elements a thru d.
- Lists may be used as arguments to predicates. $\tag{4-30b}$
- Elements of a list may be other terms, including variables, constants and other lists. $\tag{4-30c}$

Elementary list manipulation is provided somewhat implicitly (vis-a-vis LISP); that is, the head (car) and tail (cdr) of a list are referred to in PROLOG statements as X and Y and written as

$$[X|Y]. \tag{4-31}$$

The empty list is a list without any elements and denoted [ ].

The use of recursion in PROLOG programming is exemplified by developing predicates that allow manipulation of list-structured data. These are the predicates "member," which tests recursively for list membership, and "append," which appends one list to another. Both functions exhibit the use of **recursion**, which is prevalent in AI programming since it allows succinct function definitions (or descriptions). In addition, in the two applications developed below, the use of recursion allows the predicate definition to be independent of the size of the input lists. This property, as mentioned previously, is valuable due to the fact that typically the dimension of input data is unknown a priori. The recursive formulation of corresponding LISP functions "member" and "append" is considered in Chapter 8. The reader should become comfortable with the recursively-based design of these predicates, since a number of recursive definitions will be used subsequently.

Example 4.4 Predicate member. We develop a PROLOG predicate

member(X, Alist) $\tag{4-32}$

which is TRUE if element X is a member of list Alist. The overall representational concept we use in formulating the PROLOG description of member is simple and employs recursion:

> X is a member of Alist if it is in the head (i.e., the first element) or the tail (i.e., the rest of the list). $\tag{4-33}$

The first observation in (4-35) allows us to write

member(X, [$X|_$]) . $\tag{4-34}$

Thus predicate member succeeds if X is the first element of the list. (Note the use of the anonymous variable in the formulation.) To test for membership in the tail of Alist, we employ the second observation in (4-33) and recursion in the form:

$$member(X, [\_|Y]) :- member(X, Y). \qquad (4\text{-}35)$$

Note that (4-35) when invoked recursively, involves a shorter list at each invocation. Again, the anonymous variable is used for the head of Alist.

Example 4.5   Predicate append. The design of predicate "append" is more complex than example (4-32). We desire a predicate of the form:

$$append(List1, List2, Result). \qquad (4\text{-}36)$$

where Result is formed by appending List2 to the end of List1. This must be accomplished using the PROLOG unification mechanism and therefore requires a *description* or definition of what appending two lists means. Our recursive definition is based upon the successive decimation of List1, that is, forming Result by repeatedly placing the head of List1 on Result, until List1 is empty. Appending the empty list to a list yields no change, and therefore a termination condition for successful appending is:

$$append([], List, List). \qquad (4\text{-}37)$$

for any List. The case in which List1 is nonempty is treated by [Clocksin/Mellish 1987]:

$$append([X|L1], List2, [X|L3]) :- \qquad \qquad (4\text{-}38)$$

This predicate, via unification, has the following effect: if List1 is nonempty, unification will force the head of the first list to be the head of the third list. Furthermore, a more subtle result is that the tail of the first list (L1) will be appended to List2 to form L3, the tail of [X|L3]. We illustrate the operation of this predicate with a simple example. Consider the PROLOG goal:

$$append([a], [b,c], Result). \qquad (4\text{-}39)$$

Initially, in the unification process, clause (4-37) above cannot be satisfied, since $[a] \neq [\,]$. Therefore, unification using (4-38) is attempted. The variable bindings become:

$$
\begin{aligned}
X &= a \\
L1 &= [] \\
List2 &= [b, \ c]
\end{aligned}
\qquad (4\text{-}40)
$$

Variable Result is bound to [X|L3], where we note that L3 is not yet bound to a value. The subgoal in (4-38), with the current bindings, causes a recursive call to append using the tail of (4-38), that is,

$$append(L1, List2, L3) \qquad (4\text{-}41)$$

which, with the bindings on L1 and List2 indicated above, becomes:

append([], [b, c], L3).   (4-42)

This subgoal is satisfied by (4-37) if the binding on L3 is:

L3 = [b, c]   (4-43)

Thus, the goal succeeds with variable Result bound to

Result = [a | b, c] = [a, b, c]   (4-44)

which is the desired effect of the predicate.

The description of predicate append, due to the unification mechanism of PROLOG, has additional capabilities. The reader is referred to the problems to explore this.

Goals and the PROLOG Unification Mechanism

Perhaps the most important conceptual characteristic of PROLOG is the operation of the built-in mechanism that, given a database of facts and rules, and a goal (a statement whose validity is to be verified) employs repeated variable instantiation in order to return consistent values of the variables. This process is referred to as the **unification mechanism**.

An understanding of the operation of the PROLOG unification mechanism is fundamental to success in developing practical PROLOG-based systems. The rules for unification are: (4-45)

i.   The unifier proceeds from left to right in a rule.
ii. Predicates are tested in the order in which they appear in a program (the database).
iii. When a subgoal matches the left side of a rule (the head), the right side of the rule becomes a new set of subgoals to unify.
iv. A goal is satisfied when a matching fact is found in the database for all the leaves of the goal tree.
v.   When two or more clauses in the database with the same predicate name are identified as possible matches, the first clause in the database is chosen first for attempted unification. The second (and third, etc) are marked as points for possible backtracking, and are investigated subsequently if the previous (e.g., first) choice fails to unify. This is shown in Example 4.6.

Moreover, a mechanism known as backtracking is used for goal satisfaction in cases of

i. a failed unification attempt, or
ii. a search for alternative solutions.

Example 4.6   Backtracking in PROLOG. Consider the simple PROLOG database shown below:

```
/*backtrack*/
goal(A,C) :- adjacent_to(A,B),adjacent_to(B,C).
adjacent_to(r1,r2).
adjacent_to(r1,r3).
adjacent_to(r3,r4).
```
(4-46*a*)

We now follow the order of attempted subgoal unifications with the goal:

```
?- goal(W1,W2).
```
(4-46*b*)

PROLOG, in attempting to unify clause goal in (4-46*b*), makes the initial bindings

A/W1

and

C/W2
(4-46*c*)

Following this, subgoal adjacent_to(A,B) is created. Since several clauses with the predicate name adjacent_to exist in the database, adjacent_to(A,B) is marked as a clause for backtracking. The first attempted unification of adjacent_to(A,B) returns with

r1/A

and

r2/B
(4-46*d*)

The next subgoal is then adjacent_to(r2,C), where the applicable bindings in (4-46*d*) are used. Given the database of (4-46*a*), no solution for this subgoal exists, therefore PROLOG backtracks to subgoal adjacent_to(A,B), unbinds variables A and B, and considers alternative bindings by considering (in top-to-bottom order) the next clause in the database with head adjacent_to. This yields bindings

r1/A

and

r3/B
(4-46*e*)

This generates new subgoal adjacent_to(r3,C), which succeeds with binding r4/C (4-46*f*)

Therefore, the solution returned is:

W1 = r1
W2 = r4 (4-46*g*)

which is shown in example 4.7.

Example 4.7*h*   PROLOG results for backtracking example.

```
C-Prolog version 1.5
| ?- listing.

yes
| ?- consult(backtrack).
backtrack consulted 260 bytes 0.0833333 sec.

yes
| ?- system("cat backtrack").
goal(A,C) :- adjacent_to(A,B),adjacent_to(B,C).
adjacent_to(r1,r2).
adjacent_to(r1,r3).
adjacent_to(r3,r4).

yes
| ?- goal(W1,W2).

W1 = r1
W2 = r4 ;
```
(4-46*h*)

The reader should determine whether other solutions exist. An extension of this example is considered in problem 18.

PROLOG BACKTRACKING STRATEGY AS DEPTH-FIRST SEARCH. In the unification process, one fundamental property to remember is

When a goal fails, PROLOG backtracks to the nearest (most recent) clause marked for backtracking, and variables that were previously bound in an attempt to satisfy that goal become unbound after the backtrack point. (4-47*a*)

The unification procedure description in (4-46) indicates that PROLOG implements **depth-first search**, due to the backtracking mechanism employed by the unification algorithm. In addition, (4-46) indicates that the position of rules and facts in the database will affect the order in which the unification process is carried out.

Heuristically speaking, it is a good policy, in general, to place facts in the database before rules wherever possible. (4-47*b*)

(4-47) indicates that it is more efficient to organize a PROLOG program so that specific searches are attempted prior to generalized searches.

THE "CUT" PREDICATE. Backtracking is inhibited via the ! or "cut" predicate. The ! symbol is interpreted as a predicate which always succeeds, i.e, always evaluates to TRUE. In realistic or significantly more complex PROLOG descriptions, proper placement of the ! predicate often makes the difference between a program that works and one that doesn't. When a cut is encountered in the process of verifying a conjunction of subgoals in a rule, the cut forces the PROLOG unification mechanism to commit to all binding choices made from the past goal up to the cut. Thus, the cut may be viewed as a "fence" the unification mechanism may only cross once in unifying from left to right in an expression. The cut yields efficiency by signifying that only one (not all) successful unification should be found. For example, suppose we have the rule involving predicates r1, *a,b,* and *c,* of the form

$$r1 \text{ if } a \text{ and } b \text{ and } ! \text{ and } c \qquad (4\text{-}48a)$$

The application of the cut operator following clause *b* indicates we are satisfied with the first solution of subgoals *a,b*. The cut operator, in conjunction with careful placement (order) of rules and facts in the database, is useful for controlling, and often limiting, the solution search.

Example 4.8   Use of the "cut" predicate.

```
$ cat backtrack2

/*  backtrack2   5-29-89 */
/* mod to show cut */
goal(A,C)  :- adjacent_to(A,B),!,adjacent_to(B,C).
adjacent_to(r1,r2).
adjacent_to(r2,r1).
adjacent_to(r1,r3).
adjacent_to(r3,r4).

$ prolog
C-Prolog version 1.5
| ?- consult(backtrack2).
backtrack2 consulted 308 bytes 0.05 sec.

yes
| ?- goal(X1,X2).

X1 = r1
X2 = r1  ;


no
| ?- halt.
```
$$(4\text{-}48b)$$

The user should compare the results of this example with Example 4.60.

THE "NOT" PREDICATE AND NEGATION-AS-FAILURE. Furthermore, PROLOG provides the NOT operator, via a predicate that must be used with care.

> The "not" predicate, as would logically be expected, succeeds if unification of its argument fails. (4-49)

It is a useful mechanism (as we'll show in the examples in Chapter 5 and Chapter 6) that allows the programmer to encode "negative" information (what can't happen) in the PROLOG database. The operation of the `not` predicate, for example, on the following predicate:

`owns_a_gun(bob)` (4-50)

is indicated in PROLOG syntax by

`not(owns_a_gun(bob)).` (4-51)

Given statement (4-51) as a goal, the PROLOG unification mechanism proceeds first to prove the truth of statement (4-50). If a fact `owns_a_gun(bob)` does not exist in the database, the unifier fails for (4-50), consequently (4-51) succeeds. This would lead to an interpretation that "bob does not own a gun" is TRUE, however this conclusion is incorrect. A correct conclusion would be that it is not possible to prove or disprove this statement on the basis of the information contained in the database. An exception to this is the case wherein it is known that the database is all-inclusive. For example, if all gun owners are registered in some database (and therefore there existed an all-inclusive, 100% reliable database containing the name of anyone, for example, who owns a gun) then we could correctly conclude that anyone who does not own a gun is not in the database. In this case when a fact is not unified with the database we are allowed to make the conclusion that it is FALSE. The preceding argument therefore highlights one aspect of PROLOG that should be remembered in designing systems:

> Whatever is omitted from the database is treated as logically false. This is known as *negation-as-failure*. (4-52)

(4-52) is also referred to as the closed-world assumption in PROLOG.

POTENTIAL UNIFICATION CIRCULARITIES WITH SYMMETRIC AND TRANSITIVE RELATIONS

Developers of AI systems in PROLOG that incorporate relations need to be aware of another severe limitation of PROLOG, namely the lack of a built-in mechanism to handle circularity. This deficiency often manifests itself as infinite recursion (usually indicated by a "ran out of memory" error message from the system) in apparently syntactically correct PROLOG programs. It is a direct consequence of the unification mechanism incorporating depth-first search, or equivalently, proceeding from left to right in a rule, and developing and immediately pursuing new subgoals. We show this via the following example.

> **Example 4.9 Circularity in PROLOG unification.** Suppose we wished to encode the binary (two-place) relationship $next\_to$. For example, if object a were "next to" object b, we would include
>
> $$next\_to(a,b). \tag{4-53}$$
>
> in the fact base. Alternately, we would like to encode the case where object b is next to object a, that is,
>
> $$next\_to(b,a). \tag{4-54}$$
>
> is also TRUE. We could therefore attempt to represent the situation of both (4-53) and (4-54) by including the following fact and the following rule in the database:
>
> $$next\_to(X,Y) :- next\_to(Y,X). \tag{4-55a}$$
> $$next\_to(a,b).$$

The PROLOG rule (4-55) exemplifies *left recursion*. The difficulty arises when the unification mechanism attempts to unify rule (4-55a). The head would be TRUE if the tail is true, however, the tail of (4-55a) now becomes a new goal to be unified starting, as described in (4-46), with the attempted unification of the head of (4-55a). The process never converges. The example of (4-55a) concerns the PROLOG coding of a symmetric relation. Sometimes proper rule-fact placement in the database, coupled with careful use of the cut (!) operator, may alleviate this problem. Alternately, we could embed a symmetric relation in the database without using a rule by simple enumeration of the facts, with every relation of the form $next\_to(a_1,a_2)$ accompanied by another fact: $next\_to(a_2,a_1)$. This, of course, is cumbersome.

An alternate solution that allows encoding of symmetry in PROLOG is based upon the renaming of predicates to avoid circularities. This approach is shown below for the case of the relation $next\_to(\,,)$ and constants (a,b), (c,d), (e,f):

$$next\_to1(a,b).$$
$$next\_to1(c,d).$$
$$next\_to1(e,f).$$
$$next\_to(X,Y) :- next\_to1(X,Y).$$
$$next\_to(X,Y) :- next\_to1(Y,X). \tag{4-56a}$$

By renaming the predicates constituting facts as $next\_to1$, our objective is reached. The reader is left to verify that the database (4-56a), when queried with the goal

$$next\_to(A,B). \tag{4-56b}$$

returns the bindings (a,b), (c,d), (e,f), (b,a), (d,c), (f,e) on variables A and B respectively.

Infinite recursion due to the (often inadvertent) encoding of symmetry or transitivity is usually carefully embedded in more complex PROLOG programs. Often the endless unification attempt also involves a number of other rules, and thus its existence may not be apparent to the programmer (until the unification process exhausts available memory and returns an error message). Generally, problems arise when attempting to represent symmetric and transitive relations. A transitive relation would be of the form:

```
near(X,Z)  :- near(X,Y), near(Y,Z).
```
(4-57)

Further consideration of these problems is left to the exercises.

CONSTRAINTS USING VARIABLES IN PROLOG

In PROLOG, there is a distinct difference between the (sub)goals:

```
has_wheels(X), has_tires(X).
```
(4-58a)

and

```
has_wheels(X), has_tires(Y).
```
(4-58b)

In clause (4-58a) we are seeking a solution such that whatever is substituted for X has both wheels and tires, whereas in clause (4-58b) we are only requiring that the unifier return substitutions for X and Y respectively, such that X has wheels and Y has tires. Note that the second case includes the solution to the first.

CREATING, MODIFYING AND EXAMINING PROLOG DATABASES (DATABASE MANAGEMENT)

In a previous section, the built-in PROLOG predicates assert, retract, and consult were briefly considered. In this section, we introduce several more powerful predicates and their effects for PROLOG database management.

Consult

The built-in PROLOG predicate

```
consult(X)
```

reads the contents of a file, whose filename is the binding on X into the current database. If a constant is entered as the argument to consult, it must either be a PROLOG atom or enclosed in quotes. For example,

```
consult(file_1)
```

and

```
consult('file_1.pro')
```

are valid uses of consult.

It is critical to note that consult extends or augments the database with the clauses in X, therefore repetition of clauses may occur (problem 18 addresses this). Consult may also be used with arity > 1, to read multiple files into the database.

> **Example 4.10** **Repeated** consult **and PROLOG database duplication.** First, we show the effect of consulting the same file twice:
>
> ```
> | ?- consult(backtrack).
> backtrack consulted 180 bytes 0.1 sec.
>
> yes
>
> | ?- consult(backtrack).
> backtrack consulted 180 bytes 0.1 sec.
>
> yes
> | ?- listing.
>
> adjacent_to(r1,r2).
> adjacent_to(r1,r3).
> adjacent_to(r3,r4).
> adjacent_to(r1,r2).
> adjacent_to(r1,r3).
> adjacent_to(r3,r4).
>
> goal(_0,_1) :-
>     adjacent_to(_0,_10),
>     adjacent_to(_10,_1).
> goal(_0,_1) :-
>     adjacent_to(_0,_10),
>     adjacent_to(_10,_1).
>
> yes
> ```
>   (4-59a)

> **Example 4.11** **Effects of database duplication.**
>
> ```
> | ?- goal(X1,X2).
>
> X1 = r1
> X2 = r4 ;
>
> X1 = r1
> X2 = r4 ;
>
> X1 = r1
> X2 = r4 ;
> ```

```
X1 = r1
X2 = r4 ;

X1 = r1
X2 = r4 ;

X1 = r1
X2 = r4 ;

X1 = r1
X2 = r4 ;

X1 = r1
X2 = r4 ;

no
| ?- halt.

[ Prolog execution halted ]
```
                                                                    (4-59b)

Reconsult

Built-in PROLOG predicate "reconsult" is syntactically similar to "consult;" however,
in reading a file "reconsult" supercedes or overwrites all existing database clauses with
the same predicate name. This is shown below.

> **Example 4.12 Use of "reconsult."** First, we consult file "backtrack" from examples
> 4.46h and 4.59a.

```
$ prolog
C-Prolog version 1.5
| ?- consult(backtrack).
backtrack consulted 260 bytes 0.0666667 sec.

yes
| ?- goal(X1,X2).

X1 = r1
X2 = r4 ;

no
```

File "backtrack1" is a revised version of "backtrack" as follows:

```
$ cat backtrack1
/*  backtrack1  */
goal(A,C) :- adjacent_to(A,B),adjacent_to(B,C).
adjacent_to(r1,r2).
adjacent_to(r2,r1).
adjacent_to(r1,r3).
adjacent_to(r3,r4).
```

```
| ?- reconsult(backtrack1).
backtrack1 reconsulted 36 bytes 0.0833333 sec.

yes
| ?- goal(X1,X2).

X1 = r1
X2 = r1  ;

X1 = r2
X2 = r2  ;

X1 = r2
X2 = r3  ;

X1 = r1
X2 = r4  ;

no
| ?- halt.                                                    (4-60)
```

Retract and Listing

Predicate "retract" is used to remove single clauses from the PROLOG database. For example,

retract(X)

removes the first occurrence of the clause whose predicate name is the binding on X. Similarly,

retractall(X)

removes all occurrences of this predicate. Retract and retractall may be used with nonvariable arguments.

Predicate

listing(A)

lists all predicates in the database whose predicate name is the binding on A. This is a useful interactive debugging tool.

In many PROLOG implementations, listing used without arguments causes a listing of the entire current database.

A DETAILED LOOK AT THE UNIFICATION PROCESS AND SEARCH

Given the previous description of the PROLOG unification strategy, we now seek to follow the process for the "tenure" example of (4-14)–(4-18). A graphical construct based on Fig. 4.1 will aid in following this process.

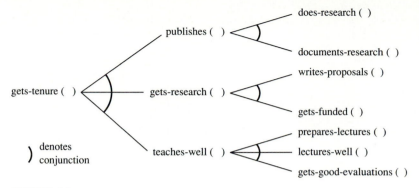

FIGURE 4.1
PROLOG clause relationships (from database of example 4.13).

Recall that the PROLOG program that embedded the logic of assigning tenure is the following database, consisting of rules and facts:

Example 4.13   PROLOG "tenure" formulation.

```
does_research(rjs).
documents_research(rjs).
writes_proposals(rjs).
gets_funded(rjs).
prepares_lectures(rjs).
lectures_well(rjs).
gets_good_evaluations(rjs).                                    (4-61)


gets_tenure(Faculty) :- publishes(Faculty),
         gets_research(Faculty), teaches_well(Faculty).
                                                               (4-62)


publishes(Professor) :- does_research(Professor),
                        documents_research(Professor).
                                                               (4-63)


gets_research(Researcher) :-
    writes_proposals(Researcher), gets_funded(Researcher).
                                                               (4-64)


teaches_well(Educator) :-
             prepares_lectures(Educator),
             lectures_well(Educator),
             gets_good_evaluations(Educator).                  (4-65)
```

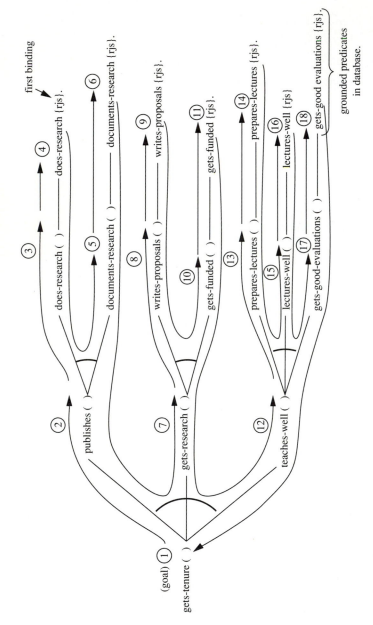

first binding

grounded predicates
in database.

FIGURE 4.2
PROLOG goal satisfaction (unification) sequence (from Fig. 4.1).

114

The database is queried with the inquiry (the goal):

?—gets_tenure(Who) .   (4-66)

The query to the database as to who gets tenure, according to the PROLOG approach, forces attempted unification of statement (4-66) with the database. We now follow the process step by step, paying particular attention to

1. The order in which unification is attempted;
2. The generation of subgoals; and
3. The substitutions that occur and their effect upon subsequent unification.

This is shown in Fig. 4.2.

REFERENCES

[Clark 1978] Clark, K.L., "Negation as Failure," *Logic and Databases*, Plenum Press, New York, 1978, pp. 293–322.
[Clark/Tarnlund 1982] Clark, K.L., and S.A. Tarnlund, *Logic Programming,* Academic Press, New York, 1982.
[Clocksin/Mellish 1984] Clocksin, W.F., and C.S. Mellish, *Programming in PROLOG*, (Third Edition), Springer-Verlag, New York, 1987.
[Covington 1985] Covington, M., "Eliminating Unwanted Loops in PROLOG," *SIGPLAN Notices*, (ACM Spec. Interest Group), Vol. 20, No. 1, January. 1985 pp. 20–26.
[Hogger 1984] Hogger, C.J., *Introduction to Logic Programming,* Academic Press, New York, 1984.
[Kowalski 1979] Kowalski, R.A., *Logic for Problem Solving*, Elsevier-North Holland, New York, 1979.

PROBLEMS

Chapters 3 and 4 (AI Language Concepts and PROLOG)

4.1. Consider the following two database formulations in PROLOG:

formulation #1:

father(bob, bernard).
mother(bob, anne).
father(jesse, bob).
mother(jesse, leslie).

formulation #2:

bernard(father, bob).
anne(mother, bob).
bob(father, jesse).
leslie(mother, jesse).

Note: In both formulations, the first fact is interpreted as "bernard is the father of bob." In each formulation, it is desired to form a rule (or set of rules, if necessary) that allows queries to the PROLOG system to determine who is the grandparent of whom. We wish to consider the suitability of each formulation, as well as the applicable rule(s).

(a) Formulate the inquiry in each case.

(b) Formulate the rules, if possible. If not possible, state, as rigorously as possible, why, and show a suitable modification to the database (excluding either of the above) that would allow this determination.

4.2. This problem provides some experience with recursive PROLOG descriptions and list manipulation. It is based upon the list membership predicate member, defined in examples 4.32, 4–33, and 4–34.

(a) Consider two possible formulations of member

```
$ cat member.pro
/* member.pro  5-29-89 */
/* example of lists, recursion */

member(X,[_|Y]) :- member(X,Y).
member(X,[X|_]).                                            (P2-1)


$ cat member1.pro
/* member1.pro  5-29-89 */
/* example of lists, recursion */
/* this example has clauses reversed */

member(X,[X|_]).
member(X,[_|Y]) :- member(X,Y).                            (P2-2)
```

(i) For the inquiry

$$?\text{- member } (a, [b, c, a, d]).$$

show, in detail, the sequence of attempted unifications. (This may be done by hand or by showing a PROLOG trace.)

(ii) Is one formulation more efficient?

(iii) Is your answer to (ii) always true?

(b) In our development of a predicate member, membership of item X in the head of the list was tested via:

$$\text{member}(X, [X|_]).$$

Consider the alternative formulation:

$$\text{member}(X, [Y|_]) :- X= Y$$

(i) Is this valid?

(ii) If so, comment on the practicality of this approach vis-a-vis the former.

(c) What is the result of the following queries:

(i) ?- member (X, [b, c, d, a]).

(ii) ?- member (a, [b, X, d, a]).

4.3. A PROLOG programmer wished to incorporate information regarding parent/child relationships in a database. Two clauses were:

$$\text{parent } (X, Y) :- \text{child}(Y, X).$$

and

$$\mathtt{child(A,B) :- parent(B,A)}.$$

(*a*) Are these valid PROLOG clauses?

(*b*) Will they cause any difficulty with the PROLOG unification mechanism? (Show why or why not).

4.4. Consider an application of PROLOG to a simple problem in computational geometry. This is an interesting problem, since problems such as determining spatial coincidence, intersections, shapes, etc., are easily handled by humans, yet often take tremendous programming resources to automate.

We address the problem of linking the edges of line segments to form a connected "chain" or 2-D curve. Fig. P4.4 shows an example of the process. The (only) data structure to be used is of the form:

$$\mathtt{chain\ (A,\ B,\ L)}$$

where *A* is the name of the first vertex, *B* is the name of the last vertex, and *L* is a list of vertices in the chain from the second to the last.

We start with the database containing each edge, or segment, separate, and finish when only one chain remains (in this example; other cases where two or more chains result may be handled in a similar way). From Fig. P4.4, the initial data-base is

$$\mathtt{chain(a,b,[b])}.$$
$$\mathtt{chain(d,e,[e])}.$$
$$\mathtt{chain(c,d,[d])}.$$
$$\mathtt{chain(b,c,[c])}.$$

The final database is

$$\mathtt{chain(a,e,[b,c,d,e])}.$$

Develop this PROLOG program, and show the results using the above data.

(This problem should give you some exposure to the assert, retract, and fail predicates as well as list manipulation).

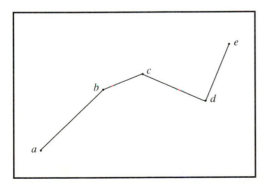

FIGURE P4.4
Line segments to be linked.

4.5. Consider the representation of the binary relation "larger than;" e.g., in PROLOG we could represent the fact that a house is larger than a person via:

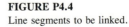

larger_than (house, person).

(*a*) Anwer "yes" or "no" to each: Is this relation
   (i) reflexive?
   (ii) symmetric?
   (iii) transitive?
(*b*) For each "yes" answer in part (*a*), show a corresponding PROLOG rule that implements the property.

4.6. Recall our development of the PROLOG predicate append with the form:

append(List1, List2, Result)

Due to the PROLOG unification mechanism, can "append" be used to do more than concatenate two lists? For example, can append be used to determine if Result is the concatenation of lists List1 and List2? Show your conclusions via examples.

4.7. Cite examples of coupled computing where:
   (*a*) it makes sense for the symbolic process to dominate, or control the overall system;
   (*b*) it makes sense for the numeric process to dominate, or control, the overall computation;
   (*c*) it is not clear whether either dominates; the computations are "equal" partners in system control.

4.8. Show, in detail, the operation of the PROLOG unification mechanism for the recursive factorial predicate description when the input is *n* = 3; i.e., the goal is

factorial(3, Answer).

Specifically, show the order in which subgoals are investigated and the variable bindings at each step. Show the recursion graphically in a form similar to Fig. 3.3 in Chapter 3.

4.9. Consider an application of the descriptive power of PROLOG in representing knowledge about music. Develop a PROLOG program that "understands" (through labeling) a sequence of piano keys.

Description: Western music divides octaves (integer relationships between fundamental note frequencies) into 12 steps (5 black keys per 7 white keys). Therefore, the piano keyboard has the familiar visual structure shown in Fig. P4.9. You will need to encode the following in a PROLOG representation:

FIGURE P4.9
Keyboard visual structure showing white/black keys.

1. The 7 white keys of the 12 total keys in each octave are sequenced using the following letter names:

C D E F G A B C . . .

2. Therefore, keys that are one octave apart have the same letter name.
3. Adjacent keys (black or white) are 1/2 step apart.
4. Note E & F and B & C are the only adjacent white keys.
   (*a*) Develop a formulation which allows the PROLOG system to label all the white keys (Key_*i*) of an unlabelled keyboard segment represented in using list notation:

[Key_1, Key_2, Key_3, . . . , Key_n]

Show results, and draw accompanying examples of test cases.

(*b*) Modify the previous goal to allow the user to specify the name of any white key (Key_i). The system should then label the key that is a major 3rd (2 full steps) above Key_i (e.g., E is the major 3rd of C). The system should also label the key that is a perfect 5th (7/2 steps) above Key_i (e.g., G is the perfect 5th of C). (Extra Credit for music buffs: Can you revise the second formulation to identify all major triads with Key_i as the root?)

4.10. This problem is similar to #9. We consider identification of the letter names of notes on open strings of a 6-string guitar in "standard tuning." We graphically designate the open guitar strings as:

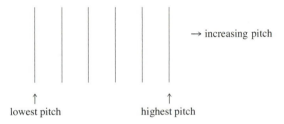

In PROLOG you should consider BOTH using the list notation

[String_1,String_2, String_3,

String_4, String_5, String_6]

or the predicate

tuning (S1, S2, S3, S4, S5, S6).

Referring to the 12-tone scale in Problem #9, we are given the fact that adjacent strings (i.e., S1 and S2) are tuned a perfect 4th (the distance from C to F) apart, except S4 and S5, which are tuned a major 3rd apart.

Develop a PROLOG database and goal, and, using PROLOG, determine the note names of a guitar in standard tuning for the cases we are given:

1. S1 is an "E"; and
2. S3 is a "D."

4.11. The following PROLOG program illustrates several aspects of PROLOG programming (including recursion, assignment and the "cut"), and may be used in benchmarking systems. A predicate "repeat(N)" is defined as follows:

```
repeat(N) :- N > 0,
             from(1, N).
from(I, I)  :-!.
from(L, U)  :- M is U-1, from(L, M).
```

Show, using examples, the operation of each step of this function.

4.12. Denoting the universe of variables X and Y as the set $A = \{$house, person, dog, cat, mouse$\}$, develop a PROLOG implementation that encodes the relation "larger-than." Use a rule to specify the transitivity property of larger−than.

For the query

$$? - \text{larger-than}(X, Y).$$

(a) How many solutions are there (this may be calculated without programming)?
(b) What are they?

4.13. The purpose of this problem is to consider PROLOG for symbolic manipulation of expressions, specifically related to the calculation of integrals. Given the following PROLOG database:

```
/* integral.pro */

integral(Variable,Function,Lowerlimit,
         Upperlimit,Var_of_integ,Value) :-
    Variable = Var_of_integ,
    integral_function(Function,IF),
    function_value(IF,Lowerlimit,V1),
    function_value(IF,Upperlimit,V2), Value is V2 - V1.


integral(Variable,Function,Lowerlimit,
         Upperlimit,Var_of_integ,Value) :-
    integral_function(Function,Var_of_integ),
    Variable = Function,
    product_value(Function,Var_of_integ,Lowerlimit,V1),
    product_value(Function,Var_of_integ,Upperlimit,V2),
    V3 is V2 - V1,
    integral(Variable,Var_of_integ,Lowerlimit,
             Upperlimit,Function,V4),
    Value is V3 - V4.


function_value(x,Argument,Value) :- Value is Argument.
function_value(sqrx_div_2,Argument,Value)
                :- Value is Argument*Argument/2.
function_value(cubex_div_6,Argument,Value)
                        :- Value is Argument*
                           Argument*Argument/6.
integral_function(x,sqrx_div_2).
integral_function(sqrx_div_2,cubex_div_6).

product_value(F1,F2,Argument,Value)
        :- function_value(F1,Argument,V1), function_value
                          (F2,Argument,V2), Value is V1 * V2.
```

If we

```
; ?- consult('integral.pro').
```

what is returned by PROLOG for the following two inquiries? If successful unification is possible, only indicate the first variable bindings that are returned.

(*a*) | ?- function_value(x,1,Y). $\longrightarrow Y = 1$
(*b*) | ?- integral(x,x,0,1,x,Y).
(assume that floating point arithmetic is used).

4.14. This problem investigates the not predicate. Given a PROLOG database and a goal, specifically

$$?-my-goal \ (X).$$

PROLOG will either succeed or fail to unify the database with this query. Consider, instead, reformulating (P14-1) as

$$?- not(not(my-goal \ X)).$$ *Yes*

Will the result of the query of (P14-2) be the same as that of (P14-1)? Verify your answer with some examples. *But first will bind X, second will not.*

4.15. The purpose of this problem is to consider the development of a PROLOG program that determines the "world's best guitarist." Since "best" is highly subjective, we leave details of the formulation to the reader.

(*a*) Formulate a database, in PROLOG, that incorporates the relevant aspects of at least five well-known guitarists. For example,

$$plays\_fast(eddie\_van\_halen).$$
$$plays\_with\_emotion(eric\_clapton).$$
$$\vdots$$
$$plays\_country(chet\_atkins).$$

(*b*) Formulate a corresponding goal.
(*c*) Experiment with the performance of your system.
(*d*) Consider the formulation of goals that lead to no solution. Modify the goal for these cases such that:
  (i) the goal is modified (constraints are relaxed), or
  (ii) the user is queried for a possible entry into the database.

4.16. Given the following PROLOG database:

```
pass_exam(Who1)  :- study_hard(Who1), not(fool_around(Who1)).

pass_exam(Who2)  :- do_homework(Who2), fail, study_hard(Who2).

study_hard(class).
fool_around(some).
do_homework(others).
do_homework(some).
```

what is the result of querying the PROLOG database with

| ?- pass_exam(Anybody). *— clos*

Specifically, does this goal succeed, and, if so, what are the resulting bindings on variable Anybody?

4.17. Which of the following are logically valid PROLOG representations:

(*a*) *q:–p.*
  p.
  q.
(*b*) *q:–p.*
  q.
(*c*) *q.*
  q:–not(p).
  p.
(*d*) *q:–not(p).*
  q.

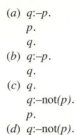

all are syntactly carr

4.18. This problem illustrates difficulties that may be encountered in PROLOG databases with (inadvertently) repeated predicates. This may occur, for example, with improper choices of predicate consult vs. reconsult. Consider a revised version of the PROLOG database of example 4.7 as shown.

```
goal(A,C)  :- adjacent_to(A,B),adjacent_to(B,C).
adjacent_to(r1,r2).
adjacent_to(r1,r3).
adjacent_to(r3,r4).


adjacent_to (r3, r4). /* repeated predicate */         (P18-1)
```

(*a*) Given the goal

```
    ?- goal(W1, W2).
```

what is returned by the PROLOG unification mechanism? Discuss why this occurs, and contrast this result with using the database of (P18-1) without the repeated predicate. Will this type of behavior cause problems?
(*b*) Where in (P18-1) could the cut (!) predicate be inserted to inhibit this behavior?
(*c*) (This problem is also related to Chapter 16.) Could you develop a predicate filter that, given a PROLOG database of the form of (P18-1), removes the redundant predicate?

4.19. (This problem provides valuable experience in interpreting the not and cut predicates.) PROLOG provides two built-in predicates defined as follows:

var (*X*)   succeeds if *X* is currently an unbound variable.
nonvar (*X*)   succeeds if *X* is currently not an unbound variable
         (the opposite of var (*X*)).

(*a*) In [Clocksin/Mellish 1984] a PROLOG description of nonvar (*X*) is offered as follows:

```
nonvar(X)  :- var(X), !, fail.

nonvar(_).                                              (P19-1)
```

Show how the use of the cut and fail predicates, together with the anonymous variable and the correct ordering of the above two statements, leads to proper operation of predicate nonvar in (P19-1).
(*b*) Contrast the description in (P19-1) with the following:

nonvar (*X*)   :− not (var (*X*)) .   (P19-2)

    Does (P19-2) accomplish the same thing?

4.20. The factorial, as shown in Example 3.4, provides a good example of recursive programming. Considering factors such as processing speed (number of overall operations) and memory utilization, compare the efficiency of iterative implementations of the factorial vis-a-vis recursive implementations.

CHAPTER
5

CONSTRAINT SATISFACTION PROBLEMS AND PROLOG APPLICATION TO IMAGE LABELING

"Vision is the art of seeing things invisible."

Jonathan Swift 1667–1745

CONSTRAINT SATISFACTION PROBLEMS

The sample PROLOG implementation in this chapter illustrates two important AI concepts:

1. Satisfaction of constraints via unification as an AI solution procedure; and (5-1a)
2. Implementation of solutions to (5-1a) using the built-in PROLOG unification procedure as well as the incremental development and refinement of the PROLOG solution. (5-1b)

We consider both the theory (5-1a) and implementation (5-1b) of AI solutions related to constraint satisfaction problems (CSPs). The PROLOG unification mechanism is a particular case of implementation of logical constraints with explicit representations. The mathematical basis and alternate formulations to constraint satisfaction is shown in further detail in Chapter 7 of [Schalkoff 1989]. Other implementations using constraint satisfaction languages (CSLs) are possible. A fundamental aspect of CSPs is that observations are unified with a constraint-based knowledge representation.

Constraint Satisfaction Problem Formulations

The important and recurring AI problem of constraint satisfaction, although solved in this chapter using the representational capability and unification mechanism of PROLOG, may be formulated and solved in a variety of ways. Many AI tasks may be explicitly formulated using a constraint satisfaction approach, consisting of a set of variables, and a set of predicates, the conjunction of which the instantiated variables must satisfy. As shown in [Mackworth 1977], one way to view this task, using our previous formulation of predicate logic, is as the problem of providing a constructive proof for the wff:

$$(\exists X_1)(\exists X_2) \ldots (\exists X_n)[P_1(X_1) \cap P_2(X_2)$$
$$\cap \ldots \cap P_n(X_n) \cap P_{12}(X_1, X_2) \cap P_{13}(X_1, X_3)$$
$$\cap \ldots \cap P_{n-1,n}(X_{n-1}, X_n) \quad (5\text{-}1c)$$

where the X_i are the variables and the P_i and P_{ij} are unary and binary constraints, respectively. (Note the above formulation only considers unary and binary constraints). One of the major concerns that emerges from formulation of AI problems as constraint satisfaction problems in the above form is efficiency of the solution procedure. Solutions (or verification of the lack of a solution) to problems that require reasonable (perhaps even finite) computational resources or time are of practical significance.

To show the suitability of this formulation, recall the basic premise of the labeling problem:

> Given feature information extracted from a problem domain in terms of a set of (unlabeled or variable) entities and observed relations, use a set of (known a priori) constraints (which the labels of objects satisfying these relations must satisfy) to map labels to objects such that a valid, that is, globally consistent, labeling is obtained. (5-2)

Relation to Numerical Constraint Satisfaction Problems

The previous formulation yielded a solution set of valid labelings based upon satisfaction of a set of local (i.e., adjacency) constraints. We observe the similarity of this symbolically based approach to numerical cases that are familiar to engineers.

> **Example 5.1   Numerical constraint satisfaction.** Consider the solution of a set of linear equalities of the form
>
> $$X + Y = 6$$
> $$3X - Y = 2 \quad (5\text{–}3)$$

Each of these equations constrains the numerical solution of assignment of values to variables X and Y. Furthermore, each equation alone is insufficient constraint information for a unique solution. More precisely, each equation constrains the n-dimensional numerical solution space to an $(n - 1)$-dimensional subspace. In this example, with $n = 2$ variables, each equation therefore constrains the solution to a line. The satisfaction of the conjugation (AND-ing) of these constraints (in this example, the intersection of the constraint lines), yields the global solution space. (In this example, if the constraint equations are linearly independent, these constraint lines are forced to be non-colinear, thus a unique solution is obtained at their intersection. This is shown in Fig. 5.1.) We note in passing that although formalized and efficient algorithms from linear algebra are available to solve this problem, search techniques are also applicable. An example is the use of Hough transform techniques [Schalkoff 1989].

Interpretation as Search

A relation-based description in the form of (5-1) where features are cast as variables imposes constraints on possible interpretations. In order to obtain a consistent interpretation, features (variable bindings) must satisfy the relational constraints in (5-1).

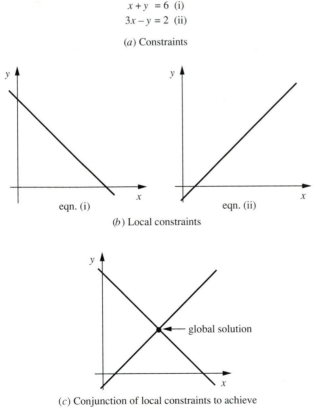

$$x + y = 6 \text{ (i)}$$
$$3x - y = 2 \text{ (ii)}$$

(a) Constraints

eqn. (i)   eqn. (ii)

(b) Local constraints

global solution

(c) Conjunction of local constraints to achieve
global solution

FIGURE 5.1
Numerical constraint satisfaction example. (a) Constraints; (b) Local constraints; (c) Conjunction of local constraints to achieve global solution.

Suppose there are n variables, each from a discrete universe (domain) of size a, and r relations among the n variables. The problem of determining all globally consistent solutions or interpretations could be viewed as that of finding all possible n-tuples, where each n-tuple represents a set of bindings on the n problem variables that satisfies (5-1). This problem is known to be NP complete [Mulder/Mackworth 1988] and therefore the computational complexity is significant (Chapter 15).

REGION LABELING AND SEGMENTATION IN IMAGE PROCESSING

The segmentation and labeling of image regions using constraint satisfaction (in addition to being an important problem in digital image processing) is an important illustration of the power of declarative programming in PROLOG, since the user need merely pose the problem; the PROLOG system determines the steps necessary to achieve a constrained labeling. Furthermore, it illustrates the important concept of constraint satisfaction, which underlies many AI formulations. (5-4a)

Labeling serves as one basis for an image description, since after we have determined the identity of each image region we are in a position to describe the overall image on the basis of the nature and interrelationships of the labeled regions.

The approach we show here may be extended to the general case where the identity of objects is to be determined based primarily upon the extraction of observed relations between unlabeled objects and a set of known allowable relations that could be obtained from a semantic net.

The reader may query: "Why segment images?" Although our objective here is to explore AI, we note that image understanding is an application (or subarea) of AI that encompasses many AI-related concepts in addition to labeling. Examples are feature extraction and description.

General Labeling Formulation

In contrast to a numerical constraint satisfaction problem (Example 5.1), the objective of labeling problems in general is to obtain one or more allowable assignments of labels to a set of entities. The following quantities are defined:

$$U = \{u_1, u_2, \ldots, u_n\} \text{ is the set of } n \textbf{ objects} \text{ to be labeled} \tag{5-4b}$$

$$\Omega = \{\lambda_1, \lambda_2, \ldots, \lambda_m\} \text{ is the set of } m \textbf{ possible labels} \tag{5-4c}$$

Two levels of compatibilities are to be addressed in the formulation:

1. The compatibilities of labels with individual objects; and (5-4d)
2. The compatibilities of labels on two or more related objects. (5-4e)

Using the definitions of (5-4b) and (5-4c), a succinct definition of the labeling problem becomes

Determine one or more mappings between elements of Ω and those of U such that the compatibility constraints of (5-4d) and (5-4e) are satisfied. (5-4f)

Note that if there are n objects to be labeled and m possible labels on each object, without constraints m^n labeling possibilities exist.

Image Labeling Example

The input of a data type "image" implies, at a low level, the acquisition of a spatially distributed array of intensities from an image sensor (often a vidicon camera). Given this raw, or low level data, many approaches to segmentation exist. For example, one may "grow" regions by lumping together regions with common intensities or other attributes, or, alternately, one may seek to extract outlines (edge information) and connect edges to form closed regions. Regardless of the approach, we assume the output is a segmented image of the form shown in Fig. 5.2.

As Fig. 5.2 indicates, we consider the labeling of six regions, denoted as $R_1, R_2, \ldots, R_6$, which compose U. There are five possible labels for each of these regions:

car

road

trees

grass

sky (5-4g)

Note that an exhaustive enumeration of the unconstrained labeling of these regions thus yields $5^6 = 15,625$ possibilities.

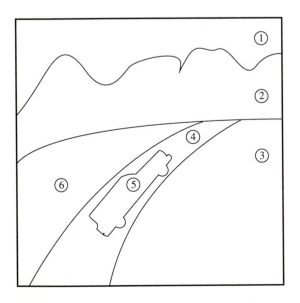

FIGURE 5.2

Sample segmented image (for PROLOG labeling example).

We should note that seldom are the results of segmentation as subjectively pleasing and simple as in Fig. 5.2. In addition, the problems of segmentation and labeling are not required to be solved sequentially; iterative applications of labeling and segmentation are possible. We ignore the particular approach used for segmentation and concentrate on labeling of the segmented image provided.

Constraint Determination

We seek to formulate the labeling problem of image regions as one of **constraint satisfaction**. We will consider only two types of constraints in this problem, namely:

1. **Unary constraints** or single argument restrictions or relations. These are most easily thought of as properties. For example, "color-of(a)" is an example of a 1-place relation or a property.   (5-4h)
2. **Binary constraints** or relations, involving two arguments or entities. "Next-to(a,b)" is an example of this type of constraint.   (5-4i)

We begin our approach to the labeling of the image with the determination of a number of constraints that make sense. This is the empirical aspect of the problem formulation; there are perhaps many formulations (employing differing constraints) that lead to satisfactory solutions. The determination of a set of constraints that make sense implies that we seek to examine the situation and extract implementable constraints based upon extractable features that do not violate human intuition. For example, rarely is it the case where an image region bearing the label "sky" appears at the bottom of an image (unless, of course, we are dealing with aircraft cockpit images and the aircraft is allowed to maneuver in an inverted position).

We now proceed to formulate the image labeling problem constraints. For simplicity, let us first consider a single binary constraint, namely that of **region adjacency**. Two regions that share a boundary are said to be adjacent. This is an easily extracted relation involving the image regions of Fig. 5.2.

Adjacency is a symmetric relation that is easily depicted graphically via an adjacency graph. The region adjacency graph (in terms of unlabeled regions R_i) for the sample segmented image of Fig. 5.2 is shown in Fig. 5.3. We note in passing that adjacency, while a symmetric relation (which, as we mentioned, implies trouble in the PROLOG representation if we are not mindful of the unification mechanism), is not transitive; i.e., a adjacent to b and b adjacent to c does not imply a adjacent to c (since we may have to go "through" region b to get to region c from region a). We indicate the symmetry of the adjacency relation by an undirected arc in the figure.

Our choice of the adjacency relation and representation of the adjacency graph for the sample image has not led to much of a solution; we still have no constraints

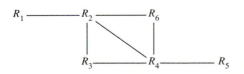

FIGURE 5.3
Observed region adjacency graph.

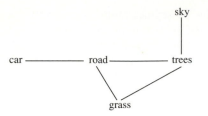

FIGURE 5.4
Allowed (constrained) adjacent region labels.

on allowable region adjacencies as a function of labels, nor have we formulated the problem in a form suitable for PROLOG. In other words, what are the predicates, what is the goal, and what are the facts and rules in the PROLOG database? We now address both concerns.

The first problem is developing a set of constraints on allowable labels as a function of whether the regions are adjacent or not. For example, it makes sense to allow two adjacent regions to have the labels "car" and "road"; that is, human intuition is not violated by viewing an image wherein a car is adjacent to a road. On the other hand, if a labeling indicated a car were adjacent to grass (the driver is driving off the road) in the image, we would not allow this labeling (or at least suspect its occurrence is atypical).

We therefore generate the set of compatible labels listed below and shown graphically in Fig. 5.4. Since adjacency is a symmetric relation, we do not show the symmetric version of each allowable adjacency in the following list.

Allowable labels on adjacent regions
"car" is adjacent to "road"
"road" is adjacent to "grass"
"grass" is adjacent to "trees"
"road" is adjacent to "trees"
"sky" is adjacent to "trees"
(symmetry of relation not enumerated)   (5-5)

PROLOG IMPLEMENTATION OF CONSTRAINT SATISFACTION

The Positive Approach

An appropriate PROLOG formulation for the constrained labeling problem formulated in the previous section is developed. In particular, this requires

1. Programming (representing) unary region label predicates (after an initial solution set has been generated).
2. Programming (representing) the allowable adjacency graph labels as predicates.
3. Satisfying the conjunction of adjacency constraints involving variables as a labeling goal.

The solution to item 2, using the preceding table of allowed labels on adjacent regions, is given by the following PROLOG database:

Example 5.2   Sample problem database using adjacency constraint (database #1).

```
adjacent_to(car,road).
adjacent_to(road,car).
adjacent_to(road,grass).
adjacent_to(grass,road).
adjacent_to(road,trees).
adjacent_to(trees,road).
adjacent_to(sky,trees).
adjacent_to(trees,sky).
adjacent_to(grass,trees).
adjacent_to(trees,grass).                                  (5-6)
```

This database of facts, based upon the predicate "adjacent_to," incorporates the constraint of Fig. 5.3. Note that in order to avoid the symmetry problem and concentrate on illustrating a solution approach, we have explicitly coded the symmetric relation as a predicate with region labels as arguments in both orders. Consequently, the five undirected arcs in Fig. 5.3 yield ten facts in the database. (Problem 5.9 explores the encoding of the symmetry of the "adjacent_to" relation via a rule.)

We can view the problem of constraint satisfaction in our example as the search for suitable bindings (assignment of labels) on the region variables such that the observed adjacency graph (with the labeling substitutions) does not violate the allowable label adjacency graph. The beauty of the problem is that we let PROLOG determine the necessary operations to achieve this; we merely worry about setting up the problem.

To formulate a goal, we need to incorporate two additional entities:

1. The coding of the *observed* region adjacency graph (incorporating the region variables) as a conjunction of clauses involving the predicate adjacent_to; and

2. Our instructions to the PROLOG system that a valid labeling will be the instantiation of these region variables with values (labels) such that the conjunction of these clauses is TRUE, i.e., satisfied through unification.

One (not necessarily unique) way to accomplish this is via the formulation of the following goal:

Example 5.3   Goal for sample problem (simplified).

```
adjacent_to(R1,R2),
adjacent_to(R2,R6),
adjacent_to(R2,R3),
adjacent_to(R3,R4),
adjacent_to(R2,R4),
adjacent_to(R4,R6),
adjacent_to(R4,R5).                                        (5-7)
```

Figure 5.5(*a*) shows the results of all possible unifications of this goal with the database. It is interesting to note that the system is still underconstrained; there are 42 possible solutions. Lest the reader suspect these are erroneous solutions, we emphasize that each of these satisfies the allowable adjacency graph. The fact that most of these solutions, when displayed on Fig. 5.2, counteract human intuition is a result of the PROLOG system not "seeing" the figure, only the database.

```
region 1 is bound to  sky
region 2 is bound to  trees
region 3 is bound to  road
region 4 is bound to  grass
region 5 is bound to  road
region 6 is bound to  road


region 1 is bound to  sky
region 2 is bound to  trees
region 3 is bound to  road
region 4 is bound to  grass
region 5 is bound to  trees
region 6 is bound to  road


region 1 is bound to  sky
region 2 is bound to  trees
region 3 is bound to  grass
region 4 is bound to  road
region 5 is bound to  car
region 6 is bound to  grass
```
} Correct solution

```
region 1 is bound to  sky
region 2 is bound to  trees
region 3 is bound to  grass
region 4 is bound to  road
region 5 is bound to  grass
region 6 is bound to  grass
```

```
region 1 is bound to  sky          region 1 is bound to  sky
region 2 is bound to  trees        region 2 is bound to  trees
region 3 is bound to  grass        region 3 is bound to  grass
region 4 is bound to  road         region 4 is bound to  road
region 5 is bound to  trees        region 5 is bound to  car
region 6 is bound to  grass        region 6 is bound to  grass
```

(*a*)   (*b*)

FIGURE 5.5
PROLOG labeling results: (*a*) Results using a single unary constraint (*b*) Results with two unary constraints.

The 42 solutions generated include the correct one (the one a human observer would return by applying additional interpretations to the sample image). Note, even though we have not generated a subjectively satisfactory unique solution (or set of solutions), we have reduced (via only five symmetric constraints) the set of possible labelings from 15,625 to 42. Thus, with merely the five simple adjacency-based constraints, we have eliminated 99.73% of the possible labelings, retaining only 0.27%.

As an aside, the normal procedure of generating these solutions with the PRO-LOG system would involve 42 separate queries from the system regarding additional solutions. Instead, as a convenience (and a way to introduce the built-in PROLOG predicate fail) we show the additional clauses that may be appended to this goal. Therefore the conjunction of these clauses must be TRUE for the PROLOG system to report success. The additional clauses are given in Example 5.4.

Example 5.4 Extended goal (output and all solutions).

```
write('region 1 is bound to   '), write(R1),
nl,
write('region 2 is bound to   '), write(R2),
nl,
write('region 3 is bound to   '), write(R3),
nl,
write('region 4 is bound to   '), write(R4),
nl,
write('region 5 is bound to   '), write(R5),
nl,
write('region 6 is bound to   '), write(R6),
nl,nl,nl,
fail.                                                    (5-8)
```

(Note: A multiple-argument "write" predicate is available in some PROLOG implementations).

The operation of the write predicate is relatively self-explanatory; it merely evaluates to TRUE and has the side effect of indicating a set of bindings on the variables R_1 through R_6. Note that the PROLOG system, due to the order in which unification occurs, must have achieved success prior to encountering the write statements; thus the problem of printing the values of unbound variables does not appear.

More interesting, however, is the use of the fail predicate as the last predicate. This predicate is built into PROLOG and always evaluates to FALSE; that is, it always fails. Incorporating fail as the last predicate in the goal statement forces all possible backtracking and consequently the generation of all possible unification solutions.

Although we have considerably reduced the solution space , we have not reached our goal of a consistent labeling that would be produced by a human observer. To do this, additional constraints must be employed to further constrain the solution space.

We consider first the incorporation of the unary constraint that the region labeled "sky" must be the uppermost region in the segmented image. We add this observation, or assumed extracted information, to the goal statement (assuming that image processing techniques may be used to extract this information) and to the database as a fact, indicating a second relation (or in this case a property) "highest."

Example 5.5 Goal modification #1.

```
adjacent_to(R1,R2),
adjacent_to(R2,R6),
adjacent_to(R2,R3),
adjacent_to(R3,R4),
adjacent_to(R2,R4),
adjacent_to(R4,R6),
adjacent_to(R4,R5),
highest(R1).
```
(5-9)

Example 5.6 Database modification #1 (database #2).

```
highest(sky).
adjacent_to(car,road).
adjacent_to(road,car).
adjacent_to(road,grass).
adjacent_to(grass,road).
adjacent_to(road,trees).
adjacent_to(trees,road).
adjacent_to(sky,trees).
adjacent_to(trees,sky).
adjacent_to(grass,trees).
adjacent_to(trees,grass).
```
(5-10)

The results of unification in this case are shown in Fig. 5.5(*b*). Note there are now five possible solutions; the problem is still undetermined. The correct solution is still included in the five that are possible.

Finally, we seek to employ an additional unary constraint. In this case, assume several time observations or samples of the image were available. Using this data, it is possible to determine if a region exhibited motion; that is, it was moving. (As an aside, this is nontrivial with "real" images). We return to our objective of formulating constraints that "make sense" and thus recognize this motion as an attribute only possible on a region labeled "car." Incorporating this second unary constraint in the database yields, we have the results shown in Examples 5.7 and 5.8.

Example 5.7 Modification for two unary constraints: "highest" and "moving" (in addition to adjacency) (goal modification #2).

```
adjacent_to(R1,R2),
adjacent_to(R2,R6),
adjacent_to(R2,R3),
adjacent_to(R3,R4),
adjacent_to(R2,R4),
adjacent_to(R4,R6),
```

```
adjacent_to(R4,R5),
highest(R1),
moving(R5).                                                    (5-11)
```

Example 5.8 Database modification #2 (database #3).

```
highest(sky).
moving(car).
adjacent_to(car,road).
adjacent_to(road,car).
adjacent_to(road,grass).
adjacent_to(grass,road).
adjacent_to(road,trees).
adjacent_to(trees,road).
adjacent_to(sky,trees).
adjacent_to(trees,sky).
adjacent_to(grass,trees).
adjacent_to(trees,grass).                                      (5-12)
```

This approach yields a single solution, which is the one a human observer would have produced.

We conclude this section with two remarks:

1. The employment of five symmetric adjacency constraints and two unary constraints eliminated all but 0.0064% of the possible (unconstrained) labelings. This is really quite surprising, since no additional image features or extracted information were necessary, and indicates the value of high-level symbolic manipulation in the image understanding process.
2. The labeling was accomplished in a "positive" fashion; we developed constraints based upon "what could happen." A more negative approach based upon "what can't happen" may significantly reduce the unification (search) process in certain problem formulations. An example of the negative approach (coding what is not allowed) using the PROLOG not predicate is shown in the following section.

The Negative Approach (Coding
What Is Not Allowed in PROLOG)

The positive approach, exemplified above, coded knowledge as facts that indicated allowable labelings in the PROLOG database. For example,

```
adjacent_to(sky, trees).                                       (5-13)
```

indicated that adjacent regions with the labels "sky" and "trees" were allowable, or made sense. We now consider an approach based upon the complement of this type of reasoning, that is, determining and coding what doesn't make sense. This example also reinforces our understanding of the PROLOG unification mechanism.

We begin by retaining the previous goal, which incorporated the observed adjacency graph for the unlabeled regions in the segmented image (and the case of a single unary constraint on "sky"):

```
adjacent_to(R1,R2),
adjacent_to(R2,R6),
adjacent_to(R2,R3),
adjacent_to(R3,R4),
adjacent_to(R2,R4),
adjacent_to(R4,R6),
adjacent_to(R4,R5),
highest(R1).                                          (5-14)
```

Our design of the PROLOG database is different. It now consists of the enumeration of illegal labels, which can't exist on adjacent regions. For example, we hypothesize that it does not make sense that a car would be driving along the sky, and therefore include the fact (which is TRUE!)

```
cant_be_adjacent_to(car,sky).                         (5-15)
```

in the database. Thus, predicates such as (5-15) evaluate to TRUE, but more importantly, indicate the truth of the statement:

"A car can't (cannot) be adjacent to the sky."

We now seek a mechanism to couple the "negative database" with the positive goal. This could be done, for example, through a rule involving the predicate "adjacent_to":

```
adjacent_to(A,B) :- not(cant_be_adjacent_to(A,B)).    (5-16)
```

This rule, given (label) bindings on A and B, evaluates to TRUE if the labeling is not one of those that is disallowed. It does this by searching for a unification with the "cant_be_adjacent_to" clauses in the database. If unification fails, we conclude that the labeling is allowed. As described previously, this makes use of the negation-as-failure nature of the PROLOG unifier; that is, failure of the cant_be_adjacent_to predicate occurs if one or more matching clauses do not exist in the database.

Given the rule in (5-16) together with the set of cant_be_adjacent_to predicates (disallowed cases), and a predicate for the unary constraint on "sky" (formulated, for illustration, in the positive sense) we might be tempted to conclude a PROLOG database is as follows.

Example 5.9 Sample PROLOG database for "negative" formulation (database #4).

```
adjacent_to(A,B) :- not(cant_be_adjacent_to(A,B)).
```

```
highest(sky).

cant_be_adjacent_to(sky,road).
cant_be_adjacent_to(road,sky).
cant_be_adjacent_to(car,sky).
cant_be_adjacent_to(sky,car).
cant_be_adjacent_to(car,grass).
cant_be_adjacent_to(grass,car).
cant_be_adjacent_to(sky,grass).
cant_be_adjacent_to(grass,sky).
cant_be_adjacent_to(car,trees).
cant_be_adjacent_to(trees,car).                              (5-17)
```

Given this database and the positive formulation of the goal in (5-14), we might conclude the system design is finished. We simply invoke the PROLOG system and read the possible image labelings. However, the astute reader who understands the PROLOG unification mechanism will realize that the above PROLOG formulation does not achieve our objective. The difficulty, in this case, is not with negation-as-failure, since we assume the database is complete. The reason is relatively obvious — there is no way for bindings of variables to occur in the database (excluding the unary constraint on "sky"). The goal statement contains the predicate adjacent_to, with variables, as does the database. Furthermore, the clause that forms the tail of the rule with head "adjacent_to" — that is, not(cant_be_adjacent_to(A, B)) — succeeds if unification of cant_be_adjacent_to(A, B) fails. If A and B are unbound, however, unification is possible. The "not" predicate therefore fails, and consequently adjacent_to fails, thus failing to satisfy the goal statement.

For illustration, this situation is rectified in a somewhat clumsy way. Given that we must force variables A and B to assume nonvariable values (constant labels) prior to the attempted unification in the adjacent_to rule, we augment the database with a set of facts consisting of all labels taken pairwise and an additional clause in the antecedent of the above rule. These are given in Example 5.10.

Example 5.10 Modified (forced) unification formulation of PROLOG (negative) database (database #5).

```
adjacent_to(A,B):-
              attempt(A,B),
              not(cant_be_adjacent_to(A,B)).

attempt(sky,road).
attempt(road,sky).
attempt(sky,car).
attempt(car,sky).
attempt(sky,grass).
attempt(grass,sky).
attempt(sky,trees).
attempt(trees,sky).
attempt(road,car).
```

```
attempt(car,road).
attempt(road,grass).
attempt(grass,road).
attempt(road,trees).
attempt(trees,road).
attempt(car,grass).
attempt(grass,car).
attempt(car,trees).
attempt(trees,car).
attempt(grass,trees).
attempt(trees,grass).
```

$$\{(plus\ "cant\_be\_adjacent\_to"\ predicates$$
$$from\ (5-17)\ database).\}\qquad\qquad (5\text{-}18)$$

The predicate attempt forces the PROLOG system to first bind A and B to one instance of the possible pairwise combinations of all labels and then consider the "not" predicate. Note that the number of possible permutations of n labels, considered r at a time, is

$$P_r^n = \frac{n!}{(n-r)!} \qquad\qquad (5\text{-}19)$$

which in this case yields

$$P_2^5 = \frac{5!}{3!} = 20$$

Given a larger set of possible labels, the above procedure becomes unmanageable. The reader is encouraged to verify that this implementation, as modified, returns the same five valid labelings (shown in Fig. 5.5a) as the positive approach, with the single unary constraint on "sky" above.

This example has provided a useful example of the representation of facts in a negative way. The negative approach, while of academic interest, violates common sense and good PROLOG programming practice for at least two reasons:

1. Usually the number of clauses necessary to enumerate what can't happen is much larger than those enumerations of what can (a few applications contradict this).
2. The formulation doesn't let PROLOG's unification mechanism do as much as possible, that is, leaves the problem formulation to the programmer.

The computational consequences of the positive versus the negative approaches are problem dependent. As noted above, it is necessary to "kludge" the PROLOG system to force unification prior to employing "negation-as-failure." In addition, the application of this approach forced the enumeration of (i) all possible pairwise combinations of labels, and (ii) all possible "cant happen" situations. The addition of these clauses to the database (depending on the order of specific facts and rules in the database) is likely to spawn a significantly larger number of attempted unifications. As mentioned previously, a measure of the system speed will be determined by the number of unifications per time interval.

Further ramifications of the "negative" approach, and more reasonable PROLOG formulations, are considered in the problems.

REFERENCES

[Mackworth 1977] Mackworth, A. K., "Consistency in Networks of Relations," *Artificial Intelligence*, Vol. 8, No. 1., pp. 99–118.

[Mulder/Mackworth 1988] Mulder, J.A., and A. Mackworth, "Knowledge Structuring and Constraint Satisfaction: the Mapsee Approach," *IEEE Transactions on Pattern Analysis and Machine Intelligence*, Vol. 10, No. 6, November 1988, pp. 866–867.

[Schalkoff 1989] Schalkoff, R.J., *Digital Image Processing and Computer Vision*, John Wiley & Sons, N.Y., 1989.

PROBLEMS

5.1. Implement, in PROLOG, a system that produces the 42 possible valid labels for the region-segmented image given in Fig. 5.2 by employing only the binary "adjacent to" constraint.

5.2. Considering the case where any label is possible for any object, derive an expression for the total number of possible labelings of r objects with m labels (before application of inter-object constraints).

5.3. In the PROLOG labeling application examples, the question of the reflexive property of the adjacency constraint was not explicitly considered. For example, in the positive approach the clause

$$adjacent\_to(car,car)$$

or

$$adjacent\_to(road,road) \qquad\qquad (P3\text{-}1)$$

was not included in the database. Similarly, in the "negative" formulation, we did not address the suitability of including

$$cant\_be\_adjacent\_to(car,\ car). \qquad\qquad (P3\text{-}2)$$

(*a*) Discuss the suitability of the inclusion of either of these constraints. In particular, is this property reflexive, and how would these allowable (or prohibited, respectively) inter-object label compatibility constraints influence the solution?

(*b*) In each of our previous formulations (the positive and negative approaches), what is implied by the absence of clauses (P3-1) and (P3-2)?

(*c*) Where reasonable, incorporate these constraints in the previous formulations and show the revised solution. How does it differ from our previous results?

5.4. Solve for the valid image labelings for the three cases shown in Fig. P5.4 by modifying and executing the PROLOG (positive formulation) program. In each case, consider first only the binary constraint, then add the unary constraints "highest" and "moving."

5.5. Consider the application of constraint-based labeling to geometric figures in the plane. An example is shown in Fig. P5.5. The set of objects to be labeled is, U, where

$$U = \{p_1, p_2, p_3, p_4\}$$

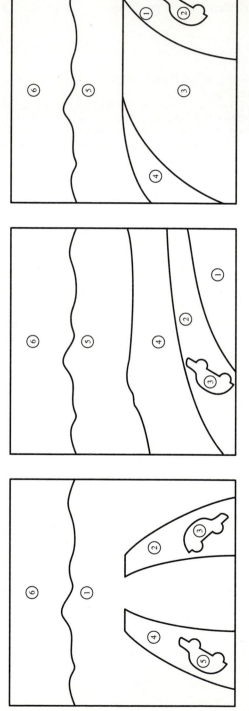

FIGURE P5.4
(Alternate labeling cases).

and the set of possible labels is

$$\Omega = \{t, b, ls, rs\}$$

corresponding to "top," "bottom," "left side," and "right side," respectively.

(*a*) Using the binary constraint "connected to" (or, equivalently, "intersects"):

    (i) Attempt labeling of this figure. Show the observed "connected to" relational graph. How many solutions exist?

    (ii) Repeat (i), but incorporate the unary constraint "topmost."

(*b*) Develop PROLOG representations for the cases in (a) and show the results.

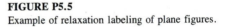

p_1

p_4 p_3

p_2

FIGURE P5.5
Example of relaxation labeling of plane figures.

5.6. ("Inversion" of the feature extraction process.) Consider the observed regional constraints for two image cases shown in Fig. P5.6. The purpose of this problem is to consider the uniqueness of this observed information in the process of going backwards to attempt to reconstruct a segmented image from these constraints. In each case (cases (*a*) and (*b*)), sketch a suitable image that may have yielded this information.

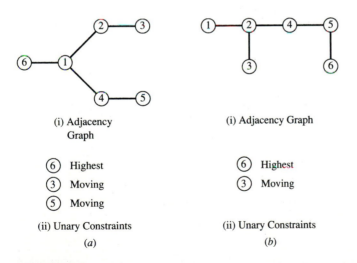

(i) Adjacency Graph   (i) Adjacency Graph

⑥ Highest   ⑥ Highest
③ Moving   ③ Moving
⑤ Moving

(ii) Unary Constraints   (ii) Unary Constraints

(*a*)   (*b*)

FIGURE P5.6
Observed region constraints (2 cases).

5.7. (This makes an excellent long-term project.) The previous PROLOG formulations of the labeling problem either generated an underconstrained (non-unique) or a unique solution. In fact, we developed a PROLOG description incrementally, working from the underdetermined case to a unique solution. In this problem, we consider the converse, by exploring the effect of overdetermined labeling problems and the corresponding PROLOG formulations. Overconstrained problems yield no solution.

(a) Suggest one or more additional constraints, which (perhaps through negation as failure) cause the labeling problem to have no solution. (Hint: consider the unary constraints "not_moving" or "lowest" or the binary relation "closer_than".) Show why and where in the unification process your solution fails.

(b) Develop an autonomous adaptation strategy, and implement this as a modified PRO-LOG goal, whereby failure to achieve a unique solution causes the goal to be amended to include additional constraints.

(c) (Corollary to (b)). Using the goal-modification concept of (b), develop an alternative strategy for the formulation of Problem 1, whereby initial generation of a non-unique solution is followed by the autonomous (the PROLOG program must do it) modification of the goal to incorporate an additional constraint until a unique solution is generated. Show program results.

5.8. How is the efficiency (from the point of view of matching, unification, or search) of our PROLOG labeling formulation affected by putting "highest" at the beginning or at the end of the goal specification?

5.9. Suppose we code a symmetric relation such as adjacency via a rule; e.g.,

```
adjacent(A,B): - adjacent_to(A,B).
adjacent(A,B): - adjacent_to(B,A).
adjacent_to(car, road).
       .
       .
       .
```
(P9-1)

rather than simply rewriting facts; e.g.,

```
adjacent(car, road).
adjacent(road, car).
```
(P9-2)

(a) Which approach is more efficient in terms of unification (search). Show some examples of your reasoning.

(b) Does the answer to (a) depend upon the number of pairs (arguments) that are adjacent?

5.10. Explore the ramifications of the following modification to the (negative) formulation of the PROLOG labeling example:

```
cant_be_adjacent_to(R1, R2): - not(adjacent_to (R1,
R2)).
```
(P10-1)

Specifically, will this rule, using Database #1 (Example 5.2), generate the same set of "cant_be_adjacent_to" clauses as in Database #4 (Example 5.9)?

5.11. We have approached the symbolic constraint satisfaction problem without requiring, for example, that all labels be used. Consider alternative formulations where we know a priori that

  (i) There is *at most one region* with the label trees.
  (ii) There is *exactly one* region with the label car.
  (iii) There is *at least one* region with the label trees.

(a) Develop revised PROLOG formulations of Database #1 (5-6) and its corresponding goal (5-7) that incorporate (in addition to "adjacent_to"):

  (i) All three of the above constraints.
  (ii) Each of the above constraints individually.

(b) Repeat (a) for

  (i) Database #2 (5-10) and its associated goal (5-9); and
  (ii) Database #3 (5-12) and its associated goal (5-11).

(c) Show how to modify the negative formulation to incorporate the constraints (i)–(iii) above.

In each of the above cases, quantify the number and "correctness" of possible solutions.

5.12. Suppose we reformulate the image labeling problem using *only* the constraints

  (i) highest
  (ii) moving
  (iii) highest and moving

How many solutions exist in each case?

5.13. (a) Why, in the labeling problem goal specification, are we allowed to specify the observed relation

$$\text{adjacent\_to(R1, R2)}$$

without specifying also

$$\text{adjacent\_to(R2, R1) ?}$$

(b) Suppose the database only contained clauses of the form "adjacent_to (car, road)"; i.e., we did not enumerate also "adjacent_to (road, car)," or use a rule to encode symmetry. How would (or could) you modify the goal specification to allow for the symmetry of the adjacency relation with this database?

CHAPTER 6

AN AI APPLICATION USING PROLOG: ELECTRIC POWER SYSTEM PROTECTION ANALYSIS

Far better never think of investigating truth at all than to do so without a method.

René Descartes

OVERVIEW

Objectives

In this chapter we consider another PROLOG application for the manipulation of symbolic information in a manner that emulates human reasoning. This particular example concerns, like Chapter 5, constraint satisfaction. However, it provides a rich, in-depth look at the use of PROLOG to develop a problem description. The particular example used also illustrates an AI application to diagnosis or trouble shooting. In addition, it also provides a look at a more sophisticated PROLOG database (developed incrementally), as well as some of the more advanced PROLOG constructs.

The application concerns the development of a reasoning system for power system protection. Protection of an electric power system involves developing a strategy to operate ("open") appropriate circuit breakers in the event a fault occurs. For simplicity, a fault may be considered a shorting of a circuit to ground, usually resulting in abnormally high currents through various power system circuit elements. These currents can cause significant mechanical and thermal damage to elements of the system. A simplistic model of a circuit breaker is that of a robust switch, which is used to isolate the faulted section of the system by removing one or more sources of current. We address our efforts in this example specifically to the automated identification of situations wherein operation of protective elements has occurred. Thus, given a PROLOG description of (i) a specific power system and (ii) breaker operation fundamentals, an explanation of the state of the system is desired from PROLOG.

Simple Power Protection Background

The basic arrangement of a simple electric power generation and distribution network is shown in Fig. 6.1. This graphical representation is used throughout the chapter and is denoted a one-line diagram. The system has sources of power (generators) and lines that interconnect generators and loads. Loads, for example, may be large industrial plants, or residential customers. Each line is protected by a circuit breaker at each end. It is important to note that each breaker only "sees" in one direction, as shown in Fig. 6.2. It is also important to note that this "sight" (or domain of protection) may extend, directionally, beyond the corresponding breaker and thus enable some overlapping of protection to other lines.[1] This is referred to as **backup**.

We begin our analysis with a detailed word description of the problem, noting that this type of generic problem is not restricted to the power system scenario; in fact it represents a form of reasoning common to other applications such as fault tolerant

---

[1]The "sight" of the breaker is not inherent in the breaker, but due to associated instrumentation known as relays. These relays have directional voltage-current characteristics, and are the "brains" of the protection system in the sense that they control breaker operation. The coordination of relaying (especially the development of autonomous systems to design this coordination) is a challenging problem in power systems engineering. In practice, the sight of the protection scheme extends behind the breaker to include the "bus" that interconnects the lines; however, we ignore all but the simplest schemes in our presentation.

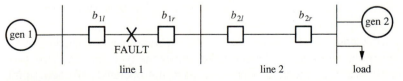

FIGURE 6.1
Simple case of protection system operation.

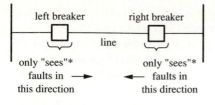

*"sight" may extend beyond corresponding breaker at other end; based upon system design

FIGURE 6.2
Simplified circuit breaker directional protection characteristics.

computing. It is an excellent medium to show the power of the declarative language PROLOG, in the sense that all we need to do is describe the power system topology and the operation (both primary and backup) of the protection scheme to enable the PROLOG system to determine the possible fault locations and interpretations of the type of protection system operation.

PROBLEM FORMULATION

Overall Goals

The operation of our massive, highly interconnected, and surprisingly reliable electric power system is complex, and requires the attention of many skilled engineers. However, electromechanical devices such as relays and breakers can and do fail to operate correctly; therefore, redundancy or "backup" is designed into the protection scheme. In particular, when elements of the protection system operate (specifically relays and their corresponding breakers), it is necessary for a power system protection engineer to determine the location of the fault in order to correct the situation and restore service to customers. More importantly, it is necessary for the engineer to examine and interpret the overall operation of the protection system to determine if any elements failed to operate (and thus required backup from other elements). In a complex system, when many interpretations are possible, this is a nontrivial problem.

Our goal in the development of an AI system to observe and "reason" about these aspects of power system protection is therefore to emulate the reasoning of the power system engineer, specifically:

1. To identify all possible fault scenarios, given (i) the power system network topology, (ii) the locations of generators, and (iii) the breaker status information—either in service (s) or operated (o). This includes fault locations (lines) and cases of circuit breaker primary operation or backup.
2. To identify correct vs. incorrect operation. Correct operation means that the appropriate breaker(s) has operated; incorrect means either the incorrect breakers have operated or (logical OR) the correct breakers have not operated. We henceforth assume that incorrect breaker operation is restricted to failure of a breaker to operate. It is highly unlikely that breakers that are not supposed to operate incorrectly do so; i.e., rarely do breakers simply decide to open for no reason

and electrically isolate a section of a line. In essence, we want to take the same information available to a power system protection engineer and automatically generate the same conclusions. As we will see, the unification mechanism in PROLOG allows us to examine this situation from several viewpoints.

3. To identify the elements that are in error (faulty).

We begin, as in most AI problems, by considering a subcase of the problem and then attempting decomposition of the larger problem into one that is solvable via the subcase. Consider the simple one-line example of Fig. 6.1. We begin our description of the protection problem to be converted to a PROLOG representation with the following knowledge.

PROLOG Description of System Topology

First, consider the case of a single (transmission) line. A line is protected by two circuit breakers; one at each end. In the normal state, there is no reason (except for scheduled maintenance, which we ignore) for either breaker to be in a state we refer to as "operated" or, electrically speaking, open. We refer to this case as a line in service, or in the normal state and denoted via a capital "S" on the one-line diagram. When a fault occurs on the line, if the line is connected to a source of generation at either end (a source of generation includes connection to another line that is in service and connected to a generation source), the breaker at that end is designed to operate. This status is denoted via "O" on the one-line diagram. Note that this takes into account the directionality of the protection scheme. Thus, at this point we could summarize the state of line_x with the following sample PROLOG description, which relates lines and breaker labels (names or numbers), corresponding operational states (O, S), and the existence of a fault. These are meant to be simple examples that are refined in the succeeding sections. This is done by the incorporation of the following facts in the PROLOG database.

Example 6.1   Simple PROLOG line description.

```
protected_by(Line_x, Breaker_l, Breaker_r).
generation(Breaker_l).
generation(Breaker_r).                                    (6-1)
```

By way of example, a sample interpretation rule for the left line breaker might be the following.

Example 6.2   Simple PROLOG predicate to assess breaker operation.

```
correct_oper_left(Line_x, Breaker_l, Breaker_r) :-
      protected_by(Line_x, Breaker_l, Breaker_r),
      fault(Line_x),
      generation(Breaker_l),
      operated(Line, Breaker_l).                          (6-2)
```

Since each line has two circuit breakers, we consider the rightmost one similarly via

```
correct_oper_right(Line_x, Breaker_l, Breaker_r)  :-
    protected_by(Line_x, Breaker_l, Breaker_r),
    fault(Line_x),
    generation(Breaker_r),
    operated(Line, Breaker_r).                              (6-3)
```

Breaker Backup

To fully appreciate the complexity of the situation, we now add additional facts.

1. Breakers are designed to provide backup for other breakers that may fail to operate. Recall the assumption that the only type of operational failure of a breaker is failure to operate when required. Backup for this type of operational failure is accomplished by modifying the time-current characteristics of the protection system; it is not imperative that this be understood in the context of the current example. Referring to Fig. 6.1, we merely note that if a fault exists on line 2 and breaker b_{2l} fails to operate (we denote this by "m" for malfunction) then breaker b_{1l} operates, providing backup for b_{2l}. A similar remark may be made for b_{2r} and b_{1r}; the directionality of the protection must still be observed.

2. The breakers will operate only if sufficient current causes an alarm. This requires that the line containing the breaker be supplied with a source of current or "generation," which may occur in either of two ways:
    i. The line is directly connected to a generator; or
    ii. The line is connected to an adjacent line that supplies current; i.e., the adjacent line has generation. This, in turn, requires the adjacent line to be either connected to a generator or itself connected to a line supplying current. (The reader may notice the beginning of a recursive definition of "generation" and a transitive relation).

   Thus, to develop a PROLOG representation for the system, we need the following.

1. The network topology, that is, the line interconnection. This representation, due to the directionality of the protection scheme, needs to account for the left-right relationship of lines.
2. An indication of the location of generators.
3. An indication of the status of all breakers in the system.

Temporarily, we assume that only a single fault is under consideration. More complex cases are considered in the problems.

An Extended Example of PROLOG Description Derivation

In this section we revise and extend our approach from that above, and develop a more general framework in PROLOG, for fault location and protection system operation interpretation. To take the development further, assume the two-line system shown

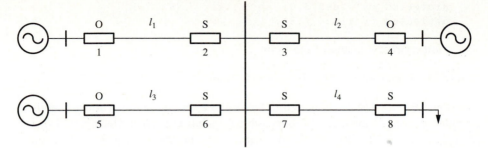

FIGURE 6.3
Sample power system topology used in Examples 6.3 and 6.4.

in Fig. 6.3 is used. Recall our objective is to develop a strategy, through description, to enable the PROLOG system, through unification, to determine all possible fault locations.

In addition, the important assumptions used in the description development are

1. Only one breaker malfunction is possible;
2. The malfunctioned breaker has backup breaker(s);
3. Only a single line fault is possible; and
4. The relays (breakers) have the aforementioned directional protection characteristics. (6-4)

Thus, in the PROLOG formulation we seek to represent

1. The topology of the network;
2. The current breaker status; and
3. Rules regarding correct (primary and backup) breaker operation.

Note we also embed a goal (run) in the PROLOG database , to avoid entering large amounts of data at the PROLOG interpreter prompt.

General Network Topology Description

First, we consider development of a general topology description. A clause of the form

```
protected_by(Line,Breaker1,Breaker2)                    (6-5)
```

means the line with variable name Line is protected by breakers with variable names Breaker1 and Breaker2. The system of Fig. 6.3 therefore contains the following facts:

Example 6.3   Line/Breaker associations for Fig. 6.3.

```
protected_by(line1,1,2).
protected_by(line2,3,4).
```

```
protected_by(line3,5,6).
protected_by(line4,7,8).
```
(6-6)

Furthermore, a clause of the form:

```
connect(Breaker1_name,Breaker2_name)
```
(6-7)

means that $Breaker1$ is connected to $Breaker2$ through a bus. (In our simplistic formulation, we assume that it is not possible for a bus to become electrically isolated from lines; that is, it is assumed to be "hardwired" into the system. In real systems, the bus itself has another special type of differential protection. This extension is addressed in the problems). From the sample network of Fig. 6.3, the PROLOG database contains the following.

Example 6.4   Description of line connections for Fig. 6.3.

```
connect(2,3).
connect(2,6).
connect(2,7).
connect(3,6).
connect(3,7).
connect(6,7).
```
(6-8)

Similarly, the fact

```
generation(Breaker_name)
```
(6-9)

means that there is a source of generation directly connected to the breaker. Note that this is only a part of the representation, since we later show how generation propagates via line interconnections and breaker status. In our example, the facts regarding generator locations are as follows.

Example 6.5   Description of (direct) sources of generation (generators).

```
generation(1).
generation(4).
generation(5).
```
(6-10)

Breaker status is indicated via the fact

```
operate(Breaker_name)
```
(6-11)

meaning that the given breaker has operated. In our system, we choose the following scenario for illustration.

Example 6.6   Breaker status (operated).

```
operate(1).
operate(4).
operate(5).
```
(6-12)

Note that this formulation implies negation-as-failure; that is, breakers that are not specified as "operated" are assumed in service. The reader is encouraged, using the previous description of breaker operation and fault locations, to manually determine all possible fault locations and corresponding protection system interpretations before proceeding. We now turn our attention to the development of PROLOG database rules.

SIGNIFICANT RULES IN DESCRIPTION

The previous PROLOG description elements (clauses) were restricted to facts. In this section we develop the significant rules that allow automated inference from the power system protection scenerio.

Connectivity Rules

The rule "connection" is used to represent the symmetric property of connectedness; that is, the relation "breaker1 connected to breaker2" implies that the relation "breaker2 connected to breaker1" also exists. This is accomplished via the scheme shown below (and cited in Chapters 4 and 5). Note that connection is a symmetric relation that must be encoded carefully.

```
connection(B1,B2)  :- connect(B1,B2).
connection(B1,B2)  :- connect(B2,B1).
```
(6-13)

Locating Corresponding Breakers via Rules

It is useful to be able to locate, given the topology of the network and the names of a specific line and one of the line's breakers, the name of the other breaker. The rule head (clause)

```
other_breaker(known_breaker_name,unknown_breaker_name)
```
(6-14)

gives the unknown breaker's name, using the following approach (note the use of the anonymous variable so the rule will work for any line):

```
other_breaker(B1,B2)  :- protected_by(_,B1,B2).
other_breaker(B1,B2)  :- protected_by(_,B2,B1).
```
(6-15)

Two rules are included in (6-15) so that we are not forced to consider which end of the line the known breaker is on.

Generation Rules

One of the most important rules, i.e., the rule head (clause)

```
has_gen(B)
```
(6-16)

is used to indicate that breaker B has a (direct or indirect) source of generation. Therefore, B may need to operate under certain fault conditions. A "generation-less" breaker does not need to consider operation; there is no current to interrupt. The first rule deals with the case in which breaker B is connected directly to a source of generation. The second rule deals with the case of generation transitivity in which breaker B is connected to breaker B1 of line L, line L is protected by breakers B1 and B2, and breaker B2 has generation. This is stated as a two-rule set.

Example 6.7   Generation transivity and examples.

```
has_gen(B)  :- generation(B), !.
has_gen(B)  :- connection(B,B1),
               other_breaker(B1,B2),
               has_gen(B2), !.                          (6-17)
```

Note that we employ the cut ("!") operator to achieve an efficient solution. A breaker may have generation from many sources; we only care about the first time we establish (through unification) that a breaker has generation.

The operation of the "has_gen" rule is quite interesting. For example, given the systems of Figs. 6.4a and 6.4b, we show the system dialog regarding using this rule as a goal, in Figs. 6.4c and 6.4d, respectively. In addition, this type of checking of intermediate representation results is fundamental in the incremental development of AI systems, and is strongly encouraged.

Review of the PROLOG Cut Predicate

Chapter 4 introduced a way to control backtracking via the "cut" predicate. The "cut" predicate (indicated by the ! symbol) appears in (6-17) and in what follows. Recall for example, in the rule

```
r1  :- a,b,!,c.                                          (6-18)
```

we indicate that the first solution for variable bindings in clauses a and b is acceptable, and that only c should be marked as a point for possible backtracking.

Backup Breaker Description

The role of a **backup breaker** is described in the PROLOG database, using predicate backup. For example,

```
back_up(B1,B2)
```

is used to represent the fact that breaker B2 is one of B1's backup breakers. Note that B1 may have any number of backup breakers, which are a function of the power network topology. **Backup operation** is specified via the following rule.

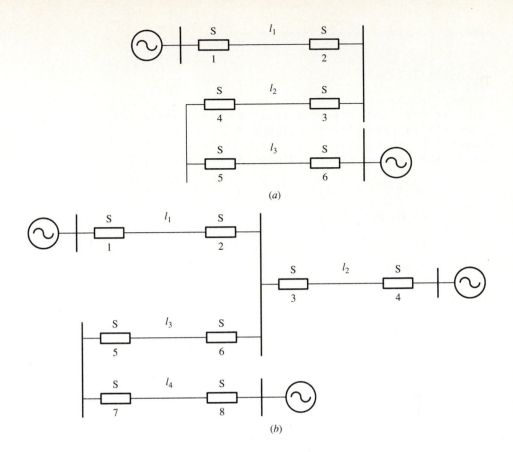

(a)

(b)

```
?- consult(gen_r).
yes
?- has_gen(1).
Breaker 1 is connected to a generation directly.

yes
?- has_gen(2).


Breaker 2 is not connected to a generation directly,
    but it is connected to breaker 3
    and breaker 3 protects a line with breaker 4.
Breaker 4 is not connected to a generation directly,
    but it is connected to breaker 5
    and breaker 5 protects a line with breaker 6.
Breaker 6 is connected to a generation directly.

yes

END OF PROLOG EXECUTION
```
(c)

FIGURE 6.4
Example of finding "generation" (all breakers in service): (a) System topology (case a); (b) System topology (case b); (c) Dialog for system of (a).

```
?- consult(gen_r2).
yes
?- has_gen(2).
Breaker 2 is not connected to a generation directly,
   but it is connected to breaker 3
   and breaker 3 protects a line with breaker 4.
Breaker 4 is connected to a generation directly.

yes

END OF PROLOG EXECUTION
```

(d)

```
protected_by(line1,1,2).
protected_by(line2,3,4).
protected_by(line3,5,6).

connect(2,3).
connect(4,5).

generation(1).
generation(6).

/* 3) rules */

connection(B1,B2)  :- connect(B1,B2).
connection(B1,B2)  :- connect(B2,B1).

other_breaker(B1,B2)  :- protected_by(_,B1,B2).
other_breaker(B1,B2)  :- protected_by(_,B2,B1).

has_gen(B)  :- generation(B),
               write('Breaker '),write(B),
               write(' is connected to a generation directly.   '),nl.

has_gen(B)  :- connection(_,B,_,B1),
               other_breaker(B1,B2),
               write('Breaker '),write(B),
               write(' is not connected to a generation directly,'),
               nl,write('  but'),
               write(' it is connected to breaker '),write(B1),nl,
               write(' and breaker '),write(B1),
               write(' protects a line '),
               write(' with breaker '),write(B2),write('.'),nl,
               has_gen(B2), !.
```

(e)

FIGURE 6.4 (continued)
(*d*) Dialog for System of (*b*); (*e*) PROLOG code for results shown in part (*c*) (note only change for part (*d*)
is system topology description).

Example 6.8   Rule for backup operation.

```
back_up(B1,B2)  :- not(generation(B1)),
                   connection(B1,B3),
                   other_breaker(B3,B2),
                   has_gen(B2).                          (6-19)
```

(6-19) indicates B2 correctly operated as B1's backup. The reader is encouraged to draw a simple one-line diagram of the scenario constrained by (6-19). In assessing protection system operation, the rule `backup_did_not_work(B1,B2)` signifies that backup breaker, B2, of breaker B1 did not correctly operate as a backup breaker. The rule is

```
backup_did_not_work(B1,B2)  :- back_up(B1,B2),
                   not(operate(B2)).                     (6-20)
```

DETERMINATION OF FAULT LOCATIONS THROUGH ELECTRICAL ISOLATION

In order to determine a possible fault location, we assume that **electrically isolated lines** (those with generation cutoff) are candidates for fault locations. This is done via the rule `no_source_coming(B1)`, which is true when the generation source is cut off from the side of the line containing breaker B1.

Example 6.9   Determining one-sided line electrical isolation.

```
no_source_coming(B1)  :- not(has_gen(B1)).
no_source_coming(B1)  :- has_gen(B1),
                         operate(B1).
no_source_coming(B1)  :- back_up(B1,_),
                         not(backup_did_not_work(B1,_)).
                                                         (6-21)
```

is used for this specification.

Rule `elect_isolated` is used to find possible fault locations, with the constraint that a fault location has generation cutoff by breaker operation. The rule employs the previously derived rule `no_source_coming` and is simply

```
elect_isolated(L,B1,B2)  :-
                   no_source_coming(B1),
                   no_source_coming(B2), !.              (6-22)
```

RULES FOR INTERPRETATION AND DISPLAY

Rule `printout` gives the interpretation of correct and incorrect (primary) breaker operation.

```
printout(B)  :- has_gen(B),
                operate(B),
```

```
                  write('Breaker '),
                  write(B),
                  write(' operated correctly.'),nl, !.
printout(B)  :- has_gen(B),
                  not(operate(B)),
                  write('Breaker '),
                  write(B),
                  write(' malfunctioned.'),nl,
                  not(printbackup(B)), !.                    (6-23)
```

For output, the rule printbackup(B) prints all correct operations corresponding to backup breakers. Note that it always evaluates to FALSE due to the final fail predicate in the body. As shown in Chapter 5, this is a way to force the PROLOG unification mechanism to exhaustively find, and enumerate, all possible successful unifications. The rule is

```
printbackup(B)  :-
                  back_up(B,B1),
                  operate(B1),
                  write('Breaker '),
                  write(B1),
                  write(' operated correctly as a back-up
                  breaker.'),
                  nl,fail.                                    (6-24)
```

Overall Goal (Incorporated in Database, for Simplicity)

Finally, we incorporate our overall goal into the database:

```
run   :-  protected_by(L,B1,B2),
          elect_isolated(L,B1,B2),
          write('Possible Fault Location is on line '),
          write(L),nl,
          printout(B1),
          printout(B2),
          nl,nl,
          fail.                                              (6-25)
```

Notice again the use of predicate fail, which, together with predicate protected_by in (6-25) as well as the topological description, forces an assessment of the status of each line.

Example 6.10 Listing of PROLOG program.

```
source:power_r.pro


/* This program finds the fault locations in a power system
network and gives the interpretation of the breaker operation.
```

The assumptions are
   1) only one possible breaker malfunction,
   2) the malfunctioned breaker has to have backup breakers.
   2) only line fault is possible,
   3) the relay has direction characteristic.

In the data base we have
   1) topology of the network,
   2) the current breaker status,
   3) rules,
   4) goal. */

/* 1) topology data for system of Figure 6.3*/

```
protected_by(line1,1,2).
protected_by(line2,3,4).
protected_by(line3,5,6).
protected_by(line4,7,8).
connect(2,3).
connect(2,6).
connect(2,7).
connect(3,6).
connect(3,7).
connect(6,7).
generation(1).
generation(4).
generation(5).
```

/* 2) breaker status */

```
operate(1).
operate(4).
operate(5).
```

/* 3) rules */

```
connection(B1,B2)  :- connect(B1,B2).
connection(B1,B2)  :- connect(B2,B1).
other_breaker(B1,B2)  :- protected_by(_,B1,B2).
other_breaker(B1,B2)  :- protected_by(_,B2,B1).
has_gen(B)  :- generation(B), !.
has_gen(B)  :- connection(B,B1),
               other_breaker(B1,B2),
               has_gen(B2), !.
back_up(B1,B2)  :- not(generation(B1)),
                   connection(B1,B3),
                   other_breaker(B3,B2),
                   has_gen(B2).
back_up_not_work(B1,B2)  :- back_up(B1,B2),
                            not(operate(B2)).
no_source_coming(B1)  :- not(has_gen(B1)).
```

```
no_source_coming(B1)  :-  has_gen(B1),
                          operate(B1).
no_source_coming(B1)  :-  back_up(B1,_),
                          not(back_up_not_work(B1,_)).
fault(L,B1,B2)  :-  no_source_coming(B1),
                    no_source_coming(B2),  !.


/* printbackup(B) prints all operate correctly backup breakers and
returns false */

printbackup(B)  :-  back_up(B,B1),
                    operate(B1),
                    write('Breaker '),
                    write(B1),
                    write(' operated correctly as a back-up breaker.
                    nl,fail.


/* printout gives the interpretation of breaker operation */

printout(B)  :-  has_gen(B),
                 operate(B),
                 write('Breaker '),
                 write(B),
                 write(' operated correctly.'),nl, !.

printout(B)  :-  has_gen(B),
                 not(operate(B)),
                 write('Breaker '),
                 write(B),
                 write(' malfunctioned.'),nl,
                 not(printbackup(B)), !.
/* 4) goal */
run   :-  protected_by(L,B1,B2),
          fault(L,B1,B2),
          write('Possible Fault Location is on '),
          write(L),nl,
          printout(B1),
          printout(B2),
          nl,nl,
          fail.                                              (6-26)
```

Sample Results

Using the sample system of Fig. 6.3, with the breaker status as shown, the PROLOG formulation of (6-26) generates the dialog shown in Fig. 6.5.

CONCLUSIONS

It is fundamental to note in the long examples presented above, that we never considered specification of the control mechanism or sequence of steps to achieve a PROLOG solution; i.e., we were concerned only about development of an adequate

```
?- consult(power_r.pro).

yes
?- run.
Possible Fault Location is on line1
Breaker 1 operated correctly.
Breaker 2 malfunctioned.
Breaker 4 operated correctly as a back-up breaker.
Breaker 5 operated correctly as a back-up breaker.


Possible Fault Location is on line2
Breaker 3 malfunctioned.
Breaker 5 operated correctly as a back-up breaker.
Breaker 1 operated correctly as a back-up breaker.
Breaker 4 operated correctly.


Possible Fault Location is on line3
Breaker 5 operated correctly.
Breaker 6 malfunctioned.
Breaker 1 operated correctly as a back-up breaker.
Breaker 4 operated correctly as a back-up breaker.


Possible Fault Location is on line4
Breaker 7 malfunctioned.
Breaker 1 operated correctly as a back-up breaker.
Breaker 4 operated correctly as a back-up breaker.
Breaker 5 operated correctly as a back-up breaker.
```

FIGURE 6.5
Sample results of power example (using Fig. 6.3).

description. The PROLOG unification mechanism was therefore left to find (the correct) solutions to our problem, as shown in Fig. 6.5.

Note also the uses of problem decomposition and incremental development and refinement of the description. The PROLOG description we have shown is probably not the simplest nor the most direct; however, this was done in order to allow a flexible and extendable solution. The solution presented above is also not unique–the reader is encouraged to develop alternative (and perhaps more efficient) solutions. Further extensions and refinements are left to the exercises.

REFERENCES

[Fukui/Kawakami] Fukui, C., and J. Kawakami, "An Expert System for Fault Section Estimation Using Information from Protective Relays and Circuit Breakers," *IEEE Trans. Power Apparatus and Systems*, to appear.

[Johns/Girgis/Schalkoff 1987] Johns, M.B., A.A. Girgis, and R.J. Schalkoff, "An Application of an Expert System to Power System Protection," *Proc. 19th Southeastern Symposium on Systems Theory*, Clemson, S.C., March, 1987, pp. 121–124.

PROBLEMS

6.1. Modify the PROLOG power system protection example to include differential relaying on buses, to detect busfaults. For example, in Fig. P6.1, bus B1 is defined as the interconnection of breakers 1, 2 and 3. A fault on bus B1 yields operation of breakers 1, 2 and 3.

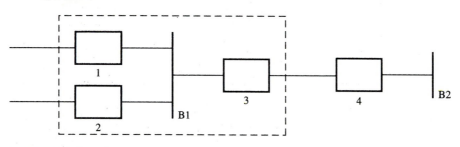

FIGURE P6.1
Power system protection modification for differential protection

The modification should be to the existing program that detects line faults, and allows

1. location of potentially faulted buses; and
2. interpretation of the corresponding breaker operation.

Show operation of your program with examples using the topologies of Figs. 6.3, 6.4(*a*) and (*b*), and Fig. P6.3.

Hints : **(i)** Continue the approach in the line protection derivation and describe a faulted bus as one which is electrically isolated.

(ii) It is not required that PROLOG determine the location of each bus. Rather, specify buses as part of your network topology; e.g., a reasonable description predicate might be protected_bus (Bus1, Bset) where Bus1 is the name of a Bus and Bset is a list of all breakers connnected to the bus. For the example of Fig. P6.1, this yields:

protected_bus (b1, [1, 2, 3]).

6.2. (This problem extends Problem 1.)

(*a*) Consider the topology of Fig. P6.1. A portion of the topological description is derivable via the transitivity of the relation connect (meaning electrically connected). For example, given the description

$$connect(1, 3).$$ (P6.2-1)
$$connect(2, 3).$$ (P6.2-2)
$$connect(1, 2).$$ (P6.2-3)

notice that (P6.2-3) is derivable from (P6.2-1) and (P6.2-2).

(i) Modify the PROLOG program to incorporate this.

(ii) What is the minimum description necessary for any bus that enables derivation of a complete description, for example, (P6.2-1)–(P6.2-3)?

(b) Extend the bus protection of problem 1 to include the operation of bus backup breakers. The backup for B3, for example, is now B4; i.e., bus protection breakers are not directional, as they were for lines. Show your results using Fig. P6.2 with the following cases:

(i) case a - breakers operated 4, 5, 8

(ii) case b - breakers operated 3, 7, 8

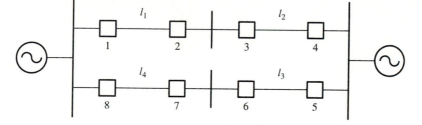

FIGURE P6.2
Modified system topology.

6.3. For the system shown in Fig. P6.2,

(a) modify the PROLOG topological description in power_r.pro for the following cases:

Breaker status

Breaker	Case 1	Case 2	Case 3	Case 4
1	0	0	0	5
2	5	0	5	5
3	5	5	5	0
4	0	5	5	5
5	5	5	0	5
6	5	5	5	0
7	5	5	5	5
8	5	5	5	5

(b) For each of the cases in (a), show the PROLOG system results (fault locations and breaker interpretations).

6.4. For the system topology shown in Fig. 6.4(a), with the following breaker status cases:

Breaker status

Breaker	Case 1	Case 2	Case 3
1	5	5	0
2	5	5	5
3	5	0	0
4	5	5	5
5	0	5	5
6	0	0	5

represent the system topology in PROLOG and

(a) find all breakers with generation; and

(b) modify power_r.pro to determine fault locations and breaker operations.

6.5. Repeat problem 4 using Fig. 6.4(b) with the following data:

Breaker status

Breaker	Case 1	Case 2	Case 3
1	0	0	5
2	5	5	5
3	5	5	5
4	0	5	5
5	5	5	0
6	5	5	5
7	5	5	5
8	5	0	0

(Problems 6 and 8 make excellent long-term projects.)

6.6. Consider a major revision of power_r.pro which, given system topology descriptions consisting of breaker status and one-line diagrams excluding generator locations, i.e., no "generation" predicates, finds all possible generator locations. Show your results using the systems of Fig. 6.3, 6.4(a) and (b), and Fig. P6.3.

6.7. What happens if our PROLOG formulation (power_r.pro) that was developed under the assumptions stated is applied to cases where these assumptions are violated? Consider specifically:

(a) multiple (> 1 faults) and

(b) backup breakers need not be those "closest" to the malfunctioning breaker.

Verify your answer with PROLOG examples.

6.8. (This problem extends problem 7.) Extend power_r.pro to handle:

(a) multiple faults; and

(b) an extended description of "backup," as shown in Figure P6.8, where breaker ($n + 2$) is backup for breaker n. If breaker $n + 2$ fails to correctly operate (as a backup breaker), then breaker $n + 4$ is used for backup.

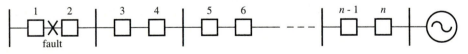

FIGURE P6.8
Extending backup.

6.9. Revise the power example to allow for the case of (at most 1) incorrect breaker status indicators. **Incorrect status** is defined to be the case of a breaker that actually operated, but is shown in service. Note that you will need to develop and incorporate PROLOG descriptions of fault locations and corresponding breaker interpretations with possibly one incorrect status indication. Test your PROLOG program on the system example in the text.

PROLOG APPLICATION TO STRUCTURAL OBJECT DESCRIPTION, FORMAL LANGUAGES, AND PARSING

. . . the man determines what is said, not the words.

Henry David Thoreau
Journal

INTRODUCTION

In this chapter we consider the use of structural descriptions in a number of application areas, including natural language processing. Our examination of modeling in Chapter 1 indicated the strong dependence of a number of models on a clearly defined structure. It is this structure that often leads to the recognition, or, more importantly, the determination of the *meaning* of an entity. For example, on one level, an English sentence is merely a string of words. (These can and have been randomly generated by computer, leading to "nonsense" prose.) On a higher level (one that implies "intelligence") once the structure of the sentence (the noun and verb phrases) has been identified, it is possible to ascertain "who did what to whom." Thus, in the interpretation of the sentence, we identify key entities (the subject), relationships or action (the verb) and interpret the sentence in the context of other a priori information about these entities.

We develop a general and formal mathematical description of languages below. It is worth noting that the descriptor's "language" and "sentence" connote a far broader meaning than "spoken words." For example, we consider computer languages as well as languages used to describe music and the structure of visible objects. An excellent example of the latter is the picture description language (PDL) due to Shaw [1970].

In this chapter we will emphasize natural language applications and string grammars. Formal grammars may be viewed as procedural representations. In a manner similar to that of Chapter 5, they may be used for unification with observed data (such as a specific sentence) in order to obtain a description. Several PROLOG tools, including language generators and parsers, are developed. The syntactic description and analysis approach, however, is easily extended to more complex knowledge representations, including relational approaches.

PARSING AND APPLICATIONS

> **Parsing** is a fundamental concept related to the syntactic or structural approach of object analysis. It is the process of determining the structure of a sentence produced in the language of some grammar.   (7-1)

Parsing is a technique inherent in syntactic pattern recognition, where one of the goals is to determine the sequence of rules or productions that were applied to some basic features or primitives to yield a combination that is interpreted as a higher-level entity such as a sentence or an object.

Parsing is common to many applications, including the following.

Compilation of High-Level Languages

High-level computer languages are written using a set of reserved words (primitives) and rules (productions) for combining these reserve words to form programs according to the syntax of the language. For example, in Pascal this may be shown in BNF (Backus Naur Form) as

    function-identifier ::= identifier
    identifier ::= letter {letter-or-digit}
    letter ::= a | b | c | ... | z | ... | A | ... | Z
    digit ::= 0 | 1 | 2 | 3 | 4 | ... | 9
    letter-or digit ::= letter | digit

where the BNF meaning of the symbol

::= means "is defined as"

| means "or"

{} indicates items that may be repeated zero or more times

A compiler or interpreter for a high-level language attempts to generate lower-level machine instructions by determining the desired structure of the input high-level language program through parsing the input or source code.

Understanding of Natural Language

The autonomous understanding of natural language (speech) is an active area of current research. Applications for this capability include "keyboardless" document preparation (the system user narrates, in contrast to typing), voice actuated machine control (freeing the operator's hands and eyes for other tasks), and operator-less information and reservation systems.

Research in this area proceeds on two levels:

1. The determination of suitable hardware and signal processing techniques to extract the basic components from speech signals necessary to form words; and
2. The autonomous determination, via AI techniques, of the meaning of the group of words (the phrase or sentence) that is produced as the result of 1.

The latter task again fits the AI/parsing mold since these basic extracted words (primitives) are combined by the speaker according to the grammar (allowable productions) of the particular language. It is fundamental to note that the use of and often correct interpretation of grammatically incorrect or imprecise (ambiguous) sentences makes this task quite challenging.

Historically, students learned the grammar of (American) English aided by the process of diagramming sentences. This process of diagramming is a graphical tool used to show the relationships among specialized classes of words, such as nouns, pronouns, adjectives, adverbs, verbs, etc., and thus illustrates correct sentence structure.

The process of diagramming also reveals the meaning of a particular sentence on a higher level. For example, after determining the case of nouns and the verb in a particular sentence, it is clear who did what to whom. This process of diagramming is really the process of parsing the sentence, using the syntax or grammar of the language to reconstruct the set of allowable productions or combinations of words to ultimately determine the meaning of the sentence.

We will investigate the process of parsing of a sentence in depth, using the PROLOG language.

One of the first and most popular examples of simplistic natural language analysis is Weizenbaum's ELIZA program, which emulates conversation with a Rogerian psychologist [Weizenbaum 1966]. Figure 7.1 shows an example of a conversation with ELIZA. (Note: In Fig. 7.1, "D" indicates "doctor," or program output, "P" indi-

D: I am at your service; just tell me anything that troubles or concerns you.
P: I am having a great deal of trouble writing an AI textbook.

D: Is it because you are having a great deal of trouble writing an AI textbook that you came to see me?
P: Yes.

D: Is there something bothering you?
P: The work in the AI textbook.

D: I am not sure I understand you fully.
P: I hate to write AI texts.

D: What else do you hate?
P: Rogerian therapists.

D: Please go on.
P: Rogerian therapists are for fools.

D: Suppose rogerian therapists were not for fools.
P: Yes.

D: Why are you so sure?
P: No.

D: Can you be more informative?
P: No.

D: Very well.
P: Tell me how to write an AI text.

D: Are you still having a great deal of trouble writing an AI textbook?
P: Yes.

D: I see.
P: This doesn't seem to be leading anywhere.

D: What does that suggest to you?
P: This program is not as intelligent as it seems.

D: Possibly that is for the better.
P: I agree.

D: You say you agree?
P: Yes.

D: I understand.
P: Goodbye.

D: I hope I have been of some service, let's get together again sometime.

FIGURE 7.1
Example of ELIZA language "understanding" program (Rogerian therapist).

cates "patient" or user input.) Unfortunately, ELIZA's responses are not determined through understanding of user input, but rather a simple pattern-matching approach is used to determine system response.[1] The program recognizes particular patterns in the user input and then selects and modifies one of a stored set of replies for response. This behavior is evident in the "shallow" conversation of Fig. 7.1.

---

[1] For this reason, many consider ELIZA a prime instance of a program that only fakes intelligence.

APPLICATION OF GRAMMARS TO MUSIC REPRESENTATION. The perceived audio structure and repetition inherent in music suggests that it is comprised of carefully ordered patterns. This becomes even more evident when viewing a transcription of a musical composition (sheet music). Patterns of notes or primitives such as scale fragments are clearly evident. Thus, music, like spoken language, may be viewed as a language. Unfortunately, as in speech, even though the primitives are well recognized, the contextual nature of the patterns contains significant information, and is often difficult to identify.

Clearly, rules of music composition such as harmony theory have existed for some time. Listeners and composers speak of "phrases," AABA structure, "12-bar blues," verse/chorus/bridge, etc. Each of these relates to the structural content of a piece of music. Although the application of AI techniques to music may have less commercial appeal (vis-a-vis industrial and military applications), it nonetheless provides another opportunity to model human perception within the framework of a structural, grammar-based representation.

Numerous authors have attempted to apply the theory of formal grammars to music interpretation and composition [Holtzman 1981, Roads 1979]. We briefly survey these efforts here, and hope that readers interested in this topic will consult the references for further direction.

The music representation example is a good example of the use of hierarchy and instance in data structures. Figure 7.2 shows this structure [Roads 1979].

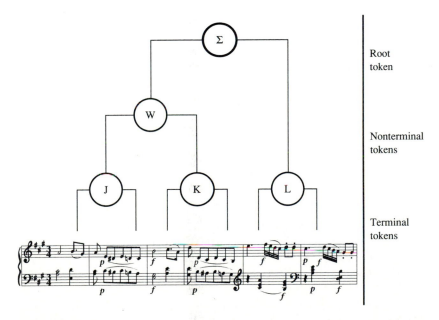

FIGURE 7.2
A simple parsing of a fragment of music, showing a hierarchical structure [Roads 1979]. Reprinted by permission.

Description and Interpretation of Image (Visual) Data

This is a topic strongly related to both applications 2 and 4 above. A good overview of the current situation is found in Bolc [Bolc 1984].

An AI application related to formal grammars, structural analysis and description, and parsing is the development of automated systems that allow a human operator to converse, in natural language, with an image or pictorial database system equipped with both image and language understanding capability. This "intelligent" capability is useful for systems including automated weather forecasting, satellite imagery interpretation, pictorial information archiving, and medical diagnosis assistance. For example, these systems may allow a physician to call up a patient's digitized chest X-ray and type into the system: "Does Mr. X have a small tumor on his left lung?" To respond to such an inquiry, the system must be able to interpret the above sentence as well as determine the pictorial significance of "tumor," "lung," "left," and "small." Clearly, for generalized cases, this system requires a significant amount of "artificial" intelligence. Inherent in emerging systems of this type are two subsystems: one is used to preprocess (correct spelling errors), parse, and determine the meaning of the input phrase, and a second is used to apply image processing and analysis techniques to the image(s) in question and extract sufficient information such that a response to the input phrase may be determined. These subsystems may, of course, be interactively related.

Picture query languages are based upon choosing, extracting, and manipulating pictorial features or data structures, thus creating a pictorial database management system. Recently developed image query and description languages are MIDAS (Multi-sensor Image DAtabase System) and PICCOLO (PICture COmputer LOgic). These languages are significant because they may be transformed from a given set of natural languages via an ATN (Augmented Transition Network), thus allowing natural language communication with the pictorial information system.

Major software components of these systems are (1) a preprocessor and parser to determine the dependency structure of the input phrase, (2) a translator, query generator and evaluator, which, together with (3) an analyzer, take the output of (1) and, through the answer generator, (4) query the pictorial database and formulate the system response in natural language form. This is shown in Fig. 7.3.

Syntactic Pattern Classification

Statistical pattern recognition attempts to classify patterns (or entities) based upon a set of extracted features and an underlying statistical (perhaps ad-hoc) model for the generation of these patterns.

Alternately, syntactic pattern recognition differs in two ways:

1. The structure (determined application of productions or rules) of the entity is used for classification. For example, one could discriminate between two classes of entities based upon derived structure, as opposed to more superfluous extracted features. This is accomplished by defining two suitable and distinct grammars.

I/O

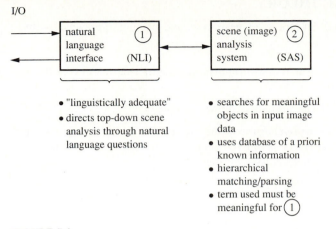

FIGURE 7.3
Example of an image analysis program with natural language interface.

2. The fact that structure is used allows syntactic pattern recognition to be used for description of an entity, in addition to classification.

While it is not mandatory, many structural pattern recognition approaches are based upon generation and analysis of complex patterns by a hierarchical decomposition into simpler patterns. For example, notice that

a paragraph may be decomposed into sentences,

sentences may be decomposed into words,

words may be decomposed into letters, and

letters may be decomposed into strokes.   (7-2)

Thus, like many AI endeavors, dealing with complex entities is best achieved by successive decomposition into more manageable entities. To generate a paragraph using some grammar, one need not begin with the problem of generating the entire paragraph. Rather the generation of appropriate strokes, which form letters, which form words, and so on, is a suitable plan. Conversely, when analyzing a paragraph, it is not necessary (or typical) to attempt analysis of the paragraph as a whole; one first decomposes the paragraph into sentences, then words, then letters, and so on.

The use of grammars in pattern recognition and AI applications is reasonable under the following set of assumptions:

1. A decomposition of the entity under consideration into a set of elements (primitives) that lend themselves to automatic identification or extraction is possible; and
2. The problem upon which (1) is employed has a discernible structure that may be employed in the solution process.

FORMAL LANGUAGE THEORY

We begin a study of formal definitions of grammars and parsing approaches with a simple example.

> **Example 7.1 Sentence formation as productions (rewrite rules).** Consider the following sentence:
>
> $$\text{The quarterback throws accurately.} \qquad (7\text{-}3a)$$
>
> Let us temporarily ignore the significance of the capital letter at the beginning and the period at the end and concentrate on the formation and structure of this sentence. The sentence was produced according to the following "rewriting" rules involving successive replacement as follows:
>
> **1.** ‹sentence›
> **2.** ‹noun phrase› ‹verb phrase›
> **3.** ‹article›[2] ‹noun› ‹verb phrase›
> **4.** the ‹noun› ‹verb phrase›
> **5.** the quarterback ‹verb phrase›
> **6.** the quarterback ‹verb› ‹adverb›
> **7.** the quarterback throws ‹adverb›
> **8.** the quarterback throws accurately $\qquad (7\text{-}3b)$
>
> More specifically, the sentence of $(7\text{-}3a)$ was formed using a sequence of rewrite or production rules. Note also the gradual elimination of intermediate entities such as "noun" and "adverb." This sequence could be determined by cataloging each of the above rewrites or substitutions. We now seek a formal definition of the above process.

Formal Definitions

A **grammar** consists of the following four entities:

1. A set of terminal or primitive symbols (**primitives**), denoted Σ (or, alternately, V_T). In many applications, the choice of this set is one of the most difficult aspects, since the process has a large component of "art", as opposed to "science."

2. A set of non-terminal symbols, or **variables**, which are used as intermediate quantities in the generation of an outcome consisting solely of terminal symbols. Often this set is denoted as N (or, alternatively, V_N).

3. A set of **productions** (production rules or rewriting rules) that allow the previous substitutions. It is this set of productions, coupled with the terminal symbols, which principally gives the grammar its "structure." The set of productions is denoted P. We will explore the ramifications of this set in detail later.

---

[2]We will also refer to this as a modifier or determiner; it may be an adverb or adjective.

4. A starting (or root) symbol, denoted S. S is a member of N. In the previous example, S = ‹sentence›. (7-4)

Having defined such a grammar, it may be used in one of two modes:

1. Generative: The grammar is used to create a string of terminal symbols using *P*; a sentence in the language of the grammar is thus generated.
2. Analytic: Given a sentence (typically, but not always, in the language of the grammar), together with Σ and P, one seeks to determine:

  i. If the sentence was in fact generated by this grammar; and, if so,
  ii. The structure (usually characterized as the sequence of productions used) of the sentence.

Thus, using the above definitions, we formally denote a grammar, G, as

$$G = (\Sigma, N, P, S) \qquad (7\text{-}5)$$

The language generated by G, denoted L(G), is the set of all strings subject to the following conditions:

1. Each string consists solely of terminal symbols; and
2. Each string was produced from S using P.

The use of graphical constructs for a grammar in either the generative or analytic mode is common. In the generative mode we show a derivation tree, whereas in the analytic mode we use a parse tree. Given a sentence, for practical purposes (and as long as the sentence is in the language of the grammar), these entities are the same; it is merely a question of whether we start from the root node or the leaves in application of the tree. These constructs are shown in the following examples.

SYNTAX/SEMANTICS/CONTEXT. In our initial work, we consider **context-free grammars**, which allow use of the productions in P independent of the *context* of the symbols. A higher-level grammar imposes constraints on the meaning of strings produced, that is, it enforces semantics. This is a more complex concept, some ramifications of which are considered in the problems.

GRAMMAR TYPES AND PRODUCTIONS. The applications we cite below typify **string grammars**, where P is used to generate sentences that consist of linear or 1-D strings of terminals. Note that this does not restrict the representation to 1-D, as shown in the following section. Thus, the production or rewrite rules in G for a string grammar are of the general form

$$S_1 \rightarrow S_2 \qquad (7\text{-}6)$$

which means string S_1 "is replaced by" string S_2. In several, S_1 and S_2 contain terminals and/or nonterminals.

Four types of grammars have been specified by Chomsky [1957].

Type 0 (Free)   (7-7a)

This grammar has no restrictions on the rewrite rules, and is of little practical significance.

Type 1 (Context-Sensitive)   (7-7b)

This grammar restricts productions to the form

$$A \, S_1 B \rightarrow A \, S_2 B$$

meaning S_2 replaces S_1 in the context of A and B. Here, all symbols may be $\in \Sigma$ or V_N.

Type 2 (Context-Free)   (7-7c)

A type 2 grammar expands, or replaces only one nonterminal token on the left-hand side of a rule. For example,

$$A \rightarrow a \, B$$

is a type 2 rewrite rule. This grammar is typified by G_1 in (7-9).

Type 3 (Finite-State)   (7-7d)

Finite-state grammars allow at most one nonterminal symbol on each side of the production. For example,

$$A_1 \rightarrow b$$

or

$$A_1 \rightarrow b \, A_2$$

are allowed in this type grammar. A_1 and A_2 are nonterminals and b is a terminal.

Grammar types other than string grammars exist and are characterized by their terminals and nonterminals (as opposed to constraints on P). These are useful in 2-D and higher-dimension applications, in that the structure of the terminals and nonterminals is higher than one dimensional. Thus, productions in these grammars are more complex, since rewriting rules embody operations more complex than simple 1-D string modifications. For example, in 2-D cases, standard "attachment points" are defined. Two of the more popular are tree grammars and web grammars [Fu 1982].

Example of a 2-D Language Application—A Line Drawing Description Grammar [Shaw 1970]

We have primarily restricted our analysis to the grammars of spoken languages. We seek now to show that this is an unnecessary restriction by showing the application of a grammar-based approach to the description of line drawings.

Suppose an image may be preprocessed (via a sequence of steps involving noise minimization, edge detection, enhancement and connection) to provide a line drawing of some object or set of objects in a scene. We ignore the complex problems of occlusion for immediate purposes. This line drawing is the input to our grammatically-based analysis of the scene.

Example 7.2   Line drawing (cylinder) description grammar. We consider the cylinder description grammar, G_{cyl}, as follows:

$$G_{cyl} = (\Sigma_{cyl}, N_{cyl}, P_{cyl}, S_{cyl}) \qquad (7\text{-}8a)$$

where:

$\Sigma_{cyl} = \{t, b, u, o, s\}$ as described in Fig. 7.4

$N_{cyl} = \{\text{Top, Body, Cylinder}\}$

P_{cyl}

Cylinder $\rightarrow$ Top $*$ Body

Top $\rightarrow t * \neg b$

Body $\rightarrow \neg u + b + u$ $\qquad (7\text{-}8b)$

$+$ represents head to tail concatenation

$*$ represents head-head and tail-tail attachment

$\neg$ represents head and tail reversal

$\rightarrow$ means may be replaced by

and

$$S_{cyl} = \text{Cylinder}$$

This grammar allows the representation of the class of cylinders shown in Figs. 7.4 and 7.5. Note the use of 2-D directed features with "attachment points" denoted head and tail.

The utility of the above approach is principally in two applications:

1. Classification of line drawings. The problem, for example, of discriminating between a line drawing of a cube and a cylinder is handled. It translates into the problem, given a suitable description, denoted d_x, of the line drawing of a scene, and given the cylinder and cube grammars G_{cyl} and G_{cube} respectively, of determining whether $d_x \in L(G_{cyl})$, $d_x \in L(G_{cube})$, or $d_x \in$ some other language. This would be accomplished via parsing.

2. Determination of the structure of the entity under observation, perhaps for descrip-

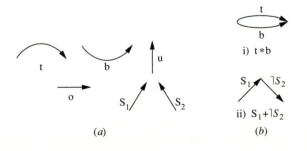

i) $t * b$

ii) $S_1 + \neg S_2$

(a)

(b)

FIGURE 7.4
(a) Picture description grammar primitives. (b) Attachment examples.

Line Drawing Grammar
  Description

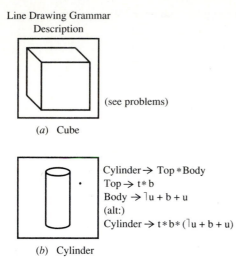

(see problems)

(*a*) Cube

Cylinder → Top * Body
Top → t * b
Body → ⌐u + b + u
(alt:)
Cylinder → t * b * (⌐u + b + u)

(*b*) Cylinder

FIGURE 7.5
Sample line drawings for the grammar-based approach
(*a*) cube (*b*) cylinder.

tive purposes, or perhaps as a prelude to some operation on the structure (such as moving it). In this example, the identity and spatial relationship of "side," "top," and perhaps the shape of the entity (cylindrical or cubical) is useful. Again, a parse of the description provides this. It is also crucial to note that the structural description and recognition of an entity avoids many of the problems due to varying orientations; that is, it should be possible to recognize a cylinder in any orientation. Conversely, the approach (the grammars) could be revised to be directionally as well as entity sensitive; in this case a description of the entity as well as its corresponding orientation may be obtained.

SENTENCE GENERATION AND PARSING IN PROLOG

Prolog Sentence Generation

To construct a parser for any language, it is first necessary to quantify the language to be parsed, in terms of primitives and allowable productions, as described in the introduction to formal analysis of grammars and languages.

Prior to our analysis of sentences using PROLOG, and to show the similarity of generative and analytic applications in PROLOG, we consider the specification of a grammar and the use of PROLOG to generate the language of the grammar.

Example 7.3   Grammar G1. Consider the following grammar, G1:

$$G1 = (\Sigma, N, P, S) \tag{7-9a}$$

where

$$\Sigma = \{\text{the, program, crashes, computer}\} \tag{7-9b}$$

$$N = \{\text{sentence, adj, np, vp, noun, verb}\} \tag{7-9c}$$

P:

$\quad$ (i) sentence $\rightarrow$ np + vp

$\quad$ (ii) np $\rightarrow$ adj + noun

$\quad$ (iii) vp $\rightarrow$ verb + np

$\quad$ (iv) noun $\rightarrow$ computer | program

$\quad$ (v) verb $\rightarrow$ crashes

$\quad$ (vi) adj $\rightarrow$ the $\hfill$ (7-9d)

in P the symbol + stands for "concatenation of," but may be thought of in terms of "string summation" (the joining of two strings). Similarly, the symbol "$\rightarrow$" stands for "may be replaced by." The symbol | has the meaning "or," from the BNF syntax.

$$S \rightarrow sentence \hfill (7\text{-}9e)$$

Given the productions and symbols (terminal and nonterminal) above, it is relatively simple to develop a PROLOG language generator. We begin with a simple version. Structure of the following PROLOG database mirrors that of G1. Clauses are numbered on the left for reference. Note that we are generating sentences entered, for simplicity, in **list form**. Each word (terminal) in the generated sentence is an atomic element of a list.

Example 7.4   Sample PROLOG language generator database (grammar G1).

```
create(sentence, [X, Y]):-create(np,X),create(vp,Y).    (7-10a)
create(np,[X1, X2]):-create(adj,X1),create(noun,X2).    (7-10b)
create(vp,[Y1, Y2]):-create(verb,Y1),create(np,Y2).     (7-10c)
create(noun,computer).                                  (7-10d)
create(noun,program).                                   (7-10e)
create(verb,crashes).                                   (7-10f)
create(adj,the).                                        (7-10g)
```

It is fundamental to observe the similarity of structure between (7-9) and (7-10), specifically:

PROLOG clause (7-10a) and G1 production (7-9d) (i).

PROLOG clause (7-10b) and G1 production (7-9d) (ii).

PROLOG clause (7-10c) and G1 production (7-9d) (iii).

PROLOG clauses (7-10d) and (7-10e) and G1 production (7-9d) (iv).

PROLOG clause (7-10f) and G1 production (7-9d) (v).

PROLOG clause (7-10g) and G1 production (7-9d) (vi). $\hfill$ (7-11)

Given the PROLOG goal:

```
?-create(sentence, A_sent).                             (7-12a)
```

the PROLOG system returns the set of all possible unifications (all possible productions), as shown in Fig. 7.6. As indicated, the language of G1 is quite restricted, in

```
/* generator_r.pro  6-2-89  */
/* Prolog Sentence Generator */

/* productions using nonterminals */

create(sentence, [X,Y]) :- create(np,X),create(vp,Y).
create(np,[X1,X2]) :- create(adj,X1),create(noun,X2).
create(vp,[Y1,Y2]) :- create(verb,Y1),create(np,Y2).

/* productions using terminals- the "dictionary" */

create(adj,the).
create(noun,program).
create(verb,crashes).
create(noun,computer).
```
(a)

```
| ?- create(sentence, A_sent).

A_sent = [[the,program],[crashes,[the,program]]] ? ;

A_sent = [[the,program],[crashes,[the,computer]]] ? ;

A_sent = [[the,computer],[crashes,[the,program]]] ? ;

A_sent = [[the,computer],[crashes,[the,computer]]] ? ;

no
| ?- create(vp, Verb_ph).

Verb_ph = [crashes,[the,program]] ? ;

Verb_ph = [crashes,[the,computer]] ? ;

no
| ?- create(noun, Noun).

Noun = program ? ;

Noun = computer ? ;

no
| ?- create(What, [crashes, [the,program]]).

What = vp ? ;

no
| ?- halt.
```
(b)

FIGURE 7.6
Sample results using PROLOG sentence generator (G1). (a) PROLOG database; (b) sample results.

fact only four sentences are generated. This is only due to our intentional limitation of P and Σ in G1. We will examine the significance of the list notation later. As the output indicates, our use of the list construct in (7-10) yields output with scattered brackets ([or]), used to indicate the list structure of the sentences produced. For example, note that a sample sentence production is now of the form

$$[\,[\,the\,,program]\,,[\,crashes\,,[\,the\,,computer\,]\,]\,]$$ (7-12*b*)

The noteworthy aspect of this form is that the PROLOG unification mechanism, in addition to creating the sentence, has created it in diagrammed or structural form; that is, the sentence is displayed in list form with this structure:

$$[\,[np]\,,\,[verb,\,[np]]]$$

(7-12*c*)

vp

    This result, while useful, causes some concern in our development of a parser, since the sentence is not typically entered in this form, as discussed below.

    The "context free" nature of our productions is significant. Note that the only restrictions on productions thus far have consisted of substitutions that did not involve the context or meaning of the variables and/or terminals involved in the substitutions. In a sense, the terminals in the sentence are forced to be only weakly related. Thus, for example, the production of nonsense-meaning sentences in an extended G1 could be of the form

the red computer ran a quick circuit breaker

or

the circuit breaker had a nice time at the beach

    More sophisticated variants and extensions of the grammars in this chapter are explored in the exercises.

Context-Free Parsing in PROLOG

The sentence generator of (7-10), based upon grammar G1, served well as an introduction to the representation of a formal context-free language in PROLOG. We now seek to develop a more structured view of how sentences are generated, which leads to an approach for the parsing of sentences, given a prespecified grammar. We note that the process of parsing (i.e., determining the structure of a sentence by determining the sequence of productions that led to the sentence) is not accomplished "in a vacuum," but rather parsing takes place in the context of a given grammar. Parsing a sentence without a grammar is meaningless; there is no structure since there are no productions.

    Recall, as in Chapters 4, 5, and 6, the development of a parsing program in PROLOG does not involve determination of the program flow of control; only problem specifications or descriptions are enumerated as PROLOG clauses. The PROLOG system uses the process of unification to determine the structure of the input words (terminals). In fact, the beauty of a descriptive approach such as in PROLOG is that one essentially describes the production rules of the grammar to the PROLOG system, then, given a production in the language of the grammar, the PROLOG system uses unification to determine the applicable sequence of rules.

To be efficient, the parser should be of hierarchical structure. For example, the initial decomposition of the sentence to be parsed should be in terms of smaller entities (such as phrases). Following this, the parsing of the phrases could occur. We note in passing that one simplistic approach to parsing might be to use the language generator to generate all possible sentences (and perhaps tag each with its structure). Then, to test for membership of a given sentence in the language of a given grammar, it is only necessary to match the sentence with all possible generated sentences. This approach is usually impractical for realistic grammars, due to the potentially large (or perhaps infinite) number of unique sentences produced.

Graphical Constructs: The Derivation Tree

As a prelude to the development of a parser for grammar G1, let us enumerate the steps used to construct the sentence

$$\text{the program crashes the computer} \tag{7-13}$$

Recall this is a valid sentence in the language of G1.

Figure 7.7 shows this sequence, and is referred to as a **derivation tree**. The process starts at the topmost portion of the tree with the root or starting symbol S (in N), and terminates with the final substitutions of terminals (constants in Σ) at the leaves of the tree. The productions occur by traversing the tree from the root to the leaves.

Proceeding from the top of the derivation tree, we notice that in all but the last substitutions (which yield the leaves), nonterminals (noun phrases, verb phrases, verbs, adjectives, and nouns) have been involved in the productions.

An Abstract View of the Parsing Problem

Given a string of terminals comprising a sentence x, and a grammar G, specified as:

$$G = (\Sigma, N, P, S) \tag{7-14}$$

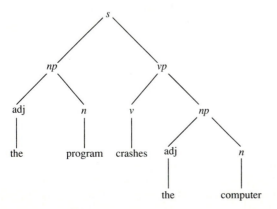

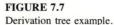

FIGURE 7.7
Derivation tree example.

we construct a triangle of the form:

The process of filling the interior of this triangle with a tree of productions that links S to x is called a parse. If we are successful, x is a member of L(G) and we determine the structure of x; otherwise it is not.

Top-Down versus Bottom-Up Parsing

If we fill the interior of the triangle from the top down (from the root of the tree), a top-down parse results. Alternately, if we work from the bottom up (x) and begin with the terminal symbols, a bottom-up parse results. Note that a bottom-up parse (so-called **parse tree**) may be obtained from a derivation tree, where the productions, P, are applied in reverse order.

Development of the G1 Parser

As noted above, we seek a paradigm that uses grammar G1 (and hopefully reflects the structure of the G1 sentence generator) together with a given sentence (which yields success in the parsing process if it is $\in$ L(G1)) to generate a structural description of the sentence. The achievement of this is akin to recreating the derivation tree by attempted traversing in either the top-down or bottom-up fashion to "fill in" the triangle shown above.

Parser/Generator Similarities

Application of a grammar in the generative mode is usually far easier than in the analytic mode (parsing). Thus, while generation and parsing are strongly related, it is not a "two-way street."

Referring to the modified sentence generator above, we note that if we use the generator in a somewhat different mode by applying the PROLOG query

```
create(sentence, [[the,program],[crashes,[the,computer]]]
```
                                                                        (7-15*a*)

the PROLOG system would respond with TRUE; i.e., unification is possible. Thus, given the ability to query the database with a sentence, we might assume that the sentence generator serves as the parser. This is incorrect for the following reason:

> In the query of (7-15*a*), it was necessary to input the sentence in structured (the way it would be output) form. This is what we are seeking, not what is known.   (7-15*b*)

In other words, although the above query succeeded, it only did so because the desired result was input. It is another realization of the dilemma that things (questions) are always trivial when you know the answer.

Desired Parser Input Structure

Alternately, we seek a parser that will take input sentences of the form

$$[\texttt{the, program, crashes, the, computer}] \qquad (7\text{-}15c)$$

(or any other equivalent unstructured form) and return the sentence structure, perhaps in the above form. This introduces two concerns:

1. Inputting the sentence to be parsed in unstructured form as part of a query to the sentence generator fails (the reader is encouraged to verify this) due to the generator's attempt to deal directly with the first member of the sentence (written as a list) as the entity "np." In practice, the parser must determine the extent of the list elements that comprise the nonterminals "np" and "vp." This is not simple, given a more sophisticated grammar. It also suggests that parsing is accomplished with a contextual component, which makes sense since the parser ultimately seeks the "structure" of the entity it is parsing.
2. The parser must find a use for all of the sentence; it cannot simply identify parts of the sentence with some structure and discard the rest. Thus, in a sense, the sentence must be "consumed" in the parse.

We now seek a way to satisfy these constraints.

Our parser development begins at the top, that is, we attempt to define the conditions under which predicate `parse` succeeds, given an arbitrary, unstructured sentence as input and the formal specifications of grammar G1. Consider the following parsing rule:

```
parse(sentence, Before, After)  :-
                        parse(np, Before, Not_np),
                        parse(vp, Not_np, After).
```
$$(7\text{-}16)$$

For a successful unification using predicate `parse`, variable `Before` must satisfy the requirement as a noun phrase (np) AND the unused portion of `Before`, namely `Not_np`, must be useful to predicate `parse (vp, Not_np, After)`. Notice the structure of predicate `parse` reflects the structure of the predicate sentence `create` with the exception of the addition of a generator third term. This term passes along to other predicates the elements of a list not used (the so-called difference list), and, in addition, forces the "consumption" constraint described above.

Rule (7-16) will then be used to begin the process of parsing, and the head of rule (7-16), forms the PROLOG goal statement. If we query our (as yet incomplete) database with the goal:

`parse(sentence, [the,program,crashes,the,computer],[]).`

$$(7\text{-}17)$$

we will interpret a positive response from the unification mechanism as an indication that the parse succeeded. Note the use of the empty list, [ ], to force "consumption" of the input sentence. Figure 7.8 indicates this structure.

Notice the structure in rule (7-16) that allows predicate `parse`, used recursively first with argument `np`, to use or "consume" part of the input list (sentence) `Before`, and pass on the unused (i.e., not used to unify with the structure of a noun phrase) portion, denoted `Not_np`. The predicate `parse` with argument `vp` then uses this "leftover" list and returns the unused portion as `After`.

As with most of our AI problem decompositions, we now look at the antecedents of rule (7-16) (the tail). We consider them in the same order PROLOG would, namely left to right. The predicate that is the head of rule (7-18), namely `parse`, that is,

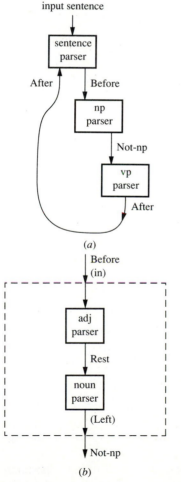

FIGURE 7.8
Parser "consumption" structure.

```
parse(np, In, Left)  :—
                     parse(adj, In, Rest),
                     parse(noun, Rest, Left).                (7-18)
```

takes in a list (I n), returns the "unused" portion (Le f t), and evaluates to TRUE when its antecedents are TRUE. Notice that this rule again recursively employs parse (with first arguments set to adj and noun respectively) with the same "used" and "unused" connotation on the second and third arguments.

Similarly, we consider the decomposition of the second antecedent to rule (7-16):

```
parse(vp, In, Left)  :—
                     parse(verb, In, Rest),
                     parse(np, Rest, Left).                 (7-19)
```

This structure follows that of rule (7-18), therefore we do not repeat the design justification. We conclude with a look at the decomposition of the remaining predicates, which involves substitution of terminals:

```
parse(adj, [A|B], B)  :— word(adj, A).
parse(noun, [C|D], D)  :— word(noun, C).
parse(verb, [E|F], F)  :— word(verb,E).               (7-20a)
```

In addition, the G1 parser needs the G1 "dictionary," for example,

```
word(verb, crashes).
word(adj,the).
word(noun, program).
word(noun, computer).                                 (7-20b)
```

We have therefore developed the parser in a systematic and somewhat recursive fashion. The reader should note the strong similarity between the parser development and the sentence generator. We now show the operation of the parser, and then proceed to make a final improvement.

Figure 7.9 shows a sample operation of the parser. Relative to the figure, the following observations may be made:

1. The parser operates correctly, however only a TRUE or FALSE indication is returned. Thus, while we are able to establish language membership, we originally sought the structure of the sentence. We modify the parser to accomplish this below.

2. The parser, due to the PROLOG unification mechanism, actually has two ancillary applications:

   (i) It is able to serve as a sentence generator (we show this in the modified parsing example and Fig. 7.10).

   (ii) As shown in part (*b*), the parser also generates sentences by filling in portions entered as variables.

```
/* oldparser_r.pro 6-2-89*/
/* first parsing program with database of generator_r  */

parse(sentence, Before, After) :-
 parse(np, Before, Not_np),
 parse(vp, Not_np, After).

parse(np, In, Left) :-
 parse(adj, In, Rest),
 parse(noun, Rest, Left).

parse(vp, In, Left) :-
 parse(verb, In, Rest),
 parse(np, Rest, Left).

parse(adj, [A|B], B):- word(adj, A).
parse(noun, [C|D], D) :- word(noun, C).
parse(verb, [E|F], F) :- word(verb, E).

word(verb, crashes).
word(adj, the).
word(noun, computer).
word(noun, program).
```
(a)

```
| ?- consult('oldparser_r.pro').

yes
| ?- parse(sentence, [the, program, crashes, the, computer], []).

yes
| ?- parse(sentence, [M, What, Did, M₂, What₂], []).
```

$Did = crashes,$
$M = the,$
$M_2 = the,$
$What = computer,$
$What_2 = computer$? ;

$Did = crashes,$
$M = the,$
$M_2 = the,$
$What = computer,$
$What_2 = program$? ;

(b)

FIGURE 7.9
Results using first PROLOG parser for G1: *(a)* Parser implementation; *(b)* results.

```
Did = crashes,
M = the,
M₂ = the,
What = program,
What₂ = computer ? ;

Did = crashes,
M = the,
M₂ = the,
What = program,
What₂ = program ? ;

no
| ?- parse(sentence, [crashes, the, computer], []).

no
| ?- parse(vp, [crashes, the, computer], []).

yes
| ?- parse(What_is_it, Generated, []).

Generated = [the,computer,crashes,the,computer],
What_is_it = sentence ? ;

Generated = [the,computer,crashes,the,program],
What_is_it = sentence ? ;

Generated = [the,program,crashes,the,computer],
What_is_it = sentence ? ;

Generated = [the,program,crashes,the,program],
What_is_it = sentence ? ;

Generated = [the,computer],
What_is_it = np ? ;

Generated = [the,program],
What_is_it = np ? ;

Generated = [crashes,the,computer],
What_is_it = vp ? ;

Generated = [crashes,the,program],
What_is_it = vp ? ;

Generated = [the],
What_is_it = adj ? ;
```

(b)

FIGURE 7.9 (continued)

```
Generated = [computer],
What_is_it = noun ? ;
Generated = [program],
What_is_it = noun ? ;
Generated = [crashes],
What_is_it = verb ? ;
no
| ?- halt.
```

(b)

FIGURE 7.9 (continued)

We now seek to modify the parser to output the sentence structure as well. This is done by adding an additional argument to predicate parse, namely a list that serves to record the result of a particular stage in the parse. As shown below, the PROLOG program is thus modified to return the unification of the last argument as the input sentence in the form that predicate create used in the generation process. The bracket or [ ] notation thus serves to "diagram" the input sentence.

The form of the modified PROLOG program is shown in Fig. 7.10. Notice from Fig. 7.10, that even a simple set of productions and "dictionary" leads to a relatively large (L(G). In this case, 6 words (2 adjectives, 1 verb, 3 nouns) generate 36 unique sentences. These are shown in part *(b)* of Figure 7.10.

It is left as an exercise to further refine the parse predicate-based PROLOG program to display "np = . . ." and so on. In fact, many PROLOG systems that permit graphics output may be used with an enhancement of the previous program to diagrammatically indicate the sentence structure. Such a device may be useful in the computer-aided teaching of the basic concepts of English grammar.

We conclude by noting the structure of the parser from a different viewpoint, namely the list input/output of each application (unification) of predicate parse. Notice the input sentence (a list) is successively decimated by each attempted unification involving predicate parse, with each parse looking for a certain entity (sentence, np, vp, noun, det, verb). The decimation takes place in returning, via the last argument of parse, the unused portion of the list. This process (particularly the "consumption" operation) is analogous to the operation of the Augmented Transition Network (ATN), described in the following section.

(AUGMENTED) TRANSITION NETWORKS (ATNs)

Transition Networks

A **transition network (TN)** is a digraph used to show the (context free) productions of a grammar. TN's are used to facilitate parsing and, as a practical matter, easily map into finite state machines. A TN consists of a set of nodes, representing **states**, and a set of labeled arcs, representing either **nonterminals** (classes of words such as

```
/* parser_r.pro 6-2-89 */
/* parsing program with database of generator_r */

parse(sentence, Before, After, [Np_result, Vp_result]) :-
         parse(np, Before, Not_np, Np_result),
         parse(vp, Not_np, After, Vp_result).

parse(np, In, Left, [Adj_result, Noun_result]) :-
         parse(adj, In, Rest, Adj_result),
         parse(noun, Rest, Left, Noun_result).

parse(vp, In, Left, [Verb_result, Np_result]) :-
         parse(verb, In, Rest, Verb_result),
         parse(np, Rest, Left, Np_result).

parse(adj, [A|B], B, A) :- word(adj, A).
parse(noun, [C|D], D, C) :- word(noun, C).
parse(verb, [E|F], F, E) :- word(verb, E).

word(verb, crashes).
word(adj, the).
word(noun, computer).
word(noun, program).
```

(a)

```
| ?- consult('parser_r.pro').
{parser_r.pro consulted, 110 msec 1552 bytes}

yes
| ?- parse(sentence, [the, program, crashes, the, computer],[], Struct

Struct = [[the,program],[crashes,[the,computer]]] ? ;

no
| ?- parse(sentence, [the,program, crashes, the, computer, [], _).

yes
| ?- parse(sentence, A_sent, [], Struct).

A_sent = [the,computer,crashes,the,computer],
Struct = [[the,computer],[crashes,[the,computer]]] ? ;

A_sent = [the,computer,crashes,the,program],
Struct = [[the,computer],[crashes,[the,program]]] ? ;

A_sent = [the,program,crashes,the,computer],
Struct = [[the,program],[crashes,[the,computer]]] ? ;
```

(b)

FIGURE 7.10
Modified parser (parses and shows sentence structure): (a) PROLOG database; (b) sample results.

```
A_sent = [the,program,crashes,the,program],
Struct = [[the,program],[crashes,[the,program]]] ? ;

no
| ?- parse(What_is, Genned, [], Struct_genned).

Genned = [the,computer,crashes,the,computer],
Struct_genned = [[the,computer],[crashes,[the,computer]]],
What_is = sentence ? ;

Genned = [the,computer,crashes,the,program],
Struct_genned = [[the,computer],[crashes,[the,program]]],
What_is = sentence ? ;

Genned = [the,program,crashes,the,computer],
Struct_genned = [[the,program],[crashes,[the,computer]]],
What_is = sentence ? ;

Genned = [the,program,crashes,the,program],
Struct_genned = [[the,program],[crashes,[the,program]]],
What_is = sentence ? ;

Genned = [the,computer],
Struct_genned = [the,computer],
What_is = np ? ;

Genned = [the,program],
Struct_genned = [the,program],
What_is = np ? ;

Genned = [crashes,the,computer],
Struct_genned = [crashes,[the,computer]],
What_is = vp ? ;

Genned = [crashes,the,program],
Struct_genned = [crashes,[the,program]],
What_is = vp ? ;

Genned = [the],
Struct_genned = the,
What_is = adj ? ;

Genned = [computer],
Struct_genned = computer,
What_is = noun ? ;

Genned = [program],
Struct_genned = program,
What_is = noun ? ;
```

(b)

FIGURE 7.10 (continued)

```
Genned = [crashes],
Struct_genned = crashes,
What_is = verb ? ;
no
| ?- halt.
```

(b)

FIGURE 7.10 (continued)

nouns, verbs, and determiners in our examples) or **terminals** (specific words such as dog, computer, etc.).

A TN parses an input string by starting at an initial state, denoted S, and sequentially checking each word in the input string against the label of each arc emanating from the present node. When a match is found, the attention focuses on the new node, or state, of the parse and the matching process is repeated until a node representing the goal state (a successful parse) is reached. Goal states are typically indicated by a node labeled "end" or a double circle.) Thus, the TN parses by "consumption" of the input string, just as in the G1 parser. Furthermore, when the parser is in a specific state, the existence of several arcs emanating from this node indicates that several productions are potentially applicable. Thus, each arc represents a condition under which the arc may be traversed. Note that a TN may be employed recursively, thus providing a space-efficient parsing machine. Productions (P) of G map directly into elements of the TN. Referring to the productions of G1, Fig. 7.11 shows the corresponding TN elements.

Given a TN to be parsed, top-down parsing corresponding to a grammar, G, and an input string proceeds by traversing the TN to a goal state, while "consuming" the input string. An arc may be traversed under one of the following conditions:

1. The arc is labeled with a terminal and the next entry in the input string is the same terminal. This terminal is "consumed."
2. The arc is labeled with a nonterminal. In this case, control passes to one or more TNs related to this nonterminal.

If the parser reaches a state (node) in the TN where no outgoing arc is applicable, a failure is encountered. This invokes backtracking, which may be implemented in a number of ways. If we simply backtrack to the previous node, that is, the last TN state, we are employing depth-first search.

Augmented Transition Nets (ATNs)

An ATN is derived from the basic TN by adding several features, especially recursion. Arcs in ATNs may be labeled with the names of other TNs. These arcs are used to let an arc "call" or pass control (and the string) to another TN. For example, in an ATN corresponding to the TNs of Fig. 7.11 (part 1), the nonterminal arc labeled "np" is not simply traversed, but rather TN "np" (part 2) is called or used to check for

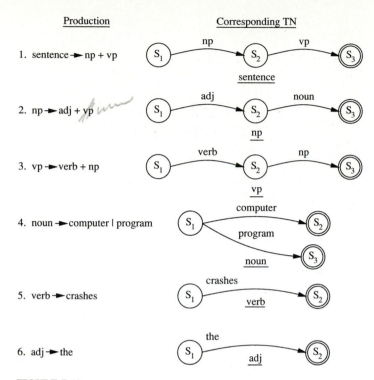

FIGURE 7.11
Transition network elements for sample grammar G1.

a noun phrase in the input string. This allows the parser to progress to a new node (consider a new production, without "consuming" additional input).

Readers will notice that the recursive invocation of TNs, and the use of back-tracking upon failure, make top-down parsing with ATNs analogous to the previous PROLOG implementation of the G1 parser.

Other features of ATNs distinguish them from TNs. This includes the embedding of conditional tests and corresponding actions (such as jump to another ATN under certain conditions) to an arc. Actions include the ability to record previous actions ("take notes") and refer to these notes at a later point. This includes attaching linguistic properties or features to a node.

CONCLUDING REMARKS

Parsing Computational Complexity

Parsing of sentences in formal languages involves the matching of substructures to form and recognizes an overall or global structure. The potential search complexity suggests that other a priori information (including heuristics) may be useful in the development of practical parsers. The reader is encouraged to develop alternative parsing techniques. We have just touched the "tip of the iceberg" in parsing. While

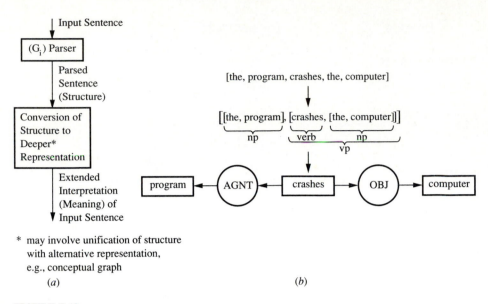

* may involve unification of structure
  with alternative representation,
  e.g., conceptual graph

     (*a*)   (*b*)

FIGURE 7.12
Using parser as a basis for deeper (semantic) sentence interpretation (*a*) Concept (*b*) Example using G1.

we have developed a functioning parser, we have done so without regard to efficiency or complexity.

From Parsing to Meaning

Parsing (particularly when applied to spoken/written languages) provides a potential first step in recognizing the structure and, consequently, meaning of an input sentence. As shown in Fig. 7.12, a parsed sentence may subsequently be converted into a "deeper" representation (a conceptual graph) forming the basis for a higher-level interpretation. This is continued in the problems.

REFERENCES

[Allen 1987] Allen, J., *Natural Language Understanding*, Benjamin Cummings, Reading, MA, 1987.

[Bolc 1984] Bolc, Leonard (ed), *Natural Language Communication With Pictorial Information Systems*, New York, Springer-Verlag, 1984.

[Chomsky 1957] Chomsky, N., *Syntactic Structures*, Mouton, 1957.

[Derouault/Merialdo 1986] Derouault, A.M., and B. Merialdo, "Natural Language Modeling for Phoneme-to-Text Transcription," *IEEE Trans. PAMI*, Vol. PAMI-8, No. 6, pp. 742–749, Nov. 1986.

[Fu 1982] Fu, K.S., *Syntactic Pattern Recognition and Applications*, Prentice-Hall, New York, 1982.

[Holtzman 1981] Holtzman, S., "Using Generative Grammars for Music Composition," *Computer Music Journal*, Vol. 5., No. 1, 1981. pp. 51-64.

[Moll 1988] Moll, R., M. Arbib, and A. Kfoury (eds.), *An Introduction to Formal Language Theory*, Springer-Verlag, New York, 1988.

[Roads 1979] Roads, Curtis, "Grammars as Representations for Music," *Computer Music Journal*, Vol. 3, No. 1, 1979, pp. 48–55.

[Shaw 1970] Shaw, A.C., "Parsing of Graph-Representable Pictures," *J. Assoc. Comp. Mach.*, Vol. 17, No. 5, pp. 453–481, 1970.

[Weizenbaum 1966] Weizenbaum, J., "ELIZA—A Computer Program for the Study of Natural Language Communication between Man and Machine," *Communications ACM*, Vol. 9, No. 1, 1966, pp. 36–45.

[Woods 1970] Woods, W., "Transition Network Grammars for Natural Language Analysis," *Communications ACM*, Vol. 13, No. 10, (1970), pp. 591–606.

PROBLEMS

7.1 Modify the PROLOG language generator (G1) grammar such that:
  (*a*) Questions are generated;
  (*b*) The noun phrase following a verb is optional;
  (*c*) The formation of compound sentences using "and" is allowed; and
  (*d*) Paragraphs are generated.

7.2 (*a*) Suggest a mechanism to modify G1 to create a context sensitive language generator. Consider two approaches:
  (i) Constraining nouns and verbs to agree; or
  (ii) Developing a Type 1 (context sensitive) grammar as described in the text (7-6).

  (*b*) Implement your solution and show PROLOG results.

7.3 In the G1 parser (parser_r.pro) presented in the text, what would be the effect of the following goal modifications:
  (*a*) ? – parse (sentence, [the, program, crashes, the, computer, and, this, extra], _).
  (*b*) ? – parse (sentence, Y, _).
  (*c*) ? – parse (X, Y, [ ]).
  Verify your answers using the PROLOG system.

7.4 The following problem makes an excellent long-term homework or project assignment. It concerns the development of a "production generator" or "system identification" program. Recall that we are given a grammar in the form

$$G1 = (\Sigma, N, P, S)$$

Our previous efforts concerned the specification of these entities in PROLOG, whereupon we could generate and parse productions in G1. Consider an alternative problem:

  Given Σ, N, and S, design a module that, given valid sentences in G1, returns all possible valid P.

Clearly, the design of such a module is nontrivial and an interesting exercise in "learning." Two immediate concerns arise:
  (*a*) How to "hypothesize" valid P.
  (*b*) How to limit the set in (*a*), given a large number of valid sentences as input.

7.5 For the following line drawing of a house, use the picture description grammar to develop a description.

7.6 Show how the picture description language may be used to generate alphanumeric characters. For example, an uppercase "A" may be written as

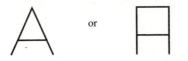

How would we develop a parser to interpret each character?

7.7 This problem considers many of the useful features of the syntactic approach for 2-D pattern representation. In particular, insensitivity to size (scale), location and rotations are achievable, since we are only considering structured representations. Consider the use of the PDL for pattern classification through parsing. Specifically, consider the case of a square, rectangle and rhombus as three possible classes. Allow each geometric primitive, for example, o, u, s1, s2, to have unit length.

(a) Develop a grammar for each class, G_{square}, $G_{rectangle}$, and $G_{rhombus}$.

(b) Develop, in PROLOG, a generator for each class and show its operation with sample results. (Can you allow for the generation of these figures with arbitrary scale without a separate production for each size?)

(c) Develop a parser for each grammar based upon (b).

7.8 Discuss the relationships between labeling using constraint satisfaction generation, and parsing of objects using formal grammars. In what ways are they similar? In what ways are they different? Illustrate your solutions using the framework problem 5 (Chapter 5) and problem 7 (Chapter 7).

7.9 (a) Modify the parser (parser_r.pro) in Fig. 7.10 by adding additional write predicates so that the sentence structure, when parsed, is then output to the user in a "natural" form. For example, sample output could be

```
for sentence : [the, program, crashes, the, computer]
with structure : [[the, program], [crashes, [the,
                  computer]]

the subject of this sentence is : program
the verb of this sentence is : crashes
the object of this sentence is : computer                    (P9-1)
```

(b) Using the results of part (a), can you further refine the output such that the meaning or an interpretation of the sentence is provided? For example, can a conceptual graph (Chapter 1, Fig. 1.7) be generated?

7.10 Modify the G1 sentence generator and corresponding parser such that sentences are generated (and parsed) with an optional adverb and optional noun phrase as part of the verb phrase. For example, the following are examples of the type of sentences produced:

the quarterback *accurately* throws the ball

the quarterback throws *accurately*.

Begin your solution by showing the revised productions in the form of (7-9d).

7.11 Modify the sentence generator so that sentences with adjectives describing nouns are possible. For example, include a sentence such as

the faulty computer crashes the esoteric program.

7.12 This problem explores the limitations of syntactically correct parsing approaches in context-free grammars. Consider interpretation(s) of the following sentence:

Flying over New York City, I saw the Statue of Liberty.

(*a*) Give two possible interpretations of this sentence.
(*b*) Why is ambiguity possible?
(*c*) How is the ambiguity removed by the human interpreter?
(*d*) How could an unambiguous interpretation be achieved autonomously?

CHAPTER
8

FUNDAMENTALS
OF LISP

"Logical consequences are the scarecrows of fools and the beacons of wise men."

Thomas Henry Huxley 1825–1895
Animal Automatism [1874]

INTRODUCTION

Artificial Intelligence programming applications generally require the processing of symbolic data, whether that data represents rules, logic functions, semantic relationships between objects, or input in human-recognizable form. Since each of these entities may be represented as lists of symbols with corresponding properties, values, and relationships, list manipulation languages such as LISP are receiving renewed attention. LISP, as is often noted, is the second oldest computer language still in common use. The proliferation of numerous dialects of LISP (for example, MacLisp, FranzLisp, and Interlisp versions are all popular with various interests) has been one obstacle to its widespread acceptance. Another nontrivial obstacle is the difficulty that many programmers, fluent in a more widespread imperative language (such as Pascal), have had in converting their thought processes to LISP programming.

Getting Started in LISP

Whereas Chapter 3 explored the "why" aspects of LISP, this chapter emphasizes the "what." The simple examples presented are intended to provide a relatively painless introduction to a quite elaborate and powerful language. A primer on the philosophy of LISP programming is provided and important LISP constructs (functions) are highlighted. The reader interested in additional detail concerning the LISP programming language and the details of a specific dialect is referred to the many excellent references cited, as well as the comprehensive summary of commonly-used LISP functions in Appendix 3.

In this chapter, an attempt has been made to show "quasi-generic" LISP code. Specifically, FranzLISP and CommonLISP examples are used. While these dialects (as cited in Chapter 3) differ principally in the scoping of variables, the reader will note a strong similarity between the syntax of most functions (see Appendix 3).

THE LISP PROGRAMMING CONCEPT. The basic idea of the LISP programming language is actually quite simple—*the language enables the manipulation of (symbolic and numeric) entities that comprise lists.* We note that PROLOG allowed the manipulation of lists, however LISP provides a much richer variety of built-in manipulation capabilities. Furthermore, the syntax of PROLOG is relatively simple (it does not take a very long discussion to summarize it). Due to the additional capabilities of LISP, however,

> LISP is a much more sophisticated language than PROLOG; its syntax is far more complicated.

Additionally,

> LISP has no built-in unification mechanism nor built-in structure for predicates and rules. If one wants one like that provided in PROLOG (it is not always needed) it must be developed in LISP.   (8-1)

IS LISP SUITABLE FOR AI? Prior to beginning a study of LISP, one obvious question the reader should ask is "Can LISP be used for implementation of the representation and manipulation strategies required by AI?" In other words, can relations, semantic nets and rules be represented and inference strategies be implemented using LISP? Are the resulting implementations straightforward and efficient? The answer is a qualified yes. This is shown via the examples in this chapter, Chapters 9 and 10, and the extensive implementations of rule-based systems and planners in Chapters 11–14.

For example, we may wish to encode predicate calculus representations in LISP, as in Chapter 2. This may be done by writing predicates in list form, for example,

```
(move A B)
(is-adjacent-to C D)
```

where the first element (the "car") of each list is the predicate name and the remainder of the list are the arguments.

PURE LISP AND EXTENSIONS. LISP is noteworthy in that it provides a solid base, via a small set of built-in functions comprising a "basic," "pure," or "mini-LISP" system, for almost unlimited extension. This is done by *creating new functions using built-in functions as building blocks.*

OVERVIEW OF LISP CONCEPTS. The concepts of LISP list processing become more complicated when one considers

1. The underlying data or knowledge structure the list represents.
2. The frequent use of recursion in function definitions.
3. The distinctions between a variable, the variable's name, the binding of the variable with a *value*, and the *scope* of a variable.
4. The concepts of LISP program control, involving conditional evaluation of expressions, looping, and so on.
5. The concept of programs built around applying functions to arguments, function definitions, and the consequences of returned function values.

At first these concepts (and a plethora of significant parentheses) may seem overly cumbersome. After some experience, the necessity and utility of these entities in AI applications become apparent.

PROGRAMS AND DATA STRUCTURES AS LISTS. A LISP program is structured in list form; therefore, *a LISP program, from a structural viewpoint, is indistinguishable from a list*. A consequence of LISP facility with list manipulation is the ability of a LISP program (or function) to manipulate a LISP program (or function), *thus providing the capability of generating self-modifying code*. While this capability must be used carefully, it may be one of the most useful features of a language designed to implement intelligent behavior. For example, this self-adaptive language system capability might be used to implement a form of learning. (Note that PROLOG, via built-in predicates such as "assert" and "retract" also has this capability, albeit to a lesser degree).

FUNCTIONAL APPROACHES AND DATA DEPENDENCIES. LISP is (loosely speaking) a functional language. Therefore, we need to become comfortable with the concept of *computation as defining and applying functions to arguments and returning values*. In a functional language, the program structure and order of execution are determined by the *data dependency* in function definitions. This is important for both creating and debugging programs and considering LISP implementations.

BASIC LISP CONCEPTS AND EXAMPLES (EVAL, LISTS, AND FUNCTION DEFINITIONS)

A note to aid in reading and understanding LISP programs (four "easy questions" to guide LISP interpretation). Newcomers to LISP tend to view the language as horribly complex and hidden behind an obscure syntax. In the same way that most things appear formidable at the outset, neither of these is true. In fact, once understood and appreciated, the syntax of LISP seems consistent, reasonable, and even desirable for AI applications. One useful approach to reading large LISP programs is to first break down the code into manageable segments that are then analyzed and understood.

An understanding of LISP is facilitated if the programmer approaches LISP with the following concepts in mind:

1. What is the underlying data structure involved? (i.e., if rules are formulated in list form, how are the antecedent(s) and consequent(s) arranged in list form?)
2. Is *evaluation* of an entity involved?
3. What are the *arguments* of a particular function, and what is the *value* the function returns?
4. What is the *flow of control* (i.e., of function evaluation) within each function, and how are functions related? (i.e., what are the overall program data dependencies?)

In some cases, this involves reading and interpreting the LISP code "from the inside out" (particularly where nested functions and recursion are involved). As the examples in the text show, indentation and the use of comments (preceded by a semicolon) lead to more readable LISP code.

The eval **Function**

The first concept LISP programmers should understand is the interface with the built-in eval function (or what is commonly referred to as the read—eval—print loop). *Anything typed at the interpreter prompt, denoted* —>, *is considered input to the* eval *function (and is usually input in list form).* eval, as its name suggests, evaluates the input and, like any function, returns a value. By learning to "think like the eval function," beginning LISP programmers will have less difficulty in developing LISP functions and programs.

The operation of eval is straightforward. After printing the prompt at the user's terminal, eval waits for a user-input expression. eval accepts expressions (s-expressions as defined in 8-14) and provides a returned value by performing the evaluation specified by the s-expression. If the expression is an atom (not a list), it is evaluated and its value is printed. If the s-expression is quoted, eval returns the quoted string as its value. If the expression is a list, eval assumes the car of the list is either a built-in (system) or previously defined (user) function. eval evaluates this type of expression by applying this function to the remainder of the list, which is assumed to be arguments. This is the general form of a LISP *function call* or evaluation. The car of a list may be a LISP function such as defun (function definition) or setq (assignment), which have *side effects*, in addition to returning a value.

Elementary List Manipulation

We begin with a few definitions. The basic structures of LISP are simply *atoms* and *lists*. In LISP (as noted in Chapter 3) data structures are both dynamic and untyped.

- An **atom** is a data structure in LISP that is "atomic" or indivisible and that is not a list. (8-2*a*)
- A **list** is a collection of atoms or other lists, enclosed by parentheses. (8-2*b*)

For example,

(this is a list)   (8-2*c*)

((this is a list) within a list)   (8-2*d*)

and

(defun both—empty (a b) (and (null a) (null b)))   (8-2*e*)

are examples of lists. In (8-2*c*), the list consists solely of atoms, whereas in (8-2*d*) and (8-2*e*) the list contains other lists as elements or members. Interestingly, the list in (8-2*e*) is also a LISP code fragment (see Chapter 10, example 10.14) that comprises a function definition.

car AND cdr AND nth. The most elementary capability of LISP is *list manipulation*. The built-in functions car and cdr facilitate this. The function car applied to a list returns the first element or member of the list; cdr similarly returns a list consisting of all but the first element. In the examples that follow, the interpreter prompt is shown as –>. The nature of assignment can get complicated in LISP. We may use the functions set and setq for assignment of values and putprop for property lists. LISP provides the setf macro, which is an "all purpose" assignment form which expands into the appropriate function for assignment, as shown later.

> **Example 8.1   Evaluation (eval) of car and cdr.**
> The command
>
> –>(car '(a b c d))   (8-3)
>
> instructs eval to apply built-in function car to the list (a b c d) and therefore eval returns the element
>
> a
>
> whereas
>
> –>(cdr '(a b c d))   (8-4)
>
> returns the list
>
> (b c d).

Similarly, the built-in function nth may be used to extract any element of a list, as shown below. Given lists that are knowledge representation data structures, these, and other LISP functions may be used to query the data base.

> **Example 8.2   List-based rule structure and LISP manipulation.** Consider the following example of a list-structured production or rule, perhaps characterizing an automobile:

```
-> (setq a_rule

'(rule 43

(concerns (car auto mobile_home))

(applicable_if (in vehicle_frame))

(antecedent_is (if (? entity) (has (wheels owner roof))))

(production_is (then ((? entity) isa auto)))))              (8-5)
```

In (8-5), the LISP assignment function setq was used to assign symbol name a_rule to the list following the single quote. The following examples show we may access parts of rule 43 or a_rule by using nested function calls or evaluation in the following manner:

```
-> (cdr (nth 3 a_rule))                        ->CADDDR
((in vehicle_frame))

-> (cdr (nth 4 a_rule))
((if (? entity) (has (wheels owner roof))))

-> (cddr (nth 4 a_rule))
nil

-> (nth 2 a_rule)                       ->     CADDR
(concerns (car auto mobile_home))

-> (cdr (nth 2 a_rule))
((car auto mobile_home))

-> (cdr (nth 4 a_rule))
((if (? entity) (has (wheels owner roof))))

-> (cadr (nth 4 a_rule))
(if (? entity) (has (wheels owner roof)))

-> (cdadr (nth 4 a_rule))
((? entity) (has (wheels owner roof)))           (8-6)
```

The last function call in (8-6) illustrates a notational shorthand provided in most LISP implementations for combining the car and cdr functions. For example,

```
->(car (cdr (cdr a_list)))
```

may be replaced with

```
->(caddr a_list)
```

n^m   1   <->   CADR

n^m   0   ->   CAR

Often, for ease of reading, the function n t h is used to extract a specific element of a list (rather than c a d . . . . d r).

It is of historical significance that the LISP function names c a r and c d r are derived from the register names of an IBM 704 computer used in an early LISP implementation; CommonLISP provides the more easily remembered names f i r s t and r e s t. Fortunately, we may achieve renaming of any function via definition of a new function. For example, we could achieve CommonLISP names for the elementary list manipulation functions using the "pure" LISP functions via

```
->(defun first (alist)
(car alist))
```

and

```
->((defun rest (alist)
(cdr alist))                                              (8-7)
```

Notice a key aspect of these three examples is that *a list was entered to* e v a l at the LISP system prompt. The c a r of the list is the symbol name of a built-in LISP function. The c d r of the list entered is the arguments and body of this function.

> **Example 8.3**   n i l **and** n u l l. The empty list, that is, ( ), is denoted n i l. LISP contains a large number of functions, used as *predicates*, which facilitate the control of function evaluation. One of these is n u l l, which checks for the empty, or n i l, list. For example,
>
> ```
> -> (null nil)
> t
> -> (null (a b))
> -> nil                                                  (8-8)
> ```

Function Definition

Built-in LISP function d e f u n is used to define new functions. As noted in Chapter 3, LISP programs (meaning LISP functions) are developed and refined incrementally. d e f u n has three parts:

1. The function name, entered to e v a l as the c a r of the function definition list
2. A list of arguments to the function
3. A function body, indicating how the returned function value is determined. The following extension to the previous example illustrates this concept.

> **Example 8.4   Function definition.** Instead of using the composite (c a r, c d r, n t h, etc.) functions in example 8.2, we may define a new function that returns various portions of RULE 43. For example,
>
> ```
> -> (defun get_antecedent (any_rule)
> (cdadr (nth 4 any_rule))
> get_antecedent                                         (8-9a)
> ```

Thus, we can determine the antecedent of any rule in this form via

```
-> (get_antecedent a_rule)
((? entity) (has (wheels owner roof)))
```
(8-9*b*)

A general function definition may contain multiple expressions in the body of the function, in which case the syntax is

```
-> (defun <name> <args> <expr₁> <expr₂> ... <exprₙ>)
```

where the body consists of $<expr_1>...<expr_n>$. When function $<name>$ is invoked, each of the $<expr_i>$ is evaluated and the value returned is that of the last expression evaluated, namely $<expr_n>$.

(FranzLISP) help

In FranzLISP implementations, the built-in function help is available to facilitate recall of the specifics of a built-in function (e.g., the order of the input arguments, or value returned). It is invoked via

```
->(help <function_name>)
```
(8-10)

where $<function\_name>$ is the name of the function about which information is desired. Other LISP implementations may have similar help facilities.

Simple LISP Assignment and I/O

set, setq **AND THE QUOTE** ('). Assignment of a value to a variable in LISP is accomplished in several ways. The set and setq functions are typically used. The quote operator inhibits expression evaluation. Many functions that are eval-type may be made to exhibit other than eval behavior by preceding the argument(s) with the quote. In addition, since many functions are useful in both modes, with perhaps one of the arguments quoted and another evaluated, functions usually ending in "q" are provided. The most typical of this is the set of assignment functions set and setq. set is strictly a two-argument eval-type function whereas setq inhibits evaluation of its first argument but evaluates the second. As an example,

```
(setq bob 33)
```

and

```
(set 'bob 33)
```

are equivalent assignment operations using the variable bob. The reader should recall that set and setq, being functions, return a value. Appendix 3 describes this in more detail.

In keeping with the functional philosophy of LISP, the use of setq in the form
-> (setq a 'b) should not be thought of simply as forcing a := b, but rather
applying function setq to two arguments, a and 'b respectively, returning a value
b, and having the side effect that a variable with symbol name a is bound to a value,
namely b.

Since LISP distinguishes between the name of a variable and its value, care-
lessness in using set and setq can lead to unexpected results. The reader should
study the following example.

Example 8.5   LISP variable assignment.

```
-> (setq bob 'gary)
gary
-> bob
gary
-> (setq gary 'a-symbol-name)
a-symbol-name
-> (setq bob gary)
a-symbol-name
-> bob
a-symbol-name
-> (set bob 35)
35
-> bob
a-symbol-name
-> a-symbol-name
35
```
(8-11)

It is common in LISP to assign the result of a function application to the value of a
variable with some symbol name. For example,

-> (setq result (car my_list))   (8-12)

is equivalent to the typical assignment statement

result := car(my_list)

in an imperative language.

A third assignment utility, namely the built-in macro setf, is described in the
section on property lists.

READING AND PRINTING IN LISP. Like any language, interaction with the outside
world during execution of a LISP program is usually necessary. This is accomplished
through the use of built-in functions for input-output (I/O). Reading from and writing to
the user's console is often necessary to allow the LISP program to prompt the user for
input or to display intermediate results. I/O is an area where the differences between
different LISP implementations become more pronounced. We consider FranzLISP
and CommonLISP separately.

In FranzLISP, reading is accomplished via the built-in function read. read, with no additional arguments, returns the value of the s-expression read from the terminal. For example

```
->(setq in_value (read))
```
(8-13)

assigns the value of the terminal input to the variable in_value. *Notice that, like most languages, there is no "automatic" prompting of the user for input.* This may be accomplished by preceding read with an appropriate print.

To read from a file, a two step process is necessary:

```
->(setq input_port_name (infile '<infile name>))
```

whereupon the file is read via

```
->(read input_port_name)
```

Both FranzLISP and CommonLISP provide printing functions that, in addition to returning values, enable the display of results through side effects. Output, as shown below, is achieved in FranzLISP using the print function. *As a side effect*, print sends the *value* of its argument to the output device, in the simplest case the user's terminal. To print strings of text, it is necessary to precede the string with the quote (') to inhibit attempted evaluation. The function terpri (which has no arguments) is used to generate a carriage return and line feed, and is useful for formatting output.

CommonLISP, on the other hand, provides the built-in functions read—line and read—char for the reading of line and character data, respectively, from the terminal. Similarly, CommonLISP provides several print functions similar to the FranzLISP print. These include prin1 and print. Formatting of the output is possible via the format function.

OTHER NOTES. The specific operation of any dialect of LISP is liable to vary. For this reason, the examples presented below, although they were implemented on both FranzLISP and CommonLISP systems, may not run in a specific implementation. Most are compatible with FranzLISP and CommonLISP, as noted.

COMMENTS AND THE SUPERPARENTHESIS (]). Comments in LISP begin with a semicolon (;) and are fundamental to good program development and maintenance. The superparenthesis (]) is used to close any number of open (i.e., left) parentheses.[*]

LISP SYNTAX IN GENERAL

There are ongoing attempts to standardize the LISP programming language and allow a more user-friendly and structured set of control constructs. CommonLISP, a dialect that evolved principally from MacLISP and ZetaLISP, appears to be the winner. This standard is designed to facilitate program portability, consistency, efficiency, and stability. All aspects of the standard are thoroughly documented in Steele [Steele

---

[*] Where available; not all LISP systems provide the superparenthesis.

1984]. It is recommended that readers who are easily frightened or are new to LISP start with the more educationally-oriented coverages of LISP programming, such as [Winston 1985] or [Willinsky1 1984].

The Basic Function Groups

LISP, being close to a functional language, may be subdivided into classes of function types, including:

1. Those that define functions and apply functions to arguments (defun, apply, map),
2. Those for program control (cond, if, do),
3. Those for assignment (set, setq, setf),
4. Those which are *predicates*, and used in 2. (equal, listp, null, member, the logical predicates and, or, not, and arithmetic predicates >, <, > =, =, etc.),
5. Those useful for I/O and their returned values versus "side effects" (read, print),
6. Those which provide arithmetic (sum or +, minus or −),
7. Those for error handling, debugging and tracing (catch, trace).
8. Those for manipulation of data structures, including (not surprisingly) list manipulation (append, cons, list, car, cdr). This class includes those for property management.

Functions and Variables

Symbolic-expressions or **s-expressions** consist of atoms or lists and are the basic data object manipulated by LISP. **Function definitions** have a list structure, and therefore are s-expressions. (8-14)

A **function**, as the classical definition indicates, is an entity that takes in arguments (perhaps following evaluation, if these are variable names) and returns a value. A returned value may not be as simple as an atom; it may be a list. (8-15)

The fundamental concept of application of functions to arguments and returning a value generates many questions. Some are

1. How does the function interface to its arguments; that is, given an argument, is the value of the argument or (literally) the argument passed (verbatim) to the function?
2. What values do functions like print and setq, which are principally used for side effects, return?
3. What happens when the value of a variable is changed in the process of execution of a function, and the variable is later used by another function (i.e, what is the scope of the variable)?

The answer to question 1 relies on the operation of eval and the quote or ' operator. The major classes of LISP functions are eval or expr type functions, which evaluate the arguments (i.e., determine values) and then pass these values to the function.

SCOPING OF VARIABLES IN LISP.

The formal parameters of a function are specified in defun. The actual parameters (usually evaluated) are computed when the function is invoked, and they are discarded after the function has returned a value.   (8-16)

The following is an important note regarding the design (definition) of LISP functions for AI applications:

Since the size of various knowledge representations (usually some structured list form in LISP) is rarely known a priori, and in fact grows and shrinks during execution of a program, we will attempt to define functions where the list arguments are of variable length. This will lead to the use of recursion, in conjunction with a check on the remaining list, in many cases.   (8-17)

Control Functions

FUNCTION EVALUATION AND BRANCHING. The flow of control in the application of functions is achieved with several LISP constructs (functions, either directly or indirectly). These include cond, if, let and do.

ELEMENTS OF LOGICAL EXPRESSIONS. Prior to considering control functions, it is necessary to define LISP predicate functions or predicates. Recall that a predicate in conventional logic is a function that maps its arguments into TRUE or FALSE. LISP is similar, except we associate a truth value of nil (FALSE) or non-nil with a predicate. In LISP, a predicate that returns nil is one case, but many returned values are non-nil, that is, something other than nil. Thus, *non-nil does not connote* TRUE, *but rather not* FALSE.

Example 8.6   and. The function defined below (used in the matching functions in Chapter 10) tests for the simultaneous end of two lists using the and function.

```
(defun both-empty (a b)
       (and (null a) (null b)))
```
                                                                          (8-18a)

Predicates are used for both logical manipulations and as a means to test for function evaluation branching. LISP provides the built-in logical predicate functions and, or, and not, which evaluate arguments as logical expressions and return non-nil or nil. In addition, built-in arithmetic predicates such as greater than ($>$), less than ($<$), equal to ($=$), and others, are provided. A much broader class of functions may be used as predicates, however, namely those that return nil or some other value. This latter class is of significance in cond, if, and do structures.

LISP provides the built-in symbol t, (for TRUE), which always evaluates to TRUE.

cond. Perhaps the most widely used branching function in LISP is the cond function or the conditional. The arguments to the cond function are a list (often a list of lists, as shown below). The general form of a cond is

```
(cond
(<pred₁> <expr₁₁>  . . .  <exprₙ₁>)
(<pred₂> <expr₁₂>  . . .  <exprₙ₂>)
                        .
                        .
                        .
(<predₘ> <expr₁ₘ>  . . .  <exprₙₘ>)                                    (8-18b)
```

Evaluation of a cond proceeds sequentially. The car of each list is a predicate, $<pred_i>$. If $<pred_i>$ evaluates to non-nil, the remainder of the list $(<expr_{ij}> \ . \ . \ . \ <expr_{pq}>)$ is evaluated and the value of the last expression, $<expr_{pq}>$, is returned as the value of cond. Notice cond checks (<predicate> <expression>) lists *serially*, and returns a value when <predicate> evaluates to non-nil. If function cond runs out of arguments before finding a non-nil predicate, nil is returned. Good programming practice, however, suggests this default be used sparingly, if at all. Most commonly, a "bailout" list is placed at the end of the cond, whose car (the predicate) is t. (Note: in LISP, functions used as predicates do not necessarily return t. Rather, success is indicated by returning non-nil (including t).)

> **Example 8.7   The cond function.** We define a simple function whose body consists of the LISP cond function as shown below:
>
> ```
> ->(defun cond_example (arg)
>     (cond ((= arg 1) (print '(the argument is 1)))
>           ((= arg 2) (print '(the argument is 2)))
>           ((> arg 2) (print '(the argument is > 2)))))     (8-18c)
> ```
>
> A sample operation of the cond function follows:
>
> ```
> -> (cond_example 1)
> (the argument is 1)nil
> -> (cond_example 2)
> (the argument is 2)nil
> -> (cond_example 3)
> (the argument is > 2)nil
> -> (cond_example -2)
> nil
> ```

if. Another notable and somewhat familiar LISP control structure is the if construct. The form is

```
(if <predicate>
    <then statement> <else statement>)                                (8-18d)
```

Note the do structure in LISP is a *macro*, which is expanded into a cond form. Thus,

```
(if  a  b  c)
```
(8-18*e*)

expands to

```
(cond
  (a  b)
  (T  c))
```
(8-18*f*)

The clarity of i f-based LISP programs makes this macro useful.

Example 8.8   if.

```
(defun  iftest  (arg)
        (if  (eql  arg  0)  arg
        (iftest  (-  arg  1))))
```
(8-19*a*)

The reader is encouraged to verify the purpose and recursive characteristics of i f test. A trace of the operation of this function follows.

Trace of i f test

```
->  (iftest  3)
1|  iftest  [ARG:  3]
2|  iftest  [ARG:  2]
3|  iftest  [ARG:  1]
4|  iftest  [ARG:  0]
4|  iftest  =  0
3|  iftest  =  0
2|  iftest  =  0
1|  iftest  =  0

0
```
(8-19*b*)

MACROS

A **macro** is a (function-like) construct used to return an expression (in place of itself) to eva l. This is referred to as macro expansion, in the sense that the macro saves us the writing of a lot of code by 1) being defined as that code and 2) returning that code to eva l when invoked. Macros are allowed to have arguments.   (8-20)

THE let MACRO. Let is a useful macro which facilitates the creation of local variables and often yields code which is both more compact and efficient. The general form is

```
(let  (<var_bindings>)  <body>)
```
(8-21)

where <var_bindings> is a list of variable symbol names and corresponding bindings. <body> is a sequence of expressions, each of which is evaluated with the previous variable bindings (in the so-called environment of the let). The value of the last expression is returned. If <var_bindings> is empty, the let may be used to simply evaluate a sequence of expressions, thus allowing an imperative programming style. A more detailed example of let is shown below.

Example 8.8   let **macro.**

```
-> (defun my_let ()

(let ((var1 1)

(var 2 2))

(print 'var1= )

(print var1)

(terpri)

(print 'var2= )

(print var2) (terpri)))                                    (8-22a)
```

The reader is encouraged to verify the operation of function my_let as follows:

```
-> (my_let)

var 1=1

var 2=2

nil                                                         (8-22b)
```

To allow iteration (particularly if the creation of local variables is involved) LISP provides the do macro [Brooks 1985] shown below. The reader, once familiar with the structure of let, should find do an extension to that structure.

THE do MACRO. The do construct has the following form:

```
(do ((var-1 init-1 step-1)
     (var-2 init-2 step-2)
      . . .
     (var-n init-n step-n))       {this initializes and steps
                                    variables}
     (end-test                    {test to see if done;
      end-form-1                    has cond-like structure}
      end-form-2
```

```
        .   .   .
      end—form—k
      return—value)
    body—1                          {body of the do}
    body—2
      .   .   .
    body—q)                                                    (8-23)
```

do **EVALUATION.** The following steps occur in evaluation of the do form of (8-23):

1. Variables are initially bound in the car of the do body to init—i values. This form of the do macro assumes "parallel" binding of all variables at each iteration. The init—i and step—i specifications are optional.
2. end—test s—expr is examined (if present). If the car of end—test is nil, then
   a. Each of body—j expressions is evaluated (if any s—expr of the form (return value) is encountered, do is exited and its value is the returned value).
   b. Note that the only utility of the body is for exiting or side effects.
   c. Next iteration starts by binding each of the var—i to the value of the corresponding step—i. If any step—i is omitted, the var—i is left unchanged.
   d. Proceed as in 2.
   else {i.e., if car of end—test returns non-nil} go to 3.
3. Each of (optional) end—form—i are evaluated (note same remark as in 2(b)).
4. return—value is evaluated and returned as the value of do.

(Note 3 and 4 behave like a cond.)

The FranzLISP and CommonLISP versions of do are the same.
The following example uses the do macro to iteratively print n integers.

Example 8.10   do.

```
->(defun do_test (limit)
    (do ((index 1 (+ 1 index)))       ; variable creation and binding
        ((equal index limit) t)        ; the end-test
        (print index)))                ; the body              (8-24a)
```

Sample results.

```
-> (do_test 15)
1234567891011121314t                                          (8-24b)
```

THE MAPPING FUNCTIONS. It is often useful to repeatedly apply a function to a list of different arguments (which themselves may be a list) and to obtain the result as another list, each element of which is the result of the function applied to a specific set of arguments. For example, we may wish to scan a database and identify the position (in a list) of all arguments that satisfy some criteria. This is done via the mapcar function, as shown in the two examples below:

Example 8.11 mapcar.

```
-> (setq test_list '(a (a b) (c d) e f))
(a (a b) (c d) e f)

-> (mapcar 'listp test_list)
(nil t t nil nil)                                              (8-25a)
```

Example 8.12 mapcar.

```
-> m_list
((a b c) (d e f) (g h i))

-> (mapcar 'car m_list)
(a d g)

-> (mapcar 'cdr m_list))
((b c) (e f) (h i))                                           (8-25b)
```

List Manipulation (Construction) Functions (and Distinctions)

Three principal constructs are used to form lists. These are cons, append, and list. The LISP programmer must be aware of the subtle distinctions in their operation, however, since they do not generally accomplish the same things.

(cons exp_1 exp_2) : returns a list whose car is exp_1 and whose cdr is exp_2. The second argument should evaluate to a list. Function cons returns a new list by "consing" together the evaluations of the first argument (exp_1) and the second (exp_2). The first argument may be either an atom or a list. (Note: function append1[*] is similar to cons, but instead places the first argument to append1 at the end of the list.)

(8-26a)

(append $list_1$ $list_2$ . . . $list_n$) : returns a list by joining the elements of the $list_i$ together. (8-26b)

(list exp_1 exp_2 . . . exp_n): returns a list consisting of
(exp_1 exp_2 . . . exp_n) (8-26c)

Note that cons, append, and list all return *lists*. The operation of each of these list construction functions is illustrated in the examples below. The reader should note and understand the differences in the values returned by cons, list and append.

---

[*] Available in some LISPs.

Example 8.13   cons, append, **and** list.

Initial Lists

```
> (setq list_a '(a b c))
(a b c)

-> (setq list_b '(c d e))
(c d e)                                           (8-27)
```

cons *example*

```
-> (setq list_c (cons list_a list_b))
((a b c) c d e)

-> (car list_c)
(a b c)

-> (cdr list_c)
(c d e)
```

append *example*

```
-> (setq list_d (append list_a list_b))
(a b c c d e)

-> (car list_d)
a

-> (cdr list_d)
(b c c d e)
```

list *example*

```
-> (setq list_e (list list_a list_b))
((a b c) (c d e))

-> (car list_e)
(a b c)

-> (cdr list_e)
((c d e))
```

Composite Applications.

```
-> (setq list_f (list (cons list_a list_b)))
(((a b c) c d e))
```

```
-> (car list_f)
((a b c) c d e)
-> (cdr list_f)
nil
-> list_a
(a b c)
-> list_b
(c d e)
-> list_c
((a b c) c d e)
-> (setq list_g (list (cons (car list_a) (cdr list_b))
     (cdr list_c)))
((a d e) (c d e))
```

Properties and Property Lists

Many dialects of LISP provide a built-in mechanism to give variables (a number of) properties. The use of and manipulation of properties of entities is fundamental to many AI problems.

FRANZLISP PROPERTY FUNCTIONS (OPTIONAL). FranzLISP provides mechanisms for the manipulation of properties, including putprop and get. The syntax of putprop is

$$(putprop <var\_name> <value> <prop\_name>) \qquad (8\text{-}28)$$

putprop puts the value of value on the property list of variable var_name under the property prop_name and returns <value> as the value of putprop.

Similarly, using the get function, with the form

$$(get <var\_name> <prop\_name>) \qquad (8\text{-}29)$$

get returns the value of the property prop_name, on the property list of var_name.

Example 8.14   Property lists (FranzLISP).

```
->(putprop 'bob 'leslie 'wife)

->((putprop 'leslie '(roland shirley) 'parents)

-> (get 'bob 'wife)

leslie
-> (get 'leslie 'parents)
(roland shirley)                                              (8-30)
```

COMMONLISP PROPERTY FUNCTIONS. In CommonLISP, the use of property lists is somewhat different. The accessing of properties is similar to FranzLISP in that function get is used, with the same syntax as (8-29):

->(get <variable> <indicator>)   (8-31)

Invocation of the property list management function get in CommonLISP causes a search of the property list of <variable> for the indicator or property <indicator>, returning its value. Note that if <indicator> does not exist, nil is returned. The significance of this is that we can't distinguish between the value of a certain property being nil and the non-existence of the property.

USING setf. CommonLISP does not specifically provide a putprop form like that of (8-28) (of course, the programmer could define this function, as shown below). Instead, a "generalized" set function, setf, is used, in conjunction with get, to achieve putprop functionality. This involves either creating a new property or replacing an existing property value. The form is

->(setf <place_ind> <value>)   (8-32a)

where <place_ind> is a piece of LISP code that accesses some component of a LISP data structure and <value> is what (through evaluation) replaces the value of this component. Thus,

(setf x 3)   (8-32b)

is equivalent to

(setq x 3)   (8-32c)

The value returned by setf is <value>.

   Using (8-30), the value of the property wife for the variable bob could be set to leslie via

->(setf (get 'bob 'wife) 'leslie)   (8-32d)

where <place> in (8-32a) is, in (8-32d), the location of the value of property wife for variable bob.

   The utility of the property list feature in succinctly keeping track of a variable's attributes is apparent from the following example, which is a continuation of (8-30).

Example 8.15   Property list utility.
Q: What is the name of Bob's wife's parents?
A: Phrase in LISP as

-> (get (get 'bob 'wife) 'parents)

(roland shirley)   (8-33)

Note that the property list implementation of (8-32*d*) is also usable in FranzLISP. In fact, it is recommended (over putprop) for compatibility.

ARITHMETIC AND NUMERICAL FUNCTIONS. LISP provides a number of functions which facilitate numerical computing. They are shown below in Table 8.1 and Example 8.16.

Example 8.16   Sample uses of LISP arithmetic functions.

```
-> (+ 1 2)
3
-> (+ 1 2 3)
6
-> (- 1 2)
-1
-> (* 4 5)
20
-> (* 4 5 6)
120
-> (= 6 (/ 60 10))
t
-> (> 7 6)
t
-> (> 6 7)
nil
-> (>= 7 6)
t
-> (> 6 6)
nil
-> (>= 6 6)
t
-> (max 3 5 2 4 1)
5
-> (min 3 5 2 4 1)
1
```

TABLE 8.1
Sample LISP arithmetic functions

Function name	Operation
+	addition
−	subtraction
*	multiplication
/	division
=	equality
>	greater-than
<	less-than
> =	greater-than or equal to

```
-> (exp 1)
2.718281828459045
-> (sqrt 9)
3.0
-> (abs -10)
10                                                              (8-34)
```

Scoping of LISP Variables

We noted the importance of scoping of variables in Chapter 3. The **scope** of a variable refers to the conditions under which reference may be made to a variable. In both FranzLISP and CommonLISP the scoping of variables is significant. Due to the importance of functions, variable scope in both dialects is with respect to functions; however, the approaches are decidedly different.

GLOBAL VS. LOCAL VARIABLES. Variables in LISP may be either global or local. The only variables we have seen so far were introduced either in the argument list of a function or as part of a do construct, where they were "created for local use" (i.e., within the do iterations). In a manner similar to the variable declarations of Pascal, a variable that can be referenced in any function is said to be a **global** variable. Due to the possibility of multiple global variables appearing in a single LISP program, it is often good programming practice to give global variables special designators. For example, global variable names are often prefaced with easily recognizable characters. The global variable all_over might be designated *allover*. CommonLISP allows global variables to be declared as **special variables**, using the (optional)

```
(declare (special <varname>))                                  (8-35)
```

construct. In addition, a large number of global variables are predeclared in CommonLISP. For example, *print-pretty*, when set to non-nil, causes pretty-printed output. FranzLISP interprets global variables as those that are not local.

The use of global variables in LISP programs is not necessarily bad, *but must be done with care.* This is especially important in programming situations where multiple programmers are providing program fragments that are later assembled into an overall program. On the other hand, global variables are useful when implementing a database which will be accessed by many functions, or when the level of function calls becomes so deep it would be cumbersome to pass the variable from function to function.

On the other hand, **local** variables may only be referred to in the function in which they are introduced. They are typically those variables that appear in the argument list of a function definition (and, of course, not declared special). Variables that do not appear in the argument list of a function are considered **free** variables with respect to that function. Variables that appear in the argument list of a function are **bound** to that function.

SCOPING. Having developed the concepts of global and local and free and bound variables, we consider the *scoping* of variables. There exist two predominant types of scoping in LISP dialects, namely *dynamic* and *lexical* scoping.

> FranzLISP (as do many of the early LISPs) uses **dynamic scoping**, meaning the formal parameters of a function are bound when the function is invoked and remain bound until the function returns a value.   (8-36*a*)

> CommonLISP, on the other hand, employs **lexical scoping**, or what is sometimes referred to as **static** scoping. Thus, the allowed bindings of a functions' local variables are only within the program text that defines that function.   (8-36*b*)

In CommonLISP, a function may not refer to the local variables of other functions. Two functions may have local variables with the same name; however, they are considered different or distinct variables.

Lexical scoping may be preferable to dynamic scoping due to the ease with which the scope of a variable may be determined (i.e., by simply looking at the program listing).

Note that CommonLISP, while it typically uses lexical scoping, allows dynamic scoping if the variable is **declared special**. Thus, global variables in CommonLISP are equivalent to dynamically scoped special variables.

Another simple way to remember the difference between dynamically scoped and lexically scoped variables is that in dynamic scoping we need to know the calling sequence of functions during program execution in order to determine the scope of a variable. In contrast, with lexical scoping the scope of a variable may be determined simply by looking at the LISP code where the variable is defined.

More is said about LISP scoping in Appendix 3.

EXTENDED EXAMPLE OF RECURSION USING LISP

The use of recursion is fundamental to many programming applications in LISP, due to the ease with which many (symbolic) computations may be recursively decomposed, and the hierarchical (list) structure of many knowledge representations. Since many of the functions to be developed in Chapters 10 through 14 employ recursion, we take time to explore the concept fully in an extended example. A sample program for recursive list reversing is shown below.

Example 8.17   List Reverser Definition

```
(defun rev (lst)
(cond
((null lst) nil)
(t (append (rev (cdr lst))
                  (list (car lst) ]
```
(8-37)

This list reverser function returns the empty list, n i l, if the input list (the function's argument) is empty. Otherwise, the function recursively reverses the order of the input list elements.

To see the operation of the rev function, consider how we might reverse the order of the following list:

(a b c d)

One approach is to define a function that does one part of the reversing task at a time; that is, the following series of steps (the {} indicates remaining "reversing" work to be done) could be used.

Example 8.18 Recursive list reverser steps.
initial list = (a b c d)

Step	Intermediate result	
1	({b c d} a)	
2	({c d} b a)	
3	({d} c b a)	
4	(d c b a)	(8-38)

Notice in step 1 the car of the list was reversed with the cdr. In step 2 this process is repeated with the reduced list (shown in { }); this resulting list is appended to the previous one. In step 3 note that the reverse of a list of a single element (a list with a nil cdr) is the list itself. This process explains the definition in (8-37).

Example 8.19 Trace of recursive function evaluation. A sample trace of the recursive behavior of the rev function is shown below.

```
-> (rev '(a b c d))
  1;  rev [lst: (a b c d)]
  2;   rev [lst: (b c d)]
  3;    rev [lst: (c d)]
  4;     rev [lst: (d)]
  5;      rev [lst: nil]
  5;      rev = nil
  4;     rev = (d)
  3;    rev = (d c)
  2;   rev = (d c b)
  1;  rev = (d c b a)
(d c b a)
->                                                              (8-39)
```

We now extend the trace of this example with the operation of function append in the recursion.

```
-> (trace 'append)
T
```

```
-> (rev '(a b c d))
 1|  rev [lst: (a b c d)]
 2|   rev [lst: (b c d)]
 3|    rev [lst: (c d)]
 4|     rev [lst: (d)]
 5|      rev [lst: nil]
 5|      rev = nil
 5|      append [nil, (d)]
 5|      append = (d)
 4|      rev = (d)
 4|      append [(d), (c)]
 4|      append = (d c)
 3|      rev = (d c)
 3|      append [(d c), (b)]
 3|      append = (d c b)
 2|      rev = (d c b)
 2|      append [(d c b), (a)]
 2|      append = (d c b a)
(d c b a)                                                    (8-40)
```

DETAILED ANALYSIS OF RECURSION (OPTIONAL). A more detailed analysis of recursion is provided using function rev, defined in (8-37). Given the desired function evaluation

$$\text{-> (rev '(a b c d))} \tag{8-41a}$$

tracing of the operation of this recursive function begins at the top, or first, level.

$$\text{1| rev [lst: (a b c d)]} \tag{8-41b}$$

At this time, the argument to rev, that is, lst, is not null; therefore rev appends (or more correctly, rev causes the application of function append to) two arguments. The first, which yields the recursive property of the function rev, is the value returned by rev applied to the cdr of lst; the second is the list consisting of the car of lst. Since the first value needed to append, however, is the result of applying rev to the cdr of lst, this involves a second (a recursive) call to function rev, with a modified argument. Thus, at the second level we have

$$\text{2| rev [lst: (b c d)]} \tag{8-41c}$$

Notice again, since lst (now only the list (b c d)) is non-null, append is applied to the result of the application of rev to the cdr of a new argument, that is, the list (cd). Thus, this need for argument evaluation in turn causes another call to rev of the form

$$\text{3| rev [lst: (c d)]} \tag{8-41d}$$

We are now at the third level in the recursive process. However, as the reader will probably surmise by now, the argument to rev (the list (cd) is still non-null, and therefore append is again applied to the value returned by rev applied to the cdr of the argument as shown:

4| rev [lst: (d)]   (8-41e)

Since the list d is not null, this copy of rev still cannot return a value. Notice that all the recursive function calls to rev up to this point (i.e, in levels 2 through 4) are needed solely to generate a value for append, which was invoked in the top level.

Thus, append is again applied to the result of rev applied to the cdr of the list (d). This then involves the final recursive application of rev, at the fifth level:

5| rev [lst: nil]   (8-41f)

Notice that in this case, the cdr of the list (d) is the null list; therefore, rev is able to return a value to append. This value, from the function definition, is nil, or the empty list. Appending an empty list to any list does not change the list.

We have now reached an important point in our analysis of this particular recursion process. Since we now have a function (i.e., append) returning a value to be used as an argument to another function (i.e., rev), instead of generating further recursive function calls, no further levels of recursion are necessary. Thus, the evaluation of the value returned by rev begins to work upwards ("unwind") towards the top-most (i.e., 1st) level. This will involve evaluation of lower-level functions whose invocation led to the higher-level recursive function calls. This starts with

5| rev = nil   (8-41g)

Thus, the arguments to function append at the most recent (i.e., the 5th) level of recursion are

5| append [nil, (d)]   (8-41h)

Thus the invocation of append at the fifth level returns the list consisting of (d):

5| append = (d)   (8-41i)

This value of append is the value returned by rev at the fourth level of recursion:

4| rev = (d)   (8-41j)

It also becomes one of the arguments for the function append, which was invoked at the third level of recursion in (8-41d):

4| append [(d), (c)]   (8-41k)

Thus append returns

4 | append = (d c)   (8-41*l*)

yielding the value returned by rev at the 3rd level:

3 | rev = (d c)   (8-41*m*)

This value is then, in turn, the first argument to append, which was invoked by function rev at the 2nd level of recursion, that is,

3 | append [(d c), (b)]
3 | append = (d c b)   (8-41*n*)

The result of (8-41*n*) yields the returned value of rev at the second recursion level:

2 | rev = (d c b)   (8-41*o*)

This, finally, is the first argument to append, which was invoked by rev at the top (1st) level. Although we have concentrated on the recursive process, notice also that the function append has a second argument, which is the list consisting of the elements of the car of lst. Notice this is different from saying simply "the car of lst" since the latter may be comprised of sub-lists, as opposed to a single list of individual elements.

At this level, the list of elements comprising the car of lst is the list (a). Thus, append's arguments are

2 | append [(d c b), (a)]   (8-41*p*)

Function append therefore returns

2 | append = (d c b a)   (8-41*q*)

which, from the definition of the function rev, is the value returned by rev, that is,

1 | rev = (d c b a)   (8-41*r*)

This is the value returned by the LISP system in the above example, that is,

(d c b a)

Notice while our lengthy analysis provided a specific look at a recursion example, we also succeeded in reversing the elements of a list! Due to its recursive design, the LISP list reverser (rev) function definition works for any length list of elements.

The number of function calls, however, and consequently the program execution time, will be a function of the list size.

A NOTE ON TAIL RECURSION. Note in the example above that after the function reached the deepest or highest (denoted "5") level of recursion (where the n i l list was reversed), the recursively-created copies of r e v e r s e began to pass values upward to lower levels of recursion. Thus, in this example the recursively-defined function r e v e r s e "unwinds" and passes values upwards, ending at the top level. A function that passes values upward without alteration as the recursion unwinds is denoted *tail recursive*, as described in Chapter 3.

REFERENCES

[Anderson/Corbett/Reiser 1987] Anderson, J.R., A. T. Corbett, and B. J. Reiser, *Essential LISP*, Addison-Wesley, Reading, MA, 1987.

[Barrett/Ramsay/Sloman 1985] Barrett, R., A. Ramsay, and A. Sloman, *POP-11: A Practical Language for Artificial Intelligence*, John Wiley, NY, 1985.

[Brooks 1985] Brooks, Rodney A., *Programming in Common Lisp*, John Wiley, NY, 1985.

[D'Ambrosio 1985] D'Ambrosio, Bruce, "Golden Common Lisp," *Byte*, Vol. 10, No. 13, December 1985, pp. 317–321.

[Steele 1984] Steele, G.L., Jr., *Common Lisp: The Language*, Digital Press, Burlington, MA, 1984.

[Tatar 1987] Tatar, D.G, *A Programmers Guide to COMMON LISP*, Digital Press, Maynard, MA, 1987.

[Willinsky1 1984] Willinsky, R., *LISPcraft*, Norton, NY, 1984.

[Willinsky2 1986] Willinsky, R., *Common LISPcraft*, Norton, NY, 1986.

[Winston 1985] Winston, P.H., "The LISP Revolution", *Byte*, Vol. 10, No. 4, April 1985, pp. 209–222.

[Winston/Horn 1984] Winston P.H., and B.K.P., Horn, *LISP*, Addison-Wesley, NY, 1984.

[Yuasa/Hagiya 1986] Yuasa, T. and M. Hagiya, *Introduction to Common LISP*, Academic Press, N.Y., 1986.

PROBLEMS

8.1. Given the following LISP assignment and program definition,
  (*a*) What does the program do? (Describe clearly and unambiguously).
  (*b*) What is the result of the application of r e c u r to friends?

```
->(setq friends '(D1 D2 D3))

(defun recur (alist)

  (cond

    ((not (null (cdr alist)))

      (recur (cdr alist)) )

    (t alist)))                                    (P8-1)
```

8.2. The purpose of this problem is to test your understanding of LISP concepts involving flow of control, function arguments, and returned values. Referring to LISP function r e c u r, defined in problem 8.1 (P8-1), (*a*) Locate the corresponding matching right parenthesis for each left parenthesis.

(*b*) Consider indicating functions with a "black box" representation of the form:

Draw a function box for each function used and its interrelation with other functions used. This resulting block diagram illustrates the structure of function `recur`.

8.3. In Chapter 3, a LISP recursive definition of the factorial function is presented.

(*a*) Repeat part (b) of problem 8.2 (the box-like structural diagram) for this function definition.

(*b*) Show each step of the process used to determine a returned value from function factorial with the input of $n = 3$. In other words, show every function invocation and returned value for

$$->(factorial\ 3)$$

(*c*) Check your results of part (a) using the LISP "trace" function[*].

8.4. For each of the following statements entered at the LISP interpreter prompt, fill in the interpreter response (shown here as `x1x?`, `x2x?`, etc.).

```
-> (setq bob 34)
x1x?
-> (setq gary 36)
x2x?
-> (setq bob 'gary)
x3x?
-> (setq bob gary)
x4x?
-> (setq gary bob)
x5x?
-> (setq list_a '(a b c d))
x6x?
-> (setq a 10)
x7x?
-> (setq b (sum a 1))
x8x?
-> b
x9x?
-> (setq c (times a b))
x10x?
-> (setq d (cons a 1))
x11x?
-> (car d)
x12x?
-> (cdr d)
x13x?
```

```
-> (defun factorial (n)
(cond
((equal n 1) 1)
(t (times n (factorial (diff n 1]
x14x?
-> (factorial 3)
x15x?
```

8.5. (a) This problem is a continuation of problem 8.4. For each of the following LISP statements, fill in the interpreter response (shown here as x1x?, x2x?, etc.).

```
->(setq a_list '(a b c d e))
x1x?
-> (nth 3 a_list)
x2x?
-> (equal (nth 2 a_list) 'c)
x3x?
-> (print a_list)
x4x?
-> (member 'c a_list)
x5x?
-> (member 'c 'a_list)
x6x?
-> (reset)
x7x?
-> a_list
x9x?
-> (setq b_list '(f g h i j))
x10x?
-> b_list
x11x?
-> a_list
x12x?
-> b_list
x13x?
-> (mapcar 'car '((a b) (c d)))
x14x?
-> (mapcar 'car (list a_list b_list))
x15x?
```

8.5. (b) For extra credit—try these additional statements.

```
->(setq m—list nil)
nil
-> m—list
x16x?
-> (null m—list)
x17x?
```

```
-> (atom m-list)
x18x?
-> (listp m-list)
x19x?
-> (car m-list)
x20x?
-> (cdr m-list)
x21x?
-> (cons 'a m-list)
x22x?
-> m-list
x23x?
-> (setq m-list (cons 'a m-list))
x24x?
-> m-list
x25x?
-> (car m-list)
x26x?
-> (cdr m-list)
x27x?
-> (setq m-list nil)
x28x?
-> m-list
x29x?
-> (setq m-list (cons m-list 'a))
x30x?
-> m-list
x31x?
-> (car m-list)
x32x?
-> (cdr m-list)
x33x?
-> (setq m-list nil)
x34x?
-> m-list
x35x?
-> (setq m-list (cons m-list '(a)))
x36x?
-> (car m-list)
x37x?
-> (cdr m-list)
x38x?
-> (cadr m-list)
x39x?
-> (exit)
```

8.6. Show, by examples using the LISP system, the distinction between the cons, append, and list functions.

8.7. Show, by example, the difference between the map, mapcan, mapc and mapcar functions.

8.8. Develop and implement a LISP function (or set of functions) that converts a function definition containing the cond to one that uses
(*a*) The if construct.
(*b*) The do construct.

8.9. This problem considers the development of LISP function contained—in, a useful function for (among other things) specificity-order conflict resolution (Chapter 11).
(*a*) Show a LISP function contained—in which returns t if a—list is contained—in another—list, that is,

```
->(contained-in '(a c) '(b c d a))
    t


->(contained-in '(a b) '(b c d b))
     nil
```

(Hint: recursion and matching are involved)
(*b*) Show how contained—in may be used to determine set equality, where the elements of two sets are in list form.

8.10. Develop a LISP function change notat which converts statements entered in infix notation to prefix notation, that is,

```
-> (change-notat '((x + y) / z))
```

returns

```
(/ (+ x y) z)
```

8.11. The function considered in this problem may be useful in specificity-ordered conflict resolution, that is, when we try to "focus" our inference strategy by finding rules that are more specific. Develop a LISP function size—of—biggest—list which, given an argument another—list consisting of a list of lists, returns the size (number of elements) of the largest list. The desired operation is shown below.

```
-> another-list
((d e f r) (a b) (c) (d e f) (g h)
-> (size-of-biggest-list   another list)
     4
```

(A succinct solution to this problem should give you some exposure to the apply, max, mapcar, and length functions.)

8.12. Rewrite each of the following composite functions using only nth and cdr:
(*a*) caar
(*b*) cdaar
(*c*) cadadr
(*d*) cdddr
(*e*) cadddr

8.13. This problem tests your understanding of the mapcar function. Given

```
-> (setq test_list '(a (a b) (c d) e f))
(a (a b) (c d) e f)
```

what is the value returned by

```
-> (mapcar 'listp test_list)
```

8.14. Which of the following functions are tail-recursive?
   (*a*) recur (P8-1)
   (*b*) rev ((8-37) in text)
   (*c*) factorial ((3-16) in Chapter 3)

8.15. Design and implement a LISP function putprop2 which has the argument structure and effect of the FranzLISP function putprop ((8-28) (8-30)) but uses setf.

8.16. This problem illustrates the effect of the quote. For each case, show the LISP system response.

```
-> (setq a_list '(a b c))
(a b c)

-> (setq b_list '(d e f))
(d e f)

-> (setq c_list '(g h i))
(g h i)
```

(*a*)
```
-> (set q m_list (list 'a_list 'b_list c_list))
?? _____
```

(*b*)
```
-> (setq m_list (list a_list b_list c_list))
?? _____
```

8.17. For the LISP function defined below:

```
->(defun quick (arg)
(if (equal arg 0) (print 'arg=0)
(print 'arg<>0)]
```
                                                        (P17-1)

What is the result of using this function with the arguments shown below?

(*a*)
```
->(quick 0)
?? _____
```

(*b*)
```
->(quick 1)
?? _____
```

8.18. Show the similarities and differences between the structure and operation of the let (8-21) and do (8-23) macros.

8.19. Develop LISP functions that, given two lists, return
    (*a*) The union of two lists.
    (*b*) The intersection of two lists.
    (*c*) The difference between two lists.
    Where possible, use recursive function definitions and verify your results using LISP.

8.20. This problem tests your understanding of several LISP control functions, functional dependence, and recursion. Parts (a) and (b) should be done sequentially. For the following LISP program (function definitions)

```
(defun cond_function_2 (arg)
  (cond((= arg 1) (- arg 1))
              ((= arg 2) (aux_fun (+ 1 arg)))
              ((>= arg 3) (aux_fun (- arg 2)) (aux_fun (- arg 3)))
              ((< arg 1) (cond_function_2 (+ 1 arg)))))

  (defun aux_fun (arg2)
      (if (> arg2 0) arg2 (aux_fun (+ arg2 1))))            (P20-1)
```

(*a*) What is the result of the following LISP function evaluations?

```
t
-> (cond_function_2 10)
??_____
-> (cond_function_2 -100)
??_____
-> (cond_function_2 1)
??_____
-> (cond_function_2 2)
??_____
-> (cond_function_2 3)
??_____
-> (cond_function_2 4)
??_____
-> (cond_function_2 5)
??_____
-> (cond_function_2 6)
??_____
```

(*b*) Verify your answers to (*a*) using a LISP system. If you have one or more mistakes in (*a*), trace the relevant functions to resolve the disparity.
(*c*) After completing parts (*a*) and (*b*), test your understanding of function cond_function_2 by rewriting this program in a more compact form.

CHAPTER
9

LIST STRUCTURES — RATIONALE AND COMPUTER REPRESENTATIONS

"Common sense is not so common."

Voltaire [Francois Marie Arouet] 1694–1778
Dictionnaire Philosophique [1764]. Self-Love

INTRODUCTION

In this chapter, several concepts are explored, particularly

1. The utility of lists in developing representations.
2. The utility of LISP in manipulating the list-based representations in (1).
3. The details of the internal computer representation of a general list.

In general, the answer to the question "Why lists?" involves the subgoals of answering three underlying questions:

1. Why graphs?
2. How do I represent and manipulate relations among symbolic entities on a computer?
3. How do I accomplish (2) efficiently? (Here "efficiently" concerns, among other things, adding, deleting, modifying, and searching AI data structures.)

WHY GRAPHS, RELATIONS, AND LISTS?

In Chapter 1 we noted (without considering implementation details) that AI approaches in knowledge representation and manipulation are characterized by the attempt to represent higher level, often non-numerical, *relationships* between symbolic entities, features, or "objects." These relationships may be represented and manipulated by considering

1. Constraints or relations among the extracted features or primitives, including adjacency, connectedness, contained−in, and a part of.
2. A set of syntactically-defined productions belonging to a grammar or perhaps set of grammars.
3. A set of rules and facts.

STORING RELATIONS AS LISTS. In Chapter 2 we considered the (binary) relation, R, between two entities x, y. Note x and y may be numbers or symbols. Given the description

$$x \text{ is related to } y \text{ by } R \qquad\qquad (9\text{-}1a)$$

or, graphically,

$$\begin{array}{l} R, \\ x \rightarrow y \end{array} \qquad\qquad (9\text{-}1b)$$

In PROLOG it is possible to encode this using the predicate r, that is, a suitable representation is

$$r(x, y) \qquad\qquad (9\text{-}2)$$

Alternately, we can represent this relation as the ordered triple

$$(R, x, y) \qquad\qquad (9\text{-}3)$$

which is referred to in Attribute, Object, Value, or (A, O, V) format.

LIST MANIPULATION. Removing the commas in (9-3) yields a suitable list structure for a relation. Numerous functions in Chapters 8 and 10 may then be used for LISP manipulation of this list. This list may be stored in computer memory and a specific element of a specific triple may be accessed by specification of the other two, using a matching process. As we show later, the graphical structure of the relation (or more generally, groups of relations, e.g., a semantic net) is not preserved in memory. Knowledge manipulation with the representations of (9-1), (9-2) or (9-3) often involves matching and binding of representation symbols (variables) to obtain a model-consistent structure (Chapter 13). This action implies potential problems with the "curse of dimensionality" and leads to our detailed examination of search in Chapter 15.

OPERATIONS ON STORED
REPRESENTATION(S) DESIRED

Before we are able to define the operations possible with a chosen representation structure, it is necessary to define or choose the structure(s). This is accomplished by considering first our overall goals (i.e., potential applications and approaches). Fundamental to this is the choice of knowledge representation and manipulation schemes, which were considered in the introduction.

Consider specification of a higher-order set of goals, namely, "What is it we wish to do?" Let us first take some examples.

CLASSIFICATION/MODEL UNIFICATION. We are given a grey-level image and asked to develop an autonomous system to answer the question,

$$\text{Is there a 1957 Chevy or a Russian tank in the image?} \qquad (9\text{-}4)$$

Let us assume we have algorithms that extract low-level image features such as edges, line segments, regions, and so on. (Note that in reality these low-level algorithms would not work independently of the higher-order model.) From this set, we wish to answer the above question. To make the example workable, let's further assume that we are able to convert the above English-language inquiry into a more computer-manipulable, but still high-level, concept. From Chapter 1, recall the description is as follows:

```
auto         has—part             wheels
             has—id               owner
             has—locations        exterior and interior
             has—part             roof
             has—for propulsion   engine

wheel        has—part             tire
             may—have—part        spokes
             may—have—part        fancy—hub—cap
             is                       round
                  unless
                       is   flat

and

roof
             location—is          (usually) highest—point
             may—be—type          convertible                  (9-5)
```

The above entity in (9-5) may be alternately represented in rule-based form, where the relationships cited above may be encoded as a set of rules in antecedent-consequent form. An example of this might be

```
if    (? entity)      has—part spokes and is round
```

```
or    (? entity)      has-part fancy-hub-cap and is-round
```

```
then (? entity) may be wheel.
```

and

```
if (? entity)
```

```
has-attributes wheels owner roof . . .
```

```
then (? entity) isa auto
```

```
or (? entity) isa mobile-home
```

```
or (? entity) isa ...
```

```
or (? entity) is unknown.                          (9-6)
```

As an aside, the relationships postulated above may also be encoded for PROLOG implementation. For example, a predicate of the form

```
is-auto (Entity)  :- has_wheels_attributes(Entity),
                     has_roof_attributes(Entity)...        (9-7)
```

is possible.

A LOOK AHEAD TO LISP (LIST-BASED) REPRESENTATIONS AND VARIATIONS. Alternative inference mechanisms (a superset of those available in PROLOG) may be used in conjunction with the rule-based representation in (9-6) to conclude (or hypothesize and prove) that the entity under observation belongs to the class auto. For example, suppose we formulated our description of the above *facts* in list form:

```
(auto  (has-part wheels)
       (has-id owner)
       (has-location exterior interior)...)             (9-8)
```

As shown in Chapter 16, alternate, more structured and more readable and manipulable forms are possible. For example, the following rule-based structures are possible.

Example 9.1 Possible fact structure.

```
(fact 27  (entity auto)
          (has  (wheels  owner  exterior interior
                 roof engine))
          (other_entries (car truck vehicle))
          (used_for (transportation status_symbol)))]    (9-9)
```

Example 9.2   Possible rule structure.

```
(if ((? entity) has (wheels and owner and roof...))
     (then ((? entity) isa auto)
         or ((? entity) isa mobilehome)...]                          (9-10)
```

Of course, just as in the previous list-based fact example, the list-structured rules may be more complex. For example, an alternate is

Example 9.3   Extended rule (production) structure.

```
(rule 43 (concerns (car auto mobilehome))
         (applicable_if (in vehicle frame))
         (antecedent_is
             (if ((? entity) has (wheels and owner
                                     and roof...))
         (production_is
             (then ((? entity) isa auto)
         (alternate_productions
             (then ((? entity) isa mobilehome)...
         (further_information
             (top_down (see transportation status_symbol))
             (bottom_up (see wheels driver owner ...)) )
         (confidence (use function auto_confidence))
         (update_rule (apply learning_function
                         (number 32))))))                            (9-11)
```

CHARACTERIZATION OF THE PREVIOUS EXAMPLES. Notice the list-based representations in (9-5) through (9-11) share a number of common characteristics:

1. The representation consists of generally non-numeric data.
2. The representation spans a considerable "representation complexity" range. The description of the car can proceed in bottom-up fashion from elementary primitives to a high-level concept, that is, from image edge points to a structural description of an automobile.
3. The representation concerns objects (spokes, wheel, car, owner, tire, roof).
4. The representation concerns the relationships between objects (has, is, has—spokes, may—be).
5. The representation concerns properties (is—round, convertible).
6. The representation is ambiguous if it does not provide enough context (allowable relationships that must satisfy a consistency criteria) to distinguish between objects, properties, and/or relationships (e.g., convertible may be either an object, or a property).
7. The representation consists of entities that (a) reflect a structure and (b) are easily discernable by humans since either the graphical or text-based models consist of English-like constructs in list form.

8. The representation (even for this innocuous case) is quite complex.

9. The representation allows the logical representation and manipulation of (perhaps) illogical data. For example, the fact that the sky is green could be entered into the database, without any "automatic" protest from the computer.

10. The representations were all achieved using lists.

REPRESENTATIONAL GOALS. We desire a list-based representation that includes the above entities, and is suitable for efficient searching and matching. More specifically, we desire representations that are isomorphic to graphical and logical structures. In particular we will show

1. That it is quite easy to represent lists with the computer memory model (shown in the next section), and that to manipulate lists (e.g., add and delete elements) is the fundamental operation.

2. That trees and lists may be made isomorphic to one another by developing the concept of the linked list representation. In fact, the availability of an alternate list notation, that is, the so-called dot notation provides a more graphic reminder of this.

3. That the capability of representing entities as lists or members of a list (perhaps with a number of associated properties) yields an efficient structure for semantic net and frame representations.

TREES

EXTENDED RELATIONS AND DIGRAPHS AND "DEGREE." In the digraph representation of a relation, R, recall from Chapter 1 a node exists for every a $\in$ A where (a, b) $\in$ R. Furthermore, a (directed) arc from node a to node b appears in the digraph.

- The number of b such that (a, b)
  $\in$ R or the number of arcs emanating from node a in the digraph representation is called the **out-degree** of node a. Similarly, the number of arcs in the digraph terminating at node b is the in-degree of node a. (9-12)

- A **tree** is a data structure that is a finite acyclic (containing no closed loops or paths or cycles) digraph. One node, called the root, has in-degree equals 0, and every other node has out-degree $\geq$ 1. Nodes called leaf-nodes have out-degree equals 0. There exists exactly one path between any two (distinct) nodes. (9-13)

Trees are extremely useful data structures for both the representation and visualization of many of the object-relationship forms we will encounter in knowledge models. The fact that they are acyclic and may be derived from a general digraph makes trees suitable for studying search. Development of the standard data representation called the *binary tree* is fundamental in efficient searching methodologies.

COMPUTER MEMORY MODEL(S)

"STANDARD" MEMORY MODEL. The memory model for the "memory" of a typical (1989) computer (for either read or write) may be simply shown as

$$\text{address} \Rightarrow \boxed{\begin{array}{c}\text{memory}\\ \text{model}\end{array}} \Leftrightarrow \text{data} \tag{9-14}$$

Thus, we may view memory as a (large) lookup table or 1-D array that is indexed by an address. Elementary computer operations using this model are simply the reading (fetching) and writing (storing) of data.

ASSOCIATIVE/CONTENT-ADDRESSABLE MEMORY. Another useful memory structure or model (which may be implemented either in hardware and/or software) is that of an *associative* or *content-addressable* (AM or CAM, respectively) memory. CAM has the following structure:

$$\text{data} \Rightarrow \boxed{\begin{array}{c}\text{memory}\\ \text{model}\end{array}} \Leftrightarrow \begin{array}{l}\text{(possibly empty) set of}\\ \text{addresses containing data}\end{array} \tag{9-15}$$

Note that the CAM model in (9-15) is, loosely speaking, a kind of "inverse" of the conventional model of (9-14). In traditional computer design, CAM finds application in the design of memory management schemes. More importantly, CAM may be used to facilitate search through a data structure.

COMPUTER REPRESENTATION OF GRAPHS AND RELATIONAL INFORMATION

LINEAR ARRAYS. Storing a list in memory is relatively straightforward under certain conditions. The obvious, simplest, and most common approach to storing a list in computer memory is to arrange the list into a simple linear array of memory locations. If the size of the list is known a priori, and little manipulation (i.e., modification) of the list is anticipated, the linear array is a useful data structure. A slot, or entry, of fixed size is created for each of the list entries. This is shown in Fig. 9.1a. Note two potential problems with the linear array data structure for lists:

1. Adding or deleting data, or changing the size, structure, or type of the data is cumbersome. (9-16*a*)
2. The linear structure in memory does not reflect any relationship or structure among the elements of the list. (9-16*b*)

Retrieval of an item from a list of m elements, in linear array form, can be done through a binary search of the array with at most

$$n_{\text{linear array}} = \log_2 (m) \tag{9-16c}$$

comparisons.

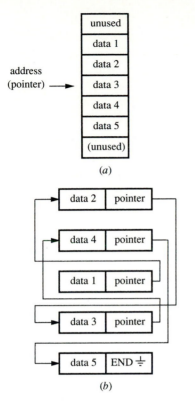

(a)

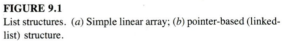

(b)

FIGURE 9.1
List structures. (a) Simple linear array; (b) pointer-based (linked-list) structure.

LINKED LISTS. An alternative data structure that facilitates the representation described above as well as overcomes the two deficiencies in (9-16a) and (9-16b) is the **linked list structure**. This is shown in Fig. 9.1b. Each member of the linked list structure contains a data cell as well as a pointer to (the address of) the next member.

Thus, memory for the linked list data structure can be allocated dynamically. In addition, ordered insertion and removal of data in this structure is possible by use of an unallocated memory location and modification of pointers.   (9-17)

Other aspects of the linked list structure include

1. The number of comparisions, on average, necessary to insert a new element (with currently m members) in a linked-list structure is

$$n_{\text{insert/remove}} = m/2 \qquad (9\text{-}18a)$$

2. Random retrieval of an element requires, on average,

$$n_{\text{retrieval}} = m/2 \qquad (9\text{-}18b)$$

comparisons.

3. The end of the list is indicated by a special type of pointer.   (9-18c)

Conversion of Graphical
Representations into Trees and Lists

MATRIX REPRESENTATION OF RELATIONS. Assume the entities, objects, concepts, and the relations that form a desired representation have been identified. One approach to developing a structured computer representation for the relations among objects is then to proceed as follows:

1. Number each object (which is a node) and thereby develop a set of numbered graph nodes indexed by [1...numobjects].
2. To represent the existence or absence of an edge between any two nodes in the set under relation R, develop an adjacency matrix with entries

$$ADJ[i,j] = \begin{cases} 1 \text{ if (i,j) in R} \\ \\ 0 \text{ if (i,j) not in R} \end{cases} \tag{9-19}$$

A 2-D data structure (specifically a numobjects × numobjects binary matrix) results from the 2-D structure defined in (9-19). Of course, the matrix will be converted to a 1-D or vector representation (usually by row or column concatenation) for storage in computer memory. Note that the implied directionality of the relation R precludes the adjacency matrix from being, in general, symmetric, unless R is a symmetric relation. If relation R is symmetric, we may store the corresponding symmetric adjacency matrix in upper or lower triangular form, thereby saving memory space.

The approach of (9-19), while conceptually straightforward, has several disadvantages:

1. The addition of new nodes to the representation is complex. (9-20a)
2. The representation only allows the storing of an *unlabeled digraph* (unless multiple matrices are used, one per relation). (9-20b)
3. Search through this structure is difficult. (9-20c)
4. The adjacency matrix, if sparse, occupies a lot of memory and stores little information. (9-20d)

ADJACENCY MATRIX EXTENSIONS. One modification, based upon (9-20d), is to develop a representation similar to the adjacency matrix that only keeps track of *edges*. This may not require the storing of all nodes. If we number the edges in the digraph, and create two 1-D arrays denoted from[] and to[] we store the digraph representation by filling in the above arrays according to the rule

if edge$_i$ (or arc$_i$) represents member (x, y) of relation R
then {make the following assignments}
```
        from [i]  := x;
        to [i]  := y
```
(9-21)

A structure may then be generated for all arcs in the digraph. Notice the direction relation R controlled by the from and to assignments. A horizontal "slice" through the representation of (9-21) introduces an important data structure, depicted below:

$$\text{arc}_i \Rightarrow \boxed{\quad \text{from node} \quad | \quad \text{to node} \quad} \qquad (9\text{-}22)$$

The data unit in (9-21) is defined as a "cell," and has two properties:

1. The cell is pointed to, indexed, or addressed by an arc or edge number.
2. The cell itself contains two data entries: the source (from) and destination (to) node names.

The difficulty with the representation of (9-22) is that it is not easy to determine what edges emanate from a certain node. Considerable (time-consuming) search may be necessary. Recall with the adjacency matrix approach of (9-19) that this could be determined by simply looking for entries along a certain row (or column, if it were necessary to find the edges that terminate at a particular node). A solution to this problem is to append a next [i] column to the representation for every from[i] to[i] entry.

next [i] contains the number of the next edge or arc after i or 0 if no such edge exists. (9-23)

Thus, each cell in the modified representation would look like

$$\text{arc}_i \Rightarrow \boxed{\quad \text{from node} \quad | \quad \text{to node} \quad | \quad \text{next node} \quad}$$
$$\quad (1) \qquad\qquad (2) \qquad\qquad (3) \qquad\qquad (4) \qquad (9\text{-}24)$$

Notice the middle two columns ((2) and (3)) in (9-24) are node numbers, whereas the outer two columns ((1) and (4)) contain arc (edge) numbers.

(9-24) is the traditional *linked list* approach for relation representation. It possesses several desirable features, the foremost of which is the capability to easily add and remove data items (in this case, edges). Thus, the size of the data structure need not be known a priori; it is able to grow or shrink as processing proceeds. Extensions to this concept, which facilitate other computations, are possible [Kolman/Busby 1984].

THE cons CELL AND BUILDING LISTS

The aforementioned linked-list approach has one shortcoming; it is "edge-centric," that is, the representation is built around the arcs or edges. We introduce a more useful linked-list structure which may be thought of as "node-centric." We begin by assuming the graphical representation is a type of binary tree. In terms of previous definitions, a binary tree is a tree where the maximum out-degree of any node is 2.

THE cons CELL.

Assume the existence of a particular cell-based entity called a cons. The cons is a two-element record structure consisting of two cells, a car cell and a cdr cell, respectively, as shown below: (9-25)

$$\boxed{\text{car} \mid \text{cdr}}$$

(9-26)

Note that we have implied that something (another cell, perhaps) may point to a cons. The car of the cons in (9-26) may contain anything (i.e., it may hold a symbol name, a value, or be a pointer) and the cdr of this cons is a pointer to other conses. In this extended representation, the basic element or cell may contain two pointers. A cdr cell that does not point to anything is said to contain nil. Conses containing nil in their cdr cells are the leaves of a binary tree.

A cons cell, represented graphically as a pair of pointers, forms the building block for a binary tree. (9-27)

Before looking at general ramifications of this data structure, an example is provided to help the reader gain familiarity with the concept.

Example 9.4 cons-**cell representation of "Jesse."** Suppose we wish to represent the cons consisting of the symbol name, Jesse, and his age, 3.5. Assume we derive a memory management strategy to accompany the cons structure and allow the "pointing" in terms of absolute memory addresses. For example, we could store the symbol name Jesse beginning at memory location 4, his age 3.5 at location 2, and beginning at location 5 we could store a cons consisting of the pair of addresses 4 and 2. The map of computer memory would appear as follows:

Address:	1	2	3	4	5	6
Contents:		3.5		Jesse	4	2

(9-28)

The diagrammatic representation of a cons shown in (9-29) suppresses the memory storage (i.e., address) details from (9-28). We hereafter assume those details are handled by the LISP compiler or interpreter.

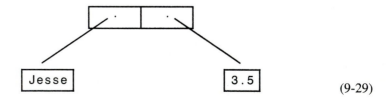

(9-29)

We may also represent cons es by a dot at the vertices in diagrams. This is an alternative representation used in LISP. For example,

(9-30)

conveys the same information as (9-29).

LISP "DOT" OR DOTTED-PAIR NOTATION. One of the linear representations recognized by most versions of LISP is the so-called dot notation. In **dot notation**, a cons is represented by a left parenthesis, a data item, a period, a data item, and a right parenthesis. For example, the cons in (9-30) is represented in dot notation as

(Jesse . 3.5) (9-31)

and in list notation as

(Jesse 3.5) (9-32)

A MORE COMPLETE REPRESENTATION (TERMINATING THE LIST WITH nil). At this point, the initial concept and utility of the cons construct has been explored. The above data structure and graphical interpretation are slightly incomplete, however. Note that due to the linked list structure, the computer implementation needs one additional feature, namely, a way to indicate when the end of a list has been reached. This is done by indicating the end of the list by a cons cell whose cdr points to nil. For example, the list

(a (b c) d) (9-33)

is more precisely represented as the following cons-based structure:

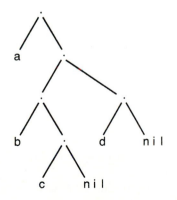

(9-34)

RELATIONSHIP TO LISP car AND cdr FUNCTIONS. With the modification of (9-34), the operation of the LISP list manipulation functions car and cdr is now less mysterious. With a cons-based internal representation, the car and cdr functions simply manipulate the pointers to the internal representations. For example, when we pass the s-expression

$$(\mathsf{cdr} \quad ' \quad (1 \quad 2 \quad 3))$$ (9-35)

to the eval function, all eval does is return what is pointed to by the right pointer of the cons node that represents this list. Thus, the left element of a cons is called the car of the cons and the right element is called the cdr of the cons.

EXTENSIONS USING THE cons CELL.

The elements of a cons can be any data object including another cons. (9-36)

For example, Jesse's last name can be included in our binary tree as

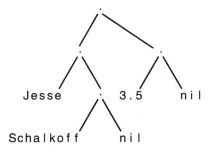

(9-37)

The equivalent dot notation representation of this tree is

$$((\mathsf{Jesse} \quad . \quad \mathsf{Schalkoff}) \quad . \quad 3 . 5)$$

and the list notation is

$$((\mathsf{Jesse} \quad \mathsf{Schalkoff}) \quad 3 . 5)$$ (9-38)

Notice in LISP nomenclature, the list

$$(\mathsf{Jesse} \quad \mathsf{Schalkoff})$$ (9-39)

is the car of the list represented in (9-37) and the list (3.5) is the corresponding cdr.

If we add the fact (or property) that **Jesse** is a dog to the binary tree:

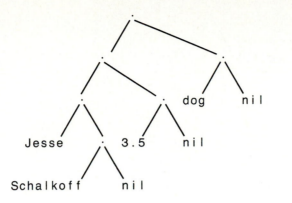

(9-40)

The tree is represented in dot notation as

$$(((Jesse \; . \; Schalkoff) \; . \; 3.5) \; . \; dog) \qquad (9\text{-}41)$$

An alternative binary tree structure for this information is the one corresponding to

$$((Jesse \; . \; Schalkoff) \; . \; (3.5 \; . \; dog)) \qquad (9\text{-}42)$$

which is shown below:

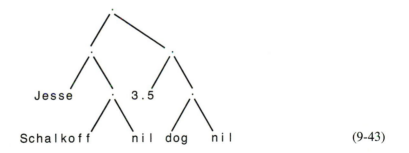

(9-43)

COLLECTIONS OF cons CELLS AS LISTS. From this discussion it should be clear that linked conses can be used to represent virtually any tree structured data. It is often most natural to represent a collection of conses as a list of data objects rather than as a deeply nested binary tree. Most versions of LISP represent a list as a linked collection of conses whose car cells point to the members of the lists and whose cdr cells point to the next cons. The linked list is terminated by a cdr cell that points to the symbol nil. For example, when the following binary tree—

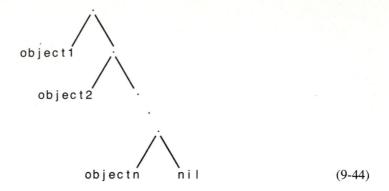

(9-44)

—is rearranged by a rotation, it is straightforward to see how it can be transformed into a cons-based list of data objects:

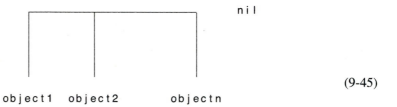

(9-45)

LISP (PRINTED) LIST REPRESENTATIONS. The linear structure of lists suggests an external printed representation that is much more readable than the equivalent dot notation representation. Thus most versions of LISP will automatically display the above object using list notation:

(object1 object2 ... objectn)   (9-46)

as opposed to the dot notation form

(object1 . (object2 . ... (objectn . nil) ...)) (9-47)

Most versions of LISP object display functions use list notation for both input and output. Dot notation is available, but it is cumbersome to a programmer who cares little about the internal representation. Thus, dot notation is used infrequently. It is useful to note:

> Any list can be reexpressed in dot notation. The converse is not true, that is, there are dotted pairs with no equivalent lists (the pair (a.b) is an example).   (9-48)

SUMMARY. Our look at binary relations spawned an interest in binary trees, which led to the linked list data representation concept. Hopefully, it is now clear that a list manipulation facility will lead to symbolic representations of relations that only require the computer to keep track of lists, represented internally as conses. Using the cons cell construct, the list structures necessary in LISP are implemented in a direct fashion.

MEMORY MANAGEMENT AND GARBAGE COLLECTION cons **CELLS IN LISP (OPTIONAL).** The dynamic nature of variable and function creation in LISP demands an efficient mechanism to determine if certain structures (variables and functions) are no longer applicable, and consequently the memory space they require may be released for use by other structures. This is a process known as **garbage collection** and is included in most LISP environments as an operation that is transparent to the programmer.

The creation (i.e., storage) of a cons cell requires computer memory. For example, hardware implementation of LISP statements such as

$$(setq \ name\_var \ some\_value) \qquad (9\text{-}49)$$

requires the allocation of memory to store the symbol name, value, and perhaps properties of the named LISP variable in (9-49). Furthermore,

$$(cons \ list1 \ list2 \ ...) \qquad (9\text{-}50)$$

involves creation of a new list, thereby requiring additional memory and/or modification of cons cells. In addition, statements such as

$$(defun \ name \ (... \qquad (9\text{-}51)$$

involve the reservation of memory locations to store symbol names and pointers relative to the creation (definition) of the function.

For these reasons, LISP dynamically allocates memory. At some point, given a fixed size (or upper limit) of available RAM, it is possible to run out of memory. To help alleviate this problem, LISP periodically invokes a procedure for garbage collection for deallocation of memory that is no longer needed. In the garbage collection process, (which is normally invoked automatically when the system runs out of available memory) the LISP system searches the current structure of memory looking for pointers to data structures that are no longer needed. These, for example, may represent local variables that were created using the do construct, while the corresponding function that included this do has long since been used and thus the variables have little present value. This is usually accomplished in a two stage process [Pleszkun/Thazhuthaveetil 1987] involving **garbage detection and garbage reclamation**. Garbage detection involves determining which memory cells are no longer applicable (i.e., have nothing pointing to them) and may be accomplished by using either *marking* or *reference counts*. Marking proceeds by tagging each cons cell known to be non-garbage (a so-called *root cell*). Following the pointer to other cons cells, these are in turn marked, until the nil cdr cell is encountered. At the conclusion of this process, all cons cells that have not been tagged are not accessible, and thus considered "garbage," and may be reclaimed. Note that at least one bit per memory cell must be allocated to facilitate this process. Reference counting, on the other hand, is accomplished, during the actual execution of the LISP program, by maintaining a count for every cons cell, of the number of pointers to it. When this count becomes zero, the cell is determined to be garbage. This approach requires the allocation of memory space for a counter for each cell, and involves significant overhead in that garbage collection is not aperiodic (as in marking, when, for example, the system runs out of memory space for new cons cells), but rather occurs continuously. Variations on these approaches are possible.

MONITORING MEMORY USAGE IN FranzLISP (OPTIONAL). Users of FranzLISP can observe the garbage collection process and explicitly invoke the garbage collection utility. For display, it is first necessary to set the value of the built-in FranzLISP variable $gcprint to non-nil, and then invoke the gc function, that is,

```
->(setq $gcprint t)
->(gc)                                                    (9-52)
```

whereupon garbage collection is initiated and relevant statistics are printed.

REFERENCES

[Cohen 1981] Cohen, J. "Garbage Collection of Linked Data Structures," *ACM Computing Surveys*, Vol. 13, No. 3, September 1981, p. 341–367.
[Kolman/Busby 1984] Kolman and Busby, *Discrete Mathematical Structures for Computer Science*, Prentice-Hall, 1984.
[Pleszkun/Thazhuthaveetil 1987] Pleszkun, A.R. and M.J. Thazhuthaveetil, "The Architecture of LISP Machines," *IEEE Computer*, Vol. 20, No. 3, March 1987, pp. 35–44.
[Willinsky 1984] Willinsky, R., *LispCraft*, W.W. Norton, 1984, (Chapter 15).

PROBLEMS

Problems 9.1 and 9.2 refer to the two sample fact and rule structures shown in Chapter 9 and repeated below, that is, the list-structured fact is

```
(fact 27   (entity auto)
           (has (wheels  owner  exterior interior  roof engine))
           (other_entries (car truck vehicle))
           (used_for (transportation status_symbol))]        (P9-1a)
```

and the sample rule developed in list form is

```
; Rule Structure

(setq arule

'(rule 43 (concerns (car auto mobile_home))
        (applicable_if (in vehicle frame))
        (antecedent_is
                (if ((? entity) has (wheels and owner and roof))))
        (production_is
                (then ((? entity) isa auto)))
        (alternate_productions
                (then ((? entity) isa mobile_home))
                (then ((? entity) isa truck)))
```

```
(further_information                              .
        (top_down (see transportation status_symbol))
        (bottom_up (see wheels driver owner)))
  (confidence (apply function auto_confidence))
  (update_rule (apply learning_function (number 32))]
```
(P9-1b)

9.1. Assume that the various fields of the rule in (P9-1b) may occur in any order. Derive and implement a function that returns the antecedent_is part of a rule in this form, without the if.

9.2. (a) Derive and implement a function that takes as input a rule (in the form of (P9-1b)) and returns a list consisting of the productions and the alternate_productions.
(b) Assume that a field may be repeated (e.g., alternate_productions may appear twice). Modify your results from (a) such that all occurrences of the field are returned.

9.3. Derive and implement a "user friendly" rule developer function that queries the user about the various slots of a rule and their contents and converts the user input into the rule structure shown in (P9-1b). The function returns the rule in the above form. Show your results using sample dialog with the function.

9.4. Consider the development of a LISP data and rulebase browsing function. Given either a list of facts or rules in the form of (P9-1), this function shows the user the structure of the fact or rule and then asks if a particular section should be printed.

9.5. Consider the extension of the list-structured fact in (P9-1a) to an elementary "frame," where each fact is comprised of slots, each containing values (Note: this value may be a list). A single fact may have an arbitrary ($\geq$ 1) number of slots. Each frame begins with the keyword frame, and the name of the frame. Each slot begins with the keyword slot and a slot name, and contains a list of entity-value pairs. Show a frame-based representation for the entity auto.

9.6. (Related to problem 9.5). Assume each frame has a slot entitled applicable_rules. Using the structure chosen in 9.5, develop and implement a function that, given a frame name, returns the list of applicable rules.

9.7. (Related to problem 9.5). Design and implement, as in problem 9.3, a "user friendly" frame developer function.

9.8. Consider the following structured fact representation in LISP where the descriptors has, used_for, and isa are randomly arranged in the description, for example,

```
(fact name    (has some_1    some_2    some_3 ...)
              (used_for something_1    something_2 ...)
              (isa other_1    other_2 ...)

                     .
                     .
                   . ]
```

(a) Develop and implement a function that takes as input a list of facts in the above form and returns all values of the used_for key.

(b) Develop and implement a second function that takes as input a list of facts in the above form and a value in one or more of the has slots, and returns the names of all facts that have a has slot with this value.

(c) ("Loose" implementation of inheritance). A LISP function that illustrates the use of inheritance (Chapter 16) is desired. We are given a list of facts of the form

```
->(setq facts '((fact  car  (has      wheel  owner   roof)
                            (used_for recreation
                                        tailgating)
                            (isa      vehicle))

                (fact  wheel  (has tire  lug-nuts)
                              (used_for   rolling))

                (fact  vehicle  (has driver  engine)
                                (isa
                                means_of_transportation))))]
```

(P9-8*a*)

Of the three relations has, used_for and isa, assume that has and isa are transitive. Develop a LISP function inherit (similar to that in (a) above) which takes as arguments the list of facts facts, a key which is one of the transitive relation names, and one of the fact-names (e.g., car). For example,

```
->(inherit  facts  isa  car)
```

should return

```
(vehicle  means_of_transportation)
```

and

```
->(inherit  facts  has  car)
```

should return

```
(wheel  owner  roof  tire  lug_nuts  driver  engine)   (P9-8b)
```

9.9. Consider the objective of determining whether an item is not a member of a list. Is this the same problem of determining list membership, or are there alternative formulations that are more computationally and search efficient?

9.10. Given a list of facts, each structured as in (P9-8*a*), design and implement a function that takes this fact list as input, and the name of a fact, and removes that fact from the list. (Note: this is similar to the effect of PROLOG remove predicate).

9.11. Show the binary-tree representation of each of the following:
(*a*) (this is a list)
(*b*) (this is (a list))
(*c*) ((this is) a list)
(*d*) ((this is) (a list))

9.12. Show the binary-tree representation of fact27 and rule43 from (P9-1).

9.13. The purpose of this problem is to develop a structured LISP database and related functions that are used to extract relevant facts from the database. We restrict attention here to simple queries, that is, we do not invoke relation properties or inference to generate additional facts. It also serves as a basis for several concepts in Chapter 16. Consider the following database:

```
(setq    database    '(
              (isa          ibm–pc        computer)
              (has–part     computer      terminal)
              (has–part     computer      keyboard)
              (has–part     computer      RAM      )
              (has–part     computer      ROM      )
              (isa          ncr–pc8       computer)
              (has–part     ibm–pc        proprietary–rom)
              (has–part     ncr           proprietary–rom)
              (has–part     ibm–pc        pc–dos   )
              (has–part     ncr           ms–dos   )
              (isa          pc–dos        operating–system)
              (isa          ms–dos        operating–system)]
```

Develop a LISP function (or set of functions) that allows us to query database and determine
(a) parts of entities, given a specific entity, that is,

```
(has–parts 'ibm–pc database)
```

should return

```
(proprietary–rom    pc–dos)
```

(b) entities that have specific parts, that is,

```
(what–has    'keyboard    database)
```

should return

```
(computer)
```

(c) what an entity is, that is,

```
(a–kind–of 'operating system database)
```

should return

```
(pc–dos ms–dos)
```

9.14. Develop a LISP function f f ⎽ g e t ⎽ f i e l d which allows the query of a list-structured rule in "free form," that is, a rule in which fields are optional. The general form of a rule is therefore

```
(rule name    <various fields>)
```

where the c a r of each of the <various fields> is the name of a field (e.g., antecedent⎽is). For example, if f f ⎽ g e t ⎽ f i e l d is applied to a rule seeking a field that does not exist, no⎽field is returned. Otherwise, the c d r of the field is returned by f f ⎽ g e t ⎽ f i e l d.

10

MATCHING AND UNIFICATION IN LISP—A PRELUDE TO RULE-BASED INFERENCE

"All we know is infinitely less than all that still remains unknown."

William Harvey 1578–1657
De Motu Cordis et Sanguinis [1628], dedication to
Doctor Argent and Other Learned Physicians

INTRODUCTION

The Need for Matching

As we discovered in Chapter 2 and in our use of PROLOG,

> The process of unification is fundamentally based upon a carefully designed matching algorithm. (10-1)

In this chapter, we develop and examine a myriad of possible matching functions in LISP. We do this not to simply study matching, nor for practice in LISP program development, but rather for the following reason:

> Matching is fundamental to pattern-directed inference, and is a major component of a rule-based inference system. (10-2)

Once list-based rule and fact structures have been chosen and the corresponding functions necessary to extract components of these structures (e.g., the antecedent portion of a rule) have been developed, we are ready to implement inference strategies. Matching of rule antecedents (and later, rule consequents, in the backwards chaining formulations) with a database of facts (in list form) is integral to the implementation of the inference strategy. For example, given a database of facts written in list notation, suppose we wish to determine the truth of the statement:

$$(\texttt{relay 5 is stuck}) \tag{10-3}$$

An obvious starting point is to attempt to match this list-form statement with each of the statements in a given database. This database could be a list whose elements themselves are lists of the form of (10-3). In this way, all we need to do is implement a means to look up, or "remember," a fact. In addition, suppose we wanted to know if *any* relay is stuck; this could be accomplished in a similar manner using a matching process that is insensitive to certain parts (members) of the list-based statement in (10-3).

Thus, in what follows, we explore extensively the matching of list-based structures. We begin with some preliminary notes:

1. Due to the fact that the size of the lists under consideration is seldom constant (as noted in Chapter 3, AI data structures are dynamic) or known a priori, matching approaches that allow for varying list sizes are desirable. This is one reason for the use of recursion in the matching algorithms.
2. The efficiency, computational requirements, and potential for parallel implementation of the matching algorithms warrants investigation.
3. The implementation of unification (Chapter 2) requires we match with consistent variable bindings. This complicates the development of a general matcher (i.e., a matching algorithm for all cases). Fortunately, subsets of the general matcher often suit our purposes for the type of unification required in pattern-directed inference.

A Hierarchy of Matching Problems

We will consider matching in a hierarchical manner, proceeding from easily understood, simple pattern matchers, to a set of fairly sophisticated matching schemes that are suitable parts of a rule-based inference system. A hierarchy of matching problems involves six cases:

case 1. Simple (non-variable) list matchers. $\tag{10-4a}$

case 2. List matchers with "don't cares," which allow some flexibility in the matching process. $\tag{10-4b}$

case 3. Matchers with variables. Three cases in increasing complexity are of interest: $\tag{10-4c}$

  (i) Each variable appears only once and in only one of the two lists. We return variable bindings resulting from the match, if successful.
  (ii) Variables appear only in one list, but variable names may be repeated.

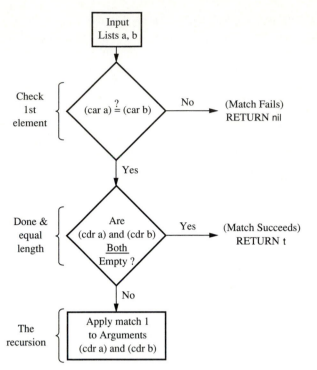

FIGURE 10.1
Strategy for simple matching algorithms-function match1.

(iii) Variables may occur in either list and also appear more than once in each list. In this (more complicated) case the consistent interpretation of variable bindings and the elimination of "circularities" in the matching process become paramount. This renews our interest in unification.

case 4. Non-variable matching of lists that are themselves members of a larger list, for example, a database of lists. (10-4d)

case 5. Variable matching in 4. (10-4e)

case 6. Matching where the matching process produces "side effects," for example, when the checking of a certain term in the matching process causes invocation of a function. (10-4f)

THE SIMPLEST MATCHER IN LISP

CASES 1 AND 4. We begin with the design of the matching algorithm required by case 1 (10-4a). Referring to the flowchart of Fig. 10.1, notice that this may be accomplished in a straightforward manner by only considering the criteria for success, that is, the lists must all have the same elements (in order) and must be of equal length. A matcher suitable for a pair of lists of arbitrary length is easily designed via recursion and checking for the (simultaneous) end of the lists.

A LISP definition of a simple function match1 is given below (note def is another name for defun):

Example 10.1   LISP matcher for case 1 (match1 **definition**).

```
(defun match1 (a b)
     (if (not (equal (car a) (car b)))
          nil
          (if (and (null (cdr a)) (null (cdr b))) t
               (match1 (cdr a) (cdr b)))))        (10-5)
```

Note the use of two nested if statements to implement the algorithm of Fig. 10.1. The operation of this matcher is shown below.

Example 10.2 match1 **operation.** First, we create several lists to be used in the matching process:

```
-> (setq a '(1 2 3))
(1 2 3)

-> (setq b '(1 2 3))
(1 2 3)

-> (setq c '(1 2 4))
(1 2 4)


-> (match1 a b)
t
-> (match1 a c)
nil                                              (10-6)
```

A trace of the operation of match1 is shown in the following example. Note the use of recursion.

Example 10.3   Detailed trace of match1.

```
-> (trace match1)
[autoload /usr/lib/lisp/trace]
[fasl /usr/lib/lisp/trace.o]
(match1)

 -> (match1 a b)
1 <Enter> match1 ((1 2 3) (1 2 3))
|2 <Enter> match1 ((2 3) (2 3))
| 3 <Enter> match1 ((3) (3))
| 3 <EXIT>  match1   t
|2 <EXIT>  match1   t
1 <EXIT>  match1   t
t

 -> (match1 a c)
1 <Enter> match1 ((1 2 3) (1 2 4))
```

```
|2 <Enter> match1 ((2 3) (2 4))
| 3 <Enter> match1 ((3) (4))
| 3 <EXIT>  match1   nil
|2 <EXIT>  match1   nil
1 <EXIT>  match1   nil
nil
```
(10-7)

Note that match1 may also be used with lists whose elements are lists (case 4). This is considered further in a later section. Examples 10.4 and 10.5 show this application of match1.

Example 10.4   Matching of lists with match1.

```
-> (setq a1 '(a (b c) d e))
(a (b c) d e)

-> (setq b1 '(a (b c) d e))
(a (b c) d e)

-> (setq c1 '(a b c d e))
(a b c d e)
```
(10-8)

Example 10.5   Detailed trace of Example (10.4).

```
-> (match1 a1 b1)
1 <Enter> match1 ((a (b c) d e) (a (b c) d e))
|2 <Enter> match1 (((b c) d e) ((b c) d e))
| 3 <Enter> match1 ((d e) (d e))
| |4 <Enter> match1 ((e) (e))
| |4 <EXIT>  match1   t
| 3 <EXIT>  match1   t
|2 <EXIT>  match1   t
1 <EXIT>  match1   t
t


-> (match1 a1 c1)
1 <Enter> match1 ((a (b c) d e) (a b c d e))
|2 <Enter> match1 (((b c) d e) (b c d e))
|2 <EXIT>  match1   nil
1 <EXIT>  match1   nil
nil
```
(10-9)

MATCHING WITH "DON'T CARES"

CASE 2. A rationale for our interest in a case 2 matcher was presented in the introduction. The design of this matcher in LISP also serves as a prelude to matching involving variables. The design is approached as an extension of the previously developed function match1, using an auxiliary function.

Example 10.6   Case 2 matching. Consider the operation of match1 on the following lists

```
A = (relay 5 is stuck)
B = (relay 6 is stuck)                                              (10-10)
```

Clearly match1 returns nil, that is, failure, given these two lists as input. Suppose, instead, we wished to match the lists

```
A = (relay (* any) is stuck)
B = (relay 6 is stuck)                                              (10-11)
```

where (* any) is an element of list A, and is used to signify that any match with this element and the corresponding element of B is acceptable. In other words, we only care about knowing if any relay is stuck, not which particular one.

MODIFICATION OF match1. Referring to the function definition of match1 in (10-5), we modify the comparison of the cars of the function arguments to be less stringent using auxiliary function matchable. This approach (i.e., the defining of a new function) may seem at first an unnecessarily lengthy extension of match1, however, it represents structured and incremental LISP program development in the sense that we develop the desired function in a hierarchical fashion and then address the details of the auxiliary functions. We thus modify match1 to create match2 for matching case 2 as follows:

Example 10.7   LISP function match2 **(case 2).**

```
(defun match2 (a b)
     (if (not (matchable (car a) (car b)))
         nil
         (if (and (null (cdr a)) (null (cdr b))) t
             (match2 (cdr a) (cdr b))))) (10-12)
```

The next task is to design function matchable that embodies the (current) notion of similarity or "matchability" in the matching process. This is done as follows:

Example 10.8   LISP function matchable.

```
(defun matchable (a1 b1)
     (if (or (equal a1 b1)
             (and (listp a1) (equal (car a1) '*))
             (and (listp b1) (equal (car b1) '*)))
         t
         nil)) (10-13)
```

As the (almost) self-explanatory code indicates, matchable works by considering both the verbatim (no "don't cares") match and the case where either corresponding element in the list (or both) is the don't care symbol, denoted by the list (* any). This notation is extended later for the matching of lists containing variables.

Operation of the newly modified matchable function is illustrated in example 10.9.

Example 10.9 **Operation of function** matchable.

```
-> (setq a '(* any))
(* any)

-> (setq b 'b)
b

-> (matchable a b)
t

-> (matchable 'c 'c)
t

-> (matchable 'c 'd)
nil

-> (matchable '(* any) '(* any2))
t

-> (matchable 'd '(* any))
t                                                        (10-14)
```

A trace of the joint operation of the functions match2 and matchable is shown in example 10.10. The reader is encouraged to become comfortable with these examples since they represent a prelude to the general matching approach.

Example 10.10 **Detailed** trace of match2 operation.

```
-> (setq a '(a b c))
(a b c)

-> (setq b '(a b (* any)))
(a b (* any))

-> (setq c '(a b d))
(a b d)

-> (match2 a b)
|1 <Enter> matchable (a a)
|1 <EXIT>  matchable   t
|1 <Enter> matchable (b b)
|1 <EXIT>  matchable   t
|1 <Enter> matchable (c (* any))
|1 <EXIT>  matchable   t
t
```

```
-> (match2 a c)
|1 <Enter> matchable (a a)
|1 <EXIT>  matchable   t
|1 <Enter> matchable (b b)
|1 <EXIT>  matchable   t
|1 <Enter> matchable (c d)
|1 <EXIT>  matchable   nil
nil                                                    (10-15)
```

Finally, we apply match2 to the problem previously stated in (10-11).

```
-> (match2 '(relay (* any) is stuck) '(relay 5 is stuck))
t                                                      (10-16)
```

A more complete picture of the matching process is shown below.

Example 10.11   **(Detailed trace of matchable).**

```
-> (trace match2 matchable)

-> (match2 '(relay (* any) is stuck) '(relay 5 is stuck))
1 <Enter> match2 ((relay (* any) is stuck) (relay 5 is stuck))
|1 <Enter> matchable (relay relay)
|1 <EXIT>  matchable   t
|2 <Enter> match2 (((* any) is stuck) (5 is stuck))
|  1 <Enter> matchable ((* any) 5)
|  1 <EXIT>  matchable   t
|  3 <Enter> match2 ((is stuck) (is stuck))
|  |1 <Enter> matchable (is is)
|  |1 <EXIT>  matchable   t
|  |4 <Enter> match2 ((stuck) (stuck))
|  |  1 <Enter> matchable (stuck stuck)
|  |  1 <EXIT>  matchable   t
|  |4 <EXIT>  match2   t
|  3 <EXIT>  match2   t
|2 <EXIT>  match2   t
1 <EXIT>  match2   t
t                                                      (10-17)
```

A subtle bug exists in this definition of match2. For example, the reader should trace the following match (see the problems):

```
-> (match2 '(a) '(a (* any)))
t                                                      (10-18)
```

MATCHING WITH VARIABLES AND BINDINGS

CASE 3. At this point, the reader may abandon further matching concerns and proceed directly to Chapter 11 for the development of rule-based inference mechanisms in

LISP (as long as facts and rules do not contain variables). In certain applications this is sufficient, and is treated as the first case in Chapter 11. However, realizing the power gained by allowing rules to represent more general cases via the incorporation of variables, we consider several additional and more complex matching scenarios. The reader is encouraged to review the unification algorithm in Chapter 2.

Matching with variables (case 3) must take into account the bindings on variables that may have occurred in previous matches. In LISP, we use a binding list to keep track of these variable bindings. New bindings augment the binding list; subsequent matching attempts involving variables require consultation of this list to check for bindings, if any.

$$(10\text{-}19a)$$

In the matching process, the current state of variable bindings is defined as the current system environment.

$$(10\text{-}19b)$$

In what follows, generalizations of the matching algorithms are analyzed.

Example 10.12   Denoting variables in lists. Hereafter, variables in lists are denoted by the structure

$$(?var? <var\_name>) \tag{10-20a}$$

where <var_name> is the symbolname of a particular variable. Note the use of ?var?, as opposed to the don't care symbol (*), to distinguish between the two cases. Therefore,

$$(?var? this\_var) \tag{10-20b}$$

is a variable and

$$(this list contains a (?var? variable)) \tag{10-20c}$$

is a sample list whose last element is, with the definition of (10-20a), a variable.

THE BINDING LIST. Recall from Chapter 2 we denoted binding variable V1 to value val_1 via

$$val\_1/V1 \tag{10-20d}$$

Similarly, binding variable V1 to variable V2 is denoted

$$V2/V1 \tag{10-20e}$$

regardless of whether V2 has a value (is itself bound). In LISP, it is convenient to record bindings via a binding list, of the form

$$((var\_name_1 \ binding_1) \ (var\_name_2 \quad binding_2) \ \dots$$
$$(var\_name_n \ binding_n)) \tag{10-20f}$$

where `var_name`$_i$ is the name of a variable (denoted by (`?var? var_name`$_i$)) and `binding`$_i$ is the binding on `var_name`$_i$. Note `binding`$_i$ may be a value or another variable name, that is, `var_name`$_j$. As we will soon show, LISP functions to manipulate the binding list are essential to the matching process.

CHARACTERIZATION OF THE EXTENDED MATCHING ALGORITHM. First, the matching of two lists (denoted a and b, below) containing variables (without any previous bindings) is considered. The function that accomplishes this matching must return

1. t (true) if the matching is successful and no bindings are created. (The binding list in this case is empty.) This may occur if only nonvariables (constants and don't cares) are members of the lists or if the same variable is matched against itself.
2. The binding list in the form of (10-20f), if the match is successful and bindings result. Thus, we not only desire a value of t or nil from the matching function, but also require a list of the resulting variable bindings if the match (unification) succeeds.
3. nil if the match is unsuccessful.

In contrast to the previous matching functions, we must now observe the constraint that a variable, once bound (either directly or indirectly) to a value must be used in subsequent attempted matches with this value. In other words, the variable may not take on a second value.

Example 10.13 Desired result.

A matching function applied to the lists

A = (the (?var? var1) is stuck)

B = (the relay is stuck)   (10-21a)

should return the binding

relay/var1   (10-21b)

or, in binding list form,

((var1 relay))

In contrast, the matcher, given the arguments

A = (the (?var? var1) is stuck)

B = (a relay is stuck)   (10-21c)

must return a value of nil.

Limited Matching Using match-var without Checking Prior Bindings

CASE 3(i). In this section a matching function is designed to accomplish the objectives stated above. We restrict the applicability of the matcher with the following assumptions:

1. Variables are only allowed in the first list.

2. Variables are not replicated (thus, inconsistent bindings are not possible).

3. A list of the variable bindings, if the match is successful, is returned.

The design of this function follows and extends the don't care matcher (match2, (10-12)), and is relatively straightforward. The overall structure is shown first via a "long" cond, in (10-22).

Example 10.14 match-var **definition.**

```
;input   lists a, b, and binding list
;output nil if match fails
        ;binding-list if non nil
        ;t if successful + no bindings
(defun match-var (a b binding-list)
    (cond ((both-empty a b); end of both lists
            (if (null binding-list) t binding-list))
                ;report success and no bindings
                                        ;otherwise
                                        return
                                        binding list
        ((or (null a) (null b)) nil) ;unequal lengths
        ((equal (car a) (car b))
                    (match-var (cdr a) (cdr b)
                    binding-list)) ;continue match
                    without more bindings
        ((atom (car a)) nil) ;must be a variable at this
                        point or fails
        ((equal (caar a) '?var?) ;check for variable
        (match-var (cdr a) (cdr b)
            (augment-binding-list (cadar a) (car b)
                        binding-list)))))
```

$$(10\text{-}22)$$

The reader should note the continued use of recursion in match-var and is encouraged to verify the operation of this function.

In match-var we employ the auxiliary function augment-binding-list:

Example 10.15 Auxiliary functions in match-var. In match-var, function both-empty checks for the simultaneous end of two lists:

```
(defun both-empty (a b)
    (and (null a) (null b)))
```

$$(10\text{-}23)$$

```
(defun augment-binding-list(var-name value prev-list)
    (append prev-list (list (list var-name value))))   (10-24)
```

Sample operation of augment-binding-list is shown in (10-25).

Example 10.16 (augment-binding-list operation).

```
-> (setq prev-list '((relay 5)]
((relay 5))

-> (augment-binding-list 'relay '6 prev-list)
((relay 5) (relay 6))                                  (10-25)
```

We now trace the operation of match-var with a few sample cases.

Example 10.17 (match-var operation).

```
-> (match-var '(a b c) '( a b c) nil)
|2 <Enter> match-var ((a b c) (a b c) nil)
| 1 <Enter> both-empty ((a b c) (a b c))
| 1 <EXIT>  both-empty  nil
| 3 <Enter> match-var ((b c) (b c) nil)
| |1 <Enter> both-empty ((b c) (b c))
| |1 <EXIT>  both-empty  nil
| |4 <Enter> match-var ((c) (c) nil)
| | 1 <Enter> both-empty ((c) (c))
| | 1 <EXIT>  both-empty  nil
| | 5 <Enter> match-var (nil nil nil)
| | |1 <Enter> both-empty (nil nil)
| | |1 <EXIT>  both-empty  t
| | 5 <EXIT>  match-var  t
| |4 <EXIT>  match-var  t
| 3 <EXIT>  match-var  t
|2 <EXIT>  match-var  t
t

-> (match-var '(a b c) '(a b d) nil)
|2 <Enter> match-var ((a b c) (a b d) nil)
| 1 <Enter> both-empty ((a b c) (a b d))
| 1 <EXIT>  both-empty  nil
| 3 <Enter> match-var ((b c) (b d) nil)
| |1 <Enter> both-empty ((b c) (b d))
| |1 <EXIT>  both-empty  nil
| |4 <Enter> match-var ((c) (d) nil)
| | 1 <Enter> both-empty ((c) (d))
| | 1 <EXIT>  both-empty  nil
| |4 <EXIT>  match-var  nil
| 3 <EXIT>  match-var  nil
|2 <EXIT>  match-var  nil
nil
```

```
-> (setq list_a '(the (?var? var1) is stuck))
(the (?var? var1) is stuck)

-> (setq list_b '(the relay is stuck))
(the relay is stuck)

-> (match-var a_list b_list nil)
1 <Enter> match-var ((the (?var? var1) is stuck)
                     (the relay is stuck) nil)
|1 <Enter> both-empty ((the (?var? var1) is stuck)
                       (the relay is stuck))
|1 <EXIT>  both-empty  nil
|2 <Enter> match-var (((?var? var1) is stuck)
                      (relay is stuck) nil)
| 1 <Enter> both-empty (((?var? var1) is stuck)
                        (relay is stuck))
| 1 <EXIT>  both-empty  nil
| 1 <Enter> augment-binding-list (var1 relay nil)
| 1 <EXIT>  augment-binding-list  ((var1 relay))
| 3 <Enter> match-var ((is stuck) (is stuck) ((var1 relay)))
| |1 <Enter> both-empty ((is stuck) (is stuck))
| |1 <EXIT>  both-empty  nil
| |4 <Enter> match-var ((stuck) (stuck) ((var1 relay)))
| | 1 <Enter> both-empty ((stuck) (stuck))
| | 1 <EXIT>  both-empty  nil
| | 5 <Enter> match-var (nil nil ((var1 relay)))
| | |1 <Enter> both-empty (nil nil)
| | |1 <EXIT>  both-empty  t
| | 5 <EXIT>  match-var  ((var1 relay))
| |4 <EXIT>  match-var  ((var1 relay))
| 3 <EXIT>  match-var  ((var1 relay))
|2 <EXIT>  match-var  ((var1 relay))
1 <EXIT>  match-var  ((var1 relay))
((var1 relay))

-> (match-var '(a) '(a (?var? any-name)) nil))
|2 <Enter> match-var ((a) (a (?var? any-name)) nil)
| 1 <Enter> both-empty ((a) (a (?var? any-name)))
| 1 <EXIT>  both-empty  nil
| 3 <Enter> match-var (nil ((?var? any-name)) nil)
| |1 <Enter> both-empty (nil ((?var? any-name)))
| |1 <EXIT>  both-empty  nil
| 3 <EXIT>  match-var  nil
|2 <EXIT>  match-var  nil
nil
```

(10-26)

Matching with Checking and Adding of Bindings

CASE 3(ii). We continue our development of matching algorithms involving variables by allowing repeated variable names in the first list. (The second list still does not contain variables). We not only *add* bindings when matching with variable elements, but also *check* bindings. We show first a simple version of the matcher, with auxiliary functions, and then proceed to a generalization.

Example 10.18   Function to check binding list (get-binding1).

```
;first binding function

(defun get-binding1 (key b-list)
;searches for key in b-list where
;key is the first element of a sublist in b-list
  (cond
    ((null b-list) nil)
    ((equal key (caar b-list)) (cadar b-list))
    (t (get-binding1 key (cdr b-list)))))))
```
(10-27)

The reader should examine function get-binding1 carefully to determine its operation. It is similar to a built-in LISP function assoc, which we will employ in the general unifier. Sample operation of get-binding1 is shown in example 10.20.

Example 10.19   match-var2 function definition—case 3(ii).

```
;the main matching function

(defun match-var2 (a b bindings)
;match two lists with possible repeated variables
;in first list
  (cond
    ((both-empty a b)
       (if (null bindings) t bindings))
;simultaneous end of both list w/o failure
    ((or (equal (car a) (car b))
         (and
           (listp (car a))
    (equal (caar a) '?var?)
           (not (null (car b)))   ;2nd list empty
           (equal (car b) (get-binding1 (cadar a) bindings)))))
     (match-var2 (cdr a) (cdr b) bindings))
;checks to see if previously bound and consistent match
    ((and
       (listp (car a))
       (equal (caar a) '?var?) ; checks to see if a variable
       (not (null (car b))) ; ran out of 2nd list
       (not (get-binding1 (cadar a) bindings)))
;no prior binding - add it and go on
       (match-var2 (cdr a) (cdr b)
                   (cons (list (cadar a) (car b)) bindings)))
;if none of the above, return fail
    (t nil)))
```
(10-28)

Example 10.20 match-var2 **and** get-binding1 **operation.**

match-var2

```
->(setq a '(this (?var? Thing) is (?var? What)))
->(setq b '(this class is boring))
-> a
(this (?var? Thing) is (?var? What))
-> b
(this class is boring)

-> (match-var2 a b ())
((What boring) (Thing class))

-> (setq a1 '(if (?var? A) is_a (?var? B) and (?var? B)
            is_a (?var? C) then (?var? A) is_a (?var? C)))

(if (?var? A) is_a (?var? B) and (?var? B) is_a (?var? C)
                then (?var? A) is_a (?var? C))

-> (setq b1 '(if flip_flop is_a chip and chip is_a
    electronic_device then flip_flop is_a electronic_device))

(if flip_flop is_a chip and chip is_a electronic_device
                then flip_flop is_a electronic_device)

-> (match-var2 a1 b1 ())
((C electronic_device) (B chip) (A flip_flop))
-> (setq c1 '(if my_flip_flop is_a chip and chip is_a
    electronic_device then flip_flop is_a electronic_device))

(if my_flip_flop is_a chip and chip is_a electronic_device
                then flip_flop is_a electronic_device)

-> (match-var2 a1 c1 ())
nil
```

Sample use of get-binding1

```
-> (setq bindings (match-var2 a b ()))
((What boring) (Thing class))
-> bindings
((What boring) (Thing class))
-> (get-binding1 'What bindings)
boring
-> (get-binding1 'Thing bindings)
class
-> (get-binding1 'Who bindings)
nil
-> (get-binding1 '(this class is boring) bindings)
nil
```
(10-29)

Function match-var2, while useful, is merely an incremental step towards the general unifier, which we now consider.

A MORE GENERAL UNIFIER STRUCTURE—CASE 3(ii). The unifier developed below unifies two lists in a prespecified binding environment (which may initially be nil). The environment is specified via a slightly modified binding list in the form of ((X a) (Y b) (empty)), where X and Y are variable names and a and b are the corresponding values. The last element in the binding list, which is a list with only one element, namely (empty), is used to distinguish the case where two lists are matched successfully without any resultant bindings and where the match of two lists fails. Thus, ((empty)) is used to signify matching success with an empty binding list. Assume, initially, only the first list contains variables.

Example 10.21   LISP functions for checking variables and bindings.

```
(defun var (x)  ;checks if ''x'' is a variable.
  (if (and (listp x) (equal (car x) '?var?)) x nil))

(defun get-binding (x bindings)
  ;get binding for ''x'' from ''bindings.''
  ;if ''x'' is not a variable, return x.
  (let ((tmp (and x (var x)
                 (get-binding (cadr (assoc (cadr x) bindings))
                              bindings))))
    (if tmp tmp x)))                                          (10-30)
```

get-binding is a more sophisticated function than get-binding1. Specifically, it tests to see if variables, bound to other variables, actually have values. The power of function get-binding is perhaps hidden in its compactness. This is illustrated in example 10.22.

Notice get-binding uses the LISP macro let and function assoc, described in Appendix 3. assoc has the general form

(assoc exp assoc-list)

where exp is an expression (which gets evaluated) and is used as a key to the search of association list, assoc-list. The first element of assoc-list whose car matches exp is returned. The assoc function is common to both FranzLISP and CommonLISP. assoc assumes assoc-list is in the form of an *association list*, where each element of assoc-list is a two-element list, whose car is matched against key. If a match is found, this element (i.e., sublist) is returned as the value of assoc.

Since our binding list is organized in this form, that is,

((<var_name_1> <value1>) (<var_name_2> <value2>) ...)

get-binding uses the LISP assoc function to retrieve the value bound to <var_name_i>, if one exists.

Example 10.22 **Sample** assoc-list **and** get-binding **use.**

```
assoc

-> (setq assoc-list '((my-computer ncr-pc6) (my-computer
                                                 ibm-pc)
(other-computer at&t&t]

((my-computer ncr) (my-computer ibm-pc) (other-computer
                                          at&t&t))

-> (assoc 'my-computer assoc-list)
(my-computer ncr)
-> (assoc 'other-computer assoc-list)
(other-computer at&t&t)                                    (10-31)
```

var *and Simple Application of* get-binding

```
-> (var '(?var? x))
(?var? x)

-> (var 'a)
nil

-> (var '(this is (?var? What)))
nil

-> (trace get-binding)

-> (get-binding '(?var? x) '((x a) (empty)))

1 <Enter> get-binding ((?var? x) ((x a) (empty)))
  {notice second check of bindings on x here}
|2 <Enter> get-binding (a ((x a) (empty)))
|2 <EXIT>  get-binding  a
1 <EXIT>   get-binding  a
a
-> (get-binding 'a '((empty)))
1 <Enter> get-binding (a ((empty)))
1 <EXIT>   get-binding  a
a
```

The recursive operation of get-binding is shown in the following example, where the binding list contains a variable bound to another variable, specifically C/B.

Example 10.23 **More complex use of** get-binding.

```
-> unify-result
((C const-2) (D const-1) (B (?var? C)) (A const-0) (empty))
-> (get-binding '(?var? B) unify-result)
const-2
```

A more complete trace of this behavior follows:

```
-> (get-binding '(?var? B) unify-result)
1 <Enter> get-binding ((?var? B) ((C const-2) (D const-1)
  (B (?var? C)) (A const-0) (empty)))
|2 <Enter> get-binding ((?var? C) ((C const-2) (D const-1)
    (B (?var? C)) (A const-0) (empty)))
| 3 <Enter> get-binding (const-2 ((C const-2) (D const-1)
    (B (?var? C)) (A const-0) (empty)))
| 3 <EXIT>  get-binding  const-2
|2 <EXIT>   get-binding  const-2
1 <EXIT>   get-binding  const-2
const-2
```

Example 10.24 unify1 **function definition.**

```
(defun unify1 (x y bindings)
;unifies lists 'x' and 'y' with 'bindings'
; only variables allowed in first list
  (cond
    ((equal (setq x (get-binding x bindings)) y) bindings)
     ; 1) get a binding for 'x'. if it is equal to 'y',
                             return with 'bindings.'
    ((var x) (cons (list (cadr x) y) bindings))
     ; 2) unbound variable 'x' is bound to 'y', revised
                             'bindings' returned.
    ((atom x) nil)
     ; 3) if 'x' is not a variable and not equal to y,
                             return nil.
    ((setq bindings (unify1 (car x) (car y) bindings))
     ; 4) unify the first element then proceed recursively.
    (unify1 (cdr x) (cdr y) bindings))))          (10-32)
```

unify1 illustrates the compactness of LISP programming that may be achieved using recursive and nested functions. Notice in the third and fourth arguments to cond in (10-32) that unify1 is used recursively, with the current binding list passed at each recursive step.

Several examples using the unifier and auxiliary functions are shown below. unify1 is a basic element of the forward-chaining system, which allows variables in rules, developed in Chapter 11 (Example 11.17).

Example 10.25 unify1 **application.**

```
-> (setq x '(this (?var? Thing) is (?var? What)))
(this (?var? Thing) is (?var? What))

-> (setq y '(this class is boring))
(this class is boring)

-> (setq bindings '((empty)))
((empty))
```

```
-> (unify1 x y bindings)
1 <Enter> unify1 ((this (?var? Thing) is (?var? What))
                                  (this class is boring)
                                         ((empty)))
;2 <Enter> unify1 (this this ((empty)))
;2 <EXIT>  unify1  ((empty))
;2 <Enter> unify1 (((?var? Thing) is (?var? What))
                                  (class is boring) ((empty)))
; 3 <Enter> unify1 ((?var? Thing) class ((empty)))
; 3 <EXIT>  unify1  ((Thing class) (empty))
; 3 <Enter> unify1 ((is (?var? What)) (is boring) ((Thing class)
                                         (empty)))
; ;4 <Enter> unify1 (is is ((Thing class) (empty)))
; ;4 <EXIT>  unify1  ((Thing class) (empty))
; ;4 <Enter> unify1 (((?var? What)) (boring) ((Thing class)
                                         (empty)))
; ; 5 <Enter> unify1 ((?var? What) boring ((Thing class)
                                         (empty)))
; ; 5 <EXIT>  unify1  ((What boring) (Thing class) (empty))
; ; 5 <Enter> unify1 (nil nil ((What boring) (Thing class)
                                         (empty)))
; ; 5 <EXIT>  unify1  ((What boring) (Thing class) (empty))
; ;4 <EXIT>  unify1  ((What boring) (Thing class) (empty))
; 3 <EXIT>  unify1  ((What boring) (Thing class) (empty))
;2 <EXIT>   unify1  ((What boring) (Thing class) (empty))
1 <EXIT>   unify1  ((What boring) (Thing class) (empty))
((What boring) (Thing class) (empty))                      (10-33)
```

THE GENERAL UNIFIER

CASE 3(iii). unify1, a derivative of match−var2, is extended in this section. Our interest is focused on the development of a more general unifier, namely one that allows input lists with the following characteristics:

1. Either list may contain variables.
2. Variables may appear more than once in either list.   (10-34)

> **Example 10.26 Desired general unifier operation.** We wish to consider a match of the lists
>
> ```
> (region1 (?var? prop1) region2 which (?var? prop2)
>                                  (?var? name1))     (10-35a)
> ```
>
> and
>
> ```
> (region1 is_connected_to (?var? name1) which (?var? prop1)
>                                  region2)
> ```
> (10-35b)

The reader should verify that the matcher should return t and the bindings

```
is_connected_to/prop1,  region2/name,  is_connected_to/prop2
```
$$(10\text{-}35c)$$

or, in binding list form:

```
((prop1 is_connected_to) (name1 region2)
                         (prop2 is_connected_to))
```
$$(10\text{-}35d)$$

The modified version of unify1, shown in example 10.27, accomplishes this.

Example 10.27   Revised (general) unifier unify and unify-lists—case 3(iii).

```
(defun unify (x y bindings)
     (cond ((equal (setq x (get-binding x bindings))
                   (setq y (get-binding y bindings)))
             bindings)
           ((var x) (cons (list (cadr x) y) bindings))
           ((var y) (cons (list (cadr y) x) bindings))
           ((or (atom x) (atom y)) (and (equal x y) bindings))
           ((setq bindings (unify (car x) (car y) bindings))
            (unify (cdr x) (cdr y) bindings))))

t
->(defun unify-lists (list_a list_b)
       (unify list_a list_b '((empty))))
```
$$(10\text{-}36)$$

Readers may question the use of setq in the first conditional predicate in the definition of function unify, that is, setq x (get-binding x bindings ...). This is necessary and explored more fully in the problems. Fig.10.2 shows the overall structure of function unify.

Example 10.28   Sample application (unify-lists).

```
-> (setq a '((?var? X) ISA computer))
((?var? X) ISA computer)

-> (setq b '((ibm-pc ISA (?var? What)))
(ibm-pc ISA (?var? What))

-> (unify-lists a b)
((What computer) (X ibm-pc) (empty))
```
$$(10\text{-}37)$$

EXTENDED EXAMPLES (unify-lists). The reader is encouraged to study these examples to become familiar with the general unification process, as implemented by function unify.

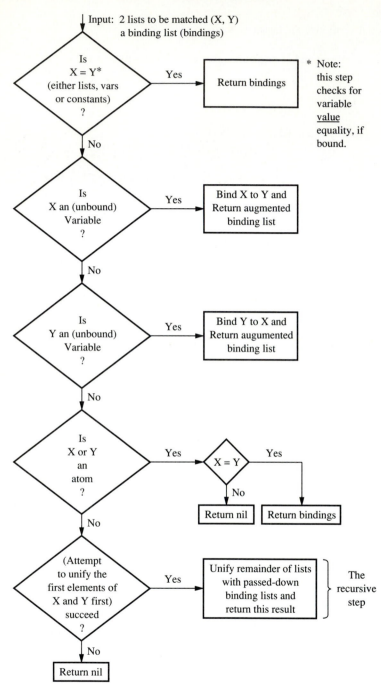

Input: 2 lists to be matched (X, Y)
a binding list (bindings)

Is X = Y* (either lists, vars or constants)? — Yes → Return bindings

* Note: this step checks for variable <u>value</u> equality, if bound.

No

Is X an (unbound) Variable? — Yes → Bind X to Y and Return augmented binding list

No

Is Y an (unbound) Variable? — Yes → Bind Y to X and Return augmented binding list

No

Is X or Y an atom? — Yes → X = Y — Yes → Return bindings
No → Return nil

No

(Attempt to unify the first elements of X and Y first) succeed? — Yes → Unify remainder of lists with passed-down binding lists and return this result } The recursive step

No

Return nil

FIGURE 10.2
Design of the general unifier—unify1. Compare with figure 2.7.

Example 10.29

```
-> (unify-lists a b)
1 <Enter> unify-lists ((((?var? X) ISA computer) (ibm-pc ISA
                       (?var? What)))
 |1 <Enter> unify ((((?var? X) ISA computer) (ibm-pc ISA
                     (?var? What))
   ((empty)))
 | 2 <Enter> unify ((?var? X) ibm-pc ((empty)))
 | 2 <EXIT>  unify  ((X ibm-pc) (empty))
 | 2 <Enter> unify ((ISA computer) (ISA (?var? What))
                    ((X ibm-pc) (empty)))
 | |3 <Enter> unify (ISA ISA ((X ibm-pc) (empty)))
 | |3 <EXIT>  unify  ((X ibm-pc) (empty))
 | |3 <Enter> unify ((computer) ((?var? What)) ((X ibm-pc)
                     (empty)))
 | | 4 <Enter> unify (computer (?var? What) ((X ibm-pc)
                      (empty)))
 | | 4 <EXIT>  unify  ((What computer) (X ibm-pc) (empty))
 | | 4 <Enter> unify (nil nil ((What computer) (X ibm-pc)
                      (empty)))
 | | 4 <EXIT>  unify  ((What computer) (X ibm-pc) (empty))
 | |3 <EXIT>  unify  ((What computer) (X ibm-pc) (empty))
 | 2 <EXIT>  unify  ((What computer) (X ibm-pc) (empty))
 |1 <EXIT>  unify  ((What computer) (X ibm-pc) (empty))
1 <EXIT>  unify-lists  ((What computer) (X ibm-pc) (empty))
((What computer) (X ibm-pc) (empty))                    (10-38a)
```

Example 10.30

```
-> a3
((?var? A) a b)
-> b3
((?var? B) (?var? B) (?var? A))
-> (unify a3 b3 '((empty)))
1 <Enter> unify (((?var? A) a b) ((?var? B) (?var? B)
                                  (?var? A)) ((empty)))
|2 <Enter> unify ((?var? A) (?var? B) ((empty)))
|2 <EXIT>  unify  ((A (?var? B)) (empty))
|2 <Enter> unify ((a b) ((?var? B) (?var? A)) ((A (?var? B))
                                               (empty)))
| 3 <Enter> unify (a (?var? B) ((A (?var? B)) (empty)))
| 3 <EXIT>  unify  ((B a) (A (?var? B)) (empty))
| 3 <Enter> unify ((b) ((?var? A)) ((B a) (A (?var? B))
                                    (empty)))
| |4 <Enter> unify (b (?var? A) ((B a) (A (?var? B))
                                 (empty)))
| |4 <EXIT>  unify  nil
| 3 <EXIT>  unify  nil
|2 <EXIT>  unify  nil
1 <EXIT>  unify  nil
nil                                                     (10-38b)
```

Example 10.31

```
-> a5
((?var? A) (?var? A) (?var? B))
-> b5
(a (?var? B) a)
-> (trace unify)
[autoload /usr/lib/lisp/trace]
[fasl /usr/lib/lisp/trace.o]
(unify)
-> (unify a5 b5 '((empty)))
1 <Enter> unify (((?var? A) (?var? A) (?var? B))
                 (a (?var? B) a) ((empty)))
|2 <Enter> unify ((?var? A) a ((empty)))
|2 <EXIT>  unify  ((A a) (empty)))
|2 <Enter> unify (((?var? A) (?var? B)) ((?var? B) a)
                 ((A a) (empty)))
| 3 <Enter> unify ((?var? A) (?var? B) ((A a) (empty)))
| 3 <EXIT>  unify  ((B a) (A a) (empty))
| 3 <Enter> unify (((?var? B)) (a) ((B a) (A a) (empty)))
| |4 <Enter> unify ((?var? B) a ((B a) (A a) (empty)))
| |4 <EXIT>  unify  ((B a) (A a) (empty))
| |4 <Enter> unify (nil nil ((B a) (A a) (empty)))
| |4 <EXIT>  unify  ((B a) (A a) (empty))
| 3 <EXIT>  unify  ((B a) (A a) (empty))
|2 <EXIT>  unify  ((B a) (A a) (empty))
1 <EXIT>  unify  ((B a) (A a) (empty))
((B a) (A a) (empty))
```
(10-38c)

Example 10.32

```
-> (unify b5 a5 '((empty)))
1 <Enter> unify ((a (?var? B) a) ((?var? A) (?var? A)
                                  (?var? B)) ((empty)))
|2 <Enter> unify (a (?var? A) ((empty)))
|2 <EXIT>  unify  ((A a) (empty))
|2 <Enter> unify (((?var? B) a) ((?var? A) (?var? B))
                                 ((A a) (empty)))
| 3 <Enter> unify ((?var? B) (?var? A) ((A a) (empty)))
| 3 <EXIT>  unify  ((B a) (A a) (empty))
| 3 <Enter> unify ((a) ((?var? B)) ((B a) (A a) (empty)))
| |4 <Enter> unify (a (?var? B) ((B a) (A a) (empty)))
| |4 <EXIT>  unify  ((B a) (A a) (empty))
| |4 <Enter> unify (nil nil ((B a) (A a) (empty)))
| |4 <EXIT>  unify  ((B a) (A a) (empty))
| 3 <EXIT>  unify  ((B a) (A a) (empty))
|2 <EXIT>  unify  ((B a) (A a) (empty))
1 <EXIT>  unify  ((B a) (A a) (empty))
((B a) (A a) (empty))
```
(10-38d)

The reader is strongly encouraged to explore additional examples.

MATCHING OF LISTS WITH LISTS
OF LISTS

CASES 4 AND 5. The previous effort concerned the matching of a list with another list (where either may contain two-element lists as elements, representing the cases of don't cares and variables). We now expand our matching capability to allow the matching of a given list with another (larger) list that may contain the first list as an element. Our reason for interest in this matching capability becomes apparent when we implement rule-based inference systems in LISP. The larger list serves as (part of) the database, containing facts.

Constants Only (Case 4)

We begin with the simplest case, that is, where the list and the larger list only consist of non-variables and non-don't cares (in other words, constants or lists of constants). This is easily handled by the function match−list−with−list:

Example 10.33   Function for list matching.

```
(defun match−list−with−list (fact facts−list)    ;checks to see
  (if                                            ;if fact
    (member fact facts−list) t                   ;is already
    nil)]                                        ;on fact list
```
$$(10\text{-}39)$$

In the development of inference engines (Chapters 11 and 12), this function is renamed recall−fact, due to its similarity with the process of recollection from a group (list) of facts.

The ease with which this programming task is accomplished is due to the availability of the built-in LISP function member that determines membership in lists with its first argument being either an atom or a list.

> member returns the remainder of the list from the point at which the match occurs, otherwise nil.   (10-40)

While not immediately apparent, this is a useful property. The syntax of member is

(member <expr> <list>)   (10-41)

member matches <expr> with every element of <list>.[*] Although member is a built-in function in LISP, we investigate a definition of member using our repertoire of LISP functions. This approach allows us to modify the operation of member to allow for matches that incorporate variables or don't cares.

---

[*] The CommonLISP member function uses an especially strict default test for equality (eql). To achieve the same results as that of FranzLISP (or MacLISP) member functions, it is necessary to employ an optional argument of the form (member <expr> <list> : test # 'equal)

Example 10.34 **Alternative** member **definition** (member2).

```
(defun member2 (item alist)
(cond
        ((null alist) nil)
        ((equal item (car alist)) alist)
        (t (member2 item (cdr alist)]                    (10-42)
```

Sample operation of member2 is shown below:

Example 10.35 member2 **operation.**

```
-> (print a_list)
(a b c d e)

-> (member2 'c a_list)
(c d e)                                                   (10-43)
```

List Matching with Variables

CASE 5. LISP-based databases may be expressed in the form of one or more large
lists of facts and rules. Let us assume that the database of facts is represented by a
list of the form

Example 10.36 **Sample database.**

```
;data_base.l   6-8-89
(setq database '(
(relay 4 open)
(relay 6 closed)
(line 4 energized)
(relay 7 malfunctioned)))                                 (10-44)
```

DATABASE QUERY TYPES. By developing and using a function match−
list−with−list, we could determine if a fact is in the database via

```
(match−list−with−list <some−fact> db)                     (10-45a)
```

where ‹some-fact› is itself a list, for example,

```
<some−fact> = (relay 4 open)                              (10-45b)
```

Alternately, we may only wish to determine if any relay is open by querying db
through a modified matching function that allows <some−fact> to be of the form

```
(relay (* any) open)                                      (10-45c)
```

or, if we wish to know which, if any, relay is open, we might formulate the first argument to the inquiry of (10-45*a*) as

(relay (?var? which—one) open)   (10-45*d*)

EXTENDED MATCHER. Following our development in previous sections, we expand the utility of function match—list—with—list to variable and don't care situations by replacing the test for equality, accomplished using equal in (10-42), with an alternative test of matchable. In addition, when variables are involved, the resulting bindings may be of interest. We show simple modifications in the following examples; alternative developments are left to the exercises.

Example 10.37 **List** member **modified for** don't cares (member4).

```
;the function member4 uses match2 to match a list
;which may contain a don't care against another
;list of lists

(defun member4 (item alist)
(cond
        ((null alist) nil)
        ((match2 item (car alist)) alist)
        (t (member4 item (cdr alist)]                            (10-46)
```

Example 10.38 list—with—list **matching and** don't cares.

```
(defun match—list—with—list2 (fact facts—list)
;fact— a fact in list form
;facts—list: a list of facts, each a list
;uses member4, which in turn uses match2
  (if
    (member4 fact facts—list) t
    nil)]                                                        (10-47)
```

Example 10.39 **Sample operation of modified list matchers.**

```
-> (pp database)
(setq database
        '((relay 4 open)
          (relay 6 closed)
          (line 4 energized)
          (relay 7 malfunctioned)))
t
-> (match—list—with—list '(relay 6 closed) database)
t
-> (match—list—with—list '(relay 4 closed) database)
nil
-> (match—list—with—list2 '(relay 6 closed) database)
t
```

```
-> (match-list-with-list '(relay (*any) closed) database)
nil
-> (match-list-with-list2 '(relay (* any) closed) database)
t
-> (match-list-with-list '(line (* any) energized) database)
nil
-> (match-list-with-list2 '(line (* any) energized) database)
t
-> (match-list-with-list2 '(relay (* any) green) database)
nil                                                              (10-48)
```

Example 10.40 match-var-list **definition.**

```
(defun match-var-list (a_list big_list bindings)
; checks to see if a_list matches an element of big_list,
; consistent variable bindings are checked w/ match_var2
  (do
    ((factlist big_list (cdr factlist))
     (newbindings nil))
    ((null factlist) nil)
    (setq newbindings (match-var2 a_list (car factlist) bindings))
    (if
      (not (null newbindings)) (return newbindings) nil )))
                                                                (10-49)
```

The reader is encouraged to study this LISP function. Note that match-var-list
uses the previous list matching function match-var2 and the do construct, described
in Chapter 8. As an aside, the function delete, used in

```
(delete (car factlist) big_list))
```

removes all occurrences of (car factlist) from big_list. Sample operation
is shown in example 10.41.

Example 10.41 Sample of list matching with variables. This example uses the
database of Example 10.39.

```
-> (setq inquiry '(relay (?var? which-one) closed))
(relay (?var? which-one) closed)

-> (match-var-list inquiry database nil)
((which-one 6))                                                 (10-50)
```

Summary

In this chapter we proceeded from a very simple matcher to unifiers of considerable
complexity. This allows us to begin various implementations of inference engines in
LISP, as shown in the next chapter.

REFERENCES

[Kahn/Carlsson 1984] Kahn, K.M., and M. Carlsson, "How to Implement Prolog on a LISP Machine," in *Implementations of Prolog* (J.A. Campbell, ed.), Halstead Press (John Wiley and Sons), NY, 1984.

[Nilsson 1984] Nilsson, M., "The World's Shortest Prolog Interpreter?" in *Implementations of Prolog*, (J.A. Campbell, ed.), Halstead Press (John Wiley and Sons), NY, 1984.

[Willinsky 1984] Willinsky, R., *LispCraft* (Chapter 21), Norton, San Francisco, 1984.

PROBLEMS

10.1. Modify the elementary list-matching function (10-5) (i.e., no don't cares or variables) to attempt matching the lists in reverse order, that is, the match starts at the end of each list and, if successful, successively moves backwards toward the first element. Be sure to check that the lists have equal length.

10.2. A generalization of our different matching strategies is to design a matching function that matches an expression anywhere in a list. In other words, the expression may be simply an element of the list, or an element of an element of the list, that is, it may be at any level in the list. Design and implement this function and show its operation using several examples. (Hint: a recursive approach will simplify the definition.)

10.3. This problem concerns the computational complexity and efficiency of matching. We desire estimates of the number of compares necessary in execution of matching algorithms for two lists, a and b. Compute the average "best" and "worst" case number of equality checks that must be performed in the following matching cases:

(*a*) Matching a single (atomic) element against a list of *n* elements.

(*b*) Matching a list of *p* elements against a list of *n* sublists, each of length *p*.

(*c*) Matching a list of *p* elements against a list of *n* sublists, with varying lengths, but average length *p*.

(*d*) Matching a list of *p* elements against a list of *p* elements, with at most one don't care in one of the lists.

10.4. This problem tests your understanding of the general unifier (function un i f y) repeated below:

```
(defun unify (x y bindings)
     (cond ((equal (setq x (get-binding x bindings))
                   (setq y (get-binding y bindings)))
            bindings)
           ((var x) (cons (list (cadr x) y) bindings))
           ((var y) (cons (list (cadr y) x) bindings))
           ((or (atom x) (atom y)) (and (equal x y) bindings))
           ((setq bindings (unify (car x) (car y) bindings))
            (unify (cdr x) (cdr y) bindings)))))          (P10-4)
```

(*a*) Why is s e t q used in the first conditional predicate, that is,

```
(setq x (get-binding x bindings))
         (setq y (get-binding y bindings)))
```

instead of simply writing

```
(get-binding x bindings))
          (setq y (get-binding y bindings)))
```

(*b*) Show an example, using the LISP system, of a case where the use of s e t q as the simpler alternative would matter.

10.5. Modify the matcher ma t ch-l i s t-wi t h-l i s t (Example 10.33) for sublist matching to allow both variables and don't cares. Test your result with several examples.

10.6. Apply the don ' t car e matching function ma t ch2 to the lists

```
((a *))
((a))
```

(*a*) Why does this function exhibit incorrect operation? (Refer also to (10-18).)

(*b*) Correct it and show your results.

10.7. Design, implement and check via examples a modified don't care matcher that has the don't care symbol, **, which indicates a match with one or two elements in the second list. For example, the function should work successfully in our previous cases, but also return t for sample input lists of the form

```
((** any1-2) relay is stuck)
(the repaired relay is stuck)
```

and

```
((** any1-2) relay is stuck)
(the relay is stuck)
```

Note that this allows successful matching with lists of unequal length.

10.8. Develop and implement a matching function that allows alternatives, that is, assume that a fact comprised of nonvariable elements a , b , c , . . . may be simply formulated in LISP as

```
((a or b) (c or d) e (f or g) ....)
```

For example, this list, when matched against

```
(a c e f ...)
```

or

```
(b d e g)
```

or

```
(a d e f)
```

should result in a successful match.

10.9. Repeat problem 8 for the case of variables in one list.

10.10. In Chapter 10, match−var2 is an extension of match−var. For simplicity, we developed the function with a minimum of auxiliary functions and noted that good program development methodology would be to replace many of the nested function applications with auxiliary functions. Do this. (match−var2 itself should be considerably simpler.)

10.11. Revise match−var2 to allow matching with both don't cares and variables. Verify your results using the lists

```
(relay  (* any)  is  (?var?  state))
```

```
(relay  6  is  open)
```

10.12. Modify match−var2 to use function get−binding, instead of get−binding1.

10.13. Develop, in LISP, a function apply_substitution which applies a given substitution (θ) to a statement (p) which contains variables. (Recall this is denoted pθ in Chapter 2.)

The data structures are shown in the following example:

```
->(setq p '((?var?  A)  is_left_of  (?var?  B)))
```

```
->setq  theta  '((A  block_1) (B  block_2)))
```

```
->(apply_substitution  p  theta)
```

should return

```
(block_1  is_left_of  block_2)
```

You should feel free to define or use any auxiliary functions necessary.

10.14. Develop and implement LISP matching functions for the "match a list with a list of lists or elements" cases under the following conditions:
(*a*) One list contains an element that is a don't care, for example,

```
((this) (is the) (first of) (the two) (lists))
```

```
((this) (is the) * (the two) (lists))
```

(*b*) An element of one of the sublists is a don't care, for example,

```
((this) (is the) (first of) (the two) (lists))
```

```
((this) (is the) ((* any) of) (the two) (lists))
```

(*c*) One mismatch of a sublist is allowed, that is,

```
((this) (is the) (first of) (the two) (lists))
```

```
((this) (is the) (second of) (the two) (lists))
```

is a valid match.

10.15. (Extension to Problem 10.14) Develop and implement a list-list matcher with an argument that allows specification of which element of the list is to be checked for the match, and whether the elements are atoms or sublists.

10.16. Develop a LISP function that, given a key and a list, matches the element against each of the list elements and returns a list indicating the success or failure of each attempted match. For example, given

(t h i s)

and

((t h i s)   (i s   t h e)   (e n d   o f)   (t h i s)   (l i s t))

the function returns

(t   n i l   n i l   t   n i l)

(Hint: the built-in LISP mapcar function may make this solution straightforward).

10.17. Redefine the function augment−binding−list (10-23) using the cons function, instead of append.

CHAPTER 11

RULE-BASED INFERENCE SYSTEMS PART I— PRODUCTION SYSTEMS, FORWARD CHAINING, AND LISP IMPLEMENTATIONS

"Works of art make rules, but rules do not make works of art."

Debussy

PRODUCTION SYSTEMS

Overview and Basic Structure

One of the most widely used models of knowledge representation and manipulation is the production system. Production systems represent symbolically tractable, (albeit limited by current standards) solutions to many AI applications. They are conceptually simple, and when implemented in "canned" form, allow use by non-AI programmers and professionals. An example of such a "canned" system is OPS5, a rule-based supplement to LISP which we explore in Chapter 13. Many production system features vary among implementations. In this and Chapter 12 we develop several systems, each with specific features, to explore the implementation details.

A **production system** consists of

1. A set of productions (e.g., rules) that modify the existing database and whose applicability is conditioned on the current database.
2. A database of information.
3. A control mechanism/rule interpreter that determines the applicability of the rules in the context of the current database, the selection of appropriate rules, and the resolution of conflicts that may arise when two or more productions are applicable at the same time. (11-1)

The "triad" constituting a production system is shown in Fig. 11.1.

PRODUCTION SYSTEMS TO RULE-BASED SYSTEMS (RBS). The production or production rules in production systems require specification of a set of condition-action pairs. Production systems are a subset of **pattern directed systems**, systems whose production applications are driven by input (or initial) data patterns. Representing our data or patterns in list form explains our interest in pattern or list matching in Chapter 10. The specification of production conditions in the form of IF statements and actions via THEN yields a familiar rule-based system paradigm.

Rule-based systems provide a natural means to express situation-action heuristics in problem solving. They are both a means to represent knowledge and manipulate this knowledge to emulate human behavior. They are typically

1. Based upon IF-THEN (implication) based representations (Chapter 2) that lead to easy augmenting of the system by adding additional rules.
2. Applied in narrowly defined problem domains.

The term **expert system**, while seemingly a catch-all in current AI jargon, is used to indicate a subset of production systems that are restricted to specific task domains.

PROLOG may be viewed as either a general-purpose, logic-based programming language or as a rule-based system (RBS) based upon facts and rules that solve for a given goal. In fact, the latter interpretation and PROLOG's depth-first unification strategy make it a model for backward chaining (Chapter 12).

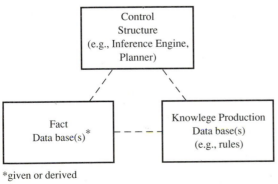

*given or derived
facts

FIGURE 11.1
The production system triad (neglects I/O).

The computer implementation aspects, in particular search requirements and parallel architecture implementations of production systems, are explored in Chapters 15 and 19.

THE INFERENCE ENGINE (IE). The heart of a rule-based production system is a database (facts and rules) and the corresponding inference mechanism or inference "engine" that manipulates this database. The inference engine (IE) (also referred to with more sophisticated names, e.g., "knowledge application structure") can be considered a finite state machine with states representing typical actions such as

1. Match rules.
2. Select rules.
3. Execute rules.
4. Check stopping conditions (i.e., goal satisfaction).

With suitable interpretations of each of these actions, the operation of a chaining-based inference engine is readily described as iteration of the above actions. The inference engine therefore exhibits *control* over the production system operation in the sense that it either regulates the production of new databases (forward chaining) or the verification of hypothetical information (backward chaining). Another view of the IE is that it generates one or more inference nets linking the initial system state to a goal state.

Fundamental to the operation of the IE is the process of matching. Since more general knowledge may be encoded with rules using variables, this often involves matching with variables and thus, a suitable unification algorithm. In addition, partial matches, or matches with don't cares, are possible. Few current systems fully utilize or provide this capability, partially because its assessment of quantitative effect on overall system operation is difficult.

RULE SELECTION. Another critical aspect of IE operation is in the selection of rules. This involves three major aspects:

1. The selection of appropriate or applicable rules.
2. The selection of good rules that enable efficient solution of a problem without exhaustive search or combinatorial explosion, as well as producing or verifying conclusions with a high degree of confidence in the validity of the conclusions.
3. The resolution of cases wherein the rules are conflicting (they produce contradictory results). This is not to be confused with the concept of a *conflict set*, which involves selection from a set of applicable rules.

Fig. 11.2 shows simplistic rule-based production system operation, indicating the "production cycle" of searching for applicable rules, selecting a particular applicable rule, applying (firing) the rule, and then restarting the cycle. A more realistic system, which takes into account practical concerns such as I/O, is shown in Fig. 11.3. The structure of a representative advanced rule-based system is shown in Chapter 13, Fig. 13.15.

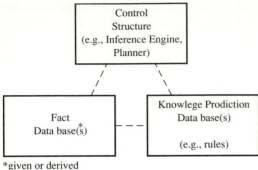

*given or derived
facts

FIGURE 11.2
Elementary rule-based system operation.

Features of Rule-based Production Systems

Characteristic of systems employing productions in rule form are the following generally positive features:

1. Ease of modification of the database (facts and/or rules may be added or removed).
2. Ease of exploring the current knowledge base contained in the system (i.e., the encoding of information is in a readable form).
3. Flexibility of processing (the inference mechanism may be chosen to suit the problem).
4. Ease in following the inference mechanism (the order in which rules were employed may be recorded and traced for an "explanation" of the system's conclusions).
5. Standardization in terms of a knowledge representation and inference approach.
6. Availability of "canned" software for implementation.

Disadvantages include

1. Inability to predict system behavior in a deterministic manner (recall this characterizes most AI systems).

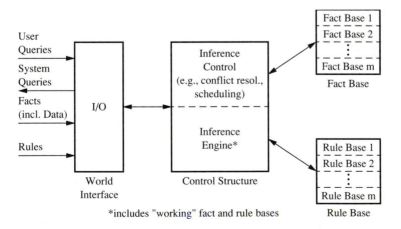

FIGURE 11.3
Extended rule-based system organization typical of "expert" systems (see also Figure 13.15, Chapter 13).

2. Inability to force a specific production sequence, as compared to imperative programming.

3. Lack of suitability for all applications.

4. Lack of ability to directly implement "deep reasoning" and "common sense." This is a representation problem (Chapter 16).

THEORETICAL ASPECTS OF THE PRODUCTION SYSTEM STRUCTURE AND INFERENCE STRATEGY

Significant Aspects of the Inference Engine (Inference Control Strategies)

The IE, coupled with the (facts and rules) database, and a goal, comprise a mechanism for a problem solution. The actions of the IE constitute a solution algorithm. Several interrelated questions regarding this view thus arise, including

1. Is this algorithm deterministic?

2. How does the order in which rules and facts are arranged (in the database), tested, and used influence the outcome and efficiency of the algorithm?

> In a general sense, nondeterminism refers to the absence of factors determining the precise course of execution. It should not be confused with the oft-used probabilistic connotation. A specific program is nondeterministic when it admits more than one computation. For example, if we allowed the inference engine to pursue a number of paths to the goal in parallel, the approach would be nondeterministic. (11-2)

CONTROL STRATEGIES. In the terminology of Nilsson [Nilsson 1980], one classification of IE control strategies is based upon the distinction between irrevocable and tentative. An **irrevocable** control strategy selects and applies applicable rules without provision for reconsideration at a later point in the inference sequence. A **tentative** strategy, on the other hand, selects and applies rules, but allows provision for reconsideration (selection and application of an alternative rule) at a later point in the inference process. A control strategy that allows backtracking (e.g., PROLOG's inference mechanism) is a good example of a tentative strategy.

A practical or generally useful control strategy is not likely to be as simple as those considered in this and succeeding chapters. This observation probably appeals to our intuition, since the control strategy is a prime component of the problem solution process; "cleverness" and "judgment" approaching that of a human problem solver are difficult to identify and easily embed in the control mechanism. Often, we enable the control mechanism with characteristics that mimic human approaches via heuristics. Furthermore, the control strategy may be intimately related to the structure of the database, for example, the use of frame-based and blackboard [Ni 1986] structures will influence control strategy design. It is entirely possible for the IE itself to be formed from a production system where **metarules** (rules about rules) are used to guide the selection of production system rules. While perhaps enabling a more sophisticated rule selection mechanism, this approach necessitates the design of another metarule-based IE.

Problem Solving, the State Space, and the Inference Engine

Whether a production system is implemented through forward, backward, or a combined chaining paradigm, the resulting inference net illustrates that the IE is used to find one or more paths from a set of facts to a goal (or vice versa in the case of backward chaining). Thus we can view this as *search through the problem state space* (Chapter 15). The IE may therefore explore a large number of redundant or unsuccessful paths through the problem state space to the goal. A good IE design uses all available a priori information (such as properties of commutativity and decomposability, if applicable), to avoid needless or unproductive searching.

Production System Properties

The general concept of a production system is theoretically and practically important enough to warrant a detailed definition and examination of several properties. Given a specific database and a set of rules, these production system properties, to some extent, guide the type of inference mechanisms we might employ in the production system. In addition, several production system properties lead to the efficient application of rules, as well as the parallel decomposition of the problem.

COMMUTATIVE VERSUS NON-COMMUTATIVE PRODUCTION SYSTEMS. Given the general production system and associated inference mechanism shown in Fig. 11.1, a significant question is

> Does the order in which the (applicable) rules are applied to the fact database(s) matter?

When the answer to the question is "no," several useful properties that lead to paradigms for rule selection and application result.

APPLICABLE RULES AND COMMUTATIVE SYSTEMS. One type of specialized production system is the commutative system. We first define a rule as **applicable** in the context of a database, denoted D, if the conjunction of the preconditions or antecedents ("IF parts") for that rule are satisfied by D, that is, the rule is eligible for firing. A commutative production system [Nilsson 1980] has three important properties:

1. Any rule applicable to D is also applicable to any database derived from D by successive applications of applicable rules. Note that this only applies to rules that are initially applicable to D. The state of the database will change over time (i.e., as productions occur and D is modified), thus possibly yielding other rules that are applicable in subsequent databases derived from D.   (11-3a)

2. If a goal is satisfied by D, then it is also satisfied by any database produced by applying applicable rules to D.   (11-3b)

3. The database generated by firing of a sequence of rules applicable to D is invariant to permutations in the firing sequence. This property should not be construed to mean that if we find a sequence of rules that move the system from the initial state

to the goal state (through a succession of intermediate system states) that we may arbitrarily reorder this entire rule sequence and find that the reordered sequence will also achieve the goal.   (11-3c)

The significance of having a production system with the commutative property is twofold:

1. The IE (as shown in the following example) does not need to consider the application of all permutations of rule order, that is, it is possible to avoid many of the solution paths that differ only in the order in which initially applicable rules are applied. For large rulebases, this may be a significant number.   (11-3d)
2. The commutative property allows use of an IE employing an irrevocable control strategy.   (11-3e)

Figure 11.4 illustrates the utility of the commutative property via a simple example involving six rules and an initial database of five facts. PROLOG-like notation is used to represent the system database. Notice that, due to the commutative property, the alternate rule order application shown in part (c) is unnecessary.

RELATION TO PLANNING SYSTEMS. A good example of a non-commutative production system is one with the capacity for fact and/or rule removal (retraction) (e.g., use of the PROLOG "retract" predicate). Our best example of a non-commutative production system, however, is a planning system, to be explored in depth in Chapter 14. In planning systems, the order in which productions are invoked is usually critical to the outcome of the system. In other words, achievement of a plan that meets the prescribed goal is highly dependent upon the chosen sequence of operations comprising the plan. Planning, as the name implies, involves not only the process of determining applicable productions, but also a careful consideration of the sequence (i.e., the "plan") of these productions.

DECOMPOSABLE PRODUCTION SYSTEMS. Whereas the commutative property of a production system facilitates a limited degree of flexibility in the sequence in which applicable rules are fired, another related property, namely that of decomposability, allows some additional freedom in the ordering of rule applications and leads to computationally efficient IE designs. We note that decomposition of problems in general is an important and desirable property of most (including AI) problems, since we may then apply a "divide and conquer" approach that involves solution of a set of (hopefully) simpler or smaller problems.

A database, D, is **decomposable** if it can be decomposed or partitioned into disjoint sets that can be processed independently (perhaps in parallel).   (11-3f)

Furthermore, for this property to be useful, it is necessary that the goal also be decomposable into components that are satisfiable by these partitioned databases. Note this does not mean that the goal must be satisfied entirely by any one partitioned

Rules (R)

1. h: – e,f,g.

2. h: – a,b,f,g.

3. e: – a,b.

4. e: – g,a.

5. f: – c,d.

6. f: – b,d.

Facts (D)

a.

b.

c.

d.

g.

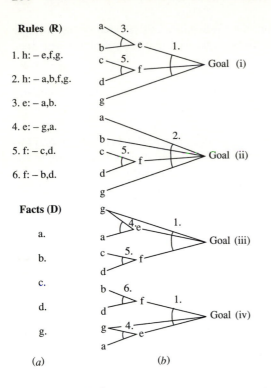

(a)

(b)

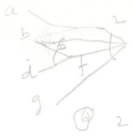

Alternate Sequences
Rules applicable to D circled

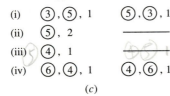

(i)   ③,⑤, 1   ⑤,③, 1

(ii)   ⑤, 2

(iii) ④, 1

(iv) ⑥,④, 1   ④,⑥, 1

(c)

FIGURE 11.4
Commutative property example. (*a*) Data bases;
(*b*) inference nets—not all possible shown (goal
= h); (*c*) possible rule application sequences
leading to goal.

system, but rather that the goal is satisfiable by some logical function of its decomposed components, each of which in turn may be the result of independent processing
in the partitioned database. Most often, this logical function is the conjunction (AND-
ing) of a set of facts.

> We define a **decomposable production system** to be one for which both the database
> and the goal are decomposable.   (11-3*g*)

The decomposability property applied to the previous example of Fig. 11.4 is shown
graphically in Fig. 11.5. Decomposability is an important production system property
for two major reasons:

1. The decomposition, as noted above, allows inferences to proceed in parallel (up
to the inputs of the goal decomposition).   (11-3*h*)

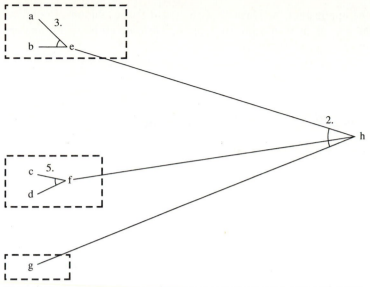

Circles indicate disjoint partitions of data base; goal decomposed using conjunction.

FIGURE 11.5
Example of decomposition system (from example of Fig. 11.4).

2. Decomposition eliminates many of the redundant solution paths and related searches that otherwise might be explored, since the entire fact and rule databases are not involved. (11-3*i*)

Given an arbitrary production system, identification of the decomposability property (as well as achievement of a suitable decomposition) is often challenging. One algorithm for this is given in [Nilsson 1980].

RULE-BASED CHAINING INFERENCE APPROACHES

Rule-based Systems as Production Systems and Control Paradigms

As noted previously, the IE is responsible for

1. Selection of relevant rules (or, in fact, sets or groups of rules, which may pertain to a specific scenario that the control mechanism determines should be "focused" upon (Chapter 16)).
2. Matching, or determining the suitability of a given rule, in the context of the current database.

3. Scheduling of the application, or "firing" of rules and the resolution of conflicts (e.g., the production of new information, on the basis of current information, which contradicts the current information).
4. Execution or "firing" of the rules, and subsequent modification of the database.
5. Determination if an overall goal has been satisfied.

Review of the Logical Basis for Forward Chaining

Example 11.1   Forward chaining. The logical basis for chaining is considered in Chapter 2. Recall we began with a series of statements connected by implication of the form

$$p1 \rightarrow p2$$
$$p2 \rightarrow p3$$
$$p3 \rightarrow q3 \tag{11-4a}$$

which formed an elementary rule base.

A paradigm known as **forward chaining** employs Modus Ponens in the following sequence:

step 1. $((p1 \rightarrow p2) \cap p1 = \text{TRUE}) \rightarrow (p2 = \text{TRUE})$ \hfill (11-4b)

step 2. (Similar to step 1) $((p2 \rightarrow p3) \cap p2 = \text{TRUE}) \rightarrow (p3 \text{ is}$
$\text{TRUE})$ \hfill (11-4c)

step 3. (Similar to steps 1 and 2) $((p3 \rightarrow q3) \cap p3 = \text{TRUE}) \rightarrow$
$(q3 \text{ is TRUE})$ \hfill (11-4d)

This sequence of deductions in the forward direction is shown in the inference net of Fig. 11.6. The action indicated by "firing" a rule is shown in the figure by enclosing

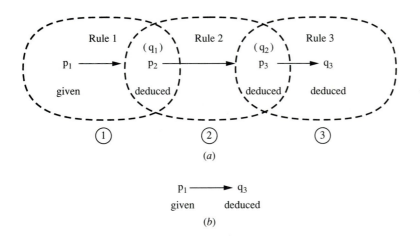

(a)

$$p_1 \longrightarrow q_3$$
given   deduced

(b)

FIGURE 11.6
Inference net for 3-Rule forward chaining (antecedents are single assertions). (a) Forward chaining sequence; (b) result.

the rule in a dotted region and labeling this region with the order in which the rule was fired. The computational process of deciding on which rule to fire (so called "conflict resolution") does not enter in this figure, due to the simplicity of the rulebase.

The derivation of a control structure for implementation of forward chaining is relatively straightforward. The database of rules is scanned for rules whose antecedents (the conjunction of statements) are satisfiable, thus allowing the rule to be employed. This use of a rule is often referred to as a "firing." Since the concentration of the inference mechanism is on the rule antecedents, this approach is referred to as antecedent-driven or **antecedent-driven inference**. As we'll explore later, the consequences of forward chaining with respect to efficiency and a more complex control mechanism are significant. It is also noteworthy that forward chaining and MP are not the only applicable solutions to a given AI problem.

IMPLEMENTATION OF A SIMPLE FORWARD CHAINING SYSTEM IN LISP

Overall System Structure

The LISP-based production systems and applications we consider here consist basically of three entities that reflect the structure of Figs. 11.1 and 11.2:

1. A set (coded here as a list) of basic facts.   (11-5*a*)

2. A set (again coded here as a list) of rules in IF-THEN form.   (11-5*b*)

3. A process (a set of functions) to systematically apply (11-5*b*) to (11-5*a*) thereby augmenting (11-5*a*) and producing high-level facts or conclusions.   (11-5*c*)

Generation of new facts proceeds by linking the THEN parts of fired rules to the IF parts of others and proceeding until the goal statement is shown to be TRUE or until no new facts may be produced. We later consider the important concept of *conflict resolution,* which is a fundamental part of the overall system structure. A general view of forward chaining is shown in Fig. 11.7.

We use global variables to represent the respective system facts and rule lists. For this reason, they are given the special names *facts* and *rules*. While this is not absolutely necessary, it is a good programming practice since the special names remind us of the global nature of the variables.

For implementation, we extend the definition of rule applicability. A rule is applicable if

1. All antecedents are in the database (on list *facts*)   (11-6*a*)

2. Not all consequents are in the database (on list *facts*); produces something new.   (11-6*b*)

The second constraint on applicability ensures the system will not repeatedly fire the same rule.

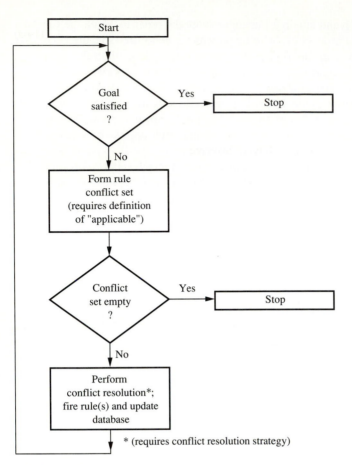

FIGURE 11.7
General strategy for rule-based forward chaining inference.

Database Structure

FACT REPRESENTATION. The LISP coding implementation of the fact information is achieved using a list structure with the following syntax (in Backus-Naur form):

$$\text{factlist} ::= \text{fact} \ \{\text{fact}\} \tag{11-6c}$$

where items enclosed in { } may be repeated zero or more times.

A simple example of such a fact list follows:

Example 11.2   Simple example of *facts*

```
(setq *facts* ' (
    (b1 = b2)
    (b2 <> 0)
```

```
(b1 <> 0)
(region1 inside region2) ))                                    (11-6d)
```

More specifically, we design LISP functions to manipulate *facts*. The following two functions check and update the *facts* list.

Example 11.3   LISP functions for manipulation of *facts*.

```
;'remember-new-fact' adds a new fact to the fact list
;input: fact
;output: nil if the fact is on the fact list,
;          otherwise the augmented fact list
;side effect: the modification of the fact list

(defun remember-new-fact (new-fact)
  (if (member new-fact *facts*)
      nil
      (setq *facts* (cons new-fact *facts*)))))             (11-7a)

;'recall-fact' checks if a fact is on the fact list
;input: fact
;output: nil if the fact is not on the fact list,
;          otherwise returns fact.

(defun recall-fact (fact)
  (if (member fact *facts*) fact nil))                      (11-7b)
```

Both remember-new-facts and recall-fact use function member. In subsequent extensions, (especially when variables and don't cares appear in rules) the more sophisticated matching strategies, developed in Chapter 10, are employed.

Rule Representation and Rulebase Structure

The system uses rules with the simple antecedent-consequent structure:

```
IF <antecedent 1>
   <antecedent 2>
         .
         .
         .
   <antecedent n>


THEN <consequent 1>
     <consequent 2>
           .
           .
           .
     <consequent m>                                          (11-8)
```

where it is assumed that the rule is fired if the logical AND of all the antecedents is TRUE. This is verified by successful unification of the antecedents with the fact base. Note in this formulation that the production of new information by the firing of a single rule is not restricted to a single new fact, that is, there may be multiple consequents in a rule. The production, however, is restricted to the addition of facts to the database. Other possible productions (or actions) include

1. Deletion of facts.
2. Addition, deletion or modification of rules.

These extensions are considered in the problems.

The LISP coding of the rule information is achieved using a list structure with the following syntax (in Backus-Naur form):

> **Example 11.4** rulelist **structure.**

```
rulelist ::= rule {rule}
rule ::= IF antecedent {antecedent} THEN  consequent
{consequent}                                          (11-9a)
```

Antecedents and consequents are of the same English-like list form as facts. A simple example of such a rulelist is

> **Example 11.5   Sample** *rules*.

```
(setq *rules* '(
  (rule REASON1 (IF (b1 <> 0) (b2 <> 0) (b1 = b2)) (THEN
    (same image motion)))
  (rule REASON2 (IF (b1<> 0) (b2 <> 0) (b1 <> b2)) (THEN
    (different image motion)))
  (rule REASON3 (IF (region1 inside region2) (b1 = b2))
    (THEN (region1 isa part of region2))) ))        (11-9b)
```

Note that individual rules contained in rule list *rules* are indexed by a name (e.g., REASON1) for identification in the chaining process as well as for practical system enhancements described later.

RULE STRUCTURE. As shown in Examples 11.4 and 11.5,

1. Each element of the rule list is a rule, itself structured as a list and consisting of four parts. (11-10a)
2. The car of each rule is the atom RULE. (11-10b)
3. The cadr (or nth 1) of each rule is an atom indicating the rulename. (11-10c)
4. The third element, caddr, (or nth 2) of each rule is a list indicating the antecedents for that rule (the conjunction of which must be TRUE for the rule to be fired). The car of this element is the atom if (not to be confused with the function of the same name); the cdr is a list of antecedents which, as shown,

could themselves be lists. The list of consequents may be extracted from a given rule via function ge t−antecedents, shown in (11-11). (11-10*d*)

5. The fourth element, cadddr, (or n t h 3) of each rule is a list containing the rule consequents; the c a r of this element is the atom THEN, the remainder or cd r of this is the list of consequents. This is extracted via function ge t−consequents in (11-12). (11-10*e*)

Example 11.6 Function ge t−antecedents.

```
; 'get−antecedents' gets the antecedents of given rule
; input: rule
; output: antecedents

(defun get−antecedents (a−rule)
  (cdr (nth 2 a−rule)))                                   (11-11)
```

Example 11.7 Function ge t−consequences.

```
; ''get−consequences'' gets the consequences of given rule
; input: rule
; output: consequences

(defun get−consequences (a−rule)
  (cdr (nth 3 a−rule)))                                   (11-12)
```

RULE ANTECEDENT CHECKING. To proceed in forward chaining, it is necessary to examine the IF part of each rule, and determine whether the conjunction of these antecedents is satisfied. In the functions we develop below, this is done recursively. Of course, the do macro provides a possible alternative formulation.

```
; 'test−antecedents' checks if all antecedents are on the
fact list
; implements (11−6a)
; input: antecedents
; output: t if all antecedents are on the fact list,
;          otherwise nil

(defun test−antecedents (antecedents)
  (if (null antecedents) t
      (if (recall−fact (car antecedents))
          (test−antecedents (cdr antecedents)))))        (11-13)
```

The tes t−antecedents function simply checks the antecedents of a rule recursively, and in conjunction with recal l−fac t (defined in 11-7*b*) determines whether the rule may be fired.

If the list of antecedents to a rule is nu l l, this implies no facts need be TRUE in order to fire the rule (i.e, the rule is a fact) or that we have reached the end of the list of antecedents without failure to unify with the facts list. (11-14)

If, during the loop, any of the AND-ed IF statements cannot be verified (via matching), function test—antecedents returns nil. If successful in checking the rule antecedents and determining that the rule firing will add something to the database (via check—consequences), we then proceed to fire the rule via function fire—a—rule. This represents a very simple, in fact almost trivial, conflict resolution strategy . We show a more complex strategy in the next section and leave additional extensions to the problems.

The use of auxiliary LISP IE functions is explored in examples 11.8–11.10.

Example 11.8.

```
; 'check—consequences' checks if any consequence is not on
the fact list
; implements (11—6b)
; input: consequences
; output: t if any consequence is not on the fact list,
;           otherwise nil

(defun check—consequences (consequences)
  (if (null consequences) nil
      (if (recall—fact (car consequences))
          (check—consequences (cdr consequences))
          t)))                                           (11-15)
```

Example 11.9.

```
; 'update—facts' adds the consequences to the fact list
; input: consequences
; output: t

(defun update—facts (consequences)
  (cond
    ((null consequences) t)
    (t (cond
         ((remember—new—fact (car consequences))
          (print (car consequences))
          (terpri)))
       (update—facts (cdr consequences)))))              (11-16)
```

Example 11.10.

```
; 'fire—a—rule' fires an applicable rule
; implements (11—6a) and (11—6b) and
; updates *facts* as a side effect.
; input: rule
; output: t if this rule is fired, otherwise nil

(defun fire—a—rule (a—rule)
  (cond
    ((and
```

```
      (test-antecedents (get-antecedents a-rule))
      (check-consequences (get-consequences a-rule)))
   (print (list (nth 0 a-rule) (nth 1 a-rule) 'IS 'FIRED))
   (terpri)
   (print 'DEDUCE)
   (terpri)                                                    (11-17)
   (update-facts (get-consequences a-rule)))))
```

EXTENSION OF RULE ANTECEDENT EXTRACTION AND CHECKING TO MORE STRUCTURED RULEBASES. The simple structure we have adopted for the rule and fact bases (and the resulting inference engine) is extendable. Rules may be more sophisticated, for example, extended rules of the form considered in Chapter 9 (and shown below in 11-18) may be used.

```
-> (setq a_rule
      '(RULE 43
             (CONCERNS (car auto mobile_home))
             (APPLICABLE_IF (IN vehicle_frame))
             (ANTECEDENT_IS (IF (? entity) (HAS (wheels
               owner roof))))
             (PRODUCTION_IS (THEN ((? entity) ISA auto)))))
                                                               (11-18)
```

Forward Chaining Inference Engine
Main Function "Chainforward"

IE CHAINING STRATEGY. Now that the data and rulebases have been established, we concentrate on the design of a forward chaining methodology that exhaustively checks rules and fires those which are applicable, according to definition 11.6a. After a rule has been fired, and thus the fact base has been augmented, it is possible that a rule checked earlier (which was not fired) is now applicable due to the production of one or more new facts. Thus, it makes sense to augment the fact list immediately after a rule firing. The application of applicable rules to the (augmented) fact base continues until no further firings are possible (if maximal fact production is the goal). Alternately, if verification of a single fact is the objective, it is necessary to check the fact list after each rule is fired (one "cycle" of rulebase application), for this fact.

FUNCTION chain-forward. The individual functions designed thus far operate only on a single (given) rule. It is necessary to search through the rulebase for applicable rules which then become arguments to these functions. This is done by

```
;'chain-forward' fires all applicable rules
;input: the rule list
;output: nil
;side effect is exhaustive *facts* augmentation
```

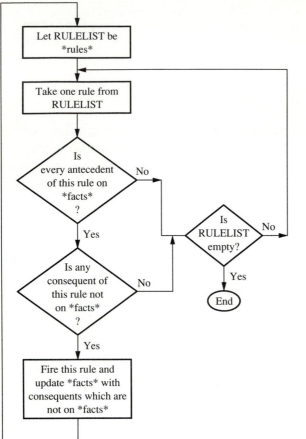

FIGURE 11.8
Flowchart for fwd_r. 1.

```
(defun chain-forward (rulelist)
 (cond
  ((null rulelist)
   (terpri)
   (print '(NO FURTHER FORWARD INFERENCE))
   (terpri))
  ((fire-a-rule (car rulelist))
   (chain-forward *rules*))
  (t (chain-forward (cdr rulelist))))))          (11-19)
```

A flowchart for this function is shown in Fig. 11.8.

Examples

A complete listing of the functions developed is shown below. In subsequent extensions, we will not repeat or re-list these functions, but rather show only new or
extended versions.

```
;fwd_r.l
;this program implements the forward chaining algorithm.
;Global Variables: *facts*, *rules*
;*facts* = (fact fact ..)
;*rules* = (rule rule ..)
;rule = (rule rule-name (IF fact fact ..)
;                        (THEN fact fact ..))

;'remember-new-fact' adds a new fact to the fact list
;input: fact
;output: nil if the fact is on the fact list,
;          otherwise the argumented fact list
;side effect: the modification of the fact list

(defun remember-new-fact (new-fact)
  (if (member new-fact *facts*)
      nil
      (setq *facts* (cons new-fact *facts*))))

;'recall-fact' checks if a fact is on the fact list
;input: fact
;output: nil if the fact is not on the fact list,
;          otherwise t.

(defun recall-fact (fact)
  (if (member fact *facts*) fact nil))

;'get-antecedents' gets the antecedents of given rule
;input: rule
;output: antecedents

(defun get-antecedents (a-rule)
  (cdr (nth 2 a-rule)))

;'get-consequences' gets the consequents of given rule
;input: rule
;output: consequents

(defun get-consequences (a-rule)
  (cdr (nth 3 a-rule)))

;'test-antecedents' checks if all antecedents are on the
fact list
;input: antecedents
;output: t if all antecedents are on the fact list,
;          otherwise nil

(defun test-antecedents (antecedents)
  (if (null antecedents) t
      (if (recall-fact (car antecedents))
          (test-antecedents (cdr antecedents)))))
```

```
;'check-consequences' checks if any consequence is not
on the fact list
;input: consequences
;output: t if any consequence is not on the fact list,
;          otherwise nil

(defun check-consequences (consequences)
  (if (null consequences) nil
      (if (recall-fact (car consequences))
          (check-consequences (cdr consequences))
          t)))

;'update-facts' adds the consequences to the fact list
;input: consequences
;output: t

(defun update-facts (consequences)
  (cond
    ((null consequences) t)
    (t (cond
         ((remember-new-fact (car consequences))
          (print (car consequences))
          (terpri)))
       (update-facts (cdr consequences)))))

;'fire-a-rule' fires an applicable rule
;input: rule
;output: t if this rule is fired, otherwise nil

(defun fire-a-rule (a-rule)
  (cond
    ((and
       (test-antecedents (get-antecedents a-rule))
       (check-consequences (get-consequences a-rule)))
     (print (list (nth 0 a-rule) (nth 1 a-rule) 'IS 'FIRED))
     (terpri)
     (print 'DEDUCE)
     (terpri)
     (update-facts (get-consequences a-rule)))))

;'chain-forward' fires all applicable rules
;input: the rule list
;output: nil

(defun chain-forward (rulelist)
  (cond
    ((null rulelist)
     (terpri)
     (print '(NO FURTHER FORWARD INFERENCE))
     (terpri))
    ((fire-a-rule (car rulelist))
     (chain-forward *rules*))
    (t (chain-forward (cdr rulelist)))))           (11-20)
```

Example 11.11 Execution of simple forward chaining LISP system. Note: In many of the examples in this chapter and Chapters 12 and 13, we represent facts on the factlist ∗facts∗ as simply atoms (e.g., ∗facts∗ could be (f1 f2 f3 ...)) for simplicity. Example 11.13 shows a more detailed example of fact and rule specification.

```
(setq *facts* '(f1 f4 f6 f7 f8 f9 f10 f11 f12 f14 f15 f16 f17
f18 f23 f24))
```

```
(setq *rules* '((rule m (IF a b c) (THEN z))
                (rule n (IF d e f g) (THEN z))
                (rule p (IF f1 f2) (THEN a))
                (rule q (IF f1 f3 f4) (THEN a))
                (rule r (IF f4 f5) (THEN b))
                (rule s (IF f6 f7) (THEN b))
                (rule t (IF f7 f8 f9) (THEN c))
                (rule u (IF f10 f11 f12) (THEN d))
                (rule v (IF f13 f14) (THEN d))
                (rule w (IF f14 f15 f16) (THEN e))
                (rule x (IF f17 f18) (THEN f))
                (rule y (IF f19 f20 f21 f22) (THEN g))
                (rule z (IF f23 f24) (THEN g))))
```

```
$ lisp
Franz Lisp, Opus 38.79
-> (load 'fwd_r.l)
[load fwd_r.l]
t
-> (chain-forward *rules*)
(rule s IS FIRED)
DEDUCE
b
(rule t IS FIRED)
DEDUCE
c
(rule u IS FIRED)
DEDUCE
d
(rule w IS FIRED)
DEDUCE
e
(rule x IS FIRED)
DEDUCE
f
(rule z IS FIRED)
DEDUCE
g
(rule n IS FIRED)
DEDUCE
z

(NO FURTHER FORWARD INFERENCE)
nil                                                            (11-21)
```

Example 11.12   Sample fact and rule databases (lists).

```
(setq *facts* '(a b g))
```

```
(setq *rules* '((rule 1 (IF a b) (THEN c))
                (rule 2 (IF b g) (THEN d))
                (rule 3 (IF a c) (THEN e))
                (rule 4 (IF e d) (THEN f))
                (rule 5 (IF d g) (THEN f))))
```

```
-> (chain-forward *rules*)
(rule 1 IS FIRED)
DEDUCE
c
(rule 2 IS FIRED)
DEDUCE
d
(rule 3 IS FIRED)
DEDUCE
e
(rule 4 IS FIRED)
DEDUCE
f
```

```
(NO FURTHER FORWARD INFERENCE)
nil                                                                    (11-22)
```

Image Motion Description Example

We consider application of a rule-based system to the case of image motion understanding. More details may be found in [Schalkoff 1986]. In this example, knowledge about image motion in terms of several geometric constraints and (incomplete) numerical estimates is used to infer (via forward chaining) higher-level conclusions about the observed image motion.

A sample run of the forward chaining system is shown below. The scenario is limited, for illustration purposes, to the rulebase shown below. In an actual application, the rule and fact bases would be considerably larger. In the example shown, the b i represent image motion translation vector estimates. A sample system dialog follows.

Example 11.13   Sample forward chaining inference application database.

```
(setq *facts* '((b1 = b2) (b2 <> 0) (b1 <> 0)
                (abs (center region1 - center region2) less
                than (extent region2 - extent region1))
                (square regions)))
```

```
(setq *rules* '((rule reason1 (if (b1 <> 0) (b2 <> 0)
                                   (b1 = b2))
                              (then (same image motion))))
                (rule reason2 (if (b1 <> 0) (b2 <> 0)
                                  (b1 <> b2))
                              (then (different image motion))))
                (rule reason3 (if (square regions)
                                  (abs (center region1 -
                                        center region2)
                                    less than (extent region2
                                    - extent region1)))
                              (then (region1 contained in
                                    region2)))
                (rule reason4 (if (region1 contained in
                                    region2)
                                  (same image motion))
                              (then (region1 is a part of the
                              object imaged as region2)))))
```

Sample Execution

```
(load fwd_mtn.l)
t
-> chain-forward (*rules*)
(rule reason1 is fired)
deduce
(same image motion)
(rule reason3 is fired)
deduce
(region1 contained in region2)
(rule reason4 is fired)
deduce
(region1 is a part of the object imaged as region2)

(no further forward inference)
nil
```

$$(11\text{-}23)$$

Thus, the augmented *facts* list obtained from the forward chaining system in example 11.13 is

```
-> *facts*
((region1 is a part of the object imaged as region2)
 (region1 contained  inregion2)
 (same image motion)
 (b1 = b2)
 (b2 <> 0)
 (b1 <> 0)
```

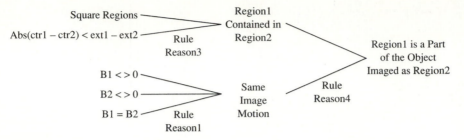

FIGURE 11.9
Sample inference net for forward chaining motion reasoning.

```
(abs (center region1 - center region2)  less  than
     (extent region2 - extent region1))
(square regions))                                        (11-24)
```

Figure 11.9 shows the resulting inference net and corresponding image motion descriptions obtained.

SUPPLEMENTAL EXAMPLES AND THE NONUNIQUE INFERENCE PATHS. In order to examine the operation of the forward chaining inference mechanism in more detail, we explore the sample rulebase in (11-25). Execution of the forward chaining inference engine with an assortment of alternative fact bases is continued in the problems.

> **Example 11.14   Rulebase for path analysis.** Consider the following simple rulebase in the form of (11-10).

```
(setq *rules* '(
                (rule 1 (IF a r) (THEN b))
                (rule 2 (IF b s) (THEN c))
                (rule 3 (IF a x) (THEN d))
                (rule 4 (IF d) (THEN c))
                (rule 5 (IF g) (THEN f))
                (rule 6 (IF h w) (THEN f))
                (rule 7 (IF f y) (THEN e))
                (rule 8 (IF c) (THEN e))
                (rule 9 (IF e) (THEN z))
                (rule 10 (IF m) (THEN i))
                (rule 11 (IF n) (THEN i))
                (rule 12 (IF o u) (THEN i))
                (rule 13 (IF i) (THEN j))
                (rule 14 (IF p t) (THEN j))
                (rule 15 (IF j v) (THEN z))
                (rule 16 (IF i) (THEN z))
                (rule 17 (IF k q) (THEN g))
                (rule 18 (IF l p) (THEN h))))       (11-25)
```

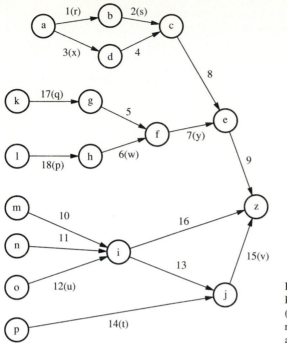

FIGURE 11.10
Possible solution paths for example 11.14
(goal is to produce "z"). Arc label indicates
rule number; other facts required to fire rule
are shown in parentheses.

Given this rulebase, together with a set of initial facts, our goal is to produce all possible facts, using forward chaining. Two important concerns arise:

1. The order in which rules are fired.
2. The nonuniqueness of the path from the initial fact base to the final fact list.

Figure 11.10 illustrates the point. All possible paths from rule antecedents to production of fact "z" (which is assumed to be the goal) are shown. Note that

1. Many paths are available.
2. The selection of applicable paths is a function of the initial database.

Further ramifications of this rulebase and initial fact lists are explored in the problems.

EXTENSIONS TO THE SIMPLE FORWARD CHAINING INFERENCE SYSTEM

The forward chaining approach of the previous section, while a useful first look at the "anatomy" of an IE, is of limited versatility, since

1. Matches of rule antecedents with the fact base are taken verbatim; statements contain no variables.

2. The matching process cannot invoke other actions, such as checking the value of a variable quantity, determining the meaning of a statement and using that for a match, or invoking a function and causing an additional (side) effect. An example is invocation of a "demon", described in Chapter 16.

3. The firing of rules occurs without considering which rules might be "preferable" or "best" (in some sense). In the implementation of (11-20), as soon as an applicable rule is found, it is fired.

For these reasons, the previous approach is extended in the remainder of this chapter.

Rule Selection, Specificity and the Conflict Set

The order in which rules are fired using function cha i n f o rwa r d (11-19) is determined by the initial database, and the path from the initial rulebase to one containing goal "z" may be predicted a priori.

RULE SELECTION AND FIRING STRATEGY FOR fwd_r . l. The previously developed inference engine of (11.20) follows the following strategy for forward chaining:

1. Find the first applicable rule. Recall applicable means that antecedents are found in the fact base and that all the consequents of the rule are not already in the fact base.

2. Fire the rule and augment the fact base; go to 1. Note that: at any given time, alternate inference nets, paths from the initial to final fact bases, are possible. It is the identification and efficient traversal of these paths that distinguish practical systems from those which simply employ exhaustive inference procedures.

$$(11\text{-}26)$$

THE CONFLICT SET. Consider the following alternative strategy for forward chaining inference:

1. Find all applicable rules.
2. From this set, choose a "good rule" or subset of "good" rules to fire (sample definitions of "good" are presented below).
3. Fire this rule or subset of rules and go to 1. $\qquad(11\text{-}27)$

The strategy of (11-27) alludes to the problem of *conflict resolution*, in the sense that a *choice* must be made in selecting rules. This selection process determines the path from initial to final databases and the solution efficiency. This, as indicated in Chapter 15, may spawn a need for search algorithms.

> The set of applicable rules constitutes the **conflict set**. Conflict resolution is thus the choosing of "good" rules. $\qquad(11\text{-}28)$

> **Example 11.15 Possible conflict resolution strategies.** Several approaches to conflict resolution exist. Examples are

1. In choosing "rule a" versus "rule b," examine the antecedents of both rules. If the antecedents of "rule a" are a superset of those of "rule b," then "rule a" is more specialized than "rule b." (Alternately, this means that more constraints must hold for "rule a" to be applicable). Consider, for example, the following two rules:

$$(\text{rule specific} \quad (\text{IF} \quad (\text{a b c d}))$$
$$(\text{THEN} \quad (\text{j k l}))) \qquad (11\text{-}29a)$$

$$(\text{rule general} \quad (\text{IF} \quad (\text{b d}))$$
$$(\text{THEN} \quad (\text{p q l}))) \qquad (11\text{-}29b)$$

One strategy is to choose the rule with the stricter precondition ("rule a" or specific in this case). We choose this rule on the grounds that it is more specialized to the current situation. This is known as **specificity-ordered conflict resolution**.

2. Examine the conflict set, and choose a rule whose firing moves the fact base (the system state) closer to the goal than any other rule. Of course, this implies we have a specific goal and some metric to measure current-state to goal-state disparity. This is the basis of search algorithm application and associated heuristics to conflict resolution.

3. Choose the rule that has the largest number of consequents, with the assumption that "more is better," that is, the more additional information produced, the closer the system is to the goal.

4. Rank rules according to "firing desirability" a priori.

If rules contain variables (the case considered below), it is possible for a rule to be used repeatedly. In this case, several additional conflict resolution strategies are possible:

5. Use the most recently used rule.
6. Use the least recently used rule.
7. Use the rule with the least (most) number of variables.

The above examples are merely suggestions for conflict resolution strategies. Other algorithms and heuristics, perhaps developed from more structured rule and fact bases, are also applicable to a given situation. In Chapter 13 we use *confidence measures* as another guide to conflict resolution. In addition, combinations of the above examples may be used. Some of these are explored in Chapter 13. Figure 11.7 shows the overall strategy of forward chaining with conflict resolution. Note this presupposes formulation of a goal, which may be as simple as "produce all possible facts" (which is usually impractical) or "prove fact z." More is said on goal satisfaction and hypothesis generation in the following chapters.

On the basis of the above reasoning, we modify the previous forward chaining algorithm to implement conflict resolution. The modified functions are shown below. In examples 11.16–11.18, the entire conflict set is identified and all the rules in the conflict set are then fired. After firing all rules in the conflict set, the new facts are printed out and another conflict set is determined, based upon the updated facts list. This step repeats until no further forward inferences are possible. Figure 11.7 summarizes the approach.

Example 11.16 Forward chaining implementation in LISP with explicit formation of conflict set.

Program listing (modified functions only)

```
;fwd_r1.l
;this program creates a conflict set which contains all
applicable rules
;and then fires them altogether.

;'form-conflict-set' finds all applicable rules
;input: the rule list
;output: the applicable rule list (conflict set)

(defun form-conflict-set (rulelist)
 (if (null rulelist) nil
     (if (check-rule (car rulelist))
         (cons (car rulelist)
               (form-conflict-set (cdr rulelist)))
         (form-conflict-set (cdr rulelist)))))



;'fire-rules' fires all applicable rules in the conflict set
;input: the applicable rule list (conflict-set)
;output: nil

(defun fire-rules (conflict-set)
 (cond
   ((null conflict-set) nil)
   (t (update-facts (get-consequences (car conflict-set)))
      (fire-rules (cdr conflict-set)))))



;'chain-forward1' gets started
;input: the rule list
;output: nil

(defun chain-forward1 (rulelist)
 (let ((conflict-set (form-conflict-set rulelist)))
      (cond
        ((null conflict-set)
         (terpri)
         (print '(NO FURTHER FORWARD INFERENCE))
         (terpri))
        (t (print '(FOLLOWING RULES APPLICABLE))
           (terpri)
           (pp conflict-set)
           (print '(NEW FACTS GENERATED FROM FIRING THESE RULES))
           (terpri)
           (fire-rules conflict-set)
           (terpri)
           (chain-forward1 rulelist)))))
```
                                                                    (11-30)

Example 11.17   Sample facts and rules databases for conflict resolution example.

```
(setq *facts* '(f1 f4 f6 f7 f8 f9 f10 f11 f12 f14 f15 f16 f17
f18 f23 f24))
(setq *rules* '((rule m (IF a b c) (THEN z))
                (rule n (IF d e f g) (THEN z))
                (rule p (IF f1 f2) (THEN a))
                (rule q (IF f1 f3 f4) (THEN a))
                (rule r (IF f4 f5) (THEN b))
                (rule s (IF f6 f7) (THEN b))
                (rule t (IF f7 f8 f9) (THEN c))
                (rule u (IF f10 f11 f12) (THEN d))
                (rule v (IF f13 f14) (THEN d))
                (rule w (IF f14 f15 f16) (THEN e))
                (rule x (IF f17 f18) (THEN f))
                (rule y (IF f19 f20 f21 f22) (THEN g))
                (rule z (IF f23 f24) (THEN g))))        (11-31a)
```

Example 11.18   Sample program results.

```
[load fwd_r1.l]
t
-> (chain-forward1 *rules*)
(FOLLOWING RULES APPLICABLE)
(setq conflict-set
        '((rule s (IF f6 f7) (THEN b))
          (rule t (IF f7 f8 f9) (THEN c))
          (rule u (IF f10 f11 f12) (THEN d))
          (rule w (IF f14 f15 f16) (THEN e))
          (rule x (IF f17 f18) (THEN f))
          (rule z (IF f23 f24) (THEN g))))
(NEW FACTS GENERATED FROM FIRING THESE RULES)
b
c
d
e
f
g

(FOLLOWING RULES APPLICABLE)
(setq conflict-set '((rule n (IF d e f g) (THEN z))))
(NEW FACTS GENERATED FROM FIRING THESE RULES)
z

(NO FURTHER FORWARD INFERENCE)
nil
-> (exit)                                               (11-31b)
```

The reader is encouraged to further verify the operation of this procedure.

Forward Chaining with Variables in Rules

We show a second modification of the previous LISP programs, with an execution example, which enables variables in rules. The logical basis for MP with variables is described in Chapter 2 and involves the determination of a *unifying substitution*.

Recall, from Chapter 2, that the strategy for forward chaining is as follows:

$$
\begin{array}{ll}
p & \text{(fact in database)} \\
p^1 \rightarrow q^1 & \text{(rules with variables)} \\
\underline{p^1\theta = p} & \underline{\text{(a unifying substitution, } \theta \text{, exists)}} \\
q^1\theta & \text{(produce new fact using } \theta)
\end{array}
\tag{11-32}
$$

Furthermore, for (11-32) to be meaningful implies there are no free variables in the implication statement.

When rules incorporate variables, the IE system design becomes considerably more complex. A unification algorithm (Chapter 10) is required to match the antecedent *list* against *facts*. In the case of an applicable rule, one or more unifying substitutions exist. This introduces additional complexity into conflict resolution. In the system shown below, functions are developed to produce and use *all* possible binding lists for an applicable rule. Of course, other strategies are possible (e.g., see the OPS5 approach in Chapter 13).

LISP IMPLEMENTATION OF FORWARD CHAINING WITH VARIABLES IN RULES.

> **Example 11.19 Program modification.** Note that this program uses functions get-bindings, var, and unify1 from Chapter 10.

```
;fwd_r2.l
;the forward chaining system using variables in rules

;'add-to-list' adds a new element to a list
;input: x -- a list
;       y -- a list of lists
;output: the list of lists

(defun add-to-list (x y)
  (if (null x) y
      (if (member x y) y
          (cons x y))))
;'combine-two-lists' adds new elements in first list to
second list
;input: x -- a list of lists
;       y -- a list of lists
;output: the list of lists
```

```
(defun combine-two-lists (x y)
  (if (null x) y
      (if (member (car x) y) (combine-two-lists (cdr x) y)
          (combine-two-lists (cdr x) (cons (car x) y)))))

;'get-binding-list' matches a variable list to a list of
lists
;input: x -- a list containing variables
;       z -- a list of facts
;output: the binding lists

(defun get-binding-list (x z)
  (if (null z) nil
      (add-to-list (unify1 x (car z) '((empty)))
                   (get-binding-list x (cdr z)))))

;'argument-binding-list' modifies the binding list
;input: x -- the list containing variables
;       y -- the fact
;       blist -- the binding list
;output: the binding list

(defun argument-binding-list (x y blist)
  (if (null blist) nil
      (add-to-list (unify1 x y (car blist))
                   (argument-binding-list x y (cdr blist)))))
;'match-with-factlist' matches a variable list with the fact
list
;given the binding list
;input: x -- the list containing variable
;       z -- the list of facts
;       blist -- the binding lists
;output: the binding lists

(defun match-with-factlist (x z blist)
  (if (null z) nil
      (combine-two-lists (argument-binding-list x (car z) blist)
                         (match-with-factlist x (cdr z) blist))))

;'find-antecedent-bindings' gets all possible bindings for
antecedents
;input: antecedents
;output: the binding list if all antecedents are on the fact
                                            list,
;                                    otherwise nil
(defun find-antecedent-bindings (antecedents)
  (do
    ((blist (get-binding-list (car antecedents) *facts*))
     (alist (cdr antecedents) (cdr alist)))
    ((or (null blist) (null alist)) blist)
```

```lisp
(setq blist (match-with-factlist (car alist) *facts* blist))))
;'substantiate' substantiates a variable list with bindings
;input: x -- a list with variables
;        bindings -- the binding list
;output: the list with variables bound to their values

(defun substantiate (x bindings)
 (if (null x) nil
     (if (var (car x))
         (cons (get-bindings (car x) bindings)
               (substantiate (cdr x) bindings))
         (cons (car x)
               (substantiate (cdr x) bindings)))))

;'check-consequences' checks if any consequence is not on the
fact list
;input: consequences and the binding list
;output: t if any consequence is not on the fact list,
;          otherwise nil

(defun check-consequences (consequences bindings)
 (if (null consequences) nil
     (if (recall-fact (substantiate (car consequences)
         bindings))
         (check-consequences (cdr consequences))
         t)))
;'update-facts' adds consequences to the fact list
;input: consequences and the binding list
;output: t

(defun update-facts (consequences bindings)
 (cond
  ((null consequences) t)
  (t (cond
     ((remember-new-fact (substantiate (car consequences)
       bindings))
      (print (substantiate (car consequences) bindings))
      (terpri)))
     (update-facts (cdr consequences) bindings))))

;'fire-a-rule' fires an applicable rule
;input: rule
;output: t if this rule is fired, otherwise nil

(defun fire-a-rule (a-rule)
 (let
  ((blist (find-antecedent-bindings
  (get-antecedents a-rule))))
  (if (null blist) nil
      (cond
```

```
((check-consequences (get-consequences a-rule) blist)
    (print (list (nth 0 a-rule) (nth 1 a-rule)
    'IS 'FIRED))
    (terpri)
    (print 'DEDUCE)
    (terpri)
    (do
      ((b1 blist (cdr b1)))
      ((null b1) nil)
      (update-facts (get-consequences a-rule)
      (car b1)))))))))
;'chain-forward2' fires all applicable rules
;input: the rule list
;output: nil

(defun chain-forward2 (rulelist)
  (cond
    ((null rulelist)
     (terpri)
     (print '(NO FURTHER FORWARD INFERENCE))
     (terpri))
    ((fire-a-rule (car rulelist))
     (chain-forward2 *rules*))
    (t (chain-forward2 (cdr rulelist)))))              (11-33)
```

Flowcharts for the strategy are shown in Figs. 11.11 and 11.12.

Example 11.20   Rule databases using variables.

```
(setq *rules* '((rule 1 (IF ((?var? a) is-a (?var? b))
                            ((?var? b) is-a (?var? c)))
                        (THEN ((?var? a) is-a (?var? c)))))))
```
                                                        (11-34)

Example 11.21   Trace selected functions of the forward chaining system with variables in rules. First, we show a simple rulelist:

```
-> (pp *rules*)
(setq *rules*
      '((rule 1
              (IF ((?var? a) is-a (?var? b)) ((?var? b) is-a
                  (?var? c)))
              (THEN ((?var? a) is-a (?var? c))))))
t
-> (setq a-rule (car *rules*))
(rule 1 (IF ((?var? a) is-a (?var? b))
((?var? b) is-a (?var? c)))
(THEN ((?var? a) is-a (?var? c))))
-> (setq ant-list (get-antecedents a-rule))
(((?var? a) is-a (?var? b)) ((?var? b) is-a (?var? c)))
```

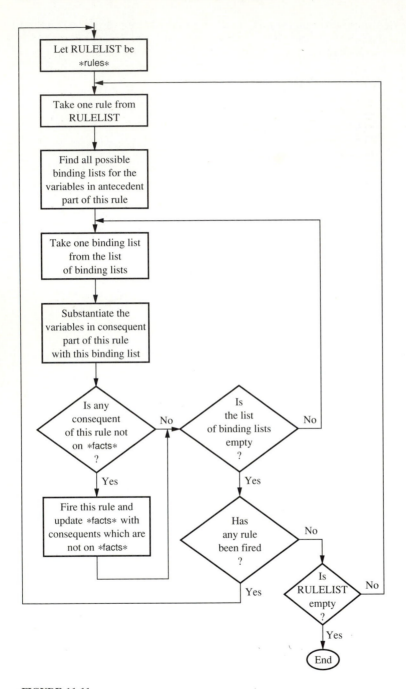

FIGURE 11.11
The flowchart of fwd_r2.1 (forward chaining with variables).

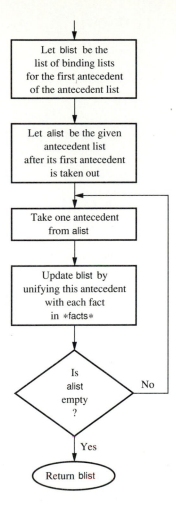

FIGURE 11.12
The flowchart for function find-antecedent-bindings (this function finds all the binding lists for given antecedent lists).

For illustration, we use an expanded list of facts:

```
-> (pp *facts*)
(setq *facts*
        '((at&t&t-pc is-a computer)
          (ncr-pc is-a computer)
          (ibm-pc is-a computer)
          (computer is-a electronic-device)))
    t
```

To show the results of finding all possible antecedent bindings:

```
-> (setq all-bindings (find-antecedent-bindings ant-list))
 :
 :
-> (pp all-bindings)
(setq all-bindings
```

```
'(((c electronic-device) (b computer) (a ibm-pc)
  (empty))
 ((c electronic-device) (b computer) (a ncr-pc)
  (empty))
 ((c electronic-device) (b computer) (a at&t&t-pc)
  (empty))))
t
```

We look at the operation of function substantiate:

```
-> (substantiate (car ant-list) (nth 0 all-bindings))
(ibm-pc is-a computer)
-> (substantiate (nth 1 ant-list) (nth 1 all-bindings))
(computer is-a electronic-device)                          (11-35)
```

Example 11.22   Sample execution of forward chaining system with variables.

```
-> (load 'fwd_r2.l)
[load fwd_r2.l]
t
-> (chain-forward2 *rules*)
(rule 1 IS FIRED)
DEDUCE
(ibm-pc is-a electronic-device)

(NO FURTHER FORWARD INFERENCE)
nil
-> *facts*
((ibm-pc is-a electronic-device) (ibm-pc is-a computer)
(computer is-a electronic-device))                          (11-36)
```

Examples of Conflict Resolution
Strategies and Resulting Rule Firing Sequences

In this section we investigate the resulting sequences of rule firings in a forward chaining system with different conflict resolution strategies. All three cases apply to the following initial database (*facts*) and rule set (*rules*):

Example 11.23   *facts* and *rules*.

```
-> *facts*
(f b g e)

-> *rules*
((rule 1 (IF f b) (THEN s i))
 (rule 2 (IF f b s) (THEN e))
 (rule 3 (IF s j q) (THEN d))
 (rule 4 (IF s e) (THEN a i)))
```

```
(rule 5 (IF g f b) (THEN j))
(rule 6 (IF s a) (THEN p q))
(rule 7 (IF s e g i) (THEN j k))
(rule 8 (IF a s j q) (THEN d p)))                    (11-37)
```

For each case explored below, we assume the goal is to fire rules until no more applicable rules are found. Specifically, we are interested in determining

1. The sequence of rule firings and the final system database (i.e., the contents of ∗facts∗ when no more rules are applicable.
2. A diagram of the database before and after each rule firing.

The conflict resolution strategies used are arranged into three cases:

case 1: Same strategy as fwd_r.l (11-20), that is, the first applicable rule is fired and the process of finding an applicable rule restarts on the modified database.

case 2: The same conflict resolution strategy as fwd_r1.l, (11-29), that is, the entire conflict set is formed and then all rules in the conflict set are fired. Following this, a new conflict set is formed using the updated database, all rules in the conflict set are fired, and the process repeats.

case 3: Specificity ordered conflict resolution. The conflict set is formed, as in case 2, but only the most specific rule is fired. Then the new database is used to find the new conflict set and, again, the most specific rule is fired. We consider "rule a" to be more specific than "rule b" if "rule b's" antecedant list is contained in the antecedent list of "rule a".

Example 11.24   Forward chaining using first applicable rule (case 1).

```
[load fwd_r.l]
t
-> (load 'database2.l)
[load database2.l]
t
-> ∗facts∗
(f b g e)
-> (pp-form ∗rules∗)
((rule 1 (IF f b) (THEN s i))
 (rule 2 (IF f b s) (THEN e))
 (rule 3 (IF s j q) (THEN d))
 (rule 4 (IF s e) (THEN a i))
 (rule 5 (IF g f b) (THEN j))
 (rule 6 (IF s a) (THEN p q))
 (rule 7 (IF s e g i) (THEN j k))
 (rule 8 (IF a s j q) (THEN d p)))
nil
-> (chain-forward ∗rules∗)
(rule 1 IS FIRED)
```

```
DEDUCE
s
i
(rule  4  IS  FIRED)
DEDUCE
a
(rule  5  IS  FIRED)
DEDUCE
j
(rule  6  IS  FIRED)
DEDUCE
p
q
(rule  3  IS  FIRED)
DEDUCE
d
(rule  7  IS  FIRED)
DEDUCE
k
(NO  FURTHER  FORWARD  INFERENCE)
nil
-> *facts*
(k  d  q  p  j  a  i  s  f  b  g  e)                          (11-38)
```

The rule sequence is thus 1-4-5-6-3-7, and the final database is shown above and in Fig. 11.13.

Example 11.25   Forward chaining using conflict set (Case 2).

```
[load  fwd_r1.l]
t
->  (load  'database2.l)
[load  database2.l]
```

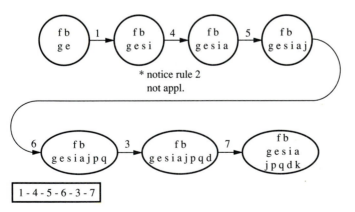

1-4-5-6-3-7

FIGURE 11.13
Case 1: fire first applicable rule.

```
t
-> *facts*
(f  b  g  e)
-> (pp-form *rules*)
((rule 1 (IF f b) (THEN s i))
 (rule 2 (IF f b s) (THEN e))
 (rule 3 (IF s j q) (THEN d))
 (rule 4 (IF s e) (THEN a i))
 (rule 5 (IF g f b) (THEN j))
 (rule 6 (IF s a) (THEN p q))
 (rule 7 (IF s e g i) (THEN j k))
 (rule 8 (IF a s j q) (THEN d p)))
nil
-> (chain-forward1 *rules*)
(FOLLOWING RULES APPLICABLE)
((rule 1 (IF f b) (THEN s i)) (rule 5 (IF g f b) (THEN j)))
(NEW FACTS GENERATED FROM FIRING THESE RULES)
(RULE: . 1)
DEDUCES:_s
i

(RULE: . 5)
DEDUCES:_j


(FOLLOWING RULES APPLICABLE)
((rule 4 (IF s e) (THEN a i)) (rule 7 (IF s e g i)
(THEN j k)))
(NEW FACTS GENERATED FROM FIRING THESE RULES)
(RULE: . 4)
DEDUCES:_a
(RULE: . 7)
DEDUCES:_k
(FOLLOWING RULES APPLICABLE)
((rule 6 (IF s a) (THEN p q)))
(NEW FACTS GENERATED FROM FIRING THESE RULES)
(RULE: . 6)
DEDUCES:_p
q


(FOLLOWING RULES APPLICABLE)
((rule 3 (IF s j q) (THEN d)) (rule 8 (IF a s j q)
(THEN d p)))
(NEW FACTS GENERATED FROM FIRING THESE RULES)
(RULE: . 3)
DEDUCES:_d
(RULE: . 8)
DEDUCES:_
```

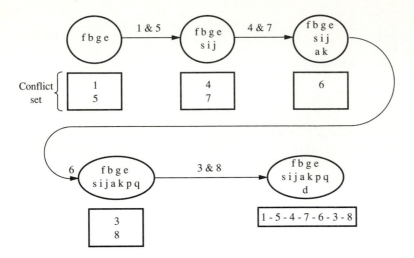

FIGURE 11.14
Case 2: form entire conflict set and fire all.

```
(NO  FURTHER  FORWARD  INFERENCE)
nil
-> *facts*
(d  q  p  k  a  j  i  s  f  b  g  e)
```
(11-39)

Thus, the rule sequence is (1-5)-(4-7)-6-3-8, and the final database is shown above and in Fig. 11.14.

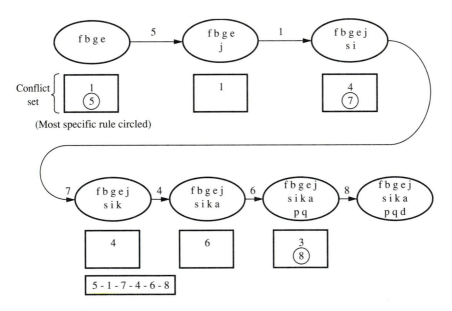

FIGURE 11.15
Case 3: Specificity ordered conflict resolution.

Example 11.26 **Specificity ordered conflict resolution (Case 3).** Results are shown in Fig. 11.15.

SUMMARY

In this chapter elements of rule-based inference using forward chaining have been explored. A number of practical and theoretical topics arose and yielded LISP implementations of increasing complexity. In the next chapter we continue our analysis of rule-based systems (in LISP) by considering the alternative strategy of *backward chaining*.

REFERENCES

[Asada/Yachida/Tsuji 1984] Asada, M., M. Yachida, and S. Tsuji, "Analysis of Three-Dimensional Motions in Blocks World," *Pattern Recognition*, Vol. 17, No. 1, 1984.
[Ni 1986] Ni, H.P, "Blackboard Systems-Blackboard Application Systems, Blackboard Systems from a Knowledge Engineering Perspective," *AI Magazine*, Vol. 7, No. 3, August 1986, pp. 82–106.
[Nilsson 1980] Nilsson, N.J., *Principles of Artificial Intelligence*, Tioga Publishers, Palo Alto, CA, 1980.
[Schalkoff 1986] Schalkoff, R.J., "Automated Reasoning About Image Motion Using a Rule-Based Deduction System," *Image and Vision Computing*, Vol. 4, No. 2, May 1986, pp. 97–106.

PROBLEMS

11.1. Referring to the fact and rule bases shown in LISP on Figs. P11.1 and P11.2 , using the forward chaining LISP program developed in this chapter (fwd_r.1) show the exact and unique sequence in which rules are fired until no further forward inferences are possible.

11.2. Notice in examples 11.24, 11.25, and 11.26 that the final facts lists are the same despite different conflict resolution strategies. Why does this happen? In general, under what conditions will this occur?

11.3. Modify fwd_r.l, fwd_r1.l and fwd_r2.l so that a goal may be specified. After each conflict resolution step, and prior to forming the new conflict set, the system checks to see if the goal has been obtained. Consider the specification of one or more facts as a goal. (Hint: a function contained−in may be useful.) Show your results using

(a) the databases of examples 11.24 and 11.25 with the goal being a database containing facts (q k).

(b) the database of Fig. P11.2 with the goal being a database containing facts (z).

(c) The database of Fig. P11.2 with the goal being a database containing facts (d f).

11.4. Modify the forward chaining system in example 11.16 (fwd_r1.l) to achieve conflict resolution via specificity-ordered conflict resolution. Test your results using the database of Fig. P11.2. Consider two cases:

(a) The "specificity" of a rule is defined simply as the number of antecedents (hint: the LISP function length and the results of problem 8.9 may be of use).

(b) rule−a is more specific than rule−b if the antecedents to rule−b are contained in those of rule−a. (The development of function contained−in may help here.)

```
(setq *rules* '(
                 (rule 1  (IF a r)  (THEN b))
                 (rule 2  (IF b s)  (THEN c))
                 (rule 3  (IF a x)  (THEN d))
                 (rule 4  (IF d)    (THEN c))
                 (rule 5  (IF g)    (THEN f))
                 (rule 6  (IF h w)  (THEN f))
                 (rule 7  (IF f y)  (THEN e))
                 (rule 8  (IF c)    (THEN e))
                 (rule 9  (IF e)    (THEN z))
                 (rule 10 (IF m)    (THEN i))
                 (rule 11 (IF n)    (THEN i))
                 (rule 12 (IF o u)  (THEN i))
                 (rule 13 (IF i)    (THEN j))
                 (rule 14 (IF p t)  (THEN j))
                 (rule 15 (IF j v)  (THEN z))
                 (rule 16 (IF i)    (THEN z))
                 (rule 17 (IF k q)  (THEN g))
                 (rule 18 (IF l p)  (THEN h))))
```

(a)

case i:

```
(setq *facts* '(a r s))
```

case ii:

```
(setq *facts* '(k g y))
```

case iii:

```
(setq *facts* '(o u))
```

(b)

FIGURE P11.1
Database for problems 11.1–11.4. (a) The rulebase; (b) sample fact bases.

Compare the inference nets for each case with those of the simplistic conflict resolution strategy of fwd_r.l.

11.5. (a) Show, using the definition of "commutative," some reasoning, and a simple example, why any PROLOG system in which facts are modified with the retract
   predicate cannot, in general, be a commutative production system.
   (b) Does this also hold for retract applied to rules?
   (c) Can a production system that uses the logical NOT in rule antecedents, for example,

   (IF (a b (NOT c)) (THEN d))

   be commutative? Show an example to justify your answer.

```
(setq *rules* '(
                    (rule 1 (IF a r s) (THEN b g c))
                    (rule 2 (IF b s) (THEN c e h i))
                    (rule 3 (IF a s) (THEN d e))
                    (rule 4 (IF r s)  (THEN c d e g b))
                    (rule 5 (IF g b s) (THEN f x y z))
                    (rule 6 (IF a g b s) (THEN r))))

(setq *facts* '(a r s))
```

FIGURE P11.2
Modified database.

11.6. A knowledge engineer suggests the following alternative for the design of an IE to produce new facts.

```
p -> (p2 -> q2 )          true
p2                        true
p                         true
_____

q2                        true
```

Give a detailed account of how the IE would function for this strategy. Show this via a flowchart. How would conflict resolution be handled? Show a simple example. Sketch the basic outline of a suitable LISP program.

11.7. (a) Show all possible solution paths for the rulebase in Fig. P11.1, where the goal state is to infer z.

(b) repeat (a) for the rulebase of Fig. P11.2.

11.8. (a) What would happen to the operation of a rule-based system if, in the determination of the conflict set, we didn't check the consequent of a rule to see if it is not already in the fact base?

(b) The logical definition of an applicable production is one whose condition elements, that is, rule antecedents, are all TRUE. For *implementation* purposes, in our LISP forward chaining implementations, we extended this definition to require a logically applicable rule to also produce something new (i.e., not all consequences are on the facts list). Given a system that, according to the logical definition of applicable, is commutative, does our implementation-based definition preserve this property? Justify your answer.

11.9. Repeat problem 11.4 for the rulebase shown in Fig. P11.2, but employ "largest number of new consequents produced" as the conflict resolution strategy.

11.10. (a) Suggest, with appropriate justification, reasonable conflict resolution methodologies other than those in the text. Indicate the utility of each.

(b) As in (a), suggest ways to combine conflict resolution strategies.

11.11. Consider the following alternative, but rule-based, inference strategy, which takes three TRUE statements and produces two results:

```
s1.        p
s2.        p → q
s3.        (r ∩ q) → s
           -----------
r1.           q
r2.        (r → s)
```

Notice that MP is a subset of this result, using statements s1 s2 and result r1.

(a) Verify the logical correctness of this more general approach.

(b) The fact that a *rule* is produced suggests this strategy could be used for learning. Indicate how this might be useful, and cite an example.

(c) How would this approach be implemented in LISP? Be as specific as possible. Indicate how the extensions would be implemented, and how chaining would proceed.

(d) (Project idea) Show a LISP implementation for (c).

11.12. Given the following database, what is the result when used with fwd_2.1?

```
(setq *facts* ' ((shirley is a parent of leslie)
                 (leslie is a parent of jesse)
                 (tom is a parent of mark)
                 (mark is a parent of peter)))
(setq *rules* ' ((rule rule1
             (IF ((?var? Parent) is a parent of
                  (?var? Child))
                 ((?var? Child) is a parent of
                  (?var? Grandchild)))
             (THEN ((?var? Parent) is a grandparent of
                   (?var? Grandchild))))))
```

11.13. We noted in PROLOG that a fact may be considered a rule with no antecedents. Is it possible, using our LISP implementations, to formulate additional facts as rules with no antecedents?

11.14. Consider an application of forward chaining to image region analysis where facts are entered as

```
(inside p1 p2)
```

```
(inside p3 p6)
```

.

.

.

The first fact indicates, for example, that region p1 is contained inside region p2. Formulate a database of rules and facts and use fwd_r2.1 to determine

(a) An augmented list of facts enumerating all information about "inside."

(b) The identity of the region that has the largest number of regions inside it.

11.15. (*a*) In this problem, we consider revision of the forward chaining rule-based system to allow computation of a value by modifying antecedents to include the keyword ACTION.
For example,

```
IF(f1  f2  (ACTION  get−f3−truth−value  RETURN  (xval))  f6)

(THEN  (f8  f9  (xval)  ]
```

Show the checking of the third antecedent which, as a side effect, causes the value <xval> to be computed. Modify fwd_r.l to allow this capability.

(*b*) Extend fwd_r.l to allow for the negation of facts, that is, the database and rule antecedents and consequents may contain facts such as

```
(not  a).
```

11.16. Using fwd_r2.l (the forward chaining system with variables), implement the positive formulation of the image-labeling problem from Chapter 5 using a rule-based approach. Include the unary constraints "highest" and "moving," and show sample results.

11.17. Using the database of Example 11.17 (11-31*a*), show the sequence of rule firings using a forward chaining approach with the conflict resolution strategy as follows:
Fire the rule in the conflict set that produces the largest number of new facts.

11.18. Consider a new conflict resolution approach that forms the conflict set and then picks a rule at random.

(*a*) Is this a reasonable conflict resolution strategy (justify your answer)?

(*b*) Modify fwd_r1.l to achieve this. (Hint: LISP provides the function)

```
(random  n)
```

Which returns a uniformly distributed random number between 0 and n.)

11.19. Modify fwd_r.1 to allow a don't care in one or more antecedents to a rule. (Hint: the results of problem 10.5 may be useful.)

11.20. Recall that function chainforward returns to the beginning of *rules* after firing an applicable rule. Revise or modify function chainforward so that, once a rule is fired, the next rule considered is the *next* rule in the database, that is, the next element of *rules* following the most recently fired rule.

11.21. Modify the rule structure and IE of fwd_r.l (11-20) to allow the following generalized productions:

```
(rule  name  (IF       ((antecedent  list)))
              (THEN     (ACTION−IS add−facts
                        ((consequent−list)))
                        (ACTION−IS delete−facts
                        ((delete−facts−list)))
                        (ACTION−IS modify  rule  ((rule−name)))]
                                                            (P11-21)
```

Note that the first ACTION−IS field in (P11-21) achieves the same effect as the previous consequent structure. The number of ACTION−IS fields should be arbitrary. Verify your results with an example.

11.22. Modify the rule structure and IE of fwd_r.l (11-20) to extend the specification of conditions for rule firing as follows:

```
... (IF (included-facts ((antecedent-list)))
       (not-included-facts ((not-antecedent-list))) ... (P11-22)
```

Note the first sublist in (P11-22) achieves the same effect as the previous rule structure (i.e., it requires checking to see that all antecedents are on *facts*). The second sublist provides a mechanism to implement the NOT operator. Verify your results with an example.

11.23. Using the modified formulation of problem 11.21 (P11-21), where *deletion* of facts is allowed, show an example where, given an initial database (*facts*), a different sequence of rule applications yields a significantly different final database.

CHAPTER 12

RULE-BASED INFERENCE SYSTEMS PART II— BACKWARD CHAINING WITH LISP IMPLEMENTATION

"Sire, I have no need of that hypothesis."

Pierre Simon de Laplace 1749–1827
Eric Temple Bell, Men of Mathematics [1937]

BACKWARD CHAINING

Backward chaining inference strategies are alternatives to forward chaining. Given a system representation with initial and goal states specified, backward chaining seeks to *derive one or more paths between the initial and goal states*. Recall from Chapter 11, forward chaining begins with the initial database and proceeds toward the goal state. Backward or consequent-driven chaining is, in essence, the "reverse" of forward chaining. It is mathematically justifiable and *not* equivalent to simply reversing the direction of implication.

> In backward chaining, the consequents, or THEN parts of rules are used to guide the search for rules to fire. (12-1)

Due to the "conditional" or "tentative" application of rules, backward chaining represents a revocable control strategy with significant emphasis on search.

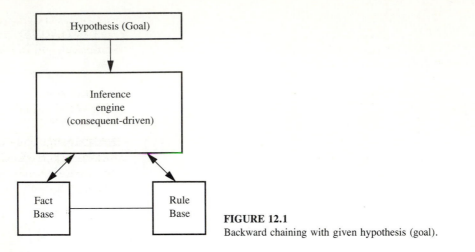

FIGURE 12.1
Backward chaining with given hypothesis (goal).

ANTECEDENT VS. CONSEQUENT DRIVEN CHAINING. Given a goal or hypothesis (a fact) to prove, backward chaining proceeds by examining the consequents of rules that contain this goal, and by making the antecedents of these rules new subgoals. This process proceeds until all the necessary rule antecedents are found in the database. Thus, unlike forward chaining, which is based upon initial examination of rule antecedents or *antecedent*-driven, backward chaining is consequent-driven. Figures 12.1 and 12.2 illustrate the overall concept.

IMPLEMENTATION STRATEGY. In developing LISP implementations for backward chaining, we proceed with an approach similar to that of Chapter 11. First, a simple

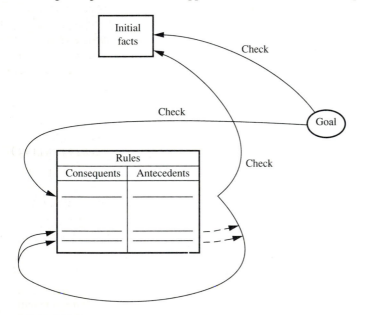

FIGURE 12.2
Overall backward chaining inference strategy.

case (with little attention to rule choice, search, and without variables) is used to develop the overall program structure. This structure is then enhanced to allow alternative search (rule selection) strategies and incorporate variables. Further extensions are considered in the problems.

The Basis for Backward Chaining

As an aid in the development of a backward chaining rule-based paradigm, the simple three-implication or three-rule system of Chapter 11, example 11.1, is used. Referring to Figs. 12.3 and 12.4, we illustrate a goal-directed strategy that allows backward chaining. Assume we are given

1. A database of implication statements (i.e., rules) and assertions that are assumed TRUE.
2. A *hypothesis*, h, which is a fact and included as part of the consequent, q, of implication (n). The goal is to prove h is TRUE.

> **Example 12.1   Three-rule example of backward chaining.** The approach is aided by the simple three-rule example of Fig. 12.4. Assume the hypothesis is q3. First, assuming that rule 3 is TRUE, the hypothesis (q3) will be verified if p3 is TRUE. The astute reader will note, from the implication truth table, that q3 may also be TRUE if p3 is FALSE. We address this concern in the problems. In other words, if p3 is TRUE, and the implication (rule 3) is TRUE, q3 must be TRUE from the implication truth table. We enclose rule 3 with a dotted curve and label its position (1) in the inference sequence to signify that rule 3 has *conditionally* fired first, as shown in Figure 12.4a. Thus, a new (sub)goal is to verify that p3 is TRUE.
>
> Repeating the process, if (implication) rule 2 is TRUE, and the goal is to prove p3 is TRUE, p3 is TRUE if p2 is TRUE. We draw a dotted curve around rule 2 and p3

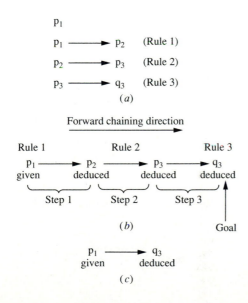

p_1

$p_1 \longrightarrow p_2$ (Rule 1)

$p_2 \longrightarrow p_3$ (Rule 2)

$p_3 \longrightarrow q_3$ (Rule 3)

(*a*)

Forward chaining direction

Rule 1   Rule 2   Rule 3

$p_1 \longrightarrow p_2 \longrightarrow p_3 \longrightarrow q_3$
given   deduced   deduced   deduced

Step 1   Step 2   Step 3

(*b*)   Goal

$p_1 \longrightarrow q_3$
given   deduced

(*c*)

FIGURE 12.3
Simple example of inference net for forward chaining (goal is to verify "q_3"). (*a*) Database; (*b*) forward chaining sequence (3 steps); (*c*) overall result.

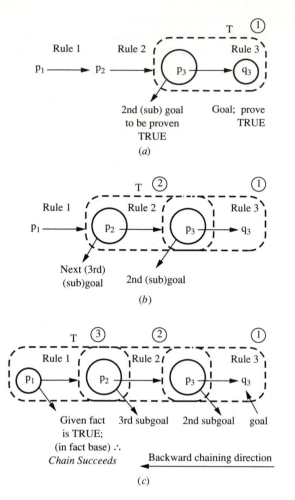

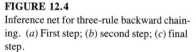

FIGURE 12.4
Inference net for three-rule backward chaining. (*a*) First step; (*b*) second step; (*c*) final step.

and p2 to indicate conditional firing of rule 2 (if p2 may be verified to be TRUE). This is shown in Fig. 12.4. Notice that these dotted regions overlap where the antecedent of one rule and the consequent of another are the same. We are thus investigating the backwards "chain" ("house of cards" might be a better description). Our goal now is to prove that p2 is TRUE.

Since rule 1 is TRUE, p2 (the consequent of rule 1) will be TRUE if p1 is TRUE. Since p1 was given (in the database) to be TRUE, by proceeding backwards we have determined the truth value of p3. A path from a database containing p3 to the initial database (p1) has been found by working in the "reverse" direction.   (12-2)

The reader should ascertain, from the above example, that we are *not* employing the converse of an implication, that is,

$$q \rightarrow p \qquad\qquad (12\text{-}3)$$

in the backward chaining process. Note:

In the backward chaining paradigm, we are employing the (assumed TRUE) implication form $(p \rightarrow q)$, contained in the rulebase. We are using this implication to establish that consequents are TRUE, conditioned upon the fact that their antecedents are TRUE. We do this in the backward direction, working from the desired hypothesis to the elementary (given) facts in the database.   (12-4)

Example 12.2   More complex example of subgoal generation and propagation.
Example 12.1 (Fig. 12.4) illustrates the backward chaining concept. The general case of backward chaining is more complex, however, because rule antecedents and goals are specified as the *conjunction* of a number of facts, all of which must be verified. This is shown in Fig. 12.5. For example, consider a simple rule such as

```
(rule r1 (IF f c q) (THEN z))
```
                                                                (12-5)

Specification of a goal, z, causes creation of a set of subgoals, namely (f c g).

```
(setq  *rules* ' (
        (rule r1      (IF      f c g) (THEN  z) )
        (rule r2      (IF      d e) (THEN  f) )
        (rule r3      (IF      a b) (THEN  c) ) )

(setq  *facts* ' (a  b  d  e  g) )
```
                                (*a*)

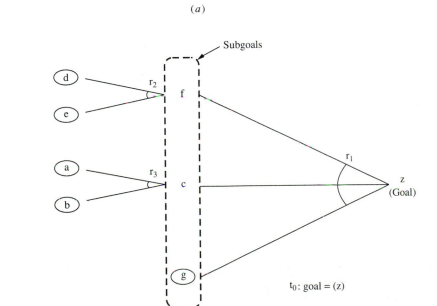

t_2: subgoals = (d e a b) t_1: subgoals = (f c g)
Progagation direction for unsatisfied subgoals
                        (*b*)

FIGURE 12.5
Backward chaining example involving multiple subgoals. (*a*) *facts* and *rules* for Example 12.2; (*b*) Backward chaining inference net showing propagation of subgoals. Goal is production of fact z. Circles indicate facts on *facts*.

TABLE 12.1
A simple backward chaining algorithm (outline)

Given: A goal (set of facts to verify). Denote these as the set of facts G, comprising the goal state, Sg.

Step 1. Check each element of G to see if it exists in the initial database (on `*facts*`). If so, consider it verified, and delete it from G. If G is empty, the goal is verified (a path from the goal state to the initial state has been found), otherwise go to step 2.

Step 2. For each element of (the filtered or modified) G, that is, g_i, find the set of rules that contain g_i in their consequents. (Note several g_i may appear in a single rule). Denote this set L_i. (Note that a specific rule may be contained in several L_i.) If any L_i are empty, this means that it is not possible to produce this g_i with the given fact and rule bases. In other words, a path between S_i and a state containing g_i does not exist. At this point it is necessary to either

    (a) Back up (if possible) and select alternative (revised) choices and corresponding subgoals. If no alternatives exist, the goal cannot be verified; or

    (b) Query the user as to the truth of facts that are not derivable along this path.

Step 3. Choose one rule from each of the L_i. The union of the antecedents to all of these rules is the new set of subgoals. This replaces G. Go to step 1.

Assuming that none of these are contained in the factbase, it is possible each of these is a consequent of one or more rules. This yields problems of

1. Rule selection (choices) or conflict resolution.
2. A possibly large and increasing set of new subgoals.

This complexity is considered further using the database of Example 12.10, after we consider the quantification of a simple backwards chaining strategy.

The reader should be aware that the choices involved in rule selection and choice of a backup point in steps 2 and 3 in Table 12.1 may significantly affect the determination of the path from the goal to initial states (provided one exists). These are aspects of the underlying search problem (Chapter 15). This algorithm is similar to that of the backward-state propagation algorithm for planning in Chapter 14.

Results using the algorithm of Table 12.1 with the database of Example 12.10 are shown in Fig. 12.6.

Hypothesis Generation and Application to Intelligent Systems

Hypothesis generation is a significant aspect of intelligent behavior. The function of a rule-based backward chaining system with hypothesis generation may be shown using the following sample application:

    Example 12.3 Hypothesis generation application. An image processing engineer wishes to develop a rule-based system for the determination of the identity of objects appearing in an image. The design should be rule based. The system employs feature extraction to guide the rulebase chaining by reducing the possible hypotheses concerning object identity to a manageable set. For example, if features extracted are circular primitives, a restricted set of object identity hypotheses may be formulated.

1. $G = \{z\}$ (step 1 of algorithm of Table 12.1)

2. $L_1 = \{m\ n\}$ (step 2)

3. Choose rule m. (step 3; possible point to backup)
   $G = \{a\ b\ c\}$

4. $G = \{a\ b\ c\}$ (step 1; none on *facts*)

5. $L_1 = \{p\ q\}$ (step 2)
   $L_2 = \{r\ s\}$
   $L_3 = \{t\}$

6. Choose rules p, r, t. (step 3)
   $G = \{f1\ f2\ f4\ f5\ f7\ f8\ f9\}$

7. $G = \{f2\ f5\}$ (step 1)

8. $L_1 = \{0\}$ (step 2)
   $L_2 = \{0\}$

(Therefore must backup to continue solution.) Suppose (for illustration brevity) we backup to 3.

9. Choose rule n. (step 3)
   $G = \{d\ e\ f\ g\}$

10. $G = \{d\ e\ f\ g\}$ (step 1)
    $L_1 = \{u\ v\}$
    $L_2 = \{w\}$
    $L_3 = \{x\}$
    $L_4 = \{y\ z\}$

11. Choose rules u, w, x, z. (step 3)
    $G = \{f10\ f11\ f12\ f14\ f15\ f16\ f17\ f18\ f23\ f24\}$

12. $G = \{0\}$ (step 1; all are on *facts*)

FIGURE 12.6a
Example of backward chaining solution using the algorithm of table 12.1 and the database of example 12.10

Interpreting circular primitives as "wheels" allows generation of cars, trucks, wagons, bicycles, and motorcycles as goals to be confirmed and narrows considerably the computational requirements of the system. Note, however, that there is a cost associated with generation of hypotheses. If all of these hypotheses are incorrect, that is, the circles are not wheels but perhaps spools of wire, then the system is not likely to (efficiently) generate the correct object identity.   (12-6)

Figure 12.7 shows a block diagram representation of the system hierarchy.

The generation of "good" (where good is interpreted to mean reasonable and likely to be confirmed) hypotheses is presently, like "good" feature extraction, an art, as opposed to a clearly tractable science.   (12-7)

Abduction

A discussion of the mathematically tractable process known as **abduction** is included here for two reasons:

1. Abduction is related to the analysis of backward chaining and implication.

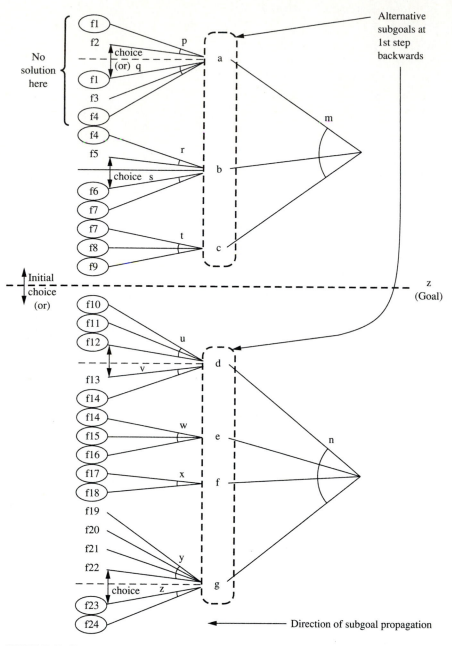

FIGURE 12.6*b*
Graphical depiction of rule alternatives or choices (search) for the backward chaining example 12.10
(circled facts are in database).

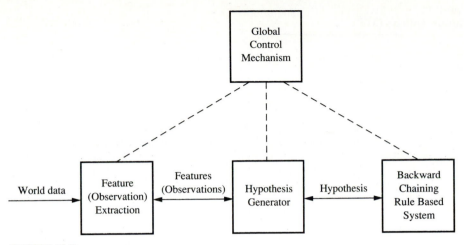

FIGURE 12.7
Hypothesis generation/backward chaining system structure.

2. Abduction is a mathematically justifiable, practical, and reasonable way to generate hypotheses.

Abduction is a modification of implication-based modus ponens (MP), shown in (12-8):

Example 12.4   MP and implication.

$$
\begin{array}{ll}
p \to q & \text{true} \\
p & \text{true} \\
\hline
q & \text{true}
\end{array}
\tag{12-8}
$$

We write abduction in a similar fashion but take considerable pains to interpret it correctly:

$$
\begin{array}{ll}
p \to q & \text{a rule; assumed TRUE} \\
q & \text{an observation ; assumed TRUE} \\
\hline
p & \text{an explanation ; possibly (but} \\
& \text{not necessarily) TRUE}
\end{array}
\tag{12-9}
$$

Thus, (12-9) provides a mechanism to explain (but not prove) an observed fact. The following example should help.

Example 12.5   Abduction.

Rule: If people are sick, they don't go to work.	(12-10*a*)
Observation: Ernie did not go to work.	(12-10*b*)
Possible Explanation (Abduction): Ernie was sick.	(12-10*c*)

TABLE 12.2
Modus Tollens (MT)

p → q

¬q
_____

¬p (an observation in the "negative sense")

Thus, the fact that "Ernie was sick" (12-10c) is one possible *explanation* for the observation of Ernie's not going to work, in the context of the above rule. However (12-10a) only explains (12-10b); it is not necessarily TRUE. For example, given the same observation and the additional rule:

Additional Rule: If people are on vacation, they don't go to work.   (12-10d)

we could also explain Ernie's absence due to his being on vacation. Either of the above explanations for Ernie's absence is plausible; neither is necessarily true. Each of these explanations provide a *hypothesis*, which could serve as a goal for verification.

EXTENDED EXPLANATION USING MODUS TOLLENS. A more rigorous logical formulation of explanation is provided by modus tollens (MT) (see Table 12.2). MT provides a logically sound explanation which is necessarily TRUE. The reader should verify the correctness of MT by showing

$$((p \rightarrow q) \cap \neg q) \rightarrow \neg p \qquad (12\text{-}11)$$

is a tautology.

LISP IMPLEMENTATIONS
OF BACKWARD CHAINING

Derivation of the Inference Engine

In this section, a sample backward chaining system is developed. In addition to the fact and rule bases, the algorithm requires specification of a goal. Note that we initially consider the case of rules without variables; extensions to this are straightforward. Many of the basic functions used are the same as, or slight modifications of, those used in the forward chaining design. Flowcharts of the program structure are used to help explain the design. An overall structure for a backward chaining strategy and flowcharts for selected LISP functions are shown in Figs. 12.8–12.10.

Lisp Implementation of Basic Backward
Chaining Algorithm

Example 12.6 LISP program listing (only modified functions shown).

```
;bwd_r.l
;this program implements the backward chaining algorithm.
```

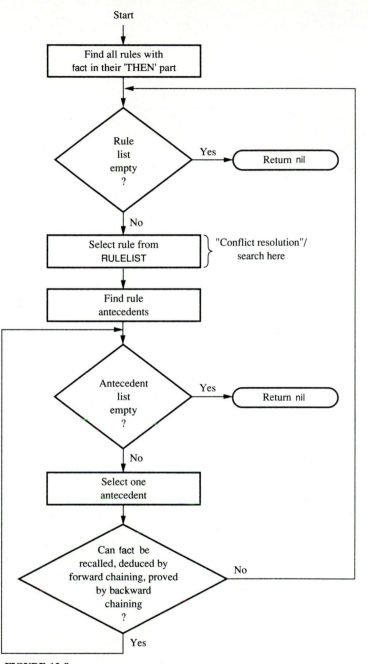

FIGURE 12.8
Function backward chaining.

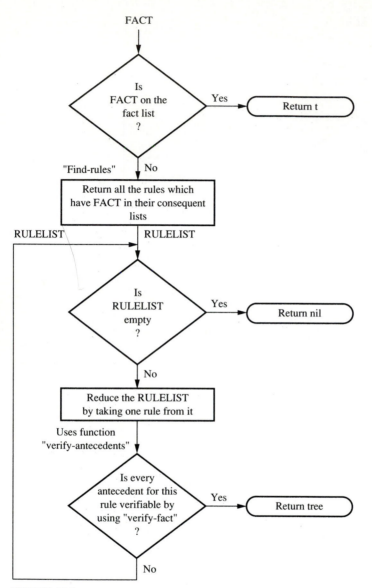

FIGURE 12.9
Flowchart for LISP function ver i fy–fact (used in backward chaining engine) .

```
;'find-rules' finds all rules with a given fact as its
   consequence.
;input: the fact and rule list
;output: the applicable rule list

(defun find-rules (fact rulelist)
  (if (null rulelist) nil
```

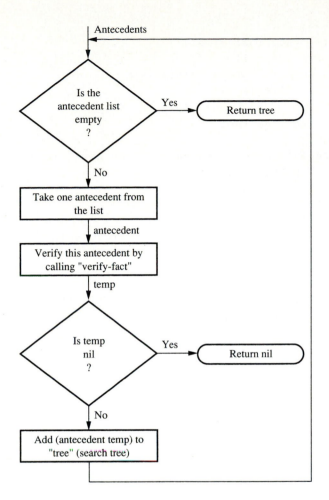

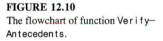

FIGURE 12.10
The flowchart of function Verify–
Antecedents.

```
(if (member fact (get-consequences (car rulelist)))
      (cons (car rulelist)
              (find-rules fact (cdr rulelist)))
      (find-rules fact (cdr rulelist)))))))


;'verify-antecedents' verifies all antecedents
;input: antecedents and the search tree
;output: the search tree

(defun verify-antecedents (antecedents)
  (do
    ((alist antecedents (cdr alist))
     (temp nil nil)
     (tree nil))
```

```lisp
     ((null alist) tree)
     (setq temp (verify-fact (car alist)))
     (if (null temp) (return nil)
         (setq tree (cons (list (car alist) temp)
                          tree)))))

;'verify-fact' verifies the fact
;input: fact
;output: nil if the fact can not be verified by backward chaining,
;        otherwise, the search tree
(defun verify-fact (fact)
 (if (recall-fact fact) t
     (do
        ((rulelist (find-rules fact *rules*) (cdr rulelist))
         (tree nil))
        ((null rulelist) nil)
        (let ((tree (verify-antecedents
                       (get-antecedents (car rulelist)))))
             (if tree
                 (return (cons (car rulelist)
                               tree)))))))

;'print-tree' prints the search tree
;input: the search tree
;output: nil

(defun print-tree (tree)
 (do
   ((temp tree (cdr temp)))
   ((null temp) nil)
   (cond
     ((equal (cadar temp) t)
       (print (append '(FACT) (list (caar temp))
                      '(IS ON THE FACT LIST)))
       (terpri))
     (t (print (append '(FACT) (list (caar temp))
                       '(CAN BE DEDUCED BY FIRING)))
       (terpri)
       (print (caadar temp))
       (terpri)
       (print-tree (cdadar temp))))))

;'chain-backward' verifies given facts
;input: the facts to be verified
;output: nil
```

```
(defun chain-backward (factlist)
 (cond
  ((null factlist)
   (terpri)
   (print '(NO MORE FACTS TO VERIFY))
   (terpri))
  (t (let ((tree (verify-fact (car factlist))))
          (cond
            (tree (setq tree (list (list (car factlist) tree)))
                  (print-tree tree))
            (t (print (append '(FACT) (list (car factlist))
                              '(CANNOT BE VERIFIED)))
          (terpri))))
      (chain-backward (cdr factlist)))))                    (12-12)
```

Example 12.7   Sample facts and rules for backward chaining.

```
(setq *facts* '(f1 f4 f6 f7 f8 f9 f10 f11 f12 f14 f15 f16 f17
                f18 f23 f24))

(setq *rules* '((rule m (IF a b c) (THEN z))
                (rule n (IF d e f g) (THEN z))
                (rule p (IF f1 f2) (THEN a))
                (rule q (IF f1 f3 f4) (THEN a))
                (rule r (IF f4 f5) (THEN b))
                (rule s (IF f6 f7) (THEN b))
                (rule t (IF f7 f8 f9) (THEN c))
                (rule u (IF f10 f11 f12) (THEN d))
                (rule v (IF f13 f14) (THEN d))
                (rule w (IF f14 f15 f16) (THEN e))
                (rule x (IF f17 f18) (THEN f))
                (rule y (IF f19 f20 f21 f22) (THEN g))
                (rule z (IF f23 f24) (THEN g))))        (12-13)
```

Example 12.8   Sample execution (chain-backward). **Assume the goal is to verify fact** z.

```
-> (load 'bwd_r.l)
[load bwd_r.l]
t
-> (chain-backward '(z))
(FACT z CAN BE DEDUCED BY FIRING)
(rule n (IF d e f g) (THEN z))
(FACT g CAN BE DEDUCED BY FIRING)
(rule z (IF f23 f24) (THEN g))
(FACT f24 IS ON THE FACT LIST)
(FACT f23 IS ON THE FACT LIST)
(FACT f CAN BE DEDUCED BY FIRING)
(rule x (IF f17 f18) (THEN f))
```

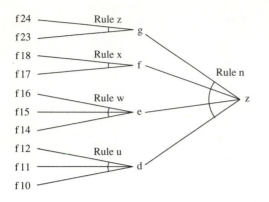

FIGURE 12.11
Inference net resulting from backward chaining example 12.7.

```
(FACT f18 IS ON THE FACT LIST)
(FACT f17 IS ON THE FACT LIST)
(FACT e CAN BE DEDUCED BY FIRING)
(rule w (IF f14 f15 f16) (THEN e))
(FACT f16 IS ON THE FACT LIST)
(FACT f15 IS ON THE FACT LIST)
(FACT f14 IS ON THE FACT LIST)
(FACT d CAN BE DEDUCED BY FIRING)
(rule u (IF f10 f11 f12) (THEN d))
(FACT f12 IS ON THE FACT LIST)
(FACT f11 IS ON THE FACT LIST)
(FACT f10 IS ON THE FACT LIST)
(NO MORE FACTS TO VERIFY)
nil
-> (exit)
```
(12-14)

Figure 12.11 shows the resulting inference nets.

Example 12.9 The motion description example (Chapter 11) using backward chaining. We continue our examination of the backward chaining paradigm by returning to the image processing example of Chapter 11.

Image motion rulebase, facts, and goal specification
```
(setq *facts* '((b1 = b2) (b2 <> 0) (b1 <> 0)
                (abs (center region1 - center region2) less than
                (extent region2 - extent region1))
                (square regions)))

(setq *rules* '((rule reason1 (if (b1 <> 0) (b2 <> 0) (b1 = b2))
                             (then (same image motion)))
                (rule reason2 (if (b1 <> 0) (b2 <> 0) (b1 <> b2))
                             (then (different image motion)))
```

```
(rule reason3 (if (square regions)
                  (abs (center region1 -
                        center region2)
                  less than (extent region2 -
                             extent region1)))
             (then (region1 contained in
                    region2)))
(rule reason4 (if (region1 contained in region2)
                  (same image motion))
             (then (region1 is a part of the object
                    imaged as region2)))))
```

```
(setq s '((region1 is a part of the object imaged as region2)))
```
                                                                                (12-15)

Sample execution
```
-> (load 'bwd_mtn.l)
[load bwd_mtn.l]
t
-> (chain-backward s)
(fact (region1 is a part of the object imaged
       as region2) can be deduced by firing)
(rule reason4 (if (region1 contained in region2) (same image
                                                  motion))
              (then (region1 is a part of the object imaged as
                     region2)))
(fact (same image motion) can be deduced by firing)
(rule reason1 (if (b1 <> 0) (b2 <> 0) (b1 = b2)) (then (same
                                                  image motion)))

(fact (b1 = b2) is on the fact list)
(fact (b2 <> 0) is on the fact list)
(fact (b1 <> 0) is on the fact list)
(fact (region1 contained in region2) can be deduced by firing)
(rule reason3 (if (square regions)
                  (abs (center region1 - center region2)
                   less than (extent region2 - extent region1)))
              (then (region1 contained in region2)))
(fact (abs (center region1 - center region2)
      less than (extent region2 - extent region1))
      is on the fact list)
(fact (square regions) is on the fact list)

(no more facts to verify)
```
                                                                                (12-16)

The reader is encouraged to compare this result with that obtained by forward chaining in the previous chapter. Additional examples are shown in [Schalkoff 1986] and [Topa/Schalkoff 1986].

Extensions to the Backward Chaining Algorithm

BACKWARD CHAINING WITH BREADTH-FIRST SEARCH. The previous examples typify *depth-first* search in the sense that new subgoals, when created, are immediately investigated prior to forming and investigating alternate subgoals. In contrast, *breadth-first* search may be used. In breadth-first search, we conditionally propagate rule application backward over all possible paths at each step. The following example illustrates the approach. Depth-first versus breadth-first search strategies are considered in more detail in Chapter 15.

> **Example 12.10   Backward chaining with breadth-first search. (Only modified functions shown.)**
>
> ```
> ;bwd_r1.l
> ;this program implements the backward chaining algorithm
> ;using breadth-first search
>
> ;'contained-in' checks if a list is contained in another list
> ;input: list a and list b
> ;output: t if list a is contained in list b,
> ;        otherwise nil
>
>  (defun contained-in (alist blist)
>  (if (null alist) t
>      (if (member (car alist) blist)
>          (contained-in (cdr alist) blist)
>          nil)))
>
>
>
> ;'verify-fact' verifies a fact
> ;input: fact
> ;output: fact if the fact is on the list,
> ;        ((antecedent lists) (rules)) if the fact is a consequence,
> ;        otherwise nil
>
> (defun verify-fact (fact)
>  (cond
>    ((recall-fact fact) (list fact))
>    (t
>     (do
>      ((rulelist (find-rules fact *rules*) (cdr rulelist))
>       (result nil)
>       (newrules nil)
>       (newfacts nil))
>      ((null rulelist) result)
>      (setq newfacts (cons (get-antecedents (car rulelist))
>                     newfacts))
>      (setq newrules (cons (list (car rulelist)) newrules))
>      (setq result (list newfacts newrules))))))
> ```

```
; 'goback-from-factset' goes one step back from a factset
; input: a fact set
; output: list of factsets and rules

(defun goback-from-factset (factset)
 (do
  ((factlist factset (cdr factlist))
   (temp nil nil)
   (newrules nil)
   (newfacts nil))
  ((null factlist) (list newfacts newrules))
  (setq temp (verify-fact (car factlist)))
  (cond
   ((not temp) (return nil))
   ((equal (length temp) 1)
     (if (not newfacts)
         (setq newfacts (list temp))
         (do
          ((alist newfacts (cdr alist))
           (blist nil))
          ((null alist) (setq newfacts blist))
          (setq blist (cons (append temp (car alist))
           blist)))))
    (t
     (cond
      ((not newfacts)
        (setq newfacts (car temp))
        (setq newrules (cadr temp)))
      (t
       (do
        ((alist newfacts (cdr alist))
         (blist newrules (cdr newrules))
         (clist nil)
         (dlist nil))
        ((null alist) (setq newfacts clist)
                      (setq newrules dlist))
        (do
         ((elist (car temp) (cdr elist))
          (flist (cadr temp) (cdr flist))
          (glist nil)
          (hlist nil))
         ((null elist) (setq clist (append glist clist))
                       (setq dlist (append hlist dlist)))
         (setq glist (cons (append (car alist) (car elist))
                           glist))
         (setq hlist (cons (append (car blist)
                                   (car flist))
                           hlist)))))))))))
```

```
;'one-step-back' goes one step backward
;input: fact sets
;output: fact sets at one step back

(defun one-step-back (factlist)
 (do
  ((alist factlist (cdr alist))
   (newfacts nil)
   (oldfacts nil)
   (newrules nil)
   (result nil))
  ((null alist) result)
  (setq result (goback-from-factset (car alist)))
  (setq newfacts (append (car result) newfacts))
  (do
   ((blist (car result) (cdr blist)))
   ((null blist) nil)
   (setq oldfacts (cons (car alist) oldfacts)))
  (setq newrules (append (cadr result) newrules))
  (setq result (list newfacts oldfacts newrules))))


;'verify-factset' verifies a factset
;input: list of factsets
;output: t if verified, otherwise nil

(defun verify-factset (status)
 (if (null status) nil
     (do
       ((factlist (car status) (cdr factlist))
        (oldfacts (cadr status) (cdr oldfacts))
        (rulelist (caddr status) (cdr rulelist)))
       ((null factlist) nil)
       (cond
        ((contained-in (car factlist) *facts*)
           (return (list (car factlist) (car oldfacts)
              (car rulelist))))))))


;'on-list' finds all facts on the fact list
;input: fact list
;output: facts which are on the fact list

(defun on-list (factlist)
 (if (null factlist) nil
     (if (member (car factlist) *facts*)
           (cons (car factlist) (on-list (cdr factlist)))
           (on-list (cdr factlist)))))

;'off-list' finds all facts not on the fact list
;input: fact list
```

```
;output: facts which are not on the fact list
(defun off-list (factlist)
 (if (null factlist) nil
     (if (member (car factlist) *facts*)
         (off-list (cdr factlist))
         (cons (car factlist) (off-list (cdr factlist)))))))


;'print-rules'

(defun print-rules (rulelist)
 (cond
  ((null rulelist) nil)
  (t (print (car rulelist))
     (terpri)
     (print-rules (cdr rulelist)))))


;'print-explanations'

(defun print-explanation (factlist rulelist)
 (cond
  ((null factlist) nil)
  (t (print '(THE CURRENT GOAL IS))
     (terpri)
     (print (car factlist))
     (terpri)
     (cond
      ((on-list (car factlist))
       (print '(FOLLOWING FACTS IN THE GOAL CAN BE RECALLED))
       (terpri)
       (print (on-list (car factlist)))
       (terpri)))
     (cond
      ((off-list (car factlist))
       (print '(FOLLOWING FACTS IN THE GOAL CAN BE DEDUCED))
       (terpri)
       (print (off-list (car factlist)))
       (terpri)
       (print '(THE RULES WHICH DEDUCE ABOVE FACTS ARE))
       (terpri)
       (print-rules (car rulelist))
       (terpri)))
     (print-explanation (cdr factlist) (cdr rulelist)))))


;'print-history' prints the inference net
;input: status and history
;output: nil if verification failed,
;          otherwise t
```

```
(defun print-history (status history)
 (if (null status) nil
     (do
       ((factlist (list (car status)))
        (pointer (cadr status))
        (rulelist (list (caddr status)))
        (alist (cdr history) (cdr alist)))
       ((null pointer) (print-explanation factlist rulelist) t)
       (do
         ((blist (caar alist) (cdr blist))
          (clist (cadar alist) (cdr clist))
          (dlist (caddar alist) (cdr dlist)))
         ((equal pointer (car blist))
           (setq factlist (cons pointer factlist))
           (if (car dlist)
               (setq rulelist (cons (car dlist) rulelist)))
           (setq pointer (car clist)))))))


;'chain-backward1' backward chaining using breadth-first approach
;input: fact list
;output: nil

(defun chain-backward1 (factlist)
 (cond
   ((null factlist) (terpri)
                    (print '(NO MORE FACTS TO BE VERIFIED))
                    (terpri))
   (t
    (do
      ((status (list (list (list (car factlist)))))
       (history (list (list (list (list (car factlist)))))))
      (nil)
      (cond
        ((print-history (verify-factset status) history)
         (terpri)
         (print (append '(FACT) (list (car factlist))
                                '(IS VERIFIED)))
         (terpri)
         (return (chain-backward1 (cdr factlist))))
        (t (setq status (one-step-back (car status)))
           (cond
             ((not status)
              (print (append '(NOT ABLE TO VERIFY)
                             (list (car factlist))))
              (terpri)
              (chain-backward1 (cdr factlist)))
             (t
              (setq history (cons status history)))))))))))
```

Facts and rules
```
(setq *facts* '(f1 f4 f6 f7 f8 f9 f10 f11 f12 f14 f15 f16 f17
                f18 f23 f24))

(setq *rules* '((rule m (IF a b c) (THEN z))
                (rule n (IF d e f g) (THEN z))
                (rule p (IF f1 f2) (THEN a))
                (rule q (IF f1 f3 f4) (THEN a))
                (rule r (IF f4 f5) (THEN b))
                (rule s (IF f6 f7) (THEN b))
                (rule t (IF f7 f8 f9) (THEN c))
                (rule u (IF f10 f11 f12) (THEN d))
                (rule v (IF f13 f14) (THEN d))
                (rule w (IF f14 f15 f16) (THEN e))
                (rule x (IF f17 f18) (THEN f))
                (rule y (IF f19 f20 f21 f22) (THEN g))
                (rule z (IF f23 f24) (THEN g))))
```

Sample execution
```
-> (load 'bwd_r1.l)
[load bwd_r1.l]
t
-> (chain-backward1 '(z))
(THE CURRENT GOAL IS)
(z)
(FOLLOWING FACTS IN THE GOAL CAN BE DEDUCED)
(z)
(THE RULES WHICH DEDUCE ABOVE FACTS ARE)
(rule n (IF d e f g) (THEN z))

(THE CURRENT GOAL IS)
(d e f g)
(FOLLOWING FACTS IN THE GOAL CAN BE DEDUCED)
(d e f g)
(THE RULES WHICH DEDUCE ABOVE FACTS ARE)
(rule u (IF f10 f11 f12) (THEN d))
(rule w (IF f14 f15 f16) (THEN e))
(rule x (IF f17 f18) (THEN f))
(rule z (IF f23 f24) (THEN g))

(THE CURRENT GOAL IS)
(f10 f11 f12 f14 f15 f16 f17 f18 f23 f24)
(FOLLOWING FACTS IN THE GOAL CAN BE RECALLED)

(f10 f11 f12 f14 f15 f16 f17 f18 f23 f24)


(FACT z IS VERIFIED)
```

```
(NO MORE FACTS TO BE VERIFIED)                        (12-17)
nil
```

Backward Chaining with Variables in Rules (Optional)

The following LISP program illustrates one implementation of a backwards chaining approach that allows variables in rules. The complexity of the code required for consistent unification and backward propagation of subgoals with variable binding constraints is evident. Note that the ultimate result is suitable for implementation of PROLOG in LISP.

Example 12.11 **(Only modified functions shown.)**

```
;bwd_var.l
;backward chaining with variables in rules.

;variable = (?var? var-name)
;bindings = (((?var? var-name) var-value) .. (end))

;'var' checks if the input is a variable
;input: x
;output: x if x is variable, otherwise nil
(defun var (x)
  (if (and (listp x) (equal (car x) '?var?)) x nil))


;'assoc1' returns var-value for (?var? var-name)
(defun assoc1 (x bindings)
  (if (equal bindings '((end))) nil
       (if (equal x (caar bindings))
            (cadar bindings)
            (assoc1 x (cdr bindings))))))

;'get-binding' returns the binding of a variable
;input: x and bindings
;output: a binding or x

(defun get-binding (x bindings)
  (let ((b (and x (var x)
                (get-binding (assoc1 x bindings) bindings))))
       (if b b x)))

;'unify' match x and y and return the binding list
(defun unify (x y bindings)
  (cond
    ((equal (setq x (get-binding x bindings))
            (setq y (get-binding y bindings))) bindings)
```

```
     ((var x) (cons (list x y) bindings))
     ((var y) (cons (list y x) bindings))
     ((or (atom x) (atom y)) (and (equal x y) bindings))
     ((setq bindings (unify (car x) (car y) bindings))
      (unify (cdr x) (cdr y) bindings)))))

;'substantiate' substantiates a variable list with bindings
;input: x -- a list with variables
;        bindings -- the binding list
;output: the list with variables bound to their values

(defun substantiate (x bindings)
 (if (null x) nil
     (if (var (car x))
         (cons (get-binding (car x) bindings)
               (substantiate (cdr x) bindings))
         (cons (car x)
               (substantiate (cdr x) bindings)))))

;'find-rules' finds rules with the fact as its consequence.
;input: the fact and rule list
;output: the applicable rule list

(defun find-rules (fact bindings)
 (do
  ((r *rules* (cdr r))
   (rulelist nil))
  ((null r) rulelist)
  (do
   ((c (get-consequences (car r)) (cdr c))
    (b nil))
   ((null c) nil)
   (cond
    ((setq b (unify fact (car c) bindings))
       (setq rulelist (cons (list (car r) b) rulelist)))))))


;'add-to-list' adds a new element to a list
;input: x -- a list
;        y -- a list of lists
;output: the list of lists

(defun add-to-list (x y)
 (if (null x) y
     (if (member x y) y
         (cons x y))))

;'combine-two-lists' adds new elements
;in first list to second list
;input: x -- a list of lists
```

```
;           y -- a list of lists
;output: the list of lists

(defun combine-two-lists (x y)
  (if (null x) y
      (if (member (car x) y) (combine-two-lists (cdr x) y)
          (combine-two-lists (cdr x) (cons (car x) y)))))

;'get-binding-list' matches a variable list to a list of lists
;input: x -- a list containing variables
;       z -- a list of facts
;       blist -- the binding lists
;output: the binding lists

(defun get-binding-list (x z bindings)
  (if (null z) nil
      (add-to-list (unify x (car z) bindings)
                   (get-binding-list x (cdr z) bindings))))


;'argument-binding-list' modifies the binding list
;input: x -- the list containing variables
;       y -- the fact
;       blist -- the binding lists
;output: the binding lists

(defun argument-binding-list (x y blist)
  (if (null blist) nil
      (add-to-list (unify x y (car blist))
                   (argument-binding-list x y (cdr blist)))))

;'match-with-factlist' matches a variable list with the fact list
;with given the binding list
;input: x -- the list containing variable
;       z -- the list of facts
;       blist -- the binding lists
;output: the binding lists
(defun match-with-factlist (x z blist)
  (if (null z) nil
      (combine-two-lists (argument-binding-list x (car z) blist)
                         (match-with-factlist x (cdr z) blist))))

;'find-antecedent-bindings' gets all possible bindings
;for antecedents
;input: antecedents
;output: the binding list if all antecedents are on the fact list,
;         otherwise nil

(defun find-antecedent-bindings (antecedents bindings)
  (do
```

```
   ((blist (get-binding-list (car antecedents) *facts* bindings))
    (alist (cdr antecedents) (cdr alist)))
   ((or (null blist) (null alist)) blist)
   (setq blist (match-with-factlist (car alist) *facts* blist))))

;'verify-fact' verifies a fact
;input: fact and bindings
;output: bindings

(defun verify-fact (fact bindings)
 (cond
  ((recall-fact (substantiate fact bindings))
    (print (append '(FACT) (list (substantiate fact bindings))
                  '(IS ON FACTLIST)))
   (terpri)
   bindings)
  (t (do
       ((rulelist (find-rules fact bindings) (cdr rulelist))
        (blist nil))
       ((null rulelist) nil)
       (cond
        ((setq blist (find-antecedent-bindings
           (get-antecedents (caar rulelist)) (cadar rulelist)))
         (do
         ((b blist (cdr b)))
         ((null b) nil)
         (do
           ((a (get-antecedents (caar rulelist)) (cdr a)))
           ((null a) nil)
           (print (append '(FACT) (list (substantiate (car a)
                                                       (car b)))
                          '(IS ON FACTLIST)))
           (terpri))
         (print (append '(RULE)
                 (list (cadaar rulelist)) '(CAN BE FIRED)))
         (terpri)
         (print (append '(DEDUCE)
                 (list (substantiate fact (car b)))))
         (terpri))
        (return (cadar rulelist)))))))))


;'chain-backward' verifies given fact
;input: fact
;output: nil

(defun chain-backward (fact)
 (cond
  ((verify-fact fact '((end)))
```

```
      (print (append '(FACT) (list fact)
                      '(IS VERIFIED))))
      (terpri))
   (t (print (append '(FACT) (list fact)
                      '(CANNOT BE VERIFIED)))
      (terpri)))))

(setq *facts* '((ibm-pc is-a computer)
                (computer is-a electronic-device)))


(setq *rules* '((rule 1 (IF ((?var? a) is-a (?var? b))
                            ((?var? b) is-a (?var? c)))
                        (THEN ((?var? a) is-a (?var? c)))))))

(setq s '(ibm-pc is-a electronic-device))           (12-18)
```

Sample execution

```
$ lisp
-> (load 'bwd_var.l)
[load bwd_var.l]
t
-> *facts*
((ibm-pc is-a computer) (computer is-a electronic-device))
-> (pp *rules*)
(setq *rules*
      '((rule 1
          (IF ((?var? a) is-a (?var? b)) ((?var? b) is-a (?var? c))
          (THEN ((?var? a) is-a (?var? c)))))))
t
-> s
(ibm-pc is-a electronic-device)
-> (chain-backward s)
(FACT (ibm-pc is-a computer) IS ON FACTLIST)
(FACT (computer is-a electronic-device) IS ON FACTLIST)
(RULE 1 CAN BE FIRED)
(DEDUCE (ibm-pc is-a electronic-device))
(FACT (ibm-pc is-a electronic-device) IS VERIFIED)
nil                                                  (12-19)
```

BACKWARD VERSUS FORWARD CHAINING (CHOOSING "DIRECTIONS")

Although our LISP examples of forward (data-driven) and backward (goal-driven) chaining are relatively simple, the computational difference between the approaches warrants investigation. In the forward chaining approach it is fundamental to note that the inference process proceeds *exhaustively* from the existing facts to a set of new facts. Thus, in a sense, all new facts are generated (unless, of course, we embedded a control or stopping mechanism in the process). A consequence of this is the checking and firing of a substantial number of rules. These rule firings may do little to advance the system state towards a goal. Thus, the utility of many of the new facts generated in forward chaining is somewhat questionable.

The backward chaining paradigm, on the other hand, seeks only to prove the validity of a chosen fact (whose truth value is not known a priori) expression. It is perhaps more computationally efficient than forward chaining, since it represents a goal-directed strategy that may eliminate checking of many superfluous paths (Chapter 15). If more than one hypothesis is involved, backward chaining (as we have formulated it) attempts to verify each one independently; the number of computations may be far less if the problem were solved with some "memory" of the truth of intermediate facts.

There exist situations where one chaining methodology may be preferred over the other. In addition, a hybrid approach that uses both forward and backward chaining (explored in the problems) may be preferable [Treitel/Genesereth 1987] and [Brownston et al. 1986].

> Forward chaining is appropriate when there exist many equally acceptable goal states, a narrow body of relevant information (facts and rules) and a single initial state.
>
> (12-20)

Moreover, data-driven inference is preferable when

1. All or most of the required facts are in the initial database.
2. It is difficult to (initially) form a goal or hypothesis to be verified.

> Backward chaining is appropriate when there exists a single goal state (such as in diagnosis, where we desire to confirm the occurrence of a single event) and a large amount of potentially relevant initial information [Brownston et al. 1986].   (12-21)

Moreover, goal-directed inference is preferable when

1. Relevant data must be acquired as a part of the inference process (e.g., "asking questions").
2. Large numbers of applicable rules exist. This potentially leads to the production of many (extraneous) facts.

An additional concern in the backward chaining approach is the generation of "suitable" hypotheses. Chapter 13 shows how a forward chaining system may be used to implement backward chaining. In Chapter 15 we explore chaining methodologies from the point of view of search.

REFERENCES

[Brownston et al. 1986] Brownston, L., et al., *Programming Expert Systems in OPS5*, Addison-Wesley, Reading, MA, 1986.

[Schalkoff 1986] Schalkoff, R.J., "Automated Reasoning About Image Motion Using a Rule-Based Deduction System," *Image and Vision Computing*, Vol. 4, No. 2, May 1986, pp. 97–106.

[Topa/Schalkoff 1986] Topa, L.C., and R.J. Schalkoff, "A Production System for Image Motion Analysis," *Proceedings 1986 Southeastern Symposium on Systems Theory*, Knoxville, Tenn., April, 1986, pp. 48–52.

[Treitel/Genesereth 1987] Treitel, R., and M.R. Genesereth, "Choosing Directions for Rules," *Journal of Automated Reasoning*, Vol. 3, (1987), Reidel Publishing, pp. 395–431.

[Winston 1984] Winston, P.H., *Artificial Intelligence*, Addison-Wesley, Reading, MA, 1984.

[Winston/Horn 1981] Winston, P.H., and B.K.P. Horn, *LISP*, Addison-Wesley, Reading, MA, 1981.

PROBLEMS

12.1. (*a*) Consider the modified problem of verification of several hypotheses concurrently. In other words, describe why it might be computationally advantageous to attempt proof of the conjunction of a set of goals rather than the goals individually. In the case that one of the goals is not satisfiable, does the concurrent solution have any disadvantages?

(*b*) Revise function chain-backward (Example 12.6) such that it returns TRUE if *all* of its arguments are provable.

12.2. In example 12.1, we verified q3 by using p3 -> q3 and back–propagated constraint or subgoal p3. Note that q3 may also be TRUE (from the implication truth table) if p3 is FALSE. On this basis, we might wish to extend the technique of backward chaining to proving p3 = FALSE. Rigorously state at least three reasons why this will not work, with an example of each.

12.3. Given identical fact and rule bases,

(*a*) If forward chaining succeeds in proving a goal, must the backwards algorithm also succeed?

(*b*) Is the path from the goal state the same in each case in (*a*)?

(*c*) (related to (*a*)) If backwards chaining succeeds, must forward chaining also succeed? (Hint: consider the importance of a commutative system.)

12.4. Discuss the suitability of using backward chaining with productions that, in addition to producing new facts,

(*a*) Remove facts.

(*b*) Employ the not operator in rule antecedents.

12.5. In the backward chaining algorithm of Table 12.1, if a solution (i.e., a path from S_g to S_i) exists, is the procedure guaranteed to find it?

12.6. Modify the backwards chaining approach so that the system, when all other approaches fail, polls the user regarding the truth of a fact (through the ask-questions function). Modify this aspect of the algorithm such that the system instead responds with "tell me something more (i.e., additional facts)" and then attempts to complete verification of the hypothesis. (This allows the system to update the facts list.) When the user enters "no," the system should then ask questions concerning a specific fact. Specifically, the system should attempt to substantiate facts by

1. Simple recollection.

2. Backward chaining.

3. Querying the user if (1) and (2) are both unsuccessful.

Develop the following functions:

unavailable-fact: Keeps track of currently unavailable facts.

ask-question: Asks the operator questions and keeps track of previously asked questions.

A sample of the desired system operation is shown in Fig. P12.6.

```
[load bwd_q.l]
t
-> (chain-backward '(f))
(IS FOLLOWING FACT TRUE)
g
((y/n)=>))y
(FACT f CAN BE DEDUCED BY FIRING)
(rule 4 (if e d) (then f))
FACT d CAN BE DEDUCED BY FIRING)
(rule 2 (if b g) (then d))
(FACT g IS ON THE FACT LIST)
(FACT b IS ON THE FACT LIST)
(FACT e CAN BE DEDUCED BY FIRING)
(rule 3 (if a c) (then e))
(FACT c CAN BE DEDUCED BY FIRING)
(rule 1 (if a b) (then c))
(FACT b IS ON THE FACT LIST)
(FACT a IS ON THE FACT LIST)
(FACT a IS ON THE FACT LIST)

(NO MORE FACTS TO VERIFY)
```

FIGURE P12.6
IE with asking questions.

12.7. Recall in forward chaining at each cycle a *conflict set* of applicable rules was identified. This set consisted of rules that could be fired. In backward chaining, suppose we define the conflict set to be the set of rules defined by step 3 of the algorithm of Table 12.1.

(*a*) With these definitions, assuming a path from the initial database to the goal state exists, is there any relationship between the forward and backward chaining conflict sets?

(*b*) Are there (perhaps different) specific conflict resolution strategies for forward and backward chaining that will yield the same path?

12.8. (This problem makes an excellent project.) Consider a new type of chaining strategy wherein the system employs a hybrid forward-backward strategy. Instead of strictly forward or backward (with the possibility of one step-forward) chaining, the system employs *both* approaches, and does not rely on either alone for goal satisfaction. An example is shown in Fig. P12.8. Thus we are trying to get the "best of both worlds" from the two chaining approaches. In other words, assume the system is given *initial* and *goal* states, denoted S_i and S_g. In this modified approach the system employs forward chaining (for some number of user-defined cycles) to move the system to state S_f, while the system also attempts backwards chaining (again to some depth), which then requires a state S_b

for goal verification. The procedure succeeds if S_f, the state produced by limited forward chaining, contains S_b, the state required for success in backward chaining. Otherwise, the system must revise its operation and proceed. (Hint: The function contained–in may be useful in examining S_f and S_b.)

(a) Discuss, in detail, the merits and shortcomings of such a scheme. In particular, what are desirable characteristics, and what would reasonable metrics for system performance be?

(b) Show the approach graphically, as the "linking" of forward and tentative backward chaining inference nets.

(c) Suggest at least two methods to continue attempted goal satisfaction if the initial attempt fails. (Note: it would make sense to suggest schemes that take into account the efforts of the previous chaining attempts, i.e., it is not desirable for the system to start all over.)

(d) Discuss methods to determine how far the system should allow each approach (i.e., the forward and the backward) to go. For example, the extremes are obvious—if the system goes too far in the forward direction it confirms or denies the hypothesis without regard to backward chaining and an analogous remark concerning backward chaining may be made).

(e) A critical aspect of the previous approach is the selection of forward and backward chaining algorithm conflict resolution strategies. We consider two subcases:

  (i) The conflict resolution algorithms must work independently (i.e., neither has any knowledge of the rules under consideration by the other).

  (ii) The conflict resolution algorithms are allowed to work cooperatively.

  For each of the above cases, discuss possible system ramifications.

(f) Implement any reasonable version of this approach and compare the result on several test cases. (You may use any of the previous sample cases we have shown.) Compare, using your metric(s) from (a), the performance of the algorithm with these test cases to the use of either the forward or backward chaining approaches alone.

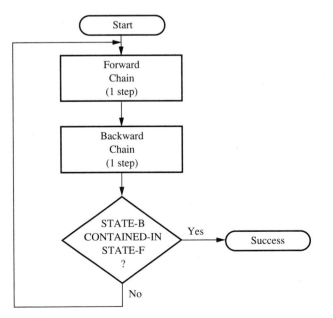

FIGURE P12.8
Hybrid chaining algorithm.

12.9. In this problem we explore the duality relationship between a commutative production system used for forward chaining and a decomposable system used for backward chaining. Referring to the database in Fig. P12.9a, below, consider the "similar" rulebases shown in Fig. P12.9(b). Notice a "reverse" rule, R_i, exists for each "forward rule" F_i. The F_i produce facts, whereas the R_i produce, or spawn, subgoals.

(a) Assume the goal is to produce a database containing fact "f." Using a forward chaining approach with S_i = *facts* and the F_i, show graphically the evolution of the problem state space for all possible orderings of rule application. In the graphical solution, use nodes (circles) containing the current database facts to represent a state and label arcs emanating from nodes with the name of the rule used. List all possible sequences of rule applications leading from S_i to a goal state.

(b) Is the forward system a commutative production system?

(c) Instead, use a forward chaining approach with the R_i and an initial database consisting of S_i = (f). Assume the goal is to produce a database containing (a b g). As in (a), show the graphical evolution of the state space for all possible orderings of applicable R_i. List all possible sequences of R_i applications leading from S_i to S_g.

(d) Do the sequences found in part (c), where reversed, have any relation to those found in part (a)? Elaborate.

(e) Repeat part (c), except revise the goal specification to be "produce a database that is a subset of *facts*." Repeat your answer to (d).

```
(setq *facts* '(a b g))

(setq *rules* '((rule 1 (IF a b) (THEN c))
                (rule 2 (IF b g) (THEN d))
                (rule 3 (IF a c) (THEN e))
                (rule 4 (IF e d) (THEN f))
                (rule 5 (IF d g) (THEN f))))
```

FIGURE P12.9a
Database for problem 12.9.

```
F1   a, b → c        R1   c → a, b,  (remove c)
F2   b, g → d        R2   d → b, g,  (remove d)
F3   a, c → e        R3   e → a, c,  (remove e)
F4   e, d → f        R4   f → e, d,  (remove f)
F5   d, g → f        R5   f → g, d,  (remove f)
        (i)                        (ii)
```

FIGURE P12.9b
"Reverse" application of rules for database of P12.9a. (i) Rules to produce new facts, (ii) Rules to produce subgoals

12.10. For the rulebase shown in example 12.10, with the database of facts modified as follows:

```
(setq   *facts*   '(f1   f2   f6   f7   f8   f9   f10
                    f11 f12 f13 f14 f15 f16
                    f17 f18 f19 f20 f21 f22)
```

(*a*) Show the rule alternatives (choices) for backwards chaining in the form of Fig. 12.6.

(*b*) Apply the algorithm of Table 12.1 (with goal z), with several different backup strategies. How many different paths from the goal to the initial database exist? Indicate each sequence.

12.11. Revise the abduction example 12.5 to generate an explanation using modus tollens (12-11). Assume we are given rules (12-10*a*) and (12-10*d*) and the revised observation:

$$\text{observation : ernie went to work} \qquad \text{(P12-11)}$$

INFERENCE
SYSTEMS—
A FURTHER
LOOK

The theory of probabilities is at bottom nothing but common sense reduced to calculus.

Pierre Simon de Laplace 1749–1827
Oeuvres, vol. VII, Théorie Analytique des Probabilités [1812–1820], introduction

In this chapter we consider several topics that are related to, or are extensions of, the previously considered rule-based inference systems. In particular, we look at the area of "expert" systems, reasoning with uncertainty, and several popular examples of automated inference systems.

EXPERT SYSTEMS

Introduction and Examples

Expert systems technology is one of the most popular and visible facets of AI. Expert system shells and knowledge acquisition systems have been developed using disparate approaches to knowledge representation and manipulation and user interfacing.

> **Expert systems** (ES's) are programs, usually confined to a specific field, that attempt to emulate the behavior of human experts. (13-1)

359

The following are typical attributes of an ES:

1. Knowledge is usually represented in declarative form to enable easy reading and modification. Most ES's use IF–THEN structures for representation; thus, rule-based ES's predominate.
2. There is a clear structure to the knowledge representation (excluding neural expert systems).
3. There is a clear distinction between the knowledge representation and the control or manipulation mechanism. Often, the control mechanism is itself rule-based (using meta-rules, Chapter 19).
4. A significant user I/O interface, to allow query, advice, explanation, and interaction with the ES is provided.
5. A user knowledge-acquisition or knowledge-modification module is often provided for extension of the ES. (13-2)

These attributes are shown in Fig. 13.1.

THE APPEAL OF EXPERT SYSTEMS. The development of ES's is motivated by a number of factors, including

1. "Expert" knowledge is a scarce and expensive resource.
2. ES's make expert behavior available to a large audience (i.e., allow more people to perform like "experts"). This is useful in applications such as systems configuration, training, and so forth.
3. The integration of the expertise of several experts may lead to ES's that outperform any single expert.
4. ES's are not motivated to leave a company for better working conditions, to demand huge salaries (although their development and maintenance costs are often substantial), or to join unions.

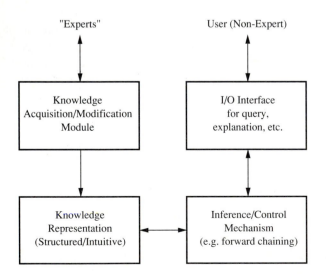

FIGURE 13.1
Structure of typical expert system (ES).

The commercial potential for expert systems is enormous [Harmon/King 1985]. Declining costs, shown in Fig. 13.2, have led to numerous efforts in developing small, easily modified ES's, as well as large systems. These trends are shown in Fig. 13.3. The expertise coded into an expert system is permanent and easily tranferable, and circumvents the payment of hourly or retainer fees. Expert systems can be put to work for long periods in difficult environments without special care. However, as noted in Chapter 1 and hereafter, the quantification coding of human insight, compassion, motivation, guessing ability, and learning capabilities is still an elusive goal. The references serve as a basis for additional exploration of expert systems. Often the ES design process requires a minimum of new technology and a large amount of engineering judgment.

EXPERT SYSTEM EXAMPLES. Approximately 50 recognized ES's are currently in operation. Examples of existing, commercially successful systems are

1. XCON from Digital Equipment Corp., which configures computer systems. XCON is written in OPS5, a rule-based programming language we explore in detail in a later section. Figure 13.4 shows the overall structure of XCON.
2. MACSYMA, which performs mathematical problem solving using symbolic manipulation rather than numerical evaluation and computation. For example,

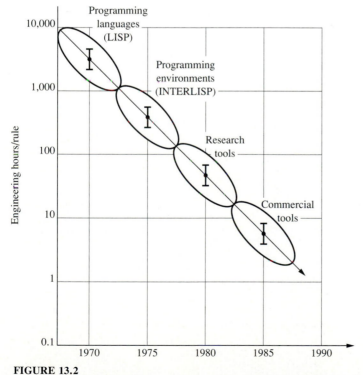

FIGURE 13.2
The declining cost of developing a knowledge system. (*From Harmon/King, 1985.*)

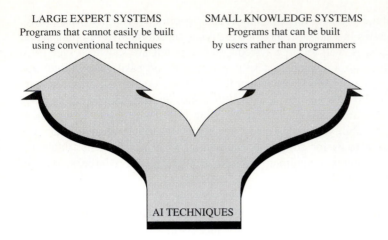

LARGE EXPERT SYSTEMS
Programs that cannot easily be built
using conventional techniques

SMALL KNOWLEDGE SYSTEMS
Programs that can be built
by users rather than programmers

AI TECHNIQUES

FIGURE 13.3
Two major trends in AI applications. (*From Harmon/King, 1985.*)

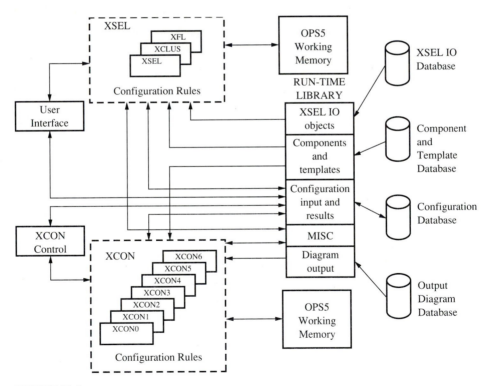

FIGURE 13.4
XSEL/XCON architecture. [Communications of the ACM, vol. 32, no. 3, March 1989.]

MACSYMA is capable of symbolic integration and differentiation of complicated algebraic expressions. Recently, MACSYMA correctly answered all but one question on a freshman calculus final exam at MIT.

3. MYCIN and CADUCEUS, which perform medical diagnosis.

4. PROSPECTOR, which guides geological prospecting. When PROSPECTOR found a molybdenum deposit worth $100 million, this application gained "respect" [Lernley 1985].

5. CATCH, which scans photographs to assist police in identifying criminal suspects in New York City.

6. DENDRAL, a chemistry-oriented ES for spectroscopic analysis. DENDRAL is one of the oldest ES's, having been developed in 1964 (in LISP!). A typical production in DENDRAL [Harmon/King 1985] is shown in Example 13.1.

Example 13.1   Dendral representation.

```
IF
the molecule spectrum has two peaks at masses x1 and x2
such that

x1 + x2 = M + 28              AND

x1 - 28 is a 'high' peak      AND

x2 - 28 is a 'high' peak    . AND

at least one of the x1 or x2 is high

THEN

The molecule contains a ketone group.
```

Expert System Limitations

One might expect the performance of expert systems, which could tirelessly and exhaustively consider every possibility associated with a problem, to outperform humans in a spectrum of applications. This is currently not the case. ES developers have discovered that knowledge acquisition can be slow and expensive. Furthermore, systems tend to be "brittle" in the sense that slight modifications in the application lead to unacceptable deviations in ES performance. It is not incidental that a human spends approximately 12 years past the age of 5 (or thereabouts) in formal schooling. Notwithstanding the possible lack of efficiency in this process, a significant amount of both *information* and *experience* (which is perhaps not as easily quantifiable) is gained over this time interval. In addition, most perceived experts have a considerable amount of additional informal and formal education past this point. Thus, we should not be surprised at even the practical difficulty of representing expert behavior.

The definition of expert systems in (13-1) did not include the term *reason*. Unfortunately, human experts do not reach conclusions solely through the application of a describable reasoning process. In fact, many experts attribute their success in reaching (what are proven over time to be) correct conclusions to "gut feel" or "instinct." This implies either a significant streak of luck, or, more likely, a subliminal reasoning process that is the result of significant experience and that defies apparent quantification. This helps to explain why ES application has heretofore been restricted to a narrow range of problem areas that are quantified in a straightforward fashion. The apparent lack of success of ES's in other areas, notably stock market forecasting, detective (criminal investigation) work, and "football picks," provides a challenge for the future.

Expert System Development

The first questions an expert system developer must ask are the following:

1. Are bona fide experts available whose performance is significantly better than that of amateurs?
2. Can their expertise be automated?
3. Does it make practical and economic sense to develop an ES?   (13-3)

EXPERT QUERY (THE ROLE OF "KNOWLEDGE ENGINEERS"). The development of expert systems involves consultation of an expert (or group of experts) with the aim of developing a manipulable knowledge base. Thus, the first phase of the process consists of the *formation of a database of domain-specific knowledge*. In the expert interrogation process, the formulation of "good" questions is paramount. Fortunately, experts often phrase problem-solving methodologies in terms of IF—THEN structures. For example,

If it looks like a duck, talks like a duck, . . . then I classify it a duck . . .   (13-4)

Moreover, an expert may volunteer rationalizations of the resulting rules, as "I conclude this *because* . . . ." This type of explanatory production is also desirable.

Note that databases resulting from the query of independent experts may not be consistent (Chapter 16).   (13-5)

ES VERIFICATION. The development of an expert system is almost always an iterative task, involving the cycle of expert query, database formation, development of the inference strategy, verification of system performance, and so on. This design process is shown in Fig. 13.5. The gap between the *concept* of an ES and a finished, delivered product may be enormous. The necessary application-specific selection of a reasoning structure, interviewing of experts, development of a prototype, refinement, user training, and documentation may take several years. A typical schedule is shown in Cupello and Mishelevich [1988].

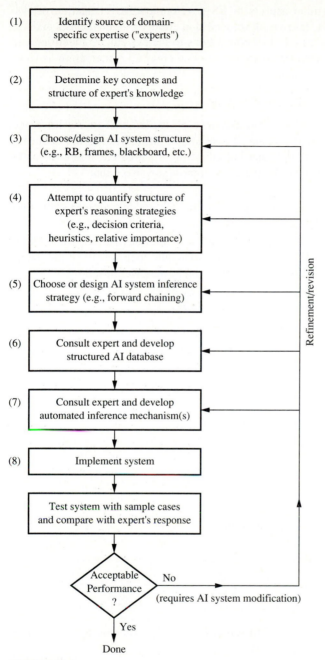

FIGURE 13.5
Example of a methodology for "Expert System" development.

One of the most important aspects of ES development is verification of system operation. A set of test cases is developed and used by both the ES and the human experts; when responses differ, modifications to the system are identified and implemented. To be useful, the system should provide good user interaction as well. A response such as

patient has disease x

is probably insufficient, even if it is correct, since no *explanation* of the inference process is provided. An explanation may be as simple as indicating the sequence of rules used, or may be as complicated as indicating all possible inference paths considered and the logic that indicates the most appropriate. Note that

1. Some measure of confidence or preference in the logic of (competing) paths may be desired. This is the subject of a later section.
2. Rules are often augmented to include a BECAUSE field or descriptor, which serves to further explain the rule. The system explanation could then consist of the output of the BECAUSE statements, in the order in which rules were used.

Example 13.2   Rule extension to include because.

```
(rule rule-17
        (IF (pinion is shiny blue color)
        (ring gear rotates below speed)
        (unit operation without load is excessively
        noisy)
        (gasket G2 is leaking))
    (THEN (bearing B5 is excessively worn))
    (BECAUSE (failure of bearing B5 causes overheating
            of the differential and warping of the
            case which causes discoloration,
            excessive tooth wear, vibration and case
            seal failure)
```

This approach is explored further in the problems.

Expert Systems Summary

In summary, note

- Expert systems are likely to succeed in some, but not all, problem domains. Often these are very narrowly defined domains.
- It may be desirable to develop hybrid systems, in an attempt to merge human and machine expertise.
- Key (sought-after) features in future generation ES's are likely to be
    - Efficient and user-friendly methods of knowledge acquisition.

- Expanded explanation-generating capability (accountability), especially in ES's used for diagnosis.
- Successful strategies for incorporating uncertainty in the representation and manipulation processes.

REASONING WITH UNCERTAINTY

In our previous knowledge-base formulations, it was implicitly assumed that facts were either absolutely TRUE or absolutely FALSE. The representation of facts and rules as axioms in a logic-based approach allows deduction to proceed as theorem proving. This is mathematically sound; however, it lacks expressiveness and leads to "brittle" reasoning strategies that do not allow uncertainty. Often, rules or facts provided by experts are accompanied by some quantification of certainty (e.g., descriptors such as "in most cases," "often," "seldom").

> Reasoning with uncertainty in AI involves the incorporation of measures of uncertainty in the *representation* as well as the inference (manipulation) strategy. (13-6)

Example 13.3   Uncertainty in statements. In Chapter 2 we considered using modus ponens to derive statements such as

$$\text{he is unhappy} \qquad (13\text{-}7a)$$

Keeping (13-6) in mind, the conclusion is perhaps more correctly, or more accurately, phrased as

> he is likely to be unhappy
> he is unhappy, except for . . .
> he is very likely to be unhappy

or

> he is unlikely to be happy

or

$$\text{he is unhappy, with a confidence measure (perhaps a probability) of } 0.85 \qquad (13\text{-}7b)$$

One of the most significant problems that arises in the representation of uncertainty in the inference process is the possibly non-unique measure of confidence that may be generated for the same conclusion through different solution paths (e.g., firing different rules). (13-8)

Therefore, if our attempt is to somehow construct a paradigm for the production of uncertain results from uncertain facts, we must either modify classical logic or append a confidence metric to the productions. We explore both.

HOW HUMANS PROCESS UNCERTAIN KNOWLEDGE. A number of significant research efforts have attempted to quantify human reasoning performance in the face of uncertainty. Examples are Cohen [1985], Garner [1975], Kahneman [1982], and Hink/Woods [1987].

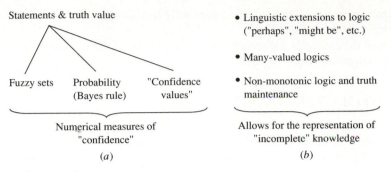

Fuzzy sets   Probability   "Confidence
              (Bayes rule)   values"

• Linguistic extensions to logic
  ("perhaps", "might be", etc.)

• Many-valued logics

• Non-monotonic logic and truth
  maintenance

Numerical measures of
"confidence"

Allows for the representation of
"incomplete" knowledge

(*a*)

(*b*)

FIGURE 13.6
Representation of uncertainty in inference techniques: (*a*) numerical approaches; (*b*) symbolic approaches.

Incorporating Uncertainty in the Inference Process

An obvious approach is to attempt the merging of logic with probability. However, other possibilities exist. As shown in Fig. 13.6, we identify two major representational techniques for incorporating uncertainty in inference techniques. These are

1. *Numerical approaches*, which attempt to associate a quantitative measure of confidence (or certainty) with the truth value of facts. This includes *fuzzy set* [Zadeh 1975] and *probabilistic* approaches.   (13-9*a*)

2. *Symbolic approaches*, which incorporate uncertainty, but in a less numerically quantitative manner. Examples are extensions to the connectives of classical logic, such as

    (*a*) *Linguistic extensions*, which allow the representation of statements using "perhaps," "maybe," and so on. An example [Pang 1987] is

    $$\text{IF} \qquad \text{symptom is-believed-to-be spots}$$

    $$\text{THEN} \qquad \text{diagnosis may-be measles}$$

    (*b*) The use of *nonmonotonic logic* and *truth maintenance approaches* to account for the possibility of incomplete or perhaps even contradictory knowledge (Chapter 16).

    (*c*) The use of *multivalued logic*.   (13-9*b*)

THE BASIC IDEA OF THE NUMERICAL APPROACH. Using probability as a guide, we begin by assigning a confidence measure (which might be interpreted as a probability) to an *event*. An event, H, could be defined as

$$H: \text{statement } S_1 \text{ is TRUE} \qquad (13\text{-}10)$$

In this manner, $P(H)$ or perhaps conf(H) and other derivable measures, such as $P(\neg H)$ or conf($\neg H$), are represented. Hereafter, we simply denote the probability of (13-10) as $P(S)$.

The previous deterministic formulation of a rule, that is,

$$p \rightarrow q \qquad (13\text{-}11)$$

given $\text{conf}(p) = 1.0$, allowed us to make certain conclusions regarding $\text{conf}(q)$. In fact, with the interpretation of (13-10), the implication truth table suggests that, given (13-11) and $\text{conf}(p) = 1.0$, then $\text{conf}(q) = 1.0$. However, two major cases occur in practice:

1. p is a simple statement and $\text{conf}(p) < 1$.

2. p is a compound statement such as $p = a \cap b \cap c \cap \ldots$, and we are given $\text{conf}(a)$, $\text{conf}(b)$, and so on, where $\text{conf}(x) \leq 1$. (13-12)

In both cases, we seek to determine $\text{conf}(q)$. In the problem formulation of (13-12), we create a "weaker" form of implication. Conclusions become more of a "hypothesis" than a certain fact.

Types of Uncertainties and Their Propagation

Consider the following types of uncertainties that could be encountered in AI applications:

Case 1. The input facts have uncertainties or probabilities associated with them; for instance,

$$\text{Breaker 4 is open} \qquad (13\text{-}13)$$

Suppose this statement is accurate (TRUE), given a particular instrumentation system, 95 percent of the time. In other words, the instrumentation system is in error (false positive) 5 percent of the time, and therefore there is a measure of uncertainty associated with (13-13).

Case 2. The rules, given facts known to be (absolutely) TRUE, generate new facts with some degree of confidence; for example,

```
IF (? organism) is a gram positive coccus
growing in chains (with 100% certainty)
THEN (? organism) is a streptococcus (with 70% certainty).
```
(13-14)

Note in this case the certainty value of the antecedents was not used in the production. This is an example of the situation where additional observations may be warranted; the rule merely states that 70 percent of all organisms that satisfy the rule antecedent are streptococcus. In this case, it is the rule that generated a confidence measure of less than 100 percent, given absolutely certain facts.

Case 3. This case combines cases 1 and 2. The confidence associated with the production of new facts is a function of both rule and fact confidence measures. A rule produces conclusions (consequents) with a certainty measure that reflects uncertainty in both facts and rules. It is left for the reader to consider (via the problems) two interesting implementation issues related to this case:

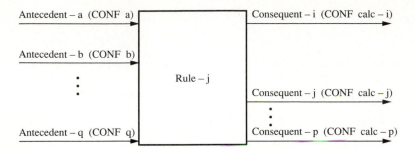

FIGURE 13.7
Modeling objective in rule-based reasoning with uncertainty (numerical approach).

    i. The rule may not be fired, due to an extremely low measure of confidence in fact(s) it produces.

    ii. A rule may produce a consequent that also happens to exist in the database prior to the rule firing. The resulting confidence measures on the same fact may not be the same.

$$\text{(13-15)}$$

Case 4 (and beyond). The firing of rules is not independent, and a confidence propagation mechanism takes this into account. For example, suppose the history of rules used to generate a particular path or inference net is recorded. The consequent confidence measure for this path is thus calculated after firing $rule-j$; it is a function of the *identity* of previously fired rules. Intuitively, we often associate confidence in a deduction with *how* the conclusion was reached. For example, we may have more confidence in the truth of an economic scenario deduced using the laws of economics than in a scenario deduced by politically-based laws (or heuristics).

Prior to a detailed analysis, note from Fig. 13.7 that our objective is to determine an input-output form for the propagation of fact-confidence measures.

LOGICAL VERSUS PROBABILISTIC INTERPRETATION OF RULES.

Given the firing of a rule, which implies verification of the antecedents, there is the *logical interpretation* of the action, which is distinguished from the *probabilistic* interpretation.

For example, given a *rule* with antecedents A and B that yields consequent C when fired, we have

$$\text{the } \textit{logical interpretation} \text{ of the rule, namely, } A \cap B \to C$$

as well as

    the *probabilistic interpretation* of the rule, that is, given
    $P(A)$ and $P(B)$ and the rule, what is (a) $P(A \cap B)$; and (b) $P(C)$?

EXPRESSING UNCERTAINTY IN STATEMENTS. As introduced earlier, uncertainty in statements or propositions may be represented in a number of ways:

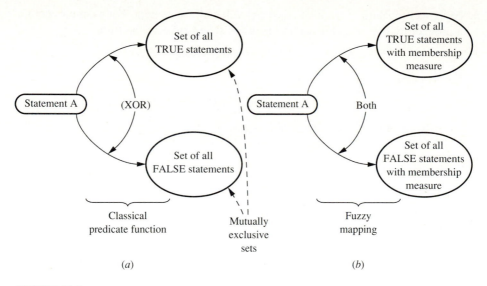

FIGURE 13.8
Conventional logic vs. fuzzy logic: (*a*) conventional logic; (*b*) fuzzy logic.

1. Allow a statement to assume a truth value other than TRUE or (exclusive "or") FALSE. One approach is to define and use a multivalued logic. For example, truth values TRUE, FALSE, and MAYBE might be used in a three-valued logic. Another approach is to expand the space of allowable truth values between definite truth and falsity, thus defining an *interval* of truth values. Within this approach there are numerous alternatives; for example,

   a. Assign to a statement a truth value that is a numerical value in the interval [0,1]. A value of 1, for example, represents absolute certainty that the statement is TRUE , whereas a value of 0 indicates absolute certainty that the statement is FALSE. A truth value of 0.75, for example, might indicate that the statement is "fairly true."

   b. Noting that in classical logic the truth value of a statement is mapped into the mutually exclusive sets TRUE and FALSE, we revise the mapping such that statements with some nonzero degree of uncertainty assume *a degree of membership in both sets*. Figure 13.8 shows this distinction, which, of course, requires extension of the classical concept of set membership. *Fuzzy sets* therefore represent an avenue to pursue this approach [Zadeh 1975] [Turner 1985]. The use of fuzzy sets requires that we develop a means to propagate set membership through conventional ("crisp") logic connectives. For example, denoting the fuzzy equivalents of the AND, OR and NOT connectives as f-AND, f-OR and f-NOT, we might derive membership values in the set of TRUE statements as follows:

$$m(a \text{ f-AND } b) = \min\{m(a), m(b)\} \qquad (13\text{-}16a)$$

$$m(a \text{ f-OR } b) = \max\{m(a), m(b)\} \qquad (13\text{-}16b)$$

$$m(\text{f-NOT } a) = 1 - m(a) \qquad (13\text{-}16c)$$

2. Assign a probability measure to the truth value of a statement. For example, define a probability-based confidence measure for statement S in the form

$$P(\text{statement } S \text{ is TRUE}) = 0.8 \text{ (or simply } P(S) = 0.8)$$

For example, if

$$P(S) = 1.0$$

we indicate absolute certainty that S is true.

Probability Review

We digress briefly to consider the manipulation of probabilities and the underlying assumptions. The probability of an event, H, is denoted as $P(H)$. (Recall we have defined an event as the occurrence of a particular statement being TRUE).

CONDITIONAL PROBABILITY. The *conditional probability* of an event H, given the information available up to this event (i.e., the knowledge of the occurrence of other events that may be related to H), is denoted

$$P(H \mid E) \tag{13-17}$$

where E is the *evidence* available. Thus, we view $P(H \mid E)$ as the conditional probability that event H is TRUE, in light of the evidence E. For example, given

$$P(H \mid E) > 0.95 \tag{13-18a}$$

we recognize that

$$1 - P(H \mid E) < 0.05 \tag{13-18b}$$

and therefore have a reasonable expectation that the probability of $P(\neg H \mid E)$ is small.

The formulation in (13-17) does not represent the attention that should be given to, or the significance of, event H, it merely reflects its probability of occurrence. For example, if H is the occurrence of an (unlikely but) deadly disease, we need an alternative formulation to indicate its *significance*.

BAYES RULE. One of the most useful formulations relates the conditional probability of an event to the joint occurrence of two events as

$$P(H \cap E) = P(H \mid E) \; P(E)$$

and

$$P(H \cap E) = P(E \mid H) \; P(H) \tag{13-19}$$

It is from this result that Bayes rule, for relating conditional probabilities, is derived:

$$P(H \mid E) = \frac{P(E \mid H)P(H)}{P(E)} \tag{13-20}$$

Another useful form is found when several pieces of evidence (E_i) condition H. Denoting the joint probability $(P(E_1 \cap E_2)$ as $P(E_1, E_2)$,

$$P(H \mid E_1, E_2, \cdots E_n) = \frac{P(E_1, E_2, \cdots, E_n \mid H) \; P(H)}{P(E_1, E_2, \cdots E_n)} \tag{13-21}$$

INDEPENDENCE. Two events, H and E, are **independent** in a probabilistic sense (denoted $H \perp E$) if

$$P(H \mid E) = P(H) \tag{13-22}$$

Thus, given the logical formulation

$$C = A \cap B$$

the assumption of independence allows us to write the following:

$$P(C) = P(A \cap B) = P(A) \; P(B) \tag{13-23}$$

The assumption of independence also allows considerable simplification in the propagation of conditional probabilities. For example, given events x, y, and z, with x and y conditionally independent, the following axioms (proofs are left to the exercises) result:

$$P(x, y \mid z) = P(x \mid z) \; P(y \mid z) \tag{13-24a}$$

$$P(x \mid y, z) = P(x \mid z) \tag{13-24b}$$

$$P(x, y, z) = P(x \mid z) \; P(y, z) \tag{13-24c}$$

Example 13.4 Sample application of Bayes rule in inference. Let

$$\begin{aligned} &H\text{: patient has lung cancer} \\ &E\text{: patient smokes} \end{aligned} \tag{13-25}$$

Suppose we are interested in developing a quantitative assessment of

$$P(H \mid E) = P(\text{patient has lung cancer} \mid \text{patient smokes}) \tag{13-26}$$

given

$P(H)$: probability of lung cancer in the general population (unconditional) (13-27)

$P(E)$: probability that a person smokes (13-28)

$P(E \mid H) = P(\text{patient is a smoker} \mid \text{patient has lung cancer})$ (13-29)

Assume $P(E \mid H)$ may be obtained from experience or history, that is, we know the percentage of all persons diagnosed to have lung cancer who are smokers. For a given patient, in the absence of *any* evidence, it is easy to show that the confidence in our diagnosis (statement H is TRUE) is $P(H)$. This is simply the probability that anyone in the general population has lung cancer. However, if we are given *evidence*, E, that the patient smokes, we may refine our confidence in the diagnosis using Bayes' rule:

$$P(H \mid E) = \left(\frac{P(E \mid H)}{P(E)} \right) P(H) \tag{13-30}$$

LIMITATIONS OF THE PROBABILISTIC APPROACH. One shortcoming of the probabilistic approach is that it does not directly lead to representations of "ignorance" (as perceived by humans). For example, if evidence E partially supports hypothesis H, through $P(H \mid E) < 1$, then according to the rules of probability, it would also have to partially support the negative of the hypothesis, $\neg H$, since probability requires

$$P(H \mid E) + P(\neg H \mid E) = 1 \tag{13-31}$$

(Verification of (13-31) is left to the problems). Humans, in contrast, tend to classify evidence as either supporting or refuting a hypothesis.

Another difficulty occurs in mapping the truth value of a statement into a probability when the statement contains variables. We could view this as spawning the need for an "extended" predicate function.

Simple Example of Two-Antecedent Rule Using Probability

Suppose a rule has two antecedents, A and B. The logical interpretation that leads to firing of the rule and generation of consequent C is $A \cap B$. We now proceed, given $P(A)$ and $P(B)$ to determine $P(C)$. Moreover, we show how the assumption of independence in the initial database facts does not lead to the assumption of independence as we get deeper in the inference net. Therefore employing the independence assumption in the calculation of probability-based confidence measures yields (probabilistically speaking) incorrect results.

THE INDEPENDENCE ASSUMPTION AND CORRESPONDING PROBLEMS. Refer to the two-level inference net in Fig. 13.9. Assuming initial facts A and B are independent (which might be a reasonable assumption), we derive $P(C)$ using rule−p:

$$P(C) = P(A)P(B) \tag{13-32}$$

Again employing the independence assumption for the second level of inference with rule−q (since $D = C \cap A$) yields

$$P(D) = P(C)\ P(A) = [P(A)]^2\ P(B) \tag{13-33}$$

We now show this is incorrect, since *the firing of* rule−p *has introduced dependence* in the antecedents (C and A) to rule−q.

CONSIDERING DEPENDENCE (CONDITIONAL PROBABILITIES). The problem is now reformulated by accounting for the dependence of propagated fact probabilities as

$$P(D) = P(A \cap C) = P(A)\ P(C \mid A) \tag{13-34}$$

Since

$$\begin{aligned}
P(C \mid A) &= P(C \cap A)/P(A) = P(A \cap B \cap A)/P(A) \\
&= P(A \cap B)/P(A) = P(A)P(B)/P(A) \\
&= P(B)
\end{aligned} \tag{13-35}$$

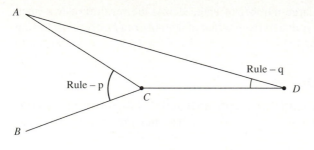

FIGURE 13.9
Example of independence assumption
for calculation and propagation of consequent probabilities.

accounting for the probabilistic dependence of the inputs to rule—q yields

$$P(D) = P(A)P(C \mid A) = P(A)P(B) \tag{13-36}$$

which is correct according to the probabilistic interpretation. It is also obvious from
the inference net of Fig. 13.9. Moreover, several important observations regarding
the intuitive correctness of this result may be made:

1. The approach based upon an assumption of independence, for a given rule, returns
   a probability-based confidence measure that is lower than one that accounts for
   dependence. Compare this result with $P^2(A)P(B)$ in the previous case.

2. The approach that accounts for dependence includes the case where the rule
   consequents are independent, that is, when $P(C \mid A) = P(C)$.

3. If all antecedents are independent, we would need to *independently* weigh their
   occurrence in firing the rule. Conversely, if it is known that all antecedents are
   dependent (with possibly varying degrees of dependence) our confidence in the
   rule conclusion might be higher since the occurrence of any input could *imply* the
   occurrence of the others. (The concept of dependence in this case is interpreted to
   mean $A \mid E$ is more likely if E occurs, i.e., the occurrence of E provides *positive
   reinforcement* of the likelihood of A. An alternate and equally valid viewpoint
   is that the occurrence of E could provide *negative reinforcement* of A, i.e., if E
   occurs then $\neg A$ is more likely.)

4. As illustrated by the example, even if the facts initially given are independent,
   the rule-based production system introduces significant dependence. Thus, at some
   level in the inference net, the assumption of independence is not reasonable. This
   introduces significant analytical and practical complexity. The rule-based inference
   net will produce facts that are dependent; thus the assumption of dependence (even
   if it is difficult to quantify) is more reasonable than that of independence.

   In closing, several characteristics of the probabilistic approach with the independence assumption are noteworthy:

1. It yields a very "lossy" system, in terms of confidence-measure propagation. Since
   the probability of any event is less than or equal to 1.0, the successive multiplication of these probabilities, as we progress through the inference net, yields
   monotonically nonincreasing confidence measures. Restoration of confidence in a
   fact is not possible without modification of the approach. $\tag{13-37a}$

2. In the case of rules with a large number of antecedents, the resulting consequent probability decreases quickly, due to the product of a number of terms, each having a value less than or equal to 1.0. $\hspace{4em}$ (13-37b)

Probabilistic Extensions (Optional)

COMBINATIONS INVOLVING CONJUNCTION AND JOINT PROBABILITY PROPAGATION DIFFICULTIES. Suppose we are asked to determine the confidence measure

$$P(S_1 \cap S_2) \hspace{4em} (13\text{-}38)$$

Furthermore, suppose the probabilities associated with the individual statements are given:

$$P(S_1) = p_1 \hspace{4em} (13\text{-}39a)$$

and

$$P(S_2) = p_2 \hspace{4em} (13\text{-}39b)$$

We seek to determine how the joint probabilities associated with logical combinations of S_1 and S_2 are related to the probabilities p_1 and p_2. More importantly, we wish to know if the probability measures in (13-39) may be used to determine the joint distributions. There are four logical combinations involving the *conjunction* of the truth states of S_1 and S_2, namely

$$S_1 \cap S_2$$
$$S_1 \cap \neg S_2$$
$$\neg S_1 \cap S_2$$
$$\neg S_1 \cap \neg S_2 \hspace{4em} (13\text{-}40)$$

Thus, we define the corresponding joint probabilities:

$$P(S_1 \cap S_2) = p_{tt}$$
$$P(S_1 \cap \neg S_2) = p_{tf}$$
$$P(\neg S_1 \cap S_2) = p_{ft}$$
$$P(\neg S_1 \cap \neg S_2) = p_{ff} \hspace{4em} (13\text{-}41)$$

The marginal probabilities of statements S_1 and S_2 may be formed from the joint probabilities. We see that

$$P(S_1) = P(S_1 \cap S_2) + P(S_1 \cap \neg S_2)$$
$$= p_{tt} + p_{tf}$$
$$= p_1 \hspace{4em} (13\text{-}42)$$

and, similarly,

$$P(S_2) = P(S_2 \cap S_1) + P(S_2 \cap \neg S_1)$$

$$= p_{tt} + p_{ft}$$

$$= p_2 \tag{13-43}$$

Given p_1 and p_2, and desiring p_{tt}, we have two equations and three unknowns. (Note also that p_{ff} was not required.) This result indicates the principal problem with the strictly probabilistic approach:

p_1 and p_2 alone are insufficient for the determination of the joint probability functions. (13-44)

Thus, we must estimate somehow and use p_{tt} to propagate probability-based confidence measures. This is impractical, since for n statements there are 2^n joint probability measures that must be considered (this is explored in the problems).

EXTENSIONS OF BAYES RULE. We begin by showing a useful extension of Bayes rule [Walpole/Myers 1972]:

$$P(A_1 A_2 A_3)/P(A_1) = P(A_2 A_3 \mid A_1)$$

$$= P(A_2 \mid A_1) \ P(A_3 \mid A_1 A_2) \tag{13-45}$$

Now consider the following problem where we have a hypothesis, C, and observed "evidence," A and B. Our objective is to combine the individual evidence and associated confidence measures; that is,

$$P(C \mid A), P(C \mid B) \text{ into } P(C \mid A, B)$$

Using Bayes rule on $P(C \mid AB)$, we see

$$P(C \mid AB) = P(A \mid BC) \ P(BC)/P(AB) \tag{13-46}$$

We make two assumptions regarding independence:

1. $A \perp B$; therefore $P(AB) = P(A)P(B)$. (13-47)
2. $P(A \mid BC) = P(A \mid C)$.

Under these conditions,

$$P(C \mid AB) = \frac{P(A \mid C) \ P(B \mid C) \ P(C)}{P(A) \ P(B)} \tag{13-48}$$

This result is even more interesting if we note that

$$\frac{P(A \mid C)}{P(A)} = \frac{P(C \mid A)}{P(C)} \tag{13-49a}$$

and

$$\frac{P(B \mid C)}{P(B)} = \frac{P(C \mid B)}{P(C)} \tag{13-49b}$$

so that

$$P(C \mid AB) = \frac{P(C \mid A)}{P(C)} \frac{P(C \mid B)}{P(C)} P(C) \tag{13-50}$$

Note that:

1. (13-50) shows the modification of $P(C)$, given "evidence" regarding A and B.
2. If C is independent of both A and B, (13-50) reduces to $P(C)$.

THE "ODDS" FORMULATION OF BAYES RULE AND UPDATING SCHEMES. Often an alternative to the preceding formulation is more convenient. The *odds* of an event E are defined to be

$$O(E) = P(E)/P(\neg E) = P(E)/(1 - P(E)) \tag{13-51}$$

The reader should recall that "even" odds $(O(E) = 1.0)$ imply that $P(E) = P(\neg E) = 0.5$. Recall also that Bayes rule allows us to write

$$P(A \mid E) = \frac{P(E \mid A)P(A)}{P(E)} \tag{13-52}$$

so that we may convert our *posterior* conditional probability $P(A \mid E)$ into an *a priori* probability $P(E \mid A)$, weighted by the ratio of the probabilities $P(A)$ and $P(E)$. To eliminate the need for $P(E)$, we often write the relation between A and E in *odds form*. Since

$$P(\neg A \mid E) = 1 - P(A \mid E) \tag{13-53}$$

and, again using Bayes rule,

$$P(\neg A \mid E) = \frac{P(E \mid \neg A)P(\neg A)}{P(E)} \tag{13-54}$$

we may write the conditional odds of $A \mid E$ as the ratio

$$O(A \mid E) = P(A \mid E)/P(\neg A \mid E) = \frac{P(E \mid A)}{P(E \mid \neg A)} \frac{P(A)}{P(\neg A)} \tag{13-55}$$

which again illustrates how the a priori unconditional odds on A $(P(A)/P(\neg A))$ are modified by the observation of E.

Heuristic Approaches Derived from Probabilistic Reasoning (Confidence Factors)

On the basis of the previous section, one might conclude that the probabilistic approach to reasoning with uncertainty, due to its rigorous foundation in mathematics and despite the aforementioned complexities, is the paradigm of choice in developing rule-based systems that reason with uncertainty. This is not the case for at least two reasons:

1. It has been observed that "experts," when faced with a problem, do not choose approaches that embody standard probabilistic approaches. (13-56)

2. The difficulty (particularly with respect to the independence assumption) in incorporating strict probabilistic approaches practically precludes their use.   (13-57)

HEURISTIC EXTENSIONS. Thus, a search for systematic techniques for the representation of uncertainties in the inference process yields two main avenues of pursuit: the identification and emulation of the (non-probabilistic) approaches observed to be used by experts; and approaches "similar" to, but not founded in, probability.

Following the first avenue (13-56), we notice that experts have been observed to use "certainty factors" in their problem solving. For example,

> In the expert system MYCIN, a confidence scale of $[-1,1]$ is used to represent the range of confidence associated with a particular fact or assertion (conclusion). A value of -1 indicates total lack of confidence (i.e., complete confidence the assertion is FALSE), whereas a measure of 1 represents complete certainty the assertion is TRUE. If, after exhausting all search possibilities, the cumulative confidence measure associated with a hypothesis is in the interval $[-0.2, 0.2]$, the hypothesis is regarded as unconfirmed. Of course, this is an empirically determined range that is subject to modification or alternative interpretation in a particular application.

> The expert system CASNET, also used for medical diagnosis (specifically for the identification of glaucoma), uses a scale of confidence factors in the range $[1,5]$, where 1 indicates "rarely causes" and 5 indicates "almost always causes." The somewhat novel feature of this approach, however, is that the numerical values of certain observations are converted into confidence factors for the associated fact. For example, if "intraocular pressure" is measured to be 15 mm Hg, the fact INCREASED INTRAOCULAR PRESSURE might have the confidence factor 3, but an observation of 30 mm Hg might yield a confidence factor of 4.

The development of confidence factors requires corresponding development of a mechanism to combine and propagate these factors. For example,

> In MYCIN, given a rule that incorporates the *conjunction* (AND-ing) of n antecedents, the confidence measure associated with the consequent obtained by firing this rule is the *minimum* of the confidence measures of the individual antecedents.

> Alternately, given a rule that incorporates the *disjunction* (OR-ing) of n antecedents, the confidence measure associated with the consequent obtained by firing this rule is the *maximum* of the confidence measures of the individual antecedents.

Notice the similarity of this approach to that of (13-16). Although there are other possible heuristic approaches, we define one as "the heuristic approach" and consider its ramifications in considerable detail.

EXAMINATION OF THE HEURISTIC APPROACH. A two-antecedent rule will be used for illustration. Given confidence measures denoted X and Y corresponding to two events A and B (i.e., $X = \mathrm{conf}(A)$, $Y = \mathrm{conf}(B)$), we compare the results for the calculation of $Z = \mathrm{conf}(C)$. Using the heuristic approach, we get Z_H, where

$$Z_H = \min\{X, Y\} \tag{13-58}$$

TABLE 13.1
Comparison of propagated
confidence factors

X	Y	$Z_p = XY$	$Z_H = \min\{X,Y\}$
0	0	0	0
0.1	0.9	0.09	0.10
0.25	1.0	0.25	0.25
0.25	0.25	0.06	0.25
0.5	1.0	0.5	0.5
0.5	0.5	0.25	0.5
0.75	1.0	0.75	0.75
0.75	0.75	0.56	0.75
1.0	1.0	1.0	1.0

whereas the confidence in the probability-based approach assuming independence, denoted Z_P is

$$Z_P = XY \tag{13-59}$$

The differing results for these two methods are shown in Table 13.1 for various values of the confidence measures.

INTUITIVE AND ANALYTICAL COMPARISON. Table 13.1 suggests a number of comparisons:

1. The heuristic approach is less conservative than the probabilistic approach; that is, the resulting confidence measures are higher than those obtained using the probabilistic approach. (13-60)
2. (Corollary to 1.) The heuristic approach *more* closely resembles the probabilistic approach with dependence considerations. This is easy to show since (13-61)

$$P(C) = P(A \cap B) \tag{13-62}$$
$$P(A \cap B) = P(A \mid B)P(B) \leq P(B) \tag{13-63}$$
$$P(A \cap B) = P(B \mid A)P(A) \leq P(A) \tag{13-64}$$

Thus,

$$P(A \cap B) \leq \min\{P(A), P(B)\} \tag{13-65}$$

so that the heuristic is a reasonable, albeit conservative, bound on the confidence of C. It also happens to have an explanation using probability.

POSITIVE AND NEGATIVE REINFORCEMENT IN THE HEURISTIC APPROACH. The reasonableness of the heuristic approach vis-a-vis the probabilistic approach is further illustrated by the following two cases:

Case 1: $P(A \mid B) \approx 1$; $P(B) < P(A \mid B)$ **(positive reinforcement).** In this case,

$$P(A \mid B) = P(A \cap B)/P(B) = 1 \tag{13-66}$$

therefore,

$$P(C) = P(A \cap B) = P(A \mid B)P(B) \approx P(B) \tag{13-67}$$

So we would be correct in choosing $P(B)$ as an estimator of conf(C). In fact, $P(A)$ in this case yields no new information; we know that

$$P(A) = \sum_i P(A \mid E_i) \tag{13-68}$$

and that $P(A \mid B) \approx 1$, so $P(A) \approx 1$, since it must hold that

$$P(A) \geq P(A \mid B) \tag{13-69}$$

We therefore correctly choose $P(B)$ as an estimator of conf(C).

Case 2: $P(A \mid B) \approx 0$ **(Negative Reinforcement).** In this case, A and B don't jointly occur; that is, $P(A \cap B) \approx 0$. Either $P(A \mid B) \approx 0$ or $P(B \mid A) \approx 0$. Suppose $P(\neg A \mid B) \approx 1$. Since $P(\neg A) \geq P(\neg A \mid B)$, we surmise that $P(\neg A) \approx 1$; therefore $P(A) = 0$, which yields the correct propagated confidence using conf(C) = min$\{P(A), P(B)\}$.

EXTENSION OF THE HEURISTIC APPROACH TO "OR" FORMULATIONS. For OR formulations, where $C = A \cup B$, MYCIN and other inference systems use the heuristic

$$\text{conf}(C) = \max\{\text{conf}(A), \text{conf}(B)\} \tag{13-70}$$

The reader is encouraged to repeat the analysis of the AND-based heuristic for this case, to verify the reasonableness of this approach as well as its relation to probability.

Many Valued Logics

Allowing a statement to assume a truth value other than TRUE or FALSE introduces *many-valued logics*. Many-valued logics have been around at least since Aristotle, who proposed four "shades" of truth:

- necessity   (13-71)
- contingency   (13-72)
- possibility   (13-73)
- impossibility.   (13-74)

The generalization to a many-valued propositional logic was shown by Post [1921]. Other comprehensive surveys appear in the references.

Example 13.5 A simple three-valued logic. Consider a three-valued logic, wherein a statement S can take on one of three truth values: TRUE (denoted 1), FALSE (denoted 0), and MAYBE (denoted $\frac{1}{2}$). Given this logic, immediate concerns include the ability to *propagate truth values using logical connectives*, specifically, AND, OR, NOT, and implication. A second issue is the combination and relation of these connectives (e.g.,

TABLE 13.2
Sample paradigm for three-valued logic

$T(\neg S) = 1 - T(S)$
$T(S_1 \cap S_2) = \min\{S_1, S_2\}$
$T(S_1 \cup S_2) = \max\{S_1, S_2\}$

recall in the classical two-valued logic of Chapter 2 that $(p \rightarrow q) \equiv (\neg p \cup q))$. An obvious choice, which parallels that of confidence-measure propagation, is shown here. Letting $T(S)$ denote the truth value of statement S, we arrive at Table 13.2.

Thus, we have an extension of two valued logic, with the addition:

$$\neg\, maybe = maybe \tag{13-75}$$

We now formalize this approach and show examples of its utility.

FORMALIZING MULTIVALUED LOGIC. We show a formulation for a many-valued logic applicable to uncertain reasoning using an Extended Post formulation [DiZenzo 1988]. We begin with the following definitions:

p: the *number* of truth values in a p-valued logic (note $p = 2$ is the conventional approach with truth values TRUE and FALSE). (13-76a)

$V(p)$: the *truth set* or set of possible truth values. Restricting *truth values* to the range [0, 1] for a p-valued logic, $V(p) = \{0, 1/(p-1), \cdots, (p-2)/(p-1), 1\}$. Note in a two-valued logic, $V(2) = \{0, 1\}$. (13-76b)

For notational convenience, we rewrite $V(p)$ to index truth values by m, where

$$V(p) = \{u(m)\}, m = 0, 1, \cdots, p - 1 \tag{13-77}$$

so the mth truth value is given by

$$u(m) = m/(p - 1) \tag{13-78}$$

For example, consider the following three-valued logic ($p = 3$) formulation:

$$V(3) = \{0, \tfrac{1}{2}, 1\} \tag{13-79}$$

(Note that truth value $u(m) = \frac{1}{2}$, i.e., the value corresponding to truth index $m = 1$, intuitively corresponds to the notion of "maybe" or "possibly.") This yields the correspondence between the truth index and the truth value for the $p = 3$ case:

m	$u(m)$
0	0
1	½
2	1

(13-80)

We denote the truth value of a statement, a, as $T(a)$. The following "weak" interpretations of the $\neg$ (not), $\cap_m$ (and) and $\cup_m$ (or) logical connectives are defined.

- *Negation* ($\neg$).

$$T(\neg a) = 1 - T(a) \tag{13-81}$$

Note that the unary negation operator is not dependent upon m.

- *Weak conjunction* ($\cap_m$).

$$T(a \cap_m b) = \max\{T(a), T(b)\} \tag{13-82a}$$

$$\text{iff } T(a) < m \text{ AND } T(b) < m \text{ OR } (T(a) \geq m \text{ AND } T(b) \geq m)$$

otherwise

$$T(a \cap_m b) = \min\{T(a), T(b)\} \tag{13-82b}$$

- *Weak disjunction* ($\cup_m$)

$$T(a \cup_m b) = \min\{T(a), T(b)\} \tag{13-83a}$$

$$\text{iff } T(a) \geq m \text{ AND } T(b) \geq m$$

$$\text{OR } T(a) < m \text{ AND } T(b) < m$$

otherwise

$$T(a \cup_m b) = \max\{T(a), T(b)\} \tag{13-83b}$$

- *Weak implication* ($\rightarrow_m$)

$$T(a \rightarrow_m b) = T(\neg a \cup_m b) \tag{13-84}$$

These connectives are summarized for the $p = 3$ case in the truth tables of Fig. 13.10. Notice that increasing m yields truth tables that are, in a sense, more conservative. Alternative truth table-based definitions for the logical connectives in a three-valued logic are explored in Chapter 3 of Turner [1984] and are summarized in Fig. 13.11.

USING MULTIVALUED LOGIC FOR INFERENCE. Notice that implied in the definitions (13-82–13-84) and in Fig. 13.10 is choice of m, which also serves as a "threshold" or "level of significance." For a p-valued logic, this enables p logically complete subsystems or "logical planes," each indexed by a particular value of m. Given some measure of desired inference significance, one conceptually obvious approach is to fix the significance measure m and use only this logical plane (with the corresponding truth tables for its logical connectives). For example, consider a logic with $p = 100$. If we were using this logic for diagnosis of cancer, we might choose a relatively high level of significance, perhaps the $m = 90$ plane. Conversely, if we are using the logic

a	b	$(m=0)$ $a \cap_0 b$	$(m=1)$ $a \cap_1 b$	$(m=2)$ $a \cap_2 b$	$(p=2$ logic$)$ $a \cap b$
0	0	0	0	0	0 (F)
0	1	1	0	1	—
0	2	2	0	0	0 (F)
1	0	1	0	1	—
1	1	1	1	1	—
1	2	2	2	1	—
2	0	2	0	0	0 (F)
2	1	2	2	1	—
2	2	2	2	2	2 (T)

(a)

a	b	$a \cup_0 b$	$a \cup_1 b$	$a \cup_2 b$	$(p=2$ logic$)$ $a \cup b$
0	0	0	0	0	0 (F)
0	1	0	1	0	—
0	2	0	2	2	2 (T)
1	0	0	1	0	—
1	1	1	1	1	—
1	2	1	1	2	—
2	0	0	2	2	2 (T)
2	1	1	1	2	—
2	2	2	2	2	2 (T)

(b)

a	$\neg a$	$(p=2$ logic$)$ $\neg a$
0	2	2 (T)
1	1	—
2	0	0 (F)

(c)

p	q	$\neg p$	$(m=0)$ $\neg p \cup_m q$	$(m=1)$ $\neg p \cup_m q$	$(m=2)$ $\neg p \cup_m q$	$(p=2$ logic$)$ $\neg p \rightarrow q$
0	0	2	0	2	2	2 (T)
0	1	2	1	1	2	—
0	2	2	2	2	2	2 (T)
1	0	1	0	1	0	—
1	1	1	1	1	1	—
1	2	1	1	1	2	—
2	0	0	0	0	0	0 (F)
2	1	0	0	1	0	—
2	2	0	0	2	2	2 (T)

(d)

FIGURE 13.10

$p = 3$ (three-valued logic: examples of weak connectives (all truth values shown using index m). (a) $a \cap_m b$; (b) $a \cup_m b$; (c) $\neg a$; (d) $p \rightarrow_m q$.

a	$\neg a$
t	f
f	t
u	u

t: TRUE
f: FALSE
u: UNDECIDED

a	b	$a \cap b$	$a \cup b$	$a \rightarrow b$
f	f	f	f	t
f	u	f	u	t
f	t	f	t	t
u	f	f	u	u
u	u	u	u	u
u	t	u	t	t
t	f	f	t	f
t	u	u	t	u
t	t	t	t	t

(*a*)

a	b	$a \rightarrow b$
f	f	t
f	i	t
f	t	t
i	f	i
i	i	t
i	t	t
t	f	f
t	i	i
t	t	t

i: indeterminate (cannot be assigned the value of t of f)

(*b*)

a	$\neg a$
t	f
f	t
m	m

a	b	$a \cap b$	$a \cup b$	$a \rightarrow b$
f	f	f	f	t
f	m	m	m	m
f	t	f	t	t
m	f	m	m	m
m	m	m	m	m
m	t	m	m	m
t	f	f	t	f
t	m	m	m	m
t	t	t	t	t

(*c*)

FIGURE 13.11
Examples of alternative definitions of logical connectives for $p = 3$. (from [Turner, 1984].) (*a*) Kleene (from [Kleene, 1952].); (*b*) Lukasiewicz ($\neg$, $\cap$, $\cup$ same as in (*a*)) (from [Lukasiewicz, 1930].); (*c*) Bochvar (from [Bochvar, 1939].).

for a very speculative mineral exploration, a lower (e.g., $m = 40$) level might be chosen. (This is explored further in the problems.)

The previous approach, while straightforward, may be improved by mixing planes, as shown in DiZenzo [1988].

LISP Implementations

Example 13.6 Sample use of LISP to implement multivalued logic and inference. A set of LISP functions is shown here that implements weak implication using a multivalued (p-valued) logic and the definitions in (13-77) through (13-84). The major function definition is as follows:

```
(defun weak-modus-ponens (a b m p)
(weak-impl (weak-conj (weak-impl a b m p) a m) b m p))
```

$$(13\text{-}85a)$$

where a, b and m are defined in (13-84). The auxiliary functions are defined next:

```
(defun negation (a p)
(- (- p 1) a))

(defun weak-conj (a b m)
(if
  (or
    (and
      (>= a m)
      (>= b m))
    (and
      (< a m)
      (< b m)))
  (max a b)
  (min a b)))

(defun weak-disj (a b m)
(if
  (or
    (and
      (< a m)
      (< b m))
    (and
      (>= a m)
      (>= b m)))
  (min a b)
  (max a b)))

(defun weak-impl (a b m p)
(weak-disj (negation a p) b m))
```

$$(13\text{-}85b)$$

We modify the fact structure to incorporate a truth value in a manner similar to that used for confidence values. The sample structure is

```
(setq a '(a 2))
(setq b '(b 0))
```
$$(13\text{-}85c)$$

The corresponding function used to extract the value from (13-85c) is

```
(defun truth-value (a)
(if (listp a) (cadr a) nil))
```
$$(13\text{-}85d)$$

LISP IMPLEMENTATION MODIFICATION FOR NUMERICAL CONFIDENCE MEASURES. For general confidence-measure propagation, the previously designed LISP fact and rule bases (and inference engines) could be modified to include additional elements in each fact representation. The *fact modification* is of the form

previous representation: $(B1 <> 0)$

modified representation: $((B1 <> 0)$ CONF conf-value)

$$(13\text{-}86a)$$

That is, each fact is now the CAR of a list whose CADR is the atom "CONF" and whose CADDR is the numerical value of the "confidence" in this fact. This confidence measure may be either

1. User input (or set by default), in the case of facts not generated by rules.
2. Propagated by the rule used to generate the fact.

The *rule modification* goes like

```
(RULE rule-name

(IF
    ((prev-fact1-repr) CONF conf-value1)
    ((prev-fact2-repr) CONF conf-value2) )

(THEN
    ((prev-concl1) CONF calc1)
    ((prev-concl2) CONF calc2) ) )
```
$$(13\text{-}86b)$$

The inference engine, in rule firing, must calculate the numerical values calc1 and calc2 in (13-86b). This may be accomplished via several of the methods illustrated previously.

Example of Numerical Confidence Propagation and Conflict Resolution in Forward Chaining

In this section, we show an example of how confidence factors are used as part of a conflict resolution strategy and may lead to a different rule-firing sequence than that using other (e.g., specificity ordered) conflict-resolution strategies. Using the conflict-resolution strategy "fire the first applicable rule and start over" (fwd_r.l), the sequence of firings is 6-7-8-10-11-13-2.

Example 13.7 Conflict resolution using confidence measures. A forward-chaining inference mechanism is used with the database shown. At each iteration, the conflict set is formed. The conflict resolution strategy is as follows:

"Fire the applicable rule that produces the consequent with the highest resulting confidence." If a tie exists, choose the more specific rule. If a tie still exists, use the rule that appears first in the conflict set.

Confidence measures in antecedents are propagated to consequents by using the minimum of the antecedent confidence measures. We show the resulting inference net for this system, the order in which rules are fired, and the fact and associated confidence measure produced at each step. Sample rule and fact bases are shown. The modification of fwd_r.l is left to the reader.

- *Database and initial confidence measures*

```
(setq *facts* '((f1  CONF  0.8)
                (f4  CONF  0.6)
                (f6  CONF  0.7)
                (f7  CONF  0.8)
                (f8  CONF  0.9)
                (f9  CONF  0.6)
                (f10  CONF  0.4)
                (f11  CONF  0.5)
                (f12  CONF  0.3)
                (f14  CONF  0.7)
                (f15  CONF  0.8)
                (f16  CONF  0.9)
                (f17  CONF  0.7)
                (f18  CONF  0.8)
                (f23  CONF  0.4)
                (f24  CONF  0.4)))


(setq *rules* '((rule 1  (IF a  b  c)  (THEN z))
                (rule 2  (IF d  e  f  g)  (THEN z))
                (rule 3  (IF f1  f2)  (THEN a))
                (rule 4  (IF f1  f3  f4)  (THEN a))
                (rule 5  (IF f4  f5)  (THEN b))
                (rule 6  (IF f6  f7)  (THEN b))
                (rule 7  (IF f7  f8  f9)  (THEN c))
                (rule 8  (IF f10  f11  f12)  (THEN d))
                (rule 9  (IF f13  f14)  (THEN d))
                (rule 10  (IF f14  f15  f16)  (THEN e))
                (rule 11  (IF f17  f18)  (THEN f))
                (rule 12  (IF f19  f20  f21  f22)  (THEN g))
                (rule 13  (IF f23  f24)  (THEN g))))
```

- *Sample Results*

Given these rule and fact bases and this conflict-resolution strategy, the following results:

```
(FOLLOWING RULES ARE APPLICABLE:)
((rule 10 (IF f14 f15 f16) (THEN e)) CONF 0.7)
((rule 6 (IF f6 f7) (THEN b)) CONF 0.7)
((rule 11 (IF f17 f18) (THEN f)) CONF 0.7)
((rule 7 (IF f7 f8 f9) (THEN c)) CONF 0.6)
((rule 13 (IF f23 f24) (THEN g)) CONF 0.4)
((rule 8 (IF f10 f11 f12) (THEN d)) CONF 0.3)

(RULE rule 10 IS FIRED)
(DEDUCES (e CONF 0.7))

(FOLLOWING RULES ARE APPLICABLE:)
((rule 6 (IF f6 f7) (THEN b)) CONF 0.7)
((rule 11 (IF f17 f18) (THEN f)) CONF 0.7)
((rule 7 (IF f7 f8 f9) (THEN c)) CONF 0.6)
((rule 13 (IF f23 f24) (THEN g)) CONF 0.4)
((rule 8 (IF f10 f11 f12) (THEN d)) CONF 0.3)
(RULE rule 6 IS FIRED)
(DEDUCES (b CONF 0.7))

(FOLLOWING RULES ARE APPLICABLE:)
((rule 11 (IF f17 f18) (THEN f)) CONF 0.7)
((rule 7 (IF f7 f8 f9) (THEN c)) CONF 0.6)
((rule 13 (IF f23 f24) (THEN g)) CONF 0.4)
((rule 8 (IF f10 f11 f12) (THEN d)) CONF 0.3)

(RULE rule 11 IS FIRED)
(DEDUCES (f CONF 0.7))

(FOLLOWING RULES ARE APPLICABLE:)
((rule 7 (IF f7 f8 f9) (THEN c)) CONF 0.6)
((rule 13 (IF f23 f24) (THEN g)) CONF 0.4)
((rule 8 (IF f10 f11 f12) (THEN d)) CONF 0.3)

(RULE rule 7 IS FIRED)
(DEDUCES (c CONF 0.6))


(FOLLOWING RULES ARE APPLICABLE:)
((rule 13 (IF f23 f24) (THEN g)) CONF 0.4)
((rule 8 (IF f10 f11 f12) (THEN d)) CONF 0.3)

(RULE rule 13 IS FIRED)
(DEDUCES (g CONF 0.4))


(FOLLOWING RULES ARE APPLICABLE:)
((rule 8 (IF f10 f11 f12) (THEN d)) CONF 0.3)

(RULE rule 8 IS FIRED)
```

```
(DEDUCES (d CONF 0.3))


(FOLLOWING RULES ARE APPLICABLE:)
((rule 2 (IF d e f g) (THEN z)) CONF 0.3)

(RULE rule 2 IS FIRED)
(DEDUCES (z CONF 0.3))


(NO MORE APPLICABLE RULES ARE AVAILABLE)
```

The reader should compare the confidence-value-based conflict-resolution strategy with alternatives discussed in Chapter 11. Further examples and extensions are considered in the problems.

A COMMERCIAL RULE-BASED SYSTEM EXAMPLE: OPS5

It is often both impractical and unrealistic to develop an ES from "scratch" in PROLOG or LISP; thus, "shells," or development environments that facilitate the development of application-customized ES's, are available. OPS5 is a popular example.

The OPS5 Production System Programming Language

OPS5 (*Official Production System, Version 5*), is a production-system language used to implement expert systems. It is often implemented as an extension to LISP. It has found considerable acceptance in the AI research and development communities, principally because of its flexibility and ease of use and the fact that it represents a standardized representation approach to rule-based inference. The initial version was written at Carnegie-Mellon University in the mid 1970s [Brownston 1986].

From a programming viewpoint, an OPS5 implementation consists of a set of suitably coded facts in *working memory* (WM) and a set of rules in *production memory*. These are shown in Fig. 13.12. Rules or productions are in IF-THEN form. A production is designated by a *list* whose car is the symbol p. The *n*th element of the list is the rule name (find−segment in Ex. 13.8), and the antecedents are a series of lists ending with the symbol -->. In the simplest form, the LHS of a rule is a set of *condition elements* that specify patterns to be matched against facts in working memory. The RHS of the rule (indicated after the arrow, as shown below) is a sequence of actions. For example, a simple rule for finding in WM a line segment whose endpoints are the values of the variables $(<x0>,<y0>), (<x1>,<y1>)$ in OPS5 is

Example 13.8 Sample OPS5 production.

```
(p find−segment
        (segment ^x0 <x0> ^y0 <y0> ^x1 <x1> ^y1 <y1>)
        (segment ^x1 <x1> ^y1 <y1> ^x2 <x2> ^y2 <y2>)
```

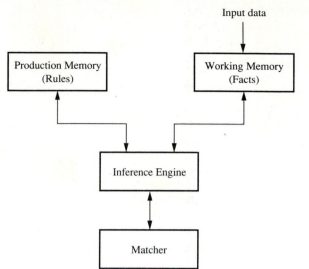

Input data

Production Memory
(Rules)

Working Memory
(Facts)

Inference Engine

Matcher

FIGURE 13.12
OPS5 production rule system architecture.

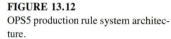

```
-->
        (write A longer segment has been found with
        coordinates
              (<x0>, <y0>, <x2>, <y2>))))                    (13-87a)
```

This rule may be paraphrased as

```
IF a segment with beginning coordinates (<x0>, <y0>)
   and ending coordinates (<x1>, <y1>) is found in working
   memory
```

```
AND another segment with beginning coordinates (<x1>,
     <y1>) and ending coordinates (<x2>, <y2>) is also
     in working memory
```

```
THEN show this by printing the longer segment endpoints
```
$$(13\text{-}87b)$$

**Example 13.9 Relating OPS5 productions to the rule structure of Chapters
11–13.** It is easy to see the structural similarity of rules in OPS5 format to those of
our previous LISP implementations (Chapters 11 and 12) via the following example:

(*a*) Structure for fwd_r∗, bwd_r∗ (Chapters 11 and 12).

```
(rule 1   (IF a r)
          (THEN b))                                          (13-88a)
```

(*b*) Corresponding OPS5 WM structure.

```
(literalize primitive element-name)                          (13-88b)
```

(*c*) Corresponding OPS5 Production.

```
(p   rule_1
        (primitive ^element−name   a)
        (primitive ^element−name   r)


-->


        (make primitive ^element−name b))
```
(13-88*c*)

This relationship is explored further in the problems.

THE RECOGNIZE-ACT CYCLE. The OPS5 IE loops through a **recognize-act cycle**, where rule antecedents are examined, a set of rules eligible for firing (the *conflict set*) is identified, and one rule is chosen for firing. This is [Brownston 1986] shown in Table 13.3.

Most versions of OPS5 allow direct embedding of LISP statements in the production system code. Prior to looking at some advanced systems, we explore the basics of OPS5 using some of the examples from Chapters 11 and 12.

OPS5 Program Structure

Not surprisingly, OPS5 uses parentheses to delineate statements. An OPS5 program consists of two major sections:

1. A *declaration section* that enumerates the data objects to be kept in *working memory*.
2. A *production section* containing the rules.

These sections must be entered in this order. An optional (third) section, consisting of "make" actions, may be used to initialize working memory.

WORKING MEMORY DATA OBJECTS. Simple declarations, as exemplified by (13-88*b*), are used to describe elementary working-memory data objects. Each element of WM is a *working element*, or *attribute-value element*, and consists of a class name and a list of attribute-value pairs. For example, the following make command creates a working-memory element of class primitive with element-class name

TABLE 13.3
OPS5 recognize-act cycle

```
repeat
        perform match
        exit if any of the following are true:
         •   the conflict set is empty
         •   a halt was performed
         •   the cycle count has been reached
         •   a breakpoint has been reached
        perform conflict resolution
        execute the selected rule
end
```
(13-89)

^element—name and value f1:

(make primitive ^element—name f1) (13-90)

The working memory element class primitive is declared in an OPS5 program via the sample statement used in (13-88*b*):

(literalize primitive element—name) (13-91)

This declares, to OPS5, that an element class named primitive exists, with a single attribute element—name. In general, elements in working memory are individually declared via a list whose car is the symbol literalize.

PRODUCTION OR RULE STRUCTURE. *Productions* are coded as a list whose car is the symbol *p* (for production). The caar of this list is the user-chosen name of the production. The rule antecedents or *condition elements* follow. They are used to specify conditions that must occur in WM for the production to be applicable. Generally, matching or unification of condition elements with WM is required. The examples that follow use simple data structures. In matching a condition element containing a compound data type (defined in 13-93) against WM, if an attribute is not specified in the condition element, it is not checked (matched). This enables, as in Chapter 10, matching with "don't cares." As in our previous rule-based analysis, the conjunction of the conditions in the production must be unified with working memory. "Not" is indicated by a *negated condition*, that is, a condition preceded by a minus sign.

Thus, the general structure for an OPS5 production is

```
(p rule_name
   (condition_element_1)
        .
        .
        .
   (condition_element_n)
-->
   (action_1)
        .
        .
        .
   (action_m)            )
```

Following the condition elements, an arrow ---> is used to signify the productions or actions that occur if the rule is fired. Each production performs some activity, usually affecting the state of the WM. Each action (there may be several) is written as a list whose car is the name of the action. Examples include

(write (crlf) <p> is a parent of <c>)

(make primitive ^element—name f1)

(remove <fact>) (13-92)

OPS5 production actions include

- modify: change one or more values in an existing WM element
- make: add an element to WM
- remove: remove an element from WM
- accept: used for input
- write: used for output
- halt: stop OPS5 execution (after current rule firing)

ADVANCED DATA STRUCTURES (WM ELEMENTS) IN OPS5. OPS5 allows *compound data types*, which are referred to as *element classes*. Compound element classes are declared via extended literalize statements of the form

```
(literalize a-class
            attribute-1
            attribute-2

            .

            .

            .

            attribute-n)                                    (13-93)
```

Example 13.10   Compound data type for line segment representation. A line segment in 2-D with endpoints $(x0, y0)$ and $(x1, y1)$ at locations $(10, 10)$ and $(30, 20)$ respectively, could be designated in OPS5 using the compound data type

```
(literalize segment
      x0
      y0
      x1
      y1)                                                   (13-94)
```

where $x0 \cdots y1$ are the *attributes* of class segment. This line segment could then be added to WM via the action

```
(make segment ^x0   10   ^y0   10   ^x1   30   ^y1   20).          (13-95)
```

VARIABLES. Variables in OPS5 are designated via angular brackets (i.e., ‹ ›). For example, variables $x0$ and $x1$ are denoted $<x0>$ and $<x1>$ respectively. This is apparent in Ex. 13.8.

WM AND TIME TAGS. Working memory elements are marked with a *time tag* or *recency attribute*, which is used as a part of conflict resolution. Larger values of the time tag indicate more recent elements. Modifying an element in WM gives the element a new time tag. When the OPS5 "examine working memory" command

```
(wm)
```

is issued, each WM element is displayed preceded by an integer, which is the time tag for the element. The reader should study the following OPS5 examples and confirm the relationship between the order in which the make action is invoked and the resulting time tags of WM elements.

Conflict Resolution in OPS5

When more than one rule may be fired, two OPS5 conflict-resolution strategies are available: LEX and MEA. LEX is the simpler of the two. The LEX strategy
  (i) Inhibits the previously fired rule (similar to the concept of "refraction" in neural networks). All instantiations (previous bindings) used to fire a rule previously are deleted from the conflict set. This prohibits a rule from continuously firing without producing anything new.
 (ii) Orders productions on the basis of recency of time tags of WM elements in condition elements and specificity (total number of tests) in rule condition.
(iii) If all else fails (i.e., (ii) yields a "tie" in conflict resolution), arbitrarily selects a production.

MEA (*means end analysis*) places additional emphasis on the recency of a working memory element that matches the first rule condition. OPS5 displays the conflict set at each cycle if the user invokes the command

```
(cs)
```

Finally, OPS5 allows several levels of IE display using the watch command. The most complete display is obtained by invoking

```
(watch 2)
```

OPS5 Examples

Example 13.11   Sample OPS5 code (using database of Ex. 11.14).

```
; ops5 program example 1

(literalize primitive element-name)

(p rule_1
        (primitive ^element-name a)
        (primitive ^element-name r)
  -->
        (make primitive ^element-name b))

(p rule_2
        (primitive ^element-name b)
        (primitive ^element-name s)
  -->
        (make primitive ^element-name c))
```

```
(p rule_3
       (primitive ^element-name a)
       (primitive ^element-name x)
-->
       (make primitive ^element-name d))

(p rule_4
       (primitive ^element-name d)
-->
       (make primitive ^element-name c))

(p rule_5
       (primitive ^element-name g)
-->
       (make primitive ^element-name f))

(p rule_6
       (primitive ^element-name h)
       (primitive ^element-name w)
-->
       (make primitive ^element-name f))

(p rule_7
       (primitive ^element-name f)
       (primitive ^element-name y)
-->
       (make primitive ^element-name e))

(p rule_8
       (primitive ^element-name c)
-->
       (make primitive ^element-name e))

(p rule_9
       (primitive ^element-name e)
-->
       (make primitive ^element-name z))

(p rule_10
       (primitive ^element-name m)
-->
       (make primitive ^element-name i))

(p rule_11
       (primitive ^element-name n)
-->
       (make primitive ^element-name i))

(p rule_12
       (primitive ^element-name o)
```

```
              (primitive ^element-name u)
-->
              (make primitive ^element-name i))

(p rule_13
              (primitive ^element-name i)
-->
              (make primitive ^element-name j))

(p rule_14
              (primitive ^element-name p)
              (primitive ^element-name t)
-->
              (make primitive ^element-name j))

(p rule_15
              (primitive ^element-name j)
              (primitive ^element-name v)
-->
              (make primitive ^element-name z))

(p rule_16
              (primitive ^element-name i)
-->
              (make primitive ^element-name z))

(p rule_17
              (primitive ^element-name k)
              (primitive ^element-name q)
-->
              (make primitive ^element-name g))

(p rule_18
              (primitive ^element-name l)
              (primitive ^element-name p)
-->
              (make primitive ^element-name h))

(make primitive ^element-name a)
(make primitive ^element-name r)
```

Example 13.12   OPS5 usage.
(*a*) We invoke OPS5 in LISP, initialize, and load the OPS5 source file:

```
-> (i-g-v)
nil
-> (wm)
nil
-> (load "example1.l")
[load example1.l]
*****************t
```

(*b*) Following this, we examine the current contents of WM:

```
-> (wm)

1:   (primitive      ^element-name a)
2:   (primitive      ^element-name r)nil
-> (watch 2)
2
```

(*c*) Add an element to WM, and then examine WM:

```
-> (make primitive ^element-name x)
nil
-> (wm)

1:   (primitive      ^element-name a)
2:   (primitive      ^element-name r)
3:   (primitive      ^element-name x)nil
```

(*d*) To initiate a recognize-act cycle, the r un command is used:

```
-> (run)

1.  rule_3  1  3
=>wm:  4:  (primitive      ^element-name d)
2.  rule_4  4
=>wm:  5:  (primitive      ^element-name c)
3.  rule_8  5
=>wm:  6:  (primitive      ^element-name e)
4.  rule_9  6
=>wm:  7:  (primitive      ^element-name z)
5.  rule_1  1  2
=>wm:  8:  (primitive      ^element-name b)
end -- no production true
18 productions (72 // 104 nodes)
5 firings (8 rhs actions)
5 mean working memory size (8 maximum)
2 mean conflict set size (2 maximum)
3 mean token memory size (3 maximum)
nil
```

(*e*) Finally, we examine WM after all production firings:

```
-> (wm)

1:   (primitive      ^element-name a)
2:   (primitive      ^element-name r)
3:   (primitive      ^element-name x)
4:   (primitive      ^element-name d)
5:   (primitive      ^element-name c)
6:   (primitive      ^element-name e)
```

```
7:  (primitive    ^element-name z)
8:  (primitive    ^element-name b)
```

Example 13.13 Sample OPS5 database (using database of Ex. 12.10, page 347).
(*a*) WM data-structure declaration.

```
(literalize primitive element-name)
```

(*b*) Productions.

```
(p rule_m
        (primitive ^element-name a)
        (primitive ^element-name b)
        (primitive ^element-name c)
-->
        (make primitive ^element-name z))


(p rule_n
        (primitive ^element-name d)
        (primitive ^element-name e)
        (primitive ^element-name f)
        (primitive ^element-name g)
-->
        (make primitive ^element-name z))


(p rule_p
        (primitive ^element-name f1)
        (primitive ^element-name f2)
-->
        (make primitive ^element-name a))


(p rule_q
        (primitive ^element-name f1)
        (primitive ^element-name f3)
        (primitive ^element-name f4)
-->
        (make primitive ^element-name a))


(p rule_r
        (primitive ^element-name f4)
        (primitive ^element-name f5)
-->
        (make primitive ^element-name b))


(p rule_s
        (primitive ^element-name f6)
        (primitive ^element-name f7)
-->
        (make primitive ^element-name b))
```

```
(p rule_t
        (primitive ^element-name f7)
        (primitive ^element-name f8)
        (primitive ^element-name f9)
-->
        (make primitive ^element-name c))

(p rule_u
        (primitive ^element-name f10)
        (primitive ^element-name f11)
        (primitive ^element-name f12)
-->
        (make primitive ^element-name d))

(p rule_v
        (primitive ^element-name f13)
        (primitive ^element-name f14)
-->
        (make primitive ^element-name d))

(p rule_w
        (primitive ^element-name f14)
        (primitive ^element-name f15)
        (primitive ^element-name f16)
-->
        (make primitive ^element-name e))

(p rule_x
        (primitive ^element-name f17)
        (primitive ^element-name f18)
-->
        (make primitive ^element-name f))

(p rule_y
        (primitive ^element-name f19)
        (primitive ^element-name f20)
        (primitive ^element-name f21)
        (primitive ^element-name f22)
-->
        (make primitive ^element-name g))

(p rule_z
        (primitive ^element-name f23)
        (primitive ^element-name f24)
-->
        (make primitive ^element-name g))
```

(*c*) Initial contents of WM:

```
(make primitive ^element-name f1)
(make primitive ^element-name f4)
```

```
(make primitive ^element-name f6)
(make primitive ^element-name f7)
(make primitive ^element-name f8)
(make primitive ^element-name f9)
(make primitive ^element-name f10)
(make primitive ^element-name f11)
(make primitive ^element-name f12)
(make primitive ^element-name f14)
(make primitive ^element-name f15)
(make primitive ^element-name f16)
(make primitive ^element-name f17)
(make primitive ^element-name f18)
(make primitive ^element-name f23)
(make primitive ^element-name f24)
```

Example 13.14   Sample OPS5 execution.

```
-> (i-g-v)
nil
-> (watch 2)
2
-> (wm)
nil
-> (load "example2.l")
[load example2.l]
*************t
-> (wm)

1:  (primitive      ^element-name f1)
2:  (primitive      ^element-name f4)
3:  (primitive      ^element-name f6)
4:  (primitive      ^element-name f7)
5:  (primitive      ^element-name f8)
6:  (primitive      ^element-name f9)
7:  (primitive      ^element-name f10)
8:  (primitive      ^element-name f11)
9:  (primitive      ^element-name f12)
10: (primitive      ^element-name f14)
11: (primitive      ^element-name f15)
12: (primitive      ^element-name f16)
13: (primitive      ^element-name f17)
14: (primitive      ^element-name f18)
15: (primitive      ^element-name f23)
16: (primitive      ^element-name f24)nil
-> (run)

1. rule_z 15 16
=>wm: 17: (primitive      ^element-name g)
2. rule_x 13 14
=>wm: 18: (primitive      ^element-name f)
```

```
3. rule_w 10 11 12
=>wm: 19:  (primitive     ^element-name e)
4. rule_u 7 8 9
=>wm: 20:  (primitive     ^element-name d)
5. rule_n 20 19 18 17
=>wm: 21:  (primitive     ^element-name z)
6. rule_t 4 5 6
=>wm: 22:  (primitive     ^element-name c)
7. rule_s 3 4
=>wm: 23:  (primitive     ^element-name b)
end -- no production true
  13 productions (107 // 149 nodes)
  7 firings (23 rhs actions)
  19 mean working memory size (23 maximum)
  3 mean conflict set size (6 maximum)
  23 mean token memory size (26 maximum)
nil
-> (wm)

1:  (primitive     ^element-name f1)
2:  (primitive     ^element-name f4)
3:  (primitive     ^element-name f6)
4:  (primitive     ^element-name f7)
5:  (primitive     ^element-name f8)
6:  (primitive     ^element-name f9)
7:  (primitive     ^element-name f10)
8:  (primitive     ^element-name f11)
9:  (primitive     ^element-name f12)
10: (primitive     ^element-name f14)
11: (primitive     ^element-name f15)
12: (primitive     ^element-name f16)
13: (primitive     ^element-name f17)
14: (primitive     ^element-name f18)
15: (primitive     ^element-name f23)
16: (primitive     ^element-name f24)
17: (primitive     ^element-name g)
18: (primitive     ^element-name f)
19: (primitive     ^element-name e)
20: (primitive     ^element-name d)
21: (primitive     ^element-name z)
22: (primitive     ^element-name c)
23: (primitive     ^element-name b)nil
-> (exit)
```

The reader should compare the sequence of rule firings in the forward-chaining OPS5 implementation with that of Ex. 12.10.

Example 13.15   OPS5 with variables in productions.

```
; ops5 program with variables in rules.
```

```
(literalize relation1
            parent
            child)

(literalize relation2
            grandparent
            grandchild)

(p rule_1
        (relation1 ^parent <p> ^child <c>)
        (relation1 ^parent <c> ^child <g>)
-->
        (write (crlf) <p> is a parent of <c>)
        (write (crlf) and)
        (write (crlf) <c> is a parent of <g>)
        (write (crlf) so)
        (write (crlf) <p> is a grandparent of <g> (crlf))
        (make relation2 ^grandparent <p> ^grandchild <g>))


        (make relation1 ^parent shirley ^child leslie)
        (make relation1 ^parent leslie ^child jesse)
        (make relation1 ^parent tom ^child mark)
        (make relation1 ^parent mark ^child peter)
```

Example 13.16   Sample OPS5 execution of Ex. 13.15 (variables in productions).

```
-> (i-g-v)
nil
-> (load "parent.l")
[load parent.l]
*t
-> (run)

1. rule_1 3 4
tom is a parent of mark
and
mark is a parent of peter
so
tom is a grandparent of peter

2. rule_1 1 2
shirley is a parent of leslie
and
leslie is a parent of jesse
so
shirley is a grandparent of jesse

end -- no production true
  1 productions (4 // 6 nodes)
```

```
2 firings (6 rhs actions)
5 mean working memory size (6 maximum)
2 mean conflict set size (2 maximum)
4 mean token memory size (4 maximum)
nil
-> (exit)
```

**OPS5 APPLICATION TO IMAGE MOTION AND STRUCTURAL IDENTI-
FICATION.** An example of a comprehensive OPS5 application is the computer vision
system of Topa and Schalkoff [1987], which determines object identity and motion
from a sequence of digital images. Rules are used for both low-level preprocessing
of the edge data (similar to the Nazif/Levine [1984] system) as well as for the
structural unification of the processed data at a higher level. A low-level preprocessing
module outputs a list of spatiotemporal edges, with attributes indicating end point
coordinates, segment length, spatial orientation, and motion direction. This input
is used to group, merge, or link segments based upon a set of similarity measures
and implemented as OPS5 rules. An example is shown in Fig. 13.13, along with sample
OPS5 code.

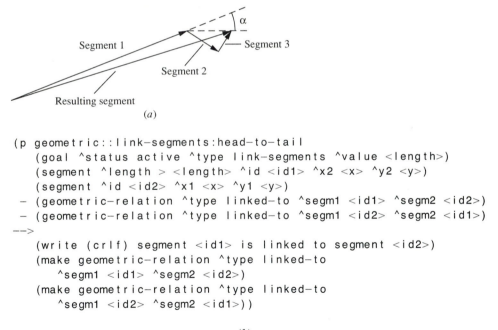

(a)

```
(p geometric::link-segments:head-to-tail
    (goal ^status active ^type link-segments ^value <length>)
    (segment ^length > <length> ^id <id1> ^x2 <x> ^y2 <y>)
    (segment ^id <id2> ^x1 <x> ^y1 <y>)
  - (geometric-relation ^type linked-to ^segm1 <id1> ^segm2 <id2>)
  - (geometric-relation ^type linked-to ^segm1 <id2> ^segm2 <id1>)
-->
    (write (crlf) segment <id1> is linked to segment <id2>)
    (make geometric-relation ^type linked-to
        ^segm1 <id1> ^segm2 <id2>)
    (make geometric-relation ^type linked-to
        ^segm1 <id2> ^segm2 <id1>))
```

(b)

FIGURE 13.13
Sample OPS5 Implementation of low-level image-processing algorithm. (a) Extending segments from the
head; (b) OPS5 production corresponding to (a).

```
(make object
        ^name airplane
        ^root fuselage
)

(make part
        ^name         fuselage
        ^cylinder     cyl1
        ^carries      right-wing left-wing
                      right-stabilizer left-stabilizer
)
(make part
        ^name         right-wing
        ^cylinder     cyl2
        ^carries      nil
)
(make part
        ^name         left-wing
        ^cylinder     cyl2
        ^carries      nil
)
(make part
        ^name         right-stabilizer
        ^cylinder     cyl3
        ^carries      nil
)
(make part
        ^name         left-stabilizer
        ^cylinder     cyl3
        ^carries      nil
)

(make attachment
          ^subject    fuselage
          ^object     right-wing
          ^where      right-side-middle
          ^how        acute angle
          ^by-what    by-the-head
)
(make attachment
          ^subject    fuselage
          ^object     left-wing
          ^where      left-side-middle
          ^how        acute-angle
          ^by-what    by-the-head)
```

FIGURE 13.14
Structure of airplane model in OPS5.

Objects in the system are modeled using a tree structured in terms of component subparts. Each object part is specified by a symbolic name, a generalized cylinder description, and a list of attached subparts. The description also constrains the possible subpart attachment, using the "where," "how," and "by-what" descriptors. Figure 13.14 shows a sample of the OPS5 make actions for creation of an airplane model. More comprehensive treatment of this example is available in Schalkoff [1989].

ADDITIONAL INFERENCE APPROACHES AND APPLICATIONS

EXTENSIONS TO SIMPLE RULE-BASED DESIGNS. Rule-based approaches have been used in numerous applications. Details of the data structures, extracted features, model complexity, and inference approaches vary with specific application. Figure 13.15 shows one example of an advanced rule-based architecture.

RULE-BASED IMAGE-SEGMENTATION EXAMPLE. As has been shown, image processing and computer vision provide a plethora of problems suitable for rule-based AI solutions. A classic example of rule-based system design applied to the problem of low-level image segmentation is found in Nazif and Levine [1984]. The system is structured as shown in Figure 13.16. The IE is itself rule-based, and consists of "meta-rules," which guide the system focus of attention. Rules are in IF-THEN form, with rule antecedents in conjunctive (AND) form. Figure 13.17 shows sample rules to facilitate region merging and region splitting.

Approaches Based upon Model Unification

The previous AI system examples illustrate typical applications and approaches. A multitude of other examples, based upon the concept of *model unification*, exist. Model-unification approaches are (model-based) attempts to unify observed (usually low-level) data with a high-level (conceptual) model. A computational paradigm is shown in Fig. 13.18.

MODEL UNIFICATION APPLICATIONS IN COMPUTER VISION. Image (scene) understanding provides a wealth of examples of model-unification applications, which may be accomplished over a spectrum of levels, ranging from raw pixel data to extracted object representations. In many cases, the algorithms rely on successive refinement of a hypothesis for model unification. This often involves a succession of feature-extraction/model-unification cycles, as depicted in Fig. 13.18.

Many challenges exist in model-unification-based computer vision. Several salient concerns are

1. Relating 2-D image data to the model representation, to constrain the selection of a 3-D model. This is dependent upon an assumed viewing direction ("viewpoint") and requires the confirmation of correspondence between image

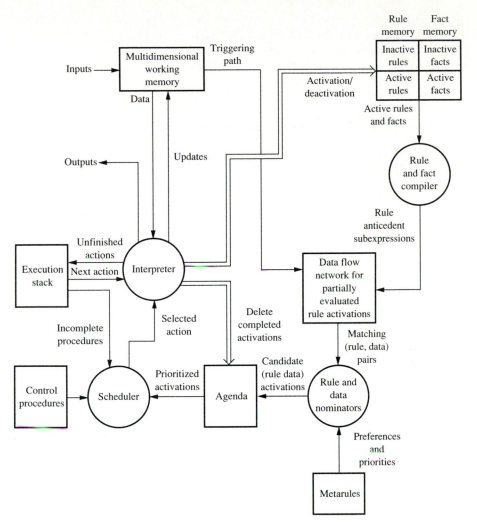

FIGURE 13.15
Representative advanced rule-based system.

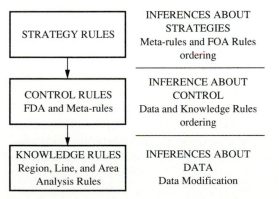

STRATEGY RULES	INFERENCES ABOUT STRATEGIES Meta-rules and FOA Rules ordering
CONTROL RULES FDA and Meta-rules	INFERENCE ABOUT CONTROL Data and Knowledge Rules ordering
KNOWLEDGE RULES Region, Line, and Area Analysis Rules	INFERENCES ABOUT DATA Data Modification

FIGURE 13.16
Hierarchical rule and control structure of the Nazif/Levine image segmentation system.

```
RULE(802):
  IF: (1) The REGION SIZE is VERY LOW
      (2) The ADJACENCY with another REGION is HIGH
      (3) The DIFFERENCE in REGION FEATURE 1 is
          NOT HIGH
      (4) The DIFFERENCE in REGION FEATURE 2 is
          NOT HIGH
      (5) The DIFFERENCE in REGION FEATURE 3 is
          NOT HIGH
THEN: (1) MERGE the two REGIONS
```

(*a*)

```
RULE (908):
  IF: (1) The REGION SIZE is NOT LOW
      (2) REGION is BISECTED BY LINE
      (3) The LINE LENGTH is NOT LOW
      (4) The LINE AVERAGE GRADIENT is HIGH
THEN: (1) SPLIT the REGION at LINES
```

(*b*)

FIGURE 13.17
Samples of "knowledge rules" from system of Figure 13.16.
(*a*) region merging; (*b*) region splitting.

features (e.g., lines, corners, circles, etc.) and the projection of the 3-D model onto the image plane. Lowe [1987] refers to this as the *viewpoint-consistency constraint*. In addition, other 3-D constraints, such as object rigidity, must be enforced.

2. The identification and grouping of observed or extracted structures in the image that are model-specific and invariant over some range of viewpoints. This is a somewhat conflicting objective, since we desire a set of model-specific features that allow some viewpoint flexibility yet this flexibility may yield intermodel ambiguity. Furthermore, the extraction of features and structures must be practical, which usually implies the use of edges, regions, surface orientation, and so forth. The grouping or organization of these features may parallel that of HVS perceptual organization, and therefore rely on similarity measures such as proximity, parallelism, and other feature attributes. A good example of the model unification process using this approach is the SCERPO system implementation of Lowe [1987].

3. Determining a plausible viewpoint on the basis of the hypothesized model and the features of 2. Often "trigger features" [Lowe 1987] are employed.

4. Incorporation of other available information in the form of (*a*) depth measurements; (*b*) stereo image pairs; (*c*) motion information (as in the previously cited example); (*d*) other a priori available information such as time of day, likely object classes to be encountered, and so on.

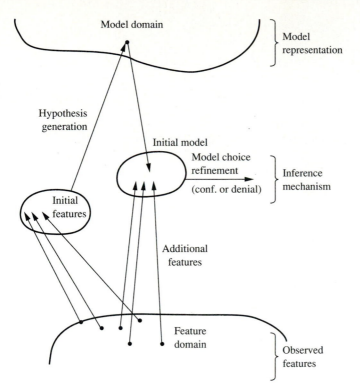

FIGURE 13.18
A paradigm for model unification.

Perhaps one of the best-known systems is the ACRONYM system of Brooks [1981]. ACRONYM stores object models in terms of component parts, which are themselves modeled as generalized cylinders. The system uses geometric reasoning with an assumption about viewpoint to predict object features that are visible, in order to unify observed data with a stored model. ACRONYM uses hypothesis generation and a backward-chaining algorithm for model confirmation.

IMAGE UNDERSTANDING EXAMPLE. A more sophisticated, frame-based implementation of an image understanding system is typified by the SIGMA system of Hwang, Davis, and Matsuyama [1986]. The SIGMA system provides an interpretation of a static image based upon an underlying scene model, as shown in Fig. 13.19. The structure of the system is shown in Fig. 13.20. The system model representation and implementation is *frame-based* as shown in Chapter 16. The SIGMA system employs both bottom up (data driven) and top down (model driven) inference. The overall objective is formation of a *maximally consistent unification* of the observed (perhaps preprocessed) image contents and an underlying scene model (Fig. 13.19). Consistency is achieved by formulation of a set of rules indicating *relational constraints* between entities.

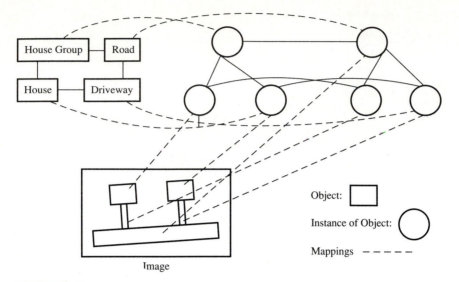

FIGURE 13.19
SIGMA system conceptual basis: mappings between the scene and the image. (From [Hwang/Davis/ Matsuyama 1986])

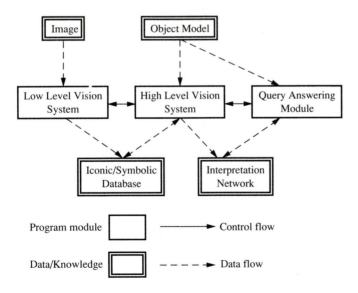

FIGURE 13.20
System architecture for the SIGMA image-understanding system.

Using a Forward Chaining System for Backward Chaining (Optional)

Many systems, such as OPS5, are designed principally for forward chaining (data-driven inference), although they can achieve (limited) backward chaining (goal-directed inference). Backward chaining, as our previous LISP developments have illustrated, generally requires more programming control. Using a forward-chaining inference engine for backward chaining requires two sets of rules [Brownston 1986]:

(i) Control rules that implement backward chaining. These are *goal-splitting* and *goal-fusing* rules.

(ii) Rules for handling immediately solvable goals.

The basis of the strategy is to split goals that are not immediately solvable into subgoals and make each of these subgoals the preconditions (antecedents) to a rule. Once the conjunction of the subgoals is satisfied, "fusing" productions return to the parent goal.

Example 13.17   Using a forward chaining system (OPS5) for backward chaining.

initial dB facts: $\{a \quad b \quad g\}$

$$
\begin{array}{lllll}
\text{rules:} & \text{IF} \quad a \quad b & \text{THEN} & c & (1) \\
& b \quad g & & d & (2) \\
& a \quad c & & e & (3) \\
& e \quad d & & f & (4)
\end{array}
$$

It is left for the reader (see the problems) to develop a forward chaining OPS5 formulation for this example.

We follow the structure of Brownston [1986] in the backward chaining formulation. The fundamental type of working-memory element is denoted goal with the specification

```
(literalize goal
        name            ;  the goal
        parent          ;  the goal which was split to yield this
                           one
        value)          ;  integer to indicate goal satisfied
                           otherwise = nil
```

The following is a sample *splitting rule* corresponding to rule 4:

```
(p split4
        (goal ^name f ^value unsat)
```

```
-->
        (make goal ^name d ^parent f ^value unsat)
        (make goal ^name e ^parent f ^value unsat))
```

This production, given a goal named *f* that is unsatisfied, creates subgoals *d* and *e* that are also unsatisfied.

Fusing is the reverse of splitting. Goals are recognized as solved by fusing all solved subgoals. Here is an example that shows the *fusing production* corresponding to rule 4 and the sample splitting production. Note the similarity between the goal-splitting and goal-fusing productions.

```
(p fuse4
        {<goal> (goal ^name f ^value unsat)}
        (goal ^name d ^value sat)
        (goal ^name e ^value sat)
-->
        (modify <goal> ^value sat))
```

Production fuse4 shows the use of a *condition element* associated with an *element variable* (<goal> in this example). An element variable is treated differently by OPS5, in the sense that it requires a match with the *entire* condition element; thus

```
(goal    ^name f    ^value unsat)
```

A value of sat is used to indicate the subgoal has been satisfied, using the modify action in production fuse4.

Example 13.18   OPS5 code for backward chaining example.

```
(literalize
    goal
    name
    parent
    value    )

(p split4
        (goal ^name f ^value unsat)
-->
        (make goal ^name d ^parent f ^value unsat)
        (make goal ^name e ^parent f ^value unsat))

(p split3
        (goal ^name e ^value unsat)
-->
        (make goal ^name a ^parent e ^value unsat)
        (make goal ^name c ^parent e ^value unsat))
```

```
(p split2
    (goal ^name d ^value unsat)
-->
    (make goal ^name b ^parent d ^value unsat)
    (make goal ^name g ^parent d ^value unsat))

(p split1
    (goal ^name c ^value unsat)
-->
    (make goal ^name a ^parent c ^value unsat)
    (make goal ^name b ^parent c ^value unsat))

(p fuse4
    {<goal> (goal ^name f ^value unsat)}
    (goal ^name d ^value sat)
    (goal ^name e ^value sat)
-->
    (modify <goal> ^value sat))

(p fuse3
    {<goal> (goal ^name e ^value unsat)}
    (goal ^name a ^value sat)
    (goal ^name c ^value sat)
-->
    (modify <goal> ^value sat))

(p fuse2
    {<goal> (goal ^name d ^value unsat)}
    (goal ^name b ^value sat)
    (goal ^name g ^value sat)
-->
    (modify <goal> ^value sat))

(p fuse1
    {<goal> (goal ^name c ^value unsat)}
    (goal ^name a ^value sat)
    (goal ^name b ^value sat)
-->
    (modify <goal> ^value sat))

(make goal ^name a ^value sat)
(make goal ^name b ^value sat)
(make goal ^name g ^value sat)
(make goal ^name f ^value unsat)
```

The WM for this example is

```
(make goal ^name a ^value sat)
(make goal ^name b ^value sat)
```

```
(make goal ^name g ^value sat)
(make goal ^name f ^value unsat)
```

Example 13.19   Using OPS5 for backward chaining.

```
-> (i-g-v)
nil
-> (watch 2)
2
-> (load 'ex3-bak.l)
[load ex3-bak.l]
********t
-> (wm)


1:   (goal      ^name a      ^value sat)
2:   (goal      ^name b      ^value sat)
3:   (goal      ^name g      ^value sat)
4:   (goal      ^name f      ^value unsat)nil
-> (run)

1. split4 4
=>wm: 5:   (goal      ^name d      ^parent f      ^value unsat)
=>wm: 6:   (goal      ^name e      ^parent f      ^value unsat)
2. split3 6
=>wm: 7:   (goal      ^name a      ^parent e      ^value unsat)
=>wm: 8:   (goal      ^name c      ^parent e      ^value unsat)
3. fuse1 8 1 2
<=wm: 8:   (goal      ^name c      ^parent e      ^value unsat)
=>wm: 10:  (goal      ^name c      ^parent e      ^value sat)
4. fuse3 6 1 10
<=wm: 6:   (goal      ^name e      ^parent f      ^value unsat)
=>wm: 12:  (goal      ^name e      ^parent f      ^value sat)
5. fuse2 5 2 3
<=wm: 5:   (goal      ^name d      ^parent f      ^value unsat)
=>wm: 14:  (goal      ^name d      ^parent f      ^value sat)
6. fuse4 4 14 12
<=wm: 4:   (goal      ^name f      ^value unsat)
=>wm: 16:  (goal      ^name f      ^value sat)
end -- no production true
 8 productions (48 // 80 nodes)
 6 firings (16 rhs actions)
 7 mean working memory size (8 maximum)
 2 mean conflict set size (4 maximum)
 8 mean token memory size (10 maximum)
nil
```

The reader should compare forward and backward formulations of this example.

REFERENCES

Expert system references

[Cupello/Mishelevich 1988] Cupello, J.M., and D.J. Mishelevich, "Managing Prototype Knowledge/Expert System Projects," *Communications of the ACM*, Vol. 31, No. 5, May 1988, pp. 534–541.

[Davis/Lenat 1982] Davis, R., and D. Lenat, *Knowledge-based Systems in Artificial Intelligence*, McGraw-Hill, New York, 1982.

[Harmon/King 1985] Harmon, P., and D. King, *Expert Systems—Artificial Intelligence in Business*, John Wiley, New York, 1985.

[Hayes-Roth/King 1983] Hayes-Roth, F., and D. King, *Building Expert Systems*, Addison Wesley, Reading, MA, 1983.

[Lernley 1985] Lernley, B., "Artificial Expertise: Intelligent Software for Problem Solving," *PC Magazine*, Vol. 4, No. 8, April 16, 1985, pp. 108–112.

[Waterman 1986] Waterman, D.A, *A Guide to Expert Systems*, Addison Wesley, Reading, MA, 1986.

References for reasoning with uncertainty

[Ackermann 1971] Ackermann, R., *An Introduction to Many-Valued Logics*, Routledge and Kegan, New York, 1971.

[Bochvar 1939] Bochvar, D., "On three-valued logical calculus and its application to the analysis of contradiction," *Matematiceskij Sbornik*, Vol. 4, 1939, pp. 353–369.

[Cohen 1985] Cohen, P.R., *Heuristic Reasoning about Uncertainty: An Artificial Intelligence Approach*, Pitman, Boston, 1985.

[DiZenzo 1988] DiZenzo, S., "A Many-Valued Logic for Approximate Reasoning," *IBM J. Res. Develop.*, Vol. 32, No. 4, July 1988, pp. 552–565.

[Duda/Hart/Nilsson 1981] Duda, R.O., P.E. Hart, and N.J. Nilsson, "Subjective Bayesian Methods for Rule-Based Inference Systems," *Readings in Artificial Intelligence*, B.W. Weber and N.J. Nilsson, eds., Tioga Publishers, Palo Alto, CA, 1981.

[Feigenbaum/Barr 1982] Feigenbaum and Barr, *Handbook of Artificial Intelligence*, Vol. II., William Kaufman, Los Altos, CA, 1982.

[Fu 1985] Fu, K.S., "Modeling Rule-Based Systems by Stochastic Programmed Production Systems," *Information Science*, Vol. 36, September 1985, p. 207.

[Garner 1975] Garner, W.R., *Uncertainty and Structure as Psychological Concepts,* Robert E. Krieger, Huntington, NY, 1975.

[Haack 1978] Haack, S., *Philosophy of Logic*, Cambridge University Press, 1978.

[Hink/Woods 1987] Hink, R.F., and D.L. Woods, "How Humans Process Uncertain Knowledge: An Introduction for Knowledge Engineers," *AI Magazine*, Vol. 8, No. 3, Fall 1987, pp. 41–53.

[Hurst 1984] Hurst, S.L., "Multiple-Valued Logic — Its Status and Its Future," *IEEE Transactions Computers* C-33, 1984, pp. 1160–1179.

[Johnson 1986] Johnson, R.W., "Independence and Bayesian Updating Methods," *Artificial Intelligence*, Vol. 29, 1986, Elsevier, NY, pp. 217–222.

[Kahneman 1982] Kahneman, D., P. Slovic, and A. Tversky, eds., *Judgment Under Uncertainty: Heuristics and Biases*, Cambridge University Press, New York, 1982.

[Kleene 1952] Kleene, S., *Introduction to Metamathematics*, Van Nostrand, New York, 1952.

[Lukesiewicz 1930] Lukesiewicz, J., "Many-valued systems of propositional logic," *Polish Logic*, S. McCall, ed., Oxford University Press, 1967.

[Pang 1987] Pang, D., et al, "Reasoning with Uncertain Information," *IEEE Proceedings*, Vol. 134, Part D, No. 4, July 1987, pp. 231–237.

[Post 1921] Post, E.L., "Introduction to a General Theory of Elementary Propositions," *American Journal of Math*, Vol. 43, 1921, pp. 163–185.

[Rescher 1969] Rescher, N., *Many-Valued Logics*, McGraw-Hill, New York, 1969.

[Shachter/Heckerman 1987] Shachter, K.D., and D.E. Heckerman, "Thinking Backward for Knowledge Acquisition," *AI Magazine*, Vol. 8, No. 3, Fall 1987, pp. 55–61.

[Shortliffe/Buchanan 1975] Shortliffe, E.H., and B.G. Buchanan, "A Model of Inexact Reasoning in Medicine," *Mathematical Biosciences*, Vol. 23, 1975, pp. 351–379.

[Turner 1984] Turner, R., *Logics for Artificial Intelligence*, John Wiley and Sons, New York, 1984.

[Walpole/Myers 1972] Walpole, R.E., and R.H. Myers, *Probability and Statistics for Engineers and Scientists*, MacMillan, New York, 1972.

[Whalen/Schott 1983] Whalen and Schott, "Issues in Fuzzy Production Systems," *International Journal of Man-Machine Studies*, No. 19, 1983, p. 57.

[Zadeh 1965] Zadeh, L.A., "Fuzzy Sets," Information and Control , Vol. 8, 1965, pp. 338–353.

[Zadeh 1975] Zadeh, L., K.S. Fu, K. Tanaka, and M. Shimura, eds., *Fuzzy Sets and their Applications to Cognitive and Decision Processes*, Academic Press, New York, 1975.

OPS5 references

[Brownston 1986] Brownston, L., R. Farrel, E. Kant, and N. Martin, *Programming Expert Systems in OPS5*, Addison Wesley, Reading, MA, 1986.

[Cooper/Wogrin 1988] Cooper, T.A., and N. Wogrin, *Rule-Based Programming with OPS5*, Morgan-Kaufmann, San Mateo, CA, 1988.

[Moskowitz 1986] Moskowitz, L., "Rule-Based Programming," *Byte*, November 1986.

Rule-based system examples and model unification

[Biederman 1985] Biederman, I., "Human Image Understanding: Recent Research and a Theory," *Computer Vision, Graphics, and Image Processing*, Vol. 32, 1985, pp. 29–73.

[Binford 1982] Binford, T.O., "Survey of Model-Based Image-Analysis Systems," *International Journal of Robotics Research*, Vol. 1, No. 1, 1982.

[Brooks 1981] Brooks, R.A., "Symbolic Reasoning Among 3-D Models and 2-D Images," *Artificial Intelligence*, Vol. 17, 1981, pp. 285–348.

[Hwang/Davis/Matsuyama 1986] Hwang, V.S., L.S. Davis, and T. Matsuyama, "Hypothesis Integration in Image-Understanding Systems," *Computer Vision, Graphics, and Image Processing*, Vol. 36, 1986, pp. 321–371.

[Lowe 1987] Lowe, D.G., "Three-Dimensional Object Recognition from Single Two-Dimensional Images," *Artificial Intelligence*, Vol. 31, 1987, pp. 335–395.

[Mackworth 1977] Mackworth, A.K., "Consistency in Networks of Relations," *Artificial Intelligence*, Vol. 8, 1977, p. 99–118.

[Nazif/Levine 1984] Nazif, A.M., and M.D. Levine, "Low-Level Image Segmentation: An Expert System," *IEEE Transactions on Pattern Analysis and Machine Intelligence*, Vol. PAMI-6, No. 5, September 1984, pp. 555–577.

[Schalkoff 1989] Schalkoff, R.J., *Digital Image Processing and Computer Vision*, John Wiley and Sons, New York, 1989.

[Shapiro 1987] Shapiro, S.C., ed., *Encyclopedia of Artificial Intelligence*, Wiley, New York, 1987.

[Stansfield 1986] Stansfield, S.A., "ANGY: A Rule-Based Expert System for Automatic Segmentation of Coronary Vessels from Digital Subtracted Angiograms," *IEEE Transactions on Pattern Analysis and Machine Intelligence*, Vol. PAMI-8, No. 2, March 1986, pp. 188–199.

[Topa/Schalkoff 1987] Topa, L.C., and R.J. Schalkoff, "A Rule-Based Expert System for the Determination of Object Structure and Motion Information from a Sequence of Digital Images," submitted to *Computer Vision, Graphics and Image Processing*, September 1987. (Also available as L. C. Topa PhD Thesis, Electrical and Computer Engineering Department, Clemson University, December 1987.)

PROBLEMS

13.1. In this problem the forward chaining implementation (fwd_r.l) is modified to allow the use of *confidence measures*.

(*a*) i. Show the revised data structures for facts and rules, and the associated LISP functions that assess them.

ii. Show explicitly the new and/or revised functions in fwd_r.l for confidence-measure propagation.

(*b*) Using the previous image-motion data example (Ex. 11.13) with modifications to allow confidence measures, implement the revised algorithm. The initial database with confidence values is

```
(setq *facts* '(((b1 = b2) conf 0.8)
                ((b2 <> 0) conf 0.7)
                ((b1 <> 0) conf 0.9)
                ((abs (center region1 -
                       center region2) less than
                   (extent region2 - extent region1))
                 conf 0.7)
                ((square regions) conf 0.7)))
```

Show the resultant goal states. Consider two cases:

i. Propagate all facts produced using the strategy of (13-58) (i.e., the minimum of the antecedent confidence values is propagated).

ii. Only consider a fact as propagated (produced) if the resulting confidence is greater than or equal to T, where T is a user-specified threshold. Show sample program results for several values of T.

(*c*) Repeat part (*b*) with the database of Ex. 13.7.

13.2. (*a*) Discuss, using an example, how incorporation of confidence measures into the chaining process affects

i. The number of alternate paths between the initial and goal states.

ii. The conflict-resolution strategy.

iii. The overall confidence produced in the goal-state facts.

(*b*) Two approaches to incorporation of uncertainty in the reasoning process cited in the text are:

i. Allowing a logic where each statement could be a member of more than one truth value set with a degree of membership in each set.

ii. Attaching a confidence measure to a fact.

Discuss, with as much analysis as possible, how or where these approaches are

- similar
- different

13.3. If we modify the previous forward chaining-algorithm conflict-resolution strategy to choose rules to be fired on the basis of highest resulting fact confidence, are we guaranteed to produce a goal state with the highest fact confidences possible? Cite examples to justify your answer.

13.4. Extend the example of probabilistic-based reasoning in the text to the case of three rule antecedents; that is, for $D = A \cap B \cap C$, formulate $P(D \mid A, B, C)$.

13.5. The application of confidence measures to backward chaining is a difficult problem. Discuss how this may be accomplished. Specifically, address the following issues:

- Cases where the only confidence measures are contained in the initial facts.
- The possible nonuniqueness of paths from S_g to S_i.
- Cases where the rules also contain (as well as propagate) uncertainties.
- The use of Bayes rule.
- Depth- versus breadth-first searches.

13.6. Show why
(a) $p_{tf} \neq p_{ft}$ in general.
(b) Given p_{tt}, p_{tf}, and p_{ft}, p_{ff} need not be specified.

13.7. Show that for n possibly dependent facts, 2^n joint probabilities must be specified for propagation of confidences. (Hint: start with $n = 3$ and follow the approach of (13-42) and (13-43).

13.8. A knowledge engineer hypothesizes that if A and B are independent, and logically $C = A \cap B$, we may simplify the propagation of confidence values using

$$P(A \cap B \mid C) = P(A \mid C)P(B \mid C)$$

Is this assertion correct in general? If not, are there specific cases where it holds?

13.9. Prove that the heuristic for propagation of confidence with the disjunction of two facts $(A \cup B = C)$, namely conf $(C) = \max \{P(A), P(B)\}$, follows from probability.

13.10. (Project idea.) The need for an expert system to justify its results to the user is described in the text. In this problem we consider the modification of the inference engine to yield an *explanation* of how a goal (z) was proved. Consider the following alternatives:
(a) The system merely restates the sequence of rule names employed in linking the initial and goal states.
(b) The system prints the entire contents of each rule (including variable bindings, if any) in the sequence used to link the initial and goal states.
(c) The system prints the BECAUSE field of each rule in the sequence.
(d) All (a) – (b) but modified to show conflict resolution and indicate alternative paths.
For each of the above approaches, modify the
(a) forward chaining
(b) backward chaining
algorithms, and show sample results.

13.11. Given that $P(A \mid E)$ is "large" (i.e., close to 1.0), does it follow that the probability of $P(A \mid \text{Other})$ is "small" (i.e., close to 0.0) where Other is the occurrence of any other event? Justify your answer.

13.12. (a) Given a probabilistic odds-based formulation and the unconditional odds on event H (i.e., $O(H)$) if $E = A \cap B$, show how A and B are used to update $O(H)$ to form $O(H \mid E)$.
(b) Repeat (a) for $E = A \cup B$.

13.13. The purpose of this problem is to compare the resulting confidence on facts produced using forward chaining and the database of Ex. 13.7 with

(a) The conflict resolution strategy of fwd_r.l.

(b) The conflict resolution strategy of Ex. 13.7.

Given that both strategies produce fact z, compare the resulting confidences.

13.14. Continuing our look at incorporating confidence, consider the following extension (this leads to an interesting project):

- A rule is *applicable* if it produces a consequent with a higher confidence value than already exists.

For simplicity, define the confidence of a fact not in the database as zero. Note this approach may "restore" confidence in facts already in the database.

13.15. Prove

$$P(\neg H \mid E) = 1 - P(H \mid E)$$

13.16. Develop several examples to show the OPS5 conflict-resolution (LEX) strategy. Include

(a) Recency.

(b) Specificity.

(c) Refraction.

13.17. Compare the sequence of rule firings using OPS5 in Examples 13.12–13.15 with those produced by fwd_r.l and fwd_r1.l.

13.18. (a) Modify the rule and fact structures of fwd_r1.l to allow the entering of rules as productions in OPS5 format.

(b) Write a LISP program that takes facts and rules in LISP in the form suitable for fwd_r1.l and converts them into a form suitable for OPS5. Show your results with an example.

13.19. Show OPS5 programs for Ex. 11.23 using both forward and backward formulations.

13.20. Suppose the knowledge base contains a rule of the form

IF   e   THEN   h

or

e --> h   (P20-1)

Suppose also we have some prior belief in h, possibly from other evidence such as another rule of the form

e$_2$ --> h   (P20-2)

We can update our belief in h (i.e. $P(h)$) using (P20-1), from

$$P(h \mid e) = \left(\frac{P(e \mid h)}{P(e)} \right) P(h)$$ (P20-3)

where we assume the term in parentheses is available.

(a) Show how this leads to a method for updating confidence values.

(b) Can the strategy of (a) be cast in terms of a "confidence-strengthening" rule of the form

$$((e \to h) \cap (e_2 \to h) \cap e \cap e_2) \to h+$$

where $h +$ denotes statement h with increased confidence?

13.21. Develop a set of truth tables for *weak modus ponens*; that is, using (13-76–13-85) formulate a set of truth tables for

$$(p \cap (p \to q)) \to q$$

each indexed by m.

13.22. Does De Morgan's Law hold for the weak interpretations of $\neg$, $\cap_m$ and $\cup_m$? That is, are the following true in p-valued logic?
(a) $\neg(a \cap_m b) = (\neg a \cup_m \neg b)$
(b) $\neg(a \cup_m b) = (\neg a \cap_m \neg b)$

13.23. (a) Derive the truth tables for $\cup_m, \cap_m$, and $p \to_m q$ for logics with i) $p = 4$ and ii. $p = 5$.
(b) Is there any way to relate truth values of statements through p and m? Hint, consider $\cap_m$, $\cup_{p-m}$, $\cup_m$ and $\cap_{p-m}$.

13.24. In Kleene's logic (Figure 13.11), do the following hold?
(a) De Morgan's Law (defined in 13.22).
(b) $(p \to q) \equiv (\neg p \cup q)$

13.25. Relate the three-valued logics of Kleene, Luckasiewicz, and Bochvar to these :
(a) The $p = 3$ EP logic for various values of m.
(b) two-valued or classical logic.

13.26. Is there a way to relate truth values in two multivalued logics through the "granularity" of the representation? For example, do truth values for the "middle" ranges of $p = 10$ relate to the "middle" ranges of $p = 5$?

13.27. Show an OPS5 (forward) implementation of the database in Example 13.17, and show the result.

13.28. Using the modified facts database of problem 12.9, show an OPS5 formulation for
(a) Forward chaining
(b) Backward chaining (the goal is "z").

13.29. PROLOG is an example of a backward chaining system. Can PROLOG be used to implement forward chaining?

13.30. (a) Show, using an example in OPS5, how the inclusion of the remove action in a production leads to a non-commutative system.
(b) If only the make action is allowed in an OPS5 production, does the use of negated conditions lead to a commutative production system? Justify your answer.

13.31. For the following OPS5 program, fill in the OPS5 system responses, where required.

```
OPS5 Program
;file: ex_5
;ops5 program for problem 31.

(literalize element name)
```

```
(p rule_f1
          (element ^name a)
          (element ^name b)
-->
          (make element ^name c))

(p rule_f2
          (element ^name b)
          (element ^name g)
-->
          (make element ^name d))

(p rule_f3
          (element ^name a)
          (element ^name c)
-->
          (make element ^name e))

(p rule_f4
          (element ^name e)
          (element ^name d)
-->
          (make element ^name f))

(p rule_f5
          (element ^name d)
          (element ^name g)
-->
          (make element ^name f))

(make element ^name g)
(make element ^name b)
(make element ^name a)
```

Responses desired:

```
-> (i-g-v)
nil
-> (watch 2)
2
-> (load ''ex_5'')
[load ex_5]
*****t
-> (wm)


---------------- (response #1)


-> (run)


---------------- (response #2)
```

```
end -- no production true
  5 productions (23 // 40 nodes)
  5 firings (8 rhs actions)
  5 mean working memory size (8 maximum)
  2 mean conflict set size (2 maximum)
  5 mean token memory size (6 maximum)

-> (wm)

----------------- (response #3)
```

Note: You must show the response *exactly* as OPS5 would. This (especially) includes time-tags.

13.32. Suppose a database includes, among other possible rules, the following:

$$p_1 \to q_1$$
$$p_1 \to q_2$$
$$p_1 \to q_3$$
.
.
.
$$p_1 \to q_n$$

In addition, suppose we observe the *evidence*

$$q_1 \cap q_2 \cdots \cap q_n \equiv T$$

Clearly, the p_1 is a common *explanation* for n of the q_i. Do the database and the evidence allow you, under any set of assumptions, to conclude:

$$(q_1 \cap q_2 \cap \cdots q_n) \to p_1$$

13.33. Discuss suitable extensions of confidence-measure propagation when rules contain multiple consequents, such as

$$\text{IF } (a \quad b \quad c) \text{ THEN } (d \quad e \quad f)$$

13.34. This problem explores one of the limitations of the rule-based approach. Consider the following rule-base segment used in an "expert system" for nuclear power plant control:

```
(Rule 406  (IF   (reactor temperature above 1800)
                 (alarm 2 active))
           (THEN (open valve PF2)
                 (resume operation)))

(Rule 407  (IF   (reactor temperature above 2000)
                 (alarm 6 active))
           (THEN (open valve PF4)
                 (activate plan EV-2)))

(Rule 408  (IF   (reactor temperature above 2200))
           (THEN (close valve PF2)
```

```
(close valve PF4)
(evacuate plant)))
```

Suppose the current system state contains the following:

```
(reactor temperature is 2300)
(alarm 2 active)
(alarm 6 active)
```

(*a*) What should the system response be?
(*b*) How could this problem be alleviated? Reformulate the database to implement your solution.

CHAPTER
14

PLANNING IN AI SYSTEMS

"When you have eliminated the impossible, whatever remains, however improbable, must be the truth."

Sir Arthur Conan Doyle 1859–1930
The Sign of Four [1890], Ch. 6

THE SIGNIFICANCE OF PLANNING

Background

Planning is a problem-solving technique that involves determining a course (or sequence) of actions that takes a system from an initial state to a desired or goal state.

(14-1)

PLANNING AND RULE-BASED INFERENCE. Planning and rule-based inference share a number of similarities. For example, given suitable representations, both problems are often pattern-directed and involve *matching* to determine applicable rules or operators. In addition, considerable complexities with search usually occur.

Several significant differences also exist, namely,

1. The representation for planning is often different and more complex.
2. Planning almost always requires a revocable control strategy due to a non-commutative production system.
3. The strong possiblity of producing conflicting subgoals due to operator interaction exists.

Planning is also closely related to a number of other topics, most significantly production systems, control, temporal reasoning, the frame problem, and search.

424

SEQUENCES AND SUBPLANS. A plan consists of a *sequence* of actions or operators or "agents" (the literature is not consistent). As in rule-based inference, this sequential, time-dependent or *ordered* set of operators is seldom unique. Like rule-based inference, planning may be accomplished by either moving the system state from an initial state, S_i, to the goal state, S_g, using forward state propagation (FSP), or by working backwards from S_g through the conditional application of operators using backward state propagation (BSP), to S_i. Parallelism in planning leads to multi-operator plans, while we consider following the development of single-operator (serial) planning.

We approach planning with a "divide-and-conquer" or problem decomposition approach. Thus, we become concerned with the development of *subplans*, or shorter (often one-step) sequences of actions, that are then merged to form the overall plan sequence.

Planning Examples

In this chapter, two "easy" examples are used to study planning algorithm development and complexities (search). As shown in Fig. 14.1, they are a "checkerboard" path planner and a "blocks-world" planner.

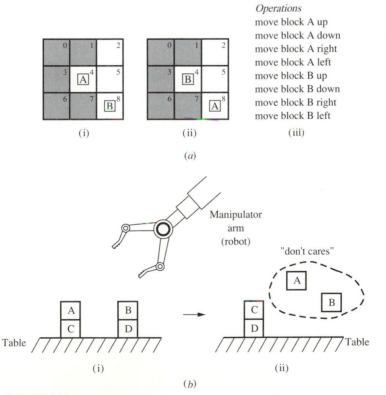

FIGURE 14.1
Planning problems used for illustration. (*a*) The "checkerboard" (path-planning) problem: (i) initial state; (ii) desired goal state; (iii) operations. (*b*) The "blocks-world" problem: (i) initial state; (ii) desired goal state.

PATH PLANNING. The first example in Fig. 14.1a illustrates *path planning* [Davis/McDermott 1984], which in its most general form, involves choosing how to move several objects in two or three spatial dimensions without collisions. In fact, one of the real-world testbeds for planning is the autonomous navigation of vehicles. The scenario consists of an area containing obstacles, object(s) to be moved, and the specified goal location(s) of the object(s). The shortest possible path is usually desired, with the additional constraint that a path should be acyclic.

BLOCKS WORLD. In Fig. 14.1b a manipulator arm is used (perhaps using vision and tactile feedback) to move blocks on a table. Given the mobility constraints of the manipulator, specification of a goal state, and specification (or autonomous recognition) of an initial situation (e.g., the present state of the blocks on the table), it is desired to generate a sequence of actions that achieves the goal state.

CLAUSES, LISTS, AND VARIABLES. In what follows, list form is used for both representations of "clauses" and operators for ease of LISP implementation. Notice that in the list-based formulation, variables are lower-case and constants (block names) are upper-case.

Representational Issues In Planning

PLANNING REPRESENTATIONS. The development of a suitable problem representation is critical for planning. This representation requires

1. A means to describe the "world" or the problem state. $\qquad$ (14-2a)
2. A means to describe how the application of an operator (an action) changes the state in (14-2a). $\qquad$ (14-2b)

Item (14-2b) is extremely significant in planning, and tends to illustrate how, practically speaking, planning differs from simple inference.

REPRESENTATIONAL DIFFICULTIES. In the application of an operator, some aspects of the previous system state are changed and some remain the same. For example, in the blocks-world problem, an operator, (pickup x), applied to block A, that is, (pickup A), changes the system state. Prior to (pickup A), the system state representation (in clause form) might have included

(on−table A) $\qquad$ (14-3)

whereas, after the action the state representation now includes

(holding A) $\qquad$ (14-4)

and

(on−table A) $\qquad$ (14-5)

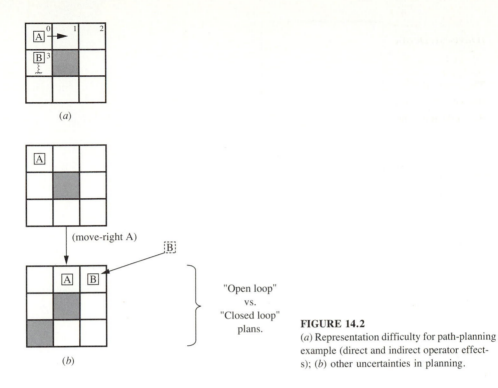

(a)

(move-right A)

"Open loop"
vs.
"Closed loop"
plans.

(b)

FIGURE 14.2
(*a*) Representation difficulty for path-planning example (direct and indirect operator effects); (*b*) other uncertainties in planning.

(14-5) indicates that (14-3) should be deleted from the representation, and (14-4) should be added. One difficulty, however, is that we have not indicated any other state changes that may have occurred due to action (pickup A), for example, if block B were initially resting on top of block A then

$$(holding \ B) \tag{14-6}$$

is also added to the resulting state. Most importantly, the states of other blocks, not affected by operator (pickup A) need either to be specified or (assumed) unchanged. It is this difficulty which brings the frame problem into planning.

THE FRAME PROBLEM IN PLANNING. The frame problem in AI (as shown in Chapter 1) involves quantifying the "persistence" of facts. Fortunately much information is persistent. Unfortunately it is inefficient to explicitly enumerate this persistence. Figure 14.2*a* provides another simple illustration of the frame problem. Movement of block A "allows" B to "spring" into location 0, that is, the statement (location B 3) is not persistent under the action of operator (move−right A). That is, there are two effects of operator (move−right A), namely the direct effect, which causes (location A 1), and the indirect or side effect, which causes (location B 0) (empty 3).
Other examples are shown in Fig. 14.2*b*.

OPERATORS, CLAUSES, AND PRECONDITIONS. To explore planning in a formal manner we distinguish between operators that represent actions with clause-based

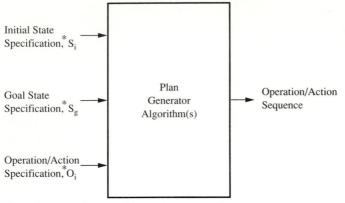

*Dependent upon chosen problem state representation

FIGURE 14.3
Entities needed for plan generation.

preconditions, and clauses, which represent facts in the system state representation and thereby constrain the application of operators.

> Operators change the system state and are applicable if certain clause-based preconditions hold. (14-7)

While we do not consider the use of rules and an inference mechanism for the production of new clauses prior to the selection of an operator, this more general formulation is both possible and desirable.

REPRESENTATION, OPERATOR SPECIFICATION, AND SEARCH

In this section, we address the requirements of (14-2) in developing representations for the path-planning and blocks-world examples. Figure 14.3 summarizes the entities needed for plan generation.

Developing a Representation

Figure 14.4a shows a graphical example of a 2-D block movement problem representation. From this description, the initial state could be described using

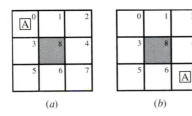

FIGURE 14.4
Sample graphical representation for path-planning example.
(a) Initial state; (b) goal state.

```
(occupied 0)
(location A  0)
(blocked 8)
(empty 1)
(empty 2)

   .
   .
   .

(empty 7)
```
$$(14\text{-}8)$$

Note that some of the information in the representation of (14-8) is (via rules) "derivable," that is, a sample rule is

```
(rule occupied—square

      (if ((location A ?var?)

      (then  (occupied ?var?)
```
$$(14\text{-}9a)$$

or simply,

```
(location A 0)  —>
                (occupied 0)
```
$$(14\text{-}9b)$$

It is important to distinguish between what the AI system "sees" through the representation, and what is seen by a human observer.

Search and Potential Computational Complexity

INTERACTING SUBPROBLEMS. The ubiquitous problem of search (involving operator selection) in AI is well illustrated by planning problems. Another concern, which we have not heretofore addressed, is that of *conflicting subgoals*. For example, in order to achieve a goal state we often require that the conjunction of a number of subgoals be satisfied via the derivation of subplans. Unfortunately, these subplans often lead to conflicts in a required state. In the following planning examples, we see this type of interacting subproblem effect where, for example, a state might be required that includes the clauses

```
(on A B)
(on B A)
```
$$(14\text{-}10)$$

From the meaning of each of these clauses, it becomes apparent that (14-10) specifies an *illegal state* which cannot exist. Figure 14.21c shows another example of an illegal state, which is of concern in parallel planning. It is important to note that the number of orderings of n operators is $n!$, and therefore the potential computational complexity in plan generation is nontrivial.

Operators and Representations

We noted that an operator "changes" the system state and, like rules, operators need to be *applicable* prior to use. In planning, the concept of "applicable" may be more complicated.

OPERATOR SPECIFICATION AS A RELATION ON THE SYSTEM STATE.

> An operator represents a relation on the system state.   (14-11)

Consider a system with only one block, denoted A, and a single operator, (move−right−A), which represents a relation on the system state. Using the locations shown in Fig. 14.1, we enumerate the relation (or mapping between sets), (move−right−A), where set members are pairs of system states, such as

(move−right−A) = {((locn A 0), (locn A 1)),

((locn A 1), (locn A 2)), ...}   (14-12)

This simplistic representation of a simple operator is probably not accurate or useful since, among other things, the state description for each element is incomplete (e.g., it does not include preconditions). An alternative is

(move−right−A) =
                {(((locn A 0) (empty 1)), (locn A 1) (empty 0))
                                  ...}   (14-13)

Whereas the formalization of (14-13) may seem somewhat unnecessary (especially since we develop simpler strategies below), it is an excellent vehicle for extension to parallel planning.

THE STRIPS REPRESENTATION. As mentioned, it would be quite cumbersome to develop a planning representation to enumerate, following every action, the state components that remain unchanged ("persist"). In many cases, especially with large representations, these "persistent" components comprise an overwhelming portion of the previous state. For this reason we adopt a planning representation in the form of GPS or STRIPS [Nilsson 1980; Fikes/Nilsson 1971] where clauses that are not subject to the "direct effect" of an action are assumed persistent. Thus, the STRIPS representation provides a solution for the frame problem by indicating state changes due to an action by specifying only which clauses in the state representation are added or deleted as a consequence of the action. All other clauses are assumed persistent. Note two shortcomings of this approach:

1. STRIPS does not allow arbitrary formulas in the add and delete lists.
2. STRIPS does not provide a convenient way to represent the effects of multiple (simultaneous) operators (i.e., parallel actions). This is considered later in this chapter.

OPERATOR CHARACTERIZATION IN STRIPS. Each operator is characterized by the following four properties:

1. An action property, which is a statement, in words, of what the operator accomplishes. This is significant only for our understanding and documentation of the operator.
2. A set of state preconditions, in the form of clauses that must be verified (TRUE) prior to application of the operator.
3. A set of clause-based ("old") facts that are to be deleted from current system description since, following operator application, they are no longer true.
4. A set of clause-based ("new") facts that are to be added to the updated system description. (Note this action was the primary basis of our previous rule-based formulation.)

Planning Difficulties (Local Actions and Global Objectives)

One of the foremost difficulties in the development of planning strategies (which parallel that of search) stems from the fact that

> Planning involves a series of local actions with the objective of achieving some global objective. (14-14)

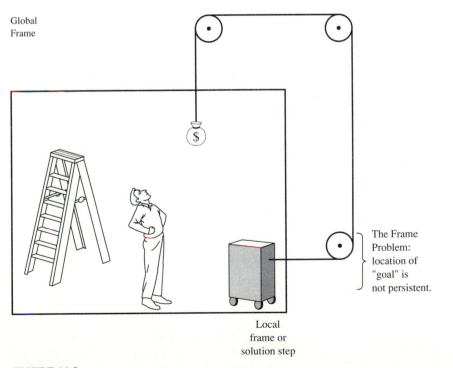

Global Frame

The Frame Problem: location of "goal" is not persistent.

Local frame or solution step

FIGURE 14.5
Inefficiency of local plan with global objective.

Often, as in optimization problems, it is not possible to "see" the goal or reliably estimate the distance to the goal at each local step. This spawns problems in operator selection. Additionally, plans often appear to contradict intuition, in the sense that they may appear to move the system state in an incorrect or opposite direction from the goal state. An example might be found in the football running back who runs backward to avoid the defense (apparently moving farther from the end zone, or goal state). The local action of running away from the goal may seem incorrect; however, if the running back avoids the defense and scores a touchdown the goal is achieved. This example illustrates the fact that local planning may be globally inefficient. This is illustrated further by the somewhat whimsical example in Fig. 14.5.

PLANNING RELATED TO A PRODUCTION SYSTEM

The Non-Commutative Nature of Planning Systems

A planning system is a non-commutative production system. Recall that (Chapter 11) a commutative production system allows limited reordering of the production rules.

> In planning systems, the order in which applicable productions are invoked is usually critical to the outcome of the system.   (14-15)

Planning, as the name implies, involves not only the process of determining applicable productions, but also a careful consideration of the *sequence*, (i.e., the "plan") of these productions. At points in plan generation it is often necessary to backtrack and consider alternative paths. The capability to backtrack requires that the history of previous system states and actions be stored. Therefore, a revocable (or tentative) control scheme is necessary in plan generation.

Plan Generation as a Control Problem

THE "CONTROL SYSTEM" PROBLEM. The problem of plan generation may be visualized using a problem (familiar to many engineers) that involves control of a system or "plant". The system state is changed through the generation of input or control signals, which may be potentiometer settings, valve positions, voltages, and so on in a physical plant. Furthermore, a closed loop or "feedback" formulation is often chosen. Reasons include robustness and ease of implementation. Characterizing the discrete closed loop control approach is the use of the current system state to form the next inputs, which in turn determine the succeeding system state. Figure 14.6a shows the typical structure, where in (i) the state error, (i.e., the deviation of the current state from the goal) is used to form the next control input. A more general controller is shown in (ii).

PLANNING ANALOGY. For comparison, a planning production system strategy is shown in Fig. 14.6b. Note the similarity—the plan generation algorithm requires the current or present state as well as the goal state and chooses the selected operator

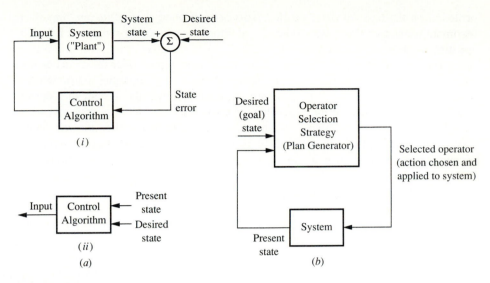

(i)

(ii)

(a)

(b)

FIGURE 14.6
Analogy of planning production system with feedback control problem. (*a*) Feedback control problem basic structure. (i) Typical implementation; (ii) generalized controller. (*b*) Planning production system structure.

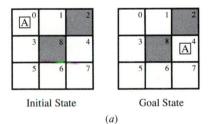

Initial State   Goal State

(a)

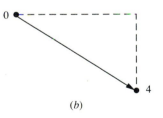

(b)

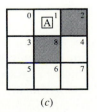

(c)

FIGURE 14.7
Heuristics for operator selection and potential problems (see also Figure 14.18. S_i and S_g; (*b*) vector difference for "best direction," leading to "best operator" (move—right A); (*c*) resulting state (backtracking will be necessary).

or action on the basis of these entities. This action, when applied (as an "input") to the system, changes the system state. In addition, the closed loop nature of the two situations in Fig. 14.6 is evident.

The *closed loop* planning or control structure shown in either (*a*) or (*b*) of Fig. 14.6. is not the only approach possible. Rather, "open loop" strategies are often used, wherein other information is used to form inputs that adjust the system to a desired state. More importantly, in the case of the control system in 14.6*a*, open loop control implies *a priori* knowledge that a specific input will result in a certain, known, output state. Correspondingly, in the case of the planning system, this implies the same type of a priori information, that is, knowledge of current state, action, and future state relationships. It is important to note here, as is the case with many human-derived plans, that this a priori information may be stored as *experience*, that is, given a situation and a goal, some action (or sequence of actions) led to the solution. Clearly, the existence of this type of a priori action-result information or experience may make plan generation simpler, and perhaps more efficient.

OPERATOR SELECTION (CONFLICT RESOLUTION REVISITED). Operator selection spawns a problem similar to conflict resolution. In developing a plan we seek operators that are both applicable and "good," "useful," or maybe even "optimal" (in some sense). Since planning involves *local* choices, consider the "flaw" of one simplistic operator selection or conflict resolution strategy (means-end), shown in Fig. 14.7. If we define a "best direction" or "best operator" according to (vector) direction of maximum state *difference* we may create local subplans that are globally inefficient in the sense they don't really move the system closer to the desired goal state (in Fig. 14.7 we would choose (`move-right A`)). Additional ramifications of state difference measures and means-end approaches are explored in a later section.

BLOCKS-WORLD SYSTEM REPRESENTATION

Problem Specification, Assumptions and Operator Representations

Consider the so-called "blocks-world problem" introduced in Fig. 14.1*b*. Given an arrangement of blocks on a table (the initial state) and the availability of a manipulator arm, the problem is that of determining an appropriate sequence of manipulator arm actions such that the goal state of Fig. 14.1*b* is achieved. We note immediately that this sequence of actions is unlikely to be unique, and some may be perceived as "better" than others.

For simplicity we assume that the relative left-right orientation of blocks on the table is inconsequential, and instead concentrate on the top-bottom relationship among the blocks. The reader should note that an extended and more realistic representation of this example should also contain operators that consider the horizontal block orientations as well. Also, assume that the manipulator arm may only grasp one block at a time and that only the top-most block of a stack may be grasped. These constraints must be converted into a manipulable operator representation.

Using Fig. 14.1*b*, the system initial and goal states are quantified using a set of self-explanatory clauses entered in list form.

Example 14.1   Blocks-world representation for Figure 14.1*b*.

Initial State S_i

```
(on A C)
(on (B D)
(ontable C)
(ontable D)
(clear A)          ;nothing on top
(clear B)
(empty)            ;state of the manipulator arm          (14-16a)
```

The clause (on x y) is used to signify the state attribute of block x being on top of block y. The predicate (clear x) indicates that there is not another block on top of block x, and "empty" signifies that the manipulator arm is empty, that is, no block is being grasped by the arm.

Goal State S_g

```
(on C D)
(clear C)
(ontable D)                                                (14-16b)
```

Notice the goal statement of (14-16b) is somewhat ambiguous in that the orientation of blocks A and B is unspecified and the arm is not constrained to be empty.

The following STRIPS representation is used for operator specification.

Example 14.2   Blocks-world operator specification.

A. Table-based block manipulation operators

1. (pickup x)   action: picks up block x (from the table)
preconditions: (ontable x), (clear x), (empty).
delete facts (ontable x), (clear x), (empty).
add facts: (hold x)

2. (putdown x)   action: puts block x down (on the table)
preconditions: (hold x)
delete facts: (hold x)
add facts: (ontable x), (clear x), (empty)

B. Block-based block manipulation operators

3. (takeoff x y)   action: takes block x off block y
preconditions: (on x y), (clear x), (empty)
delete facts: (on x y), (clear x), (empty)
add facts: (clear y), (hold x)

4. (puton x y)   action: puts block x on top of block y
preconditions: (hold x), (clear y)
delete facts: (hold x), (clear y)
add facts: (on x y), (clear x), (empty)   (14-17)

PLAN GENERATION ALGORITHMS

The details of any planning algorithm are related to the specific operator selection (search) methodology and related heuristics employed. We consider both forward state propagation (FSP) and backward state propagation (BSP) approaches. We show several examples of use of these algorithms.

GENERATE AND TEST. The first example shown exemplifies **generate-and-test** (GAT), which is a brute force, albeit systematic, procedure to generate possible solutions. GAT, as the name implies, simply generates a possible solution path and tests its feasibility. GAT is useful only when the number of possible solutions is small; otherwise, the potential combinatorial explosion of the solution space makes the approach at best inefficient, and more likely, impractical. GAT is applicable to *both* forward and backward state propagation approaches.

OPERATOR SEQUENCES AND PATHS LINKING S_i AND S_g. In the skeletal algorithms and detailed implementations and examples explored below, the choices or alternatives that occur in the tentative selection of operators and/or clauses (subgoals) indicate points for algorithm *backtracking* . Furthermore, these decisions allude to the problem of searching the plan problem state space for one or more sequences of operators that link S_i to S_g, that is, they form a path in state space. While we defer our exploration of general search problems until Chapter 15, we note that the number of potential paths to be explored, even in simple problems, suggests a need for good "decision" or operator selection strategies.

Cycles in Plans

CYCLES. In the plan generation process, it is easy for cycles to be generated. A **cycle** is defined as a succession of operators that move the system from some state, S_0, through one (or more) states and eventually back to S_0. For example, the successive application of operator (pickup A) followed by (putdown A) results in an obvious cycle, with no apparent benefit. Typically, cycles are not so easy to identify. In most practical applications, they serve no useful purpose. Identification of cycles requires keeping track of previously explored states.

HOW DO WE "BREAK" A CYCLE? Since a cycle may invoke the successive application of n operators and n corresponding states, once a cycle has been identified an obvious question is "where" to break the cycle. Given numerous operator selection alternatives along the path that led to the cycle, significant choice as to which decision(s) should be revised to eliminate the cycle exists. Unfortunately, except in simplistic cases, it is not possible to generally state a solution.

Forward State Propagation
Using Generate-and-Test

With the problem specification carefully developed, we now proceed to determine the sequence of actions (i.e., the plan) that takes the system from the initial state to the

TABLE 14.1
Planning algorithm 1: forward state propagation (FSP) without heuristics, (i.e., "generate and test")

0(a). Represent initial and goal state, S_i and S_g respectively (in clause form).

0(b). Represent operator (O_i) capability as mappings of states (in clause form).

0(c). Set the current state to be the initial state, S_i.

0(d). Check if $S_g \subseteq S_i$. If so, no plan is necessary.

1. Form L_o, where L_o only contains operators O_i, whose preconditions are satisfied by S_i. If $L_o = \varnothing$, we must backup. If no alternatives for backup exist, a path (plan) cannot be found.

2. Choose one operator, $O_i \in L_o$ (see note 1), and tentatively form S_{i+1} resulting from the application of O_i to S_i.

3(a). Check for conflicting subgoals in S_{i+1}. If one or more exists, revise operator selection.

3(b). Check for a cycle (see note 2)

   a) IF a cycle exists, backup (note 3) to a previous state and, if possible, revise a previous operator selection.

   b) IF no cycle exists, go to step 4.

4. Check if S_g is contained in S_{i+1}. If so SUCCESS, otherwise set $S_i \leftarrow S_{i+1}$ and go to step 1.

Notes:
1. This may invoke heuristics, state-difference functions, and so on (shown later).
2. A cycle is defined as a state in which the system has been previously.
3. There exist many possible ways to do this.

goal state. One aspect of this design process that contributes to its complexity is the objective of formulating a *general* plan-generator solution; we should be able to use the algorithm for any initial conditions and for any specified goal state. This also allows recursive use of the plan-generation algorithm (see Table 14.1). In general, it is desirable that the planning algorithm be independent of the chosen representation and availability of operators.

> **Example 14.3   Application of forward state propagation ("generate and test") algorithm to a simple "checkerboard" problem.** To illustrate planning algorithm 1 we choose a problem with limited operator selection choices at each step. This is shown in Fig. 14.8. In more complex problems (e.g., example 14.6) this strategy is impractical and additional constraints or heuristics must be employed to restrict the computational complexity of the search. (14-18)

Backward State Propagation

The backward state propagation algorithm below is presented for illustration purposes. It is neither unique nor optimal. For example, the algorithm does not specify that the plan be achieved in a specified or minimum number of steps, nor does it check for *cycles*. Example 14.10 illustrates how to modify a forward planning algorithm for backward state propagation.

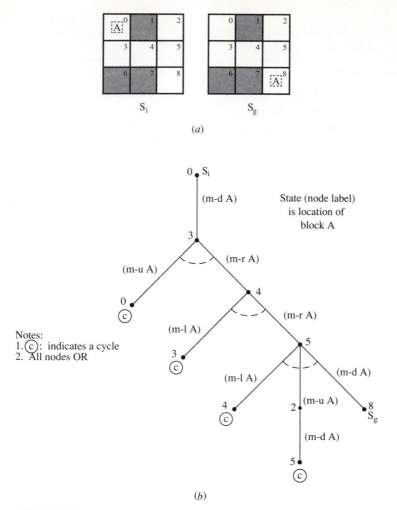

FIGURE 14.8
Simple planning example using FSP and GAT, and associated search tree. (a) Graphical representation of S_i and S_g; (b) search tree.

Example 14.4 Planning algorithm 2: backward state propagation (BSP) (single operator).

Define:

L_c: list of clauses in S_g that are not in S_i

Note: $L_c = \varnothing$ if S_g is contained in S_i.

1. Form L_c, given S_i, if $L_c = \phi$, STOP.

2. Choose one C_i from L_c. Steps 2 and 3 represent *operator conflict resolution*. Several reasonable guidelines for resolution are shown (the reader is encouraged to develop others).

3. Determine a list of all operators, L_o, that have clause C_i in their "add facts" part, that is, those operators whose application yields (perhaps among other system state changes), clause C_i. Constraints on elements of L_o are

(a) Operators should not result in the production of a conflict or contradiction in the system state following the operator application. For example, a subset of the system state after application of an operator could not be:

(on B C)
(on C B)

This happens, for example, when facts in their add facts part conflict with or contradict other subgoals.

(b) Operators should not require a conflict in the system state required prior to application of the operator. It is possible for unsubstantiated subgoals that are back propagated to introduce conflicts. An example, which appears in the following sample solution is the attempted unification of variables to create the subgoal (on A A), which cannot be substantiated.

Both situations (a) and (b) exemplify the *interacting subproblem* effect and its handling in plan generation.

4. Choose one operator, O_i, from L_o in step 3 (note 3). The preceding three interrelated steps involve *selection*, or more generally *search*. Minimization of the search space (e.g., application of "intelligence") at this stage may be rewarded with a faster (fewer steps) solution. In addition, some "experience," or previous plan generation results, may also be useful.

5. Determine, which, if any, preconditions of operator O_i chosen in step 4 are satisfied by S_i.
IF
all preconditions of O_i are satisfied
THEN
apply O_i, modify L_c, and go to step 2 (to satisfy the remaining subgoals).
ELSE { another decision is required}
        IF
other operators on L_o are available,
        THEN
(a) Choose another operator, O_j, and repeat the above procedure
OR { another algorithm decision point}
(b) Decide to attempt eventual use of the chosen operator O_i, and add the unsatisfied preconditions of O_i, to the other unsatisfied subgoals, thus producing a new set of subgoals. Thus, L_c is augmented by removing the clauses produced by O_i and adding the unsatisfied preconditions to O_i. This represents a tentative application of operator O_i. Again, conflicting subgoals and cycles need to be checked.

Figure 14.9 illustrates the alternatives possible in step 5.

6. GOTO step 2.

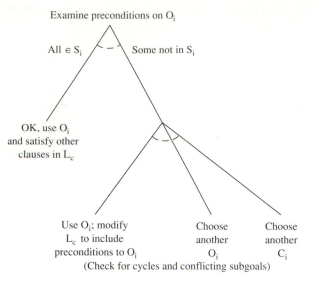

Examine preconditions on O_i

All $\in S_i$ — Some not in S_i

OK, use O_i and satisfy other clauses in L_c

Use O_i; modify L_c to include preconditions to O_i (Check for cycles and conflicting subgoals)

Choose another O_i

Choose another C_i

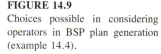

FIGURE 14.9
Choices possible in considering operators in BSP plan generation (example 14.4).

Notes

1. The algorithm is goal-driven, and bears a strong similarity to backward chaining, since we are *conditionally* using operator O_i, and then concentrating on verification of the preconditions of O_i and the remaining unsatisfied subgoals.

2. In the application of O_i, it may not be necessary to ground various clauses in the preconditions or the add facts part. It may, however, be necessary to develop and back-propagate a set of constraints on these propagated variables. This allows us to essentially search backward additional stages without making a "commitment" to a certain constant (e.g., block A) that may yield a "dead end" in subsequent attempts at subgoal satisfaction. Thus, we allow more options or flexibility at the expense of back-propagating the variable constraints. In the following example, below, a combination of grounding and constraint propagation is shown, which again substantiates the nonuniqueness of the planning algorithm.

3. A better operator selection strategy might be to select an operator that produces several of the C_i on L_o.

4. Notice the similarity of this step with that of the PROLOG unification mechanism and the backward chaining algorithm of Chapter 12.   (14-19)

This simplistic BSP algorithm fails in certain instances that are not pathological cases but (realistic) situations. Furthermore it allows cycles. We explore this effect and corresponding algorithm modifications in the examples.

APPLICATION OF BACKWARDS STATE PROPAGATION TO THE BLOCKS-WORLD EXAMPLE. We show a "hand-worked" solution for the problem shown in Fig. 14.1*b* with initial and goal states specified in example 14.1. Given the single goal clause (on C D), the applicable operators that contain (on x y) in their "add-facts" part are enumerated. Consideration of the four operators defined previously yields the list

$$L_o = \{(\text{puton x y})\} \tag{14-20a}$$

To (conditionally) employ this operator, the system must be in the state indicated in block 2 of Fig. 14.10. Also note that the application of this operator generated the additional facts (clear x) and (empty).

  Figure 14.10 also illustrates the back propagation of variable constraints resulting from the chosen operators. These are shown in the preconditions area at the bottom of each state "box." Adjacent to each box in Fig. 14.10 is the graphical illustration of the corresponding system state. This provides a visual interpretation (or confirmation) of the resulting solution sequence.

  In box 2 the new conjunction of subgoals,

subgoal 1: (hold C) $\tag{14-20b}$

subgoal 2: (clear D) $\tag{14-20c}$

must now, according to the BSP algorithm of example 14.4, be satisfied. Thus, we seek operators that contain (hold x) or (clear x) (ideally both) in their respective add-facts parts. This is true of all operators except pickup. We investigate the suitability of the operator putdown in detail to illustrate several important concerns. In the algorithm, all unsatisfied preconditions are propagated backwards to all preceding states. Furthermore, these back-propagated preconditions may involve variable constraints that are also back propagated. In the latter situation, the consistency constraint of the algorithm must be enforced by restricting variable scope.

  Suppose operator (putdown x) is chosen. To satisfy (clear D), x is bound to D. Recall from the specification of this operator that the representation of (putdown D) has add-facts: (ontable D), (clear D), and (empty).

  This choice illustrates the situation where the operator would be inappropriate, since it would generate a conflict in the system state following its application. From above, to satisfy subgoals (14-20b) and (14-20c), that is, (hold C) and (clear D), application of (putdown D), while generating (satisfying) (clear D) also generates (ontable D) and (empty). Clearly, a contradiction results in this state since a state simultaneously containing both (empty) and (hold C) cannot exist. Therefore, operator putdown is no longer considered since it generates interacting subgoals and spawns an illegal state. The reader should consider the alternative selection of operator (puton x y). This is left to the exercises.

  Returning to block 2 of the example, two operators that could be employed to satisfy the first subgoal in (14-20b), namely (hold C), are (pickup C) and (takeoff C y). The reader should verify that they do not generate conflicts. Note also that y has been left as a variable in the latter clause, which yields more flexibility in subsequent planning. However, constraints on the variable y must be determined and back propagated. Referring to box 4 in Fig. 14.10, the current constraint on y is $y \neq D$; otherwise (on C D) and (clear D) would need to be simultaneously

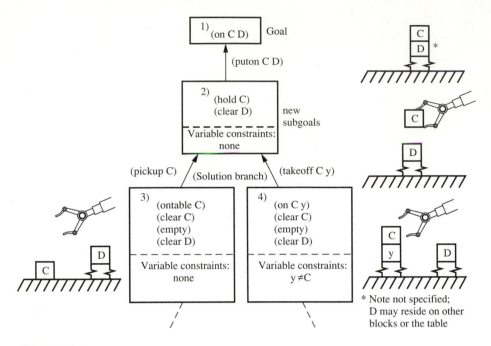

FIGURE 14.10
First and second steps in plan generation example.

TRUE.* Likewise, y ≠ C since clause (on C C), which is clearly an illegal state, would result.

Having propagated a solution two steps backward to boxes 3 and 4, as shown in Fig. 14.10, a branch (i.e., choice of alternative operators) is possible. The existence of a branch does not signify that either path guarantees a solution, but rather that we have the opportunity of exploring either (or both) paths for a possible solution. At this point we employ a "means-end" heuristic, as described later, which provides a way to automate the choice. Notice that block 3 represents a system state that is closer (in the sense of number of common clauses in the state representation) to S_i than that of block 4. Thus, we choose to pursue the subsequent path(s) involving the state in block 3. It should be noted that this heuristic does not guarantee that the overall path exists or is shorter than that involving box 4; it simply makes intuitive sense. It could be the case that the overall path (operator sequence) which involves block 4 actually is shorter, since subsequent states that lead up to block 3 may actually move away from the initial state. This is explored later.

We now consider the state succession backwards from block 3 in Fig. 14.10. Since two of the four clauses are satisfied by the initial state, the process begins (and this choice is arbitrary) by selecting operators whose add−facts specifications

---

*Note that this assumes only clause (hold C) is satisified, and therefore (clear D) is back propagated to box 4. If we use operator takeoff to satisfy *both* subgoals in box 2, then y = D.

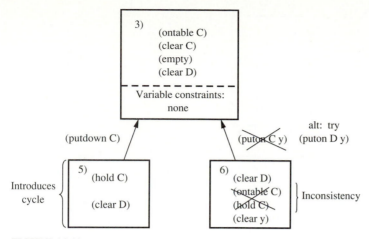

FIGURE 14.11
Succeeding steps in plan generation example (two attempted subplans; possibility of a cycle).

contain (clear C) and (clear D) and do not generate inconsistencies. Two possible approaches are shown in Fig. 14.11, involving (putdown C) and (puton C y). We notice problems with both choices, however, as shown. The application of operator (putdown C) generates the new list of preconditions shown in block 5. Strictly speaking, the more general operator (putdown x), applied to block C, may be selected and it satisfies three out of the four back-propagated subgoal clauses in block 3. However, a subtle problem has crept into the picture. Notice that to satisfy (hold C) in block 5 it is now necessary to employ (pickup C) (which contains (hold C) in its add−facts part). In addition, to employ (pickup C) requires (ontable C), which can only be generated by application of operator (putdown C). Thus, we have left the solution open to the existence of a cycle, or possibly an infinite loop, where the locally generated plan causes the manipulator arm to repeatedly pick up and put down block C. We note also the use of (takeoff x C) to substantiate subgoals in block 3 results in a dead end, since it necessitates (on C C) to occur (it is left for the reader to verify this).

One solution to the cycle dilemma is to accept a more modest change in the system state using other operators. At this point, we alternately choose to consider operator (putdown x), which we use only to substantiate the single subgoal (empty) in block 3, or, alternatively, (puton x y), which also is used only to generate the clause (empty). This is shown in Fig. 14.12. Here, since the block identity is left variable (i.e., x), we are only able to satisfy (empty) in block 3. Thus we must bring the unsubstantiated subgoals into the subsequent preconditions block for each of these operators, as shown in blocks of the figure. Additionally, we must determine the constraints on the back-propagated variables such that nonsensical states do not result. This is shown in Fig. 14.12.

Our "hand-worked" solution of the BSP algorithm with the blocks-world problem has illustrated a number of important aspects of plan generation. The remainder of the problem is left to the reader.

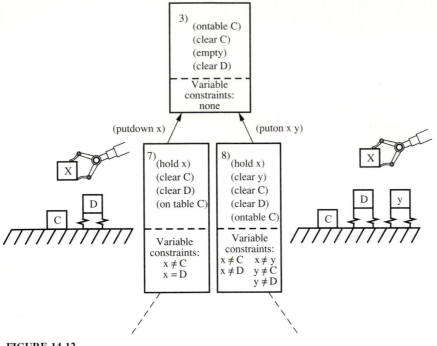

FIGURE 14.12
Alternate plan formulation (see text).

ADVANCED PLANNING STRATEGIES

We observe that humans, when faced with a goal, seldom proceed in the mechanical manner described in the previous section. In particular we note that two interrelated capabilities appear to become significant. The first is the ability to recall, or modify, a previous plan. The second is that the plans are seldom as simple as one step selections of operators. For example, in the blocks-world problem the human might effectively employ a higher-level composite operator reverse blocks, which given block A on block B, yields a resultant state of block B on block A. The individual or "atomic" actions that yield this composite operator are not recalculated, but rather stored as a result of experience. Furthermore, decomposition of the overall plan into smaller, perhaps recallable, subplans is typical.

Generation of Expertise (Remembering a Plan)

Many seemingly different goal states are merely revisions of others for which a plan is available. Thus, remembering and modification of previous plans is a significant aspect of intelligent system behavior. For example, consider the following initial and goal states for a person:

S_i: at home

S_{g1}: at work

S_{g2}: at the health club

We assume that the health club and work are at different locations and that movement between any of the above states requires driving a car. The observation is this: Given S_i and S_{g1} or S_{g2}, either resulting plan may share a large number of common operator sequences. For example, in order to drive, the person must go through the sequence of getting into the car, starting the car, and so on. This is common to either plan. It is the identification of this common sequence that makes for efficient planning, and guides, to some extent, our choice of stored or remembered plans. This reasoning suggests we need a mechanism to catalog a plan and show the operator interaction. Such a device is the *triangle table*.

The Triangle Table

A useful graphical mechanism to show plan evolution as well as "link" the succession of operators is the triangle table. We first develop the structure and rules for this table and then show an example. The triangle table has a "staircase" appearance as shown in Fig. 14.13 and provides a compact summary of plan generation. Given a resulting plan requiring the successive use of p operators, $O_1, O_2, \ldots O_p$, the table consists of $p + 1$ columns, numbered 0 through p. Similarly, the $p + 1$ rows of the table are indexed by n and numbered from the top, starting at $n = 0$ and ending with the bottom row, $n = p$. Thus, the triangle table has

$$(p + 1)^2/2 + p/2 = p(p + 3)/2 + 1$$

entries, or "cells," each of which may be empty or comprised of a subset of the system state. The columns of the triangle table, beginning with $m = 1$, are labeled with the

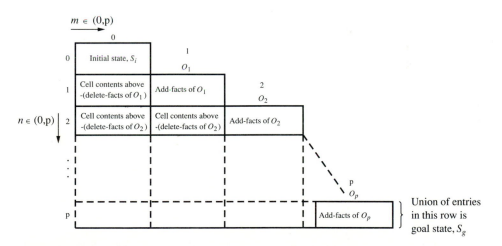

FIGURE 14.13
General form of triangle table.

m^{th} operator, O_m, in the sequence. Cell (0,0) contains the initial state. Entries are made in the table as follows:

1. The entries in cell (m,m), for $m > 0$, are the add−list facts for operator m.
2. The entries in cells (m,n) in column m, for $n > m$, are formed recursively by the following rule: cell (m,n) where $n > m$ contains the contents of cell $(m,n-1)$ with the delete−facts list of operator m removed. This procedure starts with cell (0,0). Traversing the columns from top to bottom may therefore be thought of as indicating the reduction in system state entries due to the succession of operator delete−facts application.

This is shown in Fig. 14.13. When the table is completed (it is left to the reader to prove this) the union of the facts in the bottom $(n = p)$ row represents the goal state.

Example of Plan and Corresponding Triangle Table Formation

We now show the cataloging of plan development using the triangle table. Here we use the "means-end" approach with state and operator specification in list form. (This facilitates our LISP implementation.)

From the representation of example 14.1, with initial and goal states depicted graphically in Fig. 14.1b, given initial-state S_i, in (14-16a), that is, the clauses

$$\{(\text{on A C}) \ (\text{on B D}) \ (\text{ontable C}) \ (\text{ontable D})$$
$$(\text{clear A}) \ (\text{clear B}) \ (\text{empty})\}$$
$$(14\text{-}16a)$$

and the goal state,
$$S_g = \{(\text{on C D}) \ (\text{ontable D}) \ (\text{clear C}) \ (\text{clear A}) \ (\text{clear B})$$
$$(\text{ontable A}) \ (\text{ontable B}) \ (\text{empty})\}$$

The derivation using forward-state propagation (example 14.8) in the following section yields a plan consisting of the following operator sequence:

```
(takeoff A C)
(putdown A)
(pickup C)
(puton C A)
(takeoff B D)
(putdown B)
(takeoff C A)
(puton C D)
```

The reader should verify the suitability of the derived plan. We show a quick verification while forming the triangle table:

1. If the first operator selected is (takeoff A C) the current state becomes

$$S_1 = \{(\text{hold A}) \ (\text{clear C}) \ (\text{on B D}) \ (\text{ontable C})$$
$$(\text{ontable D}) \ (\text{clear B})\}$$

   thus indicating the changes in state due to this operator.

2. The second operator selected is (putdown A) yielding the system state

$$S_2 = \{(\text{clear A}) \ (\text{empty}) \ (\text{ontable A}) \ (\text{clear C})$$
$$(\text{on B D}) \ (\text{ontable C}) \ (\text{ontable D}) \ (\text{clear B})\}$$

3. The third operator selected is (pickup C), which yields

$$S_3 = \{(\text{hold C}) \ (\text{clear A}) \ (\text{ontable A}) \ (\text{on B D})$$
$$(\text{ontable D}) \ (\text{clear B}) \ \}$$

4. If the action taken is (puton C A), then

$$S_4 = \{(\text{on C A}) \ (\text{clear C}) \ (\text{empty}) \ (\text{ontable A})$$
$$(\text{on B D}) \ (\text{ontable D}) \ (\text{clear B})\}$$
   results.

5. If the action taken is (takeoff B D), then

$$S_5 = \{(\text{hold B}) \ (\text{clear D}) \ (\text{on C A}) \ (\text{clear C})$$
$$(\text{ontable A}) \ (\text{ontable D})\}$$

   results.

6. If we select (putdown B), then

$$S_6 = \{(\text{clear B}) \ (\text{empty}) \ (\text{ontable B}) \ (\text{clear D})$$
$$(\text{on C A}) \ (\text{clear C}) \ (\text{ontable A}) \ (\text{ontable D})\}$$

   results.

7. If the action selected is: (takeoff C A)

$$S_7 = \{(\text{hold C}) \ (\text{clear A}) \ (\text{clear B}) \ (\text{ontable B})$$
$$(\text{clear D}) \ (\text{ontable A}) \ (\text{ontable D})\}$$

   results. Finally,

8. The action taken is: (puton C D), which yields the desired system goal state.

   Figure 14.14 shows a graphical illustration of the plan. The corresponding triangle table is shown in Fig. 14.15. The reader should verify the formation of this table. In particular, note that the union of all the entries in the bottom row is, in fact, the goal state.

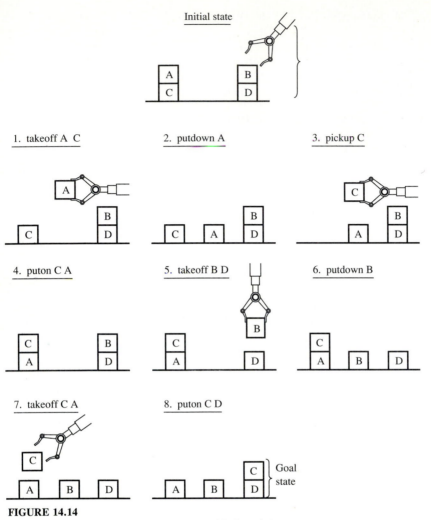

FIGURE 14.14
Plan generation for blocks-world problem (graphical results).

LISP IMPLEMENTATION OF PLAN GENERATORS

We show solutions to planning using LISP programs for both forward and backward state propagation. Note that the LISP implementation for planning is considerably more complex than that of the simple rule-based inference systems of Chapters 11 and 12.

Forward State Propagation Using Generate-and-Test (Checkerboard)

Figure 14.16 shows the structure of the LISP code for plan generation using forward state propagation. We show operation of the LISP-based planner using several

Case of p = 8 operators

m ↓   0 ——> n

	0	1	2	3	4	5	6	7	8
0	on AC on BD ontable C ontable D clear A clear B empty	**1** takeoff AC							
1	clear B on BD ontable C ontable D	hold A clear C	**2** putdown A						
2	on BD clear B ontable C ontable D	clear C	clear A empty ontable A	**3** pickup C					
3	on BD clear B ontable D	—	clear A ontable A	hold C	**4** puton CA				
4	on BD clear B ontable D	—	ontable A	—	clear C empty on CA	**5** takeoff BD			
5	ontable D	—	ontable A	—	clear C on CA	clear D hold B	**6** putdown B		
6	ontable D	—	ontable A	—	clear C on CA	clear D	empty clear B ontable B	**7** takeoff CA	
7	ontable D	—	ontable A	—	—	clear D	clear B ontable B	hold C clear A	**8** puton CD
8	ontable D	—	ontable A	—	—	—	clear B ontable B	clear A	empty on CD clear C

FIGURE 14.15
Triangle table for blocks-world plan.

examples. In both examples, notice the system checks for cycles, states that are being revisited. Cycles serve no purpose, and therefore are eliminated by the system through finding alternatives to the operator that placed the system in the cycle.

Example 14.5   Forward state propagation ("checkerboard") LISP implementation.
Figure 14.17 graphically depicts S_i and S_g for the sample case considered below.

Program Listing

```
; FILE NAME: ttt.l


;            ********** Description *******

; this program does forward state propagation planning
; for moving blocks in a tic–tac–toe path. The nine
; locations are numbered as
```

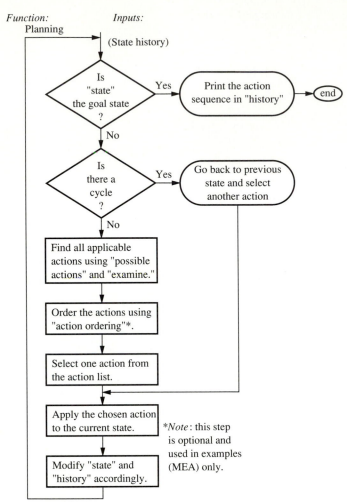

FIGURE 14.16
Overall LISP planning program structure.

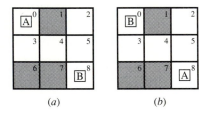

(a)　　　　　(b)

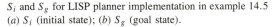

FIGURE 14.17
S_i and S_g for LISP planner implementation in example 14.5
(a) S_i (initial state); (b) S_g (goal state).

```
;                                   0  1  2
;                                   3  4  5
;                                   6  7  8
; the state is represented by a list of clauses.
;   (0 A) means that block A is at location 0.
;   (1 empty) means that there is no block at location 1.


;           ********** Initial State ******

(setq *initial-state*   '((0 A)
                          (8 B)
                          (2 empty)
                          (3 empty)
                          (4 empty)
                          (5 empty)))


;           **********  Goal State ******

(setq *goal-state*      '((8 A)
                          (0 B)
                          (2 empty)
                          (3 empty)
                          (4 empty)
                          (5 empty)))



;         *********** Operator Definitions *********

(setq *operations* '(
 (move-right x
    (precondition: ((3 4) x) ((4 5) empty))
    (added-facts: ((4 5) x) ((3 4) empty)))
 (move-left x
    (precondition: ((4 5) x) ((3 4) empty))
    (added-facts: ((3 4) x) ((4 5) empty)))
 (move-up x
    (precondition: ((3 5 8) x) ((0 2 5) empty))
    (added-facts: ((0 2 5) x) ((3 5 8) empty)))
 (move-down x
    (precondition: ((0 2 5) x) ((3 5 8) empty))
    (added-facts: ((3 5 8) x) ((0 2 5) empty)))))



;         ********** Operator Action as Function *****

; this function modifies the current state according to
; the operation definition
; INPUT: the action and the current state
; OUTPUT: the new state
```

```
(defun operator (action state)
 (add-new-facts action
                (delete-preconditions action state)))



;            *********** MAIN FUNCTIONS *******

; "examine" checks if "action" can be taken in "state".
; if it is true, finds the bindings for block name.
; INPUT: an operation definition and the current state.
; OUTPUT: action list containing all the possible bindings
;          when this action is applied to the current state.

(defun examine (action state)
 (let
  ((name (car action))                          ;action name
   (facts (get-preconditions action)))          ;preconditions
  (do
   ((xloc (get-x-loc facts) (cdr xloc))         ;block loc list
    (eloc (get-empty-loc facts) (cdr eloc))     ;empty loc list
    (xpre nil)
    (epre nil)
    (alist nil))
   ((null xloc) alist)
   (setq xpre (assoc (car xloc) state))         ;block predicate
   (setq epre (assoc (car eloc) state))         ;empty predicate
   (if (and (nequal (nth 1 xpre) 'empty)
            (equal (nth 1 epre) 'empty))
       (setq alist (cons (list name (nth 1 xpre) (car xpre)
                   (car epre)) alist))))))

; "possible-actions" finds all possible actions
; available to "state".
; INPUT: the current state
; OUTPUT: list containing all possible actions

(defun possible-actions (state)
 (do
  ((actions *operations* (cdr actions))
   (temp nil nil)
   (result nil))
  ((null actions) result)
  (cond
   ((setq temp (examine (car actions) state))
    (setq result (append temp result))))))
; "planning" generates an action plan such that the goal
   state
; can be reached from the initial-state.
;  1) stops, if goal state is reached.
```

```
;  2) goes one step back if this state has been reached
      before.
;  3) finds all possible actions.
;  4) takes one of actions, and goes back to 1.
; INPUT: the current state and the history
;        history = (((state n) (action list n)) ...
;                   ((state 2) (action list 2))
;                   ((state 1) (action list 1)))
; OUTPUT: none
; SIDE-EFFECT: result print-out


(defun planning (state history)
 (gc)
 (if (same state *goal-state*)
     (print-result state history)
     (let ((actions nil)
           (a1 nil))
      (cond
       ((cycle state history)
        (print-cycle)
        (do
         ((htemp history (cdr htemp)))
         ((cdr (get-actions htemp)) (setq history htemp)))
         (setq state (get-state history))
         (setq actions (cdr (get-actions history)))
         (setq history (cdr history))
         (print-state state)
         (terpri))
       (t
        (setq actions (possible-actions state))
        (print-actions actions)))
      (setq history (cons (list state actions) history))
      (setq a1 (car actions))
      (setq state (take-action a1 state))
      (planning state history))))


; ********** AUXILIARY FUNCTIONS ******

; "delete" deletes all the elements which are equal to
  "term"
; from "list".

(defun delete (term list)
 (cond
  ((null list) nil)
  ((equal term (car list)) (delete term (cdr list)))
  (t (cons (car list) (delete term (cdr list))))))
```

```
; "get-x-loc" gets the block location list

(defun get-x-loc (facts)
 (nth 0 (nth 1 facts)))


; "get-empty-loc" gets the empty location list

(defun get-empty-loc (facts)
 (nth 0 (nth 2 facts)))

; "get-preconditions" gets the proconditions

(defun get-preconditions (action)
 (nth 2 action))


; "delete-preconditions" deletes all preconditions from
; the current state
; INPUT: action and the current state
; OUTPUT: new state

(defun delete-preconditions (action state)
 (delete (assoc (nth 2 action) state)
         (delete (assoc (nth 3 action) state) state)))

; "add-new-facts" adds all added-facts to
; the current state
; INPUT: action and the current state
; OUTPUT: new state

(defun add-new-facts (action state)
 (cons (list (nth 3 action) (nth 1 action))
       (cons (list (nth 2 action) 'empty) state)))

; "contained" checks if list "s1" is contained in "s2".

(defun contained (s1 s2)
 (do
  ((t1 s1 (cdr t1)))
  ((null t1) t)
  (if (not (member (car t1) s2)) (return nil))))


; "same" return t if two states are same, otherwise nil.

(defun same (s1 s2)
 (and (contained s1 s2)
      (contained s2 s1)))
```

```
; "print-state" prints "state".

(defun print-state (state)
 (cond
   ((null state) nil)
   (t (print (car state))
      (terpri)
      (print-state (cdr state)))))


; "print-result" prints results after goal state is reached.

(defun print-result (state history)
 (print '(GOAL STATE IS REACHED))
 (terpri)
 (print '(THE ACTION LIST))
 (terpri)
 (do
   ((ts history (cdr ts))
    (ts1 nil))
   ((null ts) (print-state ts1))
   (setq ts1 (cons (caadar ts) ts1)))
 (terpri))


; "cycle" returns t if "state" exist in "history",
; otherwise nil.

(defun cycle (state history)
 (do
   ((ts history (cdr ts)))
   ((null ts) nil)
   (if (same state (caar ts))
       (return t))))

; "get-state" gets previous state from "history".

(defun get-state (history)
 (caar history))


; "get-actions" get previous action list from "history".

(defun get-actions (history)
 (cadar history))

; "print-cycle" print cycle message

(defun print-cycle ()
 (print '(THIS STATE HAS BEEN REACHED BEFORE)))
```

```
(terpri)
(print '(GO BACK TO PREVIOUS STATE AND TAKE ANOTHER ACTION))
(terpri)
(print '(THE CURRENT STATE IS))
(terpri))

; "print-actions" prints actions

(defun print-actions (actions)
 (print '(THE POSSIBLE ACTIONS ARE))
 (terpri)
 (print-state actions)
 (terpri))


; "take-action" applies an action to "state"

(defun take-action (action state)
 (print (list 'ACTION  action 'IS 'TAKEN))
 (terpri)
 (setq state (operator action state))
 (print '(THE CURRENT STATE IS))
 (terpri)
 (print-state state)
 (terpri)
 state)
```
                                                                    (14-21)

Example 14.6   Sample results using LISP program for forward state propagation.
The reader should be impressed (or overwhelmed!) with the significant amount of search
involved in this generate-and-test example. This is due to

1. A large problem state space.
2. The use of a brute-force (generate-and-test) planning algorithm with a simplistic
operator selection strategy. At each step, the first applicable operator is chosen. This
leads to a poorly guided and inefficient solution procedure, which should be compared
with the more sophisticated operator selection strategies of blocks-world examples
14.7 and 14.9. Note, however, a solution is found.

```
-> (load 'ttt.l)
[load ttt.l]

(Initial State)
(0 A)
(8 B)
(2 empty)
(3 empty)
(4 empty)
(5 empty)

(Goal State)
(8 A)
(0 B)
```

(2 empty)
(3 empty)
(4 empty)
(5 empty)

(THE POSSIBLE ACTIONS ARE)
(move—down A 0 3) (move—up B 8 5)

(ACTION (move—down A 0 3) IS TAKEN)
(THE CURRENT STATE IS)
(3 A) (0 empty) (8 B) (2 empty) (4 empty) (5 empty)

(THE POSSIBLE ACTIONS ARE)
(move—up B 8 5) (move—up A 3 0) (move—right A 3 4)

(ACTION (move—up B 8 5) IS TAKEN)
(THE CURRENT STATE IS)
(5 B) (8 empty) (3 A) (0 empty) (2 empty) (4 empty)

(THE POSSIBLE ACTIONS ARE)
(move—down B 5 8) (move—up B 5 2) (move—up A 3 0) (move—left B 5 4) (move—right A 3 4)

(ACTION (move—down B 5 8) IS TAKEN)
(THE CURRENT STATE IS)
(8 B) (5 empty) (3 A) (0 empty) (2 empty) (4 empty)

(THIS STATE HAS BEEN REACHED BEFORE)
(GO BACK TO PREVIOUS STATE AND TAKE ANOTHER ACTION)
(THE CURRENT STATE IS)
(5 B) (8 empty) (3 A) (0 empty) (2 empty) (4 empty)

(ACTION (move—up B 5 2) IS TAKEN)
(THE CURRENT STATE IS)
(2 B) (5 empty) (8 empty) (3 A) (0 empty) (4 empty)

(THE POSSIBLE ACTIONS ARE)
(move—down B 2 5) (move—up A 3 0) (move—right A 3 4)

(ACTION (move—down B 2 5) IS TAKEN)
(THE CURRENT STATE IS)
(5 B) (2 empty) (8 empty) (3 A) (0 empty) (4 empty)

(THIS STATE HAS BEEN REACHED BEFORE)
(GO BACK TO PREVIOUS STATE AND TAKE ANOTHER ACTION)
(THE CURRENT STATE IS)
(2 B) (5 empty) (8 empty) (3 A) (0 empty) (4 empty)

(ACTION (move—up A 3 0) IS TAKEN)
(THE CURRENT STATE IS)
(0 A) (3 empty) (2 B) (5 empty) (8 empty) (4 empty)

(THE POSSIBLE ACTIONS ARE)
(move—down B 2 5) (move—down A 0 3)

(ACTION (move–down B 2 5) IS TAKEN)
(THE CURRENT STATE IS)
(5 B) (2 empty) (0 A) (3 empty) (8 empty) (4 empty)

(THE POSSIBLE ACTIONS ARE)
(move–down B 5 8) (move–down A 0 3) (move–up B 5 2) (move–left B 5 4)

(ACTION (move–down B 5 8) IS TAKEN)
(THE CURRENT STATE IS)
(8 B) (5 empty) (2 empty) (0 A) (3 empty) (4 empty)

(THIS STATE HAS BEEN REACHED BEFORE)
(GO BACK TO PREVIOUS STATE AND TAKE ANOTHER ACTION)
(THE CURRENT STATE IS)
(5 B) (2 empty) (0 A) (3 empty) (8 empty) (4 empty)

(ACTION (move–down A 0 3) IS TAKEN)
(THE CURRENT STATE IS)
(3 A) (0 empty) (5 B) (2 empty) (8 empty) (4 empty)

(THIS STATE HAS BEEN REACHED BEFORE)
(GO BACK TO PREVIOUS STATE AND TAKE ANOTHER ACTION)
(THE CURRENT STATE IS)
(5 B) (2 empty) (0 A) (3 empty) (8 empty) (4 empty)

(ACTION (move–up B 5 2) IS TAKEN)
(THE CURRENT STATE IS)
(2 B) (5 empty) (0 A) (3 empty) (8 empty) (4 empty)

(THIS STATE HAS BEEN REACHED BEFORE)
(GO BACK TO PREVIOUS STATE AND TAKE ANOTHER ACTION)
(THE CURRENT STATE IS)
(5 B) (2 empty) (0 A) (3 empty) (8 empty) (4 empty)

(ACTION (move–left B 5 4) IS TAKEN)
(THE CURRENT STATE IS)
(4 B) (5 empty) (2 empty) (0 A) (3 empty) (8 empty)

(THE POSSIBLE ACTIONS ARE)
(move–down A 0 3) (move–left B 4 3) (move–right B 4 5)

(ACTION (move–down A 0 3) IS TAKEN)
(THE CURRENT STATE IS)
(3 A) (0 empty) (4 B) (5 empty) (2 empty) (8 empty)

(THE POSSIBLE ACTIONS ARE)
(move–up A 3 0) (move–right B 4 5)

(ACTION (move–up A 3 0) IS TAKEN)
(THE CURRENT STATE IS)
(0 A) (3 empty) (4 B) (5 empty) (2 empty) (8 empty)

(THIS STATE HAS BEEN REACHED BEFORE)
(GO BACK TO PREVIOUS STATE AND TAKE ANOTHER ACTION)
(THE CURRENT STATE IS)
(3 A) (0 empty) (4 B) (5 empty) (2 empty) (8 empty)

(ACTION (move-right B 4 5) IS TAKEN)
(THE CURRENT STATE IS)
(5 B) (4 empty) (3 A) (0 empty) (2 empty) (8 empty)

(THIS STATE HAS BEEN REACHED BEFORE)
(GO BACK TO PREVIOUS STATE AND TAKE ANOTHER ACTION)
(THE CURRENT STATE IS)
(4 B) (5 empty) (2 empty) (0 A) (3 empty) (8 empty)

(ACTION (move-left B 4 3) IS TAKEN)
(THE CURRENT STATE IS)
(3 B) (4 empty) (5 empty) (2 empty) (0 A) (8 empty)

(THE POSSIBLE ACTIONS ARE)
(move-right B 3 4)

(ACTION (move-right B 3 4) IS TAKEN)
(THE CURRENT STATE IS)
(4 B) (3 empty) (5 empty) (2 empty) (0 A) (8 empty)

(THIS STATE HAS BEEN REACHED BEFORE)
(GO BACK TO PREVIOUS STATE AND TAKE ANOTHER ACTION)
(THE CURRENT STATE IS)
(4 B) (5 empty) (2 empty) (0 A) (3 empty) (8 empty)

(ACTION (move-right B 4 5) IS TAKEN)
(THE CURRENT STATE IS)
(5 B) (4 empty) (2 empty) (0 A) (3 empty) (8 empty)

(THIS STATE HAS BEEN REACHED BEFORE)
(GO BACK TO PREVIOUS STATE AND TAKE ANOTHER ACTION)
(THE CURRENT STATE IS)
(0 A) (3 empty) (2 B) (5 empty) (8 empty) (4 empty)

(ACTION (move-down A 0 3) IS TAKEN)
(THE CURRENT STATE IS)
(3 A) (0 empty) (2 B) (5 empty) (8 empty) (4 empty)

(THIS STATE HAS BEEN REACHED BEFORE)
(GO BACK TO PREVIOUS STATE AND TAKE ANOTHER ACTION)
(THE CURRENT STATE IS)
(2 B) (5 empty) (8 empty) (3 A) (0 empty) (4 empty)

(ACTION (move-right A 3 4) IS TAKEN)
(THE CURRENT STATE IS)
(4 A) (3 empty) (2 B) (5 empty) (8 empty) (0 empty)

(THE POSSIBLE ACTIONS ARE)
(move-down B 2 5) (move-left A 4 3) (move-right A 4 5)

(ACTION (move-down B 2 5) IS TAKEN)
(THE CURRENT STATE IS)
(5 B) (2 empty) (4 A) (3 empty) (8 empty) (0 empty)

(THE POSSIBLE ACTIONS ARE)
(move-down B 5 8) (move-up B 5 2) (move-left A 4 3)

(ACTION (move—down B 5 8) IS TAKEN)
(THE CURRENT STATE IS)
(8 B) (5 empty) (2 empty) (4 A) (3 empty) (0 empty)

(THE POSSIBLE ACTIONS ARE)
(move—up B 8 5) (move—left A 4 3) (move—right A 4 5)

(ACTION (move—up B 8 5) IS TAKEN)
(THE CURRENT STATE IS)
(5 B) (8 empty) (2 empty) (4 A) (3 empty) (0 empty)

(THIS STATE HAS BEEN REACHED BEFORE)
(GO BACK TO PREVIOUS STATE AND TAKE ANOTHER ACTION)
(THE CURRENT STATE IS)
(8 B) (5 empty) (2 empty) (4 A) (3 empty) (0 empty)

(ACTION (move—left A 4 3) IS TAKEN)
(THE CURRENT STATE IS)
(3 A) (4 empty) (8 B) (5 empty) (2 empty) (0 empty)

(THIS STATE HAS BEEN REACHED BEFORE)
(GO BACK TO PREVIOUS STATE AND TAKE ANOTHER ACTION)
(THE CURRENT STATE IS)
(8 B) (5 empty) (2 empty) (4 A) (3 empty) (0 empty)

(ACTION (move—right A 4 5) IS TAKEN)
(THE CURRENT STATE IS)
(5 A) (4 empty) (8 B) (2 empty) (3 empty) (0 empty)

(THE POSSIBLE ACTIONS ARE)
(move—up A 5 2) (move—left A 5 4)

(ACTION (move—up A 5 2) IS TAKEN)
(THE CURRENT STATE IS)
(2 A) (5 empty) (4 empty) (8 B) (3 empty) (0 empty)

(THE POSSIBLE ACTIONS ARE)
(move—down A 2 5) (move—up B 8 5)

(ACTION (move—down A 2 5) IS TAKEN)
(THE CURRENT STATE IS)
(5 A) (2 empty) (4 empty) (8 B) (3 empty) (0 empty)

(THIS STATE HAS BEEN REACHED BEFORE)
(GO BACK TO PREVIOUS STATE AND TAKE ANOTHER ACTION)
(THE CURRENT STATE IS)
(2 A) (5 empty) (4 empty) (8 B) (3 empty) (0 empty)

(ACTION (move—up B 8 5) IS TAKEN)
(THE CURRENT STATE IS)
(5 B) (8 empty) (2 A) (4 empty) (3 empty) (0 empty)

(THE POSSIBLE ACTIONS ARE)
(move—down B 5 8) (move—left B 5 4)

(ACTION (move—down B 5 8) IS TAKEN)
(THE CURRENT STATE IS)
(8 B) (5 empty) (2 A) (4 empty) (3 empty) (0 empty)

(THIS STATE HAS BEEN REACHED BEFORE)
(GO BACK TO PREVIOUS STATE AND TAKE ANOTHER ACTION)
(THE CURRENT STATE IS)
(5 B) (8 empty) (2 A) (4 empty) (3 empty) (0 empty)

(ACTION (move—left B 5 4) IS TAKEN)
(THE CURRENT STATE IS)
(4 B) (5 empty) (8 empty) (2 A) (3 empty) (0 empty)

(THE POSSIBLE ACTIONS ARE)
(move—down A 2 5) (move—left B 4 3) (move—right B 4 5)

(ACTION (move—down A 2 5) IS TAKEN)
(THE CURRENT STATE IS)
(5 A) (2 empty) (4 B) (8 empty) (3 empty) ·(0 empty)

(THE POSSIBLE ACTIONS ARE)
(move—down A 5 8) (move—up A 5 2) (move—left B 4 3)

(ACTION (move—down A 5 8) IS TAKEN)
(THE CURRENT STATE IS)
(8 A) (5 empty) (2 empty) (4 B) (3 empty) (0 empty)

(THE POSSIBLE ACTIONS ARE)
(move—up A 8 5) (move—left B 4 3) (move—right B 4 5)

(ACTION (move—up A 8 5) IS TAKEN)
(THE CURRENT STATE IS)
(5 A) (8 empty) (2 empty) (4 B) (3 empty) (0 empty)

(THIS STATE HAS BEEN REACHED BEFORE)
(GO BACK TO PREVIOUS STATE AND TAKE ANOTHER ACTION)
(THE CURRENT STATE IS)
(8 A) (5 empty) (2 empty) (4 B) (3 empty) (0 empty)

(ACTION (move—left B 4 3) IS TAKEN)
(THE CURRENT STATE IS)
(3 B) (4 empty) (8 A) (5 empty) (2 empty) (0 empty)

(THE POSSIBLE ACTIONS ARE)
(move—up A 8 5) (move—up B 3 0) (move—right B 3 4)

(ACTION (move—up A 8 5) IS TAKEN)
(THE CURRENT STATE IS)
(5 A) (8 empty) (3 B) (4 empty) (2 empty) (0 empty)

(THE POSSIBLE ACTIONS ARE)
(move—down A 5 8) (move—up A 5 2) (move—up B 3 0) (move—left A 5 4) (move—right B 3 4)

(ACTION (move—down A 5 8) IS TAKEN)
(THE CURRENT STATE IS)
(8 A) (5 empty) (3 B) (4 empty) (2 empty) (0 empty)

(THIS STATE HAS BEEN REACHED BEFORE)
(GO BACK TO PREVIOUS STATE AND TAKE ANOTHER ACTION)
(THE CURRENT STATE IS)
(5 A) (8 empty) (3 B) (4 empty) (2 empty) (0 empty)

(ACTION (move-up A 5 2) IS TAKEN)
(THE CURRENT STATE IS)
(2 A) (5 empty) (8 empty) (3 B) (4 empty) (0 empty)

(THE POSSIBLE ACTIONS ARE)
(move-down A 2 5) (move-up B 3 0) (move-right B 3 4)

(ACTION (move-down A 2 5) IS TAKEN)
(THE CURRENT STATE IS)
(5 A) (2 empty) (8 empty) (3 B) (4 empty) (0 empty)

(THIS STATE HAS BEEN REACHED BEFORE)
(GO BACK TO PREVIOUS STATE AND TAKE ANOTHER ACTION)
(THE CURRENT STATE IS)
(2 A) (5 empty) (8 empty) (3 B) (4 empty) (0 empty)

(ACTION (move-up B 3 0) IS TAKEN)
(THE CURRENT STATE IS)
(0 B) (3 empty) (2 A) (5 empty) (8 empty) (4 empty)

(THE POSSIBLE ACTIONS ARE)
(move-down A 2 5) (move-down B 0 3)

(ACTION (move-down A 2 5) IS TAKEN)
(THE CURRENT STATE IS)
(5 A) (2 empty) (0 B) (3 empty) (8 empty) (4 empty)

(THE POSSIBLE ACTIONS ARE)
(move-down A 5 8)
(move-down B 0 3) (move-up A 5 2)
(move-left A 5 4)

(ACTION (move-down A 5 8) IS TAKEN)
(THE CURRENT STATE IS)
(8 A) (5 empty) (2 empty) (0 B) (3 empty) (4 empty)

(GOAL STATE IS REACHED)
(THE ACTION LIST)
(move-down A 0 3)
(move-up B 8 5)
(move-up B 5 2)
(move-right A 3 4)
(move-down B 2 5)
(move-down B 5 8)
(move-right A 4 5)
(move-up A 5 2)
(move-up B 8 5)
(move-left B 5 4)
(move-down A 2 5)
(move-down A 5 8)
(move-left B 4 3)

(move–up A 8 5)
(move–up A 5 2)
(move–up B 3 0)
(move–down A 2 5)
(move–down A 5 8)   (14-22)

Comparing a minimum path length solution (Chapter 15) with the solution of example 14.6 indicates the utility of a good operator selection (or search) strategy. An alternative solution, involving backward state propagation, is considered in the problems.

INCORPORATING "MEANS-END" IN THE OPERATOR SELECTION (SEARCH) STRATEGY

The search or conflict resolution method used to revise the FSP planner implementation is known as "means-end." The objective is to choose operators whose action moves the current system state closer (in some measure) to the goal state. This involves carefully choosing *state evaluation functions*.

Operator (and State) Evaluation Functions and Problem-Solving Heuristics

Determining "good" action conflict resolution strategies is the essence of successful (and "intelligent") planning. An "ideal" evaluation function would eliminate all search

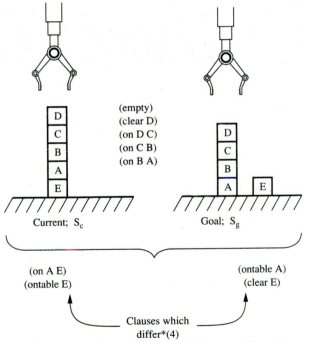

(empty)
(clear D)
(on D C)
(on C B)
(on B A)

Current; S_c Goal; S_g

(on A E)   (ontable A)
(ontable E)   (clear E)

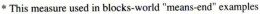

Clauses which differ*(4)

* This measure used in blocks-world "means-end" examples

FIGURE 14.18
The importance of choosing state difference measures carefully (see also Figure 14.7).

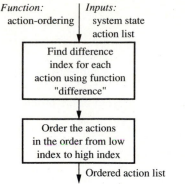

FIGURE 14.19
Function "action-ordering."

and proceed directly to the solution. Unfortunately, this is an easier problem to formulate than to solve. Figure 14.7 indicated a potential flaw in the selection of "obvious" heuristics. Figure 14.18 shows another example of a seemingly reasonable state evaluation function, namely a *state difference measure*, formed by counting the number of clauses that differ in S_c and S_g. As Fig. 14.18 shows, however, a small state difference measure is not necessarily a reliable indicator of state similarity or "closeness" to the goal. (The reader should verify this by considering the number of operators necessary to move from S_c to S_g in Fig. 14.18.)

Several possible alternatives to plan generation that avoid the pitfalls of the previous examples are

• Modify the planning heuristic to "look ahead" (more than one step).
• Develop a more global or "skeletal" plan.
• Backwards state propagation.

Forward State Propagation (Blocks-World) LISP Implementation Using Action Ordering (Means-End)

To circumvent the problem associated with the trial-and-error (GAT) based solution of example 14.6, we modify the LISP implementation such that *preferred actions* are chosen.

> **Example 14.7 Sample operation of the action ordering functions.** Due to the complexity of the LISP code in example 14.8, we take a brief look at the operation of the action ordering functions. Operation of function action−ordering is shown in Fig. 14.19. The following example demonstrates the ordering of actions in the blocks-world problem.
>
> ```
>  -> (load 'action_r.l)
> [load action_r.l]
> ```
>
> Initial State:
> (on A C) (ontable C) (ontable D) (ontable B) (clear D)
> (clear A) (clear B) (empty)

<u>Goal State</u>:
(on C D) (ontable D) (clear C) (clear A) (clear B)
(ontable A) (ontable B) (empty)

(THE FOLLOWING ARE OPERATORS WHICH ARE APPLICABLE:)
(takeoff A C) (pickup B) (pickup D)

(IF ACTION (takeoff A C) IS TAKEN)
(THE CURRENT STATE WILL BE:)
(hold A) (clear C) (ontable C) (ontable D) (ontable B)
         (clear D) (clear B)
(the difference index for this new state is 7)

(IF ACTION (pickup B) IS TAKEN)
(THE CURRENT STATE WILL BE:)
(hold B) (on A C) (ontable C) (ontable D) (clear D) (clear A)
(the difference index for this new state is 10)

(IF ACTION (pickup D) IS TAKEN)
(THE CURRENT STATE WILL BE:)
(hold D) (on A C) (ontable C) (ontable B) (clear A) (clear B)
(the difference index for this new state is 8)

(therefore, ordered operators)
(in order of min. difference indices, are:)
(takeoff A C)
(pickup D)
(pickup B)   (14-23)

Example 14.8 Forward state propagation ("blocks-world") LISP program listing (only modified functions shown).

```
; FILE NAME: plan_r3.l

; *********** Description *******

; this program does forward state propagation planning
; for a manipulator arm to move blocks.
; the state is represented by a list of clauses.
;   (on A C) means that block A is the top of block C.
;   (ontable C) means that block C is on the table.
;   (clear A) means that there is no block on the top of block A.
;   (empty) means that no block is being grasped by the arm.
;   (hold A) means that block A is being grasped by the arm.

; ********** Initial State ******

(setq *initial-state*   '((on A C)
                          (on B D)
                          (ontable C)
```

```
                                        (ontable D)
                                        (clear A)
                                        (clear B)
                                        (empty)))
```

```
;               **********  Goal State ******
```

```
(setq *goal-state*    '((on C D)
                        (ontable D)
                        (clear C)
                        (clear A)
                        (clear B)
                        (ontable A)
                        (ontable B)
                        (empty)))
```

```
;           **********  Operator Definitions ********
```

```
(setq *operations* '(
 (pickup (x)
    (precondition: (ontable x) (clear x) (empty))
    (added-facts: (hold x)))
 (putdown (x)
    (precondition: (hold x))
    (added-facts: (ontable x) (clear x) (empty)))
 (takeoff (x y)
    (precondition: (on x y) (clear x) (empty))
    (added-facts: (clear y) (hold x)))
 (puton (x y)
    (precondition: (clear y) (hold x))
    (added-facts: (on x y) (clear x) (empty)))))
```

```
;           **********  Operator Action as Function *****
```

```
; this function modifies the current state according to
; the operation definition
; INPUT: the action and the current state
; OUTPUT: the new state
```

```
(defun operator (action state)
 (add-new-facts action
                (delete-preconditions action state)))
```

```
;           ********** MAIN FUNCTIONS *******
```

```
; "examine" checks if "action" can be taken in "state".
; if it is true, finds the bindings for block names.
; INPUT: an operation definition and the current state.
```

```
; OUTPUT: action list containing all the possible bindings
;           when this action is applied to the current state.

(defun examine (action state)
 (do
  ;; LOCAL VARIABLES
  ((name (car action))                    ;action name
   (no-vars (length (cadr action)))  ;no of variables
   (act nil)                              ;action with bindings
   (pre1 (largest-vars                    ;precond with most vars
          (get-preconditions action)))
   (pres (delete (largest-vars (get-preconditions action))
                 (get-preconditions action)))
                             ; remainder of preconditions
   (fact1 nil)     ; fact in state with same name as pre1
   (result nil)    ; all possible bindings for action
   (x nil)         ; block name x
   (y nil)         ; block name y
   (tstate state)) ; temporary state
  ;; EXIT CONDITION
  ((null (assoc (car pre1) tstate)) result)
  ;; BODY
  (setq fact1 (assoc (car pre1) tstate))
  (cond
    ;; One variable action
    ((equal no-vars 1)
     (setq x (cadr fact1))
     (setq act (list name x)))
    ;; Two variable action
    ((equal no-vars 2)
     (cond
       ;; first block name in pre1 x
       ((equal (cadr pre1) 'x)
        (setq x (cadr fact1))
        (cond
          ;; two block vars in pre1
          ((equal (length pre1) 3)  (setq y (caddr fact1)))
          ;; one block var in pre1, get bindings for y
          ;; and change pre1 from (hold x)
          (t (setq pre1 (get-fact-with-var 'y pres))
             (setq pres (delete pre1 (get-preconditions
                                          action)))

            (gc)
            (setq fact1 (assoc (car pre1) tstate))
            (setq y (cadr fact1))
            (gc)))
       (setq act (list name x y)))
      ;; first block name in pre y
      ((equal (cadr pre1) 'y)
```

```
        (setq y (cadr fact1))
        (if (equal (length pre1) 3)
              ;; two block vars in pre1
              (setq x (caddr fact1))
              ;; one block var in pre1, get binding for x
              (setq x
                    (cadr (assoc (car (get-fact-with-var
                                            'x pres))
                                  tstate))))
          ;; action with variable bindings
          (setq act (list name x y)))
        (t (print '(error in variable name)))))
    (t (print '(error in number of variables to action))))
;; consistency check for variable bindings
(if (rest-prec-in-state x y pres tstate)
     (setq result (cons act result)))
(setq tstate (delete fact1 tstate))
(gc)))


; function:    largest-vars
; inputs:      clauses - list of clauses
; output:      clauses with most variables
; side effects: none

(defun largest-vars (clauses)
  (if (null (cdr clauses))
      (car clauses)
      (if
          (< (length (cdar clauses)) (length (cdadr
                                                clauses)))
          (largest-vars (cdr clauses))
          (largest-vars (cons (car clauses) (cddr
                                                clauses))))))


; function: get-fact-with-var
; input:    var - variable name
;           facts - list of clauses with variables
; output:   clause whose first variable argument has the
           same name
           as var, nil otherwise
; side effects: none

(defun get-fact-with-var (var facts)
(if (null facts)
     nil
    (if (equal (cadar facts) var)
        (car facts)
        (get-fact-with-var var (cdr facts)))))
```

```
; "possible-actions" finds all possible actions
; available to "state".
; INPUT: the current state
; OUTPUT: list containing all possible actions

(defun possible-actions (state)
 (do
  ((actions *operations* (cdr actions))
   (temp nil nil)
   (result nil))
  ((null actions) result)
  (cond
   ((setq temp (examine (car actions) state))
    (setq result (append temp result))))))
```

```
; "action-ordering" arranges the applicable operators in a
; preferred order.
; INPUT: the current state and the applicable operator list
; OUTPUT: the applicable operator list after ordering

(defun action-ordering (state actions)
 (do
  ((alist actions (cdr alist))
   (new-state nil)
   (index nil)
   (ilist nil)
   (result nil))
  ((null alist) result)
  (setq new-state (operator (car alist) state))
  (setq index (difference new-state *goal-state*))
  (do
   ((itemp1 ilist (cdr itemp1))
    (itemp2 nil)
    (atemp1 result (cdr atemp1))
    (atemp2 nil))
   ((null itemp1)
    (setq ilist (append1 ilist index))
    (setq result (append1 result (car alist))))
   (cond
    ((> index (car itemp1))
     (setq itemp2 (append1 itemp2 (car itemp1)))
     (setq atemp2 (append1 atemp2 (car atemp1))))
    (t
     (setq ilist (append itemp2 (cons index itemp1)))
     (setq result (append atemp2 (cons (car alist) atemp1)))
     (return))))))
```

```
; "planning" generates an action plan such that the goal
  state
```

```
; can be reached from the initial-state.
;  1) stops, if goal state is reached.
;  2) goes one step back if this state has been reached
;     before.
;  3) finds all possible actions.
;  4) takes one of actions, and goes back to 1.
; INPUT: the current state and the history
;        history = (((state n) (action list n)) ...
;                   ((state 2) (action list 2))
;                   ((state 1) (action list 1)))
; OUTPUT: none
; SIDE-EFFECT: result print-out

(defun planning (state history)
 (gc)
 (if (same state *goal-state*)
     (print-result state history)
     (let ((actions nil)
           (substate nil)
           (a1 nil))
       (cond
        ((cycle state history)
         (print-cycle)
         (do
          ((htemp history (cdr htemp)))
          ((cdr (get-actions htemp)) (setq history htemp)))
         (setq state (get-state history))
         (setq actions (cdr (get-actions history)))
         (setq history (cdr history))
         (print-state state)
         (terpri))
        (t
         (setq substate (diff2 state))
         (setq actions (possible-actions substate))
         (setq actions (action-ordering state actions))
         (cond
          ((null actions)
           (setq actions (possible-actions state))
           (setq actions (action-ordering state actions))))
         (print-actions actions)))
       (setq history (cons (list state actions) history))
       (setq a1 (car actions))
       (setq state (take-action a1 state))
       (planning state history))))

;         ********** AUXILIARY FUNCTIONS *******

; "get-preconditions" gets the preconditions for "action"

(defun get-preconditions (action)
 (cdr (nth 2 action)))
```

```
; "get-added-facts" gets the added-facts for "action"

(defun get-added-facts (action)
  (cdr (nth 3 action)))


; "delete-preconditions" deletes all preconditions from
; the current state
; INPUT: action and the current state
; OUTPUT: new state

(defun delete-preconditions (action state)
  (do
    ((facts (get-preconditions (assoc (car action)
                                      *operations*)) (cdr facts))
     (temp state)
     (x (nth 1 action))
     (y (nth 2 action))
     (predicate nil))
    ((null facts) temp)
    (cond
      ((equal (length (car facts)) 1)
       (setq predicate (car facts)))
      ((equal (length (car facts)) 2)
       (if (equal (nth 1 (car facts)) 'x)
           (setq predicate (list (caar facts) x))
           (setq predicate (list (caar facts) y))))
      (t
       (setq predicate (list (caar facts) x y))))
    (setq temp (delete predicate temp))))


; "add-new-facts" adds all added-facts to
; the current state
; INPUT: action and the current state
; OUTPUT: new state

(defun add-new-facts (action state)
  (do
    ((facts (get-added-facts (assoc (car action)
                                    *operations*)) (cdr facts))
     (temp state)
     (x (nth 1 action))
     (y (nth 2 action))
     (predicate nil))
    ((null facts) temp)
    (cond
      ((equal (length (car facts)) 1)
       (setq predicate (car facts)))
```

```
        ((equal (length (car facts)) 2)
         (if (equal (nth 1 (car facts)) 'x)
             (setq predicate (list (caar facts) x))
             (setq predicate (list (caar facts) y))))
      (t
         (setq predicate (list (caar facts) x y))))
    (setq temp (cons predicate temp))))
```

```
; "rest-prec-in-state" checks remaining predicates to
; see if they are in the current state
; INPUT: the variable bindings, the precondition list
;         and the current state
; OUTPUT: t if all the preconditions are in the state,
;          otherwise nil.
```

```
(defun rest-prec-in-state (x y preconditions state)
  (do
    ((facts preconditions (cdr facts))
     (predicate nil))
    ((null facts) t)
    (cond
      ((equal (length (car facts)) 1)
       (setq predicate (car facts)))
      ((equal (length (car facts)) 2)
       (if (equal (nth 1 (car facts)) 'x)
           (setq predicate (list (caar facts) x))
           (setq predicate (list (caar facts) y))))
      (t
       (setq predicate (list (caar facts) x y))))
    (if (not (member predicate state)) (return nil))))
```

```
; "diff1" gives the number of predicates which are
; not in the other state
; INPUT: two states
; OUTPUT: the number
```

```
(defun diff1 (state1 state2)
  (do
    ((index 0)
     (temp state1 (cdr temp)))
    ((null temp) index)
    (if (not (member (car temp) state2))
        (setq index (+ index 1)))))
```

```
; "difference" gives difference index of two states
; INPUT: two states
; OUTPUT: the difference index
```

```
(defun difference (state1 state2)
 (+ (diff1 state1 state2) (diff1 state2 state1)))


; "contained" checks if list "s1" is contained in "s2".

(defun contained (s1 s2)
 (do
  ((t1 s1 (cdr t1)))
  ((null t1) t)
  (if (not (member (car t1) s2)) (return nil))))


; "same" return t if two states are same, otherwise nil.

(defun same (s1 s2)
 (and (contained s1 s2)
      (contained s2 s1)))

; "diff2" finds a subset of clauses which are not included
; in goal state
; INPUT: state
; OUTPUT: subset

(defun diff2 (state)
 (cond
  ((null state) nil)
  ((and (member (caar state) '(on ontable hold))
        (member (car state) *goal-state*))
   (diff2 (cdr state)))
  (t
   (cons (car state) (diff2 (cdr state))))))          (14-24)
```

Example 14.9 Results using LISP implementation of forward state propagation blocks-world planner.

```
LISP session for plan_r3.l - Planning via
 Forward State Propagation
-> (load 'plan_r3.l)
[load plan_r3.l]
```

(a) S_i and S_g

```
(Initial State)
(on A C)
(on B D)
(ontable C)
```

```
(ontable D)
(clear A)
(clear B)
(empty)

(Goal State)
(on C D)
(ontable D)
(clear C)
(clear A)
(clear B)
(ontable A)
(ontable B)
(empty)
```

(*b*) Resulting Plan

```
(Forward State Propagation)

(THE POSSIBLE ACTIONS ARE)
(takeoff A C)
(takeoff B D)

(ACTION (takeoff A C) IS TAKEN)
(THE CURRENT STATE IS)
(hold A)  (clear C)  (on B D)  (ontable C)  (ontable D)
          (clear B)

(THE POSSIBLE ACTIONS ARE)
(putdown A)
(puton A C)
(puton A B)

(ACTION (putdown A) IS TAKEN)
(THE CURRENT STATE IS)
(empty)  (clear A)  (ontable A)  (clear C)  (on B D)
          (ontable C)  (ontable D)  (clear B)

(THE POSSIBLE ACTIONS ARE)
(pickup C)
(takeoff B D)

(ACTION (pickup C) IS TAKEN)
(THE CURRENT STATE IS)
(hold C)  (clear A)  (ontable A)  (on B D)  (ontable D)
          (clear B)

(THE POSSIBLE ACTIONS ARE)
(putdown C)
(puton C A)
(puton C B)
```

(ACTION (putdown C) IS TAKEN)
(THE CURRENT STATE IS)
(empty) (clear C) (ontable C) (clear A) (ontable A)
         (on B D) (ontable D) (clear B)

(THIS STATE HAS BEEN REACHED BEFORE)
(GO BACK TO PREVIOUS STATE AND TAKE ANOTHER ACTION)
(THE CURRENT STATE IS)
(hold C) (clear A) (ontable A) (on B D) (ontable D)
         (clear B)

(ACTION (puton C A) IS TAKEN)
(THE CURRENT STATE IS)
(empty) (clear C) (on C A) (ontable A) (on B D) (ontable D)
         (clear B)

(THE POSSIBLE ACTIONS ARE)
(takeoff C A)
(takeoff B D)

(ACTION (takeoff C A) IS TAKEN)
(THE CURRENT STATE IS)
(hold C) (clear A) (ontable A) (on B D) (ontable D) (clear B)

(THIS STATE HAS BEEN REACHED BEFORE)
(GO BACK TO PREVIOUS STATE AND TAKE ANOTHER ACTION)
(THE CURRENT STATE IS)
(empty) (clear C) (on C A) (ontable A) (on B D) (ontable D)
         (clear B)

(ACTION (takeoff B D) IS TAKEN)
(THE CURRENT STATE IS)
(hold B) (clear D) (clear C) (on C A) (ontable A) (ontable D)

(THE POSSIBLE ACTIONS ARE)
(putdown B)
(puton B D)
(puton B C)

(ACTION (putdown B) IS TAKEN)
(THE CURRENT STATE IS)
(empty) (clear B) (ontable B) (clear D) (clear C) (on C A)
         (ontable A) (ontable D)

(THE POSSIBLE ACTIONS ARE)
(takeoff C A)

(ACTION (takeoff C A) IS TAKEN)
(THE CURRENT STATE IS)
(hold C) (clear A) (clear B) (ontable B) (clear D) (ontable A)
         (ontable D)

```
(THE POSSIBLE ACTIONS ARE)
(puton C D)
(putdown C)
(puton C A)
(puton C B)

(ACTION (puton C D) IS TAKEN)
(THE CURRENT STATE IS)
(empty) (clear C) (on C D) (clear A) (clear B) (ontable B)
        (ontable A) (ontable D)

(GOAL STATE IS REACHED)
(THE ACTION LIST)
(takeoff A C)
(putdown A)
(pickup C)
(puton C A)
(takeoff B D)
(putdown B)
(takeoff C A)
(puton C D)
```
(14-25)

LISP Implementation of Backward
State Propagation

Example 14.10   Program modifications to use forward chaining LISP program for backward chaining. For illustration and simplicity, we do not develop a completely new LISP program to implement backward chaining. Instead, we show modifications of the forward state propagation program in example 14.6 to accomplish backward state propagation. Initial and goal state specification is unchanged. The modification, as the reader should verify, involves the following revisions of the corresponding LISP functions. The revised functions are shown following the description of the revision.

1. Operator definitions are unchanged.
2. Function action-ordering is revised such that the current state is compared with the *initial state* to form a difference measure:

```
; "action-ordering" arranges the applicable operators in a
; preferred order.
; INPUT: the current state and the applicable operator list
; OUTPUT: the applicable operator list after ordering

(defun action-ordering (state actions)
  (do
    ((alist actions (cdr alist))
     (new-state nil)
     (index nil)
     (ilist nil)
     (result nil)
```

```
((null alist) result)
(setq new-state (operator (car alist) state))
(setq index (difference new-state *initial-state*))
 ; Modified
(do
 ((itemp1 ilist (cdr itemp1))
  (itemp2 nil)
  (atemp1 result (cdr atemp1))
  (atemp2 nil))
 ((null itemp1)
  (setq ilist (append1 ilist index))
  (setq result (append1 result (car alist))))
 (cond
  ((> index (car itemp1))
   (setq itemp2 (append1 itemp2 (car itemp1)))
   (setq atemp2 (append1 atemp2 (car atemp1))))
  (t
   (setq ilist (append itemp2 (cons index itemp1)))
   (setq result (append atemp2 (cons (car alist) atemp1)))
   (return))))))
```

3. Function p l ann i ng is revised such that the system checks to see if the initial state
(LISP variable ∗i n i t i a l−s t a t e∗), rather than the goal state, has been reached.

```
(defun planning (state history)
 (gc)
 (if (same state *initial-state*)   ; Modified
              .
              .
              .
```

4. Auxiliary functions ge t precond i t i ons and ge t added f ac t s are modified
(the precond i t i ons and added−f ac t s parts are interchanged) to "reverse" the
effect of an operator application. Thus,

```
; "get-preconditions" gets the preconditions for "action"
(defun get-preconditions (action)
  (cdr (nth 3 action)))   ; Modified
```

```
; "get-added-facts" gets the added-facts for "action"

(defun get-added-facts (action)
  (cdr (nth 2 action)))   ; Modified
```

5. Functions p r i n t−r e su l t, p r i n t−cyc l e, and p r i n t−ac t i ons are modified
via

```
; "print-result" prints results after goal state is
    reached.
```

```
(defun print-result (state history)
 (print '(INITIAL STATE IS REACHED))   ; Modified
 (terpri)
 (print '(THE ACTION LIST))
 (terpri)
 (do
  ((ts history (cdr ts))
   (ts1 nil))
  ((null ts) (print-state ts1))
  (setq ts1 (cons (caadar ts) ts1)))
 (terpri))


; "print-cycle" print cycle message

(defun print-cycle ()
 (print '(THIS STATE HAS BEEN REACHED BEFORE))
 (terpri)
 (print '(GO BACK TO NEXT STATE AND TAKE ANOTHER ACTION))
 (terpri)
 (print '(THE CURRENT STATE IS))
 (terpri))

; "print-actions" prints actions

(defun print-actions (actions)
 (print '(THE POSSIBLE ACTIONS TO REACH THE STATE ARE))
 (terpri)
 (print-state actions)
 (terpri))
```

6. Action-ordering auxiliary function d i f f 2 is modified as shown:

```
; "diff2" finds a subset of clauses which are not included
; in goal state
; INPUT: state
; OUTPUT: subset

(defun diff2 (state)
 (cond
  ((null state) nil)
  ((and (member (caar state) '(on ontable hold))
        (member (car state) *initial-state*))   ; Modified
   (diff2 (cdr state)))
  (t
   (cons (car state) (diff2 (cdr state))))))
```

7. Finally, the example is started with the following LISP function evaluations:

```
(print '(Initial State))
(terpri)
(print-state *initial-state*)
(terpri)
(print '(Goal State))
(terpri)
(print-state *goal-state*)
(terpri)
(terpri)
(print '(Backward State Propagation))
(terpri)
(terpri)
(planning *goal-state* nil)   ; Modified                    (14-26a)
```

Example 14.11   Sample results using LISP implementation for backward state propagation.

```
LISP Session for plan_r3a.l - Planning via Backward State
Propagation


-> (load 'plan_r3a.l)
[load plan_r3a.l]
```

(*a*) S_i and S_g

```
(Initial State)
(on A C)
(on B D)
(ontable C)
(ontable D)
(clear A)
(clear B)
(empty)

(Goal State)
(on C D)
(ontable D)
(clear C)
(clear A)
(clear B)
(ontable A)
(ontable B)
(empty)
```

(*b*) Backward State Propagation Example

```
(THE POSSIBLE ACTIONS TO REACH THE STATE ARE)
(puton C D)
(putdown A)
(putdown B)
```

```
(ACTION (puton C D) IS TAKEN)
(THE CURRENT STATE IS)
(hold C) (clear D) (ontable D) (clear A) (clear B)
        (ontable A) (ontable B)

(THE POSSIBLE ACTIONS TO REACH THE STATE ARE)
(pickup C)
(takeoff C D)
(takeoff C A)
(takeoff C B)

(ACTION (pickup C) IS TAKEN)
(THE CURRENT STATE IS)
(empty) (clear C) (ontable C) (clear D) (ontable D) (clear A)
        (clear B) (ontable A) (ontable B)

(THE POSSIBLE ACTIONS TO REACH THE STATE ARE)
(putdown A)
(putdown B)

(ACTION (putdown A) IS TAKEN)
(THE CURRENT STATE IS)
(hold A) (clear C) (ontable C) (clear D) (ontable D)
        (clear B)
(ontable B)

(THE POSSIBLE ACTIONS TO REACH THE STATE ARE)
(takeoff A C)
(takeoff A D)
(pickup A)
(takeoff A B)

(ACTION (takeoff A C) IS TAKEN)
(THE CURRENT STATE IS)
(empty) (clear A) (on A C) (ontable C) (clear D) (ontable D)
        (clear B) (ontable B)

(THE POSSIBLE ACTIONS TO REACH THE STATE ARE)
(putdown B)

        (ACTION (putdown B) IS TAKEN)
(THE CURRENT STATE IS)
(hold B) (clear A) (on A C) (ontable C) (clear D)
        (ontable D)

(THE POSSIBLE ACTIONS TO REACH THE STATE ARE)
(takeoff B D)
(pickup B)
(takeoff B A)
```

```
(ACTION (takeoff B D) IS TAKEN)
(THE CURRENT STATE IS)
(empty) (clear B) (on B D) (clear A) (on A C) (ontable C)
        (ontable D)

(INITIAL STATE IS REACHED)
(THE ACTION LIST)
(puton C D)
(pickup C)
(putdown A)
(takeoff A C)
(putdown B)
(takeoff B D)
```
(14-26*b*)

The reader should note that the backward state propagation solution sequence differs from that of example 14.8.

PLANNING EXTENSIONS

Hierarchical Planning and Macro-Operators (Considering More Than One State Change)

A topic related to plan recollection is the development and use of multistep or multistate change operators. Two avenues are possible:

1. Recollection of the sequence of single step operators, combined into a composite operator. Reverse(A,B) is an example.
2. Decomposition of the goal state into a succession of (possibly abstract [Sacerdoti 1974]) subgoal states, and generation of subplans to move the system state through these subgoal states.

> Hierarchical planning reduces the search complexity by committing the planner to *sequences* of tentative actions. These sequences of actions are referred to as subplans or macro-operators and may be stored in triangle tables. This strategy facilitates *replanning*.
> (14-27)

Planning in a Changing Environment

Often, plans are generated with the assumption of a static environment, the assumption that the only changes to the system state are due to the application of operators (which we control). Unfortunately, this is often not the case, in the sense that the system state is dynamic (changing with time even without application of chosen operators), and therefore a plan may need to account for changes in assumed system states. The previous two approaches may offer some help in these types of problems. The reader is directed to the problems where this topic is continued.

FROM BLOCKS-WORLD TO REAL PROBLEMS. Blocks-world examples use simplified problem domains, a number of (simplifying) assumptions, and precisely defined ideal situations. While they are useful in introducing planning concepts, they do not provide good examples of real-world (common sense) problems [Brown 1987]. This, as mentioned in Chapter 1, is due to representational issues and the *frame problem*, among other difficulties. In addition, recall that planning problems typify AI difficulties in that *non-deterministic* (Chapter 11) algorithms result. Thus, it is quite easy to specify operators, S_i and S_g for which no plan exists. A related problem is that of *unreachable states*, as shown in Fig. 14.20. This is considered more formally in Chapter 15 when we consider the ubiquitous problem of search.

CHECKING FOR "IMPOSSIBLE" GOAL STATES. The identification of impossible (i.e., unachievable) goals (and subgoals) is critical to the practical success of a planner. Impossible subgoals include those which are (*a*) unreachable (a path does not exist) or (b) contradictory (e.g., conflicting). As mentioned above, it is desirable to check for impossible subgoals in order to avoid wasting computational resources (in the search process).

PLAN GENERATION DIRECTION. Recall in our consideration of rule-based inference that, given a specific problem, the proper choice of direction of rule selection (forward vs. backward chaining) may lead to more efficient solution procedures. An analogous remark may be made for planning direction. In some cases it is preferable to plan forward from S_i, whereas other problems are best solved by the propagation of states backward from S_g. As in rule-based inference, "hybrid" FSP and BSP strategies are also possible.

Simultaneous Application of Operators and Parallel Planning

POTENTIAL DIFFICULTIES. An interesting extension to our previous planning algorithms is to consider the generation of plans where operators may be applied simul-

(*a*)

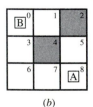

(*b*)

FIGURE 14.20
Example of an unreachable state ("checkerboard" problem). (*a*) Initial state, S_i; (*b*) unreachable state, S_u.

taneously, that is, in parallel. Often this is referred to as multi-agent or parallel planning. We explore this concept using the checkerboard example and the four operators (move−up x), (move−down x), (move−right x) and (move−left−x) where x is a variable representing the name of a specific block. For example, we could, attempt simultaneous application of operators (move−right x) (move−left x) where x takes on the values A or B. This is shown in Fig. 14.21. The difficulty, which arises initially on an intuitive level, is that certain parallel combinations of operators yield illegal states, as shown in Fig. 14.21. Note this is due to representation of the effect of each operator independently.

One of the obvious objectives of multi-operator planning is the generation of plans "superior" to those that invoke only a single action at each step. Measures of "superior" might include fewer overall steps from the initial state to the goal state. This is explored in the problems.

EXTENDING OPERATOR REPRESENTATIONS TO MULTI-AGENTS OR PARALLEL ACTIONS. To avoid the multi-operator difficulty shown in Fig. 14.21, we return to fundamental considerations in operator representation. As shown in (14-9), an operator may be formally characterized as a relation on the system state. For example, in the system state space shown for the two-block case of Fig. 14.22, consider specification of the operator move−right−A. In specifying the system state in the relation, the shorthand (A O) is used to signify that block A is at grid (single operator) location O.

Example 14.12 Characterization of move−right−A.

(move−right−A) =

$$\{((A4,\ B8),\ (A5,\ B8)),\ ((A4,\ B2),\ (A5,\ B2))\} \tag{14-28}$$

Similarly, consider the representation of move−down−B.

(a)

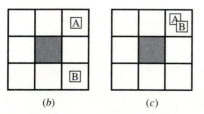

(b)   (c)

FIGURE 14.21
Example of multi-operator (simultaneous) planning difficulties. (a) Current state; (b) allowable next state: (move-right A) and (move-down B) applied simultaneously; (c) illegal next state: attempt to apply (move-right A) and (move-up B) simultaneously.

Example 14.13   move−down−B **(Single Operator).**

(move−down−B) =

{((A8, B2), (A8, B5)), ((A2, B5), (A2, B8)),

((A4, B5), (A4, B8)), (A4, B2), (A4, B5))}   (14-29)

Note in both examples 14.12 and 14.13, the location of the block *not* moved is considered persistent. In multi-operator cases, this is not necessarily true.
Consider a generalization of example 14.13 as follows:

Example 14.14   Parallel Representation of (move−right−A).

(move−right−A)p =
{
((A4, B8), (A5, B8))   ; same as before B stationary
((A4, B5), (A5, B8))   ; parallel with (m−d−B)
((A4, B5), (A5, B2))   ; parallel with (m−u−B)
((A4, B2), (A5, B2))}   ; same as before   (14-30)

Example 14.15   Parallel Representation of (move−down−B).

(move−down−B)p =

{((A4, B5), (A4, B8))   ; same as before
((A4, B5), (A5, B8))   ; parallel with (m−r−A)
((A4, B2), (A4, B5))   ; same as before
((A5, B2), (A8, B5))   ; parallel with (m−d−A)
((A8, B2), (A8, B5))   ; same as before
((A2, B5), (A2, B8))   ; same as before
((A2, B5), (A5, B8)   ; parallel with (m−d−A)
((A5, B2), (A4, B5))}   ; parallel with (m−l A)   (14-31)

Example 14.16   Extended Representation for (move−right−A) (move−down−B).
Referring to Fig. 14.22, consider the possiblity of simultaneous application of the operators (move−right−A) and (move−down−B), designated with a " | ":

(move−right−A)   (move−down−B) = {((A4, B5), (A5, B8))}
                                                                (14-32)

In this representation we assume *both* operators were applied. The result of (14-32) may be achieved by locating states wherein parallel operator application does not yield succeeding states that are illegal. It is significant that

(move−right−A)   (move−down−B) = (move−right−A)p ∩ (move−down−B)p
                                                                (14-33)

Thus, a more structured approach is to form the extended representations in (14-30)

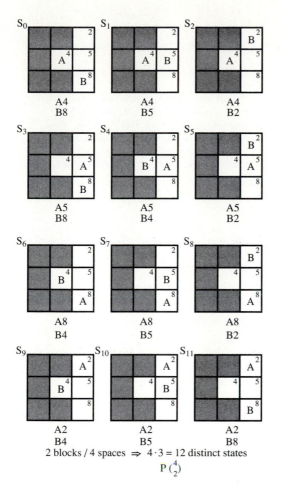

2 blocks / 4 spaces $\Rightarrow$ 4·3 = 12 distinct states

$$P \binom{4}{2}$$

FIGURE 14.22

Problem–State space for parallel actions.

and (14-31), and use the *intersection* of these relations (denoted as sets) to form the parallel operator representation.

In developing representations (move−right A)p, (move−up B)p, and soon, as relations in set form, we included state mappings (elements) which were not included in the single-operator representations. For example, ((A2, B5), (A2, B8)) appears in (move−down B), whereas new mappings

$$((A5, B2), (A4, B5)) \tag{14-34a}$$

and

$$((A2, B5), (A5, B8)) \tag{14-34b}$$

occur in (move−down B)p.

Other examples of multi-operator planning and its consequences are considered in the problems.

REFERENCES

[Brown 1987] Brown, F.M. (ed), *The Frame Problem in Artificial Intelligence*, Morgan Kaufmann Publishing, Los Altos, California, 1987.

[Davis/McDermott 1984] Davis, E., and D. McDermott, "Planning Routes through Uncertain Territory," *Artificial Intelligence*, Vol. 22, 1984, pp. 107–156.

[Fikes/Nilsson 1971] Fikes, R.E., and N.J. Nilsson, "STRIPS: A New Approach to the Application of Theorem Proving to Problem Solving," *Artificial Intelligence*, Vol. 2, 1971, pp. 189–208.

[Nilsson 1980] Nilsson, N.J., *Principles of Artificial Intelligence*, Tioga Publ. Palo Alto, CA, 1980.

[Sacerdoti 1974] Sacerdoti, E.D., "Planning in a Hierarchy of Abstraction Spaces," *Artificial Intelligence*, Vol. 5, 1974, pp. 115–135.

[Sharai/Tsujii 1984] Sharai, Y., and J. Tsujii, *Artificial Intelligence: Concepts, Techniques and Applications*, John Wiley, NY, 1984.

PROBLEMS

14.1. Complete planning example initiated in the text (and Fig. 14.12). Show a graphical description of the results by showing the succession of system states (i.e., draw the blocks and the manipulator arm) that comprise the plan.

14.2. (*a*) Redo the derivation of a blocks-world plan using backward state propagation for the following two cases:

    (i) The initial state remains unchanged, however the goal state must include

```
(ontable A)
(on B A)
(on C B)
(on D C)
(clear D)
(empty)
```

    (ii) The initial state is the state in (i); the goal state is unchanged.

  (*b*) Redo the derivation of a plan using backward state propagation with the addition of the following hierarchical or composite operator:

```
operator   :      (reverse A B)

action :          reverses the stacking of blocks A and B

preconditions : (ontable B), (on A B), (clear A), empty

add−facts :       (ontable A), (on B A), (clear B), empty

delete−facts:     (ontable B), (on A B), (clear A)
```

  (*c*) Develop complete specifications (i.e., preconditions, add−facts, etc.) in the form of part 2(*b*) for the following hierarchical operators:

```
 (i) operator:       (make_clear_on_table  x)

    action :         causes block x to be clear and on
                     table
```

(ii) operator: (stack_x_on_y_on_table   x   y)

     action :   stack block x on block y, which
            resides on table

    (*d*) Show how each of the operators in 2(*c*) could be constructed from the primitive operators in example 14.2.

14.3. Could a plan based upon the use of hierarchical or composite operators, such as in problem 14.2, lead to results where the resulting plan is less efficient (e.g., requires more steps) than one using simple, one step operators? Show your results with several examples.

14.4. Develop, and implement in LISP, a revised solution to the blocks-world planning problem with the addition of two independent manipulator arms. Specifically

    (*a*) Develop specifications for the new or revised operators, for example, (hold_1 x) and (hold_2 x), corresponding to arms 1 and 2. Notice you must develop or modify the problem constraints so, for example, (hold_1 A) and (hold_2 A) do not simultaneously occur.

    (*b*) Discuss and implement a parallel operator application strategy that will allow solution of the planning problems in problems 14.1 and 14.2(*a*). Specifically, you should attempt to solve the problem such that a minimal number of steps is required.

14.5. Suggest other ways for operator conflict resolution, that is, reasonable or intuitively appealing approaches for the selection of a O_i. Consider both FSP and BSP.

14.6. Show the complete triangle table for the plan in example 14.6.

14.7. In the hand-worked blocks-world planning example using BSP (Fig. 14.12), it was suggested that (puton x y) was applicable. Redo the solution with this choice of operator.

14.8. Given a dynamic system environment (i.e., one in which the system state changes randomly without operator application, perhaps due to other (uncontrollable) inputs),

    (*a*) Discuss planning alternatives using means-end versus generate-and-test, Be sure to indicate your assumptions. Is one approach preferable?

    (*b*) Show how a triangle table for a "similar" plan could be useful in generation of a new plan.

    (*c*) Suppose that we have some indication of likely changes in the system state (e.g., "turbine 4 is scheduled for maintenance soon"). How could the planning algorithm be modified to accommodate this information?

14.9. Given arbitrary initial and goal states, S_i and S_g, and two different planning strategies, namely,

Strategy a: uses a set of simple, one step operators.

Strategy b: uses a set of composite or hierarchical operators, composed of those in strategy a.

    (*a*) If a plan exists for strategy a, does one necessarily exist for strategy b?
    (*b*) If a plan exists for strategy b, does one necessarily exist for strategy a?
Show simple examples to verify your answers.

14.10. (*a*) Show, with as much detail as possible, why the union of the substates in the bottom row of the triangle table must be the goal state.
    (*b*) Is it possible to tell if a plan contains a cycle by examination of the triangle table?

14.11. Extend the triangle table concept to the case of problem 14.4 where there are two operators that may be applied simultaneously. Show an example of your extension.

14.12. Our derivation of a plan generator was based upon a strict observation of pre- and post-operator application system states. Notice that the complexity of the planners (e.g., examples 14.5–14.7) is considerably greater than that of the resulting plans. In this problem we consider the development of a planning methodology that is quite random. (This type of algorithm, might, for example, emulate the observed behavior of an infant.) Develop a LISP program that uses FSP and "randomly" selects applicable operators. The plan succeeds, (if one exists), when the goal state is "randomly" reached. (Note: this problem could be combined with problem 14.2(*b*) to develop and employ randomly-generated macro-operators. This makes an interesting long-term project.)

14.13. Discuss the feasibility of a hybrid planning approach that incorporates *both* means-end and FSP and BSP. The means-end approach plans forward from S_i, while the BSP algorithm plans backward from S_g. After each operator selection (or after some number of operator choices), the system states resulting (or required) are compared.

14.14. Derive and implement ways to determine if the planning algorithm is generating a *cycle*. In the case a cycle is identified, discuss several means to modify the plan generation. What information must be recorded in order to detect cycles? Should we simply modify our choice of the previous operator, or should a "cycle undoing function" backtrack several steps? Show examples of both strategies.

14.15. Show the triangle table with variables propagated backwards for the blocks-world example. Prove:
(*a*) The summation of clauses in any row is a system state.
(*b*) Partial plans are described.

14.16. Extend the problem of example 14.5 to that of more global operators (which could be composite), for example, operator (move−right−2 A) moves block A two units or locations to the right and is equivalent to (move−right A) followed by (move−right A). Develop a set of operators (including preconditions) and show the results using the initial and goal states of example 14.5.

14.17. For the planning problem of example 14.5, with the given initial and goal states, show the problem search space.

14.18. Extend the planning implementations shown to include auxiliary functions that form and display the triangle table for a completed plan. (Note: This solution is likely to be affected by the display capabilities of a specific LISP implementation.)

14.19. In our STRIPS-based representation of operators, will it always be the case that the preconditions to an operator will be identical to the delete−facts? Cite examples to justify your answer.

14.20. Discuss specific problem situations where the efficiency of plan generation is strongly influenced by choice of planning direction, that is, choice of either forward or backward state propagation is preferable.

14.21. Revise the blocks-world problem to include the following:
(*a*) The inclusion of position (horizontal) constraints. The concept of a table is expanded to mean a 2-D space that is partitioned into quadrants. A quadrant may only contain one block on its surface and blocks may still be stacked. A quadrant may also contain an obstacle indicating that no block may be placed in this quadrant and no block may be stacked on the obstacle.
(*b*) The inclusion of horizontal movement operators. Operators must be defined that will move the blocks to an adjacent grid position. If the grid is addressed by the four directions on a compass, then the operations move_north, move_south, move_east, and move_west must be defined.

14.22. Referring to Fig. 14.17
(*a*) Develop a suitable representation for the system state and operators. Assume the availability of operators:

(move−up   ?block?)

```
(move-down     ?block?)
(move-right    ?block?)
(move-left     ?block?)
```

(b) Develop a plan using means-end analysis and forward state propagation. Derive and state suitable heuristic(s) for operator selection. Assume a single operator may be applied at any step. Show each step of the plan generation, applicable operators, and the system state in the chosen representation (clause form).

(c) Repeat part (b) for the case of backward state propagation.

14.23. Figure P14.23 illustrates a situation where a state-difference measure for MEA based upon vector differences (shown in Fig. 14.7) would be counterproductive.

(a) Develop two operator selection heuristics that yield reasonable (productive) operator selections.

(b) Show your resulting plans, using FSP, based upon the heuristics in (a).

(c) Compare the efficiency of plans generated using the heuristics in (a) with those based upon the vector difference heuristic (Fig. 14.7) when there are no blocked locations.

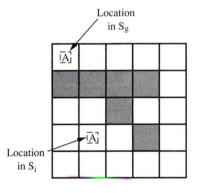

Location in S_g

Location in S_i

FIGURE P14.23
Situation where heuristics for MEA-based operator selection must be carefully chosen.

14.24. Show a triangle table for the plan generated by problem 14.22.

14.25. It was stated in the text that cycles serve no useful purpose. Can you think of examples where cycles may be advantageous?

14.26. (This makes an excellent project.) Path planning, in its most general form, is a form of planning that involves choosing how to move objects in 2- or 3-D without collisions. The scenario consists of an area containing obstacles, an object to be moved, and the specified goal location of that object. A typical case is that of navigation planning for mobile robots. The shortest possible path is usually desired, with the additional constraint that a path should be acyclic. For the situation shown in Fig. P14.26, develop a representation and show a path-planning method. Suggest heuristics that limit the search process.

14.27. (Parallel operator representation and plan generation.) The representation of the combined state effects of two operators applied in parallel is a challenging problem.

(a) Using the STRIPS representation, assume the current state satisfies the *union* of the preconditions of two operators we wish to apply in parallel. Show via example why the straightforward modification of the system state using the union of the add and delete lists for each of the parallel operators is an invalid representation strategy.

(b) Consider the following variant on the procedure in (a) — if the *intersection* of the preconditions of two operators is the empty set, may these operators be applied in parallel without causing conflicts in the system state?

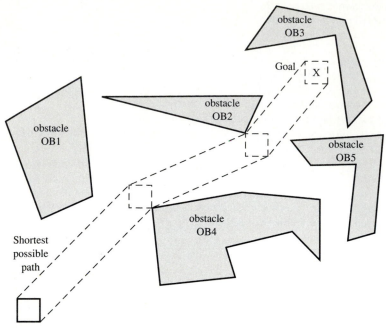

Initial position of footprint

FIGURE P14.26
Extended path-planning example.

14.28. Revise the LISP implementation of the forward state propagation-based "checkerboard" for backward state propagation, in a manner similar to that of blocks-world example 14.9.

14.29. Develop a LISP program that uses BSP and "randomly" selects operators. The plan succeeds (if one exists) when the goal state is "randomly" reached.

14.30. Do the programs in examples 14.5-14.7 check for interacting subgoals? If so, indicate which functions accomplish this. If not, suggest an efficient method(s) to incorporate this feature.

14.31. Repeat the plan derivation for the blocks-world problem of example 14.3 using FSP.

14.32. Repeat the plan derivation for the checkerboard problem of
(*a*) Figure 14.1*a*
(*b*) Figure 14.17 (Example 14.5)
using BSP and
(*c*) no variables, that is, committing the use of an operator to a specific block as early as possible.
(*d*) using variables in (conditional) operator application and back propagation of constraints on these variables.

14.33. Derive and justify several strategies for "breaking" cycles. Show their respective effect using several examples.

14.34. Referring to the system whose state space is shown in Fig. 14.22, in a manner similar to that of (14-30) through (14-33), derive relational characterizations of
(*a*) (move−left A)
(*b*) (move−up B)

(c) (move−left A)p

(d) (move−up B)p

(e) (move−left A)|(move−up B)

14.35. For the problem shown in Fig. P14.35, develop an operator representation following (14-28) through (14-32) and show

(a) a plan based on only a single operator applied at each step.

(b) a plan based on the parallel application of two operators, where possible, at each step.

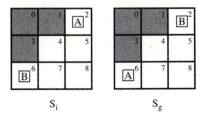

S_i S_g **FIGURE P14.35**

14.36. How could the (parallel) multi-operator formulation of (14-28) through (14-33) be extended to cases of three or more simultaneous operators? Show an example using the checkerboard problem of Fig. P14.35 with blocks A, B and C.

14.37. (How) does the formulation of (14-28) — (14-33) eliminate attempted application of multiple operations on a single block, that is, (move−right−A)|(move−up−A)?

14.38. (a) Using the state descriptions shown below each state in Fig. 14.22, develop a graphical representation of the relation represented by each of the four operators.

(b) Revise the results of (a) for multi-operator actions.

14.39. The skeletal and incomplete derivation of a plan, using the STRIPS representation and the blocks-world operators is shown in Fig. P14.39. The plan contains no cycles. Fill in responses 1-7. Be sure to be complete and specific.

14.40. This problem extends our look at the complexity of parallel planning. The state space for a checkerboard problem with two blocks (labeled A and B) and "blocked" locations (shown crosshatched) is shown in Fig. 14.22. Notice the problem space is not only finite; it is quite manageable. Each cell (location) is numbered. Each state, S_i, is specified by the locations of blocks A and B, that is, S_0 = (A4, B8). Consider the four possible operators

(move−left   ?a−block)

(move−right   ?a−block)

(move−up   ?a−block)

(move−down   ?a−block)

where ?a−block is either A or B. Blocks cannot move into "blocked" locations or into locations containing other blocks.

(a) Develop a STRIPS representation for this problem. Why is this representation more complicated than the blocks-world case?

(b) Instead of (a), consider representing each of the four operators as a *relation* on the system state. Enumerate each of the four relations (i) as a set mapping and (ii) graphically.

(c) Given four operators, what is the number of possible parallel operations? Enumerate them.

(d) Show (by example) that we cannot arbitrarily apply any of the parallel operators in (c) to the system in any S_i and achieve a valid resulting state, even if the

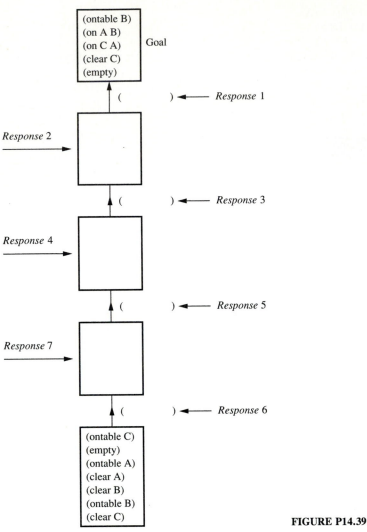

FIGURE P14.39

individual operators are valid (i.e., either operator applied alone produces a valid state mapping).

(e) Of the 120 possible parallel operator-state combinations, how many are valid? Is this to be expected? Why? Enumerate them graphically.

14.41. (This is an extension of problem 40.)

(a) For $S_i = S_0$ and $S_g = S_6$ in Fig. 14.22, use forward state propagation to derive a plan

    (i) using only serial operators.

    (ii) using parallel operators, where possible.

    Compare the resulting plans.

(b) Repeat (a) for $S_i = S_3$; $S_g = S_5$.

(c) Using the state representation of Fig. 14.22 and *only* the parallel operators derived in problem 14.41, is any state accessible from any other state (i.e., does a plan always exist if S_i and S_g are arbitrary and we may use *only* parallel operators)?

CHAPTER 15

SEARCH AND COMPUTATIONAL COMPLEXITY IN AI SYSTEMS

When you can measure what you are speaking about, and express it in numbers, you know something about it; but when you cannot measure it, when you cannot express it in numbers, your knowledge is of a meager and unsatisfactory kind: it may be the beginning of knowledge, but you have scarcely, in your thoughts, advanced to the stage of science.

William Thomson, Lord Kelvin 1824–1907
Popular Lectures and Addresses [1891–1894]

COMPUTATIONAL COMPLEXITY

As noted in Chapter 1, the concepts of search and AI have a tenuous relationship. Some view search as fundamental to AI, others view AI as a means to eradicate search from certain problems. Search comes later in this text because, in the author's opinion, the reader (or instructor) needs to be cognizant of AI problems and possible solutions before considering the solution complexity. No look at AI would be complete without an examination of the fundamental component that underlies most of the previously developed algorithms—namely the process of *search*. Search algorithms (even if they are implemented by default, i.e., without regard to optimization) are fundamental to the practical implementation of many AI paradigms. The trial-and-error nature of many of the AI approaches we have studied suggests that systematic approaches, where applicable, may be preferable to attempts to simply "fall into" or guess the solution. Inefficient ("unintelligent") algorithms often amount to brute-force search and are easily defeated by combinatorial explosion.

Quantifying Computational Complexity

Up to this point we have considered the development of AI algorithms that *work*, without regard to the efficiency or computational complexity of the algorithm. Efficiency was of limited concern in our previous examples due to the modest size of the rule and fact bases. This is not likely to be the case in real applications, where the rule and fact bases are likely to be orders of magnitude larger. A prerequisite for a successful AI system, therefore, is that it deliver a solution (or at least an answer) in a reasonable time (and perhaps using "reasonable" resources).

In order to study the efficiency and behavior of algorithms, two entities are required:

1. A model of the computation.

2. A complexity measure. (15–1)

The AI algorithms for planning, chaining, unification, and so forth that we develop are the basis for computational models. In extrapolating to larger systems many of the rule-based, unification, and planning examples we have explored, the problem of *combinatorial explosion* is apparent. Several measures of algorithm complexity are available; for example, *program length* (lines, functions, etc.). For AI, a more useful (so-called dynamic) measure is that of *execution time*. Due to the nondeterminism of AI, this measure must often be estimated or predicted. In addition, *worst-case* analysis or average-case analysis may be used in the estimation or prediction process. Following the approach of Tarjan [1983], we denote an *efficient algorithm* as one whose worst-case running time is bounded by a polynomial function of the problem size. *Tractable problems* have efficient algorithms; intractable problems do not. We note even tractable problems become gradually unusable; this is shown in Fig. 15.1. To give perspective in computing program-execution time estimates on the basis of operations per second and total required operations, it is useful to note that 10^8 sec = 3 years.

Given the mere existence of an algorithm that solves an AI problem, it is incorrect to conclude that the problem is *practically* solved. The *computational complexity* of an AI algorithm is an aspect that must be considered in practical AI applications. Algorithms may be grossly inefficient or have time and space requirements (i.e., require years of computation with potentially infinite memory space) that are unrealistic with present computing resources. We focus on solutions to the latter difficulty in Chapter 19.

PROBLEM SCALING. As a practical matter, we would like to estimate the time and space requirements for implementation of a given algorithm. To make the time measure independent of a specific computer, we measure time using the quantity *steps*. In some cases, we can characterize algorithm requirements using worst-case, best-case, and average-case estimates. Although these are useful measures, we might be more interested in the *growth rate* of algorithm complexity as a function of some problem parameter. For example, referring to the labeling (constraint-satisfaction) problem of Chapter 5, we may be interested in determining estimates of the computing time as the number of regions to be labeled increases. We would probably be surprised if it grew linearly as a function of number of regions.

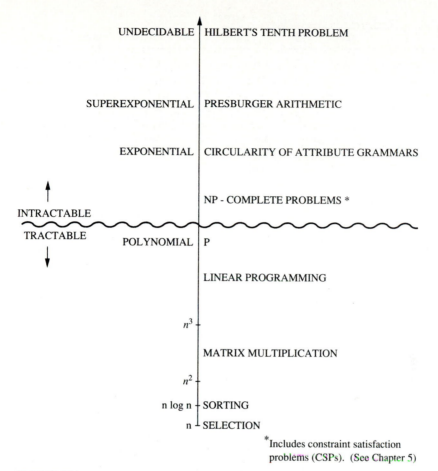

FIGURE 15.1
The spectrum of computational complexity. (From Tarjan, 1983.)

COMPLEXITY FUNCTIONS. To this end, we note that a hierarchy of complexity functions exists; this is typified in Fig. 15.2. Notice how the complexity of seemingly innocuous problems scaled to larger n often results in unacceptable computing times.

Furthermore, the issue of polynomial versus nonpolynomial complexity has been exhaustively studied [Tarjan 1983] [Witala 1987].

> We define an algorithm as *polynomial-time* (P) if its complexity function is polynomial. A *nonpolynomial time* (NP) algorithm has a complexity function that dominates every polynomial function. (15-2)

Referring to Fig. 15.2, for example, we note that the exponential function dominates any polynomial, and is thus nonpolynomial. A useful consequence of this categorization is that NP functions, when n increases, get large (unmanageable) at an alarming rate. Mathematicians have discovered a large class of problems that are nonpolynomial (often called NP-complete). Using the best methods known, the complexity of NP-complete problems grows exponentially. Examples are the "traveling

Growth	n (size)							
	1	**20**	**50**	**100**	**1,000**	**10,000**	**100,000**	**1,000,000**
n	1×10^{-6} sec	20×10^{-6} sec	50×10^{-6} sec	1×10^{-4} sec	1×10^{-3} sec	1×10^{-2} sec	0.1 sec	1 sec
n^2	1×10^{-6} sec	4×10^{-4} sec	2.5×10^{-2} sec	1×10^{-2} sec	1.0 sec	1.67 min	2.78 hours	11.6 days
n^3	1×10^{-6} sec	8×10^{-3} sec	2.5×10^{-3} sec	1.25×10^{-1} sec	16.8 min	11.6 days	3.17×10^5 CENT	—
2^n	2×10^{-6} sec	1.05 sec	35.7 years	4.02×10^{14} CENT	—	—	—	—
$\exp(n)$	2.7×10^{-6} sec	8.10 min	1.65×10^6 CENT	—	—	—	—	—

FIGURE 15.2

Execution time of processes with varying complexities. (one step $= 10^{-6}$ sec)

salesman" problem and the labeling problem shown in Chapter 5. Figure 15.2 illustrates the complexity of some problems. From this figure, it is clear that the modification of algorithms (with reasonable heuristics, for example) to avoid NP-complete (or worse) complexities is desirable. This may lead to algorithms that do not guarantee a solution, but may run with P complexity. (An interesting trade-off!)

Chapter 19 explores the use of parallel processing to reduce the time complexity (at the expense of space, or hardware complexity) of computational processes typical in AI.

SEARCH IN AI PROBLEMS

A Formal Representation for Search Problems

The first consideration necessary to the search process is problem representation. There are several scenarios that allow study of search, as a function of the chosen representation. For example, we may choose to show the problem space, given a state-space representation in terms of a graph representation. If we showed the evolution of the system using either (perhaps conditional) rule firings or operator applications, the state of a system in the graph (problem state) representation could be a position (node) in the graph. Here we have assumed specification of initial and goal states. As we shall see, many search algorithms are based upon a performance measure, which is an estimator of the distance between initial and goal states.

DEFINITION OF A SEARCH PROBLEM. A search problem, P, is characterized by

$$P = \{D, S_i, T, G\} \qquad (15\text{-}3)$$

where

D is a set of system states that represent the problem state-space.

$S_i \in D$ is a starting state.

$T = \{t_1, t_2, \ldots\}$ is a set of transformations (operators, rules).

$G \subset D$ is a set of goal states.

A solution to D, denoted T_s, is a sequence of $t_i = t_1, t_2, \ldots t_n$ with the property that

$$t_n \ldots (t_2(t_1(S_i))) \in G \qquad (15\text{-}4)$$

Note that D and T may be finite or countably infinite. (This is explored in the problems.) We may partition D into two mutually exclusive subsets:

1. Those $D_r \subset D$ where there exists some T_s such that

$$t_n \ldots (t_2(t_1(S_i)) \in D_r$$

These are *reachable* states.

2. Those $D_{ur} \subset D$ for which no T_s exists such that

$$t_n \ldots (t_2(t_1(S_i)) \in D_{ur}$$

These are unreachable states.

If

$$G \cap D_r \neq \{\varnothing\} \qquad (15\text{-}5)$$

then P is *solvable*. Unfortunately, it is difficult, at best, to ascertain if P is solvable before attempting a solution.

STATE-SPACE GRAPHS. A **state-space graph** (SSG) is a digraph that enumerates D and T. Specifically, modes of the SSG represent elements of D, and (diverted) arcs represent elements of T; that is, each $t_i \in T$ generates an arc in the SSG between modes d_i and $d_j \in D$ to indicate $d_j = t_i(d_i)$. Figures 14.8(b) and 15.3(b) show examples of SSGs.

SEARCH COSTS AND HEURISTICS. Using the SSG, a **search-cost function**, C, is a mapping of all arcs onto the set of nonnegative real numbers. More intuitively, C is a mechanism to associate a cost measure with a path through the SSG. Typically, C is used along with a search heuristic/skill algorithm to identify paths with low cost.

SEARCH AND GRAPH REPRESENTATIONS. We take a more detailed look at the graphical representations that may be employed in AI problems. Note that the principal utility of this abstraction is in conveying the complexity of the solution process and in comparing alternative solution approaches. Once a problem representation has been chosen, the problem space, within which the search process occurs, may be explored. In order to develop a unified approach applicable to a number of AI problems, often graphical abstractions are chosen. Particular states of the system are represented by nodes in a digraph, and the edges in the graph, which link nodes (or states), represent the application of a state-modification entity (i.e., a rule or operator). Note that this graphical representation does not assume certain system properties, such as decomposability or commutativity. However, if these properties

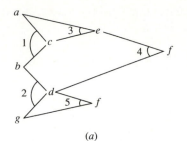

(a)

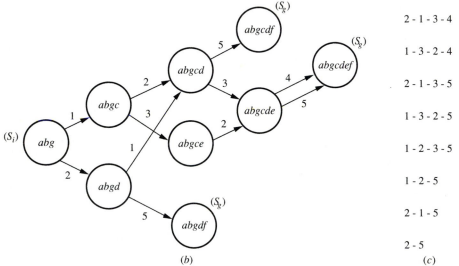

1 - 2 - 3 - 4

2 - 1 - 3 - 4

1 - 3 - 2 - 4

2 - 1 - 3 - 5

1 - 3 - 2 - 5

1 - 2 - 3 - 5

1 - 2 - 5

2 - 1 - 5

2 - 5

(b)   (c)

FIGURE 15.3
Simple example of problem search space using RB system of example 15.1: (*a*) inference net(s); (*b*) search paths through system state space using FSP (arc label indicates rule used; node shows facts comprising system state.); (*c*) possible rule-firing sequences leading to S_g's using FSP (the reader should consider BSP).

exist, modifications, partitioning, or simplifications of the graph are possible. Thus, in large scale problems, this graph is both large and complex.

Nodes (systems states) may be interpreted as the particular contents of an AI data base. Thus, all possible actions (rule firings or planning operator applications) on all possible states describe a graphical construct showing a linked sequence of system data bases. In most problems, one such data base, denoted S_i, represents the *system initial state*, and one (or more) denote the *goal state*, S_g.

Example 15.1   A graphical representation of *P***.** Consider the following simplistic rule-based system:

initial (data base) facts: $\{a\ b\ g\} = S_i$ rules:

```
rule  1      IF    a    b    THEN    c
      2      IF    b    g    THEN    d
      3      IF    a    c    THEN    e
      4      IF    e    d    THEN    f
      5      IF    d    g    THEN    f
```

Suppose our goal is to produce a state that contains fact f. Figure 15.3(a) shows a combined inference net for the system. More importantly, part (b) shows the search space and possible paths leading from S_i to (one) S_g. Note the nine possible paths (rule-firing sequences) are shown in part (c).

"GOOD" VERSUS BRUTE-FORCE SEARCH. Search strategies for practical and extendable AI solutions are usually more sophisticated (and efficient) than simple guessing (GAT). Efficiency, or "goodness," of the search strategy is dependent upon selection of a problem-dependent metric. For example, we have seen overall path length (total number of actions) used as a metric in planning examples.

> One obvious observation is that a good search strategy should avoid revisiting states already considered.   (15-6)

This condition, as shown by our planning examples, is analogous to recognizing the appearance of a cycle.

Assume we are given a rule-based system or a planning problem with intial and goal states, S_i and S_g respectively, and rule, R, or operator, O, sets specified. The AI system, in attempting to link S_i and S_g, must determine at least one sequence of rules or operators. In practice there are usually many such sequences, or paths. We note it is also possible there are none; we are not guaranteed a solution a priori. One solution procedure is to compute the entire problem space (by applying all possible sequences of operators, or firing all sequences of rules). From this, it is possible to determine if S_g is in the problem space, and, if so, the (an) operator or rule sequence that achieves the goal. Computation of the problem space may be attempted by exhaustive search. Due to the fact that the problem space for some problems may be infinite or impractically large, this is seldom possible. An efficient and practical solution does not rely on such a drastic computational approach, but rather uses "intelligent" search techniques and domain-specific knowledge to explore a subset of the problem space. The difficulty is demonstrated in Fig. 15.4.

Problem Decomposition and Searching with AND-OR Trees

TREE REPRESENTATIONS. Since two states may often be "linked" by more than one operator, the nodes in the problem state graph may have several arcs linking them. This makes analysis difficult, therefore the graph is often converted into a tree. The price of this modification is "expansion" of the graph into a structure where tree nodes are not unique (since graph nodes are replicated). One node must be specified as the root (this is usually either the initial or goal state), and the remaining nodes or

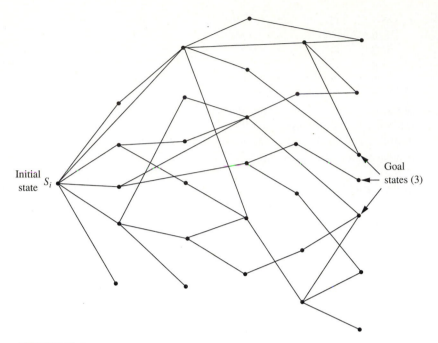

Initial state S_i

Goal states (3)

FIGURE 15.4
Example of typical problem state space and the need for "good search." Note that goal-directed search eliminates many superfluous paths.

states appear at some level in the tree. In this expansion, however, the multiplicity of sequences leading from the root state to any other specified state may easily be seen.

SEARCH PROBLEM DECOMPOSITION AND AND-OR TREES. Often, the tree representation of a search problem indicates a decomposition into search subproblems, which themselves may be (recursively) decomposed. Each goal may often be satisfied more than one way, and thus local search choices must be made. The idea of having choices to satisfy a certain subgoal and possible requirements that all subgoals must be satisfied, spawns an *AND-OR tree*. In such a tree, an OR node represents available choices for a given goal, and an AND node represents the subgoals that must all be achieved.

EXAMPLES. Figure 14.8 shows a simple example of the search tree for the checkerboard problem. Forward State Propagation (FSP) with GAT is used. Note the search tree consists solely of "OR" nodes, with the number of successors of a node indicating the number of applicable operators. Numerous potential cycles are shown.

The problem (considered in Chapter 13) of matching object model parts to extracted image data can be modeled as searching goal trees. Figure 15.5 presents an example of how model matching may be implemented by traversing an AND-OR tree. The object model is shown in part (*a*). AND nodes represent subparts that must be all present for successful object recognition. OR nodes represent the possible different subparts, contained in the image data, that can be matched to model object parts.

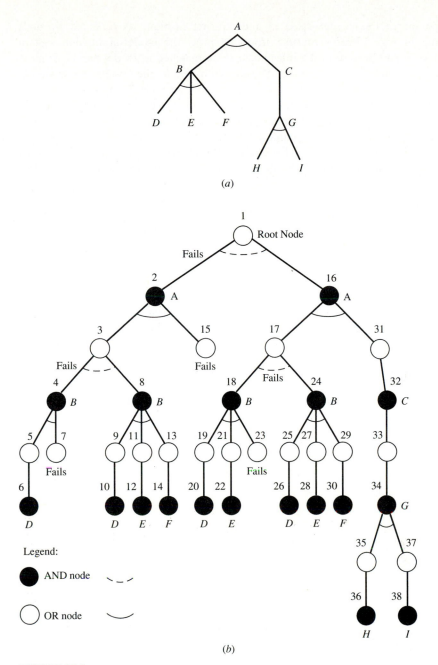

FIGURE 15.5

AND-OR searching tree for model-unification problem of Chapter 13. (*a*) Object structural model to be unified with observed data. Parts labeled *A–I*; arcs indicate "attached-to" relation. (*b*) possible search tree.

The search tree is generated in a depth-first fashion, as reflected by node numbering in Fig. 15.5(b). Starting from the root, the model-unification system chooses some part present in the image data to be matched to model part A. It must then find a match for parts B and C. Starting with part B, the system reaches node 4 and then node 6, where it finds a match for part D. At node 7, the system tries to identify part E; however, no matches are found and the system backtracks to node 3, reporting a failure for the arc from node 3 to node 4. From node 8 the system is able to identify the object subsystem composed of parts B, D, E and F; however, at node 15 it fails to identify part C. After backtracking up to the root, the system is able to correctly identify all the object parts going through nodes numbered 16, 24 and 32.

Incorporating Search in AI

SEARCH EXAMPLES IN PREVIOUSLY CONSIDERED APPLICATIONS. There are numerous examples of implied searches in the previously considered AI algorithms. For example:

1. The unification procedure employed in PROLOG involved backtracking for satisfaction of subgoals. This, as shown in the "tenure" example and figure of Chapter 4, is an example of *depth-first search*. Recall also that the unification search process is a function of the order of the rules and facts in the database (and the possible use of the "cut" operator).

2. The backward-chaining approaches (Chapter 12) in the LISP rule-based system development used implicit search mechanism to find applicable rules. The order in which rules are checked is a function of the order of the rules in the rule list as well as the success achieved in firing rules. As it was stuctured in the LISP program, the recursion represents a depth-first search. It could be easily changed (see the exercises) in order for the inference mechanism to identify the most useful or "optimal" rule to try next.

3. In the generation of plans, the order in which actions (functions) are applied determines the speed with which success (or failure) is determined. This is illustrated in the branching strategies of the "blocks-world" planning example.

HEURISTICS. Search problems, like many other aspects of AI, are often not easily described in a form that leads to immediate mathematical derivations of optimal solutions. Typically, heuristics are employed.

> A **heuristic** is a strategy (which often defies detailed analysis, such as proof of applicability in all situations) or procedure used to aid in the efficient solution of a problem. Often heuristics are developed by trial and error, in conjunction with a number of reasonable approximations, simplifications, reasonable guesses, or domain-specific problem knowledge. (15-7)

The lack of an ability to prove the worthiness of a heuristic (in all applications) does not preclude its use. Moreover, many AI problems could not be solved without the development of heuristics.

In the graphical problem-search-space description cited above, note that heuristics are used to *prune* (i.e., limit) the branches explored of the search tree. Also, heuristics are often *tuned* for a particular application; success in one AI implementation using a heuristic does not necessarily translate into success in even closely related implementations.

Search Computational Complexity and Trade-offs

When search strategies are employed for the optimization of AI algorithms, the computational cost of the search strategy must be considered in view of the efficiency gains in the overall algorithm. For example, a search strategy that led to significantly shorter or more direct paths in backward chaining is of questionable utility if the total (i.e., to completion) computation time consumed by the search algorithm far exceeds the time saved in the inference process. In other words, search algorithm effects on overall AI system computation cost must be considered.

Figure 15.6 illustrates this relationship. As an example, suppose that a backward chaining rule-based system employed a search mechanism to identify the next rule that was closest to "optimal." If the algorithm exhaustively examined the rule, referred to the past history of rule-firing success, and so on, a great deal of computational resources are expended. At some point it may be *computationally* more efficient to simply check the rule directly. Thus, there exists a point of "diminishing returns" wherein the search algorithm actually becomes counterproductive, from the point of view of overall system operation.

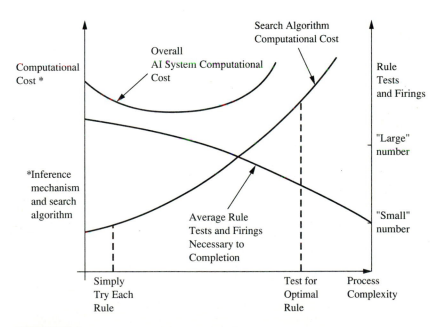

FIGURE 15.6
Search effect on overall system computation (rule-based system example).

THE COMPUTATIONAL COMPLEXITY OF SEARCHING THE PROBLEM SPACE. The primary difficulty in search is that of combinatorial explosion. Since several choices are available to the search algorithm at *each* problem step, the number of paths to be searched usually becomes unmanageable after a few steps, thereby precluding exhaustive investigation of all possibilities. For example, consider a search problem where the number of possible or alternative paths to investigate grows at an extremely rapid rate as a function of the number of problem steps (exponential or factorial growth rates are common). After a finite number of steps, the solution computational requirements may "explode," yielding a problem that is theoretically solvable, but practically infeasible. Thus, a technique to prune the possible paths is necessary, to counteract combinatorial explosion. Notice also that this pruning algorithm if it is not chosen carefully, may "prune out" an optimal solution. Thus, we are faced with an optimality-versus-practicality situation.

FORWARD PROPAGATION OF MODIFIED STATES. We present a very simple example of the combinatorial explosion that may occur in the process of generating a search tree. First, we consider the forward propagation of states; that is, starting at state S_i, we generate all possible successors to this state, by considering all applicable state-modification operators. In this example, assume we are considering a rule-based inference system, therefore the state-modification operators are rules. Suppose at state S_i, representing stage i in the problem-space-generation process, we have n_i total system facts, and m_i applicable rules. We will assume that m_i is constant with respect to i (the problems explore this further). In addition, assume the firing of each of the m_i applicable rules generates $(m_i/k_i)n_i$ new facts. Again, assume k_i is independent of i; that is, $k_i = k \forall i$. Thus, at stage $i + 1$ we have

$$n_{i+1} = n_i(1 + m_i/k) \tag{15-8}$$

total system facts. Note that it is reasonable to expect that

$$(1 + m_i/k) > 1 \tag{15-9}$$

therefore the number of system facts is monotonically increasing with i. Given n_0 facts at stage n, the number of facts propagates to stage $p(p \geq 0)$ as

$$n_p = n_0(1 + m_i/k)^p \tag{15-10}$$

For example, if $n_0 = 100$, and we assume $m_i/k = 1.3$, at stage $p = 10$ we have

$$n_{10} = 100\,(2.3)^{10} = 414,265 \text{ total facts}$$

The quantity $(1 + m_i/k)$ is referred to as the *branching factor*, denoted b, and is explored in the problems. The distance p is referred to as the *solution depth*. Referring to Fig. 15.7(*a*), we observe this effect in (15-10) graphically, in that the tree grows rapidly for succeeding stages.

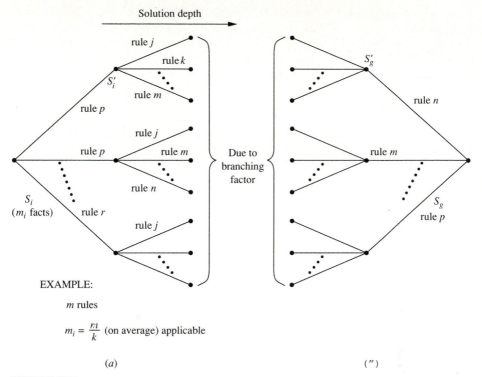

Solution depth

EXAMPLE:

m rules

$$m_i = \frac{m}{k} \text{ (on average) applicable}$$

(a)   ('')

FIGURE 15.7
Potential rule/operation combinatorial explosion (effects of branching factor in state expansion): (a) forward state propagation; (b) backward state propagation.

BACKWARD STATE PROPAGATION. Figure 15.7(b) indicates backward state propagation, which is similar to the previous case in that combinatorial explosion again may occur. Suppose we are implementing a backward chaining algorithm, are at state S_g, and therefore must identify potentially applicable rules. Selecting one clause (fact) from S_g, we consider every rule whose list of antecedents could be used to produce this fact. Since several rules may be applicable, and the preconditions to these rules introduce new clauses to verify at the next backward step, the number of rules to consider (search) working backwards may again become large after only a few steps.

SEARCH ALGORITHMS

Given S_i, S_g, a problem representation, and the set of rules or state-modification operators, numerous search strategies are possible. We highlight a few in what follows.

Trial-and-Error Approaches

This method is the most obvious and probably the least efficient. Rules or operators are randomly selected, and, following firing or application (respectively), we check to see if the goal state has been reached. In this manner, we "stumble" into a solution, if one exists and we are persistent. For simple problems (i.e., those with a very small problem space), this may be sufficient. Note, however, that the system never concentrates its "attention" in pursuit of a strategy or solution path; the selection of the next operator or rule is (almost) independent (except for the effect of new facts produced by its predecessor) of previous operator choices.

Breadth-First Search

The random approaches are systematic in their exploration of the problem space. If more systematic approaches are developed, another hard-to-quantify difficulty in the search of this space arises; it involves systematic choice or determination of a search path through the tree. This problem may alternatively be cast as determination of the order in which nodes of the problem-space tree are explored. One might suspect that many approaches are possible, and several are illustrated hereafter. Depth-first and breadth-first are two extremes in this space of possible search algorithms.

A simple problem search space and breadth-first search is illustrated in Fig. 15.8. Note that breadth-first search generates all nodes in the problem-space tree at level i prior to exploration of the nodes at level $i + 1$. We postulate that the computational complexity of any search algorithm is a function of the number of nodes investigated. The complexity of breadth-first search up to level q, therefore, is

$$C_{\text{breadth-first}} = 1 + b + \cdots + b^q \qquad (15\text{-}11)$$

where b is the branching factor. The complexity of this approach is exponential, since $e^x = 1 + x + x^2/2 + x^3/3! + \cdots$

Notice that since breadth-first search examines all nodes in the problem-space tree at level i prior to investigating level $i + 1$, the path of shortest length is found. If path length is the metric used to measure (or compare) search-algorithm performance, then breadth-first search is optimal. However, if all the goal states are a large distance

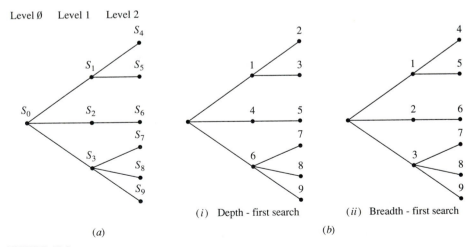

FIGURE 15.8
Sample search methodologies with simple problem space: (*a*) sample problem space; (*b*) order in which system states are expanded and searched.

from the start mode and the number of alternative paths to store is large, breadth-first search may be impractical due to both time and memory requirements.

If the search tree has b branches at each node and goes to depth d, then there are about b^d nodes. The branching factor b corresponds to the number of states adjacent to a given state, and the depth d corresponds to the path length, which is bounded by the number of legal states if the search is restricted to simple paths. For example, 2^{58} is the number of nodes in a balanced binary tree of depth $d = 58$.

As our examples show, not all searches go to the same depth, so it is often necessary to develop an estimate of d. One obvious approach involves estimating the average; however, this leads to inaccuracies. Consider, for example, a binary search of a long list of length d. Then $b = 2$ and the average depth is $d/2$, but the number of nodes in the binary search tree is $2d - 1$, which is linear, not exponential ($2^{d/2}$).

Two aspects of breadth-first search are important:

If a solution (path) exists, breadth-first search is guaranteed to find it, provided there are a finite number of branches in the search tree.

(15-12a)

Breadth-first search is memory-intensive and inefficient if even the shortest path is very long.

(15-12b)

Depth-First Search

The best example of depth-first search is PROLOG's unification mechanism, as shown in Chapter 4. It may be shown that the depth-first approach to level d generates the same number of nodes as in breadth-first search (in a different order, however), and therefore its complexity is the same. One interesting characteristic, however, is that it only requires storage of the current path, which is a function of the depth, d. For this reason, it is often preferred to breadth-first search.

Forward-Backward (Bidirectional) Search

Bidirectional search, which is considered in Chapters 13 and 14, involves starting at both S_i and S_g and working forward from S_i and backward from S_g until a common state, S_c, or a state that "links" S_i and S_g, is found. Thus, two breadth-first searches are required, although it is hoped that the combinatorial explosion in each remains limited until S_c is found. This approach is illustrated by merging parts (a) and (b) of Fig. 15.7.

Other Search Approaches (Including Heuristic Search Techniques)

Many reasonable combinations and modifications of the above algorithm are possible. For example, depth-first search could be combined with breadth-first search in a number of ways. One example of this is *depth-first with iterative deepening*. An alternative is the incorporation of *heuristics*.

Heuristic search techniques employ a measure of search cost to limit the search. Often, success is predicated upon formulation of a good cost measure. For example, a measure of the disparity or distance between the current state (S_c) and the goal state, or a state difference function, denoted $D(S_p, S_g)$ may be formulated. By choosing rules or operators that minimize $D(S_p, S_g)$ we achieve conflict resolution. In addition, intuition suggests that we would also move monotonically towards the goal. One difficulty with this approach, however, is that it does not guarantee a monotonically nonincreasing path towards the goal state. This is due to the locality of the decision process. For example, we could be on a path towards the goal that is based upon local minimization of $D(S_p, S_g)$; however, at some step we find $D(S_p, S_g)$ increasing rapidly.

THE MEANS-END APPROACH. Means-end is a valuable heuristic that may be employed in a variety of ways. The basic approach is to select operators that seem to provide a means to some end, most often the goal. Two of the planning examples of Chapter 14 illustrated this technique. Means-end assumes $D(S_p, S_g)$ exists. $D(S_p, S_g)$ is used, at each step, to choose an operator that makes the decrease in $D(S_p, S_g)$ largest. Alternatively, means-end may be used to achieve a goal by driving the system to states that allow other "more desirable" rules or operators (or perhaps previously derived subplans) to be applied.

BEST-FIRST SEARCH. Best-first search considers all the nodes that have been examined up to the current time, and proceeds by expanding the one that, according to a heuristic, is closest to the goal. In this sense, the best-first approach does not explicitly consider the cost of getting to node n, but only the estimated remaining cost. Intuitively, the search proceeds by "following the best guess." A function or heuristic to compare two operators (or their resulting states) is required.

THE A* ALGORITHM. The A* algorithm is based upon formulating a figure of merit for node n by tallying the actual (minimal or optimal) cost of the path from the initial state to node n, denoted $g(n)$, and the inferred or estimated (minimal) cost from node n to the goal, denoted $h(n)$. If there is no path from node n to the goal, $h(n)$ is infinite. Similarly, if no path between the initial state and node n exists, then $g(n)$ is infinite. Therefore, the overall metric at node n is

$$f(n) = g(n) + h(n) \qquad (15\text{-}13)$$

which represents the cost of the optimal path that includes node n. In terms of traditional optimization problems, $g(n)$ is the "cost so far" and $h(n)$ is the "cost to go." The objective is to find the optimum path, that is, one that minimizes f and links S_1 with S_g. Of course, if $f(n)$ may be explicitly formulated a priori, then the path may be found by following the nodes where $f(n)$ is minimum. Unfortunately, this is seldom the case.

REFERENCES

[Knuth 1973] Knuth, D.E., *The Art of Computer Programming, Vol. 3, Sorting and Searching*, Addison-Wesley, Reading, MA, 1973.

[Nilsson 1980] Nilsson, N.J., *Principles of Artificial Intelligence*, Tioga Publ., Palo Alto, CA, 1980.

[Pearl 1984] Pearl, J., *Heuristics*, Addison-Wesley, Reading, MA, 1984.

[Tarjan 1983] Tarjan, R.E., *Data Structures and Network Algorithms*, SIAM Publications, Philadelphia, PA, 1983.

[Witala 1987] Witala, S.A., *Discrete Mathematics, A Unified Approach*, McGraw-Hill, New York, 1987.

PROBLEMS

Note: several of these problems refer to examples and figures from previous chapters.

15.1. Given the rule base and initial facts of Ex. 11.17,

(*a*) Develop an OPS5 representation.

(*b*) Show the OPS5 solution using LEX.

(*c*) Which path of the search graph does the solution to part *b* take? Is it minimum length?

15.2. (*a*) For a $n \times n$ "checkerboard," as in Fig. 14.2, with p "blocked" locations similar to that of problem 14.22 and with q blocks ($q \le n^2 - p$), and no unreachable states, show the number of possible states C, is

$$C = \prod_{j=0}^{q-1} k - j$$

where $k = n^2 - p$. Verify the potential search complexity by computing the number of possible states for the following cases:

(i) $q = 2$, $n = 3$, $p = 5$.

(ii) $q = 6$, $n = 10$, $p = 8$.

(iii) $q = 6$, $n = 4$, $p = 10$.

(iv) $q = 10$, $n = 100$, $p = 50$.

(*b*) Repeat (*a*) for Fig 1.18, considering both reachable and unreachable states.

15.3. Refer to Fig. 14.17, assume a single operator may be applied at any step, and that the plan is developed using forward state propagation. Exhaustive search (i.e., no heuristics) is used.

(*a*) Show the search tree for this problem. (The root is S_i.) (Hint: Start with a large sheet of paper.) Identify cycles with a leaf node, *c*, and show the state of the blocks at each node.

(*b*) How many paths from S_i to S_g (i.e., how many distinct plans) exist? Enumerate them. What is the "shortest," in terms of fewest numbers of steps?

15.4. Consider the "blocks world" problem initial and goal states shown in Fig. P15.4. Assume forward state propagation is used to select operators; that is, we propagate states from S_0 (to S_g) by determining which operators are applicable.

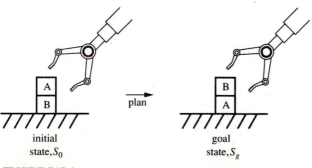

FIGURE P15.4

(a) Show the problem search space, using a digraph. Each node should contain a state description in clause form; arcs should be labeled with the operator used.

(b) What is the minimum path and corresponding plan from S_0 to S_g (assume path length = number of operators)?

(c) Identify three possible *cycles* in the search graph.

15.5. Our exploration of the generic process of search in this chapter indicated unification, rule-based inference, and planning as application areas. The purpose of this problem is to show why they are different problems.

Consider representing the blocks world problem of Ex. 14.9 using OPS5.

(a) Describe S_i in WM.

(b) Show each operator as a production.

(c) Show the result of simply invoking run.

(d) Explain in detail why the result of (c) occurs.

15.6. Using the formalisms of (15-3) through (15-5), answer the following questions:

(a) Is the blocks-world problem [Fig 14.1(b)] one where D is finite or countably infinite?

(b) Is the "checkerboard" planning problem of Ex. 14.5–14.6 one where D is finite or countably infinite?

(c) Cite examples of problems where D is countably infinite.

15.7. Consider the "checkerboard" problem shown graphically in Fig. P15.7, where each state is represented by the location of blocks A and B, (i.e., the initial state is $(A4, B8)$). Operators are designated using the following abbreviations:

uA	move block A up
dA	move block A down
rA	move block A right
lA	move block A left
uB	move block B up
dB	move block B down
rB	move block B right
lB	move block B left

(a) Enumerate the state space for this problem. How many distinct states are there?

(b) Using each state as a node and each operator as a relation, show the resulting digraph. Identify cycles (closed paths).

(c) For the three goal states

$(A2, B5)$

$(A8, B4)$

$(A5, B2)$

Identify all paths from S_i to S_g that do not contain cycles (state the sequence of operators).

Identify the shortest (in terms of steps) path.

FIGURE P15.7

15.8. For the checkerboard problem shown in Fig. 14.17(*a*), and the "move" operators described in the text, enumerate the system state space. Are there any unreachable states?

15.9. The purpose of this problem is to consider the computational complexity (scaling) of the block-movement problem of Chapter 14, as the "resolution" of the representation is increased. This is shown in Fig. P15.9.

(*a*) Show the size of the state space for each of the resolutions in the figure.

(*b*) How does this size vary with n?

(*c*) Suggest a method to use in a higher resolution space a plan developed in a lower resolution space. This should include

    1. A way to relate representations at different resolutions (e.g., (i) and (iii) in Fig. P.15.9).

    2. A way to "expand" operators at a lower resolution to a sequence at a higher resolution.

Test your strategy using a plan that reverses the block locations.

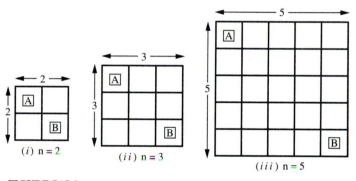

FIGURE P15.9
(*i*) $n = 2$; (*ii*) $n = 3$; (*iii*) $n = 5$.

15.10. For the "blocks-world" system shown in Fig. P15.4, consider the use of two independent *manipulator arms in parallel*. Specifically,

(*a*) Show the search space that results from the use of one or two arms in parallel. How does the path length in this case compare with that of 15.3?

(*b*) Suggest heuristics that lead to a shortest path.

15.11. Redraw the search tree for the problem of Fig. 14.8(*a*) using BSP, starting with root S_g.

15.12. Show how the CSP (labeling) problem of Chapter 5 may be cast as a search problem. Draw an AND-OR tree for a simple case.

15.13. Show examples of a problem formulation that more naturally fits depth-first search or breadth-first search. Consider best-, worst-, and average-case performance of each.

15.14. (*a*) For the two-blocks system shown in Fig. P15.14

    (i) enumerate the state space.

    (ii) given the initial state shown, enumerate all unreachable states.

(*b*) (How) does specification of an initial state for the system of Fig. P15.14 affect the unreachable states? Cite examples.

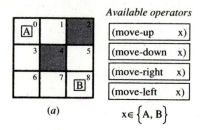

Available operators

(move-up   x)

(move-down   x)

(move-right   x)

(move-left   x)

(*a*) $x \in \{A, B\}$

FIGURE P15.14

15.15 (*a*) Distinguish the concept of an illegal state [cf. (14-10)] from an unreachable state.

(*b*) Referring to Figure P1.18 (Chapter 1), enumerate all unreachable states, if the state shown is S_i.

STRUCTURED KNOWLEDGE REPRESENTATION AND MANIPULATION (FRAMES, BLACKBOARDS, AND ADVANCED CONTROL CONCEPTS)

Let us now suppose that in the mind of each man there is an aviary of all sorts of birds—some flocking together apart from the rest, others in small groups, others solitary, flying anywhere and everywhere. . . . We may suppose that the birds are kinds of knowledge and that when we were children, this receptacle was empty; whenever a man has gotten and detained in the enclosure a kind of knowledge, he may be said to have learned or discovered the thing which is the subject of the knowledge: and this is to know.

Plato c. 428–348 B.C.
Theaetetus, 197

This chapter considers two pragmatic aspects of practical AI system development. The first concerns higher-level, structured knowledge representations such as frames and blackboards. Frames may be thought of as extensions of network or graphical representations, yielding a "network of networks," where the overall representation is partitioned in a meaningful way.

Realistic reasoning systems seldom simply develop an "ever-increasing mass of knowledge." Rather, inference must often be monitored and controlled at a level higher than simple matching of rule antecedents. It is also desirable to determine which subsets of available facts and rules are relevant to the scope of current inference. This explains the need for a structuring of the database.

Secondly, we investigate several practical aspects of inference, since

1. Assumptions upon which inferences are made may change over time or may be found to be incorrect. Thus, *nonmonotonic reasoning* with some form of possible *backtracking* may be necessary as part of a *truth maintenance system* [Doyle 1979].
2. The state of the knowledge base must be periodically examined for possible conflicts or inconsistencies.

REPRESENTATIONAL STRUCTURES

Structured Knowledge Representations and "Focusing" Inference

A central issue in the design of an efficient inference system is how to effectively concentrate the attention of the system on a salient and manageable amount of knowledge (i.e., rules and facts). This is referred to as *opportunistic problem solving*, which, as the name implies, involves automation of a "use what is most appropriate and ignore the rest" problem-solving methodology. This type of approach leads to computationally efficient inference. One risk, however, is that the potential use of incomplete information (due to the exclusion by default of other facts and rules) may lead to logically unsound conclusions. This is the subject of *nonmonotonic reasoning*.

As described previously, inference often requires a significant amount of computational effort for unification or matching of symbolic structures. If we simply represent "everything we know" in terms of massive rule and fact bases (so-called monolithic structures), a great deal of IE computational effort may be involved in searching through (and perhaps applying) rules that, although strictly applicable, do little to advance the system state towards a goal. A better strategy is to select rules and facts in our production strategy using an "information lens," so that the reasoning scenario remains focused. Subdividing a representation into manageable "packets" or frames, facilitates this objective.

Another aspect of a practical knowledge representation concerns efficient encoding of the properties of entities or objects in the representation. Often, properties of an entity are shared by all members of a class to which the entity belongs. Therefore, some representational efficiency could be achieved by representing these common properties in a generalized or stereotypical fashion in the knowledge database, and letting class membership determine properties of specific entities. The frame representation also facilitates this through *inheritance* and i s—a forms.

Classes, Structural Links, and Hierarchical Representations

In structured knowledge representations, the focus is on detailed descriptions of the *internal structure* of objects as well as their *relations with other objects*.   (16-1)

Many of the general attributes of an entity such as "Jesse" may be described in terms of more generalized entities, such as the characteristics of classes to which "Jesse" belongs. Thus, we develop representations where

1. Objects belong to classes. Each object is an *instance* of a class and all objects in a class share attributes (with generally different values for those attributes).

    (16-2*a*)

2. Classes can be subclasses of other classes. The subclass relationship is usually one of *specialization*.   (16-2*b*)

This leads to representations that indicate the structure-of-a-structure, and similar extensions, and are therefore *hierarchical*.

Structural links may be as simple as

```
is-a-part-of
has-location
occurred-while (a temporal link)
```

Commonly used structural links (which we explore later) are

```
is-a (alternatively is-an-instance-of)

could-be (alternatively is-instantiated-by)
```

The is-a link is often used to generate an *acyclic, hierarchical network*.

is-a **REPRESENTATIONS (WITHOUT EXCEPTIONS).** The logical basis for the is-a relation is easy to show. For example, the fact that all dogs are mammals may be represented by

$$(\forall X)\mathrm{dog}(X) \rightarrow \mathrm{mammal}(X)$$

or, in PROLOG

```
mammal(X) :- dog(X)
```

It is possible to have logical representations relating *class values* that are more general. For example, we could show

if the type of entity X is $t1$, then the value of property $p1$ (of X) is $v1$

as

$$(\forall X)\ \mathrm{type}(X, t1) \rightarrow p1(X, v1)$$

An example in PROLOG notation might be

$$class(X, mammal) :- type(X, dog).$$

where universal quantification (with no exceptions) on X is implied.

> **Example 16.1   Simple structured representation.** Let us return to our representation of Jesse (Chapter 10). Suppose we know that Jesse is a type of dog known as a golden retriever, is 3.5 years old, and so forth. In exhaustive query of Jesse's owner, we ascertain the facts in Table 16.1, which are based solely upon observation of Jesse.
>
> Using these facts, a hierarchical is-a-based representation is shown in Fig. 16.1. In this figure, properties of higher-order entities or classes, such as golden retriever, dog, mammal, and so on, are employed.

Inheritance

> Inheritance is used in a hierarchy to allow objects to acquire information from other objects in the representation.   (16-3)

For example, in the representation of Fig. 16.1, Jesse *inherits* properties such as having four legs from the fact that Jesse is a dog. Similarly, Jesse inherits the property of being warm-blooded due to the fact a dog is a mammal. The is-a relation shown in this hierarchy to implement inheritance has the transitive property; that is, for entities a, b, and c,

$$IF\ a\ is-a\ b\ and\ b\ is-a\ c$$

$$THEN\ a\ is-a\ c.$$

More importantly, any property possessed by entity c is inherited by entity a. Using inheritance, a particular object (or instance) inherits attributes from a general class to which the object belongs.

TABLE 16.1
Facts for representation of Jesse

owns a tennis ball
has a heavy fur coat
has a large frame
has excellent retrieving instinct
hates cats
has a water dish
has four legs
has warm blood (i.e., warm-blooded)
was born live (e.g., not hatched)
consumes food
consumes oxygen
produces waste (with any luck, outdoors)

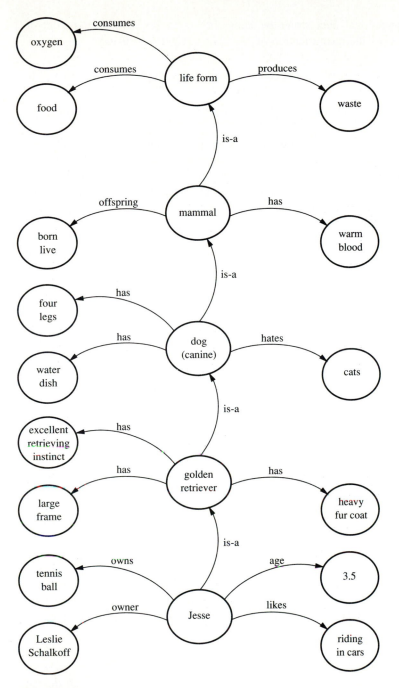

FIGURE 16.1
Is–a hierarchy for "Jesse."

A representational data structure using the is−a (or *ako*, for "a kind of") concept thus allows the quantification of Jesse's characteristics using

1. A property list (or equivalent structure), which stores properties or property values unique to Jesse.
2. A record of Jesse's membership in other classes (via is−a).

Given a set of family pets to be represented in this manner, an efficient storage mechanism results. Note that this is−a-based representation, although efficient in terms of compactness, requires some additional computational effort for property recollection. On a higher level, allowing property inheritance requires the careful design of an inference mechanism founded on a constructive proof that a certain entity has a property through inheritance.

> In many AI systems, hierarchical organization is efficient in that a great deal of "reusable" information is stored. (16-4)

FRAMES

Frame Concept

The is−a structure we just explored provides an introduction to a hierarchical and interrelated data structure we term the *frame* (also referred to in AI literature as the *schema*).

> The objective of frames is to group common knowledge together. (16-5)

A **frame** is a data structure used to represent some prototypical situation or entity. Thus, one intuitive view is that frames may be used to *stereotype* entities. For example, the prototypical automobile has four wheels. This information could be stored in a frame representing the common attributes of all automobiles. Any specific automobile description could *inherit* this information from the prototypical representation.

More specifically, a frame is a cognitive structure used to assemble information making up an entity (usually complex). This entity may be a concept (e.g., fatherhood) or physically realizable (e.g., a house). A frame is implemented as a collection of slots. Slots are frame components used to store variables that characterize the frame. Slots allow the embedding of interframe relations in the frame representation and thus provide "hooks" to link frames.

Relevant productions (e.g., rules) may be incorporated within the frame (or acquired via inheritence from another frame). In addition, *default information* or *default values* may be incorporated. The frame may also contain *procedural information* indicating how the information concerning the entity described by the frame may be used and how to calculate values needed. Finally, demons (described later) may be embedded in frames and alerted when the frame is invoked.

FRAMES FOR RECOGNITION / HYPOTHESIS GENERATION. Frames may be used for recognition, interpretation, and the prediction of entities or *situations* on the basis of information derived from the environment. Recognition is accomplished by *instantiation* or unification of observed data with a particular frame. On the basis of partial recognition, a frame could be used to encode other expected information, that is, to predict the potential appearance of other entity features. (This is explored in the problems.)

SITUATIONAL AND ACTION FRAMES. The role of frames in interpretation of situations is further enhanced by the structural information contained in a frame. We will discuss such *situational* frames first. For example, if the AI system application concerns the diagnosis of diseases, perhaps it is useful to agglomerate productions related to different classes of diseases into subsets of the overall database, and, based upon some initial productions, allow the IE to focus attention on discrimination within a specific disease class. In this manner, rules and facts not germane to the diagnosis are not involved, thus yielding a second type of efficiency. In addition, the frame provides a mechanism for identification of a situation by invoking one or more frames relevant to that situation. This suggests the need for a procedure to autonomously invoke (select) and switch frames.

Action frames (usually related to planning methodologies) consist of *slots* that specify tasks to be performed, and, like situational frames, may also be hierarchically organized through the use of *task slots*, which may point to other action frames. In either case, we see that the information is encoded in frame slots, whose general representational utility yields a versatile approach. Slots may be used to indicate rules applicable to the object, links (such as "a kind of," or *ako*) with other frames, and properties of the object itself (such as color, etc.). Furthermore, slots may be designed to incorporate a default value, to activate certain functions (such as query a human operator, or compute values of an entity). A possible further subdivision that is sometimes employed is to decompose a slot into *facets*. Facets, for example, allow the storage of changing values of an entity as well as default values. We show this by example.

Slot Types

`is–a`, `instance`, **AND OTHERS.** Slot names in frames often (but are not required to) correspond to relations. The all-important `is–a` frame link or slot (discussed above) is probably the most used slot.

A common approach to frame representation [Tichy 1987] is to create "generic" or *type* frames to represent abstractions of specific entities, and then create *instance* frames to represent specific instances of these generic types. The instance frames are linked to the type frames via the `instance` relation. This approach allows slots and their default values to be inherited by the instance frame from the type frame. Type frames may also, via the aforementioned `is–a` relation, be organized in a hierarchical fashion. Note that `is–a` and `instance` are similar relations. The major difference is that `is–a` allows a hierarchy, while `instance` may be used to efficiently represent redundant or common information at a single level.

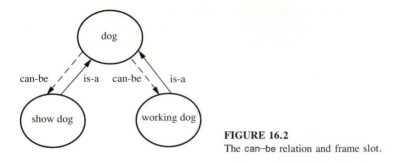

FIGURE 16.2
The can–be relation and frame slot.

can–be. Chapter 13 indicated that good hypothesis generation was often necessary. To this end, the frame is also useful in that it allows direct embedding of information useful for hypothesis formation. One example of this is the can–be slot. This type of relation, which bears some resemblance to the is–a relation, is shown in Fig. 16.2, where we have two frames, "show-dog" and "working-dog," respectively, which are linked to the "dog" frame via the is–a relation. In this hierarchical frame relation (detailed more fully later), we could also incorporate a slot in the "dog" frame of the form

```
SLOT   can–be:    show dog
                  working dog
```

OTHER SLOTS. Other frame-slot labels or relations are possible, including

- explanation–for
- revision/modification–of
- similarity–to
- causes
- more–general–than
- more–specific–than
- frame name (for identification)   (16-6)

Figure 16.3 shows a hierarchically organized frame for an automobile representation.

Inheritance with Exceptions

The is–a relation is quite useful in knowledge representation and leads to representation based on inheritance networks. Unfortunately, the generality represented using is–a often precludes its practical use, since for a is–a b to hold, all a must be of type b. In order to correctly represent the situation where almost all as are bs, we introduce the concept of inheritance with exceptions, or qualified is–a statements. For example, suppose Mr. X is a military officer, and an officer is a soldier. This holds for all cases, except the commander in chief, who is an officer, but

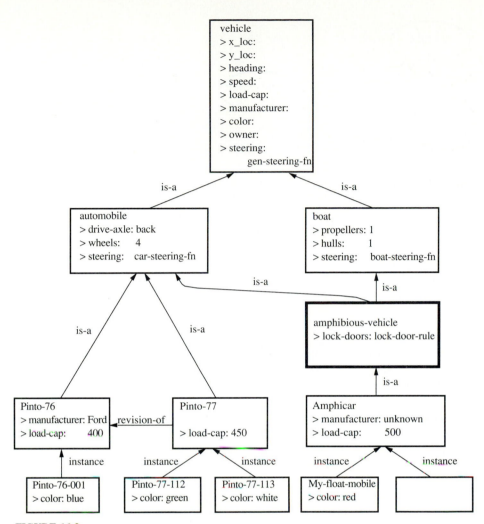

FIGURE 16.3
An inheritance network for vehicles (from Tichey, 1987).

also a civilian. Thus, if Mr. X is the commander in chief, he is an exception to the "all officers are soldiers" representation. A graphical version of this example is shown in Fig. 16.4. The exception may be handled by extension of the is−a slot.

Inheritance with exceptions has a strong similarity to the concept of generalization with exceptions. For example, see Chapter 18, (18-15) through (18-19).

Frame Networks

At the abstract level, a frame consists of a mechanism for categorizing related knowledge into *slots*. The slot is a generalized data structure that may contain both *factual* information (e.g., the type of information particular to any node of Fig. 16.1), and *procedural* or action information (i.e., what actions should be taken in a given

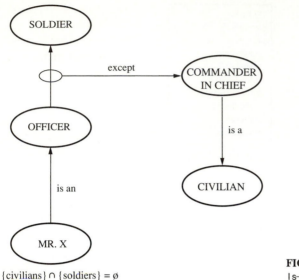

{civilians} ∩ {soldiers} = ∅

FIGURE 16.4
Is–a with exceptions example.

situation). In fact, we may decide to develop a hierarchical frame structure by allowing slots to contain other frames or perhaps pointers to other frames. We concentrate on the former here. Figure 16.5 shows the basic abstract frame structure, and a representation of the lowest-level node of Fig. 16.1.

INTERFRAME LINKS. Just as most knowledge does not exist in isolated form, isolated frames do not typically exist in a knowledge-representation application. Instead, frames are related to one another, in a manner similar to the way in which entities in a network description are related.

Structural links or relations serve as pointers among frames. Thus, frames may be used to represent linked data structures. Often, a hierarchical structure is chosen

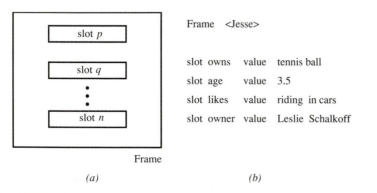

Frame   <Jesse>

slot owns   value   tennis ball
slot age   value   3.5
slot likes   value   riding in cars
slot owner   value   Leslie Schalkoff

Frame

(a)   (b)

FIGURE 16.5
Frame structure: (a) abstract model; (b) example (from Fig. 16.1): simple slot structure.

such that the data structure is acyclic. Thus, the relation between frames enables a higher-order *frame network*. The available knowledge is partitioned into situationally-related frames (e.g., dogs and cats), which themselves may be related to other frames. The result is a network of frames. The i s−a structure, when employed as a frame slot, enables the inheritance property in the frame structure. Thus, frames may be thought of as being hierarchically organized, as shown in Fig. 16.6, where we have encoded the information in Fig. 16.1. Several points regarding this figure are worth noting:

1. The hierarchical structure facilitates the inheritance property, through the i s−a relation, encoded as the slot type (or types of) and so on.   (16-7*a*)
2. The level of data representation proceeds, as shown in Fig. 16.6, from the general to the specific.   (16-7*b*)
3. In general, the frame network is more complex, with pointers from several other frames to a specific frame, which in turn may point to several other frames.
         (16-7*c*)

FRAME SELECTION. We note that a major aspect of successful frame implementation is the design of a good IE function that controls the frame selection (or deselection). This itself may be embedded as control (procedural) information within a "frame selection" frame. Clearly, it is possible in a frame-based system to focus production attention on the wrong scenario, which is, of course, self-defeating. Other practical questions regarding frame based designs, such as the need for disjoint rule and fact bases, are challenging research topics.

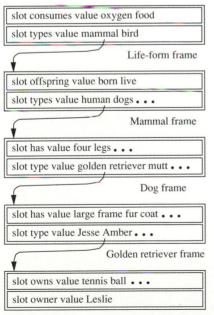

slot consumes value oxygen food
slot types value mammal bird
                    Life-form frame

slot offspring value born live
slot types value human dogs **. . .**
                    Mammal frame

slot has value four legs **. . .**
slot type value golden retriever mutt **. . .**
                    Dog frame

slot has value large frame fur coat **. . .**
slot type value Jesse Amber **. . .**
                    Golden retriever frame

slot owns value tennis ball **. . .**
slot owner value Leslie

                    Jesse frame

FIGURE 16.6
Hierarchical frame structure corresponding to Fig. 16.1.

FRAME IMPLEMENTATION AND EXAMPLES

In this section we consider the details of frame-based structure implementations. Specifically, we consider manipulation of the frame-based database (in LISP and PROLOG), as well as *maintenance* of the frame structure. The latter consists of developing facilities (functions and clauses) for the *retrieval* and *storage* (respectively) of data in the frames, and the *creation* and *deletion* of frames and slots. Finally, implementation of the inheritance property is considered. Figure 16.7 indicates the abstract-frame conceptual model and corresponding sample representations, which could be implemented in either PROLOG or LISP. Note that the use of repeated ‹facet-value› descriptors in a slot allows for the embedding of default values, units, and so forth in the frame representation.

PROLOG Frame Implementation

We use our representation of Jesse as an example. We note that although it is possible to store frames as list structures in PROLOG, we show a simpler example here.

```
jesse(is-a, value, golden_retriever, default_value, dog).
jesse(owns, value, tennis_ball, default_value, unknown).
jesse(age, value, 3.5, default_value, 0).
```

Notice that several of the arguments to predicate jesse (e.g., value) serve merely as placeholders, to facilitate reading. They may be deleted, thus reducing the arity of the predicate and yielding a simpler database.

Recall that since PROLOG clauses are restricted to represent first-order logic, this type of a frame-based database makes it difficult to determine, for example, the names of all golden retrievers older than three years, since these values are predicate names. Of course, we could revise this structure using an ancillary predicate with greater arity; for example, each of the clauses could also be represented in the form

<frame-name>
   <slot-name>
      <facet-name> : <facet-value>
     (*a*)

tank	*BMW*
ako	ako
value : vehicle	value : vehicle
has-armour	has-armour
value : yes	value : no
has-turret	has-turret
value : yes	value : yes
has-sunroof	has-sunroof
value : no	value : yes
default : option	
cost	cost
value : 10M	value : 30K
units : dollars	units : dollars

(*b*)

FIGURE 16.7
Abstract partial frame representations for "tank" and "BMW": (*a*) abstract model; (*b*) examples.

```
a_frame (jesse, is-a, value, golden_retriever,
    default_value, dog).
```

The reader is encouraged to consider alternate PROLOG representations. Mechanisms to manipulate (e.g., select) frame structures in PROLOG include using `consult` and `retract`. This is left to the exercises.

LISP Frame Implementation Example

The general data structure for a situational frame may be represented in LISP, following the structure of Fig. 16.7 as

```
(<frame name> (<slot_1> (<facet_1> (<value_1>)
                                   (<value_2>)  (<value_n>)
             (<slot_2> (<facet_1> (<value_1>)
                                   (<value_2>)  (<value_n>)
                   .
                   .
                   .
```
$$(16-8)$$

For example, we could implement a frame to store the information about Jesse as a list:

```
(Jesse (is-a (value golden_retriever))
       (owns (value tennis_ball)) (age (value 3.5))
       .
       .
       .  ]
```

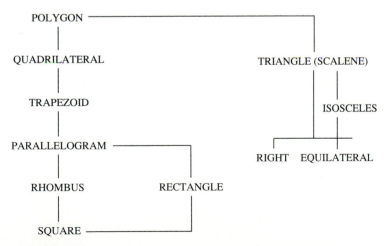

FIGURE 16.8a
Hierarchical organization of polygons (frame representation): hierarchy.

```
(FRAME: polygon

    (SLOT:      sides-connected
      (VALUE:   true)))

(FRAME: quadrilateral

    (SLOT:      is-a
      (VALUE:   polygon))
    (SLOT:      no-of-sides
      (VALUE:   4)))

(FRAME: trapezoid

    (SLOT:      is-a
      (VALUE:   quadrilateral))
    (SLOT:      no-of-parallel-pairs
      (VALUE:   1)))

(FRAME: parallelogram

    (SLOT:      is-a
      (VALUE:   trapezoid))
    (SLOT:      no-of-parallel-pairs
      (VALUE:   2)))

(FRAME: rhombus

    (SLOT:      is-a
      (VALUE:   parallelogram))
    (SLOT:      can-be
      (VALUE:   rectangle))
    (SLOT:      sides-of-equal-length
      (VALUE:   4)))

(FRAME: rectangle

    (SLOT:      is-a
      (VALUE:   parallelogram))
    (SLOT:      can-be
      (VALUE:   rhombus))
    (SLOT:      no-of-right-angles
      (VALUE:   4)))

(FRAME: square

    (SLOT:      is-a
      (VALUE:   rectangle rhombus))
```

FIGURE 16.8*b*

Hierarchical organization of polygons (frame representation): sample frames corresponding to Fig 16.8*a*.

```
(FRAME: triangle

    (SLOT:      is-a
      (VALUE:   polygon))
    (SLOT:      no-of-sides
      (VALUE:   3)))

(FRAME: right-triangle

    (SLOT:      is-a
      (VALUE:   triangle))
    (SLOT:      can-be
      (VALUE:   isoceles))
    (SLOT:      no-of-right-angles
      (VALUE:   1)))

(FRAME: isoceles

    (SLOT:      is-a
      (VALUE:   triangle))
    (SLOT:      can-be
      (VALUE:   right-triangle))
    (SLOT:      sides-of-equal-length
      (VALUE:   2)))

(FRAME: equilateral

    (SLOT:      is-a
      (VALUE:   isoceles))
    (SLOT:      sides-of-equal-length
      (VALUE:   3)))
```

FIGURE 16.8*b* **(continued)**

Example 16.2   Geometric figure representation. Figure 16.8 shows a hierarchical representation for simple 2-D geometric figures. (This example is continued in Chapter 18.) Slots used in the sample representation include:

- closed   closed form or not
- number-sides   the number of sides
- parallel_sides   the number of parallel sides
- equal_sides   the number of equal sides
- right_angles   the number of right angles
- can_be
- is_a
- instance

Figure 16.9 shows an extended frame representation for the concept "rectangle" that includes procedural information ("procedural attachment") and demons.

```
FRAME : rectangle
SLOT :  is-a          value: parallelogram
                      default-value: geometric-figure
SLOT :  side-characteristics
SLOT :  number-sides
                      value: 4
SLOT :  closed
                      value: yes
SLOT :  parallel
                      value: 2
                      units: pair
SLOT :  orthogonal
                      value: 2
                      units: pair
                       .
                       .
                       .
SLOT :  used-for      value: block-diagrams
SLOT :  relevant-procedures   name: rule-connected
                              name: rule-parallel
                              name: rule-orthogonal
                              name: rule-count-sides
SLOT :  alert-demon   demon-name: shape-analysis
                      demon-name: close-contours
```

(*a*)

```
FRAME : rectangle
          .
          .
          .
    SLOT : number-sides    value: nil
                           default: 4
                           to-calculate-value: procedure-sides
FRAME : procedure-sides
          .
          .
          .
```

(i)

```
FRAME : rectangle
          .
          .
          .
    SLOT : number-sides    value : x | procedure-sides
          .
          .
          .
```

(ii)

(*b*)

FIGURE 16.9
Frame example with inheritance, procedural attachment, and demons: (*a*) frame representation; (*b*) procedural attachment implementation: (i) using a facet for attached procedure; (ii) directly attaching procedure to value facet.

Further extensions are considered in the problems and Chapter 18, where this hierarchical representation is used to illustrate learning concepts.

FRAME MANIPULATION PRIMITIVES

The frame itself serves as a data structure for knowledge representation; therefore an inference mechanism must be developed to accommodate this representation. Numerous control and organization issues arise. Thus, frame-manipulation primitives such as the following are necessary:

1. Frame *invocation*: choosing one or more relevant frames. $\qquad$ (16-9*a*)

2. Frame *switching*: determining that one or more frames are no longer relevant.

$\qquad$ (16-9*b*)

3. Frame *modification*. This includes
   - slot addition
   - slot removal
   - value modifications $\qquad$ (16-9*c*)

4. Frame *addition* and *deletion*. This, as might be suspected, is an involved process, principally due to the interconnected nature of the frames. For example, when a frame is deleted, all links to that frame must be removed or redirected (automatically). $\qquad$ (16-9*d*)

5. Frame *linking*. Note that relations among frames serve as natural interframe pointers for this purpose. In addition, it is necessary to implement concepts such as inheritance. $\qquad$ (16-9*e*)

6. Frame *merging* or *splitting*. $\qquad$ (16-9*f*)

An Example of Frame-based Inference (SIGMA)

In the SIGMA image-understanding system [Hwang/Davis/Matsuyama 1986], the basic representation primitive is that of the frame. In SIGMA, object models are repesented by a graph structure, where the nodes are object descriptions (implemented as frames) and the arcs are relations between the objects. Figure 16.10 shows the SIGMA frame-based representation approach.

OTHER REPRESENTATION PARTITIONS

Another formalized mechanism for structuring, or specifically *partitioning*, representations is the *blackboard* model [Ni 1986]. This mechanism is so named as a result of observing how experts, confined to a room and given a problem and a blackboard, might share applicable knowledge in the solution process. In the case of humans, this knowledge might be enumeration of solution approaches, assumptions, constraints, figures, references, and so forth. Material may be added to or removed from the blackboard by one or more of the experts. The blackboard model is one vehicle for implementing opportunistic problem solving. Figure 16.11 shows the overall concept, which we now explore in more detail.

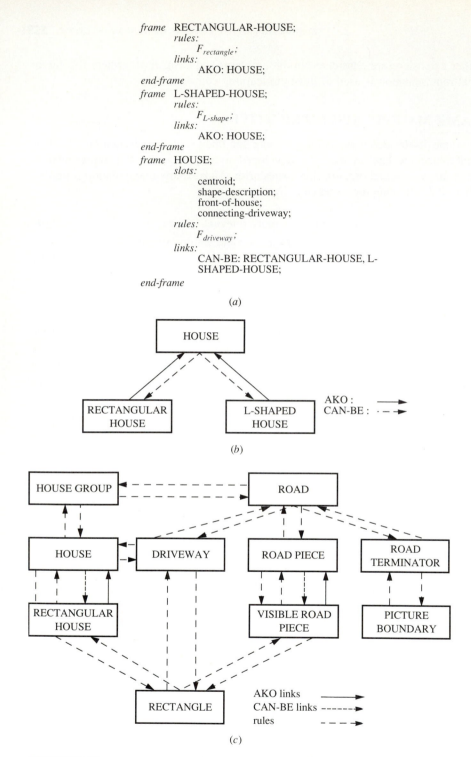

frame RECTANGULAR-HOUSE;
  rules:
    $F_{rectangle}$;
  links:
    AKO: HOUSE;
end-frame
frame L-SHAPED-HOUSE;
  rules:
    $F_{L\text{-}shape}$;
  links:
    AKO: HOUSE;
end-frame
frame HOUSE;
  slots:
    centroid;
    shape-description;
    front-of-house;
    connecting-driveway;
  rules:
    $F_{driveway}$;
  links:
    CAN-BE: RECTANGULAR-HOUSE, L-
    SHAPED-HOUSE;
end-frame

(*a*)

FIGURE 16.10
Frame representations in image analysis: (*a*) frame definitions for HOUSE, RECTANGULAR-HOUSE, and L-SHAPED HOUSE; (*b*) links between HOUSE, RECTANGULAR-HOUSE, and L-SHAPED HOUSE frames; (*c*) a model of a suburban housing development. (From [Hwang, Davis, and Matsuyama, 1986].)

530

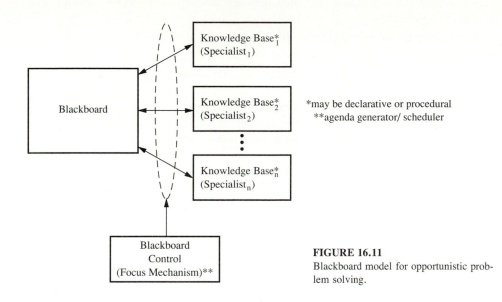

FIGURE 16.11
Blackboard model for opportunistic problem solving.

Blackboard (Theoretical Concept)

A **blackboard** is a type of globally accessible database that serves as a repository of information. In a blackboard system, domain-specific knowledge (often procedural) is partitioned into packets or specialists, which are allowed to communicate through the blackboard. These specialists are usually separate and independent. Thus, the blackboard provides a vehicle to agglomerate problem-specific information from a number of databases, without necessitating the use of the whole of each database. Only information specific to the particular state of a specific problem is extracted and communicated via the blackboard. This may include relevant data or intermediate conclusions. Note that the flow of data between the specialists and the blackboard is bidirectional—specialists may contribute knowledge to the blackboard as well as extract information from it. This allows some computationally advantageous forms of local reasoning in the specialists. In addition, the blackboard itself is a dynamic data structure, with information being added or removed over time.

CHARACTERISTICS OF A "GOOD" BLACKBOARD APPLICATION. Applications that are candidates for a blackboard solution approach share a number of characteristics, including

- A need for an opportunistic problem-solving methodology ("fusion" of expertise).
- A need to reason with incomplete and possibly inconsistent information.

- A need for extensive communication between heterogeneous representations and solution approaches.
- A need to generate and explore multiple hypotheses in parallel.
- A need to reason on multiple levels of abstraction.
- A need to consider external information that arrives sporadically.

BLACKBOARD CONTROL. In the blackboard structure, it is necessary to control the overall opportunistic reasoning that occurs; that is, using the human analogy, a "moderator" is required. This mechanism determines, among other things,

- Who is "at the blackboard" (i.e., which knowledge source is *activated*) over time.
- How long a specialist may control the inference process.
- Relative weights to be attached to statements produced by each specialist.

This "moderator" is usually implemented in the blackboard control, or focus mechanism, as shown in Fig. 16.11. For example, this control may be implemented by incorporation of a set of preconditions in each specialist, indicating the conditions that must exist for activation of that expert. The specialists may be given relative weights (just as one might choose the opinion of a more qualified person over another less qualified) that govern their activation potential. This provides, to some extent, a means of implementing some form of "common sense," by using a high-priority specialist (ofttimes referred to as a "demon" or "oracle").

Blackboard Operation

In the blackboard mechanism, the blackboard is the current global database relevant to a specific problem (or goal) containing input data, partial solutions, alternatives (tentative solution approaches), the goal, and possible control data. We do not consider here a specific data structure of the blackboard, except to note that it

1. Must be in a form accessible to the specialists.
2. May itself be partitioned into a hierarchical organization.
3. May be partitioned into multiple blackboard panels.

The control mechanism allows the specialists to respond opportunistically to the time-varying state of the blackboard. Thus, the control mechanism controls the stepwise generation of the solution.

> **Example 16.3 Typical sequence of blackboard operations.** A typical sequence of blackboard-based operations [Ni 1986] are as follows:
>
> 1. A specialist changes the blackboard.
> 2. All specialists then indicate to the control mechanism (the "moderator") their potential contribution to the problem, based on the revised problem state.

3. The control mechanism then determines the next specialist to be given access to the blackboard. If two or more are applicable, the control mechanism determines a schedule, or agenda, for their participation.

4. This specialist is allowed to revise the blackboard (and then any others on the agenda follow).

5. The control mechanism determines if the problem has been solved (or perhaps if it is unsolvable). If it has been solved, a new problem is sought; otherwise operation resumes at step 2.

This scenario indicates that the operation of the blackboard system is consistent with our concept of a general production system. The solution approach is clearly data-driven and nondeterministic. We note that the control of assertion and removal of blackboard information suggests that a tentative control strategy (i.e., keeping a copy of previous blackboard states) may be desirable. Furthermore, conflict resolution is involved. We note that the blackboard concept, as described, is easy to describe despite giving rise to a number of difficult questions in the implementation stage.

ADVANCED IE CONTROL CONCEPTS

Metarules and Demons

Our design of inference engines (IEs) has been concerned with straightforward mechanisms to manipulate facts. The efficiency of these IEs was demonstrated principally in terms of restricting the problem-space search. In this section, we consider more sophisticated IE design approaches, which are intended to embed more "intelligence" in the system inference process.

METARULES. The previously described frame concept typifies a reasonable and intuitively appealing partitioning of the knowledge representation. The use of frames requires frame-linking and frame-switching mechanisms. Thus, the IE needs the ability to accomplish a limited amount of "internal" inference, in order to guide the manipulation of rules and facts. **Metarules**, or rules about rules, provide one mechanism to accomplish this. In a system using metarules, the IE is itself a small production system, wherein facts and rules about the larger production system are used to determine the focus of system attention.

Figure 16.12 indicates this concept for the HERACLES medical-diagnosis system.

DEMONS. The inherent logic in the IE makes its behavior somewhat "cold," in the sense that it is not easy to embed common sense in the inference process. For example, logically correct, but practically unreasonable situations may arise. A human would clearly recognize these situations, and modify the inference process accordingly. To employ *common-sense reasoning*, we may incorporate the concept of demons in the inference process.

Demons are a set of procedures that are data-activated and take precedence over "normal" IE functions. (16-10)

EMYCIN

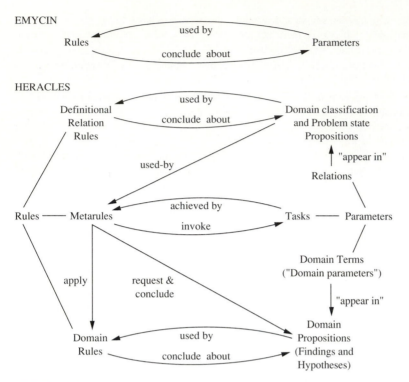

FIGURE 16.12
A higher-order IE design using metarules: how control knowledge is encoded in HERACLES. [*AI Magazine, vol. 7, no. 3, p. 53.*]

Demons monitor the state of the inference process, and, unless a state causing demon invocation occurs, are transparent to the system. They unobtrusively reside ("lurk") in the background unless an abnormal state that violates common sense is detected. Thus, from an implementation point of view, demons are like processes that are triggered by the system state and that interrupt normal processing. In this way we derive a computational mechanism that overrides normal system inference processes to ensure that common-sense productions occur. Demons in a symbolic processing scenario are analogous to internal interrupts in a high-level microprocessor, where, for example, an interrupt is generated if an abnormal or illegal operation (e.g., division by zero) is attempted.

The design and use of demons requires considerable care, for both practical and theoretical reasons. The implementation of demons requires computational resources, since the system state must be either continuously or periodically checked. Demons may be added or removed (analogous to the "masking" of interrupts) as a function of the state of the inference process. This is desirable so that irrelevant demons do not consume computational resources in the monitoring process.

VERIFYING KNOWLEDGE-BASE CONSISTENCY

The knowledge base in an expert system is typically derived from consultation with a number of different domain experts. This process may lead to the embedding of disparate information in the representation, since all the expert information is not guaranteed to be consistent. Furthermore, under some circumstances it is possible for the IE to produce conflicting information. Thus, the verification of the knowledge-base consistency is a major problem in practical AI achievement.

Description and Identification of Six Types of Rule-base Problems

For illustration purposes, we concentrate our attention on rule-based systems, and explore techniques for testing the consistency and completeness of a rule set. Our concerns are both for *static* (i.e., fixed at a certain instant of time) and *dynamic* (i.e., as the system evolves) checks of the rule base. We will use the notation of predicate calculus to represent rules.

REDUNDANCY. In this case, two rules may be equivalent in the sense that they satisfy the same preconditions and produce the same conclusion. For example,

$$p(X) \cap q(X) \rightarrow r(X)$$

and

$$p(Y) \cap q(Y) \rightarrow r(Y)$$

are redundant. Redundancy is seldom this easy to spot, due to the use of alternative, but logically equivalent, statements.

CONFLICTS. In this case the system contains two or more rules that are applicable, but that produce conflicting conclusions. For example,

$$p(X) \rightarrow r(X)$$

and

$$p(Y) \rightarrow \neg r(Y)$$

SUBSUMED OR SUBORDINATE RULES. In this case, two or more rules produce the same consequents, but one has additional preconditions (antecedents). For example, in a system containing both

$$p(X) \cap q(X) \rightarrow r(X)$$

and

$$q(Y) \rightarrow r(Y)$$

it is only necessary to have the second rule. Note, referring to the conflict-resolution strategies of Chapter 11, that the first rule is more specific.

UNNECESSARY CONDITIONS. Consider the following two rules:

$$p(X) \cap q(Y) \rightarrow r(Z)$$

$$p(X) \cap \neg q(Y) \rightarrow r(Z)$$

Application of resolution to this pair yields

$$p(X) \rightarrow r(Z)$$

UNREACHABLE CONDITIONS. This situation implies that rules exist in the rule base that, in light of the facts, can never be fired. Clearly, for a rule to be fired, its antecedents must be satisfied. The unreachable condition dilemma occurs in two ways:

1. No subset of the facts in the database will allow firing of the rule.
2. There is no combination of rule consequents that is able to produce the preconditions necessary to fire the rule.

CIRCULAR RULES. This is perhaps one of the most common problems encountered. In fact, we saw an example of this situation involving the careless representation of transitive or symmetric relations in PROLOG in Chapter 4. In a more general sense, the problem occurs when the inference net forms a cycle. The following set of rules exemplifies this problem:

$$p(X) \rightarrow q(X)$$

$$q(Y) \rightarrow r(Y)$$

$$r(Z) \rightarrow p(Z)$$

NONMONOTONIC REASONING

In many situations, inference must be conducted in light of information that is imprecise, unavailable, or of questionable validity. Often, further inferences are based upon assumptions of default values. In this section we consider *nonmonotonic reasoning*, or *nonmonotonic logic*, which are tools intended to facilitate reasoning with incomplete information; a necessary feature is revision of previous reasoning scenarios when new or more complete information becomes available. We note the following:

> A mode of reasoning is **monotonic** if it reaches conclusions that are never retracted on the basis of new information. (16-11)

Nonmonotonic conclusions are reached using currently available information. Thus, they are tentative conclusions, and may be proven incorrect (FALSE) on the basis of subsequently available information. Therefore, the uncertain appropriateness or suitability of a nonmonotonic conclusion must be weighed against the cost of being unable to otherwise reach a conclusion. In other words, is a "bad" plan better than no plan at all?

MONOTONIC VERSUS NONMONOTONIC LOGIC. The simplest way to see the distinction between monotonic logic and nonmonotonic logic is the following:

> In (classical) monotonic logic, anything that follows from inferences using a knowledge base also follows from an enlarged knowledge base. Nonmonotonic logics do not have this characteristic. (16-12)

Nonmonotonic reasoning is related to many other concepts, such as temporal logic; common-sense reasoning; database consistency; inheritance and exceptions; database completeness (e.g., the negation-as-failure concept in PROLOG); reasoning with uncertainty; and modal logic (Chapter 18).

Situations Involving Nonmonotonic Reasoning

DEFAULT REASONING. There are many examples of the reasoning process with incomplete data. For example, suppose in a frame-based implementation a number of slots contained default values that were used to verify a number of hypotheses. At some later time it is determined (on the basis of new or updated information) that the actual values of entities used in the inference process differed significantly from those assumed previously. Humans employing "common-sense" seem to know (how) to check the reasonableness of assumptions and adjust the inference process accordingly.

NEGATION-AS-FAILURE. Another example of the logical implications of incomplete data is found in the use of the PROLOG not predicate where whatever is not contained in the database is assumed logically FALSE. This is the negation-as-failure concept, or the "closed-world" assumption; that is, we assume the database (or at least the portion of the database we are using to solve a problem) is complete. Suppose a goal is proved, using the not predicate and negation-as-failure in the proof. If the database is, in fact, incomplete, and it is determined at some later time that certain facts that are missing from the database are actually true, then the validity of the goal is questionable.

Nonmonotonic Reasoning Formalisms

Modifications to classical first-order logic that enable proofs in the face of incomplete or default information are, in general, quite complicated and the subject of continued research. First, we view the distinction with two simple examples:

1. The "black and white" representation and modus ponens.

$$\text{IF } a, b, c$$
$$\text{THEN } d \tag{16-13}$$

2. An advanced or "common-sense" representation.

$$\text{IF } a, b, c$$
$$\text{ASSUMING } e, f, g$$
$$\text{THEN } d$$
$$\text{UNLESS } h, i, j \qquad\qquad (16\text{-}14)$$

The difficulty arises when attempting to develop a logic and a sound corresponding inference strategy based upon the representation in (16-14). Approaches to the implementation of nonmonotonic reasoning are just emerging; several are cited in the references.

REFERENCES

Artificial Intelligence , Vol. 13, No. 1, 1980, Special Issue on Nonmonotonic Logic.

[Clancey 1986] Clancey, W.J., "From GUIDON to NEOMYCIN and HERACLES in Twenty Short Lessons," *AI Magazine*, Vol. 7, No. 3, Summer 1986, pp. 40–60.

[Doyle 1979] Doyle, J., "A Truth Maintenance System," *Artificial Intelligence*, Vol. 12, No. 3, 1979, pp. 93–116.

[Filman 1988] Filman, R.E., "Reasoning with Worlds and Truth Maintenance in a Knowledge-Based Programming Environment," *Communications of the ACM*, Vol. 31, No. 4, April 1988, pp. 382–401.

[Hayes-Roth 1985] Hayes-Roth, F., "Rule-Based Systems," *Comm. ACM*, Vol. 28, No. 9, 1985, pp. 921–932.

[Hayes-Roth 1985a] Hayes-Roth, B., "Blackboard Architecture for Control," *Journal of Artificial Intelligence*, Vol. 26, 1985, pp. 251–321.

[Hwang/Davis/Matsuyama 1986] Hwang, V.S., L.S. Davis, and T. Matsuyama, "Hypothesis Integration in Image Understanding Systems," *Computer Vision, Graphics, and Image Processing*, Vol. 36, 1986, pp. 321-371.

[McCarthy 1980] McCarthy, J., "Circumscription: A Form of Nonmonotonic Reasoning," *Artificial Intelligence*, Vol. 13, No. 1, 1980, pp. 27–39.

[McDermott/Doyle 1980] McDermott, D., and J. Doyle, "Non-monotonic Logic I," *Artificial Intelligence*, Vol. 13, No. 1, 1980, pp. 41–72.

[Minsky 1975] Minsky, M., "A Framework for Representing Knowledge," *Psychology of Computer Vision*, P.H. Winston, ed, McGraw-Hill, New York, 1975.

[Nguyen 1987] Nguyen, T.A., et al, "Verifying Consistency of Production Systems," *Proc. 3rd Conf. on AI Applications,* Washington, DC, IEEE Computer Soc. Press, 1987.

[Ni 1986] Ni, H.P., "Blackboard Systems: The Blackboard Model of Problem Solving and Evolution of Blackboard Architectures," *AI Magazine*, Vol. 7, No. 2, 1986, pp. 38–53.

[Reiter 1980] Reiter, R., "A Logic for Default Reasoning," *Artificial Intelligence*, Vol. 13, No. 1, 1980, pp. 81–132.

[Sharkey 1986] Sharkey, N.E., *Advances in Cognitive Science*, John Wiley, New York, 1986.

[Tichy 1987] Tichy, W., "What Can Software Engineers Learn From Artificial Intelligence?," *IEEE Computer*, Vol. 20, No. 11, November 1987, pp. 43–54.

[Winograd 1975] Winograd, T., "Frame Representations and the Declarative/Procedural Controversy," *Representation and Understanding*, Bobrow and Collins, eds., Academic Press, New York, 1975.

[Winston/Horn 1989] Winston, P.H., and B.K.P. Horn, *LISP*, 3d ed., Addison-Wesley, Reading, MA, 1989.

PROBLEMS

16.1. This problem concerns the `is_a` and `can-be` relations.

    (*a*) What properties does each relation have?

(*b*) Derive the relationship between statements using `is_a` and statements using `can-be`.

16.2. Discuss implementation in PROLOG of the six frame-manipulation primitives listed in the text.

16.3. Develop a hierarchical frame representation for the entity "house." Include entities such as door, window, street address, driveway, etc. Consider value inheritance and default values in your representation.

16.4. Discuss how to use the frame representation of problem 16.3 (perhaps together with an inference procedure) for object recognition. Suppose entities (or features) corresponding to "door," "window," and so on, have been extracted from input data. How would a frame representation for "house" be used to facilitate
(*a*) Further feature extraction.
(*b*) Recognition.

16.5. Consider the two structural links "is-a" and *ako* (a-kind-of). Are they the same? Hint: consider the destination between membership in a class versus subclass of a class.

16.6. Develop, in PROLOG, a frame representation for the entity "microcomputer."

16.7. Discuss methods of implementing *value inheritance* and *default inheritance* in frame representations.

16.8. Consider the following database (used for Problem 9.13):

```
(setq   database   '(
    (isa            ibm-pc          computer)
    (has-part       computer        terminal)
    (has-part       computer        keyboard)
    (has-part       computer        RAM     )
    (has-part       computer        ROM     )
    (isa            ncr-pc8         computer)
    (has-part       ibm-pc          proprietary-rom)
    (has-part       ncr             proprietary-rom)
    (has-part       ibm-pc          pc-dos  )
    (has-part       ncr             ms-dos  )
    (isa            pc-dos          operating-system)
    (isa            ms-dos          operating-system) ]
```

(*a*) Draw a semantic net for this database.
(*b*) Develop a LISP function (or set of functions) that allows us to query this database and determine, given the name of a specific entity (e.g., ibm-pc), all the parts belonging to the entity. Implement inheritance.
(*c*) Develop a function `could-be` that implements the `could-be` relation; that is,

```
(could-be   'computer   database)
```

returns

```
(ibm-pc   ncr-pc8)
```

16.9. (This problem makes an excellent long-term project.) Recall one of the principal limitations of logic is that it leads to a formal and "brittle" proof of statements, in the sense that inexactness could not be represented. Consider the use of extended rules to embed sense or *intension* in a database. For example, given the brief fact "?x kills ?y," we may elaborate on the meaning of this via a rule:

```
IF  ?x kills ?y
  THEN ?x will cause ?y to be no longer living
       ?y will need to be buried
       ?x will need a lawyer
       ?x will probably go to jail
       the family of ?y will mourn
```

.
.
.

16.10. One knowledge-base inconsistency, discussed in the text, concerns the subsumption of rules. This condition is indicated by the following statements:

$$p \cap q \rightarrow r$$

$$q \rightarrow r$$

(*a*) Does $\neg p \rightarrow r$ logically follow?

(*b*) What constraints do the two statements jointly place upon p?

16.11. As shown in the text, a prototypical "automobile" frame could contain, among other information, the fact that an automobile has four wheels. However, there may be exceptions where we have reason to believe otherwise, and therefore wish to override this inherited information. Discuss and compare several alternatives for implementing exceptions; these might involve

- Additional frame slots.
- Demons.
- Attached procedures.
- Multiple defaults.

16.12. Consider the use of a frame-structured representation with slots labeled "more-general" and "more-specific." Discuss how this structure could

(*a*) Lead to a hierarchical representation structure.

(*b*) Facilitate the focusing of diagnostic inference.

16.13. Show, using *resolution*, that the following database contains an inconsistency:

$$a$$

$$a \rightarrow b$$

$$c$$

$$c \rightarrow \neg b$$

16.14. For the LISP frame implementation shown in Ex. 16.2 and Fig. 16.8, develop and implement LISP functions to

(*a*) Access slots and return the value or list of values found.

(*b*) Use default values, if present.

(*c*) Compute default values using procedures referenced within the frame.

(*d*) Inherit values if possible.

Show examples using the LISP functions.

16.15. (*a*) Develop a LISP function that identifies demons that should be activated, if they are encountered during access to a particular frame.

(*b*) Discuss how the activation of demons should be integrated with overall AI system control.

(*c*) How should demons be represented?

16.16. Comment, with explanation, on the following observation:

- Most realistic descriptions of commonplace entities possess properties that have at least one exception.

16.17. Consider an alternative structured representation based upon the *typical* attributes of an entity. For example, instead of representing "all elephants are grey," or equivalently

$$(\forall X)\text{elephant}(X) \to \text{grey}(X)$$

we choose to represent

typical elephants are grey

Can this approach be quantified and extended? How are exceptions handled?

16.18. Show the nonmonotonic nature of the following database:

> initial database (at t_0)
> quantifying AI is difficult
> quantifying AI is worthwhile
>
> additional statement (at $t > t_0$)
> if ‹something› is difficult, then ‹something› is not worthwhile

16.19. Can you distinguish a logic that is nonmonotonic from one that is inconsistent?

16.20. Another concept related to hierarchical structures is that of *encapsulation*. Encapsulation concerns the "hiding" of unnecessary or irrelevant information from users of an object. Discuss how encapsulation may be beneficial in developing and using structured representations.

16.21. This problem concerns alternatives for implementing structured representations. Consider two approaches faced by an AI system developer in attempting to link objects:

approach 1. The system incorporates a special data structure for object representation. The data structures (e.g., using slots such as i s−a) are linked. The IE is modified to include special functions used to access data structures and implement inheritance.

approach 2. Simple rules are used together with a simple IE. For example,

$$\text{IF}((?x)\text{IS-A}(?y))\text{AND}$$

$$((?y)\text{IS-A}(?z)))$$

$$\text{THEN}((?x)\text{IS-A}(?z))$$

Compare approaches 1 and 2. Specifically, address representational efficiency, complexity, extendability, and the computational complexity of inference.

16.22. Refer to the 2-D geometric figure representation of Fig. 16.8. Develop LISP functions to implement each of the six-frame manipulation primitives listed in the text.

16.23. Refer to the frame example of Fig. 16.9.

(*a*) Convert this into a suitable LISP structure and design functions for frame access.

(*b*) In cases where procedural attachment is represented (see Fig. 16.9(*b*)), develop LISP functions for obtaining slot information involving these attached procedures.

CHAPTER 17

TEMPORAL LOGIC AND REASONING IN ARTIFICIAL INTELLIGENCE

"The mind of man is capable of anything—because everything is in it, all the past as well as all the future."

Joseph Conrad 1857–1924
Heart of Darkness [1902], II

INTRODUCTION

Time and Logic

This chapter concerns the fundamental concepts of reasoning with time (RWT). Up to this point, our examination of knowledge representation and manipulation has neglected the concept of time; for example, we ignored the ramifications of tense in statements (or simply considered all statements atemporal). Clearly, this has left us ill-equipped to implement AI-based solutions to a number of realistic problems wherein the temporal ramifications of events are fundamental. The temporal change of the database, the need to consider previous and future states in plan generation, and other considerations as well, all point to the need to incorporate the effects of time in reasoning. For example,

- Statements that were true yesterday *may* still be true today, but perhaps not tomorrow. Thus, temporal reasoning is a *dynamic* process.
- Things we do (and don't do) today *cause* other things to be in some state at a later time.
- Humans reason and plan in a world with history, calendars, wristwatches, deadlines, predictions, and other temporal constraints.

A number of fundamental topics are related to RWT including temporal logics, interval-based temporal representations, causality, and modal logic.

Tools for formal reasoning with time are needed to achieve realistic AI implementations. For example, the development of a rule-based logic that employs a when construct, as compared to an if-based antecedent designator, illustrates the point. In our previous reasoning we formulated rules in the form

$$IF < statement > \ldots THEN < consequent > \qquad (17\text{-}1)$$

versus the form

$$WHEN < statement > \ldots THEN \ldots \qquad (17\text{-}2)$$

Statement (17-2) is quite useful in a number of representations. The connotation in statement (17-2) is different from (17-1) in the sense that (17-2) implies that eventually the antecedent is true. More specifically, there is some time after which the rule is applicable. Other possible connectives include

```
henceforth (subsequently)
until
never
eventually
previously
before, after, and during
```

One viewpoint is that time is a parameter that governs the truth of statements. Thus,

> The concept of time is a parameter in the reasoning process that must be carefully interpreted and that constrains most practical reasoning. (17-3a)

In addition,

> Temporal reasoning may involve *predictions* about what will happen based upon knowledge of past events. (17-3b)

However, the concept of time as applied to reasoning is much deeper for several reasons:

1. There exist situations (or reasoning scenarios) other than the "current" one. The situation existing at the present time may influence future states and itself be influenced by events occurring in the past. Temporal reasoning systems therefore must keep a *record* (or history) of the occurrence and characterization of events to be used for *future* reasoning.

2. Humans (and some signal-processing algorithms) have a limited memory capacity in the sense that over time they forget; that is, information is removed from the data base. This attribute is not necessarily completely good or bad; forgetting irrelevant (or possibly no longer TRUE) details frees the reasoning process to concentrate on currently important events. However, forgetting may be a detrimental property in other situations.

3. There exist many realistic situations wherein human reasoning capacity is *incomplete* with respect to time. For example, we may not be able to establish either the validity of the rule or truth of the antecedent in the following statement without an unreasonable observation interval.

> IF humans are exposed to excessive levels of radon gas for 300 years
> THEN cancer will develop

4. The process of *planning* is intimately related to the concept of time since a plan is comprised of a *sequence* of actions with a temporal precedence. Another way to see the relevance of time to planning is through the concept of a *deadline*, which requires that some action(s) occur prior to a specified time.

5. The database of a realistic system is often a function of time and must allow for state changes (either controllable or uncontrollable) over time. The representation is checked to eliminate those facts (or rules) which are no longer true and to add those facts and rules which are now true (as a result of the advance of time). An obvious example is the updating of information regarding the age of individuals in a database; this must be updated on (or near) the birthday of each individual.

6. We (usually) must employ causal reasoning where knowledge of events in the future is not required to enable reasoning in the present.

Recall in classical logic, anything that follows from a set of facts also follows from an enlarged set of facts (the monotonic property). Intuitively, the reader should verify that this is not true in temporal reasoning.

Example 17.1 Temporal overlap and chaining. The significance of reasoning with time is further exemplified by the following "misapplication" of MP (assume we are reasoning in the present):

IF relay 5 is open
　　　THEN line 5 is not energized　　　　　　　　　　(TRUE)
relay 5 was open yesterday　　　　　　　　　　　　　(TRUE)

line 5 is not energized today　　　　　　　　　　　(?)　　　　(17-4a)

This inference is neither intuitively sound (would you work on the line?), nor can our simple formulation of symbolic logic represent the intent of this logic without modification. Note in (17-4) that the consequent involves a different (today) time frame than that of the antecedent (yesterday).

17-4(a) illustrates the concept of temporal overlap and chaining, as shown below:

$$p \rightarrow q \qquad \text{(TRUE} \quad \text{for } t \in T1)$$

$$p \qquad \text{(TRUE} \quad \text{for } t \in T2)$$

$$q \quad \text{(TRUE for } t \in (T1 \cap T2)) \tag{17-4b}$$

CONCEPTS AND APPROACHES FOR REASONING WITH TIME (RWT)

Time Concepts

Reasoning with time (RWT) may be point or interval-based. In other words, we quantify time as a *point* (or moment) or an *interval* (or period). For example, our language allows for both of these concepts using phrases such as "at this point in time" and "within the time frame allocated." This dichotomy is easily explained by recalling that (fortunately) time is a 1-D concept with an ordering which is universally accepted, as shown in Fig. 17.1. The three major subdivisions of time, relative to a chosen point (which is not stationary), are

1. The present or "current time," denoted t_c. Although it is defined as a point, loosely speaking we may wish to think of the present as an interval including t_c. For example, the present might be "today" or "this week." The present may be affected by the past.
2. The past is defined by all values of $t < t_c$ and is available to us in the form of "history" or experience. The past cannot be changed (but it may be "reinterpreted"). There is one "past."
3. The future is defined by all values of $t > t_c$ and may be affected by events occurring in the past or present. Furthermore, the occurrence of events (statements and their associated truth values) in the future is predictable with varying degrees of accuracy, but not certainty. (At least initially) we postulate that there exists an infinite number of "future" scenarios.

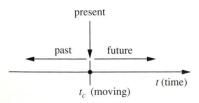

FIGURE 17.1
Major subdivisions of the time concept (point and intervals).

BEFORE AND AFTER. The "before" and "after" relate *temporal domains*. In addition, we usually refer to *events* in these temporal domains, thereby implying "occurs before" or "begins before."

LINEAR VERSUS BRANCHING TEMPORAL LOGICS. Temporal logic systems have different methods for treating the concept of the future. In **linear temporal logic**, the future is unique. Conversely, in **branching temporal logic**, there exists a set of possible evolutions or futures. In the latter, a time instant which spawns more than one future is a **branching time**. In either approach, there is a *single* or *unique* past.

CAUSAL REASONING. The above characterization of time embodies a *causal* reasoning scenario in that the present and the future are inhibited from affecting the past.

> Causal reasoning does not allow reasoning in the present to require facts in the future.
> (17-5)

THE CLOCK WE CAN'T STOP. It is especially important to note that the concepts of past and future are of relatively little *absolute* significance; they are *relative* concepts and determined by the the the choice of t_c. Equivalently, specification of any one uniquely determines the other two. Furthermore, none of these concepts is static; t_c is continually increasing. This suggests that the temporal-based inference engine will need to have some method to account for the time at (or during) which reasoning is occurring; that is, the IE has an internal "clock." RWT problems are always, in a sense, "moving."

TEMPORAL PRIMITIVES AND REPRESENTATIONS. Association of the truth value of atemporal statements with time is fundamental to development of RWT strategies. One of the major dichotomies of RWT approaches concerns *point-based* versus *interval-based* temporal reasoning. In other words, are temporal primitives in RWT time points or intervals? In current AI research, there seems to be approximately equal attention given to both as well as attempts to unify the two. An interval-based logic formulation (e.g., [Allen 1981]) might denote that properties or events are valid over an interval by clauses of the form

$$valid\_event(e,i) \qquad (17\text{-}6a)$$

where e is a specific event and i is a time interval.

By contrast, a point-based logic (e.g., [McDermott 1982]) could form a representation with clauses of the form

$$\begin{aligned} &is\_true\\ &is\_true\ (t,p) \qquad (17\text{-}6b) \end{aligned}$$

indicating that a fact, denoted p, is true at time t. By specifying end points, the truth of statements over time intervals may be represented in this form.

Modal temporal logics (discussed later) accommodate point-based representations with little modification due to the indexing of a world with a point in time, that is, t_1. This is due to the accessibility relation being that of temporal precedence of points (i.e., the accessibility relation between world t_1 and t_2 holds if and only if $t_2 > t_1$). Note that temporal precedence only requires that we consider the relation "after" (or its inverse "before"). Interval-based temporal logic, on the other hand, requires that we develop formalisms to represent and manipulate other relations between time intervals. This includes before, during, overlapping, abutting, and so on.

TIME INTERVALS AND POINTS. With respect to the concept of a **time interval**, we note that an interval (*i*) is defined as a *set of points* and therefore (*ii*) may or may not contain a specified point, and that intervals (*iii*) may *overlap*, that is share common points; or (*iv*) may be *disjoint* (e.g., the past and future intervals always are).

Although we often speak of a "time frame" in terms of an interval, the concept of a **temporal frame** (which we develop below) is a more complex and constrained entity. Temporal relations involving intervals may be developed by considering interval-based relations involving "overlapping," "coincident," and so on. For example, given intervals I1 and I2, the following predicates are TRUE under the stated conditions:

```
during (I1, I2)    : interval I1 is (completely) contained
                     within interval I2.
before (I1, I2)    : I1 exists before I2 and there is no
                     overlap.
overlap (I1, I2)   : I1 begins before I2, and I1 and I2
                     overlap.
equal (I1, I2)     : I1 ≡ I2.
meets (I1, I2)     : before (I1, I2) ≡ T and I2 starts
                     where I1 ends (i.e., no interval
                     between I1 and I2).
```

These are shown in Fig. 17.2.

In order to relate the truth value of statements to intervals, we use predicates of the form of (17-6a), that is,

```
holds (A, I)
```
(17-6c)

where A is a statement and I is an interval. Note also we may implicitly develop the notion of a temporal point from the interval-based formulation by "shrinking" an interval I, perhaps using a limiting argument. This is explored in the problems.

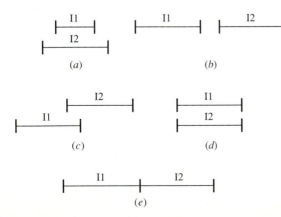

(a) (b) (c) (d) (e)

FIGURE 17.2
Graphical description of temporal interval relations: (*a*) during (I1, I2); (*b*) before (I1, I2); (*c*) overlap (I1, I2); (*d*) equal (I1, I2); (*e*) meets (I1, I2).

REPRESENTING COLLECTIONS OF STATIC STATES.

A temporal *frame, world,* or *situation* is a system state, defined over some time interval, where the truth value of facts is constant (persistent). (17-7)

Graphical Representations for RWT

Adding time as a parameter to a representation increases the "dimensionality" of the representation. Recall from Chapter 1 (Fig. 1.7) that actions and events could be represented using conceptual relations and corresponding graphs. In this way, the agent, act (action), and object were identified.

We seek a similar graphical structure for situations involving temporal reasoning. This includes

1. Graphical representations of temporal relations between simple elements (e.g., "event a at time t_1 causes event b at time t_2").
2. Graphical representations of relations between temporal frames (e.g., a relation of temporal precedence).

A simple method to indicate causation in temporal reasoning could be using the relation "causes-later"; that is, the occurrence of event a "causes-later" event b. This relation, depicted graphically, generates a time-map. Other temporal relations such as "must occur before" also generate graphical representations (e.g., a PERT-chart). The difficulty in employing relations of this sort is that "later" is a *relative* concept, and the temporal precedence of objects in a graphical relation may be ambiguous. For example, given

$$\text{causes-later (event\_a, event\_b)}$$
$$\text{causes-later (event\_a, event\_c)} \qquad (17\text{-}8a)$$

we are unable to determine the temporal precedence of `event_b` and `event_c`.

APPLICATION OF SEMANTIC NETS—APPROACHES AND PROBLEMS. Labeling an arc with the relation "causes-later" is one example of extending the semantic net to temporal representations. Figure 17.3a shows a simple example using "before." Another simple approach is to let a single semantic net represent a current system state, thus spawning a family of semantic nets indexed by time. This is shown in Fig. 17.3b. Viewing any "plane" gives a semantic net representation at that time; viewing an event or statement-specific "slice" through the planes yields historical information. Since the temporal reasoning involves keeping track of previous events (history), a single, extended semantic net may not be able to satisfy our need for a graphical representation involving time. Moreover, it raises the question of whether a natural separation of temporal representations is desirable.

SEPARATION OF TEMPORAL REPRESENTATIONS. The difficulty in developing a combined representation for a state at several different times (e.g., before, during, and

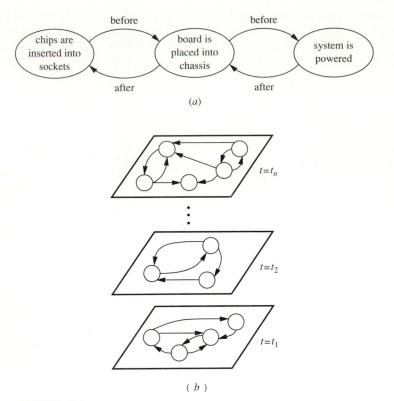

FIGURE 17.3
(*a*) Graphical representation of the temporal relations "before" and "after"; (*b*) "family" of semantic nets, indexed by time.

after some event) suggests the utility of separating the representations. One method of achieving this is through *modal logic*, which is treated later.

POTENTIAL IMPLEMENTATIONS OF RWT (WITHOUT THEORY). The fundamental property of temporal logic, in contrast to the classical logic we employed previously, is this:

> In temporal logic, the same statement may have different truth values at different times, that is, in different worlds, situations, or "time frames."   (17-8*b*)

For example, statements true in the past are not required to be true for all time, as the example in (17-4) shows.

There exists a multitude of conceptually obvious (and simplistic) implementations of RWT. In studying the RWT literature, the reader should note that most current implementations do not use all of the formalisms presented in this chapter. Rather, a carefully-chosen subset is implemented. Indeed, many approaches are simple extensions to atemporal logic. In most cases, the resulting inference mechanisms are considerably more complex than those that (explicitly) ignore time. Two major approaches to RWT are [Camurati/Prinetto 1988]:

1. Explicitly introducing time as a variable in predicate logic. In Chapter 2 the truth values of statements were represented using predicate functions to allow variables in statements. One result was that the truth value of a statement varied, depending upon the value(s) taken on by variable(s) in the statement. This suggests one possibility, namely, to increase the arity of predicate functions by one and thus make time a variable in the statement. Thus, temporal predicates arise. The temporal index, or variable, is most-often considered a continuous variable whose universe is the set of positive real numbers, and is therefore countably infinite. This fact (again) complicates the representations.

2. Generalization or augmentation of atemporal logic to modal logic.

AN EXAMPLE OF A SIMPLISTIC RWT IMPLEMENTATION: MODIFICATION OF PROLOG PREDICATES. A time interval (or other equivalent measure) could be added to each PROLOG predicate, and, in conjunction with the value of a current or "present" clock (time value), the "retract" and "assert" predicates used to modify the database. Equivalently, we could include a time interval in all predicates, and force the PROLOG unification mechanism to use this argument in the matching process.

Simple Prolog Example of RWT Implementation

We use PROLOG to show a simple system that employs some of the above ideas. The scenario used is one that involves RWT and is familiar to most humans, namely the concept of a finite lifetime for living organisms. Relative to any choice of current time, there exist three designators regarding a specific person's lifetime: unborn, alive, and dead. These represent three moving (with t) intervals associated with each person in the database. Furthermore, the relative position of the intervals on the time axis determine who preceded or survived whom, and so on. We employ a (fictitious) database involving the lifetimes and chronology of family pets. A simple example of a PROLOG program is shown in Fig. 17.4.

A RWT THEORETICAL FRAMEWORK

The notion of RWT in various capacities may be achieved by augmenting our previous application of logic with the concept of associating time with events or the truth value of statements and a set of relations of temporal significance, that is, the concepts of causality, the precedence of events in time, the past as fixed knowledge, and the future as time- and event-varying.

DEPICTING THE TRUTH VALUE OF STATEMENTS OVER TIME. A convenient tool for exploring temporal logic is shown in Fig. 17.5a. The "history" of the truth value of statement A is plotted over time. This graphical approach may be extended to include more than one statement, as well as compound statements.

TEMPORAL OPERATORS (F, P, G, H). Using the terminology of [Turner 1984], we develop an alternative and rigorous definition of a temporal frame, to develop a minimal temporal reasoning methodology. Our attention is restricted to four possible

```
/* database */

current(1989).
born(morris,1974).
born(jesse,1983).
born(ruffie,1979).
born(ralphie,1965).
born(harry,1981).
born(rasp,1980).
born(tiger,1960).
killed(ruffie,1983).
died(ralphie,1971).
died(tiger,1964).
died(morris,1985).

/* examples of rwt predicates */

was_alive(X) :- born(X,_),
                dead(X).

unborn(X) :- born(X,Date),
             current(Now),
             Now < Date.

unborn(X) :- not(born(X,Date)).

will_die(X) :- born(X,Then),
               current(Now),
               Then =< Now,
               not(dead(X)).

dead(X) :- died(X,When),
           current(Now),
           Now > When.

dead(X) :- killed(X,When),
           current(Now),
           Now > When.

age(X,Years) :- born(X,Date),
                current(Now),
                Years is Now - Date,
                Years > 0,
                not(dead(X)).
alive(X) :- born(X,_),
            not(dead(X)).
```

FIGURE 17.4
Example of temporal reasoning in PROLOG.

```
same_age(X,Y)  :- not(X=Y),
                  alive(X),
                  alive(Y),
                  age(X,A1),
                  age(Y,A2),
                  A1 == A2.


/* Sample Predicates for Interval-Based RWT */


lifespan(X,Begin,End)  :- born(X,Begin),
                          killed(X,End).
lifespan(X,Begin,End)  :- born(X,Begin),
                          died(X,End).


lifespan(X,Begin,_)  :- alive(X),
                        born(X,Begin).


alive_at_same_time(X,Y)  :- lifespan(X,Bx,Ex),
                            lifespan(Y,By,Ey),
                            not(X = Y),
                            overlap(Bx,Ex,By,Ey).


/* utility predicates */


overlap(Bx,Ex,By,Ey)  :- contained_in(Bx,By,Ey).
overlap(Bx,Ex,By,Ey)  :- contained_in(Ex,By,Ey).
overlap(Bx,Ex,By,Ey)  :- contained_in(By,Bx,Ex).
overlap(Bx,Ex,By,Ey)  :- contained_in(Ey,Bx,Ex).


contained_in(A,B,C)  :- bound(A),
                        B =< A,
                        bound(C),
                        A =< C.


contained_in(A,B,C)  :- bound(A),
                        B =< A,
                        not(bound(C)).


not(P)  :- call(P),!,fail.
not(P).


bound(X)  :- nonvar(X).
```

FIGURE 17.4 (continued)

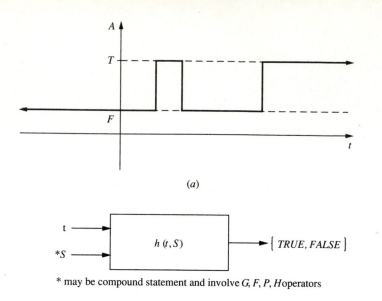

(a)

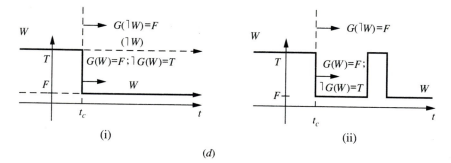

(b)

* may be compound statement and involve G, F, P, H operators

(c)

(d)

FIGURE 17.5

(a) Graphically depicting the truth value of statement A over time; (b) using the h function to map (possibly compound) statements into truth values as a function of time; (c) history of A over time (from 17.5a) and the corresponding truth values of the G, F, H, P operators at selected times. Note how the truth value of these operators varies with t, the current time; (d) graphical analysis of why G(¬ W) ≠¬ G(W). (i) History of W where G(¬ W) = ¬G(W); (ii) history of W where G(¬ W)≠¬ G(W) (counterexample to (i)).

time-specific aspects of the truth value of a statement, A, which are conveyed by four temporal operators, denoted F, P, G, and H. When necessary, the truth value of A at time t is denoted $A|_t$. Denoting the current time as t_c, they are

1. $F(A)$: A is TRUE at some future time; that is, $\exists$ a nonempty set of values $\{t_f\}$ where $t_f > t_c$ such that $A|_{t_f}$ is TRUE for each value. $\qquad$ (17-9a)
2. $P(A)$: A was TRUE at some time in the past; that is, $\exists$ nonempty set of values $\{t_p\}$ where $t_p < t_c$ such that $A|_{t_f}$ was TRUE for each value. $\qquad$ (17-9b)
3. $G(A)$: A is TRUE at all future times; that is, $(\forall t > t_c)\, A|_t$ is TRUE $\qquad$ (17-9c)
4. $H(A)$: A was TRUE for all past time; that is, $(\forall t < t_c)\, A|_t$ is TRUE $\qquad$ (17-9d)

Note the relationship between the F and G and the P and H operators, respectively. G and H are used to form stronger (in the sense of constraints) statements, and therefore F and P are always applicable in situations where G and H, respectively, apply. Fig. 17.5c serves as a prelude to the more formal characterizations of F, G, H, P in (17-16), (17-21), and (17-22). Note that the truth value of $F(A)$, $G(A)$, $P(A)$, or $H(A)$ depends upon the notion of the current time, t_c.

Example 17.2 Utility of temporal operators. Consider the following statements:

A: person X will die (i.e., is $\neg$ alive)
B: person X is alive $\qquad\qquad\qquad\qquad\qquad\qquad\qquad\qquad$ (17-10)

Given B is TRUE at t_c, we may correctly assert $F(A)$. Furthermore, given B is TRUE at t_c, we may also correctly assert $P(B)$ but not $H(B)$.

Example 17.3 Manipulation of compound statements using G, F, A, and P. Manipulation of compound statements involving the G, F, A and P operators is both possible and desirable. Often, this is facilitated by a sketch of the truth values of individual statements along the time axis as shown in Fig. 17.5. For example, we might wish to consider distributing the F, P, G, H operators over compound statements such as $G(A \cup B)$. The reader should verify that

$$G(A \cup B) \not\equiv G(A) \cup G(B) \qquad\qquad (17\text{-}11)$$

Similarly,

$$G(A) \cup G(B) \rightarrow G(A \cup B) \qquad\qquad (17\text{-}12a)$$

and

$$G(A) \cap G(B) \equiv G(A \cap B) \qquad\qquad (17\text{-}12b)$$

are easy to verify.

Other valid statements (tautologies) are shown in Table 17.1. From Table 17.1, two TRUE implications are

$$G(A) \rightarrow F(A) \qquad\qquad (17\text{-}13a)$$

and

$$H(A) \rightarrow P(A). \qquad\qquad (17\text{-}13b)$$

TABLE 17.1
Valid statements in temporal logic

1. $G(A \rightarrow B) \rightarrow (G(A) \rightarrow G(B))$
2. $H(A \rightarrow B) \rightarrow (H(A) \rightarrow H(B))$
3. $A \rightarrow H(F(A))$
4. $A \rightarrow G(P(A))$
5. $G(A) \equiv \neg F(\neg A)$
6. $H(A) \equiv \neg P(\neg A)$
7. $G(\neg A) \rightarrow \neg G(A)$

These may be verified using the definitions of (17-9). The F, P, G, and H operators, combined with the tautologies of Table 17.1 and a notion of temporal relations, form the basis of a manipulable and quantifiable RWT strategy.

TEMPORAL FRAMES. Notice that the truth value of (possibly compound) statement A (or of any operator applied to A, e.g., $G(A)$) may not be determined without explicit knowledge of the current reasoning time (which therefore determines the notions of "past" and "future"). To accomplish this, we introduce the concept of a *temporal frame*. We extend atemporal logic to achieve a *propositional* temporal logic by first adding to the previous atomic sentences and connectives a set of temporal operators. An additional step in the extension is the development of a function, h, which assigns truth values to statements over time.

A **temporal frame** consists of three entities:

1. A nonempty set of time points, T.
2. A relation of temporal precedence, denoted R. R enables an interpretation of the ordering of time. Properties of significance, such as transitivity of this precedence relation, are considered below. The simplest and least constrained relation of temporal precedence is to stipulate

$$R(t, t') = \text{TRUE for } t < t' \tag{17-14}$$

3. A function, denoted h, to map the truth value of statements, tagged with respect to time (i.e., time is always an explicit argument in application of h) into the values TRUE or FALSE. Function h has two arguments, t (time) and a (possibly compound) statement. This function continually updates and guides RWT. This is shown in Fig. 17.5b.

RELATING h TO F, P, G, H, AND COMPOUND STATEMENTS. The following are consequences of the mapping function, h, which are consistent with our notation and concepts previously discussed in (17-9). Note A and B are statements; equivalence is denoted using the iff operator, depicted as "$\equiv$," and "such that," indicated by "s.t." The current time is denoted simply by t.

1. $[h(t, A \cap B) = \text{TRUE}] \equiv$
$$[h(t, A) = \text{TRUE}) \cap (h(t, B) = \text{TRUE}] \tag{17-15a}$$

2. $h(t, \neg A) = \text{TRUE} \equiv$
$$h(t, A) = \text{FALSE} \tag{17-15b}$$

The meaning of (17-15a) and (17-15b) is relatively obvious. However, incorporating the F, P, G, and H operators gives more purpose to h.

3. $h(t, F(A)) = \text{TRUE} \equiv$
$$(\exists t_f) \text{ s.t. } (t < t_f) \cap h(t_f, A) = \text{TRUE} \tag{17-15c}$$

Alternately, using our definition of $R(t, t_f)$ above, this may be written

$$h(t, F(A)) = \text{TRUE} \equiv$$
$$(\exists \ t_f) \text{ s.t. } (R(t, t_f) \cap h(t_f, A)) = \text{TRUE} \tag{17-15d}$$

The left hand side of (17-15d) says that from the point of view of some time, t, A will be TRUE at some time in the future. This is equivalent to using $R(t, t_f)$ and h to temporally constrain the truth value of A. Similarly,

4. $h(t, P(A)) = \text{TRUE} \equiv$
$$\exists t_p \text{ s.t. } [(t_p < t) \cap h(t_p, A)] = \text{TRUE} \tag{17-15e}$$

Equivalently,

$$h(t, P(A)) = \text{TRUE} \equiv$$
$$(\exists \ t_p) \text{ s.t. } [R(t_p, t) \cap h(t_p, A)] = \text{TRUE} \tag{17-15f}$$

Furthermore, we note two useful corollaries and an important distinction with respect to the above results. First,

$$G(A) \equiv \neg F(\neg A) \tag{17-16}$$

which equates the truth of the statements "A will always be TRUE in the future" with "there is no future time at which A will be FALSE." Second,

$$H(A) \equiv \neg P(\neg A) \tag{17-17}$$

which equates the truth of statement "A has always been TRUE in the past" with "there is no past time for which A is (was) FALSE."

We need to be careful to avoid superficially developing or interpreting temporal logic. For example, there is a clear distinction between statements such as

$$H(\neg A) \tag{17-18a}$$

and

$$\neg H(A) \tag{17-18b}$$

(17-18a) indicates A has always been FALSE, whereas (17-18b) stipulates A has not always been TRUE. Clearly, these are *not* equivalent statements.

Similarly,

$$G(\neg A) \neq \neg G(A) \tag{17-19}$$

as shown graphically in Fig. 17.5d.

Several other questions regarding the equivalence of RWT-related statements are left to the exercises.

Additionally, the following are equivalences in this temporal logic:

$$h(t, G(A)) = \text{TRUE} \equiv$$

$$(\forall t_f)(R(t, t_f) \rightarrow (h(t_f, A) = \text{TRUE}) \tag{17-20}$$

and

$$h(t, H(A)) = \text{TRUE} \equiv$$

$$(\forall t_p)(R(t_p, t)) \rightarrow (h(t_p, A) = \text{TRUE}) \tag{17-21}$$

Some (not all) axioms of RWT, using this temporal logic, are

1. $G(A \rightarrow B) \rightarrow (G(A) \rightarrow G(B))$ (17-22)

   which is equivalent to saying that $(A \rightarrow B)$ being TRUE for all future times implies (the implication) that A being TRUE for all future times implies B being TRUE for all future times.

2. $A \rightarrow G(P(A))$ (17-23)

   which indicates that if A is TRUE we are guaranteed that there is a time in the past when A is TRUE.

PROPERTIES OF $R(t, t')$. We now consider several important properties that must accompany the above RWT formulation. The first is the existence of the transitivity property of $R(t, t')$:

$$(\forall t)(\forall s)(\forall r)\ [(R(t, s) \cap R(s, r)] \rightarrow R(t, r) \tag{17-24}$$

This is shown in Fig. 17.6a. The second deals with the (assumed) continuous (non-discrete) nature of time, namely, that given two non-equal values of time there is a continuum of time values between them. This is forced via

$$(\forall s)(\forall t)(\exists r)R(s, t) \rightarrow [R(s, r) \cap R(r, t)] \tag{17-25}$$

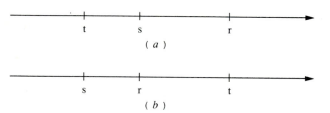

FIGURE 17.6
Properties of $R(t, t')$. (a) Transitivity $(R(t,s) \cap R(s,r)) \rightarrow R(t,r)$; ($b$) continuous and open
$(\forall s)(\forall t)(\exists r)R(s, t) \rightarrow (R(s, r) \cap R(r, t))$
$(\forall s)(\exists t)R(t, s) = \text{TRUE}$ (infinite past)
$(\forall s)(\exists t)R(s, t) = \text{TRUE}$ (open future).

which is related to the transitivity concept and shown in Fig. 17.6*b*. Finally, to achieve the concept of time not having a beginning (start) or an end (finish), we assert

$$(\forall s)(\exists t)(R(t, s) = \text{TRUE}) \tag{17-26a}$$

and

$$(\forall s)(\exists t)(R(s, t) = \text{TRUE}) \tag{17-26b}$$

indicating we can always go farther into the past and are always guaranteed a future. The properties of (17-26) may be restricted in the implementation of RWT systems, perhaps due to the finite temporal extent of the database.

The preceding exemplifies (but does not completely specify) a temporal logic from which consistent inference strategies may be implemented. Several nuances, such as the forcing of a unique past, but "open" future, need also to be addressed. However, we leave the formal logic and proceed to a simple example.

Modal Logic as a RWT Framework (Optional)

In modal logic [Chellas 1980], [Shoham 1987], we create worlds in which to interpret (i.e., assign a value to) the truth of a statement, A. Such worlds are connected by directed links, which indicate temporal relations between worlds. (17-27)

The relation of *accessibility* (or reachability) is of utmost importance. In modal logic, the truth value of statements interpreted in one world is related to other worlds, specifically those that are accessible (i.e., related by the accessiblity relation).

If A is a statement, then we may interpret A in a particular world, W_1. A may be true in W_1, as well as in other worlds, W_i. We adopt the following two lemmas. For any formula, A,

L1:   ■ A ("necessarily" or "box" A) is TRUE in W_1 iff A is TRUE in all worlds that are accessible from W_1.

L2:   *A ("possibly" or "diamond" A) is TRUE in W_1 iff $\exists$ a world accessible from W_1 in which A is TRUE.

Based upon L1 and L2, the following equivalence (the proof of which is left to the problems) results:

$$*A \equiv \neg \blacksquare (\neg A) \tag{17-28}$$

The previous abstract concept is, surprisingly, useful in temporal logic. Often world W_1 is the "time frame" or point in time at which current reasoning is taking place. The world accessibility relation used, denoted R, is that of *temporal precedence*. By indexing relating worlds to time, world t_2 is accessible from world t_1 iff $t_2 \geq t_1$. Notice at this point it is not necessary to define worlds as time points or time intervals. Furthermore, note the relation $\geq$ is both reflexive and transitive. The world concept and temporal precedence relation are shown in Fig. 17.7.

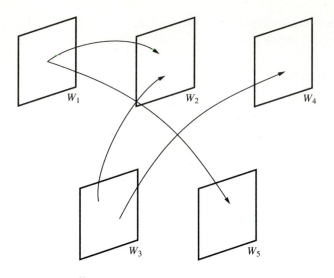

FIGURE 17.7
Worlds in modal logic for RWT (accessibility relation shown)

Example 17.4   Modal logic versus first order logic.

$$\neg \text{ likes\_cats} \rightarrow \blacksquare \neg \text{ likes\_cats} \tag{17-29}$$

means if I don't like cats (now), then I'll never like cats (in the future). Interestingly, this statement in modal logic may be replaced by the more familiar

$$\neg \text{ likes\_cats}(t_1) \rightarrow ((\forall t_2) \ (t_2 \geq t_1) \rightarrow \neg \text{ likes\_cats}(t_2)) \tag{17-30}$$

Thus, modal logic is merely a more compact formalism for reasoning with time.

REFERENCES

[Allen 1981] Allen, J.F., "An Interval Based Representation of Temporal Knowledge," *Proc. 7th Int. Joint Conf. on Artificial Intelligence,* Vancouver, Canada, 1981, pp. 221–226.

[Allen 1984] Allen, J.F., "Towards a General Theory of Action and Time," *Artificial Intelligence*, Vol. 23, No. 2, July 1984, pp. 123–154.

[Camurati/Prinetto 1988] Camurati, P., and P. Prinetto, "Formal Verification of Hardware Correctness: Introduction and Survey of Current Research," *IEEE Computer*, July 1988, pp. 8–19.

[McCarthy 1987] McCarthy, J., "The Frame Problem Today," in *The Frame Problem in Artificial Intelligence*, (F. M. Brown, ed.), Morgan Kaufman Publ., Los Altos, CA, 1987, p.3.

[McCarthy/Hayes 1981] McCarthy, J.M., and P.J. Hayes, "Some Philosophical Problems from the Standpoint of Artificial Intelligence," *Readings in Artificial Intelligence*, Tioga Publ., Palo Alto, CA, 1981.

[McDermott 1982] McDermott, D., "A Temporal Logic for Reasoning About Plans and Actions," *Cognitive Science*, Vol. 6, 1982, pp. 101–155.

[Shoham 1988] Shoham, Y., *Reasoning About Change*, MIT Press, Cambridge, MA, 1988.

[Turner 1984] Turner, R., *Logics for Artificial Intelligence*, John Wiley, NY, 1984.

PROBLEMS

17.1. Consider the following temporal indicators as relations: "is," "was," "will be."
   (*a*) Cite examples of their application.
   (*b*) What properties do they have?

(c) For each case that makes sense, repeat (a) and (b) for the complement of each of these indicators, (i.e., "is-not," etc).

17.2. Implement each of the G, F, P, A operators from (17-9) in PROLOG.

17.3. Implement the axioms for temporal reasoning from Table 17.1 in PROLOG.

17.4. Show whether each of the following statements is TRUE or FALSE in temporal logic. (Hint: in many cases proof by contradiction is an efficient solution procedure.)

(a) $(G(A) \rightarrow F(A)) \cap (H(A) \rightarrow P(A))$

(b) $H(A \rightarrow B) \rightarrow (H(A) \rightarrow H(B))$

(c) $G(A) \rightarrow F(A)$

(d) $H(A) \rightarrow P(A)$

(e) $H(A) = \neg P(\neg A)$

(f) $G(A) \equiv \neg F(\neg A)$

17.5. Show $A \rightarrow H(F(A))$ is TRUE.

17.6. (a) Prove

$$G(\neg W) \rightarrow \neg G(W)$$

(i) Graphically

(ii) Algebraically

(b) Show why

$$G(\neg W) \not\equiv \neg G(W)$$

(i) Graphically

(ii) By showing a counterexample

17.7. Discuss RWT and *negation as failure*, in light of the finite (temporal) extent of a database.

17.8. Referring to the definitions in L1 and L2, prove

$*A \equiv \neg (\blacksquare(\neg A))$

17.9. Determine the truth value of each of the following:

(a) alive $(X) \rightarrow F(\text{die } (X))$

(b) $P(\text{born } (X)) \rightarrow F(\text{die } (X))$

(c) alive $(X) \rightarrow P(\text{born } (X))$

17.10. (The following problem is a good way to "exercise" your thinking about temporal intervals.) Which of the following statements using interval-based logic are TRUE? (Show justification for each answer.)

(a) before (I1, I2) $\equiv$ after (I2, I1)

(b) before (I1, I2) $\equiv \neg$ after (I1, I2)

(c) overlap (I1, I2) $\cap$ overlap (I2, I3) $\rightarrow$ overlap (I1, I3)

(d) before (I1, I2) $\cap$ overlap (I2, I3) $\rightarrow$ before (I1, I3)

(e) before (I1, I2) $\cap$ overlap (I2, I3) $\rightarrow$ overlap (I1, I3)

(f) before (I1, I2) $\cap$ overlap (I2, I3) $\rightarrow$ overlap (I2, I3)

(g) overlap (I1, I2) $\cap$ during (I1, I2)

(h) before (I1, I2) $\rightarrow \neg$ during (I1, I2)

(i) before (I1, I2) $\equiv \neg$ during (I1, I2)

17.11. Certain types of temporal reasoning lead to *circularities*. For example, consider the following rules:

```
IF     person_x can't sleep well
THEN   person_x doesn't work effectively          (P17-11a)


IF     person_x doesn't work effectively
THEN   person_x can't sleep well                  (P17-11b)
```

Show

(a) through causation, the circularity;

(b) a graphical representation of (P17-11a) and (P17-11b);

(c) a way to remove the circularity by making time a point process.

17.12. Verify (17-4b).

17.13. (This problem makes an excellent long-term project.) Develop a system that allows reasoning in the sense that if we know an event occurred in the past, there exists a rule (applied either in the past or the present) that says that something *will* happen (in the future, relative to the occurrence of the initial event). We need to check the present time to see if the latter event has happened (yet). Conversely, we may develop rules that check for the occurrence of events (sufficiently in the past, relative to the present) to determine the truth value of a present event.

An obvious example involves the planting of flower seeds in a garden, where at the time the seeds are planted we may formulate a hypothesis that mature flowers will exist in some number of days in the future. The truth of this hypothesis is a function of events at the time of planting (i.e., the seeds were fresh and planted in soil, not concrete) as well as future events (such as the weather in the succeeding interval). Conversely, if, at the present time, we are reasoning about the existence of flowers in the garden, the IE must check the past for the occurrence of a group of events (the planting of the seeds, the intervening weather) as well as quantitative information regarding the difference between the present time and the time of planting.

17.14. Is the temporal relation "causes-later" transitive? Cite an example to justify your answer.

17.15. Develop a representation for each of the following temporal statements:

    (i) If my homework is handed in before noon Friday and my grade is above 70, then I will receive a grade of B or better at the end of the semester.

    (ii) Before the circuit board is inserted into the chassis and before the chassis is energized, the integrated circuits (chips) must be inserted in their sockets, which must have been previously inserted into the circuit board.

    (iii) Interest on a savings account is compounded quarterly at an annual rate of 12 percent, starting on the day of deposit, using:

(a) point-based temporal logic

(b) interval-based temporal logic

17.16. An engineer suggested the following procedure to relate interval-based temporal reasoning with a point-based representation:

$$\text{point (I)} = \lim_{I2 \to I} \{\text{during (I, I2)}\}$$

Show, by example, why this procedure does not yield the desired result and show a revised procedure that does.

17.17. Give an example, in words, of the utility of RWT axioms such as

$$\neg G(A) \equiv F(\neg A)$$

17.18. Prove

(a) $G(A) \cap G(B) \equiv G(A \cap B)$

(b) $G(A) \cup G(B) \to G(A \cup B)$

(c) $G(A \to B) \to (G(A) \to G(B))$

17.19. An extension to the propositional temporal logic we developed in this chapter is to allow variables in statements, thus yielding sample statements such as

$$G \text{ (alive (Who))}$$

Discuss, in detail, the problems this extension generates in RWT.

17.20. Discuss, both informally and using definitions, the (composite) operator $F(F(A))$. Is it the same as $F(A)$?

17.21. Given that the world accessibility relation is that of temporal precedence, relate modal logic lemmas L1 and L2 defined in (17-28) to the G, H, F, P operators. Is modal logic statement (17-29) a restatement of one of the equivalences derived using G, H, F, P?

17.22. Consider a database consisting of the following statements, which, at the current time, are TRUE:

$$\text{(airplane 3 landed)} \tag{P17-22a}$$

$$\text{(airplane 4 took-off)} \tag{P17-22b}$$

On the basis of (P17-22a) and (P17-22b), which of the G, H, F, or P operators, applied to the following statements, yields TRUE statements?

$$\text{(airplane 3 took-off)} \tag{P17-22c}$$

$$\text{(airplane 4 landed)} \tag{P17-22d}$$

17.23. Suppose we modify Example 17.1, specifically (17-4a), by including the additional (TRUE) rule

IF (? relay) was open yesterday

$$\text{THEN (? relay) is open today} \tag{P17-23}$$

(a) Is the conclusion reached in (17-4a) now
  (i) TRUE?
  (ii) Sound, in the sense of logically supported?
(b) Which of the RWT temporal operators in (17-9) does the modified formulation of (P17-23) attempt to implement? Can other rules be derived that implement the other operators in (17-9)?

CHAPTER
18

LEARNING
IN AI
SYSTEMS

"What one knows is, in youth, of little moment; they know enough who know how to learn."

Henry Brooks Adams 1838–1918
The Education of Henry Adams, ch. 21

"Learning is not attained by chance, it must be sought for with ardor and attended to with diligence."

Abigail Adams 1744–1818
Letter to John Quincy Adams [May 8, 1780]

INTRODUCTION

The Concept of Learning

In earlier chapters, knowledge bases were designed by "programming-in" the knowledge. Thus, "concepts" are formulated by the database developer. In many applications, it is desirable for the AI system to develop or modify its internal knowledge representation on the basis of "experience," thus facilitating "learning." The concept of learning is both fundamentally important and difficult to precisely define or quantify. Some might argue the concepts of AI and learning are indistinguishable; for a system to be considered "artificially intelligent," it should have the capacity for learning. As application areas mature, the automation of human learning will become necessary to achieve adaptable and robust systems that can aggregate experience in an opportunistic manner. Autonomous learning is probably one of the least developed or least mature subareas of AI, and therefore it is likely that learning will receive a good deal of future research attention.

Systems that can automatically formulate new high-level concepts (such as rules), modify old concepts, and improve their performance gradually through acquired experience are typical of learning systems. The current generation of AI systems almost exclusively employ *deduction*, in the sense that they are able to prove goals or verify facts. They do not, however, have the ability to generate new knowledge (or facts) autonomously; that is, they are unable to make *constructive* inductive inferences. Humans, on the other hand, are quite adept at synthesizing new knowledge from existing evidence or information. The development of self-adaptive or learning systems with predictable or controllable properties is a formidable task.

Conceptually, learning usually is related to

1. Self-improvement.
2. Adaptation to new or different circumstances.
3. Behavior modification.
4. Concept formulation and refinement, including generalization or specialization of the conceptual model.

LEARNING AS MODEL REFINEMENT. In this chapter, we emphasize that the implementation of automated learning involves learning as model formulation or refinement. Specifically, we may view learning as refinement of the representation, perhaps on the basis of experience. Experience may be gained by interaction with the existing system and the outside world. For example, when the representation contains rules, the modification (e.g., generalization) of rules based upon cumulative experience is a form of learning.

Historical Learning Research

The study of learning, like the study of intelligence itself, is not new. The German psychologist Johann Friederich Herbart in 1816 formulated an intuitively plausible conjecture that is referred to as the **apperceptive mass** explanation of learning. Paraphrased [Watson 1963], "Combined ideas form wholes and a combination of related ideas form an apperceptive mass, into which relevant ideas are welcomed but irrelevant ones are excluded."

Conversely, psychologists supporting the *behaviorist* notion promoted *conditioning*. Conditioning may be an unconscious process wherein behavior changes after a number of examples of correct behavior, that is, accumulated evidence. Behaviorism attempts to characterize and achieve correct stimulus-response (S-R) action. A neural network that adapts its interconnection structure on the basis of a training set typifies this approach.

Piaget [Piaget 1968] proposed a categorization of learning based on the type of change in the stored knowledge representation. Assimilation of new information into an existing and unchanged structure (e.g., a schema) is differentiated from accommodation, wherein the existing structure is modified on the basis of new information. This taxonomy has been extended to three categories [Rummelhart/Norman 1978]:

- *Accretion:* basically the same as assimilation.
- *Schema tuning:* minor changes to the structure (e.g., addition of new properties or defaults, generalization) are allowed.
- *Restructuring:* major reorganization of schemata allows induction of new concepts (similar to accommodation).

Thus, accommodation encompasses both tuning and restructuring.

The hypothesis generation necessary for new or modified concept induction requires a hypothesis generator. As in Chapter 13, the process of *abduction* is useful.

Learning Definitions

A reasonable interpretation of machine learning is the following:

> The development of systems capable of learning involves the development or identification and implementation of algorithms ("learning algorithms") that enable other algorithms (AI algorithms) to improve their performance or to adapt on the basis of past experience or information.
>
> (18-1a)

On the basis of definition (18-1a), note that a general notion of learning is not simply the acquisition of additional raw data (e.g., additional explicit programming). There is a distinct difference between *reasoning* and *recollection*. Nevertheless, rote learning or direct knowledge acquisition (memorizing) is one of the earliest identifiable signs of intelligence. For example, an elementary school student is considered more educated, that is, to have learned more, when the multiplication tables have been successfully memorized. This occurs even in the absence of an understanding of the concept of multiplication.

Another possible definition of learning is

> (Inductive) learning systems form plausible internal descriptions that explain observed evidence and are useful for prediction of new evidence.
>
> (18-1b)

Examples of Current Automated Learning Research Paradigms

At least four major research approaches to machine learning are identifiable:

1. *Neural Modeling:* In this approach, learning (or training) takes place via adaptation of network connection strengths.
2. *Decision Theoretic Techniques:* Evidence, that is, $A_1 A_2 \ldots A_n$ is used to update $P(E \mid A_1 A_2 \ldots A_n)$ from $P(E)$.

3. *Symbolic Concept Acquisition (SCA):* Proceeds by constructing or modifying stored representations of concepts. Representations may be in the form of logic, production rules, or semantic networks.

4. *Constructive Induction [Michalski 1986]:* This major area includes learning from examples or observations (as in concept acquisition) and learning by analogy.

A long-term objective of automated learning research is the development of precise computational models for the learning mechanism. As with other aspects of AI, research into learning methodologies must consider the potential contribution of the human behavior model. Through the study and attempted modeling of the cognitive development of babies and young children in key areas such as the development or acquisition of language understanding [Selfridge 1986], development of the capacity to understand humor, and the ability to count, key aspects related to the automation of learning capability may result.

Learning must be facilitated by the observation of information. Note that this may be achieved in several (not really disparate) ways:

1. Through sources external to the AI system, that is, through I/O with the external world. This is analogous to everyday human experience.

2. Through investigation of new information sources. This is analogous to a human reading (and comprehending) a new book.

3. Through assessment of past actions (e.g., previously generated inference nets, plans, etc.).

Learning Approaches

Several learning approaches are known to exist and behavioral classification of these learning paradigms may be achieved in several ways. We describe each below:

Rote learning. This is equivalent to memorization of facts and actions. Understanding of the data (in the sense of any action other than recollection) is not required. In this context the "opposite" of learning is "forgetting." We equate rote learning with explicit programming.

Advice taking. Given control information, for example, heuristics, the system IE is modified. This is also simplistic in the sense that it represents the creation of additional rules; for example, advice may be phrased as "IF . . . THEN . . . . " The possibility of advice that conflicts with information in the current database must also be considered. Furthermore, if we allow the "advice generation" mechanism to examine past inference results and perhaps to incorporate performance evaluation or provide "criticism," we arrive at performance-driven learning.

Learning concepts from examples (or evidence). This is a common and powerful learning paradigm and may be implemented in a variety of ways. Figure 18.1 shows the general structure. Several aspects of this approach are

1. Learning from examples directly exemplifies *generalization* of knowledge as

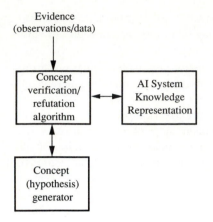

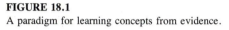

FIGURE 18.1
A paradigm for learning concepts from evidence.

learning. In particular, the process of induction is used to generalize a portion of the existing knowledge structure using the "example" information.

2. Learning from examples may be used to generate totally new rules.

3. Learning from examples allows the potential of learning by analogy, in the sense that new actions or conclusions are based upon the similarity of structure with previous actions or conclusions. The autonomous recognition of analogy, however, is a challenging problem.

4. Learning from examples may be further subdivided into two categories, which are often employed in pattern recognition applications. They involve searching the information space for concept clustering and, on a higher level, concept description. We assume the set of examples is pre-interpreted (or pre-classified) and refer to this process as supervised learning.

5. The related *apprenticeship learning techniques*, a form of "learning by watching," facilitate the automatic transfer of human problem-solving expertise.

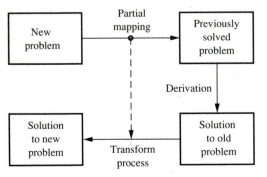

1. Match old problem similar to new one.
2. Recall final solution to the old problem.
3. Transform recalled solution to satisfy
   the constraints of the new problem.

FIGURE 18.2
Learning by analogy (from [Carbonell/Langley 1987] by permission).

Learning by exploration. Nature provides the best example of this paradigm for adaptation (or learning) through the random perturbations or adaptation of a system and consequent survival of those systems whose perturbation is beneficial.

Learning by analogy. We saw in the plan generation of Chapter 14 that, once a problem has been solved, the solution (in this case a plan) could be applicable to other similar situations. In addition, the solution to a specific problem may often provide useful guidelines on how to approach related problems. Past experience, perhaps in the structure of the solution, may be modified or adapted to solve a new problem. Several approaches to analogical problem solving have been postulated [Carbonell/Langley 1987]. These are depicted in Fig. 18.2. Learning by analogy is a way to relate knowledge between domains.

LEARNING ALGORITHMS

Much of the behavior of learning in an AI system involves a transition from the specific to the general (or vice versa). The generalization/specialization dichotomy of knowledge is one vehicle through which to explore learning.   (18-2*a*)

From (18-2a) we note that *induction* involves the agglomeration of information, or organization, or rule development, from specifics to generalities. For example, the application of mathematical induction to logic usually involves showing (through some induction rule) that if predicate p_k is TRUE, then p_{k+1} is TRUE ("and so on"). Generalization-based learning paradigms may involve

1. The elimination of constraints in certain expressions (this makes them more general); or
2. The substitution of variables for constants. This is due to the observation that constants are specific, whereas variables are general. On this basis, we formulate the definition [Dietterich/Michalski 1981]:

Inductive learning may be viewed as a search for plausible general descriptions (inductive assertions) that explain the previously encountered data (experience) and that are likely to correctly explain new data.   (18-2*b*)

LEARNING FORMALISMS FOR AI IMPLEMENTATION. Learning algorithms could be integrated into AI systems as a "shell" around the AI system or developed as an integral part. The amount of choice an AI system designer has in this respect is due to the potential coupling of the chosen knowledge structure and the learning algorithm. In some cases it may be inappropriate to separate these functions. Figure 18.3 indicates a global definition of learning, which is independent of the precise learning or knowledge representation methodology employed. For example, one learning approach may be predicated upon the modification of the knowledge structure. This could involve adding nodes and arcs to a previously stored semantic network. In the case of a frame-based representation, we may add new slots, new is_a hierarchies, or update default values. Recalling one approach in Chapter 11 where the IE contains "rules about rules" (metarules), Fig. 18.3 permits the extension of this concept one step

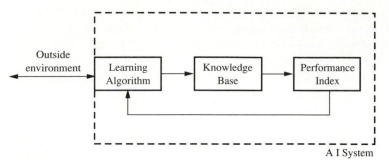

FIGURE 18.3
Elementary model for a learning paradigm.

further. A learning algorithm that directly modifies a rule-based IE may be cast as "rules about rules about rules."

The learning performance index or measure shown in Fig. 18.3 allows a generalized interpretation of learning. For example, this performance index may take into account

1. The *volume* of information (facts and rules) in the database.
2. The *specificity* of the information in the database.
3. The *generality* of the information in the database.
4. The *conceptual organization* of the information in the database.

LEARNING THROUGH DESCRIPTION GENERALIZATION/SPECIALIZATION

General-to-Specific (G-S) and Specific-to-General (S-G) Approaches

Learning through generalization or specialization may be cast in a number of ways. In some instances, the ability to derive more specific information may be desirable, where the generalization of existing information is also useful. In specific-to-general (S-G) approaches, the goal is to find a minimal description that includes (generalizes) all possible instances of some concept in the database, without including any negative instances. One difficulty with this approach is stated below.

> Often, learning (in non-constructive inductive inference) involves *search* through *concept space*. The examples or evidence used may consist of labeled samples, which may be *positive instances* (i.e., exemplars of a given concept) or negative instances. The concept space in realistic problems is likely to be large. (18-3)

Example 18.1 Generalization from evidence.
(Hypothesis) *h*: all birds can fly

> *Evidence*
> *(e-1): sparrows are birds*
> *(e-2): sparrows can fly*   (18-4*a*)

Evidence *(e-1)* and *(e-2)* may be used to conclude *h*. However, if the database contained negative instances of this, for example

>   *(e-3) newborn sparrows cannot fly*
>   *(e-4) newborn sparrows are birds*   (18-14*b*)

the generalization would fail. This type of reasoning, particularly with respect to the exceptions, is related to *nonmonotonic reasoning* (Chapter 16). Generalization of this type may also be categorized as *instance-to-class* or *part-to-whole*.

  The achievement of generalization through application of inductive reasoning involves a transformation of less general descriptions into more general ones. This is accomplished via *generalization operators*.   (18-5)

Typical generalization operators are shown in (18-12).

A Detailed Look at G-S and S-G Algorithmic Approaches

REPRESENTATIONS AND DESCRIPTIONS. Assume we begin with

1. A chosen *problem representation* that includes   (18-6*a*)

2. A set of elemental descriptors (primitives). For example, a representation could consist of descriptors forming a semantic net or a predicate calculus formulation. Alternately, a set of clauses using this chosen representation develops concept descriptions, denoted c_i. A set of concept descriptions is denoted C.   (18-6*b*)
3. A set of generalization/specialization operators.   (18-6*c*)

The key to this type of learning is modification of the concept descriptions through generalization (or specialization). This may involve elimination, addition, and/or modification of descriptors in the c_i in C.

THE TRAINING SETS. To initiate training or learning, we assume we are given sets of exemplars or instances. The positive exemplar set, denoted P, consists of positive examples, whereas the negative exemplar set, denoted N, consists of negative examples (or counterexamples). Note that C, P, and N consist of descriptors in a chosen representation.

CONSISTENCY, EXPLAINING, AND "COVERING." A description, c_i, "covers" an exemplar iff:

1. It is consistent with (i.e., unifies) a positive exemplar.   (18-7*a*)
2. It is inconsistent with a negative exemplar.   (18-7*b*)

The determination of "consistency" in (18-7*a*) and (18-7*b*) requires a matching process. This is shown in Fig. 18.4. A set of descriptions, C, covers an exemplar iff each member of C covers the exemplar. On this basis, a minimal goal for concept

Concept (c_i): parallelogram

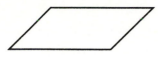

(sides 4)
(closed TRUE)
(parallel 2-side-pairs)
(equal–length 2-side-pairs)

Graphical description

Implementable description
Note: some of this information,
as in any representation, may
be derivable.

(a)

(sides 4)
(closed TRUE)
(parallel 2 - side - pairs)
(equal - length all - sides)
(right - angle all - vertices)

(b)

(sides 4)
(closed TRUE)
(right - angle one vertex)
(parallel 1 - side - pair)
(equal - length 0 - side - pairs)

(c)

FIGURE 18.4
Positive and negative exemplars and "covering" ("semi-abstract" representation). (a) Concept description;
(b) positive exemplar p_i (square); (c) negative exemplar n_i (quadrilateral).

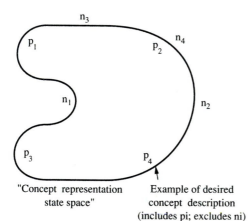

"Concept representation
state space"

Example of desired
concept description
(includes pi; excludes ni)

FIGURE 18.5
Example of desired learning algorithm results.
Note in G-S the coverage "shrinks," whereas in
S-G the coverage "grows."

learning from examples is to derive C such that all exemplars in the training set are covered. This is shown in Fig. 18.5.

ALGORITHMIC GOALS FOR GENERALIZATION/SPECIALIZATION-BASED LEARNING. Specifically, using the given exemplars (the training set), goals of the two approaches are as follows:

specific-to-general (S-G) : produce a set of general concept descriptions

$$(18\text{-}7c)$$

general-to-specific (G-S) : produce a set of most specific concept descriptions

$$(18\text{-}7d)$$

In both cases, the resulting descriptions must cover all the positive and negative exemplars in the training set. It is also desirable that the resulting descriptions possess the property that they are praobable to cover probable future (extended) data. This is shown in Fig. 18.6.

DESCRIPTION MODIFICATION. Description modification occurs through descriptor modification. We adopt a "conservative" approach to the modification of descriptions in the sense that a description is only extended (generalized) or specialized as much as is needed at each step in the process. By modifying descriptions as little as possible, we (attempt to) avoid the generation of modified descriptions that are easily disproved. The issue of non-constructive versus constructive description modification is addressed in a subsequent section.

SPECIFIC-TO-GENERAL (S-G) ("OPENING" THE DESCRIPTION) APPROACH. Given C, a set of (possibly empty) current concept descriptions, and a set of positive exemplars (instances), P, where

$$P = \{p_0, p_1 \ldots p_n\} \qquad (18\text{-}8a)$$

and a set of negative exemplars, N, where

$$N = \{n_0, n_1, \ldots n_n\} \qquad (18\text{-}8b)$$

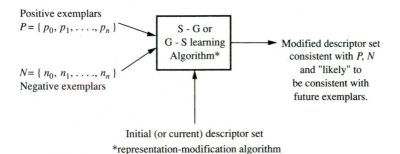

Positive exemplars
$P = \{p_0, p_1, \ldots, p_n\}$

S - G or G - S learning Algorithm*

Modified descriptor set consistent with P, N and "likely" to be consistent with future exemplars.

$N = \{n_0, n_1, \ldots, n_n\}$
Negative exemplars

Initial (or current) descriptor set
*representation-modification algorithm

FIGURE 18.6
General structure of S-G or G-S learning approach.

- Boundaries denote constraints.
- The boundary partitions the set of all possible descriptions such that descriptions that satisfy the constraints are enclosed within the boundary and tuples that do not are excluded.

(a)

p_1 p_2 Sample training sets (exemplars) (P, N)
n_1 p_3

1. Initialize c_1 to cover p_1.

2. Generalize C to cover one or more of the remaining elements of P. (Six possible generalizations shown.)

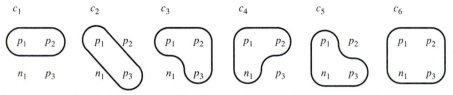

3. Remove any c_i which includes any n_i. (Thin C by removing c_4-c_6).

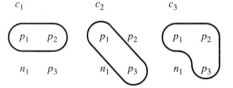

4. If any c_i covers both P and N, STOP. If more than 1 c_i covers P and N, choose the most specific.

c_3

$$
\begin{array}{cc}
p_1 & p_2 \\
n_1 & p_3
\end{array}
$$

(b)

FIGURE 18.7
S-G algorithm—graphical description. (a) Graphical concepts used for illustration; (b) illustration of procedure.

there exist many strategies for the sequential use of elements of P and N to refine C. Given the goal of (18-7c), a skeletal algorithm for S-G is as follows:

Example 18.2   S-G algorithm.

1. If $C = \varnothing$, initialize C to cover one (or more) of the p_i that have not previously been elements of C.

2. Generalize C to cover one or more remaining elements of P.

3. Thin C by:

    (**a**) removing generalizations, c_i, that include any element n_i of N; and

    (**b**) removing any c_i that are overly general; that is, they are more general than (or subsume) another element in C.

    If C becomes empty, go to 1.

4. If every c_i covers both P and N, STOP, else go to 2.

This is shown graphically in Fig. 18.7.

GENERAL-TO-SPECIFIC (G-S) ("NARROWING" THE DESCRIPTION) AP-PROACH. Using the definitions above, an alternative learning strategy is shown. The G-S approach begins with an overly general description and successively refines C using P and N.

Example 18.3   G-S algorithm.

1. If $C = \varnothing$, initialize C to the most general p_i, or another (a priori known) set of general descriptions.

2. Using N, specialize each c_i so that it does not include any n_i.

3. Thin C by

    (*a*) eliminating any c_i that does not cover a p_i (it is overly specific);

    (*b*) eliminating any c_i that is more specific than another c_i.

1. Initialize c to cover all p_i.

$$c_1$$

$$\begin{pmatrix} P_1 & P_2 \\ P_3 & n_1 \end{pmatrix}$$

2. Using N, specialize each element of C so it excludes every n.

c_1 c_2 c_3 c_4 c_5

$\begin{pmatrix} P_1 & P_2 \\ P_3 & n_1 \end{pmatrix}$ $\begin{pmatrix} P_1 & P_2 \\ P_3 & n_1 \end{pmatrix}$ $\begin{pmatrix} P_1 & P_2 \\ P_3 & n_1 \end{pmatrix}$ $\begin{pmatrix} P_1 \end{pmatrix} P_2 \\ P_3 \quad n_1$ $P_1 \begin{pmatrix} P_2 \end{pmatrix} \\ P_3 \quad n_1$ $P_1 \quad P_2 \\ \begin{pmatrix} P_3 \end{pmatrix} n_1$

$$c_6$$

3. Remove any c_i that does not cover all p_i.

$$c_1$$

4. If several c_i cover both p and n, then select the c_i that is most specific and that covers P and N.

FIGURE 18.8
Graphical illustration of the G-S algorithm using "boundaries" as described in Fig. 18.7a.

TABLE 18.1
Utility of exemplars in generalization formulations

	positive exemplar (p_i)	negative exemplar (n_i)
specific-to-general (S-G)	generalize C	filter C (eliminate overly general alternatives)
general-to-specific (G-S)	filter C (eliminate overly specific alternatives)	make C more specific

If C becomes empty, go to 1.

4. If every c_i in C covers both P and N, STOP, else go to 2.

This is shown graphically in Fig. 18.8.

COMPARISON OF THE S-G AND G-S APPROACHES. The S-G approach leads to the set of most general concept descriptors, whereas the G-S approach leads to the most specific set. The choice of one approach over the other, like many AI choices, is probably application-dependent. Table 18.1 summarizes the role of the exemplars in each approach. Of course, hybrid approaches [AI encyl], explored in the problems, are possible. Note also that both algorithms invoke *choices* of different concept description-modification paths. Thus, an underlying search problem is also present in the formulation.

> **Example 18.4   Learning 2-D geometric descriptors.** The following extended example is intended to illustrate the overall approach. Figure 18.9 indicates the hierarchical arrangement of 2-D geometric figures used. Figure 18.10 shows the chosen representation and the training sets (P and N). The desired concept to be learned is "parallelogram." Figure 18.11 shows sample results for the S-G algorithm. Figure 18.12 shows application of the G-S approach. This approach is extended in the problems.

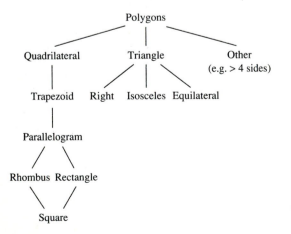

FIGURE 18.9
Sample hierarchical arrangement of 2-D figures (used for learning example).

(closed ?status?)   ; is the figure closed?
(sides ?number?)   ; number of sides
(right_angles ?number?)   ; number of right angles
(parallel ?number? or ?number-pairs?)   ;parallel sides (pairs)
(equal_length ?number?)   ; number of equal_length sides

(*a*)

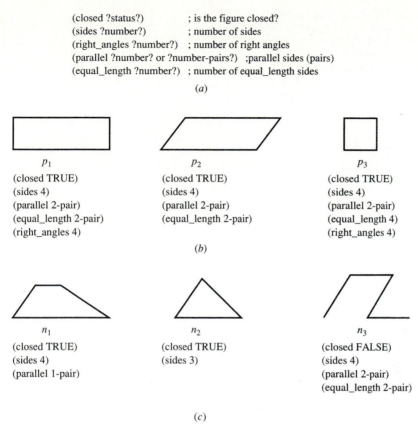

*p*₁

(closed TRUE)
(sides 4)
(parallel 2-pair)
(equal_length 2-pair)
(right_angles 4)

*p*₂

(closed TRUE)
(sides 4)
(parallel 2-pair)
(equal_length 2-pair)

*p*₃

(closed TRUE)
(sides 4)
(parallel 2-pair)
(equal_length 4)
(right_angles 4)

(*b*)

*n*₁

(closed TRUE)
(sides 4)
(parallel 1-pair)

*n*₂

(closed TRUE)
(sides 3)

*n*₃

(closed FALSE)
(sides 4)
(parallel 2-pair)
(equal_length 2-pair)

(*c*)

FIGURE 18.10
Representation and training sets used for geometric figure learning example (desired concept: parallelogram). (*a*) Representation; (*b*) positive exemplars, *P*; (*c*) negative exemplars, *N*.

Inductive Reasoning and Truth/Falsity Preservation

One difficulty with inductive inferences [Michalski 1983], for example, generalization, is that the process is only falsity preserving, not truth preserving. For example, if we declare the statement

$$(\forall X)\ \texttt{electronic\_device(X)} \ :- \ \texttt{computer}\ \texttt{(X)},\texttt{has\_chips(X)} \qquad (18\text{-}9a)$$

is TRUE, we are able correctly to *deduce* that if X is a computer and has chips, then X is an electronic device. An inductive generalization of (18-9*a*) is:

$$(\forall X)\ \texttt{electronic\_device(X)} \ :- \ \texttt{computer(X)} \qquad (18\text{-}9b)$$

1. Assume $C = \varnothing$. Initialize C to be equal to p_1.

   ```
   C = {c₁} = { ((closed TRUE)
                 (sides 4)
                 (right_angles 4)
                 (parallel 2-pair)
                 (equal_length 2-pair))}
   ```

2. Generalize C to cover one or more of the remaining elements of P.

   Generalize c_1 to cover p_2 by deleting the (descriptor) clause

   ```
   (right_angles x) where x = 4
   ```

   since from p_2, one of the possible values of x is 0.

   ```
   C = {c₂} = { ((closed TRUE)
                 (sides 4)
                 (parallel 2-pair)
                 (equal_length 2-pair))}
   ```

3. Thin C by removing any c_1 that does not cover any N_i (i.e., any c_1 that is consistent with N).

   ```
   c₂ does not cover any element of N, so go to 4.
   ```

4. If every c_i covers both P and N, Stop. Else go to 2.

   ```
   c₂ does not cover p₃, so generalize c₂:
   ```

   ```
   C = {c₃} = { ((closed TRUE)
                 (sides 4)
                 (parallel 2-pair)
                 (equal_length x)
                     where x ∈ (2,4))}
   ```

5. Since every c_i covers both P and N, STOP.

   ```
   c₃ is the minimal description that covers all pᵢ.
   ```

FIGURE 18.11
An example of the S-G algorithm applied to Fig. 18.10.

which may or may not be TRUE. However, if (18-9a) is FALSE, then (18-9b) must also be FALSE (hence the falsity preserving characteristic). This is explored further in the problems.

Generalization Operators

In the examples above, the set of generalization or specialization operators was left unspecified. In this section, using nomenclature of [Dietterich/Michalski 1981], the process of generalization is viewed as the application of generalization operators to intermediate descriptions. The application of a generalization operator, denoted G, to an expression S_1 produces a more general expression S_2. Of course, the operator is applied to S_1 based upon some subset of the cumulative knowledge and experience available, collectively denoted E. In other words, denoting this generalization operator

1. Initialize

$C_1 = \{ ((\text{closed } x)$
   $(\text{sides } a)$
   $(\text{right\_angles } b)$
   $(\text{parallel } c)$
   $(\text{equal\_length } d))$
     where a, b, c, $d \in I$ and $x \in \{\text{TRUE}, \text{FALSE}\}\}$

This is the most general description available.

2. Using N, specialize each element of C (c_1) so it covers (i.e., is inconsistent with) each n_i. (Not all possible specializations shown).

Generalize c_1 to cover p_2 by deleting the (descriptor) clause

$C1 = \{ ((\text{closed TRUE})$
  $(\text{sides } x)$ $x \neq 4$
  $(\text{right\_angles } y)$ $y \in I$
  $(\text{parallel } z)$ $z \neq 1$ pair
  $(\text{equal\_length } z)$ $z \neq 0, 3)\}$

$C2 = \{ ((\text{closed TRUE})$
  $(\text{sides } x)$ $x \neq 3$
  $(\text{right\_angles } y)$ $y \in I$
  $(\text{parallel } z)$ $z \in I$
  $(\text{equal\_length } w)$ $w \in I\}$

$C3 = \{ (\text{closed FALSE})$
  $(\text{sides } x)$ $x \neq 4$
  $(\text{right\_angles } y)$ $y \in I$
  $(\text{parallel } z)$ $z \neq 1$ pair
  $(\text{equal\_length } w)$ $w \in I\}$

$C4 = \{ (\text{closed TRUE})$
  $(\text{sides } x)$ $x \neq 4$
  $(\text{right\_angles } y)$ $y \in I$
  $(\text{parallel } z)$ $z \neq 2$ pair
  $(\text{equal\_length } w)$ $w \neq 2$ pair$\}$

$C5 = \{ (\text{closed FALSE})$
  $(\text{sides } x)$ $x \neq 3$
  $(\text{right\_angles } y)$ $y \in I$
  $(\text{parallel } z)$ $z \in I$
  $(\text{equal\_length } w)$ $z \in I\}$

$C6 = \{ (\text{closed TRUE})$
  $(\text{sides } 4)$
  $(\text{right\_angles } x)$ $x \in I$
  $(\text{parallel } 2\text{-pair})$
  $(\text{equal\_length } 2\text{-pair})\}$

3. Thin C in Step 2 by elimination of any c_i which does not cover a p_i (this eliminates c_1, c_2, c_3, c_4, and c_5).

4. Since the description of c_6 covers each p_i and each n_i, stop.

FIGURE 18.12
Sample application of G-S algorithm to problem of Fig. 18.10.

$$S_2 = G(S_1, E) \tag{18-10a}$$

means that the implication of (18-10b) (note carefully the direction of this implication) must be TRUE:

$$S_2 \rightarrow S_1 \tag{18-10b}$$

where now the knowledge contained in S_1 is a specialized case of that in S_2, as desired. Based upon this observation, we use the notation $\leftarrow$ (which may be viewed as an implication arrow reversed with a conditional bar, |) to indicate the construction. Thus $A \leftarrow B$ denotes "A may be generalized to B." For example, the operation in

(18-10*a*) is denoted

$$S_1 \leftarrow\!\!\!| \; S_2 \qquad\qquad (18\text{-}10c)$$

and read as "S_1 may be generalized to S_2".

A non-constructive generalization operator uses only the descriptors in S_1 to produce S_2.
(18-11*a*)

Conversely,

a constructive generalization operator creates one or more new descriptors in S_2, thus changing the representational space of the problem. (18-11*b*)

We note at the outset that the problem of computational complexity, that is, search for the "best" set of generalization operators in a given problem, is significant. In a learning system, at any given time there may be an enormous number of statements that may be generalized, a large number of ways (e.g., different variables) in which individual generalization operators may be applied, and a large number of applicable generalization operators.

Sample Non-Constructive Generalization Operators

A number of non-constructive generalization operators exist. We use predicate calculus to show their effect. They may be combined to form even broader generalizations. Several of these operators are

1. The *dropping condition operator*. We may relax the conditions on one or more of the components in the description, for example,

```
must_have(dec_computer), must_have(dec_terminal) |←
                              must_have(dec_terminal)
```
(18-12*a*)

2. The *constants to variables operator*.

```
must_have(dec_computer), must_have(dec_terminal) |←
              must_have(A_computer), must_have(A_terminal)
```
(18-12*b*)

(18-12*b*) includes the case of the variable that always matches (i.e., the _variable in PROLOG). For example, when the generalization to require a computer, but any computer is acceptable, we may have the generalization:

```
must_have_computer(dec), must_have(dec_terminal) |←
              must_have_computer(_), must_have(dec_terminal)
```

3. The *disjunction operator*. Allowing additional possibilities through disjunction is a form of generalization. For example, in (18-12*a*)

```
must_have_computer(dec)
```

may be generalized through disjunction in several ways. (Note that; denotes OR.) For example,

```
must_have_computer(dec)      |←
must_have_computer(dec);
must_have_computer(ibm);
must_have_computer(ti).
```
(18-12*c*)

4. The *closing interval operator*. This is an extension of the previous example and is used in (18-9). A constraint on the range of a variable is relaxed. For example,

$$num \in (lower, upper] \quad |← $$
$$num \in [lower, \quad \infty]$$
(18-12*d*)

5. The *hierarchy-generation generalization operator*. This operator is based upon generation of generalizations satisfying hierarchical relationships. For example, using the hierarchy of Fig. 18.9 yields

$$\left.\begin{array}{c} \text{square(x)} \\ \\ \text{rectangle(x)} \end{array}\right| ← \text{ polygon(x)}$$
(18-12*e*)

6. The *specialization exception operator*. If, during the process of generalization, a description becomes over-generalized, or a generalization is inhibited due to a small number of exceptions (due perhaps to the observation of frequent negative-reinforcing or counterexamples), rather than inhibit the generalization we achieve generalization with exceptions. Recall this was addressed in our examination of frames, property inheritance, and the is_a hierarchical representation. In addition, the example above of sparrows and the flying capability exemplifies this.

CREATING IF-THEN-UNLESS RULES FOR GENERALIZATION WITH EXCEPTIONS. This approach [Winston 1986] leads to augmented versions of IF-THEN rules with the form

$$\text{IF } a_1 \ldots a_n \text{ THEN } c_1, c_2 \ldots c_p \text{ UNLESS } b_1, b_2, \ldots b_m$$
(18-13)

where the a_i are antecedents, the c_i are (possibly multiple) consequents and the b_i are m **blocking conditions** that inhibit firing of the rule if their disjunction (OR-ing) evaluates to true. Thus, we say a rule application may be blocked by the UNLESS part. Note that this is, in some sense, superfluous, since we may logically reformulate the rule as

$$\text{IF } (a_1 \ldots a_n) \cap \neg (b_1 \cup b_2 \ldots \cup b_m) \text{ THEN } c_1, c_2 \ldots c_p$$
(18-14)

However, this formulation leads to "bloated" rules.

In addition, a method to formulate the UNLESS-modified rules is necessary. An example of an IF-THEN-UNLESS form is the following generalization:

```
electronic_device (X)  :— computer (X), has_chips (X).(18-15)
```

which was generalized to

```
electronic_device  ;— computer  (X).                                 (18-16)
```

The generalization of (18-16) is FALSE, for example, if we consider optical computers. One way to reformulate (18-16) is therefore

```
electronic_device (X)  :— computer  (X)|optical_dev (X)(18-17)
```

where the "|" denotes "unless."

Constructive Inductive Generalization

This type of learning is considerably more difficult to analyze and, not surprisingly, to achieve. A constructive generalization operator creates one or more new descriptors and thus changes the representational space of the problem. Examples of constructive generalization rules are given in [Michalski 1980].

Learning through Building Models and Structural Links

In learning as model building, we view experience as instances or realizations of a process that is either generated by or constrained by a model. Larger conceptual models may be built from smaller building blocks (e.g., concepts) and experience. A rule or mechanism to organize concepts into larger structures is the **schema**. This is an area of active research.

REFERENCES

[Carbonell/Langley 1987] Carbonell, J., and P. Langley, "Machine Learning," in *Encyclopedia of Artificial Intelligence*, (Shapiro, ed.), Vol. I, John Wiley, 1987.

[Connell/Brady 1987] Connell, J.H., and M. Brady, "Generating and Generalizing Models of Visual Objects," *Artificial Intelligence*, Vol. 31, 1987, pp. 159–183.

[Dietterich/Michalski 1981] Dietterich, T.G., and R.S. Michalski, "Inductive Learning of Structural Descriptions," *Artificial Intelligence*, Vol. 16, 1981, pp. 257–294.

[Glorioso/Colon-Osorio 1980] Glorioso, R.M., and F. C. Colon-Osorio, *Engineering Intelligent Systems*, Digital Press, Bedford, MA, 1980.

Handbook of Artificial Intelligence, (Cohen and Feigenbaum, eds.), Vol. III, William Kaufmann, Los Altos, CA, 1982.

[Michalski 1983] Michalski, R.S., J. G. Carbonell, and T. M. Mitchell, (eds.), *Machine Learning*, (An Artificial Intelligence Approach), Volume I, Tioga Publ., Palo Alto, CA, 1983.

[Michalski 1986] Michalski, R.S., J.G. Carbonell, and T.M. Mitchell, (eds.), *Machine Learning*, (An Artificial Intelligence Approach), Volume II, Morgan Kaufman Publ., Los Altos, CA, 1986.

[Michalski 1980] Michalski, R.S., "Pattern Recognition as Rule-Guided Inference," *IEEE Trans. PAMI*, Vol. 2, No. 4, 1980, pp. 349–361.

[Piaget 1968] Piaget, Jean, *On the Development of Memory and Identity*, Clark University Press, Worcester, MA, 1968.

[Rummelhart/Norman 1978] Rummelhart, D.E., and D.A. Norman, "Accretion, tuning and restructuring: three modes of learning," *Semantic Factors in Cognition,* (J. W. Cotton and R.L. Klatzky, eds.), Lawrence Erlbaum, Hillsdale, NJ, 1978.

[Schafer 1976] Schafer, G., *A Mathematical Theory of Evidence,* Princeton University Press, Princeton, NJ, 1976.

[Selfridge 1986] Selfridge, M., "A Computer Model of Child Language Acquisition," *Artificial Intelligence,* Vol. 29, 1986, pp. 171–216.

[Valiant 1984] Valiant, L.G., "A Theory of the Learnable," *Communications of the ACM,* Vol. 27, No. 11, Nov. 1984, pp. 1134–1142.

[Watson 1963] Watson, Robert I., *The Great Psychologists from Aristotle to Freud,* Lippincott, NY, 1963, p. 209.

[Winston 1986] Winston, P.H., "Learning by Augmenting Rules and Accumulating Censors," in *Machine Learning,* (An Artificial Intelligence Approach), Volume II, Morgan Kaufman Publ., Los Altos, CA, 1986.

PROBLEMS

18.1. Consider implementation of generalization through the following "intersection-based" approach:

initial rulebase

$$(\text{eat meat}) \rightarrow (\text{satisfy-hunger}) \qquad (\text{P18-1}a)$$
$$(\text{eat cookies}) \rightarrow (\text{satisfy-hunger}) \qquad (\text{P18-1}b)$$

generalization

$$(\text{eat}) \rightarrow (\text{satisfy-hunger})$$

$$(\text{P18-1}c)$$

Develop, in LISP, a function that accomplishes this generalization. Hint: The result of problem 8.19(b) may be useful.

18.2. Consider an implementation of specialization (again perhaps using intersection) as follows:

initial database

$$(\text{car in scene}) \rightarrow (\text{observe road wheels body sky trees})$$
$$(\text{car in scene}) \rightarrow (\text{observe garage wheels body driveway})$$

$$(\text{P18-2}a)$$
$$(\text{P18-2}b)$$

Develop a LISP function that yields a more specific description, that is,

$$(\text{car in scene}) \rightarrow (\text{observe wheels body})$$

18.3. (Learning/Generalization) Consider generalization using the following two compound statements:

$$c, a \rightarrow e \qquad (S_1)$$
$$c \rightarrow e \qquad (S_2)$$

S_2 is the generalization of S_1.

(a) Prove that generalization is *falsity preserving;* that is, if S_1 is FALSE, then S_2 must be FALSE.

(b) Prove that generalization implies specialization, that is,

$$S_2 \rightarrow S_1$$

must be TRUE.

Detailed proofs, using logic, are required.

18.4. Cite examples of several constructive generalization operators.

18.5. This problem raises an interesting learning question. What if no positive instances exist? Can learning be accomplished with only N? Does it matter if the G-S or S-G algorithm is used? Show an example.

18.6. Consider the following alternative, but rule-based, inference strategy that takes three TRUE statements and produces two results:

$s1$	$.p$
$s2$	$.p \rightarrow q$
$s3$	$.(r \cap q) \rightarrow s$
$r1$	$.q$
$r2$	$.(r \rightarrow s)$

Notice that MP is a subset of this result, using statements s1 s2 and result r1.

(a) Verify the logical correctness of this more general approach.

(b) The fact that a rule (r2) is produced via generalization suggests this strategy could be used for learning. Indicate how this might be useful and cite an example. What is the effect of variables in q?

(c) How would this approach be implemented in LISP? Be as specific as possible. Indicate how the extensions would be implemented and how chaining would proceed.

18.7. (a) Using the S-G (Example 18.2) and the G-S (Example 18.3) learning algorithms, derive a hybrid learning algorithm that uses both S-G and G-S approaches iteratively.

(b) Apply the algorithm from part (a) to the problem in Example 18.4.

(c) Discuss the merits and shortcomings of this algorithm versus the S-G or G-S approaches.

18.8. Consider, as in Chapter 16, problem 16.12, a frame-structured representation that includes slots "more-general" and "more-specific." Show, in detail, how this structure could be used to implement the G-S or S-G learning algorithms.

18.9. This problem explores some of the difficulties that can arise with subtle changes in a problem representation. In learning Example 18.4 descriptions, we chose the clause

```
(closed   ?status?)
```

where ?status? $\in$ [True, False] and indicates whether the 2-D figure is closed or not. If instead we chose the clause

```
(connected   ?num_sides?)
```

where ?num_sides? indicates the number of line segments that have *both* endpoints connected to other line segments, does this result in an equivalent representation? Show some examples to support your answer.

18.10. Humans are often said to "learn from our mistakes." Describe, as quantitatively as possible, a technique for learning from mistakes. Note that you must be able to identify a "mistake."

18.11. In Examples 18.2 and 18.3, description modification was based upon covering exemplars. Suppose instead, we knew a priori that the concept we were seeking to "learn" was part of a hierarchy of concepts. The generalization or specialization could then be guided by a corresponding hierarchy of descriptions. For example, in G-S we might start at the most general descriptor and work "down" the hierarchy, and vice versa for S-G. Consider the 2-D geometric figure representation hierarchy shown in Fig. 18.9. Derive modified G-S and S-G algorithms that implement this approach.

18.12. Develop a detailed and quantitative response to the following statement:

"Forming a triangle table for a plan is a type of learning."

18.13. (This problem makes an excellent long-term project.) Develop and discuss at least one method to implement nonmonotonic reasoning. Consider, among other factors
(*a*) the logical basis for the scheme;
(*b*) how assumptions or default values are formulated and revised;
(*c*) the "backtracking" strategy when assumptions or default values are revised.

18.14. In step 1 of the S-G algorithm (Example 18.2), (why) is it necessary to specify that the chosen p_i "have not previously been elements of c"?

18.15 Compare and contrast the concepts of *generalization with exceptions* and *inheritence with exceptions*.

CHAPTER
19

AI SYSTEM
ARCHITECTURES

"Civilization advances by extending the number of important operations which we can perform without thinking about them."

Alfred North Whitehead 1861–1947
An Introduction to Mathematics [1911], ch. 5

INTRODUCTION

AI System Architecture Components

Previous chapters addressed the theoretical, modeling, and *algorithmic* aspects of AI. The need for program efficiency and structuring was noted without considering specifics and peculiarities of AI software *implementation*. There is significant interest in developing parallel algorithms for AI implementation. Algorithms for search, optimization, constraint satisfaction, production systems, and pattern and graph matching are excellent candidates for parallel implementation. Note that the subject of how a parallel machine is to be designed and programmed is very much an open question at this time. On another level, data structures for knowledge representation that enable parallel manipulation are of significant interest. Thus, the design of *knowledge-system architectures* involves a number of interrelated components, including

- Representation primitives.
- Knowledge structures.
- Inference mechanisms.

586

This chapter assumes that the reader is familiar with the rudiments of uniprocessor architecture theory, specifically the Von Neumann computing paradigm.

HARDWARE/SOFTWARE DECOMPOSITIONS. AI implementation concerns many aspects of computer architecture, including memory structures and parallelism. In Chapter 9 we explored efficient implementation of dynamic linked structures and the associated problem of garbage collection. In this chapter, the concepts of *parallel-algorithm decomposition* and *parallel-hardware processing* are emphasized. The achievement of parallel AI implementations is not confined to hardware. A (higher level of) *software* might identify parallelism in a program and, given a knowledge of the hardware capabilities, partition or assign the tasks spawned by the AI algorithm into modules that may be executed in parallel. Alternatively, a less user-transparent approach might be to design development software for programming that enables user specification of parallelism. Examples of this are MultiLISP and Concurrent PROLOG. In this approach, programmers are forced to direct parallelism, although accompanying this responsibility is the *flexibility* allowed the programmer to conceive algorithms in parallel. Developing parallel implementations is a capability that is often unappreciated, due to our familiarity with inherently serial machines, which only support sequential programming styles.

AI parallel-processing research attention has been given both to special purpose parallel architectures and to parallel programming languages and techniques. As general-purpose parallel machines (such as systolic arrays, hypercubes, data flow designs,etc.) become available, it is likely that both economics and availability will give rise to an interest in converting AI problems to these generalized architectures.

Extension of languages to allow concurrent programming gives the programmer the ability to create concurrent activities, or *processes*. While a process is a somewhat abstract entity, unification and function evaluation are two examples of the types of processes we would like to spawn in parallel execution of AI algorithms.

POSSIBLE ARCHITECTURE EXPLORATION PATHS. Parallel AI architectures may be studied by considering parallel decomposition and corresponding architectures for

1. Generic AI computations such as search, matching, or production systems.
2. Implementations in AI languages (e.g., Concurrent PROLOG and MultiLISP).

We will consider elements of both of these categories, with an emphasis on the second.

PARALLEL PROCESSING, COMPUTATIONAL COMPLEXITY, AND NONDETERMINISM. The use of multiple concurrent processors (parallel processing) attempts to reduce the time complexity of a computational process at the expense of increased space or hardware complexity. Note that NP-complete problems (Chapter 15) cannot be solved in real time unless an exponential number of processors is used [Garey/ Johnson 1979]. Thus, problems that are solvable by a serial computer with P complexity (or less) are the ideal candidates for parallel implementation.

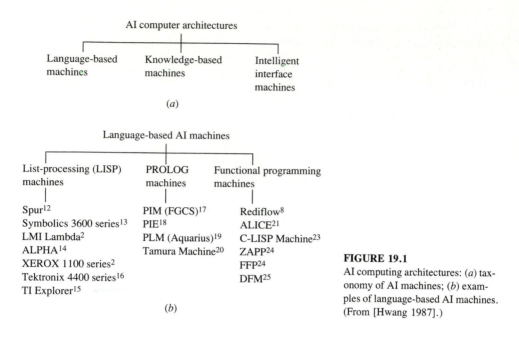

FIGURE 19.1

AI computing architectures: (*a*) taxonomy of AI machines; (*b*) examples of language-based AI machines. (From [Hwang 1987].)

Due to the nondeterminism in many AI algorithms, one alternative is to use several different *techniques* in parallel. When one of these techniques produces a solution, (parallel) execution of the remaining are terminated.

Levels of Architectural Concern

The specific representations and implementations chosen link AI applications and dedicated architectures. These models link the levels of knowledge representations, AI languages, and computing models. Figure 19.1*a* shows a simple taxonomy for AI architectures. As noted previously, we will concentrate on language-based machines, examples of which are shown in Fig. 19.1*b*.

A General Need for Parallel Computing Architectures

Despite amazing gains in processing speed and memory size, there are reasons to expect that real-time AI processing requirements will be met not via faster hardware, but rather through using radically different hardware and software architectures. In the near future, it may not be possible to speed up a particular processor by simply increasing clock speed. This is due to the fact that propagation delays of integrated circuit gates are approaching the speed of electricity in a wire, which is a theoretical limit. An obvious approach to overcoming this obstacle is based upon the following observation:

In implementing a given algorithm, if we are unable to increase processor speed to meet requirements, an alternative is to distribute the algorithm or computation over an ensemble of processors and thereby achieve speedup (over the single-processor implementation) due to the concurrency of the implementation. $(19\text{-}1)$

This is the principal subtopic of parallel processing that we explore. On the basis of this observation, we identify three issues related to the design of solutions to AI implementation problems:

1. The *design of programming languages* with a parallel capability (either under the control of or, alternatively, transparent to the programmer).
2. The *programmer's efficient* use of these languages. (This is only a concern if the parallel capability is made available to the programmer as opposed to being an "automatic" part of the system.)
3. The *implementation of these languages* on suitable hardware architectures.

Examples of Current AI-Machine Architectural Features

AI-MACHINE GENERATIONS. The evolution of computer architectures includes several generations of AI machines. The first generation comprised interpreters for AI languages running on dedicated mainframe machines. To some extent, this generation still thrives, due to the efficiency of the solution (e.g., many LISP interpreters and compilers are available for the VAX hardware family). The second generation consisted of dedicated workstations whose architecture was designed to allow the efficient implementation of one (or more) AI languages. Perhaps the best known are "LISP machines" from various vendors. A clear example is the Symbolics 3675 machine. A third generation of machines with the potential to provide realistic AI functionality is the rapidly evolving personal-computer domain. The fourth generation, which is presently emerging, involves the implementation of dedicated AI processor architectures in silicon, that is, VLSI designs. An example is the TI Compact LISP Machine (CLM), under development for DARPA, which features 60 percent of the logic of the TI Explorer LISP machine. Another example is the Xerox Common LISP Processor (CLP), which is the result of a five-year research project aimed at developing a specialized RISC machine tuned to the execution of instructions particular to LISP.

AI WORKSTATION ARCHITECTURAL FEATURES. Dedicated AI machines ("workstations") with processors and languages dedicated to AI applications are available from a number of vendors. Two popular examples are the Symbolics 3670 and the Texas Instruments (TI) Explorer. Desirable features of the software-development environment in such workstations were covered in Chapter 3. From an architectural viewpoint, typical features of the TI Explorer are that

- It is designed to support the LISP language.
- It has hardware optimized for symbolic processing, including:
  - Microprogrammed LISP processor.
  - Tagged architecture (described later) for hardware support of run-time data typing.

- Bit field hardware for manipulating data structures.
- Hardware-assisted memory management (for garbage collection, to be described later).
- Large virtual address space (e.g., 128 Mbyte).
- Large, high-speed-access physical RAM (e.g., 16 Mbyte; 300nS).
- High-resolution graphics display (e.g., 1024H $\times$ 808V pixels).
- High-performance mass storage devices.

Many of these hardware features are also desirable in a numerical processor. The above examples represent inherently serial (but fast and efficient) approaches to dedicated AI-machine development.

GENERAL CONCEPTS OF PARALLEL PROCESSING

Parallel Computer Architecture, Decompositions, and Algorithms

Even very fast uniprocessor architectures are inadequate for many current or projected AI computing tasks. This shortcoming has generated significant interest in the area of *parallel processing*, that is, identifying subtasks that may be independently implemented in a time-parallel manner. By identifying and distributing computational subtasks over physical hardware, significant time savings are anticipated. Usually, this process involves replication of the spatial or physical hardware, leading to space-time trade-offs.

In describing parallel computer architectures, the development of parallel-programming languages to accompany these hardware devices must be considered. A very real and significant problem is how to decompose (perhaps automatically) a given symbolic processing task into one that may be executed in parallel segments. It is this task that currently borders on being more of an art than an exact science, although, as we show, there are some engineering guidelines and current successes.

In numerical applications, the identification of potential processing concurrency is often quite obvious. For example, in operations involving vector and matrix quantities, this type of data structure suggests the obvious desirability of emulating the data structure in hardware, hence, *array processors* (not to be confused with arrays of processors). In contrast, problems in symbolic manipulation often do not suggest any obvious decomposition.

Area/Time Trade-offs and Decompositions

Measures of the performance of parallel-computing architectures are of fundamental importance to their systematic, structured development and application. Intuitively, one might hope that an *n*-processor implementation of an algorithm will achieve the result in $1/n$ the time required by a single processor working on the same problem. In this case, the product of the overall processing time and hardware complexity is constant. Unfortunately, this is at best *an upper bound on the achievable speedup*; the actual performance increase is less impressive. This result is due in large measure to

i. The processing time necessary for communication (e.g., sharing of data or results) between processors. (19-2a)

ii. The fact that processors may have to wait for the results of other processors (i.e., the process was not completely decomposable into a parallel algorithm). (19-2b)

iii. The fact that some area of data memory may need to be shared by several processors (and therefore contention for memory resources may occur). (19-2c)

METRICS FOR PREDICTING SPEEDUP. For a parallel implementation, we define **speedup** as the ratio

$$\text{Speedup} = \frac{\text{processing time with single processor}}{\text{processing time with } n \text{ processors}} \tag{19-3a}$$

With this definition, the theoretical maximum speedup for an n-processor implementation of an algorithm is n. Due to reasons cited in (19-2), actual speedup may be observed and/or predicted to be less than this value. One historically significant measure is *Minsky's conjecture*, which states that the actual speedup is $\log_2(n)$. This, as Table 19.1 indicates, is somewhat disappointing, especially for large processor numbers. Consequently, the economics of large processor implementations in cases where Minsky's conjecture holds favor fewer, but faster, processors. An alternate speedup measure, proposed as an upper bound in [Hwang and Briggs 1984], is $n/\ln(n)$. This is a more optimistic bound. Minsky's conjecture and the Hwang/Briggs bounds assume some (unstated) amount of necessary serial computation. Another approach, which is known as *Amdahl's law* [Amdahl 1967], explicitly predicts speedup as a function of the *fraction of required serial computations* in a given algorithm. Defining the following quantities,

s the fraction of computations that are necessarily serial.

p the fraction of computations that may be done in parallel (note $s + p = 1$).

n number of processors over which p is distributed.

Amdahl's law calculates speedup as

$$\text{Speedup} = (s + p)/(s + p/n)$$
$$= 1/(s + p/n) \tag{19-3b}$$

TABLE 19.1
Speedup comparisons

n (# processors) (Ideal Speedup)	Minsky $\log_2(n)$	Optimistic (Hwang/Briggs) $(n/\ln(n))$	Amdahl's Law $(1/(s + p/n))$ $s = 0.05$	$s = 0.20$
4	2.0	2.9	3.5	2.5
10	3.3	4.3	6.9	3.6
100	6.6	21.7	16.8	4.8
1,000	10.0	144.8	19.6	5.0
10,000	13.3	1,086.0	20.0	5.0

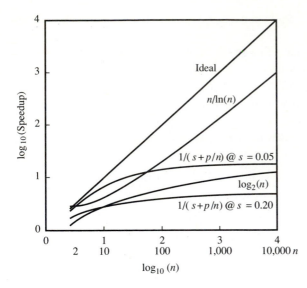

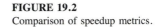

FIGURE 19.2
Comparison of speedup metrics.

In general, Amdahl's law is a very pessimistic bound on achievable speedup, even for small values of s ($s < 5$ percent). Note that, according to Amdahl's law, speedup approaches $1/s$ for large n. Recent studies [Gustafson 1988] indicate that Amdahl's law may be too pessimistic. Figure 19.2 compares these measures. The measure of speedup, therefore, is highly dependent on the desired overall operation, the decomposition chosen, and the specific architecture chosen to implement the decomposed algorithm.

It is likely that these less-than-ideal speedup measures are applicable to AI computations. In other words, there exists a certain amount of inherent non-parallel computation in AI programs. Therefore, applying more and more parallel hardware to the problem may yield little incremental benefit. We seek tools and approaches that allow us to identify parallelism in AI programming, so that parallel hardware solutions may be developed.

Algorithm Decomposition Tools (Flow Graphs)

The (data) flow graph (DFG) for an algorithm (or subset of operations of an algorithm) provides a mechanism to identify potential concurrency (and, conversely, operations that are strictly serial). We begin with the numerical example of Fig. 19.3. Assuming all operands are available simultaneously (more will be said about this later), a data flow graph for the overall computation is drawn by showing the necessary computational modules (arithmetic operators in this case) and the relationship of the inputs and outputs of these modules. Tasks or functions that may be evaluated in parallel are shown arranged vertically, whereas strictly serial tasks are arranged horizontally.

The DFG does not directly facilitate a computation of speedup. For example, we might conclude from Fig. 19.3 that the serial implementation requires five steps, (plus (times 3 4) (times (plus 7 6) (plus 5 8)))

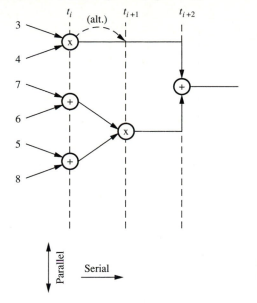

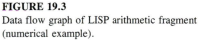

FIGURE 19.3
Data flow graph of LISP arithmetic fragment (numerical example).

whereas the parallel implementation requires three, thus yielding a speedup of $\frac{5}{3}$. This would be true if all processes required exactly the same amount of time. (This is explored in the problems.) In addition to showing data dependencies, Fig. 19.3 (as drawn) also indicates a maximum of hardware cost of three *reconfigurable* processors. Note that an alternative DFG, obtained by moving the (times 3 4) node to step t_{i+1}, only requires two reconfigurable processors, which are never idle. In the case shown, two of the processors are idle in steps t_{i+1} and t_{i+2}.

The data flow graph for a given computation is seldom unique; rearrangement may yield an alternative graph representation. In fact, ofttimes the algorithm formulation will determine the degree of decomposability. Extending the DFG to LISP function definitions is simple; each node in the DFG corresponds to a LISP function. An example is shown in Fig. 19.4.

Do We Need a Specific Architecture for AI?

A guiding principle in exploring parallel AI processing algorithms is the observation that

> If a particular AI problem suggests a certain structure for its solution, then an efficient computer implementation may be one that reflects that structure. (19-4)

For example, if the processing algorithm is based upon search, a logical problem decomposition and associated architecture might be to design a parallel computer in which each processing element independently searches a subspace of the problem solution space. (This is easier to state, however, than to achieve.)

```
(and
    (listp   (car a)
    (equal  (caar a)  '*)
    (equal  (car  b)   (assoc (car a) bindings)))
```

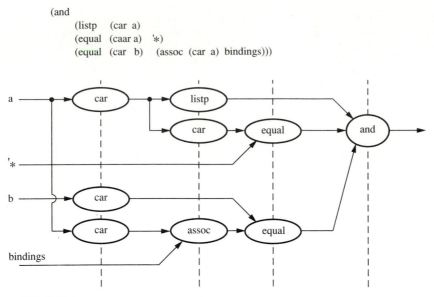

FIGURE 19.4
DFG LISP "fragment" (symbolic example).

The identification of concurrency in AI processing algorithms is often an "art," as opposed to a science. The DFG helps this task. However, the (nonunique) problem or algorithm formulation often influences the decomposability of the solution. Furthermore, even in obvious decompositions, the space complexity of the solution is considerable. Consequently the design of AI processing hardware poses a panoply of unsolved problems involving switching complexity, interprocessor communications, memory contention, and so forth.

Symbolic Processing Benchmarks

We note first that the benchmarking of any computer system is usually plagued by controversy (since business interests are at stake), nonuniqueness of interpretation, and lack of standardization. Benchmarking a computer usually involves quantifying speed of execution (although, as noted hereafter, there are other factors one might consider). In other words, a benchmark usually consists of measurement of the time it takes to accomplish some number of operations or tasks. However, benchmarks are often cited using different algorithms, which immediately raises the question of how to compare results.

Nevertheless, benchmarking, however imperfect, does occur and yields some useful results. Numerically-oriented computers are usually benchmarked in terms of number of floating point operations per second (FLOPS). Since numerical operations are of secondary interest, another measure for AI applications must be devised. To this end, the metric *logical inferences per second* (LIPS), or simply *inferences per second* (IPS), has been proposed. Of course, this definition is itself ambiguous unless a

TABLE 19.2
LIPS benchmarks for current AI machines (from [Stone 2 1987])

Machine	LIPS (thousands)
Sun 2	14
VAX 11/780	15
Symbolics 3675	53
80386 Processor with Gold-Hill "Hummingbird" co-processor	~ 14

universally accepted definition of what constitutes a "logical inference" is determined. A logical inference may be different in PROLOG or LISP implementations. For example, a logical inference might be defined as the firing of a rule. With this interpretation, however, we do not directly measure or benchmark the ability of the system to check the antecedents of a rule, which is often the time-consuming part. Loosely speaking, a logical inference is defined to be the fundamental logical operation underlying the manipulation of a given AI implementation.

Examples of benchmarks using some of the AI systems mentioned previously [Stone 2 1987] are shown in Table 19.2.

PARALLEL IMPLEMENTATIONS
USING PROLOG

In developing parallel AI languages, it makes sense to consider extension of the currently-used serial versions. This leads to Concurrent PROLOG (and MultiLISP). In a sense, Concurrent PROLOG is to PROLOG what Occam or Parallel Pascal is to Pascal.

In "conventional" PROLOG, the goal formulation and ordering of clauses in the database determine the (sequential) order in which unification-guided search occurs. In Concurrent PROLOG, commit and read—only operators are added to synchronize the parallel unification process.

Types of PROLOG Parallelism

"AND" AND "OR" PARALLELISM. Two types of parallelism that may impact PRO-LOG parallel execution are [Tanaka 1986]

1. AND parallelism.
2. OR parallelism.

In the case of two or more rule-antecedent clauses that are AND-ed, the simultaneous verification of these clauses is referred to as *AND parallelism*. Recalling the scoping of variables in PROLOG, two or more of these clauses with common variables require communication between the parallel unification processes to ensure that a successful unification (if possible) occurs with consistent variable binding. This communication

$$p(X) :- p_1(X), p_2(X)$$

(a)

$$q(X) :- q_1(X) ; q_2(X).$$

(i)

$$q(X) :- q_1(X).$$

$$q(Y) :- q_2(Y).$$

(ii)

(b)

FIGURE 19.5
AND/OR parallelism in PROLOG: *(a)* AND parallelism example (one shared variable); *(b)* OR parallelism example: (i) original database; (ii) rewritten for parallel unification.

or checking represents overhead that works against the potential speedup benefits of the parallel formulation.

Similarly, *OR parallelism* may be achieved by concurrently attempting unification on clauses that represent alternative solution paths. OR-ed clauses, in contrast to their AND-ed counterparts, do not require checks for consistency in variable bindings. (The reader is encouraged to verify this.) This is relatively easy to see, since a rule with n OR-ed antecedents may be rewritten as n (independent) rules. However, the nondeterminism of algorithms based upon the unification process combined with large numbers of possible OR-based solution paths may quickly lead to combinatorial explosion.

Figure 19.5 depicts these concepts in PROLOG.

ARGUMENT DEPENDENCE (PARALLELISM). Another concern, namely the so-called *argument parallelism*, is one of the more interesting and difficult concepts to implement; it refers to the process of unifying several predicates containing one or more variables in parallel. Such variables are referred to as *shared variables*. Checking consistency of bindings (particularly if variables may be bound to other variables) is a nontrivial problem. *Argument dependence*, or shared variables, may lead to *binding conflicts*. The generation of independent subgoals (or parallel processes) that may be explored in parallel is difficult. Two major extremes [Tung/Moldovan 1986] of dealing with AND parallelism in clauses with shared variables are possible:

1. *None-shared-variable (NSV) schemes*, wherein the presence of shared variables in subgoals forces these subgoals to be explored serially. This may be implemented during the unification process by dynamically creating and updating a *dependency network* to control subgoal exploration.

2. *Reconciliation schemes*, where all subgoals are explored in parallel, and possible conflicts are "reconciled" using an additional unification step.

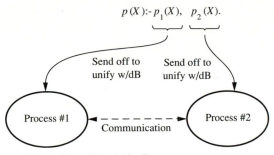

$p(X):-p_1(X),\ p_2(X).$

Send off to unify w/dB

Send off to unify w/dB

Process #1 - - - - - - - → Process #2

Communication

- Problem is "shared" variable, X
- At best, requires communication between (unification) process #1 and process #2.

FIGURE 19.6
Simple example of parallel unification with AND-ed predicates.

A more moderate approach [DeGroot 1984] is to "annotate" shared variables in one of a variety of ways to restrict the binding of variables when satisfying subgoals. A specific example is where only one subgoal is allowed to determine the value of a specific variable. This subgoal is referred to as a "producer" of its respective variable binding. This is shown in Fig. 19.7a.

Implementing PROLOG Unification (Search) in Parallel

Consider the simple PROLOG rule

$p(X)\ :-\ p_1(X),\ p_2(X).$

If, during unification, p is invoked as a subgoal with X unbound, we could attempt to spawn two parallel unification processes, one for p_1 and one for $p_2(X)$. However, p_1 and p_2 may yield unifications with different values bound to the shared variable X. Of course, one approach is to let this occur and then discard the solution in search of other independently-obtained solutions with different bindings for X. If (purely by accident) a consistent solution (i.e., one in which X is bound to the same value) is found, the process succeeds. Unfortunately, it is more likely that binding conflicts or inconsistencies arise. Figure 19.6 shows the overall problem. We look at two possible interprocess-communication schemes for parallel unification.

THE "RECONCILIATION" APPROACH. Suppose that a set of possible bindings on variable X is produced in the unification of $p_1(X)$, and another (possibly different) set of bindings on X is produced in the unification of $p_2(X)$. Denote these sets of bindings as S_X^1 and S_X^2 respectively. A *consistent* solution is the *intersection* of S_X^1 and S_X^2. Thus, after S_X^1 and S_X^2 are produced, a "reconciliation" of (possibly disparate) bindings is undertaken. Such a scheme (often denoted as "join" algorithm) is inefficient, for example, when the cardinality of S_X^1 is small and that of S_X^2 is

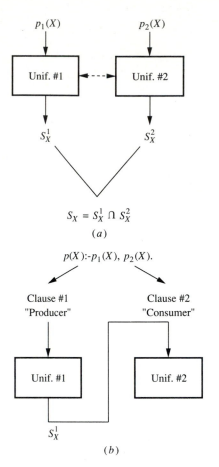

$$S_X = S_X^1 \cap S_X^2$$
(*a*)

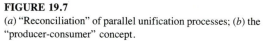

FIGURE 19.7
(*a*) "Reconciliation" of parallel unification processes; (*b*) the "producer-consumer" concept.

large and their intersection is small. In this case, computational resources are wasted in computing S_X^2. This is shown in Fig. 19.7*a*.

THE "PRODUCER-CONSUMER" APPROACH. This approach is an alternative to the reconciliation approach. As shown in Fig. 19.7*b*, it makes sense to "communicate" members of S_X^1, as they are produced, to the parallel unification process producing S_X^2. By restricting values of X in the $p_2(X)$ unification to S_X^1 (note here $p_1(X)$ is a "producer" of variable bindings), the set of common unifications (still explored in parallel, but with interprocess communications) is efficiently obtained. One of the difficulties, however, is determining which clauses should be producers.

Note that certain clauses containing variables may be unified independently. For example, the rule

```
f(X,Y) :- g(X), h(Y).
```

typifies this. Lest the reader be misled, however, consider the following *pair* of clauses:

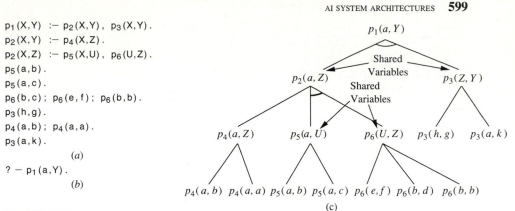

$p_1(X,Y) :- p_2(X,Y), p_3(X,Y).$
$p_2(X,Y) :- p_4(X,Z).$
$p_2(X,Z) :- p_5(X,U), p_6(U,Z).$
$p_5(a,b).$
$p_5(a,c).$
$p_6(b,c); p_6(e,f); p_6(b,b).$
$p_3(h,g).$
$p_4(a,b); p_4(a,a).$
$p_3(a,k).$

(a)

$? - p_1(a,Y).$

(b)

FIGURE 19.8
Shared variables are not always "transparent" (or simple): (a) sample database; (b) sample goal; (c) search tree of attempted unifications.

$$p_0(X) :- p_1(X,X)$$
$$p_1(Y, Z) :- p_2(Y), p_3(Z)$$

Whereas these two clauses do not *individually* exhibit shared variables, the unification of p_0 leads to a coupling of p_2 and p_3, since Y and Z become shared variables.

> **Example 19.1 Parallel unification schemes with sample PROLOG database and goal.** Consider the PROLOG database and goal shown in Fig. 19.8a and b. As shown in Fig. 19.8c, shared variables result at several stages in the attempted parallel unification process.
>
> Figures 19.9 and 19.10 show the operation of the producer-consumer and reconciliation schemes using the database of Fig. 19.8.

Concurrent PROLOG

Concurrent PROLOG is an implementation of first-order Horn clause logic, which differs from pure PROLOG in the details of the unification mechanism. As described in Chapter 3, the pure PROLOG unification process uses the order of clauses in the database and the order of subgoals in a rule body to sequentially attempt unification.

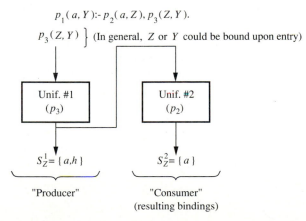

FIGURE 19.9
Producer approach for variable Z using the problem of Fig. 19.8. (Let p_3 be the producer.)

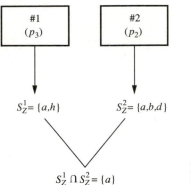

$$S_Z^1 \cap S_Z^2 = \{a\}$$

FIGURE 19.10
Reconciliation approach for problem of Fig. 19.8.

Concurrent PROLOG attempts unification in parallel through the introduction of two additional constructs, which are used to control concurrency in the unification process:

1. The `commit` operator ($|$) and a guard clause, which allow a specific unification process (i.e., one of the n that are being attempted in parallel) to attempt unification (which may involve the given operator) in a clause prior to unification of the remainder.
   For example, given the PROLOG rule

   ```
   a :- g | b.
   ```

   where a, g, and b are clauses (with g specifically a guard clause), a particular unification mechanism (one of the parallel unification processes) that has a as a subgoal will attempt to prove guard clause g is true. In this way, unification of b is prevented or postponed via g. If unification of g is successful, the unification of b is attempted; otherwise this clause is not used further. Thus, g serves as a "guard" on the clause b. Note that we can read the above clause as if it were simply

   ```
   a :- g, b.
   ```

   An empty guard clause is omitted in the notation and thus results in a clause that resembles conventional (serial) PROLOG. More importantly, once guard clause g permits the attempted unification of b, Concurrent PROLOG cannot undo the unification if it is successful. This is an example of computational behavior known as *committed-choice nondeterminism*.

2. The `read-only` operator (denoted ?) synchronizes the parallel unification processes. A process that attempts instantiation of a variable in the `read-only` mode is suspended until another process instantiates the variable (thus, the `read-only` connotation). For example, if we had the following AND-parallel clause,

   ```
   p₃(X) :- p₁(X), p₂(?X).
   ```

only clause p_1 may instantiate X. Thus, using our previous notation, p_1 is the only generator or *producer* of bindings on X, and clause p_2 is a *consumer*. The unifier for clause p_2 may obtain values for X from the unifier for p_1, if a binding exists. Otherwise, the (parallel) unification of p_2, which shares variable X, is suspended until a binding is generated by p_1. Read−only annotation of variables in Concurrent PROLOG thus enforces constraints on the order in which unification may proceed and the degree of parallelism that is achieved. Note that the read−only operator allows implementation of the producer-consumer approach of Figures 19.7*b* and 19.9.

PARALLEL IMPLEMENTATIONS USING LISP

IMPLEMENTING A PURELY FUNCTIONAL LANGUAGE. One approach towards identifying parallelism in LISP is to assume that a given LISP implementation is derived from a "pure LISP," containing only a minimal number of constructs, which may be used to generate more sophisticated LISP versions. For example, as we showed in an earlier chapter, the built-in LISP function member may be written using only the cond, null, equal, car and cdr functions. The problem with this approach arises when LISP admits large, predefined data structures, and data structures, such as function *side effects*, that are more sophisticated than those contained in the "pure" set.

> A **"black-box" model** of a function is one wherein the function is viewed as a computational entity that accepts input entities and returns one or more values (i.e., the result of the evaluation of the function, given its arguments). (19-5)

Thus, values (arguments) are passed to a function, and the *only* result or effect of the function is realized through its *returning a value*. With this definition, a function has no *side effects*.

SIDE EFFECTS. A **side effect** is a change to the system environment that occurs by some method other than through a function returning a value. Perhaps the best example of this is the case where a function changes the value of a nonlocal (i.e., global) variable. This may occur through the use of functions such as set and any of the property list manipulation functions, for example, get. Since the result of a side-effect, or "back door," operation may not be immediately apparent in the execution of the program and may significantly detract from debugging attempts, this type of operation is generally considered undesirable. One attribute of "good" LISP code is therefore that it does not contain functions with side effects. (Notice this is almost impossible to achieve in practice, since some side effects, such as printing, are desirable.) Hereafter, we restrict our attention to the decomposition of LISP programs containing only functions that are free of side effects. These are "safe" candidates for parallel execution.

Functional languages, therefore, are prime candidates for parallelism since data dependencies are explicitly shown in the DFG. Each function may be implemented by a separate process.

Parallel LISP Implementation Examples

The following LISP code fragments provide examples of possible parallel decomposition.

Example 19.2.   LISP program fragment.

```
(defun ...
          .
          .
          .
    (cond
       ((predicate_a) (evaluate_a1  a b c)
                      (evaluate_a2 d e f)
                              .
                              .
                              .
                      (evaluate_aN x y z))

       ((predicate_b) (evaluate_b1  a b c)
                      (evaluate_b2 d e f)
                              .
                              .
                              .
                      (evaluate_bN x y z)
                      .
                      .
                      .
       ((predicate_M) (evaluate_M1  a b c)
                      (evaluate_M2 d e f)
                              .
                              .
                              .
                      (evaluate_MN x y z)
```

Example 19.3.   LISP program fragment.

```
(defun ...
         .
         .
         .
    ((evaluate_a1  (evaluate_a2 (...(evaluate_aN x y z)...)]
```

Example 19.4.   LISP program fragment.

```
(defun ...
          .
          .
          .
     (cond
        ((predicate_a)
```

```
(evaluate_a1   a  b  c)
(evaluate_a2  d  e  f)
                .
                .
                .

(evaluate_aN  x  y  z)
(cond
  ((predicate_b)
          (evaluate_b1   a  b  c)
          (evaluate_b2   d  e  f)
                          .
                          .
                          .

          (evaluate_bN   x  y  z)
```

SPECULATIVE EVALUATION AND cond. The LISP program fragment in Example 19.2 is used to show several possible types of generic concurrency. Consider first the potential parallelism spawned by use of the cond construct. Recalling the implied serial nature of the cond function, we notice that LISP function evaluation is "lazy," in the sense that only evaluations that must occur actually do; that is, there are a number of possible branches in Example 19.2, whereas only one "evaluation path" through the cond function actually occurs. For example, if predicate_a evaluates to non-nil, then functions evaluate_a1 through evaluate_aN are serially evaluated. Conversely, if predicate_a evaluates to nil, then predicate_b is evaluated in order to determine if functions evaluate_b1 through evaluate_bN are to be serially evaluated.

Consider first a parallel decomposition for Example 19.2 involving *speculative* evaluation [Halstead 1986] of possible branches. The predicates predicate_a through predicate_M are all evaluated *in parallel*. The first predicate (in terms of the order in which they appear in the cond) returning a non-nil value spawns the evaluation of evaluate_?1 through evaluate_?N, where the ? is replaced by the identity of the corresponding first non-nil predicate.

PARALLEL EVALUATION OF *s*-EXPRESSIONS AND DATA DEPENDENCIES. A second parallel decomposition of Example 19.2 is possible due to the structure of the function evaluations in the cdr of each cond branch, for example, the lists ((evaluate_a1   a b c) (evaluate_a2 d e f) ... (evaluate_aN x y z)). The serial LISP syntax indicates the serial evaluation of these entities, from left to right in the list. Since in this example the arguments to these functions are independent of the functions, it is possible to evaluate each of these independently. While this is straightforward, hidden data dependencies or side effects that may limit parallel evaluation may be present and require checking. If the number of possible branches in a given function (or program) becomes large, speculative evaluation may become intractable. Example 19.4 shows this situation. Furthermore, note that in hindsight (i.e., after the program has executed) this process is not efficient, in the sense that a number of unnecessary function evaluations occurred.

The LISP program fragment in Example 19.3 shows an alternative program structure that significantly reduces concurrency potential, due to *data dependency*. In this (extreme) case the function evaluations appear nested:

```
((evaluate_a1   (evaluate_a2
                  (...(evaluate_aN x y z)...))]
```

so that the result (value) of (evaluate_aN x y z) is needed to form the input to (evaluate_a$N-1$ t u v), and so on. A decomposition is not apparent with the evaluations nested in this serial form, as shown by the DFG.

Parallelism in LISP Using the "Future" Construct

THE monoOfuture CONSTRUCT. As in Concurrent PROLOG, we seek some mechanism to signify the creation of a process (function evaluation) that may be accomplished in parallel. MultiLISP [Halstead 1986] is an example of a LISP with parallel processing capability, through the use of the MultiLISP future construct.

In evaluation of a LISP *s*-expression, the future form is used to spawn a new process that executes in parallel with other processes (assuming sufficient computing resources in LISP code). This construct has the appearance of a function. Referring to the LISP program fragment in Example 19.2, a sample use of the future construct is

```
(cond
   ((future (predicate_a)) (future (evaluate_a1   a b c))
                            (future (evaluate_a2 d e f))
                             .
                             .
                             .
                            (future (evaluate_aN x y z)))
      .
      .
      .
```

The spawning of (possibly) parallel tasks to evaluate the functions predicate_a, evaluate_a1, ··· evaluate_aN is shown. More specifically, in an application of the future construct to a LISP code fragment such as

```
(t) (setq x (future (plus y z))) (setq w (minus x v))  ...]
```

the operation LISP future construct is as follows:

future:

1. Spawns a task to evaluate (plus y z), by
2. Assigning to x a pointer to the future value of (plus y z), and
3. Continues evaluation of the cdr of the given list.

If the value for x is needed before it is available (i.e., before the spawned task has completed), such as in (minus x v), the latter task is *suspended* until a value is available. Thus, the reader will notice the future construct is aptly named; values involving this construct are "promised" at perhaps a "future" time.

RESTRICTIONS ON THE USE OF THE future **CONSTRUCT.** Notice, due to the aforementioned data dependency, that the use of future in Example 19.3, i.e.,

```
          .
          .
          .
((future (evaluate_a1 (future (evaluate_a2 (
                          ...future (evaluate_aN x y z)...)]
```

does not create any useful parallelism. In fact, due to the overhead associated with the future construct, the serial version of this program fragment may execute faster. Thus, it is important to note that

Insertion of future does not automatically lead to parallelism or faster execution.

(19-6)

Furthermore, we restrict our application of the future construct to functions without side effects.

AUTOMATIC GENERATION OF PARALLEL LISP PROGRAMS. Recall that LISP does not distinguish between program and data. LISP programs may take other LISP programs as input, since everything is list-structured. Although we have assumed that the programmer will identify potential parallelism in task generation, the future construct may be inserted by a LISP program preprocessor; that is, it is possible to write a LISP program that takes in another LISP program and applies the future construct to "safe" functions. This, of course, implies that a mechanism to detect side effects is available. The following simplistic example, which applies only to a single function evaluation (adapted from [McGehearty and Krall 1986]), shows this:

```
(defun rewrite-fn-eval (lst)
  (cond ((null lst) nil); don't modify empty lists
        (t (cons ('future lst)))))
```

OTHER PARALLEL IMPLEMENTATIONS

Parallel Implementation of Production Systems

Recall that a forward chaining production system, as defined in Chapter 11, has three operations that form a cycle:

TABLE 19.3
Sample characteristics of several production systems (from [Forgy 1984])

Attribute	R1[1]	PTRANS[2]	DAA[3]
total # productions	1932	1016	131
avg # conditions/ production	5.6	3.1	3.9
avg # consequents/ production	2.9	3.6	2.9

1. R1: VAX configuration program (forebear of XCON, which currently has over 10,000 rules)
2. PTRANS: factory management program
3. DAA: VLSI design program

1. Check rules (match).

2. Perform conflict resolution.

3. Fire rule(s) and repeat step 1.

OPS5 was an example of such a production system. Much effort has been expended in attempting to match rule antecedents and to *fire rules in parallel.* Two observations that may be used to speed up step 1 are [Forgy 1984]

1. *Working memory (wm) changes slowly.* Whereas wm may consist of thousands of elements, a typical production may only change a few. Thus, the matcher may take into account that most of the necessary matching information at the current cycle is the same as that of the previous cycle. Table 19.3 [Forgy 1984] illustrates this for several OPS5 applications.

2. Many rules contain *antecedents* (left-hand sides) that are *similar* in the sense that they contain common subexpressions.

In attempting to fire rules in parallel, the major problem encountered is that rules may interfere with each other. For example, simultaneous addition and deletion of an element from wm is probably meaningless. Therefore, determining how to partition the production memory for multiple rule-firings requires some computational effort.

Distributed Artificial Intelligence (DAI)

Recently, the area of DAI has received attention. We first define DAI:

> **"DAI (distributed artificial intelligence)** is concerned with the cooperative solution of (AI) problems by a decentralized group of agents." [Huhns 1987]   (19-7)

These "agents" range from simple processing elements to complex, distributed entities with some local and independent reasoning capability.

DAI systems are therefore characterized as a collection of logically distinct processing agents, where each agent has only partial and perhaps inexact information on the overall (composite) system state (which includes the goal state). Agents may be used to solve subproblems.

Applications for DAI include manufacturing, office automation, and man-machine interaction. DAI also offers a means to

1. Interconnect multiple expert systems with different or overlapping areas of expertise. This may enable the solution of a much broader class of problems whose domain is outside any single expert system. (This has an analogy with the opportunistic problem-solving mechanism of the *blackboard* treated in Chapter 16.)

2. Solve problems that are inherently distributed in nature such as fusion of information from distributed sensors and geographically distributed information databases.

Furthermore, DAI systems facilitate other desirable AI system characteristics such as modularity, speed (due to parallelism), and reliability. DAI is likely to be one area of significant research interest in the future.

REFERENCES

[Amamiya 1986] Amamiya, M., et al, "Implementation and Evaluation of a List-Processing-Oriented Data Flow Machine," 0884-7495/86, 1986.

[Amdahl 1967] Amdahl, G.M., "Validity of the Single-Processor Approach to Achieving Large-Scale Computing Capabilities," *AFIPS Conference Proceedings*, Vol. 30, 1967, pp. 483–485.

[Baker 1978] Baker, H.G., "List Processing in Real Time on a Serial Computer," *Communications ACM*, Vol. 21, No. 4, April 1978, pp. 280–294.

[Bic 1985] Bic, L., "Processing of Semantic Nets on Dataflow Architectures," *Artificial Intelligence*, Vol. 27, 1985, pp. 219–227.

[Ciepielewski/Haridi 1983] Ciepielewski, A., and S. Haridi, "A Formal Model for OR-Parallel Execution of Logic Programs," *Information Processing 1983*, 1983, pp. 299–305.

[Cohen 1981] Cohen, J., "Garbage Collection of Linked Data Structures," *Computing Surveys*, Vol. 13, No. 3, September 1981, pp. 341–367.

[Comp 1987] *Computer*, Special Issue on Architectures for AI Applications, (B. Wah, ed.), January 1987.

[Conery/Kibler 1985] Conery, J.S., and D.F. Kibler, "AND-Parallelism and Nondeterminism in Logic Programs," in [Wah/Li 1986].

[Crammond 1985] Crammond, J.A., "A Comparative Study of Unification Algorithms for OR-Parallel Execution of Logic Languages," *IEEE Transactions on Computers*, Vol. C-34, No. 10, October 1985, pp. 911–917.

[DeGroot 1984] DeGroot, D., "Restricted AND-Parallelism," *Proceedings of the International Conference on Fifth Generation Computer Systems 1984*, ICOT, pp. 471–478.

[Flynn 1972] Flynn, M.J., "Some Computer Organizations and Their Effectiveness," *IEEE Transactions on Computers*, Vol. C-21, No. 9, September 1972, pp. 948–960.

[Forgy 1984] Forgy, C., A. Gupta, A. Newell, and R. Wedig, "Initial Assessment of Architectures for Production Systems," *Proceedings of the National Conference on Artificial Intelligence*, August 1984, pp. 116–120.

[Garey/Johnson 1979] Garey, M.R., and D.S. Johnson, *Computers and Intractability: A Guide to the Theory of NP-Completeness*, Freeman, San Francisco, CA, 1979.

[Gustafson 1988] Gustafson, J.L., "Reevaluating Amdahl's Law," *Communications ACM*, Vol. 31, No. 5, May 1988, pp. 532–533.

[Halstead 1986] Halstead, R.H., "Parallel Symbolic Computing," *Computer*, August 1986, pp. 35–43.

[Huhns 1987] Huhns, M.N., ed., *Distributed Artificial Intelligence*, Morgan Kaufmann, Los Altos, CA, 1987.

[Hwang 1987] Hwang, K., J. Ghosh, and R. Chowkwanyun, "Computer Architectures for Artificial Intelligence," *IEEE Computer*, Vol. 20, No. 1, January 1987, pp. 19–27.

[Hwang/Briggs 1984] Hwang, K., and F.A. Briggs, *Computer Architecture and Parallel Processing*, McGraw-Hill, New York, 1984.

[McGehearty/Krall 1986] McGehearty, P.F., and J. Krall, "Potentials for Parallel Execution of Common LISP Programs," *Proc. 1986 Int'l Conf. on Parallel Processing*, University Park, PA, August 1986, pp. 696–702.

[Pleszkun/Thazhuthaveetil 1987] Pleszkun, A.R., and M.J. Thazhuthaveetil, "The Architecture of LISP Machines," *IEEE Computer*, Vol. 20, No. 3, March 1987, pp. 35–44.

[Shapiro 1986] Shapiro, E., "Systems Programming in Concurrent PROLOG, Logic Programming and Its Applications," (Van Caneghem and Warren, eds.), Ablex Publishing, Norwood, NJ, 1986.

[Shapiro 1986a] Shapiro, E., "Concurrent PROLOG: A Progress Report," *IEEE Computer*, August 1986, pp. 44–58.

[Stone 1 1987] Stone, H.S., *High Performance Computer Architecture*, Addison-Wesley, Reading, MA, 1987.

[Stone 2 1987] Stone, J., "The AAAI-86 Conference Exhibits: New Directions for Commercial AI," *AI Magazine*, Vol. 8, No. 1, Spring 1987, pp. 49–54.

[Tanaka 1986] Tanaka, H., "A Parallel Inference Machine," *IEEE Computer*, May 1986, pp. 48–54.

[Tung/Moldovan 1986] Tung, Y.W., and D.I. Moldovan, "Detection of AND-Parallelism in Logic Programming," *Proc. 1986 Int'l Conf. on Parallel Processing*, University Park, PA, August 1986, pp. 984–991.

[Wah/Li 1986] *Computers for Artificial Intelligence Applications*, (B.W. Wah and G.J. Li, eds.), IEEE Computer Society Press, Washington, DC, May 1986.

[Wah/ Li/ Yu 1985] Wah, B.W., L. Guo-jie, and C.F. Yu, "Multiprocessing of Combinatorial Search Problems," *IEEE Computer*, Vol. 18, No. 6, June 1985, pp. 93–108.

PROBLEMS

19.1. Draw the DFG for the LISP program fragment in

(*a*) Example 19.2

(*b*) Example 19.4.

19.2. Discuss the parallel implementation of LISP functions that contain side effects, such as changes to global variables. Does the presence of side effects necessarily eliminate the potential for parallelism?

19.3. Consider the following LISP function for testing list equality:

```
(defun equal2 (x y)
    (if (atom x)
        (equal x y)
        (if (atom y)
            nil
            (if (equal2 (car x) (car y))
                (equal2 (cdr x) (cdr y))
                nil)))))
```

To make things simple, consider only the execution of this function (or its parallel equivalent **EQUALPAR**) on two equal *n*-element lists.

(*a*) Where, if anywhere, would you insert the **future** construct in this function to speed up execution?

(*b*) Again using the future construct, write a new function EQUALPAR that tests for list equality but achieves maximum parallelism. Show, in time, how this parallelism is achieved.

In both cases assume that it is possible to spawn an arbitrarily large number of processes. In each case, for two equal input lists of n elements, estimate the speedup that would occur.

19.4. Can functions that are recursively defined be implemented in parallel? Consider both tail-recursive and non-tail-recursive cases.

19.5. Recall the list reversal function:

```
(defun rev (alist)
    (if   (null alist)   nil
            (append (rev (cdr alist)) (list (car alist)]
```

(*a*) Consider specifically modification of the last *s*-expression for parallel execution using future; that is,

```
(append   (future (rev (cdr alist))
            (future (list (car alist))]
```

(i) Draw the DFGs for the original and modified (parallel) *s*-expressions. (Ignore any overhead due to use of future construct.)

(ii) Assume (for specific input) the following execution times for two cases:

Function	Case 1 time (units)	Case 2 time (units)
cdr	2	2
rev	12	5
car	2	2
list	1	1
append	3	3

Calculate the speedup for both cases 1 and 2. What would be the speedup in a case where each function took exactly one time unit?

(*b*) Repeat part (*a*) for the modified *s*-expression

```
(append (future (rev (future (cdr alist)))
            (future (list (future (car alist))))))
```

19.6. Given a modified LISP code fragment similar to that of Figure 19.3, which is of the form

.
.
.

```
(t (setq x (plus y z)) (setq w (minus p v)) (setq z (minus x v)))
```

(*a*) Rewrite this code using the future construct where appropriate, and estimate the relative speedup (assume each operation takes one time unit).

(*b*) Repeat part (*a*) for

.

.

.

```
(t (setq x (plus y z)) (setq p (minus x v))
                       (setq z (minus x p)))
```

19.7. The following LISP code fragment is taken from function planning (Chapter 14):

```
(setq substate (diff2 state))
(setq actions (possible-actions substate))
(setq actions (action-ordering state actions))
(cond
  ((null actions)
   (setq actions (possible-actions state))
   (setq actions (action-ordering state actions))))
  (print-actions actions)))
(setq history (cons (list state actions) history))
(setq a1 (car actions))
(setq state (take-action a1 state))
(planning state history))]
```

(*a*) Show where it makes sense to insert the future construct.
(*b*) Show several examples of places where insertion of future is not appropriate, in the sense that it does not facilitate speedup.
(*c*) Estimate the speedup that would occur with the parallel modifications of (*a*).

19.8. For the PROLOG goal database shown, which uses the adjacency constraint,

```
goal :-

adjacent_to(R1,R2),
adjacent_to(R2,R6),
adjacent_to(R2,R3),
adjacent_to(R3,R4),
adjacent_to(R2,R4),
adjacent_to(R4,R6),
adjacent_to(R4,R5).

adjacent_to(car,road).
adjacent_to(road,car).
adjacent_to(road,grass).
adjacent_to(grass,road).
adjacent_to(road,trees).
adjacent_to(trees,road).
adjacent_to(sky,trees).
adjacent_to(trees,sky).
adjacent_to(grass,trees).
adjacent_to(trees,grass).
```

(*a*) Identify the shared variables in the goal.

(*b*) Apply the producer-consumer approach to parallel unification of this goal.

(*c*) Repeat (*b*) using the reconciliation approach.

19.9. For the following PROLOG database

```
create(sentence, [X,Y]) :-
                    create(np,X), create(vp,Y).

create(np, [X1,X2]) :-
                    create (adj, X1), create(noun, X2).
create(vp, [Y1,Y2]):- create(verb, Y1), create(np, Y2).
create(adj, the).

create(noun, program).
create(verb, crashes).
create(noun, computer).
```

(*a*) Show, as in Fig. 19.8*c*, the search tree of attempted unifications, taking shared variables into account.

(*b*) Given the goal

```
?-create(sentence, [A, B]).
```

apply the producer-consumer and reconciliation approaches to parallel unification.

19.10. Repeat the producer-consumer solution to Example 19.1 with p_2 as the producer.

19.11. Repeat Example 19.1 with the goal of Fig. 19.8*b* changed to

(*a*) $?-p_1(X, a)$.

(*b*) $?-p_1(X, Y)$.

Indicate all shared variables.

19.12. In the reconciliation scheme of Example 19.1, with the possible unifications shown in Fig. 19.8*c*, note that a second shared variable occurs in unifying p_2. Repeat the solution by using

(*a*) The producer-consumer approach on p_2.

(*b*) The reconciliation approach.

19.13. Another approach to parallel unification is to generate a separate path in the search tree for each possible set of variable bindings.

(*a*) Show the hardware requirements (processors) and speedup consequences of this approach for goal

```
?-p_1(X, Y, Z).
```

where

```
p_1(X,Y,Z) :- p_2(X, Y), p_3(Y, Z), p_4(Z, X).
```

and the remainder of the database is the same as that of Fig. 19.8*a*. Notice that you must consider all binding triples (X, Y, Z).

(*b*) The above approach may be impractical for problems with predicates with large arity and large numbers of shared variables. One suggested remedy is to force some degree of "waiting" (serial bindings) until some variables are bound. Using the results of part (*a*), determine if this is "search" and "processor" efficient, in the sense that many potential paths are eliminated.

19.14. Show the parallel unification using the PROLOG "backtrack" database example (Example 4.46, Chapter 4). Consider both producer-consumer and reconciliation approaches, and estimate the speedup in each case.

19.15. This problem attempts to relate the speedup metrics of Minsky and Hwang/Briggs to that of Amdahl (cf. Table 19.1). Recall that only Amdahl's metric explicitly considered s, the serial fraction of the computation, whereas some serial computation was implied in the others. What constraints result on s from equating speedup metrics in each case? Does this make intuitive sense? Hint: Recall that $s + p = 1$.

APPENDICES

APPENDIX 1:
DISCRETE MATHEMATICS REVIEW

In this appendix, an extended overview is presented of topics from discrete mathematics that are useful in AI. These topics include relations and logic.

Relations

Definition

If A and B are sets, a **relation** from A to B is a subset of $A \times B$. (A1.1)

Here $A \times B$ denotes the cartesian product of the sets A and B. This definition is mathematically precise and somewhat esoteric. (A1.1) defines a *binary relation* since it only involves two sets, and provides a way of "connecting" or relating members of the sets. In particular, the manner in which the sets are connected and the properties of this connection, or relation, are of interest.

SET REPRESENTATION OF RELATIONS. A relation may be represented as a set of ordered pairs. The *domain* of a relation is the set of all first elements of the ordered pairs in the relation, and the *range* is the set of second elements. Thus, the domain consists of a subset of A and the range consists of a subset of B. Many popular relations are defined on a single set; that is, $A = B$. For example, consider the ordered pair of numbers (x,y). The set of all possible values of x is the *domain*, and the set of all possible y values is the *range*. A relation may be enumerated as a set of ordered pairs; for example, relation R_1 may be defined as

$$R_1 = \{(1, 2), (2, 3), (3, 4), (4, 5)\} \qquad (A1.2a)$$

On the other hand, another relation R_2, based upon members of sets that contain symbolic entities, might be

$$R_2 = \{(\text{floor, foundation}), (\text{rug, floor}), (\text{chair, rug}),$$
$$(\text{person, chair})\} \qquad (A1.2b)$$

where the set A consists of entities that lie on something else. Relation R_2 therefore denotes "lies on," or perhaps "is supported by." From the enumeration of R_2, for example, we may represent the fact that a chair "is supported by" a floor, and so forth.

Finally, consider the relation R_3, where

$$R_3 = \{(\text{car, wheels}), (\text{car, driver}), (\text{driver, license}),$$
$$(\text{tire, tread}), (\text{car engine})\} \qquad (A1.3)$$

R_3 demonstrates the relation "has," where sets A and B consist of (perhaps different) sets of entities. A variant on this is when set B consists of *properties* of the elements of A; that is, B is composed of the values of certain predefined attributes of corresponding elements of A.

In many AI applications, enumeration of the relation as above is both necessary and practical. In other situations it is possible to specify the relation via a rule. For example, in relation R_1 the obvious rule is "next in ascending order," where A and B are sets of non-negative integers.

RELATION PROPERTIES. In representing relations as sets of ordered pairs, note that the *order* in which an entity appears in the pair is significant. For example, referring to the relation "contained in" (Chapter 1), "a contained in b" does not signify, in general, that "b is contained in a." Thus relations have a *direction*, as the graphical representation will more clearly show.

The important symmetric, reflexive, and transitive properties of relations are defined in Chapter 1 and considered throughout the text. The practical aspects of attempting to represent symmetric relations in PROLOG are addressed in Chapter 2. Two special cases of relations are the *equivalence relation* and the *function*.

Definition: Equivalence relation.

A relation that satisfies all three properties (i.e., it is reflexive, symmetric, and transitive) is termed an **equivalence relation**. $\qquad (A1.4)$

Relations as functions. Most scientists and engineers are familiar with a subset of relations called functions. Functions are not restricted to numerical quantities. A **function** from A to B is a relation (denoted by the symbol f) such that for every $a \in A$ there exists one and only one $b \in B$ such that $(a,b) \in f$. Usually we show this relation as

$$f: A \Rightarrow B \qquad (A1.5a)$$

where A is the domain of function f, and B is the range. For a particular member of f, that is, $(a,b) \in f$, we say that b is the *value* of f at a; in other words,

$$b = f(a) \tag{A1.5b}$$

Another way to view a function is as a special relation in which each $a_i \in A$ belongs to only one ordered pair in the relation. Thus, given one element of R, that is,

$$(a_i, b_i) \tag{A1.6a}$$

no other element of the form

$$(a_i, c_i) \tag{A1.6b}$$

belongs to R unless $b_i = c_i$. From (A1.5b), this is written as $b_i = f(a_i)$ to denote the function mapping.

Notice the previous definition allows f to contain pairs

$$(a_i, b_i)$$

and

$$(d_i, b_i)$$

If this occurs, the function is not one-to-one, and $f(a_i) = f(d_i)$ does *not* imply $a_i = d_i$.

BIPARTITE GRAPH REPRESENTATIONS OF RELATIONS. Given

$$A = \{a, b, c, d, \ldots\} \tag{A1.7a}$$
$$B = \{x, y, z, \ldots\} \tag{A1.7b}$$

a relation from A to B, namely R, satisfies $R \subseteq A \times B$. The relationship may be represented graphically by using an arrow to show each element of R. In this way, the "connection" between the sets is displayed graphically.

Directed graphs and intra-set relations. When $R \subseteq A \times A$, a *directed graph*, or *digraph*, is a convenient tool to represent the relationship between elements of a set. Suppose

$$A = \{a, b, c, d\}$$

Then

$$\begin{aligned} A \times A = \{&(a,a),\ (a,b),\ (a,c),\ (a,d), \\ &(b,a),\ (b,b),\ \ldots\} \end{aligned} \tag{A1.8}$$

If we assume, for example, that a relation R is defined as

$$\begin{aligned} R = \{&(a,b),\ (b,c),\ (b,d),\ (b,a), \\ &(c,c),\ (d,a)\} \end{aligned} \tag{A1.9}$$

then we may graphically represent R using the graphical construct shown in Fig. 1.4, where the elements of A are *nodes* in the graph and the elemental relationships are indicated by *arrows* from the element in the domain to the corresponding element in the range. Often we refer to these arrows as *edges*. The use of arrows in the digraph reinforces the notion of a direction to the relation.

Uniqueness of relation digraphs and isomorphism. The digraph for a specific relation is not unique, since two digraphs may be isomorphic. This is a consequence of the arbitrary choice of nodes to represent specific elements of set A. The *structure* of the graphs resulting from any choice of nodes (or "vertices") will be the same, however. The isomorphism of graphs G_1 and G_2 implies there is a one-to-one correspondence (onto function), denoted v, from the vertices of G_1 to the vertices of G_2, as well as a one-to-one correspondence (onto function), denoted e, from the edges of G_1 to the edges of G_2. Thus, for an edge e_1 connecting vertices v_1 and w_1 in G_1, an edge $e_2 = e(e_1)$ exists in G_2 and connects nodes $v_2 = v(v_1)$ and $w_2 = v(w_1)$.

Logic

STATEMENTS. A *statement* (or *proposition* or *assertion*) is a declarative sentence that is either TRUE or FALSE. Three examples of statements are

$$\text{The value of the current through resistor } R_4 \text{ is 6 mA.} \qquad (A1.10a)$$

$$\text{Many books on Artificial Intelligence exist.} \qquad (A1.10b)$$

$$\text{A system is stable if the poles are in the right half plane.} \qquad (A1.10c)$$

Not all phrases or sentences in English are statements according to the above definition. For example

$$\text{Place the wrench on the nut.} \qquad (A1.11)$$

is a *command* (it is neither TRUE nor FALSE);

$$\text{Artificial Intelligence will solve all problems in Image Processing.} \qquad (A1.12)$$

is an *opinion* (its truth or validity is subject to opinion); and

$$\text{This statement is FALSE.} \qquad (A1.13)$$

is referred to as a *paradox*: it can be neither TRUE nor FALSE.

In AI representations, the use of *open statements*, such as

$$x + 8 = y - 3$$

which are TRUE for some values of the variables x and y but FALSE for others, is significant. This type of statement leads into the study of *predicate logic*.

A compound statement is formed by using logical connectives, such as "and," "not," and "if," to connect statements. $(A1.14)$

Examples are

The current in R_4 will decrease if the voltage across R_4 is decreased. $(A1.15a)$

The block on the workstand may be moved if there is not another block on top of it and it weighs less than 10 kg and it may be grasped in the x,y-plane. $(A1.15b)$

TABLE A1.1
AND

X	Y	$X \cap Y$
F	F	F
F	T	F
T	F	F
T	T	T

If the vessel pressure exceeds 30 psi, and the temperature is between 120 and 180°F, then the alarm is to be sounded. (A1.15c)

The circuit board is inserted incorrectly and there is a missing integrated circuit chip. (A1.15d)

The *truth value* of a compound statement depends upon the truth values of the individual component statements as well as the connectives used. There are a number of techniques for manipulating and determining the truth of logical expressions, including Karnaugh maps, truth tables, and Boolean algebra. The nomenclature for compound statements follows that of the connectives used; that is, an AND statement is based upon the AND connective.

Conjunction (AND). A *conjunction* or *AND expression* is based upon the logical AND function, whose truth table is given for the case of two arguments in Table A1.1. The logical states, or truth values, of the arguments are represented by the symbols X and Y, and the AND operator, or logical connective, is denoted by the symbol $\cap$. As shown by the table, the compound statement $X \cap Y$ has value T (TRUE) only if *both* X and Y evaluate to T. The case of $n > 2$ arguments (an n-ary AND function) in compound statements is handled in one of two ways:

a) Define the conjunction of n statements to be TRUE only if all component statements are TRUE.

b) Use the association

$$A \cap B \cap C \equiv (A \cap B) \cap C$$

and the two-argument AND definition (Table A1.1).

By way of example, we may use statement (A1.15d). Letting

I = the truth value of the statement "the circuit board is inserted incorrectly"

M = the truth value of the statement "there is a missing integrated circuit chip"

C = the truth value of compound statement (A1.15d)

we could reformulate the truth value of statement (A1.15d) as the logical expression

$$C = I \cap M \tag{A1.16}$$

TABLE A1.2
OR

X	Y	$X \cup Y$
F	F	F
F	T	T
T	F	T
T	T	T

Disjunction (OR). Another useful operator is the *disjunction*, or *OR connective*, denoted as $\cup$, whose corresponding binary function truth table is shown in Table A1.2.

The OR connective yields a compound expression that evaluates to TRUE when at least one of the component statements is TRUE. Note that the use of the connective "or" in the English language does not have the logical meaning of the OR operator defined above; the reader should verify that the English "or" typically means exclusive-OR (XOR), which is FALSE if *both* operands are TRUE.

Negation (NOT). The unary NOT operator, denoted by $\neg$, is of significant use in symbolic logic manipulation. For example, consider statement (A1.15*b*). Letting

B = the truth value of "the block on the workstand
    may be moved"

A = the truth value of (the situation) "there is
    another block on top of the block to be moved"

W = the truth value of "the weight of the block
    is less than 10 kg"

G = the truth value of "the block is able
    to be grasped in the x,y-plane"

then the truth value of (A1.15*b*) may be written compactly using the AND, NOT, and IF logical connectives as

$$B \text{ if } (\neg A) \cap W \cap G \qquad (A1.17)$$

The truth table for the unary NOT connective is given in Table A1.3. A connective employing NOT is sometimes referred to as a *denial*.

Equality. The final simple connective is the *equality* connective. Given the truth value of two statements, represented by logical variables X and Y, the truth value of a compound statement with the equality connective is defined to be TRUE if both variables have the same truth value; otherwise it is FALSE. This is denoted in the truth table in Table A1.4. The equality connective is denoted using the symbol $\equiv$. Equality is an

TABLE A1.3
NOT

X	$\neg X$
F	T
T	F

TABLE A1.4
Equality

X	Y	$X \equiv Y$
F	F	T
F	T	F
T	F	F
T	T	T

important concept that has a strong relationship to (but is different from) the implication operator considered next. Note that the individual meanings of two statements connected by the equality operator to form a TRUE compound statement are not necessarily equal. (This is, in fact, one of the shortcomings of logic in AI.) It is only the *truth values* of the statements that are equal.

Implication (IF-THEN). The implication connective (denoted $\rightarrow$) is defined in Chapter 1. It is fundamental to many AI inference strategies and must be interpreted carefully. Implication is often misunderstood to mean equality; it is instead a "one-way" connective. This is shown in Example A1.1.

Example A1.1   Implication. Consider this compound statement:

If the University of Virginia's (U.Va.) football team plays Clemson University, then U.Va. will lose.

Make these truth-value variable assignments:

$P =$ the truth of the statement "U.Va. plays Clemson"

$L =$ the truth of the statement "U.Va. loses (the game)"

It is tempting, and *incorrect*, to equate the playing of Clemson with losing; that is,

$$P \equiv L$$

since there are other ways for U.Va. to lose. Viewed another way, P is a *sufficient*, but not a *necessary*, condition for L. Correctly stated using implication, the situation described is

$$P \rightarrow L$$

meaning that if P is TRUE, then L must be TRUE. However, if P is FALSE (i.e., U.Va. does not play Clemson), L may still be TRUE; that is, U.Va. may still lose. Thus, in logic, implication is used in a weak sense and forms a "one-way" logical relationship.

Example A1.2   Implication truth table derivation. Suppose Maxwell Smart is a candidate to be the next president of Clumpsen University (CU). During the interview process, he makes a promise that during his tenure as president, CU will achieve national prominence. In words, his implication-based compound statement becomes

IF

Maxwell Smart is chosen as the next president of CU,

THEN

CU will achieve national prominence.

TABLE A1.5
Implication truth table

Possible combination	Truth value of statement
1. $(p = T)$; $(q = T)$	T
2. $(p = T)$; $(q = F)$	F
3. $(p = F)$; $(q = T)$	T
4. $(p = F)$; $(q = F)$	T

Coding this logic using variables p and q, where

$p = $ the truth value of the statement "Maxwell Smart is chosen as the next president of CU" (or more simply, "he is chosen")

$q = $ the truth value of the statement "CU achieves national prominence"

The compound statement may thus be written

$$p \rightarrow q$$

We wish to consider the truth of the implication $(p \rightarrow q)$ as a function of the logical values of p and q. Consider the four possible truth-value combinations shown in Table A1.5. A practical way to determine the truth of the compound statement is by considering which, if any, of the four cases in Table A1.5 make Maxwell Smart a liar. Such cases make the compound statement $(p \rightarrow q)$ FALSE; otherwise it is TRUE.

Only case 2 in Table A1.5 makes Maxwell Smart a liar. In case 1, he is telling the truth. Furthermore, we cannot claim that combinations 3 and 4 are FALSE (i.e., he is a liar), since his original compound statement makes no claim as to what will happen to CU if he is not chosen.

An alternate viewpoint of implication, explored by examination of the Karnaugh map and Table A1.5, is that $\neg (p \rightarrow q)$ is TRUE (i.e., $(p \rightarrow q)$ is FALSE) when p is TRUE and q is FALSE. Using De Morgan's law,

$$(p \cap (\neg q)) \equiv \neg (\neg p \cup q)$$

Thus, given an implication known to be FALSE (if, for example, we know we are dealing with a liar), the truth values of the component statements in the implication are constrained.

Implication and equality. Consider the final question:

How are implication and equality related? (Alternatively—Under what conditions are they the same?) (A1.18)

This inquiry is explored again by use of either the implication truth table or Karnaugh maps. Consider the case where both $(p \rightarrow q)$ and $(q \rightarrow p)$ are TRUE. The compound statement $(q \rightarrow p)$ is known as the *converse* of the implication $(p \rightarrow q)$. The combined truth tables are shown in Table A1.6.

TABLE A1.6
Implication and equality

p	q	$(p \rightarrow q)$	$(q \rightarrow p)$	**BOTH WAYS**
T	T	T	T	T
T	F	F	T	F
F	T	T	F	F
F	F	T	T	T

The logical function

$$\text{BOTH\_WAYS} \equiv ((p \rightarrow q) \cap (q \rightarrow p)) \tag{A1.19}$$

is referred to as the *biconditional* or iff ("if and only if") connective. It is often denoted $(p \leftrightarrow q)$. Notice that the biconditional BOTH_WAYS is TRUE only when $(p \equiv q)$ is TRUE. Thus, if implication is TRUE in either direction (i.e., p implies q is TRUE and q implies p is also TRUE) then the logical relationship between p and q is stronger than implication; it is equality. This leads to the following conclusion:

> If an implication and its converse are both TRUE, then the assertion may be replaced by an equality connective. (A1.20)

STATEMENTS, VARIABLES, AND PREDICATES. In the preceding examination of *propositional logic*, statements were variable-free. There was no other explicit dependence of the truth of the statement on the individual contents (i.e., words or phrases) of the statement. In this sense, there was no mechanism that allowed the possibility of a substitution of an element in the statement with another, making the truth value of the statement a function of this substitution. In other words, there is no ability to take into account the dependence of the truth of the statement on the contents of a portion of the statement. Consider the following two statements, derived from previous examples:

U.Va. lost the game.

Clemson lost the game.

Clearly, each of these statements has a truth value that is a function of the particular team. If we assume the first statement is TRUE and the second is FALSE, we could reformulate the information as:

```
(? who) lost the game is
```

```
        TRUE if (? who) is U.VA.
```

```
        FALSE if (? who) is Clemson
```

A variable, denoted `(? who)`, has been introduced into the statement formulation. Statements whose truth values depend upon specific elements in the statement, that is, variable bindings or values, are modeled using *predicates*. The truth value of our compound statement may be represented by the predicate lost_the_game, whose argument may take on the values U.Va. or Clemson, and is defined as

lost_the_game(U.Va.) = TRUE

and

lost_the_game(Clemson) = FALSE

Predicates are considered further in Chapters 2 and 4.

QUANTIFICATION IN STATEMENTS.

The universal quantifier. The universal quantifier often appears (either implicitly or explicitly) in (possibly compound) statements involving predicates. For example, consider a database incorporating the fact that U.Va. lost *regardless* of whom they played. In other words,

For all opponents, U.Va. loses

is TRUE. Assume the set of teams U.Va. played was

Opponents = {clemson, maryland, duke, n.c.state}

This set also constitutes the universe of the variable Opponent, used in the predicate

lost_the_game(u.va., Opponent) = TRUE

IF

Opponent = clemson   OR
Opponent = maryland   OR
Opponent = duke   OR
Opponent = n.c.state

Predicate logic allows this statement to be written succinctly using the universal quantifier ∀, read "for all," together with the predicate function lost_the_game. The structure of the statement would then be

[(∀ Opponent)   lost_the_game (u.va., Opponent)] = TRUE

It is not necessary to force the universally quantified statement to be TRUE, although this is often implied. It does hold, however, that the universally quantified formulation yields a general statement about the truth of a statement containing one or more variables.

The existential quantifier. The companion to the universal quantifier is the *existential* quantifier, which specifies that "there exists" at least one instantiation of the existentially quantified variable that according to the previous convention, makes this predicate TRUE. This quantifier is denoted ∃ and written with syntax similar to that used for the universal quantifier. For example, consider the statement (assumed TRUE)

U.Va. lost a game to at least one opponent

This statement could be reformulated using the existentially quantified predicate

(∃ Opponent) (lost_the_game(u.va., Opponent) ≡ T)

Compound statements involving quantification. The representational capability of predicate logic far exceeds that shown in the simple examples. For example, suppose that we wished to represent this (assumed TRUE) statement in logic:

For all visible objects in a scene, there exists a point on each that is closest to the viewer.

One (not necessarily unique) formulation of this statement using predicates, quantification, and implication is

(∀ Object) [visible_in_scene(Object) ->

((∃ Point) (on(Point, Object) ∩ closest_to(Point, viewer)))]

In this formulation, brackets have been employed to indicate that the *scope* of universally quantified variable Object is that of the entire statement; the scope of existentially quantified variable Point is only that of the implication consequent.

APPENDIX 2: PROLOG SYNTAX SUMMARY

Given a database of rules and facts (expressed as clauses), together with a goal, PROLOG searches for a consistent binding of variables with values (the unification process). PROLOG implements a subset of logic restricted to first order Horn clauses (meaning roughly that predicates can't be variables). The basis for applications implemented in PROLOG is a set of statements containing rules and facts. Often this is viewed as the "database" of problem information. PROLOG's main utility is in searching this database with the objective of satisfying one or more goals through a process of unification that involves consistently instantiating variables with values, or "binding." When one or more consistent solutions are found, that is, when bindings yield facts that are either provable or derivable from the fact- and rule-bases, the PROLOG system returns these bindings.

Basic Program Elements

PROLOG databases are made up of clauses. The basic building block of a clause is the *predicate*, which is of the form

```
predicate_name (atom_1, atom_2, ... atom_N).
```
(A2.1)

The arity of a predicate is the number of its arguments. Two-argument predicates (arity = 2) are useful for representing *binary relations*.

ATOMS, CONSTANTS, AND VARIABLES. Atoms may be either *constants* or *variables*. Variables are denoted by capitalizing the first letter of the variable name. Constants begin with a lower case letter. For example,

> Bob is a PROLOG variable
>
> bob is a PROLOG constant

The anonymous variable (which is denoted by the underbar), matches anything; that is,

```
predicate (_).
```
(A2.2)

will unify with anything of the form

```
predicate(atom).
```

RULES AND FACTS. Facts are of the form

```
predicate_name (atom_1, atom_2, ... atom_N).
```
(A2.3)

> Rules are of the form

```
predicate_1 (atom_1, atom_2 ... atom_N) :-
```

```
predicate_2 (atom_1,...),

    predicate _3 (atom_1,...),
                        .
                        .
                        .
        predicate_R (atom_R1, ... atom_RQ).
```
$$(A2.4)$$

Predicate_1 is the *head* or *consequent* of the rule; predicates_2 through R are the *tail*, *antecedents*, or *body* of the rule.

Unification

In a Prolog database, unification proceeds from *top to bottom* in the database, and from *left to right* in a rule. When more than one clause is found in the database that represents a potential unification solution, the clause is marked for *backtracking*.

Lists

A list is delineated by square brackets. For example, [one, two, three, four] is a list. Lists are manipulated using the form $[x|y]$, where x is the first element of the list and y is the remainder (a list).

Special Symbols and Operators

?−	question (database query)
:−	"if"
,	"and"
;	"or"
.	clause terminator
is	causes binding (PROLOG's assignment operator)
!	cut operator
+	addition
−	subtraction
*	multiplication
/	division
=	equality predicate (match operator)
\=	inequality predicate
>	greater than
>=	greater than or equal to
=<	less than or equal to

Database Creation and Editing

Built-in predicates assert, asserta, assertz (see Chapter 2) are used to add single clauses to the database. Similarly, retract( ) and retractall remove one or all predicates from the current database. Predicate consult (<filename>) is used to bring the PROLOG statements in text file <filename> into the current database. <filename> is created outside of the PROLOG system by a text editor (e.g., vi). consult fails if: (1) <filename> is not found; or (2) one or more of the statements in <filename> violate the syntax of PROLOG.

Noteworthy Built-in Predicates

asserta (X)	Add clause X to database (at beginning of file).
assertz (X)	Add clause X to database (at end of file).
atom (X)	Test for list.
call (X)	X is interpreted as a PROLOG goal; succeeds if attempt to satisfy X is successful.
consult (X)	Invoke datafile X to extend database *without* overwriting current predicates.
fail	Predicate that always evaluates to NOT TRUE; that is, fails.
halt	Predicate that terminates PROLOG session and returns user to operating system.[*]
listing(X)	List all predicates whose name is X; listing. (without an argument) lists the contents of the current database.
nl	Line return (for printing).
nonvar(X)	Succeeds if variable X is bound.
not (X)	Negation operator succeeds if argument fails to unify; must be used carefully (see Chapter 4).
notrace	Stops trace.
read (X)	I/O predicate with side effect (evaluates to TRUE).
reconsult(X)	Like consult, predicates in X with same name as those in current database *supercede* or *overwrite* existing predicates.
retract (X)	Remove first occurrence of predicate whose name is X.
retractall	Remove all occurrences of predicate whose name is X.
trace	Side effect is to turn on tracing.
true	Predicate that always evaluates to TRUE.
var(X)	Succeeds if variable X is unbound.
write (X)	I/O predicate.

---

[*]The name of this predicate tends to vary among PROLOG implementations. abort and exit are popular synonyms.

APPENDIX 3:   COMMONLY USED
LISP FUNCTIONS AND EXAMPLES

We indicate here most of the frequently used LISP functions. In some cases, these are defined and explained in the text. In other cases, longer examples are provided. Most, but not all are available in FranzLISP and CommonLISP. To distinguish the availability in these dialects, the following conventions are used:

CL   denotes CommonLISP availability

FL   denotes FranzLISP availability

We note, as in the text, the following major differences between FranzLISP and CommonLISP:

1. FranzLISP is *case sensitive*; CommonLISP is not.
2. FranzLISP employs *dynamical* scoping; CommonLISP variables are *lexically* scoped.
3. Global variables must be specially declared in CommonLISP (and consequently receive dynamic scoping) using the `defvar` macro[*], i.e., (`defvar` <variable-name>) or the

    (`declare` (`special` <variable-name>))

    construct.

In both FranzLISP and CommonLISP, comments in the source code begin with a semicolon.

Predicates

Note: Each of these predicates returns either `t` or `nil`.

Function: `atom`   FL   CL
Sample Use: (`atom arg`)
Value Returned: `t` iff `arg` is not a list.

Function: `equal`   FL   CL
Sample Use: (`equal arg1 arg2`)
Value Returned: `t` iff `arg1` and `arg2` satisfy the requirements below.
Remark: This is a less stringent test for equality than `eq`. Arguments `arg1` and `arg2` are `equal` if

---

[*] This is preferred.

they are eq.

they are both f i xnums with the same value.

they are both f l onums with the same value.

they are both b i gnums with the same value.

they are both strings and are identical.

they are both lists and their cars and cdrs are equa l.

Function: not   FL   CL
Sample Use: (not arg)
Value Returned: t if arg is ni l.

Function: nul l   FL   CL
Sample Use: (nul l arg)
Value Returned: t if arg is the empty list, that is, ni l.

Function: l istp   FL   CL
Sample Use: (l istp arg)
Value Returned: t iff arg is a list.

Arithmetic predicates.

Function: =   FL   CL
Sample Use: (= arg1   arg2)
Value Returned t if arg1 = arg2

Function: > FL   CL
Sample Use: (> arg1   arg2)
Value Returned: t if arg1 > arg2

Function: < FL   CL
Sample Use: (< arg1   arg2)
Value Returned: t if arg1 < arg2

Function: >= FL   CL
Sample Use: (>= arg1   arg2)
Value Returned: t if arg1 ≥ arg2

List Manipulation

(See Chapter 8.)

Function: car   FL   CL
Sample Use: (car larg)
Value Returned: the first element of larg.

Function: cdr   FL   CL
Sample Use: (cdr larg)
Value Returned: the list larg with all but the first element.

Function: cons   FL   CL
Sample Use: (cons arg1 arg2)
Value Returned: a list whose car is arg1 and whose cdr is arg2.

Function: append   FL   CL
Sample Use: (append larg1 larg2)
Value Returned: a list containing the elements of larg1 followed by larg2.

Function: member   FL   CL
Sample Use: (member arg1 larg)
Value Returned: that part of the larg beginning with the first occurrence of arg1.
Remark: member tests for equality using equal in FranzLISP. To achieve the same effect in CommonLISP, the optional argument :test #'equal must be used; otherwise a stricter test for equality (eql) is used.

Function: nth   FL   CL
Sample Use: (nth index list)
Value Returned: the nth element of list, using zero-based indexing, for example, (nth 0 list) is the same as (car list).

Function: delete   FL   CL*
Sample Use: (delete element list)
Value Returned: a modified list with all occurrences of element removed.
Function: remove   CL
(CommonLISP equivalent of FranzLISP delete).

Function: length   FL   CL
Sample Use: (length a_list)
Value Returned: the number of elements of a_list.

length example:

```
-> one-list
((a b) (c) (d e f) (g h))

-> (mapcar 'length one-list)
(2 1 3 2)
```

---

*delete in CommonLISP must be used with care, in that it is "destructive." remove in CL is nondestructive.

Assignment

Function: setq   FL   CL
Sample Use: (setq symb1 val1 [symb2 val2 ... ...])
Definitions: the arguments are pairs of atom names and expressions.
Value Returned: the last vali.
Notable Side Effect: each symbi is set to have the value vali.
Remark: set evaluates all of its arguments, setq does not evaluate the symbi.

Function: setf (see Chapter 8)   FL   CL
Sample Use: (setf expr value)
Remark: setf is a generalization of setq.

Property and Association Lists

Function: assoc   FL   CL
Sample Use: (assoc arg larg)
Value Returned: the first element of larg whose car is equal to arg.
Remark: Usually larg has an assoc−list structure. arg thus acts as a key.

Function: get   FL   CL
Sample Use: (get symb prop_val)
Value Returned: The value associated with property prop_val of symb.

Function: putprop FL   (in CL, use setf; see Chapter 8)
Sample Use: (putprop name val ind)
Value Returned: val.
Notable Side Effect: Adds to the property list of name the value val under the indicator (See Chapter 8) ind.
Remark: putprop evaluates its arguments.

Arithmetic and Logical Functions

Function: plus, +   FL   (+ in CL only)
Sample Use: (+ arg1 ...argn)
Value Returned: the sum of the arguments. If no arguments are given, 0 is returned.

Function: diff, −   FL   (− in CL only)
Sample Use: (− arg1 ...argn)
Value Returned: the result of subtracting from arg1 all subsequent arguments. If no arguments are given, 0 is returned.

Function: minus   FL   ((− arg) in CL)
Sample Use: (− arg)
Value Returned: zero minus arg.

Function: times, *   FL   (* only in CL)
Sample Use: (* arg1   ...arg_m)
Value Returned: the product of all of its arguments. It returns 1 if there are no arguments.

Function: quotient, / FL (/ only in CL)
Sample Use: (arg1   arg2)
Value Returned: arg1 ÷ arg2

Function: and   FL   CL
Sample Use: (and arg1 ...argn)
Value Returned: the value of the last argument if all arguments evaluate to a non-nil value; otherwise and returns nil.
Remark: The arguments are evaluated left to right and evaluation will cease with the first nil encountered.

Function: or   FL   CL
Sample Use: (or arg1...argn)
Value Returned: the value of the first argument that evaluates to a non-nil value, otherwise returns nil.

Function: max   FL   CL
Sample Use: (max 'n_arg1 ...)
Value Returned: the maximum value in the list of arguments.
Remark: The function min, which is

(min 'n_arg1 ...)

is similar; the minimum value in the list of arguments is the value returned.

max example:

--> (max 3 4 5 9 1 2)
9

Printing Functions

Function: pp   FL
Sample Use: (pp name)
Value Returned: t
Notable Side Effect: If name has a function binding, it is pretty-printed; otherwise, if name has a value then that value is pretty-printed.

Function: pprint   CL
Sample Use: (pp name)
Value Returned: N/A (side effect only)
Notable Side Effect: If symbol name has a value then that value is pretty-printed. Not applicable to functions.

Function: read   FL   CL
Sample Use: (read)
Value Returned: the next LISP expression read.

Function: print   FL   CL
Sample Use: (print arg)
Value Returned: nil in FL; arg in CL.
Notable Side Effect: prints arg on the default port.
Remark: In CommonLISP a carriage return and linefeed are added. Also, in CommonLISP a global variable *print—pretty*, when set to non-nil, is used in conjunction with print to pretty-print output.

Function: terpri   FL   CL
Sample Use: (terpri)
Value Returned: nil
Notable Side Effect: terpri is an argument-less function used to print a carriage return and line feed and used for formatting.

Function Definition and Application

Function: defun   FL   CL
Sample Use: (defun fname argl exp)
Value Returned: fname
Notable Side Effect: This defines function fname.
Remark: An example of defun is shown below (see "apply").

Function: putd   FL
Sample Use: (putd alt_name func_name)
Value Returned: func_name
Notable Side Effect: This sets the function binding of symbol alt_name to func_name.
Remark: This is an efficient method for renaming functions.

Function: mapcar   FL   CL
Sample Use: (mapcar func larg1 ...largn)
Value Returned: a list of the values returned from the functional application.

mapcar example

```
-> (mapcar 'atom '(a b '(c a) (d) e (f g)))
(t  t  nil  nil  t  nil)
```

Function: eval   FL   CL
Sample Use: (eval expr)
Value Returned: The evaluation of expr.

Function: apply   FL   CL
Sample Use: (apply func largs)
Value Returned: the result of applying function func to the arguments in the list largs.

apply example:

```
-> (apply 'plus '(1 2 3 4))
10

-> (defun size-of-biggest-list (a-list)
(apply 'max (mapcar 'length a-list)))
size-of-biggest-list

-> (size-of-biggest-list one-list)
3
```

Control Functions

Function: cond   (see Chapter 8)   FL   CL
Sample Use: (cond lclause1 ...lclausen)
Value Returned: the last value evaluated in the first clause satisfied; that is, a satisfied lclause is one whose CAR evaluates to non-nil.

Function: let   (see Chapter 8)   FL   CL
Sample Use: (let var_binds body_exp)
Value Returned: value of last expression in body_exp. Note, let and do (below) allow creation and binding of temporary variables.

Function: do   (see Chapter 8)   FL   CL
Sample Use: (do lvrbs ltest gexp1 ...)
Value Returned: the last form in the cdr of ltest evaluated, or a value explicitly given by a return evaluated within the do body.

Function: if   (see Chapter 8)   FL   CL
Sample Use: (if a b c)
Value Returned: b if a evaluates to non-nil, else c.
Remark: If is a macro that expands into a cond. For example,

```
(if a b c)
```

is equivalent to

```
(cond
   (a b)
   (T c))
```

Function: return   (see Chapter 8)   FL   CL
Sample Use: (return <expr>)
Value Returned: the value of <expr>; nil if <expr> is missing
Notable Side Effect: return is used to exit from the body of a do macro (i.e., to stop the iteration without using end-test).

Debugging and Tracing Functions

Function: trace   FL   CL
Sample Use: (trace arg1 ...)
Definitions: the form of the ls_argi is described below.
Value Returned: a list of the functions successfully modified for tracing. If no arguments are given to trace, a list of all functions currently being traced is returned.

Function: untrace   FL   CL
Sample Use: (untrace arg1 ...)

System Functions

Function: exit   FL
Sample Use: (exit)
Value Returned: doesn't matter
Notable Side Effect: exits LISP system

Function: abort   CL
(same effect as exit; see above)

Function: load   FL   CL
Sample Use: (load '<filename>) in FL; (load "<filename>") in CL
Value Returned: t
Notable Side Effect: reads and interprets contents of <filename>.

Function: help   FL
Sample Use: (help arg)
Notable Side Effect: If arg is a symbol then the portion of the FranzLISP manual beginning with the description of arg is printed on the terminal.

Function: gc   FL
Sample Use: (gc)
Value Returned: nil
Notable Side Effect: This causes a garbage collection (see Chapter 9 and 19).

APPENDIX 4:
ELEMENTARY UNIX COMMANDS AND v i

Many good PROLOG, LISP, and OPS5-based AI development environments are available on UNIX-based systems. In fact, all the examples in this text were run using such a system. For readers with access to comparable facilities, these sections will serve as an introduction for those new to UNIX commands and the vi editor, or as a review for those just needing a quick "refresher."

Basic UNIX Use

The UNIX operating system is popular due to a number of factors, including flexibility and portability. However, the potential complexity of UNIX often impedes familiarization.

The commands man −k keyword (list commands relevant to keyword) and man command (print out the manual for command) serve as the basis for getting started. Of course, these are of limited use if you don't know the names of any useful commands. The most commonly used UNIX commands are shown in Table A4.1.

For example, you could find programs about mail by the command man −k mail and print out the mail command documentation via man mail.

To logout, type control-D (if your prompt is $).

A QUICK EXAMPLE OF A UNIX SESSION (SIMPLE COMMANDS).

```
$ who
rjschal      tty19      Mar    2 10:59
hubcap       tty22      Mar    2 08:30
ece406       tty31      Mar    2 10:31
```

TABLE A4.1
Commonly used UNIX commands

apropos (string)	give info on all commands dealing with string
cat	concatenates files (and just prints them out)
chmod	sets protection on files/directories
cp	copy
finger	user information lookup program
lpr	print
ls	list contents of a directory
mail	send and receive mail
mkdir	make a new (sub)directory
passwd	change login password
pwd	print working directory (useful for "recalling" where you are in the UNIX subdirectory structure)
rm <filename>	delete <filename>
rmdir	remove a (sub)directory
who	who is on the system
write	write to another user
vi	invoke visual editor (vi)

```
$ whoami
rjschal

$ ls -al
total 757
drwxr-xr-x   2 rjschal          512 Dec  4 10:01 .
drwxr-xr-x484 root             8192 Mar  2 08:32 ..
-rwxr-xr-x   1 rjschal          281 Feb 23  1987 .cshrc
-rwxr-xr-x   1 rjschal          256 Feb 23  1987 .login
-rwxr--r--   1 rjschal           79 Feb 23  1987 .mailrc
-rw-r--r--   1 rjschal           73 Oct 14 09:14 rule
-rwxr-xr-x   1 rjschal       716303 Oct 14 09:14 rulestate

$ cat .profile
PATH=.:$HOME/bin:/usr/ucb:/bin:/usr/bin:/usr/local:/usr/new:/usr/hosts
MAIL=/usr/spool/mail/$USER
tset -n -I
export TERM MAIL PATH
biff n

$ ls>temp

$ cat temp
rule
rulestate
temp

$ cp cfile cfile.c
$ rm cfile

$ apropos directory
cd (1)- change working directory
chdir (2)- change current working directory
ls (1)- list contents of directory
mkdir (1)- make a directory
```

USING THE UNIX tee TO GET A LOG OF YOUR PROLOG OR LISP Session. One useful feature of UNIX systems is the capability for *redirection*. For example, the output of your PROLOG session (which is, by default, sent to the terminal), may be redirected to file my-output via invocation of

```
$ prolog > my_output
```

Unfortunately, the output would no longer appear in the terminal with this type of redirection. Instead, the UNIX tee may be used to send output *both* to the terminal and to a file. Invoke the LISP or PROLOG program with a UNIX tee of the form

```
$ prolog ; tee my_log.1
```

This sends your output both to the default device (the terminal) as well as a file named my_log.1.

Example A4.1. (*a*) First a PROLOG session:

```
$ prolog ; tee my_log.1
C-Prolog version 1.5
; ?- consult('parser.pro').
parser.pro consulted 868 bytes 0.1 sec.

yes
; ?- listing.

word(verb,crashes).
word(adj,the).
word(noun,computer).

yes
; ?- halt.

[ Prolog execution halted ]
```

(*b*) End of session—now look at what is in my_log.1:

```
$ cat my_log.1
C-Prolog version 1.5
; ?- parser.pro consulted 868 bytes 0.1 sec.

yes
; ?- listing.

word(verb,crashes).
word(adj,the).
word(noun,computer).

yes
; ?-
[ Prolog execution halted ]
```

This is a handy tool—you can now send my_log.1 to the printer to get a copy of your PROLOG or LISP session.

DOS TO UNIX COMMAND CONVERSION. Table A4.2 is intended to help readers familiar with DOS become accustomed to UNIX.

Elements of the Visual Editor (vi)

vi, a screen editor commonly found on UNIX systems, is used to create, modify, or view ASCII files. We will not attempt to list or describe all of the features of vi; rather our purpose is to enable the reader to create and edit typical files with a minimum of effort using the basic features of vi.

TABLE A4.2
DOS to UNIX command conversion

These DOS and UNIX commands have similar purposes and operate nearly the same way.

DOS Command	Closest UNIX Command	Description
CHDIR (CD)	cd	Change directory
COPY	cp	Copy a file or group of files
	cat	Concatenate files
DIR	ls	List a directory
ERASE, DEL	rm	Remove files
MKDIR (MD)	mkdir	Make a directory (a directory list under UNIX)
RENAME	mv	Move (rename) files
RMDIR	rmdir	Remove a directory (a directory list under UNIX)
TIME, DATE	date	Display and change the system time
TYPE	cat	Display the contents of a file (a file list under UNIX)

GETTING STARTED. To use vi to edit a file, issue the following command to UNIX:

`vi <filename>`

vi reads the file to be edited into a memory buffer or "work space" and uses the terminal screen as a window into the buffer. If `<filename>` does not exist (i.e., you are creating a new file), then vi assumes an empty memory buffer.

vi MODES
vi does its work in one of three modes or states:

1. keystroke mode
2. insert mode
3. command line mode

When vi is first invoked, it is in keystroke mode. Most keys on the keyboard have a meaning to vi and case is always important (for example, l means "move the cursor right one character position," while L means "move the cursor to the bottom of the window"). A number of the keystroke commands cause vi to change from keystroke mode to insert mode. The simplest of these is i. When vi is in insert mode, whatever characters you type at the keyboard are echoed in the window and placed in the buffer. The escape key moves vi from insert mode back to keystroke mode.

To get to command line mode, you need to be in keystroke mode and press the colon key. When you do this, the cursor will go to the line below the last line in the window and the colon will be echoed there. Then you can type in a command and press return. For example

```
:set number
```

tells vi to redraw the window with line numbers on each line. After you type a command and press return, you will be back in keystroke mode.

A simple edit session.

1. Log onto the UNIX system.
2. Edit a new file named <filename> via typing:

   ```
   $vi <filename>
   ```

   at the UNIX prompt ($).
3. Press the i button (this puts you into insert mode).
4. Insert text into your document, pressing return at the end of each line.
5. When done inserting text, press the escape (esc) button (this puts you into keystroke mode).
6. Finally, type :x (this saves the new file and returns you to the UNIX operating system).
7. To check for your saved file, use the UNIX ls and cat commands.
8. To revise the file you have just created, edited and saved, type vi filename and move the cursor to a desired point in the file buffer using the h, j, k and l keys.
9. If you don't wish to make (or save) any changes, type :q. This ends the edit session without re-saving the file.

Partial list of keystroke mode commands.

i	Causes vi to change from keystroke mode to insert mode (and inserts *before* the cursor).
a	Puts you into insert mode *after* the current cursor position.
r	Replace the character at the current cursor position with the next character typed.
R	Replace characters until encounter <esc>.
<esc>	Causes vi to change from insert mode to keystroke mode.
:	Causes vi to change from keystroke mode to command line mode (after you enter a command, vi will be back in keystroke mode).
h	Move the cursor to the left one position.
j	Move the cursor down one line.
k	Move the cursor up one line.
l	Move the cursor to the right one position.
H	Move the cursor to the first line in the window.

M	Move the cursor to the middle line in the window.
L	Move the cursor to the last line in the window.
CNTL–F	Scroll forward a window.
CNTL–B	Scroll backward a window.
$	Move the cursor to the end of the current line (the line where the cursor currently resides).
0 (zero)	Move the cursor to the beginning of the current line.
o	Open up an empty line *below* the current line and change vi from keystroke mode to insert mode.
O	Open up an empty line *above* the current line and change vi from keystroke mode to insert mode.
G	Move the cursor to a particular line. G by itself causes the cursor to go to the last line in the file. <n>G causes the cursor to go to the nth line in the buffer.
D	Deletes everything from the current cursor position to the end of the line.
x	Deletes the character that the cursor is on top of.
dd	Deletes a line (cursor positioned at beginning of line).
dw	Deletes a word (cursor positioned at beginning of word).
u	Undo. "Undoes" the last change made to the main buffer. For example, if you delete something, it may be restored by pressing the u key.
<n>Y	"Yank" <n> lines starting at cursor into buffer (1st part of "cut and paste" operation).
p	Put (insert) contents of buffer (2nd part of "cut and paste").
xp	Transpose two characters.
/<string><CR>	Search for <string>.

Partial list of command line mode commands. (Remember that you must be in keystroke mode in order for a colon to move you to command line mode.)

:x	Save the changes you have made to the file and end the edit session.
:w	Save the changes you have made to the file and continue the edit session. You could also type

:w filename

and the changes that you have made during this edit session will be saved in the file you specify.

:q   Quit (end) the edit session without rewriting the file. If you have made changes to the file during the edit session, vi forces you to type

:q!

to insure that you really want to quit.

:x,y w <filename>   Write lines numbered x through y to
                                  <filename>.

:/pattern/   Move the cursor to the next line in the buffer
                                  that contains the specified pattern. / by itself
                                  will find the next occurrence of the last pattern
                                  specified.

:g/pattern/s/pattern/newstuff/g

                                  Global replacement of **pattern** with
                                  newstuff.

:set   When the set command is given by itself, a
                                  list of the currently set options is printed at the
                                  bottom of the window. If you type

                                      :set all

:set number   a list of all possible options is printed. An example
                                  of setting an option is

:set nonumber   which causes vi to redraw the window with line
                                  numbers. The command

                                  redraws the window without the numbers.

OTHER v i **FEATURES USEFUL FOR LISP PROGRAMMING.** vi has several features that facilitate the creation and editing of LISP programs. For example, in
keystroke mode with the cursor positioned under a parenthesis, the vi % command
will move the cursor to the matching parenthesis (if one exists). This is an excellent
way to identify the extent of an s-expression. Similarly, by invoking the command

:set lisp <cr>

in keystroke mode, the (or { keys will advance the cursor backward an s-expression
({ skips over atoms). The) or } keys have a similar effect in moving the cursor
forward an s-expression.

REFERENCES

[Bourne 1983] Bourne, S.R., *The Unix System*, Addison-Wesley, Reading, MA, 1983.
[McGilton/Morgan 1983] McGilton, H., and R. Morgan, *Introducing the UNIX System*, McGraw-Hill,
      New York, 1983.

EPILOGUE

I endeavor to keep their attention fixed on the main object of all science, the freedom and happiness of man.

Thomas Jefferson
Letter to General Kosciusko, 1810

INDEX

A* algorithm, 508
Abduction, 331
Actions, 27
Adjacency graph, 129
Advanced rule-based system, 407
Agents, 425
AI
   architectures, 73
   workstation, 589
Algorithms, 7
AND and OR parallelism, 595
AND-OR tree, 500
Anonymous variable, 99
Antecedent, 41, 43
Applicable operators, 430
Applicable rules, 284
Apprenticeship learning techniques, 568
Argument dependence, 596
Arithmetic and numerical functions, 214
Assertion, 40
Association, 6, 22
Atom, 197
Attributes, 22
Augmented transition networks (ATNs), 185
Axioms, 39

Backtracking, 104
Backtracking strategy as depth-first search, 105
Backward (goal-driven) chaining, 325, 353, 411
Backward state propagation (BSP), 437, 505

Bayes rule, 373, 378
Best-first search, 508
Binary constraints, 129
Binary relation, 11
Binding, 88
   environment, 58
   list, 256
Blackboard, 514, 529
Blocks-world problem, 434
Bottom-up parsing, 179
Branching temporal logic, 547
Breadth-first search, 506
Brute-force search, 499

C + M (Clocksin and Mellish) syntax
      (PROLOG), 92
car, 198
Categorical propositions, 50
cdr, 198
Chaining, antecedent vs. consequent driven,
      326
Circularity in PROLOG unification, 108
Clause, 93
Clause form, 56
Closed formulae, 54
Combinatorial explosion, 494
Common-sense reasoning, 533
Complexity functions, 495
Compound data types, 394
Compound statement, 41

Computational complexity, 9, 493, 587
Computer
  configuration, 5
  memory model(s), 234
  vision, 5, 406
Concepts, 22
Conceptual relations, 16
Conceptualization, 16
Concurrent PROLOG, 595, 599
cond, 206
Condition elements, 390
Conditional statements, 41
Confidence factors, 305, 378
Conflict resolution, 304, 315
Conflict set, 304, 392
Conflicting subgoals, 429
cons, 210
Consequent, 41, 43
Constraint satisfaction, 22, 74, 124
Constructive inductive inferences, 565
Content-addressable memory (CAM), 234
Contradiction, 53, 55
Contrapositive, 43
Control strategies, 283
Converse, 43
Coupled computing, 75
Cut predicate, 106
Cycle, 436

Data dependency, 196
Data-directed
  inference, 353
  processing, 79
  search, 31
Declarative representation, 26–27
Decomposable production systems, 285
Deduction, 39, 46, 565
Default information, 518
defun, 200
Demons, 533
Description, 571
Digraph (directed graph), 11, 236, 615
Disagreement set, 59
Discrimination, 6
Distributed artificial intelligence, 606
do, 209
Dot notation, 242

Eliza, 165
Environment, 90
Equality, 43
Equivalence relation, 614
eval function, 197

Existential quantifier, 51, 53
Expert system, 3, 5, 280, 359
  examples, 361
Extended MP, 65

Factorial, 83
Features, 27
Fifth generation computing, 2
Floating point operations per second (FLOPS),
  594
Flow graph, 592
Formulae, ground, 54
Forward (data-driven) chaining, 42, 44, 45,
  288, 353, 411
Forward state propagation (fsp), 436, 448
Frame
  -based representations, 409
  manipulation primitives, 529
  networks, 521
  problem, 24, 427
Frames, 26, 513, 518
Function
  definition in LISP, 200
  mathematical, 614
Functors, 98
Future construct, the, 604
Fuzzy logic, 38, 371

Garbage collection, 243
Generalization operators, 571, 578
General-to-specific, 575
Generate-and-test (GAT), 436, 448
Geological prospecting, 5
Grammar, 170
  types, 171, 172

Heuristic approaches, 378
Heuristics, 502, 507
Hierarchical planning, 481
Horn clause, 91, 95
Hypothesis, 43
  generation, 330

If connective, 207
If-then-unless rules, 581
Illegal state, 429
Image motion description example, 300
Implication, 41, 43, 619
Induction, 39, 569
Inference, 28, 39
  control, 9

Inference (*Cont.*)
  engine, 281
  net, 45
Inheritance, 514, 516
  with exceptions, 520
Instance, 515
Intensional knowledge, 20
Intractable problems, 494
Inverse, 43
is-a forms, 514, 519

Knowledge
  consistency, 535
  engineers, 364
  manipulation, 4
  representation, 4, 18, 19
  system architectures, 586

Labeling, 127
Languages, 164
Learning
  by analogy, 569
  from examples (or evidence), 567
  by exploration, 569
let, 208
Line drawing description grammar, 172
Linear temporal logic, 547
Linked list structure, 235
LISP (LISt Processing), 74, 77
  functions (summary), 627
List, 98, 197, 210, 625
Lists in PROLOG, 101
Logic, 616
  first order, 39
Logical inferences per second (LIPS), 594

Machine intelligence, 3
Macro-operators, 481
Manipulable representation, 19
Matching, 9, 14, 424
Matching problems, hierarchy of, 249
Maximally consistent unification, 409
Means-end, 442, 464, 508
Medical diagnosis (mycin), 5
Metarules, 533
MFLOPS, 4
Microworld, 18
Modal logic, 550, 559
Model
  unification, 406
  -based reasoning, 17
Modeling space, 23

Modus ponens (MP), 38–39, 46
Multivalued logic, 38, 382

Natural language applications, 5, 164
Negation as failure, 49, 107
Neural computing, 21
Non-commutative system, 432
Non-constructive generalization operators, 580
Non-terminal, 170
Nonmonotonic logic, 38, 514, 536
Nonpolynomial time (NP) algorithm, 495
Not predicate, 107
NP-complete problems, 495
nth, 198

Opportunistic problem solving, 531
OPS5, 279, 390, 394
Ordered pair, 12

Parallel
  computations, 1
  planning, 484
  processing, 587, 590
Parsing, 164, 178
Path planning, 426
Pattern directed inference, 248
Persistence, 24, 26
Plan, 424
  generation direction, 482
  representations, 426
Polynomial-time (P) algorithm, 495
Power system control, 5
Predicate, 48, 624
  calculus, first order, 50
  functions, 48
Primitives, 22, 27, 170
Probabilistic logic, 38
Problem descomposition, 9
Problem space, 29
Procedural information, 26, 518
Production, 170
  memory, 390
  system, 279
  system properties, 284
Programming languages, 9
PROLOG (programming in logic), 74, 77, 91, 624
  and modus ponens, 96
  term, 98
Property, 12, 22
  functions, 213
Proposition, 40

Propositional logic, 621
Pure LISP, 195
Puzzles, 8

Quantification, 622

read-eval-print, 197
Reasoning
  processes, 6
  with uncertainty, 367
Reconfigurable processors, 593
Recursion, 8, 60, 85
Reflexive, 12
Relation, 10, 12, 236, 613
  digraph representation, 233
  properties of, 12
  ternary, 12
Relational constraints, 409
Representation, 2, 9, 23, 424
Resolution, 9, 55
Robotics, 5
Rote learning, 567
Rule firing, 45
Rule-based production systems, 27, 38
  features of, 282
Rules, 94

Scope, 53
Scoping of variables, 216
Search, 8, 9, 29, 428, 463, 493
  cost function, 497
  depth-first, 502, 507
  forward-backward (bidirectional), 507
  goal-directed, 31
  graph representations, 499
  heuristics, 74
  problems, 496
Semantic net, 13
Sentence, 54
set, setq, 201
Side effect, 601
Situations, 26, 519
Specialization, 515
Specific-to-general, 573
Speedup, 591
Stack frame, 86
State, system, 29
  preconditions, 430
  representation, 29
  space, 284
  space graph, 497
State difference, 434
  evaluation functions, 464
  measure, 464

Statement, 40
Statistical pattern recognition, 168
String grammars, 164
STRIPS representation, 430
Structural links, 515
Structural object description, 28
Structured knowledge representations, 513
Structures, 98
Subgoal generation and propagation, 329
Subplans, 425
Substitution, 58
Symbolic logic, 37
Symmetric and transitive relations, 12, 107
Syntactic description, 164

Tail recursion, 87
Tautology, 53
Temporal
  frame, 548, 556
  logics, 38, 544, 547
  operators, 551
  reasoning, 544
  reasoning, point-based vs. interval-based, 547
  representations, 549
Tentative, 283
Terminal, 170
Theorem proving, 5
Time tag, 394
Top-down parsing, 179
Trees, 233
Triangle Table, 445

Unary
  constraints, 129
  relation, 12, 49
Uncertainty, 9, 28
Unification, 9, 57–58, 92, 103, 124, 248, 597, 625
  rules for, 59
Unifier, general, 263, 266
Unifying substitution, 63
Universal quantifier, 51, 53
UNIX commands, 635
Unreachable states, 482

Values, 22
Variable scope, 88
Variables and bindings, 255
Visualization, 26

Well-formed formula, 54
Working memory, 390